Concepts, Cases, and Regulations in Financial Fraud and Corruption

Abdul Rafay
University of Management and Technology, Pakistan

IGI Global
PUBLISHER of TIMELY KNOWLEDGE

A volume in the Advances in Finance, Accounting, and Economics (AFAE) Book Series

Published in the United States of America by
IGI Global
Business Science Reference (an imprint of IGI Global)
701 E. Chocolate Avenue
Hershey PA, USA 17033
Tel: 717-533-8845
Fax: 717-533-8661
E-mail: cust@igi-global.com
Web site: http://www.igi-global.com

Library of Congress Cataloging-in-Publication Data

Names: Rafay, Abdul, 1973- editor.
Title: Concepts, cases, and regulations in financial fraud and corruption / Abdul Rafay, editor.
Description: Hershey, PA : Business Science Reference, [2023] | Includes bibliographical references and index. | Summary: "This book offers contributions that provide understanding and lessons learned in regard to all aspects of financial & technological crimes, frauds, and corruption in individual, organizational, and societal experiences with a goal to present a unique opportunity for researchers to take the shape of experience, implementation, and application in the current technological advancement"-- Provided by publisher.
Identifiers: LCCN 2022018630 (print) | LCCN 2022018631 (ebook) | ISBN 9781668450079 (hardcover) | ISBN 9781668450086 (paperback) | ISBN 9781668450093 (ebook)
Subjects: LCSH: Fraud. | White collar crimes. | Corporations--Corrupt practices.
Classification: LCC HV6691 .C665 2023 (print) | LCC HV6691 (ebook) | DDC 364.16/8--dc23/eng/20220708
LC record available at https://lccn.loc.gov/2022018630
LC ebook record available at https://lccn.loc.gov/2022018631

This book is published in the IGI Global book series Advances in Finance, Accounting, and Economics (AFAE) (ISSN: 2327-5677; eISSN: 2327-5685)

British Cataloguing in Publication Data
A Cataloguing in Publication record for this book is available from the British Library.

For electronic access to this publication, please contact: eresources@igi-global.com.

Advances in Finance, Accounting, and Economics (AFAE) Book Series

Ahmed Driouchi
Al Akhawayn University, Morocco

ISSN:2327-5677
EISSN:2327-5685

Mission

In our changing economic and business environment, it is important to consider the financial changes occurring internationally as well as within individual organizations and business environments. Understanding these changes as well as the factors that influence them is crucial in preparing for our financial future and ensuring economic sustainability and growth.

The **Advances in Finance, Accounting, and Economics (AFAE)** book series aims to publish comprehensive and informative titles in all areas of economics and economic theory, finance, and accounting to assist in advancing the available knowledge and providing for further research development in these dynamic fields.

Coverage

- Health Economics
- Economics of Intellectual Property Rights
- Internet Banking
- Borrowing and Lending
- Ethics in Accounting and Finance
- Economics of Migration and Spatial Mobility
- Investments and Derivatives
- Entrepreneurship in Accounting and Finance
- Economic Downturn
- Theoretical Issues in Economics, Finance, and Accounting

IGI Global is currently accepting manuscripts for publication within this series. To submit a proposal for a volume in this series, please contact our Acquisition Editors at Acquisitions@igi-global.com or visit: http://www.igi-global.com/publish/.

The Advances in Finance, Accounting, and Economics (AFAE) Book Series (ISSN 2327-5677) is published by IGI Global, 701 E. Chocolate Avenue, Hershey, PA 17033-1240, USA, www.igi-global.com. This series is composed of titles available for purchase individually; each title is edited to be contextually exclusive from any other title within the series. For pricing and ordering information please visit http://www.igi-global.com/book-series/advances-finance-accounting-economics/73685. Postmaster: Send all address changes to above address.

Titles in this Series

For a list of additional titles in this series, please visit: http://www.igi-global.com/book-series/advances-finance-accounting-economics/73685

Future Outlooks on Corporate Finance and Opportunities for Robust Economic Planning
Siraj Kariyilaparambu Kunjumuhammed (Modern College of Business and Science, Oman) and Nithya Ramachandran (University of Technology and Applied Science, Oman)
Business Science Reference • © 2023 • 278pp • H/C (ISBN: 9781668453421) • US $240.00

Exploring Business Ecosystems and Innovation Capacity Building in Global Economics
Mihir Joshi (Banasthali Vidyapith University, Rajasthan, India) Mohsen Brahmi (University of Sfax, Tunisia) Luigi Aldieri (University of Salerno, Italy) and Concetto Paolo Vinci (University of Salerno, Italy)
Business Science Reference • © 2023 • 325pp • H/C (ISBN: 9781668467664) • US $250.00

Considerations of Territorial Planning, Space, and Economic Activity in the Global Economy
Helmuth Yesid Arias Gomez (Masaryk Institute of Advanced Studies (MIAS), Czech Technical University in Prague, Czech Republic) and Gabriela Antošová (Institute of Education and Communication, Czech University of Life Sciences in Prague, Czech Republic)
Business Science Reference • © 2023 • 356pp • H/C (ISBN: 9781668459768) • US $250.00

Transforming Economies Through Microfinance in Developing Nations
Yahaya Alhassan (University of Sunderland in London, UK) and Uzoechi Nwagbara (University of Sunderland in London, UK)
Business Science Reference • © 2023 • 263pp • H/C (ISBN: 9781668456477) • US $250.00

Advanced Machine Learning Algorithms for Complex Financial Applications
Mohammad Irfan (CMR Institute of Technology, India) Mohamed Elhoseny (American University in the Emirates, UAE) Salina Kassim (International Islamic University of Malaysia, Malaysia) and Noura Metawa (University of Sharjah, UAE)
Engineering Science Reference • © 2023 • 292pp • H/C (ISBN: 9781668444832) • US $270.00

Exploring the Dark Side of FinTech and Implications of Monetary Policy
Sheraz Ahmed (LUT University, Finland) John Agyekum Addae (LUT University, Finland & Ghana Communication Technology University, Ghana) and Kwame Simpe Ofori (International University of Grand-Bassam, Côte d'Ivoire & University of Electronic Science and Technology of China, China)
Business Science Reference • © 2023 • 300pp • H/C (ISBN: 9781668463819) • US $250.00

IGI Global
PUBLISHER of TIMELY KNOWLEDGE

701 East Chocolate Avenue, Hershey, PA 17033, USA
Tel: 717-533-8845 x100 • Fax: 717-533-8661
E-Mail: cust@igi-global.com • www.igi-global.com

Dedication

This book is dedicated to the memory of (the late) **Hakim Muhammad Hassan Qarshi (1896-1974)**, a visionary practitioner of eastern herbal medicine in Indo-Pak sub-continent. He was a creative soul with a flair of writing and reading. His scholarly and practical contribution in the field of eastern medicine made him a person of great depth and integrity. In fact, he was an institution in himself and the history of herbal medicine is incomplete without him. Hakim Muhammad Hassan Qarshi laid the foundation of Qarshi Industries in 1968. Today in 2023 after five decades, based on indigenous research, the herbal medical products of the Qarshi Industries became household names not only in Pakistan but around the globe. On December 20, 2002, the Pakistan Postal Department issued a commemorative stamp on the occasion of his 100th birthday.

Currently, **Iqbal Ahmed Qarshi,** a chemical engineer by profession, is the torch bearer for his father's vision. He is the founder/chairman of Qarshi foundation, Chairman of Board of Governors of Qarshi University and the president of World Wide Fund for Nature, Pakistan (WWF-P). In 1994, he formed Qarshi Foundation, a non-profit welfare organization. The foundation is working with a vision of "Healthy, Educated and Happier Pakistan" to improve the quality of life of poor and underprivileged people of Pakistan. Having devoted all life for the sake of his vision and mission, the personal and professional integrity of **Hakim Muhammad Hassan Qarshi** reflects in the institution established by Qarshi Foundation in Pakistan, "the Qarshi University".

May Allah rest his soul in peace.

EDITORIAL ADVISORY BOARD

Table of Contents

Section 3
Fraud and Technology

Detailed Table of Contents

This study is designed to investigate the use of counterfeit money in the Ottoman Empire. Firstly, the concept of money and the reasons for the use of counterfeit money in the Ottoman Empire are described. Secondly, the reasons for the formation of counterfeit money are examined. Thirdly, the precautions taken against counterfeit money in the Ottoman Empire are discussed. The goal of this study is to investigate the counterfeit money printing incidents that had taken place. Moreover, the anti-counterfeit measures are identified that are implemented by Ottoman Empire to curb this crime and to remove counterfeit money from the market.

Growing corruption in Nigeria is a cause of concern for everyone. In order to strengthen the fight against corruption, the government is determined to nip the hydra-headed monster in the bud. In this regard, two anti-corruption agencies have been established and the introduction of a whistleblowing policy has been introduced. Initially, the citizens embraced the policy by blowing the whistle on fraud, bribery, looted public funds/assets, financial misconduct, and other forms of gratification/theft. This yielded fruitful results as stolen public funds and assets that run into billions were recovered. However, rather than intensify their initial zeal to exposé corruption, the citizens' desire to blow the whistle began to wane amidst large-scale corruption. Against this backdrop, this chapter proffers solutions and recommends ways for the government to get Nigerians to actively continue with the whistleblowing policy.

Several factors like cognitive attitude, norms, and behavioral control still influence corruption. Ajzen theory states that social and psychological aspects can be antecedents. This research looks into the variables of the theory of planned behavior (TPB) to anticipate the effect of perceived corruption (PC). Considering the primary entrepreneurial deterrent, the dataset is based on 400 Polish graduate students' entrepreneurial intents and behavior who graduated from higher education programs at eight universities in Poland. These three variables were examined for their influence on corrupt perception and behavior. This study explores the attitude and behavior of corruption/fraud by using Ajzen's TPB. This is accomplished by paying closer attention to the impact of cognition attitude (CA), subjective norm (SN), and perceived behavioral control (PBC), which influence the intention to commit corruption. This provides a solid theoretical basis for this research.

Corruption is one of the main causes of inefficiency and poor productivity. This chapter looks at the relationship between banking failure, corruption, financial development, and economic growth in Nigeria during the period from 1989 to 2019. The work uses the autoregressive distributed lag (ARDL) cointegration and error correction model and the Granger causality test for the analysis of data. The results of the empirical analyses show a negative relationship between corruption and both financial development and economic growth. This shows that corruption is bad for both the financial sector and the economy. The result also shows that corruption is a good reason for causing bank failures in Nigeria. Hence, for financial development and economic growth, corruption must be reduced as much as possible if not eliminated. It is recommended to put the fight against all forms of corruption in Nigeria in top gear.

Principles-based accounting standards (PBS) are imbued with high levels of flexibility that enable any company to apply accounting policies that suit its unique circumstances. The use of PBS necessarily leaves much room for extensive use of the 'ingredients or elements of accounting flexibility' including, estimates, multiple measurement types, and professional judgments to select accounting policies and make decisions around 'materiality'. By invoking these flexibilities, entities can manipulate financial numbers and perpetuate improper acts that significantly impact the fairness of published general-purpose financial statements particularly the financial position and financial performance. This chapter concluded that while flexibility embedded in PBS is inevitable and necessary in financial reporting, its unintended consequence is to facilitate aggressive optimistic or pessimistic (as opposed to neutral) reporting practices. The flexibilities inherently pervasive in PBS can constitute the slippery slope through which fraudulent actions and reporting could be perpetuated.

Several ways or tactics can be used by entities to manage disclosed information, undermining its transparency and mitigating its credibility. Even though accounting literature has covered a wide range of IM strategies and investigation lines since the seminal research from the last decade of the 20th century, this chapter demonstrates that IM remains relevant since it can be assessed and adapted from

The aftermath of the 2008 global financial crisis has led to the emergence of the OECD/G20 Base Erosion and Profit Shifting (BEPS) initiative developed in 2013. This project provides several actions plans to establish coherence and transparency and also to prevent malpractices in the international taxation system. Being a member of the OECD, Mauritius joined the inclusive framework on BEPS in 2016. This research assesses the adoption of the BEPS standards by Mauritius on Controlled Foreign Corporations (CFCs), transfer pricing, and on country-by-country (CbC) reporting. The purpose of this study is to identify any convergence and divergence between BEPS standards and the corresponding implementation measures in Mauritius. To achieve this research objective, the study has adopted the black letter approach by analyzing existing laws. A critical analysis is conducted about the implementation measures by Mauritius and assessing their implications on the domestic and the international taxation systems.

Tax frauds with fake traders have existed since the 1980s and are certainly not a new phenomenon. Likewise, ways to fight against these frauds have existed since the moment they first appeared. Just as the frauds have evolved over time, so have the proposals for solving them becoming more sophisticated and comprehensive. With the development of the VAT system in the European Union, the methods of fraud are also developing, and over time the EU member states realize that they cannot fight against these frauds alone. The directive on the common system of VAT in 2006 represents the unification and the beginning of the joint fight of the member states of the European Union against these frauds. The EU member states systematically reinforced the measures of the common fraud prevention strategy. One such measure is the transfer of tax liability between the member states of the European Union.

Corruption secures benefits for those with power, status, money, or protection. Corruption generally manifests itself in the form of a tacit convention that is put in place discreetly, gradually, and cumulatively by feeding itself and secreting its own rules, mechanisms, and intermediaries. In Morocco, social tolerance towards corruption is strong, influenced by a general feeling of impunity and the inequality of citizens under the law. The force of the political discourse displayed, and which is supposed to fight it remains unchanged without notorious effects. However, emerging technologies can serve as a remarkable lever to transform public actions in their fight against corruption through a paperless environment, the reduction of red tape, and highlighting the gray areas where corruption thrives. By focusing on the Moroccan case,

Preface

The editing of a book on financial fraud and corruption is more exciting and challenging than ever before. The past few decades have been an eventful one for this growing area of interest from G20[1] to World Economic Forum[2] to global and national economic agendas. Today the alarming prevalence of fraud/corruption and tackling this menace are being considered key issues in developed and developing countries alike. Fraud and corruption also enabled the birth of a new regulatory regime based on strict compliance and robust processes.

Fraud and Corruption have been presented throughout history and plagued societies and communities for far too long. The statute of Purveyors in 1350, made forgery and counterfeiting a treasonable offense. Fraud and corruption can have devastating financial consequences for companies and individuals. Regardless of the size of the business, industry, or country, financial fraud/corruption is one of the biggest and growing problems that countries and organizations are facing today at the macro and micro levels.

CORRUPTION

There are many paradigms of corruption like political corruption, public corruption, private corruption, and bribery to name a few. A generic definition of corruption by Transparency International is:

Corruption is the abuse of entrusted power for private gain which eventually hurts everyone who depends on the integrity of people in a position of authority. (TI, 2022)

On the other hand, various aspects of political corruption (Millar, 2018) are discussed by philosophers like Montesquieu (in *The Spirit of the Laws*), Machiavelli (in *The Prince* and *The Discourses*), Aristotle (in *The Politics*) and Plato (in *The Republic*). Similarly, Nye (1967) explained public corruption as "*the abuse of power by a public official for private gain*". Massive public corruption is the hallmark of countries with weak institutions and low levels of transparency. Rule of law is undermined by public corruption that leads to social disharmony and stifles economic development.

FRAUD

Fraud is a growing reality for over a century now. In the early 20th century, Anson (1906) defined fraud as:

A false representation of facts made, with a knowledge of its falsehood or recklessly without belief in its truth, with the intention that it should be acted upon by the complaining party, and actually inducing him to act upon it.

Regarding basic accounting frauds, Bennett (1930) discussed:

An all-inclusive definition of fraud means any intentional misrepresentation or concealment of some past or present material fact by a party in interest, such material fact not being open equally to the observation of both parties in interest, or not to be discovered through the exercise of ordinary care, and being relied upon by one party to a transaction, to his damage.... The concealment of assets by a bankrupt is a fraud upon his creditors.... Overstating the profits of a business by a vendor in a sale contract is a material misrepresentation which would constitute fraud... The utterance of a false statement of financial condition to induce credit may be a representation held to constitute fraud.

Fast forward to the late eighties, Bose and Gunn (1989) said about fraud:

Fraud is now big business. Its roots run deep into the fabric of finance and commerce, nurtured by the rapid expansion of twenty four hour electronic international trading.... It is now all too easy for the skilled fraudster to engage in shady deals (and cover his tracks) quicker than the blink of an eye. Indeed it is estimated that the amount of fraudulently converted cash swilling around the world at any one time is more than equals the Gross National Products of several third world countries.

Multiple fraud models have been introduced over a period of time. "Fraud Triangle" was the initial model that pointed out pressure, opportunity and rationalization as the factors that can lead anyone to commit fraud. The latest "Fraud Hexagon" is a powerful tool for identifying and preventing fraud. It can help you to identify potential risks and vulnerabilities, and develop measures to protect your business. The main factors of the fraud hexagon are Stimulus, Capability, Collusion, Ego/Entitlement, Rationalization and Opportunity.

In many cases, fraud/corruption is a difficult crime to talk about rather it is a taboo subject. In today's world, fraud/corruption is in the form of identity fraud, cyber fraud, phishing, hacking, Ponzi/pyramid schemes, insider trading, embezzlement of funds, window dressing, tax evasions, kickbacks, graft, influence peddling, nepotism, misuse of resources, to name a few. In 2022, 46% of the organizations experience some kind of fraud during the last twenty-four months (PwC, 2022). There are instances of high-profile frauds in the world. For example, in 2022, one of the Instagram biggest fraudsters Ramon Abbas, aka the "Billionaire Gucci Master" or Hushpuppi brought down (Liebman & Brahce, 2022). He was sentenced to 11 years in prison in the U.S. for committing wire fraud, money laundering and identity theft (Lytton, 2022).

During the current century, advances in technology have made it easier to commit, detect and prevent fraud. Cybercrimes pose the biggest threat followed by customer fraud and asset misappropriation (PwC, 2022). On one hand, the triple threat of fraud, compliance risks and cyber-attacks (KPMG, 2022) is increasing, while on the other hand environmental, geopolitical, financial and social pressures are complicating the fraud prevention measures (PwC, 2022). In order to restore public trust in general, comprehensive AI-driven anti-corruption platforms are being developed for transparency and accountability. These platforms use data analytics, artificial intelligence, and machine learning to effectively identify corruption/fraud. Using these platforms, governments and organizations can keep an eye on potential fraud and/or corruption before it happens.

CONCLUDING REMARKS

The sustainability of a transparent society is at risk. In order to ensure a safer working environment and eradication/reduction of corruption from society, effective implementation of anti-fraud/corruption policies is necessary. These may include anti-corruption strategies, transparent governance procedures, bribery laws, whistleblower systems, internal audit policies, and corporate compliance programs. The focus of anti-corruption regulators is on the detection, investigation and prosecution of white-collar crimes. For Example, in 2000, Anti-Fraud Communicators' Network (OAFCN) was formed as a cross-European network of communicators working on anti-fraud issues. Its main objectives are public/media awareness for the prevention and deterrence of fraud through a permanent dialogue, reinforced cooperation, and joint communication initiatives (OLAF, 2022). Similarly, United Nations Office on Drugs and Crime (UNODC) is also playing a key role in fight against fraud and corruption.

Confucius (or Master Kong as he was known), a Chinese philosopher in the 6th century BC, advised king Chi K'ang about how to handle the thieves in the country:

If you sir, were not covetous, although you should reward them to do it, they would not steal. To govern means to rectify. If you lead on the people with correctness, who will dare not to be correct. (Shafritz & Hyde, 2016)

CONTEXT AND ORGANIZATION OF THIS VOLUME

Regardless of whether you are a beginner or a seasoned researcher, this book will deepen the discourse about financial frauds. I am hopeful that this book is a fascinating and invaluable guide for understanding the theory, practice, and cases of finance frauds in today's world.

This book consists of fifteen chapters by writers from twelve countries. Thirty authors contributed from disparate parts of the world:

Europe: Portugal, Italy, Croatia, and Turkey

Asia: China, Mauritius, and Pakistan

Africa: Nigeria, Tanzania, Morocco, Ghana, and Uganda

The first chapter, "Mortgage Financing Frauds in the US: An Analysis of CFPB Complaint Database," by Ali Polat, Muhammad Mobeen Ajmal, and Abdul Rafay, examines the performance of Consumer Financial Protection Bureau (CFPB) in the US. Results show that predatory behaviour is more dominant in Non-Banking Credit and Lending Institutions and CFPB was not so successful in getting relief for the customer. The second chapter, "Corruption and Governance in Africa: An Insight," by Tochukwu Benedict Ezeifekwuab and Marie G. Nakitende, examines the corrupt practices conducted by Africans as well as foreigners who are collaborating with corrupt African leaders. The external and internal sources of corruption are discussed which are systemic, interrelated, and interdependent. The chapter also looks at the failure and challenges to handle or deal with the issue of corruption in various dimension. The third chapter, "Counterfeiting Money and Anti-Counterfeit Measures: The Historical Case of the Ottoman Empire," by Büşra Karataşer, investigates the use of counterfeit money in the Ottoman Empire. Important points discussed are the concept of money, the reasons for the use of counterfeit money in the Ottoman Empire and the precautions taken against counterfeit money in the Ottoman Empire. The fourth chapter, "Whistleblowing Policy Against Corruption: The Case of Nigeria," by Benjamin Enahoro Assay, describes the introduction of the whistleblowing policy in Nigeria that yielded fruitful results as stolen public funds and assets that run into billions were recovered. Recommendations are suggested to further intensify the initial zeal of public to exposé corruption. The fifth chapter, "Perceived Corruption in the Process of the Entrepreneurial Intention: An Extension into the Ajzen's Theory of Planned Behaviour," by Mohammad Heydari, Yanan Fan, Xiaoyang Li, and Kin Keung Lai, discusses that several factors like cognitive attitude, norms, and behavioral control still influence corruption. Ajzen theory states that social and psychological aspects can be antecedents. This research looks into the variables of the Theory of Planned Behaviour (TPB) to anticipate the effect of perceived corruption. The sixth chapter, "Economic Growth, Corruption, Banking Failure, and Financial Development in Nigeria," by Shafiu Ibrahim Abdullahi, Mukhtar Shuaibu, Mustapha Yusufu, Kamal Kabiru Shehu, and Abdul Rafay, looks at the relationship between banking failure, corruption, financial development and economic growth in Nigeria during the period from 1989 to 2019. The results show that corruption is a good reason for causing bank failures in Nigeria. It is suggested that for financial development and economic growth, corruption must be reduced as much as possible if not eliminated. The seventh chapter, "Principles-Based Accounting Standards: A Slippery Slope to Financial Reporting Fraud," by Clement Chiahemba M. Ajekwe, explains that Principles-based accounting standards (PBS) are imbued with high levels of flexibility that enable any company to apply accounting policies that suit its unique circumstances. It is concluded that while flexibility embedded in PBS is inevitable and necessary in financial reporting, its unintended consequence is to facilitate aggressive optimistic, or pessimistic (as opposed to neutral) reporting practices. The eighth chapter, "Impression Management in Accounting: Evolution and Trends," by Fábio Albuquerque, Vinícius Stoltzemburg, and António Cariano, depicts that accounting literature has covered a wide range of Impression Management strategies and investigation lines since the seminal research from the last decade of the 20th century. It is concluded that Impression Management remains relevant since it can be assessed and adapted from the perspective of trending accounting topics. The ninth chapter, "Enterprise Risk Management and Shadow Banking Systems: The Case of European Union," by Stefano de Nichilo, explains that during the last few years, the European Court of Auditors highlighted the importance of "special reports" that examine the economy, efficiency, and effectiveness of EU spending. The chapter discussed the fraud and management bad practice of agile marketing concepts in the context of digital transformation and international business. The tenth chapter, "Insurance Fraud and Financial Performance: The Case of Tanzania," by Pendo Shukrani Kasoga and Amani Gration Tegambwage, identified the Insurance frauds as a significant risk that undermines investor and customer trust. The findings reveal that policyholder fraud, internal fraud, and intermediary fraud have a negative effect on the financial performance of insurance companies and brokers. The eleventh chapter, "Base Erosion and Profit Shifting (BEPS) in International Taxation System: The Case of Mauritius in the Light of OECD/G20 Initiatives," by Ambareen Beebeejaun, Rajendra Parsad Gunputh, and Abdul Rafay, assesses the adoption of the BEPS standards by Mauritius on Controlled Foreign Corporations (CFCs), transfer pricing and on Country-by-Country (CbC) reporting. A critical analysis is conducted about the implementation measures by Mauritius and assessing their implications on the domestic and the international taxation system. The twelfth chapter, "Circular VAT Fraud by Transfer of Tax Liability: The Case of the EU," by Valentina Vinsalek Stipic, discusses that frauds have evolved over time and the proposals for solving them becoming more sophisticated and comprehensive. The EU member states systematically reinforced the measures of the common fraud prevention strategy, and one measure is the transfer of tax liability between the member states of the European Union. The thirteenth chapter, "Fight Against Corruption Through Technology: The Case of Morocco," by Hicham Sadok, explains that in Morocco, social tolerance towards corruption is strong and influenced by a general feeling of impunity/inequality of citizens under the law. It highlighted the role that digitalization on the moralization of public life.

The fourteenth chapter, "Financial Cybercrimes During the COVID-19 Pandemic: The Case of Africa," by Usman Sambo, Babayo Sule, Misbahu Ibrahim Zamfara, and Marie G. Nakitende, proves that although Africa witnessed low levels of infections and deaths as compared to other continents, African socio-economic life was affected tremendously. It is revealed that COVID-19 significantly increased the number of social media users in Africa and has a correlation with cybersecurity threats and cybercrime. The fifteenth chapter, "Mobile Money Frauds in the African Continent," by Adam Salifu, contends that while it may not be possible to completely eliminate mobile money fraud, some key strategies such as collective action, strong regulatory frameworks, and standardization of mobile money transaction processes are important in reducing the phenomenon.

I thank the contributors and also the external reviewers who have patiently critiqued these chapters to meet the minimum acceptable standard. While the publisher and the Editor (myself) have used their best efforts in preparing this book, they make no representations and warranties with respect to the accuracy or completeness of the contents of this book and specifically disclaim any implied warranties of merchantability or fitness for a particular purpose. The strategies or suggestions or whatsoever contained in this book may not be suitable for any specific situation for which anyone should consult with a professional, where appropriate. Neither the publisher nor the Editor shall be liable for any loss of profit or any other commercial damages, including but not limited to special, incidental, consequential, or other damages.

March 2023

Abdul Rafay
University of Management and Technology, Pakistan

REFERENCES

Anson, W. R. (1906). *Principles of the English Law of Contract and of Agency in its Relation to Contract*. Banks Law Publishing Company.

Bennett, G. E. (1930). *Fraud: its control through accounts*. Century Company.

Bose, M., & Gunn, C. (1989). *Fraud: The Growth Industry of the Eighties*. Unwin Hyman.

KPMG. (2022). Key Findings. In A triple threat across the Americas: KPMG 2022 fraud outlook. KPMG.

Liebman, J., & Brahce, A. (2022). *Fraud magazine*. Association of certified Fraud Examiner. Retrieved from https://www.fraud-magazine.com

Lytton. (2022, November 8). He got burnt': How one of Instagram's biggest fraudsters was brought down. *Vice.* Retrieved from https://www.vice.com/en/article/wxnbvz/hushpuppi-ramon-abbas-jailed

Miller, S. (2018). *Corruption.* Stanford Encyclopedia of Philosophy.

Nye, J. S. (1967). Corruption and political development: A cost-benefit analysis. *The American Political Science Review, 61*(2), 417–427. doi:10.2307/1953254

OLAF. (2022). *The OLAF Anti-Fraud Communicators' Network (OAFCN).* European Anti-Fraud Office. Retrieved from https://anti-fraud.ec.europa.eu/media-corner/olaf-anti-fraud-communicators-network-oafcn_en

PwC. (2022). *Protecting the Perimeter: The rise of external Fraud.* PwC's Global Economic Crime and Fraud Survey 2022.

Shafritz, J. M., & Hyde, A. C. (2016). *Classics of public administration.* Boston: Cengage Learning.

TI. (2022). *Corruption.* Transparency International. Retrieved from https://www.transparency.org/en

ENDNOTES

1 **Group of Twenty (G20):** It is an intergovernmental forum comprising of the European Union and nineteen industrialized and developed countries. It is a primary venue for international economic and financial cooperation.

2 **World Economic Forum (WEF):** It is an international non-governmental forum based in Switzerland, to discuss the state of the world by engaging business, political, academic, and other leaders of society.

Section 1

Theory and Practice of Fraud, Corruption, and Governance

Chapter 1
Mortgage Financing Frauds in the US:
An Analysis of CFPB Complaint Database

Ali Polat
Ankara Yıldırım Beyazıt University, Turkey

Muhammad Mobeen Ajmal
University of Management and Technology, Pakistan

Abdul Rafay
https://orcid.org/0000-0002-0285-5980
University of Management and Technology, Pakistan

ABSTRACT

In the US, the Consumer Financial Protection Bureau (CFPB) monitors the financial institutions which sell financial products and services to consumers. CFPB ensures that the consumers of financial products receive transparent and competitive services from financial institutions. The chapter contributes to the literature on state-run consumer protection organizations. The CFPB complaint database is used to analyze the performance of CFPB and to find some real-world behaviors of financial institutions from the perceptions of financial consumers. The weaknesses of CFPB are discussed in light of the current social, political, and economic changes happening in the USA. Results show that predatory behaviour is more dominant in non-banking credit and lending institutions. During COVID-19, the people took benefit of others' misery by engaging in manipulative fraud-for-profit schemes. Overall, despite creating awareness, CFPB was not so successful in getting relief for the customer.

DOI: 10.4018/978-1-6684-5007-9.ch001

INTRODUCTION

In the US, since 2011, the Consumer Financial Protection Bureau (CFPB) has provided services for the consumer to file disputes against financial service providers. CFPB ensures that the consumers of financial products receive transparent and competitive services from financial institutions. CFPB empowers, educates, and protects consumers of financial products. On the other hand, it monitors the financial institutions which sell financial products and services to consumers. If in the interaction between a consumer and a financial institution, the consumers feel that they have been deceived or defrauded, they can complain to CFPB. CFPB publishes its complaints data to educate the masses about the scams, financial frauds and other predatory behaviors affecting consumers' decision-making.

The literature on CFPB is unclear about its performance; thus, no result can be reached if CFPB has succeeded in strengthening financial consumers. This chapter analyses the performance of CFPB over the years based on customer complaints against the financial service and product providers. If CFPB had performed its duty, the complainants would find relief after the company responded to the complaints. If more customers find such relief, CFPB would efficiently fulfil one of its primary goals. Since the CFPB complaint database mostly has qualitative variables, which are nominal and categorical, most of the analysis is done using cross-tabulation, bar charts and pie charts. The narrative part of the complaint is analyzed for fraud and scams using textual analysis of keywords.

The chapter is divided into four sections. The first section explains the role of CFPB in the US ecosystem and identifies the roles and responsibilities of CFPB to the US financial consumer and the US financial markets. The section ends with a discussion of the essential attributes of the Consumer Complaint Database maintained by CFPB. In the second section, the literature review is presented. The third section has an analysis of a component of the database. Mortgage-related complaints were taken to look for patterns and discern the performance of CFPB in a product category that has existed since the inception of CFPB.

CFPB AND THE UNITED STATES FINANCIAL ECOSYSTEM

CFPB has the authority to implement and enforce federal financial consumer law as per the US Consumer Financial Protection Act of 2010. The main functions of the CFPB are (1) taking actions to reduce abusive and predatory behavior of lending companies that violate the law and (2) getting the consumers reimbursed for their damages incurred due to deceptive and unfair practices of the lending companies. CFPB also has a statutory mandate to identify and remove the structural barriers to entry of new financial institutions, strengthen competition, and encourage innovation to reduce market inefficiencies that are harmful to the consumers of these financial services. CFPB achieves this by coordinating with the federal and state governments and partnering with the American Consumer Financial Innovation Network[1], the Securities and Exchange Commission and the National Association of Attorney Generals.

CFPB also works on increasing financial inclusion and consumers' financial knowledge by disseminating information to help consumers make rational decisions. Thereby, CFPB, through monitoring, ensures that the financial transactions are fair, leading to depth in the market and thus boosting the overall economy. By monitoring, researching, educating, and empowering consumers of the financial practices, tools, and strategies, as well as their rights, CFPB can promptly disseminate information about hot scams to the public. Some common scams include the student loan relief scam, unemployment benefits scams, social security benefit scams, and advanced child tax scams, amongst others. The informed consumers and the financial institutions then can take actions to reduce exposure risk to such scams.

Figure 1. CFPB Complaint handling procedure

The CFPB complaint handling procedure is given in **Figure 1**. Any scam or predatory, abusive behavior is reported to CFPB by the aggrieved party. CFPB reviews the petition and then sends the information to the company. The company has fifteen days to respond. If the company responds positively and promptly, CFPB notifies the consumer and then the decision is passed to the consumer, who can ask for further action. In such a case, CFPB initiates an administrative adjudication proceeding or files an action in the federal district court. The Judge then holds a hearing and recommends an action following the Rules of Practice for Adjudication Proceeding published by CFPB. The judiciary holds CFPB's rulings under the Chevron Deference[2]. Thereby, any ruling, interpretation, and meaning of any provision of the Federal consumer financial law provided by CFPB is absolute and is as if CFPB is the only agency authorized to apply, enforce, interpret and administer the law. CFPB then enforces the ruling passed by the court. In some cases, CFPB may even send warning letters to pre-warn institutions of practices that may violate the law.

CFPB, in the adjudicative proceedings or civil litigation, can seek any appropriate legal or equitable relief, including damages, restitution, refund, disgorgement, rescission, notification of the violation to the public and placing limits on the defendant's commercial activities. In some of the rulings passed by the court, the financial institution has to compensate the consumers. As per the court's ruling, there are three ways to compensate the victim, as shown in **Table 1**. In all three cases, the focus is to ensure that CFPB compensates the victim to the best of its ability.

Figure 2 shows the number of enforcement cases and the amount of relief for the consumers ordered by the CFPB enforcement actions each year. The data for **Figure 2** was available from the CFPB website[3]. The figure shows that the number of enforcements of CFPB increased from 2012 to 2015, then decreased before the number started increasing again in 2018. At the same time, the relief to the consumers increased till 2015 and then took a sharp dip. From 2016, the relief was almost between \$0.6

billion and $0.8 billion. This drop in relief provided by the CFPB is attributable to the structural attacks on CFPB under the Trumps regime (McCoy, 2018).

Table 1. Ways to compensate the Victim after ruling

Method		Payee	Administrator	Explanation
Direct	Defendant Administered Redress Payment	Defendant	Defendant	The defendant directly pays the designated settlement to the victim.
Indirect	Bureau- Administrated redress payment	Defendant	CFPB	The Bureau collects the defendant's settlement and then passes it on to the victims.
Mix	Victim Payment from the Civil Penalty fund	Defendant and CFPB	CFB	If the redress paid by the defendant is insufficient to compensate the victim fully, then the Bureau adds money to the settlement from the Bureau's Civil Penalty fund.

CFPB has statutory supervision authority over certain entities, as given in **Figure 3**. CFPB has the power to protect consumers; however, it cannot force lending institutions to give credit. It is not a gatekeeper of the financial instruments offered. If a bank offers an exotic instrument and does not offer a standard or vanilla product, CFPB cannot ask the bank to issue the vanilla products. However, if the exotic instrument was created to harm consumers, CFPB can step in. Similarly, CFPB is not responsible for promoting products or asking consumers to purchase the offered products. Finally, CFPB cannot create a private right of action; thus, individuals cannot use CFPB to bring lawsuits against the companies that have harmed them.

Figure 2. CFPB enforcement and consumer relief

Figure 3. CFPB statutory supervision authority

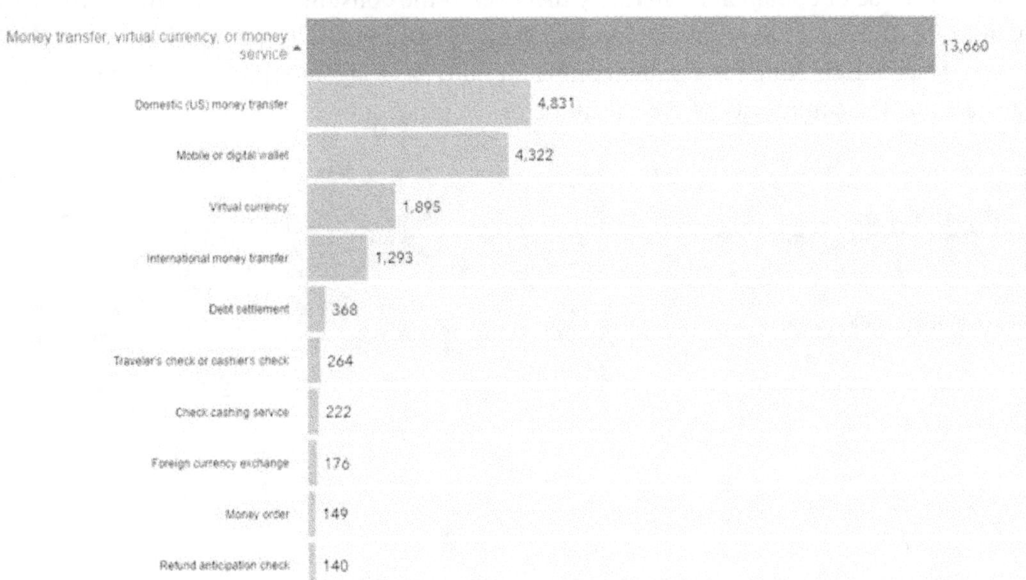

CFPB COMPLAINT DATASET

CFPB publishes the complaint data from the financial product and services consumers after verification from the financial institution on its website. This database only has complaints against companies or individuals; complaints against other regulators are not in the CFPB complaint dataset. This daily updated complaint database of CFPB is publicly available in an anonymized structure in which the identification of the financial customer is impossible. The dataset is publicly available to educate the users and the masses about the trends in financial complaints, scam behaviors, and predatory lending schemes.

The CFPB database is expanding rapidly; over an approximately 11-year period from December 2011 to October 2022, there have been about 3.02 million complaints.[4] The CFPB complaint dataset has complaints about 12 financial products and their multiple sub-product categories, as shown in **Table 2**. The dataset includes the name of the state where the complaint was generated, the date of the complaint, the defendant's name, and the date when the case was resolved. There are some indicator variables, like whether the company gave a timely response or whether the customer disputed the court's ruling. There are also some complaint quality variables, but no variable can link the data point with a victim of financial crime.

Table 2 shows the magnitude and variation of complaints across the 12 financial product categories. About 50% of the complaints were because of credit reporting, credit repair services, or other personal consumer reports, while only 1.0% were because of consumer loans, and about 1.0% were because of Payday loans, title loans, or personal loans.

This finding leads to the misconception that the US consumer loans market is more efficient, fair, and transparent. The consumers of these loans are least hurt by the predatory or deceptive behaviour of financial institutions offering these products. Compared to the US consumer loan market, the US Credit Reporting System is extraordinarily inefficient and biased toward consumers. This logic is faulty and does not match the ground reality. A smaller percentage of complaints for a product does not imply that the consumers are not harmed by the market's inefficiency or the institution's deceptive behaviour. This smaller volume of complaints can imply that even if the consumer was hurt, the consumer did not complain to the Bureau as the problem was not directly attributable to one institution but the market as a whole. Thus, interpreting the smaller complaint ratio has to be interpreted in light of the product's market share and the complexity of the execution of the product or service.

Table 2. Complaints by product on 8th November 2022

Sr	Product	Sub-products	Number of Complaints	Percentage of Complaints
1	Credit reporting, credit repair services, or other personal consumer reports	3	1,529,306	50.18%
2	Debt collection	17	449,608	14.75%
3	Mortgage	11	364,068	11.95%
4	Credit card or prepaid card	7	256,051	8.40%
5	Checking or savings account	4	139,648	4.58%
6	Bank account or service	5	86,206	2.83%
7	Student loan	3	70,910	2.33%
8	Money transfer, virtual currency, or money service	10	52,237	1.71%
9	Vehicle loan or lease	3	36604	1.20%
10	Consumer Loan	6	31,596	1.04%
11	Payday loan, title loan, or personal loan	5	30,441	1.00%
12	Other financial services	7	1,058	0.03%
	Total		3,047,713	

Data Source: CFPB

Extend this same logic to the cases when any particular defendant's or state's complaints are analysed. States with higher populations will have more complaints filed with the CFPB regardless of the credibility, fairness, and transparency of the financial institutions of that state. Similarly, a financial institution with more clients will have a more significant proportion of complaints than an institution with fewer clients.

LITERATURE REVIEW

CFPB in the US Consumer Financial Protection Ecosystem

Any policy that reduces financial hardship for consumers would lead to consumers' financial well-being which can only be achieved if the consumers have beneficial access to financial products and services (Huang *et al.*, 2022). On the other hand, a person's financial well-being would decrease directly when their access to financial products and services is reduced because of predatory behavior, misrepresentation or involvement in financial fraud. A person who is a victim of fraud loses his self-confidence in financial matters. The decrease in confidence in a person's ability to manage financial matters is even more than the loss incurred by the person facing the scam or financial fraud (Brenner *et al.*, 2020). An increase in wealth and technological innovations should decrease the incidence of fraud in the future (Karpoff, 2021); however, there is a chance that these would lead to a higher risk of systematic fraud if the system is not adequately designed to control it. The new products which are now available are complex and impact all the stakeholders. Thus, it is pertinent that everyone involved in the ecosystem of the products understands the risks and the returns associated with the products (Willis, 2017).

The financial consumer's ecosystem amplifies this risky situation. In a typical business situation, commercial affairs are based on the principle of repeat dealing and reciprocity. However, in the financial consumer's case, there are seldom repeat customers; their need for financial products is sporadic at best. A person will only engage in a house mortgage or a student loan a few times in their lives. Since the financial service providers provide the same facility to many customers, they can become sophisticated; thus, any transaction is skewed in their favor. This legal and financial asymmetry, with the suppliers being more powerful stakeholders, creates a need for consumer financial protection (Bradley, 2020).

Before CFPB, financial consumers were protected against fraud and misrepresentation through the state Tort and Contract law. The Usury statute guided any borrowing instrument's maximum legal interest rate. The State law restricted the state-owned enterprises' ability to issue financial instruments based on their solvency status (Levitin, 2012). Furthermore, as listed in **Table 3**, a mesh of Federal laws was passed and amended over fifty years in response to the changes in commercial practices and technological shifts to protect consumers (Peterson, 2015). Under all these laws and statutes, consumer protection was a private affair. Since no one agency focused on providing consumer financial protection, the mission was orphaned under the state government and subordinated to other priorities, such as the safety and soundness of the market and banks' profitability (Zywicki, 2013). This capture of the regulators with the industry's interest over the financial consumers or the public was primarily due to the revolving door employment opportunities where the policy maker could be employed by these financial lenders as soon as their term ended (Levitin, 2009). With a lack of regulatory expertise in this field and diffusion of regulation, the opportunistic lenders took advantage of regulatory arbitrage; they led the race to maximize their profits on the shoulders of financial consumers (Levitin, 2012). Thus, even before the establishment of CFPB, many civil society members were calling for a one-stop window for consumer protection with a focus on assisting consumers over all other stakeholders' needs.

Table 3. Federal statutes laws for consumer protection

Statute and Acts of Consumer Protection	**Year**
Truth in Lending Act (TILA)	1968
Equal Credit Opportunity Act (ECOA)	1974
Fair Credit Reporting Act (FCRA)	1970
Electronic Fund Transfer Act(EFTA)	1978
Real Estate Settlement Procedures Act of 1974 (RESPA)	1974
Fair Debt Collection Practices Act(FDCPA)	1977
Home Ownership and Equity Protection Act of 1994 (HOEPA)	1994
Interstate Land Sales Full Disclosure Act (ILSA)	1968
Credit Card Accountability Responsibility and Disclosure Act	2009
Military Lending Act (MLA)	2006
Secure and Fair Enforcement for Mortgage Licensing Act (SAFE ACT)	2008
Federal Trade Commission Act (FTCA)	1938
Consumer Financial Protection Act (CFPA)	**2010**

Source: Peterson, 2015

The CFPB's structure was designed by Congress when they initially formulated the plans for CFPB under the Dodd-Frank Wall Street Reform[5] and Consumer Protection Act 2010. Congress strengthened CFPB through approved regulations that made it more bureaucratic while giving it more independence (Zywicki, 2013). The agency had an independent agency status, with a single director, was a bureau of the Federal Reserve, had budgetary independence from the congregational appropriations process, had a higher pay scale for employees, and was not subjected to the regular cost-benefit analysis (Levitin, 2012). Thus, Congress also ensured that the director could not be fired at will and provided independent sources of revenue for the Bureau (McCoy, 2018). Further, Congress ensured that in the short run, the politicians could not use consumer finance for political gains at the cost of federal oversight of the financial product's consumers (Kennedy *et al.*, 2012). This emphasis on the bureaucratic structure ensured that the consumers of the financial products were safe from predatory behaviors and the manipulation of the financial institutions, which had higher bargaining power than individual consumers. The architect of CFPB's design was a vital issue with Congress because it wanted to ensure that the consumers were financially protected.

Even with independence, CFPB was still heavily regulated, as seen in **Table 4** from Levitin (2012), which shows the comparison of regulation on CFPB with other independent agencies operating in the US. It had to follow the APA[6], the FSOC[7], and the SBREFA[8] review panels reviewed all its rulings. The CFPB cannot put limits on usury, and it also cannot regulate non-financial businesses (Levitin, 2012). Finally, CFPB has a maximum annual spending limit and an annual financial audit by the government's auditing office (Zywicki, 2013).

Table 4. Comparison of oversight of CFPB and other agencies

	Environmental Protection Agency EPA	Federal Deposit Insurance Corporation FDIC	Federal Trade Commission FTC	Office of the Comptroller of the Currency OCC	Securities and Exchange Commission SEC	**CFPB**
APA Rulemaking	Yes	Yes	Yes	Yes	Yes	**Yes**
APA Adjudication	Yes	Yes	Yes	Yes	Yes	**Yes**
Budget Cap	No	No	No	No	No	**Yes**
Budget subject to Appropriation	Yes	No	Yes	No	Yes	**No**
SBREFA Review	Yes	No	No	No	No	**Yes**
FSOC Veto	No	No	No	No	No	**Yes**
Annual government Audit	No	No	No	No	No	**Yes**
Presidential removal of director						
-without Cause	Yes	No	No	No	No	**No**
-with congressional oversight	Yes	Yes	Yes	Yes	Yes	**Yes**
-with Moral Suasion by administration	Yes	Yes	Yes	Yes	Yes	**Yes**

Source: Levitin, 2012

The performance effectiveness of CFPB effectiveness is debatable. During the first six years of its inception, CFPB had an excellent track record under its first director Richard Cordray. It protected consumers from predatory lending and even decreased the discriminatory practices of lending institutions (Li, 2022). The trust-based relationship with financial institutions was accentuated. Banks in low-trust regions had to decrease their fees compared to banks in high-trust regions after CFPB origination and dissemination of the complaint database. This pricing discrepancy implies that the presence of the authority affected how banks interacted with their customers (Hayes *et al.*, 2021). Furthermore, evidence exists that consumers have become savvier after the complaint database was made public. Even when the banks respond more promptly, consumer complaints and post-complaint disputes have increased (Bhattacharya, 2022). However, the success of the first six years of CFPB led it to come under the line of fire from the Republican-controlled Congress, the Trumps administration, and the courts. When all structural change amendments failed, the new director Mick Mulvaney focused on changing the rules, supervision, and enforcement procedure of CFPB from within the institution, thereby rolling back the CFPB compliance oversight and giving breathing room to the financial institutions (McCoy, 2018).

However, the single-director-independent CFPB structure has been under widespread political opposition. Presidential Contender Ted Cruz called CFPB a “runaway agency” (Hiltzik, 2015), while another contender Carly Fiorina, called it “classic crony capitalism” with “no congressional oversight” (Jacobson, 2015). CFPB work has been summarized as a “nanny state mechanism” (Carson,2015) that "continuously oversteps its bounds" (Ratcliffe, 2015). This opposition to CFPB exists because the laws and rulings of the CFPB have a direct effect on the bottom line of the financial institutions. In response to the change in their earnings, the financial institutions countered the situation by turning pro-business politicians against the CFPB (Bradley, 2020). Unfortunately, such changes do not only play out in the political arena. Complaining behavior is part of social identity. The application of social identity theory implies that people are more likely to complain to CFPB if they associate with the democrats and are less likely to complain to CFPB if they associate with the republicans and view the other party's actions unfavorably. Thus, Cho *et al.* (2023) used the student loan complaining behavior to show that the states which were more prop democratic had significantly more complaints lodged to CFPB compared to the pro-republican states in the same duration. Thus, the overall success and efficiency of CFPB across states have been affected by the political dissension around it.

CFPB is effective in two ways. The first success factor relates to its direct function; CFPB exists as a bridge between the financial institutions offering products and services and the consumers using these services. Consumers can complain on the CFPB portal if they have a complaint. Foohey (2017) and Ayres *et al.* (2013) gave examples of successful cases of CFPB and analyzed the timeliness of response. The second benefit of CFPB to the public is indirect; the consumers are at least satisfied that an independent third party hears their complaints, and someone is working towards resolving their issues at the macro level (Porter, 2012). Many researchers have suggested ways to improve the CFPB complaint database management and help the CFPB make proactive, effective decisions using the database. Shivaprasad (2019) suggested a qualitative text classification model through which more information can be extracted from the qualitative notes to the complaints. Ayres *et al.* (2013) recommended ways to further improve the timeliness of CFPB response.

Another case study in point is the spread of the COVID-19 pandemic and the resulting business activity decline, which led to thousands being unemployed and facing a sharp decline in income. In such a scenario, there was also a financial crisis apart from the health and macroeconomic crisis. Financial scams were on the rise (Cordray *et al.*, 2020). For instance, scammers tried to take advantage of the uncertainty by conning the people. Such cons included offering unauthorized COVID test kits, taking payments for phony COVID-19 tests and vaccinations, and stealing personal care information by deceiving the masses by impersonating government officials. Furthermore, such predatory behavior included raising funds in the name of actual or alleged charities. Another trick used in those high uncertainty periods was an identity scam. The scam callers first claimed familial association, such as a grandchild, friend, or relative. Once the person had accepted that the call was from a relative, the scammers then established a need for immediate fund transfer because the relative was either stranded or had to pay for COVID treatment. In all such scams, the imposters collected money from hundreds of unsuspecting US citizens. In such turmoil, CFPB should have taken aggressive action to reduce widespread consumer harm. CFPB should have collected and disseminated information in four key areas, which would reduce mass panic and decrease systematic risk. These four areas are foreclosure prevention, oversight of debt collectors, forbearance of non-mortgage debt and supervision of credit reporting agencies (Cordray *et al.*, 2020).

However, in the pro-business setup of Trump's regime, the complaints from low socioeconomic zip codes, with a higher proportion of poor and minority borrowers and a higher proportion of Afro-Americans, were less likely to be resolved. A similar difference existed in the distribution of restitutions; the complaints from higher socioeconomic zip codes were more likely to get restitution (Haendler & Heimer 2021). Furthermore, retail banks provided poor customer service, misrepresentation, predatory pricing and mis-selling in lower socioeconomic zip codes (Begley & Purnanandam, 2021). Thus, while these people from lower socioeconomic zip codes get worse services than higher socioeconomic zip codes, their complaints are also not resolved. Another piece of evidence against CFPB's efficiency comes from the scams involving military veterans. Veterans are significantly more likely to be scammed (Shadel & Pak, 2017) even when CFPB emphasizes complaints from older citizens and veterans.

Fraud is the blood in the Mortgage Loan Ecosystem

In the mortgage industry, there are numerous instances of fraud. Reurink (2018) differentiates between frauds because of false financial disclosures, financial scams and fraudulent financial mis-selling. These frauds occur because of the increasing complexity of the transactions due to legal, financial, and technological innovations. As per Carswell and Bachtel (2009), in the mortgage industry, there are two prevalent types of fraud: fraud for property and fraud for profit. Fraud for property focuses on situations where a mortgage loan is given to high credit-risk personnel. In such cases, the families do not have the capacity to pay their obligations and thus are set up for failure. The originator is paid upfront and gets the maximum benefit from such deals. The only reason such deals are allowed is that there is a social justice connotation, as in this way, some underprivileged families can afford and maintain a house. On the other hand, fraud-for-profit schemes are primarily predatory. Most such schemes involve the manipulative behavior of industry insiders (Carswell & Bachtel, 2009). **Table 5** lists some of the fraud-for-profit schemes. These are the schemes against which CFPB is open to hearing complaints.

The underlying property is the base on which a financial fraud pyramid, **Figure 4**, can be laid, as explained by Reurink (2018). Every step in the mortgage ecosystem can lead to potentially fraudulent activities. At the base, the borrowers were exposed to fraud for housing schemes and the mortgage-based financial intermediaries' predatory lending behavior. Then these intermediaries passed the risk onto the banks and other lending institutions by planning and executing fraud-for-profit schemes.

When the banks write instruments with the mortgages as underlying, they misrepresent information about portfolio formation and risk to the security underwriters. Through securitization, nonprime and liar's loans were packaged with prime loans and then bundled into residential mortgage-backed loans (RMBS). The collateralized debt obligations (CDOs) were the riskier tranches of RMBS and had high credit risk; however, even the independent credit rating agencies gave them investment-grade ratings (Griffin, 2021). Since the originators could sell almost all such securitized mortgages, they bared minimum prepayment risk, interest rate risk and default rate risk, which were all passed on to the investors (Edwards, 2020). Since the underwriters were buying or underwriting such originate to distribute securities, to pass the risk forward as quickly as possible to increase their turnover, they also started being financially negligent about the underlying. Thus, they passed on this misrepresentation risk to the investors, especially the institutional investors. Financial fraudulent mis-selling is possible because of the informational asymmetry between the underwriters and the investors. This asymmetry in mis-selling is not because of the transaction but because of the speculative and misleading statements about the future expected performance of the portfolio in a manner that the investor may feel the product is suitable for its risk profile need when it is not (Reurink, 2018).

While the complaints from the lower socioeconomic zip codes are predominantly about debt collection and credit reporting, the mortgage complaints are higher from the higher income zones (Gimpel, 2021). In such a system, where risk is part of the ecosystem, the consumers are more sensitive to the risk, and a higher number of complaints is a proxy for higher risk. Banks and institutions with more mortgage-related complaints have seen a reduction in mortgage applications. Thus, CFPB provided market discipline and transparency to the ecosystem (Dou & Roh, 2020).

Table 5. Common fraud for profit schemes

Fraud offense	Description
Illegal flipping	Seller inflates the value of the property using an illegitimate appraisal. Once the mortgage is delivered, the home is then sold with the mortgage taken over by another buyer, who unwittingly believes that the house is of higher quality than it truly is. Ultimately, the buyer is left to repay a high mortgage on a property whose market value exceeds the mortgage value, a situation which usually results in default.
Real estate title fraud	Through identity theft, a mortgage fraud perpetrator is able to secure a mortgage loan using an assumed identity and presumably an untarnished credit file and history.
Straw buyers	Similar to the title fraud offense, a straw buyer is someone who has knowingly given credit information to an interested party for a fee, usually totalling several thousand dollars. Months after the mortgage fraud has been committed, the straw buyer is left with the outstanding mortgage, much to his or her surprise.
Silent second mortgage	Buyer of the property borrows the down payment through an undisclosed second mortgage (usually through the seller). If the second mortgage is not recorded, this can allow the seller to inflate the actual value of the house, beyond its market value.
Foreclosure rescue/equity skimming	This situation occurs when a financially-strapped homeowner is urged to sign over the deed of the property to a "specialist" who can help sell the house quickly, sometimes with an up-front fee involved. The rescue buyer may collect rents on the property without making any mortgage payments. This forces the lender to foreclose on the property, holding the original owner and mortgage holder liable in the process.
Air loans	The property in question is either misrepresented, does not exist, or is not what the loan says it is. The dishonest broker fabricates borrowers and properties, creates accounts for payments, and maintains custodial accounts for escrows.
Double sales scam	This form of fraud occurs in areas where the recording of the transaction takes several weeks to several months. In essence, the owner of the house (who may operate under the guise of a shell company) takes advantage of this delay in deed recording to sell the home more than once. When the ruse is uncovered, actual title to the property becomes cloudy as a result.

Source: Carswell and Bachtel, 2009

ANALYSIS OF THE DATABASE

CFPB classifies complaints on two pivots. The first categorization is regarding products and then divides these products into different sub-product categories related to the product. The second categorization concerns the issues faced by consumers. While credit reporting, credit repair services and other personal consumer reports account for about 50% of the complaints, there are only three subcategories, with 90% of the complaints of the category focused on credit reporting. Furthermore, this category was started in 2017, and prior to 2017, the complaints about this category could have been labelled as credit reporting or even other personal services. Thus, a full-duration analysis of this category would understate the results. Similarly, the second biggest category, debt collection, started in June 2013 and has the same problem discussed above.

In this analysis, complaints against mortgages are considered. About 12% of complaints are due to mortgages. Furthermore, mortgages as a category label have been in the CFPB database since the start. Further, it has six subcategories and a rich dataset to analyze the CFPB performance. On average, from December 2011 to October 2013, there were 2779 monthly complaints about Mortgages with a standard deviation of 884 complaints. **Figure 5** shows the variation in Mortgage-related complaints over time. The average monthly complaints were more in the first five years since CFPB's inception, and since then, the average monthly complaints have decreased.

Figure 4. Frauds in Mortgage Ecosystem

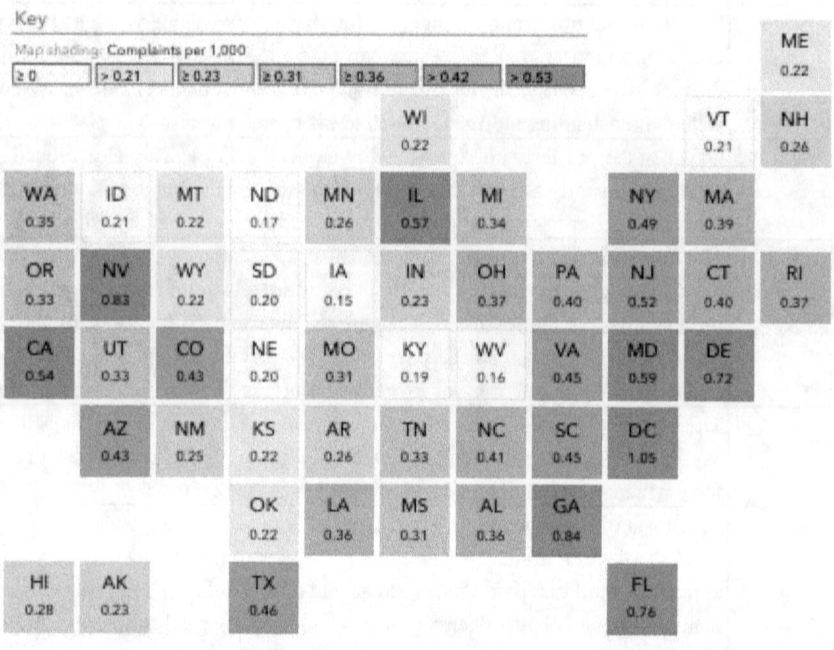

Figure 5. Number of mortgage complaints across time

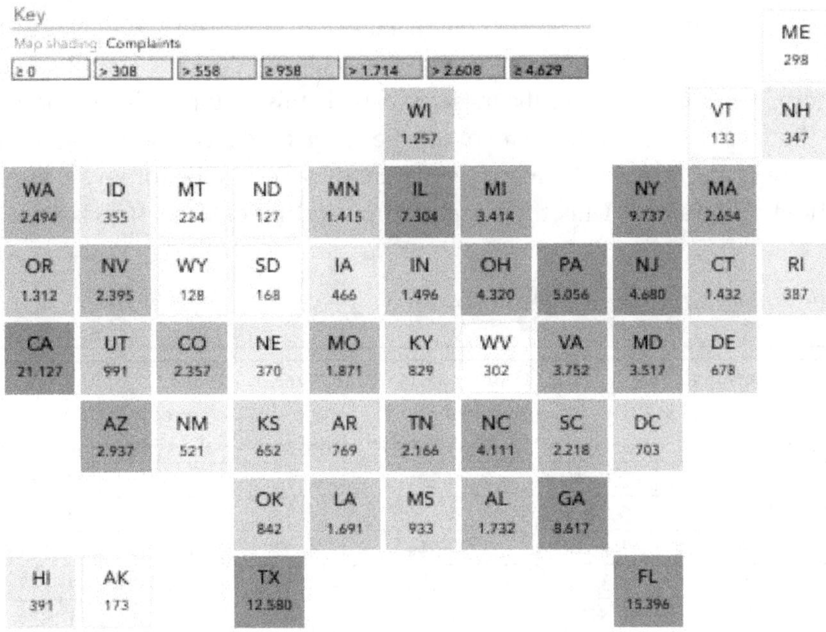

The mortgage complaints are related to six sub-product categories. **Table 6** shows the subcategory complaints as a percentage of total mortgage complaints over the years. About 42% of the mortgage-related complaints concern conventional home mortgages, the more vanilla type of mortgage option available to the consumer. In any given year, the complaints about conventional mortgages are consistently between 3.75% and 4.0% of all the complaints.

The number of complaints against other specialized subcategories of mortgages follows. The second most complaints are about FHA mortgages, backed by the Federal Housing Administration (FHA) and issued by FHA-approved institutions. FHA mortgage is for consumers with lower credit ratings and is a special type of product for the lower strata of society. After FHA mortgage, the following higher number of complaints are regarding Home Equity Loans (HELOAN) or lines of credit (HELOC), secured loans that keep the house as a mortgage, and money borrowed against the equity the borrower owns in the house. Unlike a conventional mortgage, where the lender takes a loan to buy or construct, the HELOAN or HELOC loan is taken against the house's equity. VA mortgages are guaranteed by the United States Department of Veteran Affairs. The fewest subcategory complaints are about reverse mortgages, a liquidation deal in which the elderly convert their home equity into an income stream.

The percentage of complaints about these mortgage products is consistent with the origination of the mortgages. As per the Home Mortgage Disclosure Act, data collected and disseminated by CFPB, about 19 million conventional mortgages originated in 2021, as opposed to 1.27 million FHA mortgages, 1.19 million VA mortgages and 0.85 million reverse mortgages. Thus, the more mortgages sold in the subcategory, the more complaints registered with CFPB.

Not all mortgage complaints were directed toward banks. **Table 7** shows the mortgage-related complaints from different financial service providers. 20.22% of the conventional mortgage complaint were against banks, and about 38.5% were against specialized mortgage companies. HELOAN and HELOC mortgage owners also complained most about the banks. However, for all other Mortgage categories, the specialized mortgage institutions have the maximum number of complaints, followed by the banks. This high volume of complaints against banks and mortgage companies could be justified in two ways. First, the banks and mortgage companies have the most business in this sector, while the Non-Banking Credit and Lending Institutions have a smaller share of the mortgage products industry. Secondly, the number of people who invest in mortgages is far more significant than the number of investors of products with mortgage-based underlying assets. Thus, the complaint from institutional investors is comparatively fewer.

Table 6. The sub-product categories over the years

Row Labels	Conventional home mortgage	FHA mortgage	Home equity loan or line of credit (HELOC)	Other type of mortgage	Reverse mortgage	VA mortgage	Grand Total
2011	0.13%	0.03%	0.02%	0.16%	0.00%	0.01%	0.35%
2012	2.77%	0.74%	0.41%	6.35%	0.06%	0.14%	10.47%
2013	4.03%	1.20%	0.53%	7.51%	0.08%	0.21%	13.57%
2014	3.91%	1.34%	0.62%	5.59%	0.10%	0.24%	11.80%
2015	3.94%	1.51%	0.66%	5.07%	0.13%	0.32%	11.63%
2016	3.76%	1.50%	0.75%	4.83%	0.15%	0.39%	11.39%
2017	3.87%	1.11%	0.56%	2.39%	0.13%	0.33%	8.40%
2018	3.85%	0.94%	0.47%	1.06%	0.10%	0.32%	6.75%
2019	3.86%	0.94%	0.40%	0.57%	0.10%	0.37%	6.24%
2020	4.40%	0.99%	0.37%	0.44%	0.07%	0.51%	6.77%
2021	4.74%	1.09%	0.33%	0.50%	0.11%	0.52%	7.29%
2022	3.35%	0.93%	0.27%	0.29%	0.10%	0.40%	5.35%
Grand Total	**42.61%**	**12.34%**	**5.39%**	**34.77%**	**1.13%**	**3.76%**	**100.00%**

Data Source: CFPB

Table 7. The mortgage subproduct categories complaints against different financial service providers

Type of Company	Conventional home mortgage	FHA mortgage	Home equity loan or line of credit (HELOC)	Other type of mortgage	Reverse mortgage	VA mortgage	Total
Bank	20.22%	24.48%	40.11%	31.13%	12.40%	13.08%	25.26%
Credit or lending Institution	7.83%	8.02%	6.38%	4.13%	0.41%	12.51%	6.58%
Investment or Holding Institution	7.71%	3.50%	6.91%	6.96%	3.66%	5.15%	6.75%
Mortgage Company	25.73%	31.67%	13.35%	21.09%	43.80%	38.30%	24.86%
Other	38.51%	32.33%	33.25%	36.68%	39.72%	30.96%	36.56%
Total	**100.00%**	**100.00%**	**100.00%**	**100.00%**	**100.00%**	**100.00%**	**100.00%**

Data Source: CFPB

Table 8 shows the top ten banks with the highest percentage of mortgage products-related complaints against each. Of the banks, the most mortgage products related complaints are against Bank of America, followed by Citi Bank. The Banks with the most complaints are big, famous banks with a high trust factor from the customers. This table suggests that the bigger banks have more leeway in customer interaction. However, like all the previous results, a caveat also exists. There is a possibility that the higher complaint volume could be correlated with more transaction volume.

For about 68.7% of the mortgage-related complaints, the alleged company did not provide a reply or did not permit a public reply. For another 18.61% of the complaints, CFPB did not post a public reply even when the company granted the permission since the reply had a chance to affect the market negatively. For the remaining complaints, the top four public replies are summarized in **Table 9**. For 30.86% of the conventional mortgage-related complaints, the defending companies argued that they followed the law and acted appropriately; therefore, they did not try to misrepresent the information or scam the customer. Another 3.7% of conventional mortgage complaints were claimed to be isolated errors, while 2.75% were brushed off as misunderstandings.

Table 8. Top ten banks with most mortgage related complaints

Bank	Conventional home mortgage	FHA mortgage	Home equity loan or line of credit (HELOC)	Reverse mortgage	VA mortgage	Total
BANK OF AMERICA, NATIONAL ASSOCIATION	44.19%	47.64%	41.17%	24.07%	34.75%	50.48%
CIT BANK, NATIONAL ASSOCIATION	13.82%	9.47%	11.64%	69.47%	12.07%	13.04%
U.S. BANCORP	9.04%	12.36%	8.09%	1.17%	9.78%	7.96%
PNC BANK N.A.	7.84%	4.35%	14.25%	0.39%	6.31%	6.67%
FLAGSTAR BANK, FSB	5.01%	8.58%	0.70%	0.39%	12.85%	4.04%
SUNTRUST BANKS, INC.	4.23%	3.24%	3.43%	0.78%	4.19%	4.04%
M&T BANK CORPORATION	3.19%	6.12%	1.78%	1.57%	8.16%	3.31%
SANTANDER BANK, NATIONAL ASSOCIATION	1.56%	0.37%	3.23%	0.20%	0.17%	1.22%
HUNTINGTON NATIONAL BANK, THE	1.13%	0.78%	1.57%	0.00%	1.01%	0.87%
ARVEST BANK GROUP, INC.	1.12%	0.21%	0.06%	0.20%	0.22%	0.68%
Total	**100.00%**	**100.00%**	**100.00%**	**100.00%**	**100.00%**	**100.00%**

Data Source: CFPB

Table 9. Top four company responses for mortgage products

Mortgage Product	Company believes it acted appropriately as authorized by contract or law	Company believes complaint is the result of an isolated error	Company believes the complaint is the result of a misunderstanding	Company believes complaint represents an opportunity for improvement to	Total
Conventional home mortgage	30.86%	3.70%	2.75%	1.91%	50.07%
Other type of mortgage	12.77%	0.92%	0.86%	0.39%	26.74%
FHA mortgage	5.88%	0.76%	0.71%	0.61%	12.94%
VA mortgage	2.97%	0.37%	0.28%	0.35%	5.21%
Home equity loan or line of credit (HELOC)	1.47%	0.14%	0.12%	0.09%	4.00%
Reverse mortgage	0.63%	0.02%	0.13%	0.01%	1.05%
Total	54.58%	5.92%	4.85%	3.35%	100.00%

Data Source: CFPB

Table 10. The relief provided with respect to mortgage products

Mortgage Product	Closed with relief	Closed without relief	Unclosed	Total
Conventional home mortgage	3.36%	39.18%	0.06%	42.61%
FHA mortgage	0.95%	11.37%	0.02%	12.34%
Home equity loan or line of credit (HELOC)	0.66%	4.71%	0.02%	5.39%
Other type of mortgage	2.79%	31.97%	0.01%	34.77%
Reverse mortgage	0.03%	1.10%	0.00%	1.13%
VA mortgage	0.30%	3.45%	0.01%	3.76%
Total	8.09%	91.78%	0.12%	100.00%

Data Source: CFPB

Therefore, the public has to rely on a small set of resolutions and make their decisions to complain or take the company to court based on the minimal set of complaints that have a resolution posted online. This lack of serious commitment from the alleged company to reduce and facilitate the customers also translates into the minimal relief provided to the customers. The company could accept a problem existed that led to the complaint or refuse the existence of any such problem. If the mistake is accepted, the company can provide monetary or non-monetary relief against the complaint. On the other hand, the company could accept its mistake and provide an explanation or an apology without providing any restitution to the customer. **Table 10** shows the trend of providing relief for mortgage-related complaints. In 91.78% of the total mortgage-related complaints, no relief was provided. Relief was only provided in 8.09% of the cases, of which about 3.4% were related to conventional mortgages. In all such cases, monetary relief was only provided against 3.08% of mortgage-related complaints.

Of these limited situations where CFPB successfully got relief for financial consumers, the performance of the first six years outperformed the relief-generating ability in the next six years. **Figure 6** shows the trend of CFPB getting monetary relief for financial product consumers of mortgage products over the years. From 2012 to 2017, CFPB performed better. However, after the regime change and under the pressure of Trump's pro-business policies, CFPB did not provide the consumers with the same safeguard it initially provided.

Figure 6. Monetary relief provided over the years

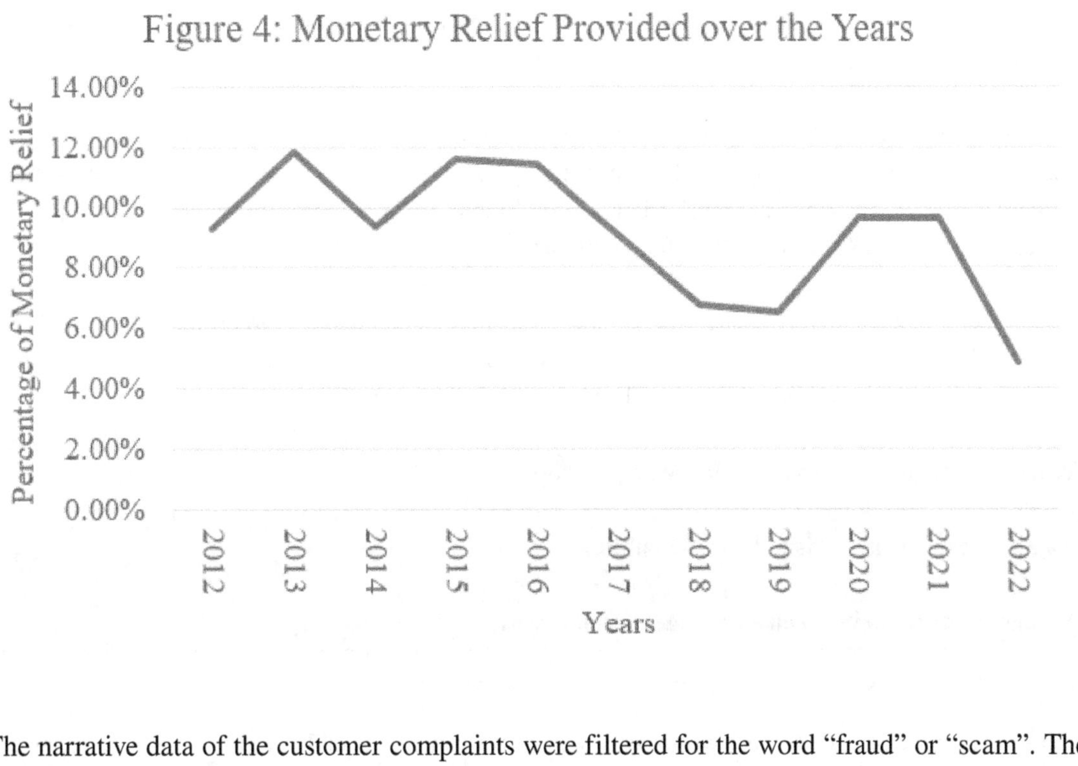

The narrative data of the customer complaints were filtered for the word "fraud" or "scam". There were 112734 complaints in total in the CFPB complaint database with either or both the words used in the narrative. In only 5% of these instances, these words were used in conjunction with a mortgage. Furthermore, there are 2372 complaints about predatory lending during mortgage origination, 311 about forgery, 239 about perjury, 1568 of illegal foreclosure of a mortgage, and 1403 complaints about identity theft, 1154 about misrepresentation, apart from many other indicative complaints. A typical homeowners complaint launched on May 8, 2020, against PNC Bank with complaint Number 3643294 is given in **Table 11**. Any unique identifier of the customer has been replaced with XXXX by CFPB.

Table 11. An account of scam narrative during COVID

I am a single homeowner, solely responsible for my mortgage. I unexpectantly became unemployed due to no fault of my own. I requested a forbearance and received it. After the forbearance period, I started making payments again. In desperation, I had to take jobs that were not suitable for me. I lost my job again, and then I started having symptoms of COVID, and I have not been able to look for new employment. My mortgage servicer started the foreclosure process. They gave me false hope that they wanted to help me. Their solution is a scam that takes advantage of a person's hardship. I have been paying for my mortgage since XXXX. I used the money I made from the home I owned since XXXX to help pay a down payment on this loan. So, everything I've paid as a homeowner is tied to this home and loan. The servicer's or XXXX XXXX solution is to modify the loan to a 40-year loan. That is a scam that will never allow a person with a mortgage to get on their feet and one day own their home. It's unethical and needs to be regulated and scrutinized. Congress set up XXXX XXXX. There should be oversight into this type of homeownership scam. How can this be allowed? Why is there no help for a person in my situation? I do not want to lose my home, but a 40-year mortgage is ridiculous. I'd be XXXX before I could pay it back. The money that goes toward housing counsellors is a joke. It has wasted money that would be better spent with an Ethics committee overseeing the housing industry and services. XXXX and PNC are using unscrupulous immoral practices to hang desperate homeowners. Where is Congress? Where is help? Where is hope? It's all a scam! This needs to be made public. No one deserves to be taken advantage of in this way."

Interestingly, before 2014, these words were sparingly used; however, later, these words were repeatedly used in the complaints to describe the problem. In this regard, CFPB has successfully raised consumer awareness about Frauds and Scams that consumers could face. Thus, the consumers are more willing to report suspected frauds or scam and even describe it as such in the narrative.

Table 12 lists the percentage of fraud complaints against the different financial institutions for each mortgage product. Of the complaints about a bank with a "scam" or "fraud" narrative, 34.12% are about conventional home mortgages. Across conventional mortgages, the highest fraud narrative was about non-banking credit or lending institutions scamming their customers. This relationship indicates that even though the mortgage product portfolio of Non-Banking Credit and Lending Institutions is smaller than the portfolios of banks and specialized mortgage institutions, they tend to have a higher percentage of scam or fraud complaints, indicating that their behavior may be predatory.

Table 12. Fraud narrative by mortgage products and financial institutions

Mortgage Products	Bank	Credit	Investment	Mortgage	other	Total
Conventional home mortgage	34.12%	50.69%	48.69%	44.10%	44.89%	42.61%
FHA mortgage	11.96%	15.04%	6.40%	15.72%	10.91%	12.34%
Home equity loan or line of credit (HELOC)	8.56%	5.23%	5.53%	2.90%	4.90%	5.39%
Other type of mortgage	42.85%	21.82%	35.89%	29.50%	34.88%	34.77%
Reverse mortgage	0.56%	0.07%	0.61%	1.99%	1.23%	1.13%
VA mortgage	1.95%	7.15%	2.87%	5.79%	3.18%	3.76%
Total	100.00%	100.00%	100.00%	100.00%	100.00%	100.00%

Data Source: CFPB

Similarly, about 48.69% of the frauds reported in the investment and holding institutions category are for conventional home mortgage products. These transactions reflect the misrepresentation between the lending institutions, the underwriters, and the securitizes.

Finally, using textual analysis of keywords from all the complaint narratives, the indicative words of "Fraud for Profit" schemes were analyzed. While the textual analysis is highly informative about the "Fraud for Profit" schemes, it should be noted that while some narrations fit a general category, others could be classified in more than one way. In all such cases, judgements were made based on the narration and other information. So, there are chances that a few of the complaints are mis-specified; however, for this work, the general inferences are essential and thus, the slight loss of accuracy is accepted.

Figure 5 shows the proportion of "Fraud for Profit" schemes for mortgage-related fraud and scam narratives. Most mortgage consumers complained about Foreclosure Rescue type schemes, which ultimately led the homeowners to take extra risks and offer to pay for a longer duration, in most cases, at a higher rate. This scheme was most prevalent during COVID when the homeowners had a challenging time making their payments and were trapped by their mortgage provider or consultant.

The second biggest scheme complained about was Identity theft leading to real estate titles frauds. Unlike the Foreclosure Rescue scheme, this was more prevalent even before COVID, though there was a slight post-COVID increase in complaints referring to Real Estate Title Frauds.

Figure 7. Narrative for fraud-for-profit schemes

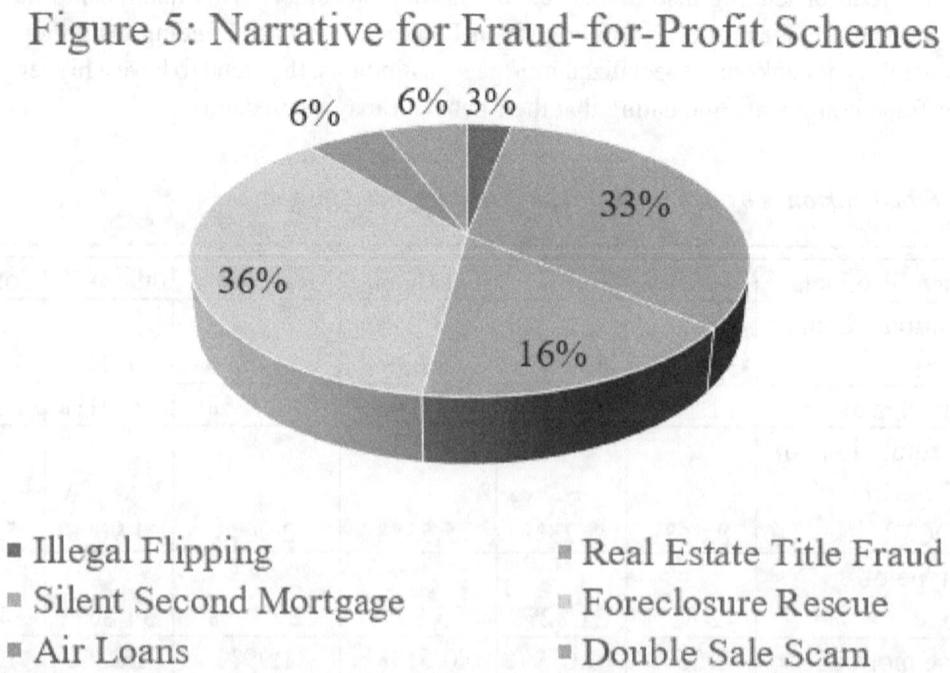

As per **Table 13**, of the fraud or scam cases, only about 6.46% were closed with any relief, while the other 93.54% of cases were closed without relief. Of the cases closed with relief, about 1.88% of the customers disputed the company's response and dragged the case. On the other hand, most of the complainers did not pursue the case if they received any relief. On the other hand, of those who did not get relief, a majority did not contest the future, and the dispute ended. A third of the people did not agree with the company's first response and disputed it.

Table 13. Fraud, relief, and consumer dispute

Customer Disputed the Company's response	Closed with relief	Closed without relief	Total
No Dispute	4.58%	56.56%	61.15%
Dispute	1.88%	36.98%	38.85%
Total	6.46%	93.54%	100.00%

Data Source: CFPB

Table 13 first strengthens the association that CFPB did not effectively get relief for the customers even if the customers self-reported a scam or a fraud. However, the customer's tendency not to dispute the company's verdict and end the complaint also indicates that for the US financial consumers, CFPB is an organization they trust would listen to their grievances and ensure that the company responds to their problems. However, they do not expect CFPB to get closure or any relief for them; thus, they prefer not to continue the dispute.

CONCLUSION

The well-being of financial consumers is essential for a solid financial system to function. Some players in the industry would use their strong bargaining power to prey on the rights of the weaker financial consumers. For the protection of consumers, the US has formed the Consumer Financial Protection Bureau (CFPB). The Bureau works towards increasing transparency in financial transactions and reducing informational asymmetry. CFPB is working towards creating awareness about predatory behavior and disrupting the financial system players from engaging in fraudulent activities.

The complaints against the Mortgage related services providers in the CFPB complaint database were analyzed. Three key findings are reported. *Firstly*, banks are less prone to fraudulent activities than non-banking credit and lending institutions when they offer mortgage-based products. Banks have the most complaint concerning mortgage products; however, fraud and scams are not usually associated with Banks. On the other hand, Non-banking Credit and Lending Institutions have a smaller portfolio in the mortgage market; however, the number of frauds and scams is much higher. This finding indicates that predatory behavior is more dominant in Non-Banking Credit and Lending Institutions. *Secondly*, fraudulent activities and scamming behavior increased during the COVID. Evidence of Fraud for Profit Schemes was found using textual analysis of the complaint's narrative. The people took benefit of others' misery by engaging in manipulative Fraud-for-Profit schemes or variants of schemes. The most identified schemes were Foreclosure Rescue and Real Estate Title fraud. *Thirdly,* the CFPB has generated awareness among financial consumers, who have become savvier. However, at the same time, CFPB has failed to get relief for the customer, and over time, the amount of monetary and non-monetary relief is decreasing. The consumers have accepted that CFPB will make their complaints audible to the critical stakeholders while it would not get them any financial relief.

DECLARATION

The authors declare that the manuscript follows ethical standards and there are no potential conflicts of interest with respect to the research, authorship and/or publication of this chapter.

DISCLAIMER

The contents and views of this chapter are expressed by the authors in their personal capacities. It is not necessary for the Editor and the Publisher to agree with these viewpoints, and they are not responsible for any duty of care in this regard.

ACKNOWLEDGMENT

The authors extend sincere gratitude to

• The Editor and the International Editorial Advisory Board (IEAB) of this book who initially desk reviewed, arranged a rigorous double/triple blind review process, and conducted a thorough, minute, and critical final review before accepting the chapter for publication.

• All anonymous reviewers who provided very constructive feedbacks for thorough revision, improvement, extension, and fine tuning of the chapter.

• All colleagues, assistants and well-wishers who assisted to complete this task.

REFERENCES

Ayres, I., Lingwall, J., & Steinway, S. (2013). Skeletons in the database: An early analysis of the CFPB's consumer complaints. *Fordham Journal of Corporate and Financial Law*, *19*, 343. doi:10.2139srn.2295157

Begley, T. A., & Purnanandam, A. (2021). Colour and credit: Race, regulation, and the quality of financial services. *Journal of Financial Economics*, *141*(1), 48–65. doi:10.1016/j.jfineco.2021.03.001

Bhattacharya, A. (2022). Consumer, bank, and stock market reaction to CFPB's complaint data disclosure. *Journal of Financial Services Marketing*, 1–18. doi:10.105741264-022-00143-2

Bradley, C. G. (2020). The consumer protection ecosystem: Law, Norms, and technology. *Denver Law Review*, *97*(1), 35.

Brenner, L., Meyll, T., Stolper, O., & Walter, A. (2020). Consumer fraud victimization and financial well-being. *Journal of Economic Psychology*, *76*, 102243. doi:10.1016/j.joep.2019.102243

Carson, B. S. (2015, July 28). The perfect example of government overreach. *The Washington Times*. Retrieved from https://www.washingtontimes.com/news/2015/jul/28/ben-carson-perfect-example-government-overreach/

Carswell, A. T., & Bachtel, D. C. (2009). Mortgage fraud: A risk factor analysis of affected communities. *Crime, Law, and Social Change*, *52*(4), 347–364. doi:10.100710611-008-9186-5

CFPB. (2022). *Resources to help you avoid scams*. Retrieved from https://www.consumerfinance.gov/coronavirus/avoiding-scams/

Cho, J., Krush, M. T., Walker, D., & Nowlin, E. L. (2023). An Examination of Student Loans, Partisanship and Complaining Behavior: The Consumer Financial Protection Bureau. *Journal of Consumer Satisfaction, Dissatisfaction & Complaining Behavior*, *36*(1), 1–18.

Cordray, R., Thompson, D. E., & Peterson, C. L. (2020). *Consumer Financial Protection in the COVID-19 Crisis: An Emergency Agenda* (University of Utah College of Law Research Paper No. 370). University of Utah. Retrieved from https://papers.ssrn.com/sol3/papers.cfm?abstract_id=3569357

Dou, Y., & Roh, Y. (2020). Public Disclosure and Consumer Financial Protection. SSRN *Electronic Journal*. Retrieved from https://papers.ssrn.com/sol3/papers.cfm?abstract_id=3647491

Edwards, M. A. (2020). The Concept and federal crime of mortgage fraud. *The American Criminal Law Review, 57*, 57.

Foohey, P. (2017). Calling on the CFPB for help: Telling stories and consumer protection. *Law and Contemporary Problems, 80*(3), 177–210.

Gimpel, J. G. (2021). Citizen contacting in response to crisis: Voicing grievances to the Consumer Financial Protection Bureau. *American Politics Research, 49*(2), 198–214. doi:10.1177/1532673X20962414

Griffin, J. M. (2021). Ten years of evidence: Was fraud a force in the financial crisis? *Journal of Economic Literature, 59*(4), 1293–1321. doi:10.1257/jel.20201602

Haendler, C., & Heimer, R. (2021). The Financial Restitution Gap in Consumer Finance: Insights from Complaints Filed with the CFPB. SSRN *Electronic Journal*. Retrieved from https://papers.ssrn.com/sol3/papers.cfm?abstract_id=3766485 doi:10.2139/ssrn.3766485

Halvorsen, J. L., & Møkkelgård, P. J. (2018). *Financial literacy and other determinants of consumer complaint behavior: An empirical study utilizing the CFPB's complaint database*. Retrieved from https://openaccess.nhh.no/nhh-xmlui/handle/11250/2585500

Hayes, R. M., Jiang, F., & Pan, Y. (2021). Voice of the customers: Local trust culture and consumer complaints to the CFPB. *Journal of Accounting Research, 59*(3), 1077–1121. doi:10.1111/1475-679X.12364

Hiltzik, M. (2015, July 23). Consumer protection: Why do republicans hate the CFPB so much? *Los Angeles Times*. Retrieved from https://www.latimes.com/business/hiltzik/la-fi-mh-cfpb-republicans-20150723-column.html

Huang, J., Sherraden, M., Sherraden, M. S., & Johnson, L. (2022). Effective finance to increase financial well-being for low-income families: Empirical examination and policy implications. *The Journal of Consumer Affairs, 56*(4), 1638–1657. doi:10.1111/joca.12484

Jacobson, L. (2015, Nov 14). Carly Fiorina Says Consumer Financial Protection Bureau has 'No Congressional Oversight. *Politifact*. Retrieved from https://www.politifact.com/factchecks/2015/nov/14/carly-fiorina/carly-fiorina-says-consumer-financial-protection-b/

Karpoff, J. M. (2021). The future of financial fraud. *Journal of Corporate Finance, 66*, 101694. doi:10.1016/j.jcorpfin.2020.101694

Kennedy, L. J., McCoy, P. A., & Bernstein, E. (2011). The consumer financial protection bureau: Financial regulation for the twenty-first century. *Cornell Law Review, 97*, 1141.

Levitin, A. J. (2009). Hydraulic Regulation: Regulating Credit Markets Upstream. *Yale Journal on Regulation, 26*, 143.

Levitin, A. J. (2012). The consumer financial protection bureau: An introduction [Review]. *Banking and Finance Law, 32*, 321.

Li, X. (2022). *Bank Competition and Entrepreneurial Gaps: Evidence from Bank Deregulation*. Royal Economic Society. Retrieved from https://res.org.uk/wp-content/uploads/2022/11/11.pdf

McCoy, P. A. (2018). Inside job: The assault on the structure of the Consumer Financial Protection Bureau. *Minnesota Law Review*, *103*, 2543.

Peterson, C. L. (2015). Consumer Financial Protection Bureau law enforcement: An empirical review. *Tulane Law Review*, *90*, 1057.

Porter, K. (2012). The complaint conundrum: Thoughts on the CFPB's complaint mechanism. *Brooklyn Journal of Corporate and Financial & Commercial Law*, *7*, 57.

Ratcliffe, J. (2015, July 30). Abolishing the Consumer Financial Protection Bureau. *The Washington Times*. Retrieved from https://www.washingtontimes.com/news/2015 /jul/30/john-ratcliffe-abolishing-the-consumer-financial-p/

Reurink, A. (2018). Financial fraud: A literature review. *Journal of Economic Surveys*, *32*(5), 1292–1325. doi:10.1111/joes.12294

Shadel, D., & Pak, K. (2017). *Under Fire: Military Veterans and Consumer Fraud in the United States*. AARP Research. doi:10.26419/res.00182.001

Shivaprasad, V. M. (2019). *Analysis of customer complaint data of Consumer Financial Protection Bureau using different text classification methods*. Dublin Business School. Retrieved from https://esource.dbs.ie/bitstream/handle/10788/4224/msc_Shivaprasad_vm_2020.pdf?sequence=1&isAllowed=y

Willis, L. E. (2017). The consumer financial protection bureau and the quest for consumer comprehension. *RSF: The Russell Sage Foundation Journal of the Social Sciences*, *3*(1), 74-93.

Zywicki, T. (2013). The Consumer Financial Protection Bureau: Savior or menace. *The George Washington Law Review*, *81*, 856.

ADDITIONAL READING

Delisle, J. D., & West, L. (2019). *Student Loan Servicers: Scammers or Scapegoats?* American Enterprise Institute. Retrieved from https://luminafoundation.org/wp-content/uploads/2019/11/student-loan-servicers.pdf

Garz, S., Giné, X., Karlan, D., Mazer, R., Sanford, C., & Zinman, J. (2021). Consumer Protection for Financial Inclusion in Low- And Middle-Income Countries: Bridging Regulator and Academic Perspectives. In Annual Review of Financial Economics (Vol. 13). Academic Press.

Markov, S. C. (2022). Open Banking: The CFPB Should Follow the European Regulatory Regime. North Carolina Banking Institute, 26(1), 269.

Odinet, C. K. (2018). Consumer BitCredit and Fintech Lending. *Alabama Law Review*, *69*(4), 781.

Pappalardo, J. K. (2022). Economics of Consumer Protection: Contributions and Challenges in Estimating Consumer Injury and Evaluating Consumer Protection Policy. *Journal of Consumer Policy*, *45*(2), 201–238. doi:10.100710603-021-09482-4

The World Bank. (2014). *Global Survey on Consumer Protection and Financial Literacy: Oversight Frameworks and Practices in 114 Economies.* Retrieved from www.worldbank.org

ENDNOTES

1 ***The American Consumer Financial Innovation Network (ACFIN)***: It is a network of US Federal and State officials and regulators seeking coordination to facilitate innovation and further shared objectives such as competition, consumer access, and financial inclusion.

2 ***Chevron Deference***: It is a principle of administrative law requiring courts to defer to interpretations of statutes made by those government agencies charged with enforcing them unless such interpretations are unreasonable. The "Chevron deference" was coined after a landmark case, Chevron U.S.A., Inc. v. Natural Resources Defense Council, Inc., 468 U.S. 837 (1984).

3 Consumer Financial Protection Bureau. (2022). Enforcement by the numbers.[Datasets]. https://www.consumerfinance.gov/enforcement/enforcement-by-the-numbers/

4 Consumer Financial Protection Bureau. (2022). Consumer Complaints.[Datasets]. https://www.consumerfinance.gov/data-research/consumer-complaints/

5 ***Dodd-Frank Act:*** Enacted in 2010, it is an Act to promote the financial stability of the United States by improving accountability and transparency in the financial system, to end "too big to fail", to protect the American taxpayer by ending bailouts, to protect consumers from abusive financial services practices, and for other purposes.

6 ***The Administrative Procedure Act (APA):*** Codified in 5 U.S.C. §§ 551–559, it is a US Federal Act that governs the procedures of administrative law. The core pieces of the Act establish how federal administrative agencies make rules and how they adjudicate administrative litigation.

7 ***Financial Stability Oversight Council (FSOC):*** An Authority created by Dodd-Frank to supervise the safety and soundness of the US financial system. The council has the mandate to identifying risks and respond to emerging threats to financial stability.

8 ***The Small Business Regulatory Enforcement Fairness Act (SBREFA):*** This Act was enacted in 1996 in response to concerns expressed by the small business community of the US that Federal regulations were too numerous, too complex and too expensive to implement. SBREFA was designed to give small businesses assistance in understanding and complying with regulations and more of a voice in the development of new regulations.

Chapter 2
Corruption and Governance in Africa: An Insight

Tochukwu Benedict Ezeifekwuaba
South America University, Nigeria

Marie G. Nakitende
Uganda Martyrs University, Uganda

ABSTRACT

Corruption is a challenge and problem for governance in Africa. The existence of anti-corruption institutions and legislation in Africa is the result of the questioning of the commitment and dedication of African leaders to combat and tackle corruption. There are corrupt practices conducted by Africans as well as foreigners who are collaborating with corrupt African leaders. The aim of this chapter is (1) to highlight the types of corruption in Africa, (2) to highlight the anti-corruption efforts and moves in Africa, and (3) to suggest workable and suitable solutions. The external and internal sources of corruption are discussed which are systemic, interrelated, and interdependent. The chapter also looks at the failure and challenges to handle or deal with the issue of corruption in various dimensions.

INTRODUCTION

Anyone that has had the privilege to count the numbers of times African countries have been "labelled" being "corrupt" in the international media will have miscounted. Therefore, without any obscurantism, there can be no scepticism that all charges are factual as there are both international and also domestic investigations of corruption and fraudulent scenarios in Africa. Each of these reports has questioned the willingness of African Heads of State to manage cases of corruption. Also, governance in Africa plays a tremendously essential role and responsibility in determining and examining the relationship between the followers and the leaders, especially when state endowments (resources) are being allocated so as to enhance the socio-economic welfare of Africans. It is on this ground that government concentrates

DOI: 10.4018/978-1-6684-5007-9.ch002

and focuses on the citizens to embark on its constitutional obligations and duties as well as to ensure the required platform for social participation between citizens and leaders when tackling socio-economic issues such as poverty (Nnoli, 2003).

Thus, the issue of poverty in Africa has been connected to corruption at the institutional level. Therefore, to get Africa out of corruption, motives need to change and efforts to stop corruption at the institutional level must now be made. A nation that is affected by corruption cannot develop and nurture its citizens to their maximum capabilities and capacities. Corruption thus results in underdevelopment (Momoh, 2013). In addition, vast resources lost to corruption, both externally or internally, that should have been channelled to tackle the scenario of underdevelopment in Africa is a major worry to those that view corruption as a challenge to the globe that must be emphasized and tackled.

Also, the severe nature and level of corruption in Africa, particularly at the institutional level, question the ability and willingness of African nations to manage the issue of corruption in which enormous amounts of resources are lost, especially when the global extent of poverty is on the rise.

THEORETICAL PERSPECTIVE

Many theories have been presented in order to explain the extent of corruption and the inferior quality of governance in Africa. Some of the findings of the research conducted, which are presented in this book support the theories that have been written about. This book's perspective originated from the public choice mechanism of human behaviour that distinguishes a society into Private and Public spheres, based on the writings and thoughts of several authors and on research conducted by institutions. Rather than trying to introduce any innovative ideas or new theories, or to conduct any new research, this book attempts to cobble together, by borrowing and copying, the works of others in order to present a coherent and comprehensive perspective. The concentration of this book's point of view is on the public and general issues in which decisions or policies on governance are ensured.

An evaluation of corruption usually categorizes between bureaucratic, political and also economic corruption (Nakitende, Rafay & Waseem, 2021) A study of corruption also usually distinguishes between incentive settings or theories in these three domains (Chipkin, 2013). Furthermore, the focus on political corruption in this book is essential because major advanced scenarios of corruption in Africa emerge from the political sphere. This perspective has been supported and backup by the American and British Intelligence Report in Ezeoha and Uche (2005) which found that in a Nation such as Nigeria; 60 percent of corruption comes from the presidency. It, therefore, falls within the scenario of this book's theoretical perspective to give an insight into what has and is transpiring in Africa when it comes to corruption.

Lastly, this book could be antagonized for only focusing and depending on the structure and not the individuals that coordinate, control, and regulate the activities of these institutions. Although the individuals who coordinate and regulate the activities of these institutions do have access to the means to engage and involve in corruption, the instance and scenario of corruption in Africa are so severe at the institutional level, that the concentration first is on institutions and not on the people in them.

CORRUPTION AND GOVERNANCE IN AFRICA

Since Africa achieved independence from colonial rule, corruption has been a major issue and worry because it siphons already limited or scarce funds. It impedes and also prevents policy changes (transformations) needed for development and undermines economic progress.

Africa depicts an actual scenario of nations in the globe whose development has been retarded and undermined by the rot of corrupt and fraudulent activities or practices. A series of modifications and transformations have been conducted and embarked in every African nation in order to ensure that the systems implemented in African nations are efficient as well as result oriented. The required benefits of such reforms and motives have not been glaring due to numerous conditions and reasons that entail corruption. Corruption has entered deeply into the African nations and anyone that says that corruption in Africa has not yet become disastrous is either a crook or a fool, or does not exist on this globe (Achebe, 1988). The situation or events has actually gotten out of hand to the extent that, whichever way a person sees corruption, it entails a deviation from increased moral standards in exchange for, and in anticipation of, private pecuniary benefits. It has added effects of violating the public trust, abdication from public responsibility, and also a dereliction of duty being committed by those in power. It is associated with dishonest and immoral acts (Ayo, 1995).

However, the direct costs of corruption can be seen in the ever-increasing diversion of funds from their intended use, in lost revenue, and in the indirect costs of economic distortions, waste, and inefficiencies emanating from corrupt practices. Long-term corruption is even more challenging to address as it has become systemic. Corruption maximizes the costs of conducting business and wastes resources, thus severely minimizing revenues owned by the state. Also, it leads to a deficient and weak service delivery, various concurrent sources (means) of employment, and "moonlighting" including the refusal to conduct obligatory routine activities without extra or additional payment.

Also, corruption maximizes poverty and makes it challenging for ordinary or common individuals to forge ahead solely due to their personal efforts. There is increasing or rising evidence that the economic and also social costs of corruption also affect the poor such that they not solely suffer from the absence of efficient government or services but are helpless to antagonize the requirements of corrupt authorities. Various arguments and debates have been brought forward to highlight further and emphasize the pervasiveness of corruption in Africa. These arguments and debates involve the personalization of public posts, poverty, and political culture. The arguments include the unwillingness of leaders to withstand their colonial mentality and perspective in regard to their perspective of public position (Lawal, 2007). To this end, the wealth of some African leaders as well as heads of state was published back in time, such as those published by French Weekly on May 1977, as shown by (Ayittey, 2002). Below are a few:

President Hissene Habre of Chad – $3 Million
President Mariam Haite of Ethiopia – $30 Million
President Paul Biya of Cameroon– $70 Million
President Bongo Omar of Gabon – $80 Million
President Denis N'Gnesso of Congo – $200 Million
President Henri Bedie of Ivory Coast – $300 Million
President Mouza Traore of Mali – $2 Billion
President Mobutu of Zaire – $4 Billion
General Ibrahim Babaginda of Nigeria – $5 Billion
President H. Boigny of Ivory Coast – $6 Billion

General Sani Abacha of Nigeria – $20 Billion

Two parties often conduct theft: thief and "receiver" who is the "dishonest" individual to whom the thief sells the stolen products or commodities, and without whose service thievery cannot be a booming business. An insight into corruption in Africa, given without recourse to the external and internal perspectives of corruption in Africa, has done no justice nor brought about solutions for the issue of corruption.

According to Transparency International (TI), corruption is functionally defined as "the wrong use of bestowed power for personal purpose and gain. It further categorizes corruption as "against the protocol" corruption and "according to protocol" corruption. The "against the protocol" corruption is corrupt acts not permitted by the legislation of a nation, while the "according to protocol" corruption is corrupt acts permitted by the legislation of a nation (Momoh, 2013). Governance determines and examines the relationship between the ruled and the rulers in a society. It is also a means of social interaction between the ruled and the rulers (Nnoli, 2003).

Corruption has received global blasting, particularly through the United Nations Declaration and Action Plan against Money Laundering, and United Nations Convention against Corruption and Regional Anti-Corruption Programme of Africa (2011-2016) which is a principle and ideology of the United Nations Economic Commission for Africa (UNESCA) in partnership with the African Union (AU) Advisory Board on Corruption, through African Union (AU) Convention on Combating and Preventing Corruption, launched on the 11th of July 2003. This provides and creates various-track strategic techniques which combine policy analysis and research, including peer learning, capacity and training development, including information ideology sharing, and the recording of the appropriate practices on policy dialogue, anti-corruption, and special or unique scenarios on corruption in Africa (UNECA, 2015)

Corruption also ostensibly serves the purpose and aim of lubricating and promoting commerce (Momoh, 2013). Furthermore, corruption also transpires in Africa because its systems lend themselves to it. Transparency International (TI) states that where temptation attains permissiveness, corruption takes root on large and vast dimensions. It is against this notion that this book evaluates the external and the internal perspectives, including the impediments in tackling corruption in Africa, and also ensures recommendable and better solutions.

EXTERNAL PERSPECTIVES ON CORRUPTION IN AFRICA

The external perspective entails corrupt acts conducted by internationals in collaboration and partnership with corrupt Africans so as to participate in different illegal capital flows and to bribe government authorities in Africa so as to obtain contracts. For example, in 2009 New African Magazine emphasized that on the 25th of September 2009, a United Kingdom (UK) individualized firm called Mabey & Johnson (M & J), whose business was to construct bridges in African nations such as Angola, Ghana, Mozambique, and Madagascar, pleaded guilty at Southwark Crown Court in London, for bribing governments in these African nations so as to seek out and get contracts. Also, there was an allegation of bribery against BAE Systems for the role they and others played in the international weapons industry in South Africa's largest ammunition deal in 1994, involving sales of Gripen and Hawk Warplanes for GBP 1.67 billion.

Between 1993 and 2002 in Nigeria, there was a serious investigation conducted that exposed Halliburton Co executive Jack Albert Stanley. He pleaded guilty to "*accepting more than $200 million in bribes from major government authorities so as to seek contracts*" (Aghedo & Osumah, 2013).

What is more, Global Witness (2018) has stated that some British high-street financial institutions ensured and coordinated money laundering between Nigeria and United Kingdom between 1998 and 2005. The financial institutions also made it attainable for late General Sanni Abacha, and former governor of Plateau State, Chief Joshua Dariye Chibi, and Bayelsa State DSP Alamieyeseigh to launder funds (Aghedo & Osumah, 2013).

Finally, the inability or unwillingness of foreign countries to monitor complex and cumbersome activities conducted by their "blue chip" firms that functioned in Africa, has resulted in those firms being involved in bribing an array of national government authorities and money laundering and participating in illegal capital flows (Rafay, 2021a).

INTERNAL PERSPECTIVES OF CORRUPTION IN AFRICA

The internal perspective of corrupt practices in Africa entails every corrupt practice conducted by African leaders. For instance, in 2004, a former Head of the Kenya Anti-Corruption Commission was prohibited by the Attorney General from unveiling evidence of corruption when an anonymous firm, referred to as "Anglo Leasing," was awarded various projects by the Government of Kenya that were not implemented (Honson, 2009).

In Malawi, the Malawi Newsweek reported that corrupt parliament members had siphoned the State Wealth to the tune of US $ 3.5 million. They reported that the Head of the Agricultural Development Marketing Corp used his portion of the loot to establish an expensive hotel in Malawi (Ojo, 2007). Also, in Congo (Zaire), the late Mobute Seko Sese was not innocent of the allegations of corruption as he was accused of employing a Concorde jet for a shopping trip, as well as building a palace equipped with the nuclear gadget (Ojo, 2007).

In Nigeria, the military junta led by the late dictator General Sani Abacha was accused of having stolen millions in foreign currency of which former Head of State General Abubakar Abdusalami's regime retrieved almost US $780 million. Former Head of State Olusegun Obasanjo Aremu Matthew's era lured Swiss banking officials to freeze more than US $700 million in General Abacha's bank accounts, and to return almost US $150 million to the Nigerian Treasury (Momoh, 2013). Nigeria as a failed nation has lost an approximated US $450 billion to corruption.

In addition, the edition of the African News Online of 2nd November 1998 emphasized that General Abacha possessed real estate worth between three to six billion US dollars. This comprised of five hundred properties including some government facilities that he unlawfully transformed in Nigeria. What is more, his regime was accused of outright theft, shady dealings, bribery, and kickbacks. It was also emphasized that the Minister of Finance during the General Abacha period, Anthony Ani, was labelled of corrupt, as was the then National Security Adviser, Gwarzo Ismail, who it is alleged had confiscated almost US $1.5 billion worth of foreign reserves and placed them in his private bank account (Ojo, 2007).

NATURE OF CORRUPTION

Political Corruption

Corruption is a major obstacle to the political transparency of African nations. As the outcomes of the GCB Survey of 2019 emphasize, many Africans attest that there is an enormous amount of political corruption in their nations, conducted especially by parliamentarians, and government officials, including the heads of governments and the heads of state (Transparency International 2019).

State of Capture

This actually entails "a situation or instance where powerful and influential individuals, groups or companies, outside or within a nation, uses corruption to disrupt a country's initiatives, principles, guidelines, legal environment, and economy, to their personal benefit, and to advance their personal interests. State capture is achieved by first capturing high-placed officials and heads of state. They in turn influence, on behalf of private individuals and other politicians, especially those responsible for running parastatals entities with large procurement budgets. Such capture of state agencies by private or personal individuals, in order to change and alter state decisions or policies for their personal benefit, has become a major worry in Africa (Lodge, 2018). Its major consequences are that the interests of a particular group are prioritized over public interests in the activity of the state. In South Africa, the word was applied to emphasize the connection between the Gupta Family, from India, and the former president, Jacob Zuma. The report on the State of Capture by the Public Protector found that Gupta Family unduly gained from corrupt connection with the past president and affected executive decisions such as the dismissal or the appointment of ministers including the awarding of government deals or projects to the family's enterprises (Public Protector South Africa, 2016).

State Capture may entail a more unclear proximate combination of interests between the political elites and state businesses through friendship, family relationships including business relationships (Martini 2012:2). In such scenarios, state parastatals are manipulated, and policies are manufactured, to favour the personal interests of those related to political elites. An instance of this entails Isabel Dos Santos, the Daughter of the Former Angolan President Eduardo Jose Dos Santos, and Africa's wealthiest woman. It is alleged that she exploited her father's position and authority for her personal benefit. In Luanda Leaks documents, the Dos Santos family's emphasized State Capture entailed the misuse of executive power to award government projects for telecom permits and diamond mining rights to themselves.

Conflicts of Interests

Some government and political authorities see themselves in a situation where they stand to accumulate personal benefits and opportunities from decisions they make in their formal capacity. During the Presidency of Al-Bashir in Sudan, members of the ruling National Congress Party, and government officials including senior security members, had bestowed interests in state- accumulated and funded ventures, leading to lucrative opportunities and benefits. Also, senior security officials and members of the ruling party who possessed private entities gained favouritism from the government in form of being awarded public projects (US Department of State, 2015).

Vote Buying

Vote buying by political individuals remains an obstacle in a number of African Nations. The 2016/2017 Somalia presidential and parliamentary elections were strewn with, and impaired by, allegations of heavy corruption (Burke, 2017). Fartaag Abdirazak, a former Somali government authority, alleged that the electoral system that entailed and entitled only 14000 individuals to vote members of parliament, which would then choose a president, led to "corruption inflation" as candidates purchased votes to secure a seat in the parliament (Gettleman, 2017). It was alleged that at least US $25 million was fraudulently applied in the parliamentary elections. It was also followed by presidential candidates accusing each other of purchasing votes from parliamentarians. Local (Native) anti-corruption campaigners termed it "the most costly election, a vote" in the history of the nation (Burke, 2017). In Nigeria, vote buying is rampant. Vote buying has long been a major problem in Nigeria. With the 2023 elections fast approaching, Nigerian politicians will be using vote buying to massively rig the election. International community observers need to watch out for this.

Opaque Political Funding

Another obstacle to political transparency is the general or overall opaque financing of political parties. In regard to a report by the International Institute for Electoral Assistance and Democracy, there is inadequate regulation of electoral campaigns and political financing in numerous African nations, making it simpler for corrupt exercises, linked to political funding, to continue unmonitored (Check *et al.* 2019).

For example, Burkina Faso does not control personal political financing, which heightens the exposure of political actors to corruption risks (IDEA, 2018). Undisclosed and unveiled political financing puts political parties and also stakeholders at risk (hazard) of capture as secret financiers will demand "payback" once their financed candidates come to authority. In Somalia, there have been allegations of Qatar, United Arab Emirates, Saudi Arabia, and Turkey funding the campaigns of wanted candidates, and therefore triggering corruption (Burke, 2017)

Individuals accused of severe corruption, have participated in election manifestoes (campaigns), thereby providing more corruption hazards or risks. "Dirty" funds have been used to purchase votes and finance electoral campaigns. In the DRC's previous elections, the campaign funding team for presidential candidate Emmanuel Shadary Ramazani comprised of Albert Yuma, CEO of Gecamines, which is the DRC's biggest state-controlled corporation, and Lushyma Ekanga Moise, the director of Sino-Congolese Corporation Initiative. Both have been accused and labelled with corruption and fraud allegations related to the stealing or siphoning of public wealth (Global Witness, 2018).

Role of Foreign Actors

Numerous present scenarios of serious corruption have entailed multinational organizations. In 2017, the United Nations Department of the Treasury sanctioned and penalized Israeli billionaire Gertler Dan in connection with accusations of him making a fortune through fraudulent oil and mining transactions in the DRC. Dan was in collaboration and alliance with Glencore, a British-Swiss multinational mining and commodity trading company, in their mining exercises at the DRC. It is emphasized that Dan functioned as an intermediary for multinational firms to get and ensure mining rights in the nation, as a result of his intimate connection and linkage with the former president Kabila Joseph. The United States Treasury stated that between 2010 and 2012 solely, almost US $1.36 billion in revenue was lost and wasted through the sale of mining assets and rights sold to offshore organizations connected to Gertler Dan.

Another major profile scenario is the United States formal accusation of five business leaders and three Mozambican public officials over allegations of running a money-laundering scheme and committing fraud estimated at US $2 billion (US Department of Justice, 2019). It was stated and emphasized that the indicted individuals conspired in a dubious and unlawful loan initiative with a foreign investment firm that allegedly paid out US $200 million in kickbacks and bribes. In 2019, three credit Suisse operators attested to their responsibilities in the bribery allegation and pleaded guilty (Ljubas, 2019).

Nations hosting multinational firms accused of and participated in corruption scandals in Sub- Saharan Africa are vindicated to be not doing better to sanction and prohibit foreign bribery. Transparency International's 2018 report: Exporting Corruption, emphasised that most of the corruption-exporting nations have little, constrained, or no legislation implementation against the bribery of international (external) public authorities (Dell & McDevitt, 2018).

Foreign nations also play a responsibility in keeping the proceeds of political corruption from Sub- Saharan Africa. It is anticipated that Africa loses at least US $55 billion yearly through unlawful financial channels (UNECA, 2015). Just 5% of the illegal outflows that are characterized by corruption, result in nearly US $2.5 billion in revenue being lost annually by African nations through corruption (UNECA, 2015). The channels of these proceeds entail extortion, kickbacks, bribery, embezzlement of public funds/self-dealing and conflicts of interest. Illegal finances are then kept in foreign or offshore jurisdictions with the help of lawyers, bankers and banks (FATF, 2011). The Financial Secretary Index of 2020 provides an emphasis of the destinations of the proceeds of corruption from Africa, the major five jurisdictions being Cayman Islands, Hong Kong, Switzerland, USA and Singapore (Tax Justice Network, 2020).

Patronage Networks

Government dependence on extensive and various patronage networks is a major reality in a few African nations. These patronage networks are aspects of the informal power settings that decide who gets access or linkage to public resources. The patronage networks comprise three C's which are: Camouflage, Control and Co-option (Camargo & Koechlin, 2018).

Camouflage

Camouflage entails the concealment of the realities or the facts about control and co-option behind formal policies and facades that are coherent with a dedication to democratic accountability including good and better governance. For example, such policies may allow for sanctioning a detractor in order to publicly demonstrate a commitment to tackling corruption. It is a charade of note.

Control Mechanisms

Control Mechanisms are unwritten or unrecorded management tools for managing undisclosed interests and conflicts of interest, to protect elite cohesion including imposing and ensuring discipline among corrupt allies.

Co-option

Co-option entails the strategic recruitment of political opponents and associates who are granted immunity for their misappropriation of state resources or power, in exchange for loyalty and mobilizing support for the regime.

Empirical evidence shows the occurrence of such power networks in Uganda, Tanzania, and Rwanda (Camargo & Koechlin, 2018). In Nigeria, powerful and vibrant patron-client networks and connections in the electricity sector create and provide privileges and benefits for rent capture (Roy *et al.* 2020). Furthermore, patronage networks occur across Sub-Saharan Africa and have affected the distribution of resources including health system governance (Hutchinson *et al.* 2019).

Before the exit of Burkina Faso president Compaore, the executive had a significant and huge effect on and influence over the majority of the appointments of public figures. The executive also regulated the payment for, and dissemination of, resources to local governments (Hagberg *et al.* 2017). Such "Clientelistic" and strategic recruitment practices and regulation over local government funding were major electoral strategies applied by Compaore to stay in authority (Hilgers & Loada, 2013).

In the DRC, patron-client connections were attributed to the presidency of Kabila Joseph, as allegations were raised of fraudulent government elites and cabinet ministers channelling or diverting unlawful gains and benefits to the president, in exchange for holding their positions (posts) as well as ensuring safeguard from prosecution and prison (Titeka & Thamani, 2018). Therefore, the president, as well as the family at the helm of an organized and enormous form of graft, accumulated great wealth at the expense of the masses. For example, the family of the former president allegedly possessed more than eighty firms, had strong and deep interests in banking, farming, airlines, mining, telecoms, and real estate, and possessed almost 71000 hectares of land (Kavanagh & McCarey, 2017).

Corruption, Conflict and State Fragility

The least peaceful and conducive nations in Africa have maximum levels of corruption. For example, nations close to the bottom or beneath the 2019 CPI such as South Sudan, Sudan and Somalia (rated 173, 179 and 180) have witnessed violent and serious conflicts in present years as they are ranked 3rd, 8th and 2nd respectively among the fragile nations in the globe (Fragile States Index, 2019).

Corruption dissolves state legitimacy, authority, power and capacity in fragile or weak nations. For example, maximum levels of corruption in Somalia have resulted in weak or deficient institutions and corruption in the security area known to be "organized and systematic." There have been scenarios of security forces harassing, stealing, torturing, and intimidating individuals (Mubarak, 2017).

Corruption creates or provides the conditions for criminality to occur, as well as arms trading, illicit mining, and narcotics dealings. Criminal Networks in Mali use an amalgamation of networks of corruption and threat of violence to safeguard the illegal dissemination of cigarettes, arms and also narcotics (Reitano & Shaw, 2015). As emphasized in a current document, "The pervasive extent of corruption within Sahelian Nations, as well as their security structure and system, have allowed criminal and dubious markets to thrive and occur at the first place as well as allowed for their expansion" (Micallef & Bish, 2019).

The unlawful exploitation and trading of natural resources are recognized by the United Nations as triggering continuous conflicts and in the DRC. The security sector in the DRC is majorly engaged in the mining firm and the report emphasized the participation of Major General Gabriel Kumba Amisi, who was the Commander of the Primary Defence Zone, which was an unlawful gold exploitation zone (UN Security Council, 2017). On the other side, Mai-Mai groups and a number of rebels regulates their personal mines (Matthysen *et al.* 2019). These cater to them the financial resources to sustain and maintain their activities. The United Nations emphasized that gold emanating from conflict-affected areas is still being smuggled out and traded on international markets. Funds from the sale of smuggled gold benefit criminal associations (UN Security Council, 2017)

The Agenda of the African Union (AU) to restrict or stop guns in 2020 risked being crippled by the maximum extent of corruption on the globe. In South Sudan, one of the most delicate countries on the globe, a present United Nations report stressed corruption as the reason for the challenge in South Sudan, as millions of dollars have been siphoned or embezzled from public treasures (UN Commission on Human Rights, 2020). In 2019, a lot of individuals went to the streets chanting against severe economic conflict as well as endemic corruption (Maclean & Boley, 2019). Gbowee Leyman, a Liberian Nobel Peace Prize Winner in 2011, emphasized that silencing the guns in Africa will entail prohibiting corruption as it is a serious challenge resulting in serious catastrophe in the region (UN African Renewal, 2019).

Corruption in Development Assistance

Development Assistance Funds are a major target and aim of corruption in a few nations and sectors. The Nation Report for Somalia, by Bertelsmann Stiftung (2018), highlighted serious misappropriation of foreign and internal revenues at the federal level. Also, the United Nations Monitoring Group emphasized Misappropriation and also the Diversion of Humanitarian funds in Somalia (UN Security Council, 2016). In Uganda, there was corruption aspersion in its refugee initiatives, as funds went untraceable (Gitta & Froehlich, 2019). The aspersion also unveiled the rise or emergence of the number of refugees by almost 350,000. As a result of the aspersion, some nations as Japan and the United Kingdom suspended their assistance to Zambia after recognition by the Zambian Government that finances meant for poor and suffering families are nowhere to be found (Papachristou, 2018)

Gender-Based Corruption

Corruption and Gender have become a theme of concentration in current years. For example, Rwanda Transparency International conducted statistics on gender-based corruption in general settings and places of work in Rwanda. It discovered that at least 2 in 11 respondents are conscious of someone who had encountered gender-based corruption at their place of work during the past twelve months. Also, it discovered that cases of gender-based corruption are hardly reported to superiors as a result of the fear of retaliation and other repercussions. The few respondents or repliers interested in sharing their encounters revealed that ignoring gender-based corruption was met by an unfriendly and aggressive response or resulted in a harsher work environment, as well as threats of termination of their employment contracts and denial of annual leave. Even after reporting their situations to superiors, some respondents or repliers were exposed to harassment and humiliation (Transparency International Rwanda, 2018a, b).

Some research had indicated that men are more probably to pay bribes than the women (Boehm & Sierra, 2015). This is backed up by data from the GCB survey that indicated that men (32%) paid more bribes than women (25%) in Sub-Saharan Africa (Transparency International, 2019). Experimental research studies have shown that women tend to be more honest and transparent than men and are more interested in fairness and faithfulness in their actions (Rivas 2015). This has been attributed to the traditional role of men being financial providers for the family. That makes them susceptible to paying bribes or inducements for essential amenities or services (Transparency International, 2019).

In regard to Transparency International, "*Regardless of if women are less or more corrupt or unscrupulous than men, they witness and encounter corruption or dishonest dealings in more various manners than men, as a result of political inequalities as well as due to the difference or inequality in their involvement in domestic versus public life.*" (Rheibay & Chene, 2016)

In Somalia, research studies have indicated that gender inequality and corruption have traces in some cultural traditions or practices (Ahmed, 2016; Carver, 2017). For example, traditional male superiors, which play a responsibility in the choice of initial political contenders, have been indicted of wrongly selecting male candidates, thus downsizing the anticipated female candidates (Carver, 2017).

Another form of gendered corruption entails sextortion. Another trending report by Transparency International showed that sextortion is rampant in various areas, as well as the police, education, civil and judiciary, including the refugee camps (Transparency International, 2020). There are numerous documented situations of sextortion in the African continent. For example, an inquiry in the refugee settlements in Yemen, Kenya, Uganda, Ethiopia and Libya unveiled fraudulent acts by an employee from the office or seat of the United Nations High Commissioner for Refugees (UNHCR), who collected bribes or inducement from refuges for listing and uploading them for resettlement (relocation) in a better nation (Hayden 2019). It was reported and documented that few refugee girls and women were compelled to pay bribes or inducements in the form or means of sex. The United Nations High Commissioner for Refugees (UNHCR) repudiated the allegations in the report as well as cautioned them on untruthful agents (UNHCR, 2019).

Sextortion is also rampant in the supply of essential services such as water and food. In 2019, after Cyclone Idai in Mozambique had wrecked livestock and homesteads, a lot of individuals became focused on food initiatives rendered by public officials and local or regional leaders. A report by Human Rights Watch in 2019 emphasized that these leaders or superiors had sought bribes to include families on the aid and support list. Women without funds were subdued to sextortion as local heads wanted intercourse in exchange for food. A Survey conducted by Zimbabwe Transparency International emphasized that 57% of respondent women encountered and witnessed sextortion in various areas of the neighbourhood or community. As one of the cultural conspirators from civil society put it, "Sex is a legal tender in numerous corrupt dealings in Zimbabwe. Sexual intimidation is institutionalized, and women have been withstanding for a long period of time" (Transparency International Zimbabwe, 2013, 2019).

Land Corruption

The land is the cornerstone of political, economic and also social living in Africa although it is majorly inclined to corruption. In a document report by Transparency International, one in every two individuals witnesses corruption in land issues in Africa in comparison to one in five individuals for the rest of the globe (Transparency International, 2013).

Another document by Transparency International on land corruption in Sierra Leone, Zambia and Liberia, emphasizes that sextortion, fraud; kickbacks, patronage, and bribery are major types of corruption in land issues. The challenge is triggered by structural problems in administrative frameworks or legislations that have to do with land governance. For example, the surveyed nations do not have standardized land tenure regulations or policies, and their land administration departments lacked accountability and also transparency (Wadström & Tetka, 2019).

Women are worst hit by land corruption as a result of their major dependency on land. Transparency International's Land and Corruption in Africa Initiative conducted a baseline survey on land corruption and women, together with eight national chapters: Zimbabwe, Uganda, Kenya, Sierra Leone, Cameroon, Madagascar, Ghana, and Liberia. It documented the experiences of women, including every obstacle, in accessing land as well as their continuous exposure to sextortion and bribery by land officials and community leaders For instance, at least 65% of surveyed rural and native women in Zimbabwe have been requested for a bribe by a community head. In Kenya, 40% of surveyed women had been subjected to demands for bribes or inducements in similar land matters in the past decade. In Liberia, at least 10% of surveyed women had either been exposed and victim to sextortion to settle a land problem, or they are conscious of other women and ladies that had been (Transparency International, 2018a, b).

Women remain exposed to land dispossession, especially in nations with land grabbing activities. In Zimbabwe, Almost 65% of urban women surveyed and also 40% of rural women scrutinized, stated their exposition to land denial and deprival. In Chisumbanye, community or neighbourhood land was seized by ethanol firm Green Fuel, which collected the land through bribing top politicians. The firm wrecked crops or pastures in the farmlands and individuals were compelled to collect half hectare's plots that were smaller or lesser than the acreage they had previously had. A discussion with the expelled or overridden community highlighted how women from the displaced regions bargained sex for land, and how any rejection of sexual demands led to a forfeiture of land (Transparency International, 2018a, b).

Private or Individualized sectors are also involved in fraudulent transactions to get land, as well as schemes bypass deliberations with those in disrupted regions. In Zambia, chiefs are paid off to use their native authority for the transformation of customary land to long leaseholds and state assets, without any assistance from the affected community and village heads, in breach of the recognized and identified proposition of "*prior, free and informed consent.*" This also is the scenario in Liberia and, in some cases; research indicated that organizations give bribes or gifts to Liberian officials to obtain acres of acreage, without any demarcations and surveys conducted (Wadström & Tetka, 2019).

CHALLENGES FOR ANTI-CORRUPTION IN AFRICA

The manner in which the extents of corruption in Africa have exterior and interior influences and sources presents big challenges for those who are anti-corruption. Here follows a look at both the external and internal challenges.

External Challenges to Anti-Corruption in Africa

Exterior problems are those fraudulent practices conducted by foreigners or outsiders as well as their associated entities that function in Africa (Rafay, 2023). One major aspect is money laundering that the United Nations Development Programme (UNDP) Thematic initiative on Anti- Corruption Document, recognized that Africa lost approximately US $150 billion yearly to fraudulent activities, while the United States approximated that Africa lost $148 billion yearly to corruption which is 25% of the whole Global Gross Domestic Product (GDP). Within this sum, between US $20 to US $ 50 billion is missing as a result of the payment of inducements or bribes to government authorities.

Whilst the occurrence of different foreign instruments used in tackling corruption are protocols and procedures (Rafay, 2021b), in the appropriate path, there entail other major factors which comprise corruption which some of the instruments fail to apprehend, such as the scenario of ill-gotten funds from heinous crimes such as tax evasion, and from funding terrorism, among others. The ratification of continent-wide legislation is retard or slow. For example, when the African Union (AU) Meeting on Combating and also Preventing Corruption was applied on the 11th of July 2003, only forty-seven member nations became signatories, while twenty-seven member nations only ratified the convention on the 29th of September 2008, five years later.

Finally, the formation of the Advisory Body on Corruption under the African Union Convention on Combating and also Preventing Corruption is an appropriate step, but launching an international governmental agency that will ensure the necessary room to check and evaluate the extent of corruption in governance at the regional stage, that requires states to approve it conventions/treaties, so that its resolutions or verdict will be legal on it participating nations, is hitherto deficient. Such an institution would support the exercises of the Advisory Body under the African Union (AU) gathering on Combating and Preventing fraudulent activities, and the Transparency International (TI) benchmark for evaluating corruption in governance will ensure an annual basis, a Nation Perception Index and also appropriate results to nations thriving, to tackle corruption at the internal stage.

Internal Challenges to Anti-Corruption in Africa

Varied reasons have caused serious challenges in tackling corruption at the internal level in Africa. Momoh (2013) categorized the challenges as environmental, technological, sociocultural, economic, and also political reasons. The problem is that each of these factors re-enforces the others. For example, there is a connection between economic and political corruption in some regard. Although the classification of politics in Africa since independence (self-rule) has been majorly politically debatable, such that triumph in major elections is seen as life or death, contenders will participate in every form of political altercation so as to capture political power, by any means necessary. Mbaku (2000) emphasizes that corruption in Africa is the primary outcome of weakly crafted institutional patterns, as well as poor frameworks. The effect of this is that African state agencies are poor, as the majority of these agencies do not have the ability to cater to the fundamental general services needed by citizens. Instead, they are "confused" as they tend to look "inward," instead of "outward" in their management of general services. It has contributed to major nations in Africa lacking the ability, or even the desire to manage the scenario of corruption.

Another obstacle in tackling corruption in Africa is the discretionary nature of anti-corruption legislation. The majority of anti-corruption legislation in African Nations, in States such as Nigeria, South Africa and also Kenya, permits certain immunities and privileges to some political figures by ensuring that the procedure and protocol for dealing with such leaders, when discovered guilty of corruption charges, are malleable. This depicts that the African community has hastened the way for immunity in a few African nations, as political immunities provide or create ways for corrupt public figures to avoid prosecution. Besides, there are specific acts in law that Transparency International says promote corruption. For example, the legislation which allows constructors to the Nigerian Government to seek aid at contract sum rates, 10% of the project allocated and apportioned by public authority standing on behalf of the government, also constitutes corruption (Momoh, 2013). The constrained independence provided to anti-corruption agencies in African countries particularly in nations such as Botswana, Guinea, Liberia, Zimbabwe, South Africa, Malawi, Kenya, and Nigeria amongst others, to effectively tackle corruption, poses a major problem with regard to the workings of these anti-corruption agencies. Also, anti-corruption agencies are usually labelled as behaving in accordance with the "mannerism of the President." This results in anti-corruption agencies in major African nations either solely prosecuting the individuals that the President deems to be corrupt or victimizing those that he/she sees as "political tyrants or foes." This was the actual basis for what President Olusegun Obasanjo of Nigeria did in his period as the Head of State in Nigeria.

Furthermore, the poor perception of governance in Africa has made the majority of African political superior's view governing, and therefore governance, as a means of amassing wealth. This migration in the demands of the majority of African leaders, from encouraging economic growth and development through the provision of public services which will enhance the welfare of the citizenry, to raiding the State Purse to the disadvantage of the citizenry, is a critical factor and it is the cause for the hesitant level of development in Africa. Flimsy procedures and protocols for prosecuting severe cases of corruption are other major areas of concern. They have negatively affected the potential prosecution of corrupt African leaders. For example, in Nigeria, Section 52 (1) of the ICPC Act demands that the commission present any petition against the President or Vice President to the Chief Justice of Nigeria (CJN). They will as well permit Independent or Sole Counsel to check the allegations and then tell the National Assembly while, at the state level, any charges against the Deputy Governor or the Governor will be sent to the Commissioner of Justice that will appoint an Independent (Sole) Counsel, whose discoveries will be sent to the State House of Assembly.

RECOMMENDATIONS

External Mechanisms for Tackling or Fighting Corruption in Africa

The United Nations Declaration and Action Plan against Money Laundering including the United Nations Convention against Corruption 2004, as well as the African Union (AU) Meeting on Combating or Preventing Corruption, adopted on 11th July 2003, are protocols in the appropriate path and they are only the essence for foreign motives aimed at fighting fraudulent activities. They need to culminate in a specialized international governmental organization hosted by the AU, the UN, the ECOWAS, or SADC. Such an international organ would be responsible for and capable of fighting corruption, in whichever member nation that will ratify their convention/treaties against corruption.

Foreign financial institutions, as well as donor organizations, such as International Development Agency (IDA), International Monetary Fund (IMF), World Bank, United Nations Development Programme (UNDP), International Development Agency (IDA), Department for International Development (DFID), and United States Agency for International Department (USAID), among others, need to offer technical aid including offering loans to African nations where fraudulent activities are severe and hinders transparency in governance and hinders performance in regards to the extent of accountability or transparency in their political systems.

Moreover, the United Nations must ensure that it advises its participatory nations to control funds transfers from one nation to another by categories and individuals and that they must be aware of the purpose for which such funds will be used. This will help to check and monitor illegal capital flows which, between 2002 and 2012, lost Nigeria approximately US $8160.50 billion, exceeding South Africa misplaced approximately US $8125.30 billion due to fraudulent or illegal mis-invoicing of trade activities.

Internal Mechanisms for Tackling and Fighting Corruption in Africa

Africa Civil society groups must do more in the aspect of coercing governments at the internal stage to ensure accountability and also transparency in governance, by permitting anti-corruption legislation to be implemented. They should also function as whistleblowers against any form of fraudulent activities, to prevent corruption from being swept under the carpet.

The absence of stiffer penalties for corruption culprits in Africa means that there is no deterrent for those looking at corruption as a "lucrative or booming venture." Stiffer penalties and sanctions are necessary to deal with scenarios of corruption. Whilst the death sentence has been emphasized, suitable penalties would be forfeiture and the confiscation of all assets, and the payment of compensation for being involved in corruption in proportion to the crime perpetrated.

Governments at the domestic stage should also concentrate on the financing of political parties, by ensuring that financing of political parties is made general, and by ensuring that the state financing of political parties is optimal. This is due to the fact that the majority of the ruling parties in African countries such as Cameroun, Botswana and also Nigeria are financed by fraudulent and greedy politicians who, after financing the ruling and major parties that go on to win elections, will not be checkmated by governments formed by the winning political party. The funding of parties by corrupt politicians increases the extent of corruption in these nations as politicians that siphon the State Funds usually collaborate with the ruling party, so as not to be dealt with.

Furthermore, the anti-corruption legislation on the African globe needs to be evaluated and strengthened so as to manage major problems such as tax evasion, the funding of terrorism, drug trafficking, and the inflation of contracts and dealing with illegal proceeds derived from other heinous crimes. A Code of Conduct and Asset Declaration are paramount and imperative for tackling Africa's institutional corruption. This needs to be completed by politicians before taking the political post and after exiting the post.

In addition, the anti-corruption agencies in Africa must also be categorized from the executive organ of government. Preferably, anti-corruption agencies must have a primary budgetary apportion from the yearly budget including an independent government agency that will select its staff, and that will provide a yearly report to the legislature. In addition, there should be an independent corruption court, set apart from the conventional court system, for the sole purpose of fast tracking corruption cases, without the influence of the regular court system or politicians. This would alleviate the setback in ensuring of justice in the traditional court system.

Lastly, a political determination is necessary for tackling corruption in Africa. African leaders need to move beyond rhetoric by taking realistic steps to institute procedures to enable tougher anti-corruption laws to be implemented and ensuring that anti-corruption agencies are permitted to function better, without any type of political hindrance.

FURTHER SUGGESTIONS

Restoration of Traditional Cultures and Institutions

African traditional systems including values were for a major part dismissed, first by the missionaries, followed by colonialists, in a much coercive way. Traditional elucidation for fraudulent activities needs to be once again abided, applied by re-establishment of traditional systems of administration. Rwanda has effectively conducted the latter through the Umudugudu, Umuganda, Abunzi, including Gacaca, as well as other indigenous systems.

Religion as a Nation-Building Agency

Africans pay heeds to their spiritual superiors much more than they do to policymakers and politicians. The podium needs to be activated as a faith-based learning platform for converting African souls and aiming them for National Building.

Revitalizing Anti-Graft Agencies

Vibrant anti-graft agencies are paramount in African nations as in any other part of the globe; African government need to select determined and also credible persons that could be from other African nations, to start the fight against corruption in low and major places.

Africans must be encouraged to migrate vastly across the globe so as to withstand the ethnic hostilities and stigmas which were ignited by colonialism, and then exacerbated by the post-colonial struggle for power and authority among the ruling upper class, as well as being strengthened and enhanced by geographic claustrophobia and xenophobia.

Formal and Informal Learning

The essential tool for the cultural evolution of predominating social paradigms is education. Informal learning situations such as camps, workshops, and conferences, as well as other informal learning instances, need to be applied to re-tutor or tutor citizenry on the fact that actual living thrives when persons have better moral values, and principles or, consistently intend to have them. In formal education settings, the curriculum across Africa must be worked on to ensure actual intellectual and mental independence.

International Agencies or Organizations such as the IMF, UN, ECOWAS, WHO and other agencies must be careful in the way they give out loans, grants or whatever assistance or aid to African nations. When they do, they must monitor how such funds and aid are being expended and, if possible, come to see and audit the projects that are being implemented or executed, as well as demand financial documentation to ensure transparency and accountability.

Whistleblowing policy should also be another best and appropriate practice in tackling corruption in Africa (Assay, 2023). Thus, there should be an introduction and full execution in Africa as it will be a unique and a perfect measure, particularly in the exposure as well as the recovery of looted assets and funds. In order to have sustainability or ensuring of a free corrupt society in Africa, whistleblowing policy must be accommodated by the citizens by taking ownership of the policy. The practical and major successes by whistleblowing policy in the exposure and the recovery of stolen assets and funds must be consolidated by successive administrations so as to get rid of or save Africa from the shackles of corruption. Any nation that upholds accountability and transparency would not fold her hands while corruption and poor governance thrive. Whistleblowing is another international best approach applied in combating corruption. It is suggested that public awareness must be conducted so as to tutor the citizens on the essence of correcting and exposing corruption. A whistleblower is an employee that reports their employer's wrongdoing or evil deeds to a Law enforcement agency or government.

The present form of whistleblowing exceeds beyond the walls of an organization to the general political settings. The whistleblower must also be given enough protection for this is essential to the success of this initiative. Also, there must be superbly detailed provisions emphasizing the available remedies to a whistleblower when they are victimized. Lastly, Payment of Compensation must also be provided statutory deadline with specific attention to the quantum of reward including the period upon which such payment needs to be made.

CONCLUSION

The case of corruption in Africa must primarily be emphasized at the Institutional Stage. This is because corruption on the African continent emanates from the institutional level. African political institutions have been characterized as weak and as not having the political will or strong enough politicians, to deal with corruption. This remains a challenge and an obstacle to governance which is therefore the cause for the hesitant level of development on the globe.

For African nations to successfully tackle corruption, it needs to be combated externally and internally. It will place an emphasis on and address the domestic conditions which allow corruption to thrive and encourage African countries to demand external support from each other and from the international community. This is due to the fact that corruption is permitted to thrive at the institutional stage to the extent that it does on the continent. The implication for and repercussion of not arresting institutional corruption will be total and absolute institutional decline.

The adoption and application of the United Nations Convention against Corruption in 2004, the African Union's Convention on Combating and Prohibiting Corruption 2003, and also the United Nations Declaration and Action Plans or Initiative against Money Laundering should have come decades ago.

DECLARATION

The authors declare that the manuscript follows ethical standards and there are no potential conflicts of interest with respect to the research, authorship and/or publication of this chapter.

DISCLAIMER

The contents and views of this chapter are expressed by the authors in their personal capacities. It is not necessary for the Editor and the Publisher to agree with these viewpoints, and they are not responsible for any duty of care in this regard.

ACKNOWLEDGMENT

The authors extend sincere gratitude to

• The Editor and the International Editorial Advisory Board (IEAB) of this book who initially desk reviewed, arranged a rigorous double/triple blind review process, and conducted a thorough, minute, and critical final review before accepting the chapter for publication.

• All anonymous reviewers who provided very constructive feedbacks for thorough revision, improvement, extension, and fine tuning of the chapter.

• All colleagues, assistants and well-wishers who assisted to complete this task.

REFERENCES

Achebe, C. (1988). *The trouble with Nigeria*. Fourth Dimension Publishers.

Aghedo, I. & Osumah, O. (2013). Prospects and challenges of Anti-Corruption crusade in Nigeria's fourth republic. *Ilorin Journal of Business and Social Science, 15*(2).

Ahmed, S. K. (2016). *European Union Somalia Gender Analysis Study*. Garowe: Somali Institute for Development and Research Analysis (SIDRA). Retrieved from https://sidrainstitute.org/wp-content/uploads/2018/04/Report_EU_Gender_Analysis_Somalia_Study-SIDRA_Final_2016.pdf

Assay, B. (2023). Whistleblowing Policy against Corruption: The Case of Nigeria. In A. Rafay (Ed.), *Concepts and Cases of Illicit and Illegitimate Finance*. IGI Global. doi:10.4018/978-1-6684-8587-3.ch004

Ayittey, G. (2002). *Biting their own Tails: African Leaders and the Internalist intricacies of the Rape of a Continent*. A Keynote address to SORAC.

Ayo, S. B. (1995). The Evolution of the Nigerian Local Government System. In A. M. Awokotun (Ed.), *New Trends in Nigerian Local Government*. Obafemi Awolowo University Press.

Bertelsmann Stiftung. (2018). *BTI 2018: Country Report – Somalia*. Gutersloh: Bertelsmann Stiftung. Retrieved from https://docslib.org/doc/9506976/bti-2018-country-report-somalia

Boehm, F., & Sierra, F. (2015). *The gendered impact of corruption: Who suffers more-men or women?* Bergen: Chr. Michelsen Institute. Retrieved from https://www.cmi.no/publications/5610-the-gendered-impact-of-corruption

Burke, J. (2017). Somalis greet 'New Dawn' as US dual national wins presidency. *The Guardian*. Retrieved from https://www.theguardian.com/world/2017/feb/08/somali-presidential-election-won-mohamed-abdullahi-mohamed

Camargo, C. B., & Koechlin, L. (2018). Informal governance: Comparative perspectives on Co-optation, control and camouflage in Rwanda, Tanzania and Uganda. In African Cities and the Development Conundrum (pp. 78-100). Brill.

Carver, S. (2017, March 5). Somali elections: How women still fight for political space in African polls. *The Conversation*. Retrieved from https://theconversation.com/somali-elections-how-women-still-fight-for-political-space-in-african-polls-73213

Check, N. A., Madise, T., Majozi, N., & Hamada, Y. (2019). *The Integrity of Political Finance Systems in Africa: Tackling Political Corruption* (International IDEA Policy Paper No. 20). Africa Institute of South Africa. Retrieved from https://www.idea.int/publications/catalogue/integrity-political-finance-systems-africa

Chipkin, I. (2013). Whither the state? Corruption, institutions and state-building in South Africa. *Politikon, 40*(2), 211–231. doi:10.1080/02589346.2013.798457

Dell, G., & McDevitt, A. (2018, September 12). Exporting Corruption: Progress Report 2018: Assessing Enforcement of the OECD Anti-Bribery Convention. *Transparency International*. Retrieved from https://www.transparency.org/en/publications/exporting-corruption-2018

Ezeoha, A., & Uche, C. (2005). *South Africa, NEPAD and the African Renaissance* (ASC Working Paper 64). African Studies Centre. Retrieved from https://vdocument.in/south-africa-nepad-and-the-african-south-africa-nepad-and-the-african-renaissance.html?page=1

FATF. (2011). *Laundering the proceeds of corruption*. Financial Action Task Force. Retrieved from https://www.fatf-gafi.org/documents/documents/launderingtheproceedsofcorruption.html

Fragile States Index. (2019). *Fragility in the World 2019*. Retrieved from https://fragilestatesindex.org/

Gettleman, J. (2017, February 7). Cash flows freely as Somalia holds 'fraudulent' election. *Irish Times*. Retrieved from https://www.irishtimes.com/news/world/africa/cash-flows-freely-as-somalia-holds-fraudulent-election-1.2966543#:~:text=Cash%20flows%20freely%20as%20Somalia%20holds%20%E2%80%98fraudulent%E2%80%99%20election,corruption%20Expand%20Swimmers%20among%20boats%20in%20Mogadishu%2C%20Somalia

Gitta, A., & Fröhlich, S. (2019, May 24). *Germany withholds aid money from Uganda*. Retrieved from https://www.dw.com/en/germany-withholds-aid-money-from-uganda/a-48862574-0

Global Witness. (2018, November 16). *DRC: Anti-Corruption organizations question make-up of candidate's campaign finance team*. Retrieved from https://www.globalwitness.org/en/press-releases/drc-anti-corruption-organisations-question-make-up-of-candidates/

Hagberg, S., Kibora, L., Barry, S., Gnessi, S., & Konkobo, A. (2017). *Transformations sociopolitiquesburkinabè de 2014 à 2016: Perspectives anthropologiques des pratiques politiques et de la culture démocratique dans" un Burkina nouveau"*. Uppsala University. Retrieved from https://www.semanticscholar.org/paper/Transformations-sociopolitiques-burkinab%C3%A8-de-2014-%C3%A0-Hagberg-Kibora/d3e44808d5ffc8eb53006994d3f60892a044f397

Hayden, S. (2019, April 6). Asylum for sale: Refugees say some U.N. workers demand bribes for resettlement. *NBC News*. Retrieved from https://www.nbcnews.com/news/world/asylum-sale-refugees-say-some-u-n-workers-demand-bribes-n988351

Hilgers, M., & Loada, A. (2013). Tensions et protestations dans un régime semi-autoritaire: croissance des révoltespopulaires et maintien du pouvoir au Burkina Faso. *Politique Africanise, 3*, 187-208. Retrieved from https://www.cairn.info/revue-politiqueafricaine-2013-3-page-187.htm

Honson, S. (2009, August 6). *Corruption in Sub- Saharan Africa.* Council on Foreign Relations. Retrieved from https://www.cfr.org/backgrounder/corruption-sub-saharan-africa

Human Rights Watch. (2019, April 25). *Mozambique: Cyclone Victims Forced to Trade Sex for Food.* Retrieved from https://www.hrw.org/news/2019/04/25/mozambique-cyclone-victims-forced-trade-sex-food

Hutchinson, E., McKee, M., & Balabanova, D. (2019). What Drives Health Workers to Break the Rules and Use Public Resources for Private Gain? A Review of the Literature on sub-Saharan Africa. *LSHTM Research Online*. Retrieved from https://researchonline.lshtm.ac.uk/id/eprint/4659912/

IDEA. (2018). *Burkina Faso: Latest available data.* International Institute for Democracy and Electoral Assistance. Retrieved from https://www.idea.int/es/data-tools/country-view/61/55

Kavanagh, M., & McCarey, D. (2017). *All the president's wealth: the Kabila family business.* Congo Research Group. Retrieved from https://pulitzercenter.org/stories/all-presidents-wealth-kabila-family-business

Lawal, G. (2007). Corruption and development in Africa: challenges for political and economic change. *Humanity and Social Sciences Journal, 2*(1), 1-7.

Ljubas, Z. (2019, July 24). *US: Another guilty plea in Mozambique financial scam.* Organized Crime and Corruption Reporting Project (OCCRP). Retrieved from https://www.occrp.org/en/daily/10304-us-another-guilty-plea-in-mozambique-financial-scam

Lodge, T. (2019). State Capture: Conceptual Considerations. In M. Meirotti & G. Masterson (Eds.), *State Capture in Africa: Old Threats, New Packaging?* EISA Publications.

Maclean, R., & Boley, T. (2019). Protests in Liberia over George Weah's failure to tackle corruption. *The Guardian.* Retrieved from https://www.theguardian.com/world/2019/jun/07/thousands-protest-in-liberia-against-failure-to-tackle-corruption

Martini, M. (2014). State Capture: An Overview, Anti-Corruption Helpdesk. *Transparency International.* Retrieved from https://www.transparency.org/files/content/corruptionqas/State _capture_an_overview_2014.pdf

Matthysen, K., Spitaels, S., & Schouten, P. (2019). *Mapping artisanal mining areas and mineral supply chains in eastern DR Congo: Impact of armed interference & responsible sourcing.* International Peace Information Service. Retrieved from https://ipisresearch.be/publication/mapping-artisanal-mining-areas-mineral-supply-chains-eastern-drc/

Mbaku, T. M. (2000). *Political Corruption and Bureaucratic in Africa: The Public Choice Perspective*. Kriag.

Micallef, M., & Bish, A. (2019, November 21). *After the storm: Organized crime across the Sahel-Sahara following upheaval in Libya and Mali*. Global Initiative against Transnational Organized Crime. Retrieved from https://globalinitiative.net/analysis/after-the-storm/

Momoh, Z. (2013). *Faces of Corruption in Nigeria, Jos*. New Africa Magazine.

Mubarak, M. (2017, February 7). State of Accountability in Somalia in 2016: Unrestrained Corruption. *Marqaati*. Retrieved from https://marqaati.org/en/2017/02/state-of-accountability-in-somalia-in-2016-unrestrained-corruption/

Nakitende, M. G., Rafay, A., & Waseem, M. (2021). Frauds in Business Organizations: A Comprehensive Overview. In A. Rafay (Ed.), *Handbook of Research on Theory and Practice of Financial Crimes* (pp. 21–38). IGI Global. doi:10.4018/978-1-7998-5567-5.ch002

Nnoli, O. (2003). *Introduction to Politics*. SNAAP Press Ltd.

Ojo, O. (2007). A Political Economy Technique to comprehending Corruption and the obstacle of Human Development. In A. Aina (Ed.), *Corruption and the Challenge and Obstacle of Human Development*. Babcock University.

Papachristou, L. (2018). *UK pulls aid to Zambia over corruption report*. Organized Crime and Corruption Reporting Project (OCCRP). Retrieved from https://www.occrp.org/en/daily/8598-uk-pulls-aid-to-zambia-over-corruption-report

Public Protector South Africa. (2016). *State of Capture: A Report of the Public Protector* (Report No 6 of 2016/17). South African Government. Retrieved from https://www.gov.za/documents/state-capture-14-oct-2016-0000

Rafay, A. (Ed.). (2021a). *Money Laundering and Terrorism Financing in Global Financial Systems*. IGI Global. doi:10.4018/978-1-7998-8758-4

Rafay, A. (Ed.). (2021b). *Handbook of Research on Theory and Practice of Financial Crimes*. IGI Global. doi:10.4018/978-1-7998-5567-5

Rafay, A. (Ed.). (2023). *Concepts and Cases of Illicit and Illegitimate Finance*. IGI Global. doi:10.4018/978-1-6684-8587-3

Reitano, T., & Shaw, M. (2015, June 11). *Fixing a Fractured State? Breaking the Cycles of Crime, Conflict and Corruption in Mali and Sahel*. Geneva: Global Initiative Against Transnational Organized Crime. Retrieved from https://globalinitiative.net/analysis/fixing-a-fractured-state-breaking-the-cycles-of-crime-corruption-and-governance-in-mali-and-the-sahel/

Rheibay, J., & Chêne, M. (2016). *Gender and Corruption: A Topic Guide. Anti-Corruption Helpdesk*. Transparency International. Retrieved from https://knowledgehub.transparency.org /assets/uploads/kproducts/Topic_guide_gender_corruption _Final_2016.pdf

Rivas, M. F. (2013). An experiment on corruption and gender. *Bulletin of Economic Research, 65*(1), 10–42. doi:10.1111/j.1467-8586.2012.00450.x

Roy, P., Iwuamadi, K. C., & Ibrahim, J. (2020). *Breaking the cycle of corruption in Nigeria's electricity sector: A political settlements analysis* (Working Paper 20). ACE SOAS Consortium. Retrieved from https://eprints.soas.ac.uk/32532/1/ACE-WorkingPaper020-NigeriaPowerSector-200319.pdf

Tax Justice Network. (2020). *Financial Secrecy Index 2020*. Retrieved from https://fsi.taxjustice.net/en/

Titeka, K., & Thamani, J. (2018, December 18). How to get ahead in DR Congo politics: a flatterer's guide. *African Arguments*. Retrieved from https://africanarguments.org/2018/12/18/how-get-ahead-dr-congo-politics-guide/

Transparency International. (2018a). *The Impact of land corruption on women: Insights from Africa*. Retrieved from https://www.transparency.org/news/feature/impact_of_land_corruption_on_women_insights_from_africa

Transparency International. (2018b). *Women, Land and Corruption: Resources for Practitioners and Policy-Makers*. Retrieved from https://www.transparency.org/en/news/impact-of-land-corruption-on-women-insights-from-africa

Transparency International. (2019). *Global Corruption Barometer Africa 2019: Citizen's Views and Experiences of Corruption*. Retrieved from https://www.transparency.org/whatwedo/publication/gcb_africa_2019

Transparency International. (2020). *CPI 2019: Sub-Saharan Africa*. Retrieved from https://www.transparency.org/news/feature/cpi_2019_sub_saharan_africa

Transparency International Rwanda. (2018a). *Gender-based corruption in public workplaces in Rwanda*. Retrieved from https://tirwanda.org/IMG/pdf/gender_based_corruption_1_.pdf

Transparency International Rwanda. (2018b). *Promoting Transparency and Accountability in Climate Change Finance in Rwanda*. Retrieved from https://tirwanda.org/IMG/pdf/climate_change_mapping_report_final.pdf

Transparency International Zimbabwe. (2013). *Enforcement of Anti-Corruption laws: Zimbabwe*. UNCAC Civil Society Review 2013. Retrieved from https://uncaccoalition.org/files/cso-review-reports/year2-zimbabwe-report.pdf

Transparency International Zimbabwe. (2019). *Gender and corruption in Zimbabwe: Debates and policy options*. Retrieved from https://www.tizim.org/gender-and-corruption-in-zimbabwe-debates-and-policy-options/

UN African Renewal. (2019). *Silencing the Guns in Africa*. UN department of Global Communication. Retrieved from https://www.un.org/africarenewal/sites/www.un.org. africarenewal/files/A_R33_3_EN_0.pdf

UN Commission on Human Rights. (2020). *Deliberate starvation and corruption hallmarks of conflict in South Sudan say UN human rights experts*. Retrieved from https://www.ohchr.org/EN/HRBodies/HRC/Pages/NewsDetail.aspx?NewsID=25583&LangID=E

UN Security Council. (2017). *Letter Dated 8 August 2017 from the Group of Experts on the Democratic Republic of the Congo Extended Pursuant to Security Council Resolution 2293 (2016) Addressed to the President of the Security Council*. S/2017/672/Rev.1

UN Security Council. (2016). *Letter Dated 7 October 2016 from the Chair of the Security Council Committee Pursuant to Resolutions 751 (1992) and 1907 (2009) Concerning Somalia and Eritrea Addressed to the President of the Security Council*. S/2016/919.

UNECA. (2015). *Illicit financial flow: Report of the High Level Panel on Illicit Financial Flows from Africa*. Retrieved from uneca.org/handle/10855/22695

UNHCR. (2019, April 6). *UNHCR strongly rejects widespread allegations against workforce*. Retrieved from https://www.unhcr.org/news/press/2019/4/5ca8a2594/unhcr-strongly-rejects-widespread-allegations-against-workforce.html

US Department of Justice. (2019). *Three Former Mozambican Government Officials and Five Business Executives Indicted in Alleged $2 Billion Fraud and Money Laundering Scheme that Victimized U.S. Investors*. Retrieved from https://www.justice.gov/usao-edny/pr/three-former-mozambican-government-officials-and-five-business-executives-indicted

US Department of State. (2015). *Investment Climate Statement – Sudan*. Retrieved from https://2009-2017.state.gov/e/eb/rls/othr/ics/2015/244456.htm

Wadström, A., & Tetka, J. B. (2019). *Understanding land corruption as a basis for prevention: Findings from Liberia, Sierra Leone and Zambia*. Transparency International. Retrieved from https://www.transparency.org/en/publications/understanding-land-corruption-as-a-basis-for-prevention

Chapter 3
Counterfeiting Money and Anti-Counterfeit Measures:
The Historical Case of the Ottoman Empire

Busra Karataser
Tekırdag Namık Kemal, Turkey

ABSTRACT

This study is designed to investigate the use of counterfeit money in the Ottoman Empire. Firstly, the concept of money and the reasons for the use of counterfeit money in the Ottoman Empire are described. Secondly, the reasons for the formation of counterfeit money are examined. Thirdly, the precautions taken against counterfeit money in the Ottoman Empire are discussed. The goal of this study is to investigate the counterfeit money printing incidents that had taken place. Moreover, the anti-counterfeit measures are identified that are implemented by Ottoman Empire to curb this crime and to remove counterfeit money from the market.

INTRODUCTION

Money has had an important place in the economic field since the moment it was invented. It is recognized as certain coined metals or paper in assorted colors carrying varying symbols (Bülbül, 2013). Money has three primary functions within an economic structure. These functions are being distinguished as a medium of exchange, as a unit of account, and as a store of value (Bülbül, 2013). Monetary variable mechanisms were analyzed to determine the effects of monetary variables on economic activity and on the general level of prices. (Mishkin, 1994; Rafay & Farid, 2017). It was seen that the effects of monetary variables on total output and price level mostly affected the money market (Akdeniz & Çatık, 2019).

Like all traditional economies, the Ottoman economy was based on the coin system. The basis of this system is the use of money, that is, gold and silver, as a medium of exchange while minimizing its use as goods so that the money supply is at a level that will meet the need for exchange. This system brought a stable monetary regime to the Ottoman economy (Tabakoğlu, 2016). The first Ottoman currency, the *akçe*, was struck in 1326. The geometric average of the total depreciation of the *akçe* in 414

DOI: 10.4018/978-1-6684-5007-9.ch003

years between 1326 and 1740 was 2%, suggesting an inflation-free economy (Tabakoğlu, 2016). The Ottoman State coined its first currency as a symbol of independence in its establishment and started to use it within its borders. Although the coining began in the central regions, the State kept coining in places close to the mines over time, facilitating its circulation. The Ottoman Empire paid attention to protecting the value of the money coined in the mint and to its circulation within the State. Various laws were enacted to protect the circulation of money. Penal sanctions were applied to those who acted against the law (Baytimur, 2016).

The 19th century is a unique period in terms of economy and money in Ottoman history. A feature of the period is the reforms inspired by the West, which were undertaken to strengthen the central state in the fields of economy, finance, and money, as well as administration, education, and justice. Another key feature of the period is its opening up to world markets through the rapid expansion in European trade. In this way, the Ottoman economy gained an identity that specialized in exporting agricultural goods and importing manufactured goods. Between 1820 and 1914, there was a 15-fold increase in foreign trade by Macedonia, Anatolia, Syria, and Iraq, which were within the empire's borders until 1911. This increase was supported by the construction of ports and railways, causing an expansion in trade volume (Pamuk, 1999). Policymakers need to take various measures on monetary policies to ensure economic growth in the country. Economic growth forms the basis of increasing welfare in society. Investments in human and physical capital, the adaptation of new production techniques, and the development of new products are considered indispensable elements of the growth process. (Çetin & Ecevit, 2016).

Money is used as a medium of exchange, and the State must only carry out the minting of money. However, in all societies throughout history, some individuals placed counterfeit money on the market (Kılıç, 1999).

Kalpazan (transl. counterfeiter) is an expression that means liar or unreliable, and it is used for people who counterfeit money (Pakalın, 1972). Ottoman documents mainly include words such as *kallab* (transl. fraud*), kalbzen* (transl. liar), and *sikkezen* (transl. coiner) (Kılıç, 1999). To maintain balance in the circulation of money within its borders, the Ottoman Empire attempted to implement the monetary system in an orderly manner by issuing laws stating the mintage methods of the coins and the steps to be taken by officials (Akgündüz, 1990).

Counterfeit *akçe* is the money used as an imitation of the *akçe*. Counterfeiting activities occurred in various regions during different periods. Counterfeiting events were concentrated in Central and Western Anatolia and Rumelia in the 16th century. One hundred forty-three incidents occurred in 108 separate locations. The mints were one of the areas in which counterfeiting activities were found to be intense. For example, there were 13 counterfeiting incidents in Skopje, 10 in Edirne, seven in Novo Brdo, and six in Bursa (Kılıç, 1999). Counterfeit coins were obtained by pouring them into a mold and could easily be distinguished due to their rough and damaged surfaces. Other coins, which could not easily be detected as counterfeit, were coins that could not be detected by measuring their weight unless their components were weighed. (Öztel, 2018). To distinguish these counterfeit coins from the real ones, it was necessary to divide the counterfeit coins into two groups. Those in the first group were counterfeit coins made by inexperienced manufacturers, and those in the second group were skillfully made. These coins were manufactured and placed on the market by organized crime groups. Some looked even better than the real coins. This counterfeit money was impossible to recognize without using a chemical method. The observational approach, the contact method, recognition by a sound test, a chemical test, and a specific gravity test were used to distinguish coins from each other (Arat, 1985). Various methods were followed while taking precautions regarding counterfeit money in the Ottoman Empire. One of these methods included following the counterfeiter and the counterfeit money. This method was one of the most common methods of reaching the counterfeiter by detecting counterfeit money. The second method involved informing the public about the counterfeit money, and when the public encountered the counterfeit money, they immediately informed the police station. Due to this issue's importance, the police authorities conducted the investigation in secrecy until it was concluded (Öztel, 2020).

Another type of counterfeit money was commercially minted counterfeit money by foreigners that was identical to real money. These coins were made to facilitate trade in the regions where Ottoman coins were in circulation. Another example of counterfeiting was the imitation of gold- and silver-plated jewelry produced in the last period of the State (Öztel, 2018). The main reasons for the spread of imitation jewelry and coins were the influence of the West and to weakening the power of the sultans in the last period of the empire (Mikeska, 1988). There were some factors that facilitated counterfeiting and the spread of counterfeit currency, namely the effects of monetary and fiscal policies, the problem of detecting counterfeit money and coins, the difficulty of detecting counterfeit banknotes, and the lack of deterrent laws.

One of the punishments inflicted on counterfeit-money criminals in the Ottoman Empire was rowing, i.e., sentences of those convicted of various crimes were converted to rowing on ships in the Ottoman Empire. Apart from the rowing penalty, shackling (i.e., executing the prison sentence with leg cuffs) was also one of the punishments. Another punishment for counterfeiting was the death penalty.

BACKGROUND

This study investigates counterfeiting and anti-counterfeit methods during the historical Ottoman Empire. Since money is one of the main trade methods, many studies have been conducted on the topic. Especially in the 19th century, the modernization movements that started in the world led countries to new financing needs. For this reason, the problem of counterfeit money emerged in almost every country in the world. Key studies have been conducted on money, including studies on Turkish economic history (Tabakoğlu, 2007) and counterfeit money and counterfeiting in the Ottoman Empire (Öztel, 2018). Since counterfeit money and the measures taken were key in the Ottoman Empire, many new study topics emerged. Using the Ottoman archive's precious resources for the first time, this study examines the problem of counterfeit money in the Ottoman Empire, how it dealt with the issue and its fight against counterfeiting. This study, unlike previous studies, initially examines the economic background of the Ottoman Empire in cases where counterfeit money spread. The aim of this study is to show in detail the negative view of counterfeit money in the Ottoman Empire and the efforts made to prevent it.

COUNTERFIET MONEY: FAULTS AND SOLUTIONS

This study investigates the problem of counterfeit money, which is one of the biggest problems in history, and how the Ottoman Empire fought against the problem of counterfeiting. The effectiveness of the measures taken by the Ottoman Empire to solve the problem of counterfeit money was officially examined using Ottoman Archive sources.

MONETARY AND FINANCIAL SYSTEM OF THE OTTOMAN STATE

Money has a dynamic structure. It shows a variable structure from society to society and over time. While the functions of money have changed over time, the form of money has also begun to change. Different objects are used as a means of exchange in various cultures, which can be identified as commodity money and fiat money in the basic sense. Commodity monies are objects that have value when used as commodities and can also be used as a medium of exchange. Gold is a good example of commodity money. For centuries, gold has served as a medium of exchange for purchasing goods and services. Gold also has an important value in other areas of use as a commodity. Another type of commodity money is silver. Silver has also been used for many years. Another type of money is fiat money, which has no value as a commodity but is used to purchase goods and services. Although the paper money used today has no tangible value, it is used because of its nominal value (Pamuk, 1999).

Classical Period Ottoman Monetary System

The Ottoman economy was based on the coin system like all other traditional economies. The Ottomans employed the flexible attitude that Islam displayed during the first spreading period in the face of local traditions, and they did not force the change of tradition. In fact, the essence of this system was to minimize the use of money, that is, gold and silver, as a means of exchange. The coin system was different from today's money system. There was no monetary policy that was applied differently in the face of price movements or unemployment (Tabakoğlu, 2014).

The Ottoman State continued the practice inherited from the Seljuks and encouraged the entry of precious metals into the country while prohibiting its exit. This application aimed to improve the money supply (Koçi (bey) & Danişman, 1972). The Ottoman system utilized money as a financing tool in three ways. Firstly, the State increased the money supply by minting new coins out of precious metals and old coins, effectively financing various expenditures. Secondly, the new sultan who ascended the throne used to mint his own coins and forbade the circulation of old coins. Starting from *Süleyman I,* the sultans put an end to this policy. Thirdly, the policy of changing the settings of the coins (coin correcting) had to be followed from time to time, which meant increasing the copper ratio in gold and silver coins and scaling down these coins (debasement and devaluation) (Tabakoğlu, 2019).

The coins could be made of either gold or silver, the weight of these coins was considered and the money was minted in mints. Mints were operated as *Muqata'ah* for a period of three years using the tax farming method. Mints were generally established in places with mines or where a region needed circulation. It was necessary to accumulate the mine to cover the costs of minting the mints (Açıkgöz, 2010). The coin system was in effect in the Ottoman economic system in the classical period. Although the value of *akçe* had decreased recently, it was used as the money of account between 1326 and 1757. Representative money began to be widely used in the *Tanzimat* period (Tabakoğlu, 2019).

Counterfeit Money Minted in the Ottoman State

There were many reasons for counterfeiting money in the Ottoman Empire. Therefore, it is necessary to understand the economic conditions of the period. When the conditions of the Ottoman Empire in the 19th century were combined with the outside world, significant negativities were experienced. The mentality of the politicians who served in this period, the *Tanzimat* reforms, and the wars adversely affected the state economy. On the one hand, these developments increased the demand for money and the speed of circulation along with the expanding trade volume in the 19th century. The Ottoman Empire established monetary policies to meet its financial and economic needs with the effect on both internal and external factors (Öztel, 2018).

A disintegration started in the country during this period with the mobilization of ethnic elements, starting from the Balkans. The Ottoman Empire had to lean on Europe to maintain its power under central control. The constant increase in external debt also worsened the country's financial situation. The '93 war that suddenly broke out made the financial conditions of the country even more difficult. As the trading volume was growing, new market conditions were shaped for counterfeiters as well. Being able to earn more with less risk became important in society. Under these conditions, paper money was seen as a new source of finance in addition to the coins in circulation in the country at the time. Although the State considered this situation as a source of financing, counterfeiters considered it a new opportunity (Öztel, 2018).

For the first time, "*Kaime-I Nakdiye-iMutebere*" (*Kaime* in short, transl. interest debt securities) were issued by the State in 1840. The only reason forcing the State to issue *Kaime* was the urgent need for financial resources. Funding required for the *Tanzimat* reforms was at the forefront of the resource needs. The other resource needed was the increase in military financing expenditures due to the wars that took place during that time. *Kaime's* began circulating in the market after they were first printed inside and outside the country (Erol, 1970).

Counterfeit money began to be printed due to problems in the monetary system, especially in the 19th century in the Ottoman Empire. Official institutions were constantly warned about counterfeit money, so necessary precautions were taken. In the Ottoman Empire, both money and coins were counterfeited. This money circulating in the market looked real unless the coins were analyzed. However, it was revealed as counterfeit as a result of the analysis made in the laboratories. For example, the fake Ottoman gold coins produced by an international band of counterfeiters composed of Hungarians and Americans captured in 1859 were a work of mastery and were indistinguishable from the real coins. If the gang had not been reported, it was inevitable that these coins would have continued to circulate in the market (Öztel, 2020).

A letter was delivered to *Sadaret* (transl. the Grand Vizier) from Darphane Nazırı (transl. the Minister of Mint) on 2 December 1815, mentioning that a person who minted counterfeit gold, similar to Egyptian Ruby on copper, was found in his house in the vicinity of *Kıztaşı in Istanbul.* Realizing that he would be caught, this person tried to escape by changing his clothes. However, his crime was detected by officials, and he was taken to the Mint. In his interrogation there, he admitted to the crime of minting counterfeit money. He was handed over to the Mint after taking out the necessary tools from his stash that he used to print counterfeit money. These tools were sent to *Bâb-ı Âli* (transl. the Ottoman Porte). He also delivered some minted and rough copper in addition to these tools. This person was arrested and sentenced to rowing for some time to set an example to other counterfeiters.

The letter written by *Sadaret* to *Darphane Nazırı* stated that the counterfeiter should be punished according to the will of the Sultan. Addressing the letter of *Darphane Nazırı*, the Sultan stated that this problem could not be prevented unless the counterfeiters were punished and that it was not appropriate to pass it over only with the rowing punishment. He demanded that this issue be punished following the Sharia provisions after the Sheikh al-Islam made a fatwa on it (Prime Ministry Ottoman Archive HAT 409/21264).

The State focused greatly on the crime of counterfeiting money because it harmed the economy, so it tried to take every measure to prevent it. For this purpose, the situation was controlled by catching people red-handed. While the Mint was conducting its investigations meticulously, a consent order was requested from the Sultan. Due to the seriousness and importance of the issue, it was requested that, instead of glossing over the issue with light penalties, punishments be given as an example to other counterfeiters. The request has great importance as it shows how seriously the Ottoman Empire approached this issue.

While the Ottoman Empire continued to take precautions against counterfeit money, it tried to inform its provinces to reduce the criminal act. On July 22, 1899, a letter was sent from *Dahiliye Nezareti* (transl. the Ministry of Internal Affairs) to the provinces, the sanjaks that were not affiliated with a province, the *Şehremaneti* (transl. the Municipality*), Rüsumatemaneti* (transl. the Tax Administration), *ZabtiyeNezareti* (transl. the Ministry of the Police), and *Posta ve TelgrafNezâreti* (transl. the Post and Telegraph Ministry), stating that: "It has been determined that a person from the Tirana district with twenty gold coins sent the coins to the *Shkodër* Province. As a result of the examination and analysis carried out by the *Meskukat-ı Şahane* administration (transl. a unit in the Ministry of Finance), it was determined that these twenty gold coins were composed of two rotten pieces and their raw materials were copper and zinc. It was also determined that the *tughra* and inscriptions had nothing to do with the original coins. It had been revealed in the investigation that there were more of these counterfeit coins, and they would be released into the market. For this reason, the Ministry of Finance announced measures to be taken in this regard with the letter dated 15 July 1899 and notified all provinces to prevent the circulation of counterfeit money. The *Shkodër* Governorate, where the incident occurred, was asked to focus on preventing counterfeit money from being placed on the market and imported from abroad" (BOA, DH.MKT.2237/54).

The Ottoman Empire tried to fight against counterfeit money during the 19th century. However, while fighting against this crime domestically, counterfeit money imported from abroad caused the problem to grow even more in the process. The remarkable aspect of counterfeit money in the Ottoman Empire in the 19th century was that gold and silver coins called *Mecidi* began to be counterfeited. As mentioned in the inscription written by *Bab-ı Ali Daire-iUmur-ı Dahiliye*(transl. Ministry of the Interior of the Ottoman Porte) on 4 December 1901, one *Mecidi* was sent from the *Bank-ı Osmani* (transl. the Ottoman Bank), which was considered to be counterfeit. According to the analysis and control made by *Meskukat-ı Şahane*, it was understood that the metal composition consisted of 812-carat silver and copper, which was produced by pouring it into a mold. On October 22, 1901, *Maliye Nezareti* (transl. the Ministry of Finance) stated that the issue needed attention since *Mecidis* reached the banks in the market (BOA, DH.MKT. 2564/127). The Ottoman State kept informing all provinces and sanjaks of every problem related to counterfeit money to prevent the proliferation of the crime.

Involvement of Public Officials in Counterfeit Money Processes

The letter written by *Dahiliye Nezareti* (nowadays, referred to as ministry) to the *Huzur-ı Sadaret office* and *Posta ve Telgraf Nezâreti* on 14 December 1901, mentioned that the investigation revealed that Aleppo Post Manager, *Osman Efendi*, was part of a counterfeiter group. He then confessed to the crime. The Chief Post Office was asked to appoint a deputy in place of the Post Manager, *Osman Efendi*, due to his crime. The molds and other tools belonging to the counterfeiting group that he was caught with were found and delivered to *Sadaret*. The incident was reported to *Posta ve Telgraf Nezareti*. In addition, *Posta ve Telgraf Nezareti* in Aleppo was asked to investigate other employees in case they were also involved in any counterfeiting activity. *Sadaret* investigated the issue in detail and reached some conclusions. There were several incidents that involved the employees. The suggestions by *Sadaret* regarding the appointment of someone to *Posta ve Telgraf Nezareti* in Aleppo were as follows: "It would be appropriate to dismiss the Chief Director from the job since the truth could not be revealed as long as he was on duty, or an officer should be sent to *Posta ve Telgraf Nezareti* in Aleppo, and the inspection and investigation should be conducted urgently" (BOA, DH.MKT 2568/116).

While the Ottoman State took various measures to prevent counterfeit money, the involvement of some State officials in the crime made the process even more difficult. The involvement of civil servants in the crime disturbed *Sadaret*, so the officers found guilty were dismissed from their jobs, and it was attempted to prevent causing further harm to the public.

While the Ottoman State was sensitive about counterfeit money, it was frequently encountered that public officials were involved in or accused of these crimes. One of these incidents was experienced with one of the *Beyoğlu* administrators, Bahri Pasha (*Süleyman Bahri*). Bahri Pasha was an administrator that the Palace and *Bab-ı Ali* favored. He was rewarded with medals at different times in the Ottoman Empire (Öztel, 2020).

Bahri Pasha had close relatives among top government officials in the State. Bahri Pasha could speak Turkish, Kurdish, Persian, and Armenian. He started his civil service in 1864 at the age of 19. He became the Governor of *Beyoğlu* in 1878 after successfully serving in civil service for many years and he was rewarded with long-service medals (Öztel, 2020). However, Bahri Pasha, the governor of *Beyoğlu*, had as many enemies as he had friends. While he was serving as the highest civilian authority, he was accused of counterfeiting in 1883 and placed in the spotlight. After Bahri Pasha was accused of counterfeiting, he was dismissed and charged (BOA, DH. SAID 1/146).

While Bahri Pasha was on trial, a telegram was sent to *Nusret* Pasha, the aide-de-camp of *II. Abdülhamid*, with three signatures from Beyoğlu, contains inappropriate statements about Bahri Pasha. In response to the telegram written to *Sadaret* on September 23, 1883, *Nusret* Pasha stated that the court process of Bahri Pasha regarding counterfeiting should be settled as soon as possible. Additionally, *Nusret* Pasha stated that Bahri Pasha was still one of the Ottoman State officials, that there was no final decision about him yet, and that malicious people would not be allowed to intervene, referring to those who wrote the letter. He requested that inappropriate speeches be avoided since such malicious people's unreliable statements would harm the State's reputation. While hoping that Bahri Pasha would never commit a crime related to the issue of the counterfeiting in question, it was asked that the issue be settled quickly by the Ministry of Justice in a righteous and just manner according to the will of the Sultan (BOA, İ.DH. 895/71227).

Unfortunately, it was revealed that counterfeit gold was in circulation and had spread in the market as well, despite the measures taken regarding counterfeit gold. The emergence of these events usually occurred as a result of denunciations or police pursuits. On 20 July 1902, a letter presented to the Governor from the *Erzincan Eğin* District Commissioner mentioned that *Nalband Mehmedoğlu* found twenty gold coins suspected of being counterfeit on an Armenian in the *Egin* bazaar. People reported that these twenty gold coins were given to a Kurd while trading and that the coins were returned by the Kurd. Upon noticing this, *Police Lombo Efendi* accompanied the informant and brought the Armenian and the Kurd to the police for questioning about the gold. When the seized gold was examined, it was understood to be missing carats and new gold. When the Kurdish citizen with whom he traded was asked about the situation, he said that he bought the gold from a tailor, *Toskiyan Kirkor Efendi*, for 24 *kuruş*. When the tailor was questioned, he said that he received this gold from trading with his partner *Eşkizade Lütfü Efendi*. Upon investigation, the clothes and shop of the Armenian tailor were searched. A crucible made of white gypsum soil, which was placed by *Lütfü Efendi*, was found in a drawer in the shop. *Lütfü*

Efendi was also questioned, and he confessed that he had provided the gold. When the investigation was deepened and *Lütfü Efendi's* interrogation continued, he admitted that he had given the gold to the other people. He also said that he bought six gold coins from the goldsmiths in *Istanbul Balıkpazarı. Lütfü Efendi* accepted that the crucible (the tool used in making counterfeit coins) belonged to him. The investigation was deepened to detect the widespread use of counterfeit coins in trade. The proceedings expanded in this way and showed that these counterfeit gold coins were plentiful in Istanbul, and the people who traded from *Erzincan Egin* bought these gold coins from Istanbul to make jewelry for the women in *Eğin*. Although various measures were taken to prevent counterfeiting in the country, it was also stated that this gold might have come from Europe. The above-mentioned persons were arrested by *Zaptiye Nezareti* (transl. the Ministry of Security), and their statements were recorded and handed over to the district governor's office.

While the Ottoman Empire fought against counterfeit coins and gold, full control could not be achieved for various reasons. *Zabıta Nezareti* (transl. the Police Department) tried to catch criminals through informants. Even if inter-provincial control was ensured, no results were obtained as gold from Europe could not be controlled (BOA, DH.MKT 545/44).

Table 1. The List of counterfeit gold and the places it was sent on 25 July 1903

	Origin	# of Pieces	Type	How is it made?	Weight		Made of	Carat	Evaluation
					Dirhem	Grad			
1	*Deputy of Edirne Governor*	1	*Quarter Mecidi*	Casting	1	9½	Copper Tin Zinc	0	The sultan's monogram, calligraphy and decoration are not like the original
2	*Deputy of Edirne Governor*	1	*Mecidi*	Casting	6	9½	Silver Copper	875	The sultan's monogram, calligraphy and decoration are not like the original
3	*Aydın Province*	1	*Mecidi*	Casting	14	5	Antimony, Tin, Copper, Zinc	0	The sultan's monogram, calligraphy and decoration are not like the original
4	*Aydın Province*	1	*Mecidi*	Casting	12	5	Tin Antimony Lead Copper	0	The sultan's monogram, calligraphy and decoration are not like the original
5	*Aydın Province*	1	*Mecidi*	Casting	13	5	Tin Antimony Lead	0	The sultan's monogram, calligraphy and decoration are not like the original
6	*Aydın Province*	1	*Mecidi*	Casting	0	6	"		The sultan's monogram, calligraphy and decoration are not like the original
7	*Tripoli Province*	1 17	*Quarter Mecidi Double*	Casting	0 Misc.		Silver Copper Silver Copper	825 850	The sultan's monogram, calligraphy and decoration are not like the original
8	*Tripoli Province*	3 8	*Quarter Mecidi Double*	Casting	0 Misc.		Silver Copper Silver Copper	830 840	The sultan's monogram, calligraphy and decoration are not like the original
9	*Tripoli Province*	1 48	*Mecidi Double*	Casting	12 Misc.	6	Silver Copper Silver Copper	560 850	The sultan's monogram, calligraphy and decoration are not like the original
10	*Tripoli Province*	38	*Double*	Casting	Misc.		Silver Copper	870	The sultan's monogram, calligraphy and decoration are not like the original

Continued on following page

Table 1. Continued

	Origin	# of Pieces	Type	How is it made?	Weight		Made of	Carat	Evaluation
					Dirhem	Grad			
11	*Tripoli Province*	26	*Double*	Casting	"		Silver Copper	850	The sultan's monogram, calligraphy and decoration are not like the original
12	*Shkodër Provincial Revenue Office*	1	*Mecidi*	Casting	4½	6	Silver Copper	480	The sultan's monogram, calligraphy and decoration are not like the original
13	*Ministry of Monastery Revenue Office*	1	*Mecidi*	Casting	9	1	Tin Copper Antimony Silver	0	The sultan's monogram, calligraphy and decoration are not like the original
14	*Ankara Revenue Office*	1	*Mecidi*	Casting	8½	5	Tin Copper Antimony Copper	0	The sultan's monogram, calligraphy and decoration are not like the original
15	*Sivas Province*	1	*Mecidi*	Casting	14	6	Silver Copper	625	The sultan's monogram, calligraphy and decoration are not like the original
16	*Kastamonu Province*	1	*Mecidi*	Casting	10½	5	Tin Antimony Zinc Lead	0	The sultan's monogram, calligraphy and decoration are not like the original
17	*Aleppo Provincial Revenue Office*	1	*Mecidi*	Casting	8	7	Silver Copper	830	The sultan's monogram, calligraphy and decoration are not like the original
18	*Yemen Province*	1 1	*Mecidi*	Casting	7½	6	Copper Tin Silver	260260	The sultan's monogram, calligraphy and decoration are not like the original
19	*Baghdad Province*	1	*Mecidi*	Casting	11½ 0	6 7	Tin Zinc Lead Silver Copper	0 450	The sultan's monogram, calligraphy and decoration are not like the original
20	*Izmid Governor's Office*	1	*Mecidi*	Casting	7	5	Antimony Tin Copper	0	The sultan's monogram, calligraphy and decoration are not like the original

Continued on following page

Table 1. Continued

	Origin	# of Pieces	Type	How is it made?	Weight		Made of	Carat	Evaluation
					Dirhem	Grad			
21	*Gum Governor's Office*	1 1	*Mecidi*	Casting	11 11	5 5	Tin Antimony Zinc Lead Tin Antimony Zinc Lead	0 0	The sultan's monogram, calligraphy and decoration are not like the original
22	*Konya Province*	1	*Mecîdî*	Casting	8	7	Silver Copper	620	The sultan's monogram, calligraphy and decoration are not like the original
		161							

The letter sent from *Dahiliye Nezareti* to all provinces, independent sanjaks, *Zabtiye Nezareti, Posta ve Telgraf Nezareti,* and *Şehremaneti* on 25 July 1903, included a list of the counterfeit gold caught between 1900 and 1901, where they originated, and their weights. According to this:

1 and a quarter *Mecidi* were sent from the Edirne Province. The full *Mecid*i weighed six dirhams, was nine and a half carats, and it consisted of silver and copper. The quarter weighed one dirham, was nine and a half carats, and it consisted of copper, tin, and zinc.

4 *Mecidis*[1] were found in the Aydın Province. Each *Medici* weighed five dirhams, they were either fourteen, twelve, or thirteen carats and consisted of antimony, lead, zinc, and copper.

137 double *Mecidis*[2], 4 quarter *Mecidis*, and 1 *Mecidi* were sent from the Tripoli Provincial Revenue Office, and they were made of copper and silver.

1 *Mecidi* was sent from the Monastery Province Revenue Office. It weighed one dirham, was nine carats, and was made of tin, copper, antimony, and a small amount of silver.

1 *Mecidi* was sent from the *Ankara* Province Revenue Office. It weighed five dirhams, was eight and a half carats, and was made of tin, antimony, and a small amount of copper.

1 *Mecidi* was sent from the *Sivas* Province. It weighed 16 dirhams, was 14 carats, and was made of silver and copper.

1 *Mecidi* was sent from the *Kastamonu* Province. It weighed five dirhams, was ten and a half carats, and was made of tin, antimony, anode, and lead.

1 *Mecidi* was sent from the Aleppo Provincial Revenue Office. It weighed seven dirhams, was eight carats, and was made of silver and copper.

1 *Mecidi* was sent from the *Yemen* Province. It weighed six dirhams, was seven and a half carats, and was made of copper, tin, and silver.

2 *Mecidis* were sent from the Baghdad Province. The weight of one *Medici* was seven dirhams, the others weighed six dirhams, they were eleven and a half carats and made of silver, copper, tin, zinc, and lead.

1 *Mecidi* was sent from the *Izmir* Governor's Office. It weighed five dirhams, was seven carats, and was made of antimony, tin, and copper.

2 *Mecidis* were sent from the *Chios* Governorate. They weighed five dirhams, were eleven carats, and were made of tin, antimony, zinc, and lead.

1 *Mecidi* was sent from the *Konya* Province. It weighed seven dirhams, was eight carats, and was made of silver and copper.

What made it possible to understand that these gold coins were counterfeit was that the Sultan's signature, calligraphy, and ornaments were not the same as the coins in circulation. This finding resulted from the analysis and examination made by the *Meskukat-ı Şahane* Administration[3]. A letter was sent from *Maliye Nezareti* to all provinces to prevent the circulation of such counterfeit coins and prevent their import from abroad (BOA, DH.MKT.545/44).

While the Ottoman Empire fought against counterfeit money and gold, it sought to take precautions against counterfeit money by informing the provinces and districts of the places from where this counterfeit gold and money originated.

The letter written by *Maliye Nezareti* to *Dahiliye Nezareti* on September 8, 1903, mentioned that five-lira Ottoman gold shown to the Ottoman Bank cashier and examined by the *Meskukat-ı Şahane* Administration was found to be counterfeit. A letter written on January 13, 1903, specified the details of the production of the counterfeit money and requested an investigation if this money was brought to the Commodity Fund.

Some of the counterfeit money and gold were detected by Meskukat-ı Şahane and sent to the Beyoğlu Bidayet Court Penal Department to determine (inspect) whether the gold was counterfeit. It was revealed that the two Ottoman liras that were sent were found to be counterfeit. It was reported to Zabtiye Nezareti to conduct the necessary investigation about these gold coins. As a result of the investigation, it was ordered that these counterfeit gold pieces be published in the newspapers so that the shape and production method would be known to the public so that they would not be released to the market. The letter sent to Dahiliye Nezareti by Meclis-iMaliye (transl. the Ministry of Finance), mentioned that counterfeit gold started to be seen quite frequently in the Istanbul market. Especially since it was used in the form of jewelry, the public was made aware of these counterfeit products and that they should not be purchased if they were fake. For this purpose, this form of counterfeit gold was published in Istanbul newspapers. However, this jewelry was not only spread within the Istanbul market, but also in other provinces and independent sanjaks, and it was requested that the counterfeit gold be withdrawn from the market. It was also stated that the counterfeit gold detected by Meclis-iMaliye should be sent to Hazine (transl. the Ministry of Treasury). It was recommended to investigate those who placed the counterfeit gold in the market and to impose legal penalties (BOA, DH.MKT.545/44).

While the Ottoman Empire fought against counterfeit money, it tried to inform the public about this issue by notifying the places from where the counterfeit money originated. The imports arriving between June and August 1903 were inspected. Incoming gold types were known as Mecidiye and double gold. It was realized that this gold came from abroad and spread to the domestic market. For example, 6 Mecidiyes that came from Jeddah arrived at the Ports of Thassos (today, on the borders of Greece) and Moldova.

Table 2. The List of places that sent counterfeit gold to the ministry of the navy in 1903

# of Pieces	Type	Date	Origin
1	*Mecidi*	11 June 1319 (24 June 1903)	Sile Port
1	*Double*	11 June 1319 (24 June 1903)	Thasos Port
4	*Mecidi*	3 July 1319 (16 July 1903)	Jeddah Port
1	*Mecidi*	5 July 1319 (18 July 1903)	Moldovan Port
1	*Mecidi*	12 July 1319 (25 July 1903)	Mihaliç Port
1	*Mecidi*	24 July 1319 (6 August 1903)	Silivri Harbor
2	*Mecidi*	2 August 1319 (5 August 1903)	Marmara Port
1	*Mecidi*	18 August 1319 (31 August 1319)	Bartin Port
1	*Mecidi*	28 August 1319 (10 September 1903)	Mudanya Port
TOTAL	17	17 September 1319 (30 September 1903)	Giresun Harbor

The letter sent by *Dahiliye Nezareti* to the Thessaloniki Province on 17 June 1903, mentioned that when the expenditures of the Thessaloniki Province in May 1902 were examined, 1919 kuruş and 30 liras were sent from the districts to the city centers, in return for fifteen debt securities that were provided to some individuals by the finance officers for their debts. In the census, there were missing carat coins among these coins. However, since this money was received for debt, the large number of missing funds drew the center's attention. These missing funds would have caused damage to both the public and the State treasury. *Maliye Nezareti* requested that the public be cautious around counterfeit money placed into the market (BOA, DH. MKT 725/50).

A telegram was sent to *Sivas Emniyet-i Umumiye Müdüriyeti* (transl. the General Directorate of Security of *Sivas*) by the *Sivas Police* Chief *Mehmed C*elal on February 28, 1911. It mentioned that *Topuzoğlu Agop* from the house of *Ohannesoğlu Doğramacı Kasartik* in the *Akdeğirmen* district of *Sivas* carried a small but heavy chest to his house. The situation was suspect as the circulation of counterfeit money became widespread in the market. As a result of the investigation, the house of *Topuzoğlu Agop* was searched. During the search, 414 counterfeit two-*kuruş*, 2-quarter *Mecidiye* molds, scales, a wheel-composite machine, a gear-wheel compound machine, a fixing plate, a screwdriver, three rasps and handles, a hammer, twenty-five iron tools, and some scraps were found (BOA, DH.EUM.KADL 9/46).

Since counterfeit money began circulating in the market, authorities tried to prevent the problem by considering all kinds of notices. For this purpose, every suspicious situation was carefully examined, and the related reports were considered. Telegrams regarding money counterfeiting were being sent from almost every province of the Ottoman Empire.

Counterfeit gold coins were sent from *Sadaret* to *Maliye Nezareti* for inspection on August 1, 1913. The five-piece gold coins were sent to the *Meskukat-ı Şahane* Administration for examination from the First Penal Department of the *Beyoğlu Bidayet* Court, and it was determined that these gold coins were counterfeit and mostly used for adornment (jewelry). For this reason, *Zabtiye Nezareti* was requested to investigate on the subject on 1 August 1903. Since these gold coins were mostly used for jewelry, public awareness was raised, and purchases were prevented. Advertisements were published in the newspapers, the shapes and production forms of the gold were shown with pictures, and these counterfeits five-piece gold coins were not allowed to be placed on the market (BOA, BEO 2132/159879).

OUTCOME

Since the earliest periods of history, money has been a widely used medium of value. Since its invention, it has played a key role in economics. Money is made of certain metals and papers, carries certain symbols, and comes in assorted colors. Money functions as a medium of exchange, a unit of account, and a store of value. Early in history, coins were mostly made of gold and silver. Since these coins were made of valuable metals, new coins were eventually required due to transportation challenges.

Coining has always been seen as an expression of power. In 1326, the *akçe*, the first Ottoman coin, was produced. The geometric average of the *akçe's* overall depreciation for the period of 414 years between 1326 and 1740 was 2%, which suggests an inflation-free economy. Although the coining started in the central regions, the State began minting coins near mines over time to facilitate its circulation.

Following the *Tanzimat* reforms, the Ottoman Empire needed new financial resources throughout the 19th century. The ethnic-based warfare escalated over time, increasing the Ottoman Empire's financial needs. As a result, paper money, known as *Kaime*, supplanted gold and silver coins. These political and economic upheavals have also shifted the direction of money printing.

The first counterfeit coins in the Ottoman Empire were made of gold and silver. A counterfeit coin is basically a forged coin or a defective *akçe*. Most of the counterfeit coins were gold jewelry pieces. However, most of these counterfeit gold coins came from abroad and were imported into Ottoman territory. Counterfeit gold in the shape of coins and jewelry was discovered in numerous Ottoman regions. The Police mostly used informants to locate counterfeit gold and coins. Most of the counterfeiters were discovered while trading. Ballot boxes carried by suspicious persons had been noted. During searches conducted at their residences and workplaces as a result of the investigation of these suspects, tools and equipment needed to coin counterfeit gold was discovered. Legal proceedings to punish these suspects were then promptly initiated. Some counterfeit gold was used to produce jewelry, which was found to be fake after an investigation by the Mint's Head. Gold was imported, sold on demand, and used as jewelry. Following the proliferation of counterfeit gold jewelry in the market, the administration implemented various measures. Initially, it was thought that publishing the shape of counterfeit (fake) jewelry in newspapers would solve the problem. One of the issues with counterfeit money in the Ottoman Empire was the involvement of some public officials in the crime. The administration was particularly saddened by the participation of the Head of the Post Office in gold counterfeiting. To resolve the incident, the manager was fired.

The Ottoman Government fiercely fought against this crime, as counterfeit gold would harm both its people and the country's economy. It attempted to control counterfeiting money activities through a variety of measures. Penalties were used as a deterrent, but these measures were ineffective. Although the Ottoman government attempted to solve the problem of counterfeit money within its borders, the problem reappeared with the arrival of counterfeit gold from abroad.

DECLARATION

The author declares that the manuscript follows ethical standards and there are no potential conflicts of interest with respect to the research, authorship and/or publication of this chapter.

DISCLAIMER

The contents and views of this chapter are expressed by the author in his personal capacity. It is not necessary for the Editor and the Publisher to agree with these viewpoints, and they are not responsible for any duty of care in this regard.

ACKNOWLEDGMENT

The author extends sincere gratitude to

• The Editor and the International Editorial Advisory Board (IEAB) of this book who initially desk reviewed, arranged a rigorous double/triple blind review process, and conducted a thorough, minute, and critical final review before accepting the chapter for publication.

• All anonymous reviewers who provided very constructive feedbacks for thorough revision, improvement, extension, and fine tuning of the chapter.

• All colleagues, assistants and well-wishers who assisted to complete this task.

REFERENCES

Açıkgöz, Ö. (2010). Osmanlı Para Politikasında Reform Çabaları:1800-1844 Dönemi Üzerine Bir Değerlendirm. *Uluslararası Yönetim İktisat ve İşletme Dergisi*, *6*(12), 36–55.

Akdeniz, C., & Çatik, N. (2019). Parasal aktarım mekanizmalarının işleyişinde finansal koşulların önemi: Tvp-var modellerinden bulgular. *Pamukkale Üniversitesi Sosyal Bilimler Enstitüsü Dergisi*, *34*, 73–96.

Akgündüz, A. (Ed.). (1990). *Osmanlı Kanunnameleri ve Hukuki Tahlilleri:Osmanlı Hukukuna giriş ve Fatih devrikanunnameleri*. FEY Vakfı.

Arat, M. (1985). Kalp Para Nasıl Tanınır. *Türk NümizmatikDerneğiYayınları*, *15*(1), 1–29.

Baytimur, S. (2016). Osmanlı devleti'nde kalpazanlık faaliyetleri ve uygulanan cezalar (1789-1808). *Bitlis Eren Üniversitesi Sosyal Bilimler Enstitüsü Dergisi*, *5*(2), 56–72.

Bülbül, Y. (2013). *Osmanlı İktisat Tarihi*. Anadolu Üniversitesi Yayınları.

Çetin, M., & Ecevit, E. (2016). Vergi yükü ve ekonomik büyüme arasındaki ilişki: Türkiye ekonomisi üzerine ampirik bir analiz (1965-2013). *Namık Kemal Üniversitesi Sosyal Bilimler Metinleri. Ekim*, *8*(30), 95–112.

Erol, M. (1970). *Osmanlı İmparatorluğu'nda Kağıt Para*. TTK.

Kılıç, O. (1999). *16.Yüzyılın İkinci Yarısında Kalpazanlık Faaliyetleri. Osmanlı Ansiklopedisi*. Yeni Türkiye Yayınları.

Koçi (bey), & Danişman, A. Z. (1972). *Koçi Bey Risalesi, 1051/1641*. Ankara: Milli EğitimBakanlığı.

Mikeska, J. (1988). *Osmanlı Paralarının Sahteleri ve Taklitleri Üstüne Bazı Düşünceler*. Türk Nümizmatik DerneğiYayınları.

Mishkin, F. S. (1995). Symposium on the monetary transmission mechanism. *The Journal of Economic Perspectives*, *9*(4), 3–10. doi:10.1257/jep.9.4.3

Öztel, M. (2018). Osmanlı Devleti'nde Kalpazanlık ve Sahte Para (1808-1914): Kalpazanlığı ve Sahte Paranın Tedavülünü BesleyenFaktörler. *Historical Studies (Melbourne, Vic.)*, *10*(1), 197–221.

Öztel, M. (2020). Counterfeit money in Circulation in the Ottoman Money Market (1811-1919). *Medeniyet Araştırmaları Dergisi*, *5*(1), 1–23.

Öztel, M. (2020). Osmanlı Devleti'nin Kalpazanlıkla İmtihanı (1818-1921). *Belleten - Türk Tarih Kurumu*, *84*(299), 315–356. doi:10.37879/belleten.2020.315

Öztel, M. (2020). Payitaht'ın Avrupalısı Beyoğlu'nda İdareci Olmak:Mutasarrıf Bahri Paşa'nın Zorgünleri. *Fatih Sultan Mehmet İlmi Araştırmalar*, *16*(1), 223–258.

Pakalın, M. Z. (1972). *Osmanlı Tarih Deyimleri ve Terimleri Sözlüğü*. Milli Eğitim Bakanlığı.

Pamuk, Ş. (1999). *Osmanlı İmparatorluğu'nda Paranın Tarihi*. TarihVakfı Yurt Yayınları.

Rafay, A., & Farid, S. (2017). Dynamic Relationship between Islamic Banking System and Real Economic Activity: Evidence from Pakistan. *Journal of King Abdulaziz University. Islamic Economics*, *30*(2), 97–114.

Tabakoğlu, A. (2016). *Osmanlı MaliTarihi*. DergahYayınları.

KEY TERMS AND DEFINITIONS

Counterfeit Money (Counterfeit Akçe): It is the expression used for money that imitates akçe. Counterfeiting activities occurred in various regions during different periods. Counterfeiting activities were concentrated in Central and Western Anatolia and Rumelia in the 16th century.

Counterfeiter (Person Who Coins Counterfeit Money): An expression used to describe the counterfeiter, a liar or unreliable person.

Double Mecidi: The minted gold coins were called Mecidiye. There were 500 kuruş (five hundred/five-piece) that weighed 11 dirhams and was 4 carats, 100 kuruş (hundreds) that weighed 2 dirhams and was 4 carats, and 250 kuruş (coined in the ninth year of Culûs) that weighed 5 dirhams and was 10 carats. In addition, 50 (half) and 25 (quarter) gold Mecidis were coined. New silver coins were minted in the sixth year of the Culûs: 1 silver Mecidi (20 kuruş) that weighed 7 dirhams and was 8 carats, 1/2 Mecidiye (10 kuruş) that weighed 3 dirhams and was 12 carats, 1/4 mecidiye (5 kuruş) that weighed 1 dirham and was 14 carats. Specifically for these silver coins, the name Mecidi became well known, and later such coins were also called Mecidi. Among the people, 10 kuruş were called a half and 5 kuruş were called a quarter. Smaller units were double (12 carats), kuruş (6 carats) and 20 paras (3 carats). Silver Mecidis were known as "white mecidi" or "silvery mecidiye" among the people.

Mecidi: It is the general name of the gold and silver coins minted in the name of the Ottoman Sultan Abdülmecid in 1260 (1844) on the occasion of the sixth year of his accession to the throne. This term was widely used to denote silver coins worth 20 kuruş.

Money: It has played a vital role in the economic field since its invention. Money is made of certain metals and papers, carries certain symbols, and comes in assorted colors.

Money in the Ottoman Empire: The Ottoman Empire focused on protecting the value of money coined in mints and its circulation within the State. Various laws were enacted to protect the circulation of money. Penal sanctions were applied to those who acted against the law.

Chapter 4
Whistleblowing Policy Against Corruption:
The Case of Nigeria

Benjamin Enahoro Assay
https://orcid.org/0000-0002-2850-1718
Delta State Polytechnic, Ogwashi-Uku, Nigeria

ABSTRACT

Growing corruption in Nigeria is a cause of concern for everyone. In order to strengthen the fight against corruption, the government is determined to nip the hydra-headed monster in the bud. In this regard, two anti-corruption agencies have been established and the introduction of a whistleblowing policy has been introduced. Initially, the citizens embraced the policy by blowing the whistle on fraud, bribery, looted public funds/assets, financial misconduct, and other forms of gratification/theft. This yielded fruitful results as stolen public funds and assets that run into billions were recovered. However, rather than intensify their initial zeal to exposé corruption, the citizens' desire to blow the whistle began to wane amidst large-scale corruption. Against this backdrop, this chapter proffers solutions and recommends ways for the government to get Nigerians to actively continue with the whistleblowing policy.

INTRODUCTION

Corruption is a global phenomenon. No region is immune from it. Most countries of the world are plagued by the hydra-headed monster. Everywhere around the globe, it is common knowledge that corruption stifles economic growth and undermines development as resources meant for the progress of a nation are stolen by a privileged few. It is for this reason, that concerned citizens in most climes often move against all known forms of corrupt practices and various strategies are deployed to combat the scourge. Though a global problem, its negative effects are more felt in underdeveloped societies.

Nigeria is a developing country endowed with abundant human and natural resources but real development has eluded the nation owing to endemic corruption and a lack of purposeful leadership. It is sad to note that almost all aspects of the nation's life are afflicted by corruption. Corruption is said to

DOI: 10.4018/978-1-6684-5007-9.ch004

be responsible for the high level of poverty in the country and Africa at large. As a result of large-scale corruption, the economy of Nigeria has over the years witnessed stunted growth; various sectors are underfunded and neglected with citizens at the receiving end (Oluikpe, 2018; Babalola, 2019).

The regime of President Muhammadu Buhari came into power with a commitment to fight corruption to a standstill having realized the enormous threats it poses to the nation's survival. During his pre-election campaign in London, the president had said "*There will be no confusion as to where I stand on corruption*", adding that "*the corrupt will not be appointed into my administration*". In one forum after another, he was always quick to point out his administration's determination to rid Nigeria of cancerous corruption and impunity in public office. How far he has been able to achieve this is a matter of conjecture.

The president's assumption of office was followed by the launch of a vigorous anti-graft campaign with an alarm that "*if we do not kill corruption, corruption will kill Nigeria*". The fear of corruption became so obvious that the "*body language*"[1] of the president assumed a warning signal to those engaged in graft. Apart from launching some strategies to tackle corruption, the Buhari's administration came up with an innovative whistleblowing policy, which was unveiled on December 21, 2016, by Mrs. Kemi Adeosun, a former minister of finance. The whistleblowing policy was one of the creative additions to the fight against corruption by the federal government.

This chapter, therefore, examines the whistleblowing policy and corruption in Nigeria. The objectives of the chapter are:

- To highlight the benefits of the whistleblowing policy to Nigeria.
- To show why Nigerians are no longer blowing the whistle.
- To stress the need for government to legalize the whistleblowing policy.

BACKGROUND

Overview of Corruption

Corruption is a complex phenomenon. As a result, it is difficult to conceptualize. Evidence has shown that it is indeed a daunting and challenging endeavor (Derin, 2007; Ajibewa, 2006, Faloore, 2010, Igbuzor, 2008). Andvig *et al.* (2001) posit that "*corruption is a complex and multifaceted phenomenon with multiple causes and effects, as it takes on various forms and functions in different contexts*". In fact, one of the major problems in conceptualizing corruption is that while it is difficult for it to go away easily, it has the capacity to take new forms (Andrig & Fjeldstad, 2001; Girling & Staff, 1997).

The difficulty of defining corruption is first a function of its being a secret and clandestine activity and secondly because it has many manifestations, dimensions, and forms. That is why Johnson argues that studying corruption is a tricky business. According to him, definitions are controversial, and solid evidence is often elusive. Descriptive accounts may be clouded by self-serving equivocations. Equally subtle is the question of the significance of a corrupt act-not by its consequences but also by its meaning as perceived by citizens and officials alike (Ogundiya, 2009). Nevertheless, Tanzi (1998) has argued that while it may not be easy to define corruption, the crisis associated with corruption is not difficult to recognize.

The word corruption is originally from the Latin verb "*rumpere*" which means to break (Abdul-Ismail, n.d). Following this, corruption means the breaking of a certain code of conduct for the personal benefit of the perpetrator. Many definitions of corruption have been put forward. For example, Sen defines it as the violation of established rules for personal gain and profit (Aluko, 2009). Osoba defines it as "*anti-social behaviour conferring improper benefits contrary to legal and moral norms, and which undermines the capacity of authorities to improve the living conditions of the people*" (Aluko, 2009). The World Bank defines corruption as "*The abuse of public office for private gains. Public office is abused for private gain when an official accepts, solicits, or extorts a bribe. It is also abused when private agents actively offer bribes to circumvent public policies and processes for competitive advantages or profit. Public office can also be abused for personal benefit even if no bribery occurs, through patronage and nepotism, the theft of state assets, or the diversion of state resources*" (Agbu, 2003).

In Nye's classical definition, corruption is "*behaviour that deviates from the formal duties of a public role (elective or appointive) because of private regarding (personal, close family, private clique) wealth or status gains*" (Nye, 1967).

What can be deduced from the foregoing definitions is that corruption entails any behaviour that deviates from accepted norms, especially in the public space. It is any behaviour that goes against established rules, regulations, and established procedures. In short, corruption is behaviour that breaks the law or aid and abets breaking the law. Such behaviour usually confers undue and/or unmerited advantages on the perpetrator. Such behaviour also expresses the notion of a betrayal of trust, especially in a democracy where public office is held in the trust of the people.

Corruption has various forms and dimensions. Aluko (2009) has identified eight forms namely:

- Political corruption (grand)
- Bureaucratic corruption (petty)
- Electoral corruption
- Bribery
- Fraud
- Embezzlement
- Favoritism
- Nepotism

Table 1. Below graphically shows the types, causes and consequences of corruption

Types of Corruption	Causes	Forms	Consequences
Political Corruption	Weak electoral commission, law enforcement mechanism, judiciary and one-party dominated state	Inflation of votes, rigging of elections and deprivation of winners from weaker political parties	Civil unrest, bad governance, incompetent rulers and bad international image and electoral violence
Economic Corruption	A weak state, poverty and a wide income gap between the rich and the poor	Bribing to win contracts, influenced service delivery, contract cut-backs, inflation of government contracts and non-payment of taxes by highly placed businessmen	The escalating cost of governance, poor or non-implementation of public contracts, poor public services delivery, the shutdown of public parastatals and loss of public revenue through tax evasion and avoidance
Bureaucratic Corruption	Lack of national commitment, weak state and complex bureaucratic process	Bribery of public officials and distortion of due process/normal procedure in the public sectors	Bad policies, non-pursuance of policy objectives, policy failures, employment of incompetent hands as public officials and poor service delivery
Judicial Corruption	Poor salary scale, greed and weak law enforcement mechanism	Free bail, distortion of judgments, acceptance of bribes by judges and delay in passing judgement	Corruption persists, the private cost of corruption is lowered or reduced to zero, civil unrest and lawlessness take stage, and decadence of rule of law
Moral Corruption	Non-taxation of property, high level of poverty and wide income distribution	Flamboyant demonstration of individual materialistic possession and exploitation of masses by the few powerful rich in the society	Desperation to acquire wealth, arm robbery (419s), civil disorder and eventually revolution for change

Other categorizations which do not differ from that of Aluko exist (Yaru, 2009, Omotola, 2006). What is important, however, is that in whatever form it manifests, corruption perverts' public interest and unlawfully elevates private gain and advantages.

Manifestation and Acts of Corruption

Corruption manifests itself in various ways (Rafay, 2023). According to the Political Bureau established in Nigeria in 1987, the manifestations of corruption include:

- The inflation of government contracts in return for kickbacks;
- Frauds and falsification of accounts in the public service;
- Examination malpractices in educational institutions including universities;
- The taking of bribes and perversion of justice among the police, the judiciary, and other organs for administering justice, and
- Various heinous crimes against the state in the business and industrial sectors of the economy, in collusion with multinational companies such as over-invoicing of goods, foreign exchange swindling, hoarding, and smuggling (Egwemi, 2012).

The African Union Convention of Preventing and Combating Corruption and Related Offences list acts of corruption including:

- The solicitation or acceptance, directly or indirectly by a public official or any other person, of any goods of monetary, or other benefits, such as a gift, favor, promise or advantage for himself or herself or for another person or entity, in exchange for any act or omission in the performance of his or her public functions.
- The offering or granting, directly or indirectly, to a public official or any other person of any goods of monetary value, or other benefits, such as a gift, favor, promise or advantage for himself or herself or for any person or entity, in exchange for any act or omission in the performance of his or her public function.
- The offering or granting, directly or indirectly, to a public official or any other person for the purpose of illicitly obtaining benefits for himself or herself or for a third party.
- The diversion by a public official or any other person, for purposes unrelated to those for which they were intended, for his own or her own benefit or that of a third party of any property belonging to the state or its agencies, to an independent agency, or to an individual, that such official has received by virtue of his or her position.
- The offering or granting, promising, solicitation or acceptance, direct or indirectly, of any undue advantage for or by any person, who directs or works for, in any capacity, a private sector entity, for himself or herself or for anyone else, for him or her to act or refrain from acting, in breach of his or her duties.
- The offering, giving, soliciting or accepting directly or indirectly, or promising of any undue advantage to or by any person who asserts or confirms that he or she is able to exert any improper influence over the decision making of any person performing functions in the public or private sector in consideration thereof, whether the undue advantage is for himself or herself or for anyone else, as well as the request, receipt or the acceptance of the offer or the promise of such an advantage, in consideration of that influence, whether or not the influence is exerted or whether or not the supposed influence leads to the intended result.
- Illicit enrichment.
- The use or concealment of proceeds derived from any of the acts referred to in this article; and
- Participation as a principal, co-principal, agent, instigator, accomplice, or accessory after the fact, or in any other manner in the commission or attempted commission of, in any collaboration or conspiracy to commit, any of the acts referred to in this article (Egwemi, 2012).

The Corrupt Practice and other Related Offences Act 2000 lists offences, which are punishable by the Act to include among other things gratification by an official, corrupt offers to public officers, corrupt demand by persons, fraudulent receipt of property, making a false statement or return, gratification by and through agents, bribery of public officers and using position for gratification (Egwemi, 2012).

Agenyi and Ameh (2009) averred that corruption covers a whole gamut of activities that are not limited to the following:

- Intentional distortion of financial records.
- Misappropriation of assets whether or not accompanied by distortion of statement.
- Payment for contracts of jobs not executed.
- Ten percent kickbacks from contracts awarded.
- Intentional loss of receipts and mutilation of accounts documents.

- Insertion of fictitious names in the payment voucher and the amount involved paid to unauthorized persons.
- Using government official letterhead paper to order goods for private use purporting that it belongs to the government.
- Paying public cheques into a private account for any reason best known to the officer.
- Paying twice the cost of the item(s) using the same document.
- Leaving ex-employees on the payroll and collecting the said amount for private use.
- Charging the public or students unauthorized fees that are not utilized for the supply of any material for the institution.
- Doctoring marks for students for personal reasons.
- Asking and receiving cash or material before approving projects.
- Having carnal knowledge of the opposite sex before transacting business.
- Receiving cash or kind to write projects for students.
- Disposal of any government assets without due approval.
- Auctioning government property to oneself at little or no cost.
- Dolling money to people to allow you to stay in an office for another term.
- Over-inflating the cost of items purchased for the public.
- Diversion of workers' salaries and allowances for personal use.

As a universal menace, corruption does not seem to have respect for geographical boundaries, creed, race, or ethnicity. However, the scope and scale of corruption vary from one country to the other. Whatever the scale and scope of corruption, the important thing about it is that corruption on any scale is bad (Obasanjo, 1994; Lash, 2003).

Cost and Consequences of Corruption

Corruption has a lot of negative impacts on every sphere of development: social, economic, and political. As Ikubaje (2004) has argued, corruption is a global phenomenon and its effects on individuals, institutions, countries, and global development have made it an issue of universal concern (Igbuzor, 2008). According to the Lima Declaration, the impacts of corruption include the erosion of the moral fabric of society, violation of the social and economic rights of the poor and vulnerable, undermining of democracy, subversion of the rule of law, retardation of development and denial of society, particularly the poor, denial of the benefits of free and open competition (Igbuzor, 2008).

In the same vein, Bello-Imam (2004) has outlined the negative consequences of corruption including:

- Retardation of economic growth: corruption lowers investment and retards economic growth.
- Misallocation of talent: Where rent seeking proves more lucrative than productive work, talent will be misallocated. People will be lured to rent-seeking rather than productive work.
- Limitation of Aid flows: Where corruption is rampant, donor agencies are unwilling to put in their money.
- Loss of tax revenue: Revenue is lost through tax evasion or claiming improper tax exemptions.
- Adverse Budgetary consequences: When corruption is rampant budgeted amounts will not deliver the required services.

- Negative impact on quality of infrastructure and public service: When public contracts are procured through a corrupt system, it results in lower quality of infrastructure and public services.
- Negative composition of government expenditure: Corruption often tempts government officials to choose government projects not on the basis of public welfare but on the opportunity, they provide for extorting bribes. Under such a situation, large projects, whose exact value and benefit are difficult to monitor, usually present lucrative opportunities for corruption while returns on teachers' salaries and textbooks could be zero for the same set of officials.

As the former chairman of Transparency International, Peter Eigen correctly noted, corruption does not just line the pockets of political and business elites; it leaves ordinary people without essential services such as lifesaving medicines and deprives them of access to sanitation and housing. In short, corruption costs lives (Igbuzor, 2008).

Evolution of Corruption in Nigeria

Corruption is not new to Nigeria. Its origin dates to the colonial era. The hydra-headed monster started to manifest in various *chiefdoms* and *kingdoms* following the introduction of the Indirect Rule System by the British colonial government whose major preoccupation at that time was to explore and exploit the amalgamated entity called Nigeria. The essence of the Indirect Rule System was to create an administration that would be effective based on the consular system with native councils and minor councils as agents of the government. Warrant chiefs and clerks or court messengers were therefore used to drive the administrative system put in place by the colonial masters to the chagrin of the local people.

The warrant chiefs in the Southern part of Nigeria and the Emirs in the North were given the authority to try cases and control forced labour such that they became very powerful and corrupt in their operations. Unachukwu *et al.* (2003) noted that these warrant chiefs became corrupt and unpopular, and notorious for the sale of justice and for using forced labour. The level of corruption and hardship perpetrated by them became unbearable and roundly criticized by the people. A 1919 report of a panel of inquiry revealed that "*application for the warrant was merely for the purpose of self-enrichment and that was the warrant system to be investigated on the issue of bribery and corruption, about ninety percent of the warrant chiefs would be imprisoned … through bribery and corruption, most of the warrant chiefs prospered in material substance.*" (Chuta, 2004). In view of this scenario, Afigbo observed that the warrant chief system was "*rotten to the core*"[2] (Ezeogidi, 2020).

The level of corruption in Nigeria especially at the local council level continue to increase so much so that in May 1954, a commission of inquiry set up to look into the affairs of Igbo-Etiti District Council indicted the council for financial scandal and indiscriminate award of contracts and staff promotion (Okonkwo, 2005). From the Local Government level, corruption gradually spread to every part of the country as those regarded as nationalists were accused of the vice. For instance, in 1954, a tribunal known as the Foster-Sutton Tribunal which investigated the activities of the African Continental Bank (ACB) came out with a report that indicted the late Dr. Nnamdi Azikiwe for abusing his position as Head of Government by diverting huge sums of Eastern Nigerian Government Funds into his own bank, the ACB, thus solving the bank's problem of a chronic shortage of operation capital and in the process greatly enriching himself. Also, in 1962, the G.B.A. Coker Commission of Inquiry which looked into the operations of six Western Nigerian Public Corporations indicted the late Chief Obafemi Awolowo and his colleagues in the leadership of the Action Group Government of Western Nigeria for enriching themselves and their party greatly at the expense of the accumulated funds of the Cocoa Marketing Board, property of the people of Western Nigeria (Austine, Charles & Raymond, 2013). These two examples of judicially investigated corrupt cases in the Eastern and Western Nigeria were not unique. It only goes to show how pervasive corruption was in the First Republic all over the country.

At the time of political independence in 1960, corruption had infiltrated the ranks of politicians as shown in the series of commissions of inquiry set up by Major General Aguiyi Ironsi to investigate the affairs of Electric Corporation of Nigeria, Nigeria Airways Authority, Nigeria Railways Corporation and Nigeria Ports Authority. The reports of the various commissions of inquiry indicted some prominent politicians like Okotie Eboh, R. Njoku, Ribanu and Ikejiani as well as Chief Dafe who was accused of not knowing the difference between Nigerian Airways and the NCNC party headquarters (Ezeogidi, 2020).

Ministers and political officeholders became notorious for corruption. Chief Festus Okotie-Eboh, minister of finance, while defending himself against corruption accusations quoted from the Holy Bible saying: "*To those that have, more shall be given ...*" (Ezeogidi, 2020). The Minister of Aviation, Dr. K.O. Mbadiwe, on his part, told the House of Representatives that his wealth came from "*known and unknown sources.*" Chief Samuel Akintola was nicknamed "*Rigging*". Ahmadu Bello was however noted for his flamboyant and expensive dressing acquired through ill-gotten wealth (Okonkwo, 2005). Dr. Ikejiani, who was the chairman of the Nigerian Railway Corporation was found guilty of misallocation of public funds and was therefore barred from further holding public office. In fact, he was found guilty of inflating the contract for the building of Railway Medical Center from 75 to 440 pounds.

The widespread corruption in the First Republic may have prompted the military to stage the first *coup d'etat* in Nigeria. The coupists led by Major Chukwuma Nzeogwu while justifying their action said:

"Our enemies are the political profiteers, the swindlers, the men in high and low places that seek bribes and demand ten percent. Those that seek to keep the country divided so that they can remain in office as ministers and VIPs, at least the tribalists, the nepotists, those that make the country look big for nothing before international circles; those that have corrupted our society and the Nigerian political calendar by their words and deeds." (Nzekwe 1994)

Prior to 1966, vocabularies like rigging, kick-back, you scratch my back, I scratch your back, ten percenters, and inducement became the language of the political class daily. In his confirmation of the ugly situation, Crowder (1978) said "*by the end of 1965 the politicians had earned almost contempt for their corruption, profligacy and lack of real concern for those they ruled and who had elected them.*" From the First Republic up till now, successive governments have continued to witness higher levels of corruption and mismanagement of public funds. Endemic corruption in Nigeria has also nurtured widespread poverty and low human development indices.

Strategies Used by Successive Governments to Curb Corruption in Nigeria

Several attempts have been made by successive regimes to wipe out corruption in Nigeria but to no avail. The colonial government, no doubt, was the first to legislate against the phenomenon in the first criminal code ordinance of 1916 (No. 15 of 1916) which elaborately made provisions prohibiting official bribery and corruption by persons in the public service and in the judiciary. This was an indication that the colonial overlords did not tacitly endorse the way and manner corruption was spreading at that time.

When Nigeria attained independence on October 1, 1960, the criminal code against corruption and abuse of office appeared in sections 98 to 116 and 404 of the code.

The government of Alhaji Tafawa Balewa who holds sway in the First Republic made no significant effort to curb corruption. Instead, his regime was sacked partly due to corruption (Dudley, 1973). Top government officials in the First Republic were said to have disregard for accountability for the public fund. For example, Dr. Nnamdi Azikiwe was accused of starching public funds in his own bank account in the African Continental Bank (ACB) while Chief Obafemi Awolowo was found guilty of financial impropriety by the G.B.A Coker Commission of Inquiry into the Western Region Government in 1962.

Major General Aguiyi Ironsi who took over from Alhaji Tafawa Balewa did not do much as his regime only lasted for seven months (January to July 1966) as a result of a countercoup that brought General Yakubu Gowon to power in July 1966. Although his regime was applauded for bringing peace to the country, it did not do much in curbing corruption. Instead, his government was accused of large-scale corruption (Okolie, 2007). Gowon's assertion that money was not Nigeria's problem but how to spend it was a pointer to his regime's corrupt tendencies (Chukwuemeka *et al.* 2012). Gowon's regime which was terminated in July 1975 was characterized by massive corruption which partly accounted for the takeover of the government by General Murtala Mohammed. In his broadcast to the nation, General Murtala Mohammed told Nigerians that, "*Gowon's leadership either by design or default had become insensitive to the true feelings and yearnings of the people. The nation was thus being plunged inexorably into chaos*" (Nzekwe 1994). On assumption of office, General Murtala Mohammed swung into action to deal with corrupt politicians both in civilian and military uniform. He displayed leadership by example through his war against indiscipline, and by so doing, according to Chuta (2004), "*set a record by being the first and so far, the only Nigerian leader who forfeited his ill-gotten wealth to the nation before carrying out war against corruption.*"

Shortly after he came to power, discipline became part of Nigerians. Many things that were wrong began to fall into place. In Lagos for instance, public servants became regular at work and were found on their seats. Military personnel were at their duty posts, the crippling *go-slow* syndrome disappeared, and sanity was everywhere. This new way of life, as Achebe (1984) puts it was a result of "*the new ruler's reputation for ruthlessness was sufficient to transform in the course of time Nigeria's unruly capital (Lagos).*" In one of the inquiries instituted by General Murtala Mohammed, all the military governors of the previous regime (and the administrator of East Central State) except two: Brigadier Mobolaji Johnson of Lagos State and Oluwole Rotimi of the Western State, were found guilty of corruption and dismissed. They also forfeited property acquired with looted funds (Chuta, 2004). Brigadier Samuel Ogbemudia had his multi-million Naira Palm Royal Motel seized. Ukpabi Asika of East Central State had his assets worth N200,689 confiscated, while Joseph Gomwalk of Benue-Plateau had his property worth over N99,000 seized. The former Governor of Northwestern State, Alhaji Usman Farouk had his property worth N264,000 confiscated (Ezeogidi, 2020).

General Murtala Mohammed's anti-graft effort could not make any meaningful impact as his regime was toppled after a few months in office through a military coup led by Lieutenant Colonel B.S. Dimka. General Olusegun Obasanjo was ushered in as the new military ruler. He started the anti-corruption fight by setting up the Federal Asset Investigation panel to probe corrupt high profile office holders and top bureaucrats. No significant progress was made in the fight against corruption as he could not sustain the tempo of his predecessor's anti-corruption crusade (Uju, 2002). Rather, his leadership was accused of corruption as shown in the award of white elephant projects (Dike, 2001). His leadership could not give an account of N2.8 billion oil money that got missing from the nation's foreign reserve between

1976 and 1979 (Dike, 2001) and the N2 billion jumbo loans from the International Finance Corporation (IFC) in 1978 (Derin, 2007).

In 1979, General Olusegun Obasanjo handed over power to a civilian government headed by Alhaji Shehu Shagari. In 1981, the Shagari government set up the Ethical Re-orientation Committee and the Code of Conduct Bureau to shore up the dwindling nation's national values characterized by fraud and corruption. His effort at curbing corruption failed woefully as the regime was neck-deep in it. No wonder Welch (1987) described Shehu Shagari's regime as uncontrollably corrupt. The massive corruption that took place under Shagari's watch was partly responsible for the military takeover of his regime in 1983 (Chukwuemeka, 2006; Dike, 2001; Ogundiya & Baba, 2004).

General Muhammadu Buhari took overpower from Alhaji Shehu Shagari. He made significant efforts to curb corruption through the War Against Indiscipline (WAI) introduced in 1984, the Public Property Decree and the Public Officers (Special provision) Decree of 1984 (Chukwuemeka *et al.*, 2012). While unfolding his plans to tackle social ills in the country, General Buhari stated "*corruption and indiscipline have been associated with our state of underdevelopment, this twin evil in our body politics have attained unprecedented heights in the past four years. We deplore corruption in all its facets-this government will not tolerate inflation of contracts and over-invoicing of imports etc. nor will it condone forgery, embezzlement, misuse, and abuse of office and illegal dealing in foreign exchange and smuggling.*" (ChijiokeUtomi, 2022). General Buhari's government took some drastic steps to prosecute corrupt officers (both civilian and military) who were forced to cough out embezzled funds that run into millions of naira (Chukwuemeka, 2006). The regime did not last long as it was overthrown after barely two years in office. The sacking of the government was attributed to the regime's highhandedness, poor human rights record and general authoritarian tendencies (Derin, 2007).

General Ibrahim Bagangida came into power through the military coup of 1985. His effort at controlling corruption started majorly through the establishment of Mass Mobilization for Social Justice, Self-Reliance, and Economic Recovery (MAMSER) in 1985. His regime did not make significant progress through this initiative. Instead, corrupt practices were said to have heightened under his leadership (Dike, 2001). As a matter of fact, his administration was roundly criticized for institutionalizing corruption in Nigeria (Derin, 2007). For instance, Babangida was indicted by the Plus Okigbo Report of 1995 for failure to account for the $12.4 billion that accrued to Nigeria from the Gulf War Oil Sales (Derin, 2007). Again, accusing fingers were pointed at him over the enormous electoral fraud and corruption involved in the transition to civil rule program initiated and organized by General Ibrahim Babangida, which he eventually annulled. The annulment of the June 12, 1993 election culminated in a political impasse that forced him to step aside and hand over to Chief Earnest Shonekan, head of the Interim National Government (ING).

However, after a few months in office, the Interim National Government was overthrown by General Sani Abacha, who assumed leadership of the country. He initiated some measures to curb corruption but without success. The most notable measure introduced by him was the War Against Indiscipline and Corruption (WAIC). Abacha's leadership, unfortunately, did not achieve much in curbing corruption as his administration was generally characterized by mismanagement and corruption of a monumental scale (Chukwuemeka, 2006). General Sani Abacha's administration was so corrupt that after his demise, over 600 million dollars and 75 million British pounds were recovered from his family members as part of the money he corruptly enriched himself with. The government of General Sani Abacha almost emptied the nation's treasury. The United Nation Industrial Development Organization (UNIDO) revealed that about $107 billion was kept in private accounts in Switzerland, the United States and Paris Club by

General Sani Abacha. The state of capital flight was unquantifiable. Under Abacha's leadership, over N400 billion was siphoned from the nation's treasury (Derin, 2007). To date, Nigeria is still recovering monies looted from the state treasury while he was head of state.

After the demise of General Sani Abacha on June 8, 1998, General Abdulsalami Abubakar took over the mantle of leadership as head of state. No significant effort was made under his leadership to curb corruption. There was no effort to probe past regimes that were accused of corruption. Even those who were accused of looting the treasury with General Sani Abacha were retained by his government (Dike, 2003). His regime lasted barely a year in office and was handed over to a democratically elected government under the leadership of Chief Olusegun Obasanjo on May 29, 1999.

On assumption of office, Chief Olusegun Obasanjo promised to wage war against corruption, noting that no society can thrive and flourish if it allows corruption to take over it. Nigeria is no exception. Consequently, the president swung into action by establishing two anti-corruption agencies namely: Independent Corrupt Practices and other Related Offences, Commission (ICPC) and the Economic and Financial Crimes Commission (EFCC). They were established in 2000 and 2004 respectively. In spite of these initiatives, corruption was rampant in Obasanjo's administration. There were allegations of corruption in high places. Some of the prominent corrupt activities in his regime include electoral fraud and corruption as seen in the 2003 and 2007 general elections, giving bribes to federal legislators before budget approval, paying large sums of money to legislators before being confirmed as a minister and the use of unreasonable money to prosecute election campaigns (Derin, 2007). Corruption allegations also trailed Obasanjo's third term bid.

The government of Alhaji Umaru Yar Adua which lasted from 2007 to 2009 did nothing spectacular to combat corruption despite promising to continue to wage war against it. He was therefore accused of being lukewarm towards the fight against graft. After the death of Yar Adua in 2009, Dr. Goodluck Jonathan assumed office as president of Nigeria. When the mantle of leadership fell on him, he promised to intensify the war against corruption. As a result, he decided to retain the two anti-graft agencies (ICPC and EFCC) established by former president Olusegun Obasanjo rather than scrap them. However, his government was also accused of monumental corruption.

In May 2015, Muhammadu Buhari took office as Nigeria's president. A former military dictator known for an austere lifestyle and a strict anti-corruption stance, Buhari was seen as the perfect man to rid the government of its excesses and instill a semblance of financial responsibility (Kazeem, 2016). Muhammadu Buhari, widely known as a man of integrity with a very strong aversion for corrupt practices (Onyeacholem, 2017) campaigned on the promise to address alleged multibillion-dollar corruption scandals, stemming largely from the mismanagement of the country's oil reserves, and weakening Nigeria's legitimacy domestically and internationally (Omilusi, 2019). A widespread concern in Nigeria prior to Buhari's election that helped to push his predecessor out of office was the billions of dollars of oil revenue that disappeared under Dr. Goodluck Jonathan's administration, in addition to credible allegations of graft and runaway illegal outflows. It is not surprising that Buhari was elected on an anti-corruption ticket and has since cracked down on graft in various sectors of the government (Omilusi, 2019).

Money Laundering and Financial Crimes are other important issues (Rafay, 2021a; 2021b). Apart from strengthening the powers of the anti-graft agencies, president Buhari also appointed a committee known as Presidential Advisory Committee on Corruption (PACAC) which he inaugurated in August 2015. Headed by Professor Itse Sagay, PACAC has wide ranging duties bordering on anti-corruption. Some of the anti-corruption laws in the country include the Advance Fee Fraud and other Related Offences Act 2006; Money Laundering (Prohibition) (Amendment) Act 2012; Miscellaneous Offences

Act; Code of conduct Act; Nigerian Extractive Industries Transparency Initiative Act; Freedom of Information Act 2011; Fiscal Responsibilities Act 2010; Criminal Code Law of Federation of Nigeria 2004; Banks and Other Financial Institutions (Amendment) Act 1991; and Failed Banks (Recovery of Debts) and Financial Malpractices in Banks (Amendment) Act 1994; Proceeds of Crime (Recovery and Management) Act 2022 and Terrorism Prevention Act 2022.

Corruption and the Nigerian Society

As mentioned earlier in the introductory section, Nigeria is deeply troubled by widespread corruption. Despite concerted efforts to tame the monster, it has taken a firm root in the socio-political and economic systems of the nation, so much so that the majority sees it as a way of life with only a few despising it.

The global anti-corruption watchdog, Transparency International, has consistently rated Nigeria among the most corrupt countries in the world. If the 2021 Corruption Perception Index (CPI) by TI is anything to go by, then Nigeria deserves a lot of pity having ranked abysmally low out of the countries appraised. The country dropped five places in the 2021 Corruption Perception Index (CPI) released in late January 2022 by Transparency International. Auwal Rafsanjani, Country Representative of Transparency International and Executive Director, the Civil Society Legislative Advocacy Centre (CISLAC) disclosed that Nigeria scored 24 out of 100 points and was rated 154 out of 180 nations measured, pushing it back five places from the rank of 149 in 2020. This was Nigeria's second successive year of a downward movement on TI's CPI rating, having dropped from 26 in 2019 to 25 in the 2020 assessment, and further to 24 in the 2021 exercise.

Transparency International assessment showed that Nigeria was ranked thus: 136 (2015); 136 (2016); 148 (2017); 146 (2019); 144 (2018); 149 (2020) and 154 (2021). The country performed poorly in the 2021 CPI due to several factors including security sector corruption, failure to investigate high profile corruption cases and prevent illicit financial flows, absence of asset recovery and the protection of whistleblowers and other key anti-corruption legal frameworks. Others are judicial challenges, corruption in the COVID-19 response, the ban on Twitter, shrinking civic space and intimidation of human rights defenders. The 2021 CPI ranking placed Nigeria as the second most corrupt country in West Africa after Guinea that was ranked 150 on the global index. With the recent CPI, the claim by the Nigerian government of reducing corruption in the country is by no means doubtful. Nigeria's woeful performance according to TI's report is an indication that the strategies deployed to tackle corruption are not effective. Newspaper reports of May 17, 2022, of the arrest of Mr. Ahmed Idris, Accountant General of the federation (AGF) and subsequent trial alongside his cohorts by the Economic and Financial Crimes Commission (EFCC) in connection with the alleged diversion of funds and money Laundering to the tune of N109bn has confirmed the fears of many concerned citizens that corruption is getting worse in the country.

Today, many ministries, departments and agencies (MDAs) of government reeks of corruption. In an audit report by the office of the Auditor-General of the Federation (AUGF) 2022, it was discovered that these federal MDAs failed to account for N323.5 billion in 2019. Many offices reportedly violated rules on payments, remittances and tax. To help tackle some of these corrupt tendencies, the Federal Executive Council (FEC), on July 5, 2017, approved what is known as the National Anti-Corruption Strategy (NACS). It directed the Attorney-General of the Federation (AGF) and Minister of Justice, Abubakar Malami, to come up with a robust implementation plan for it. NACS was established in compliance with Nigeria's national and international obligations on tackling corruption. It was to fulfill the United Nations Convention Against Corruption (UNCAC), which Nigeria signed in 2003 and ratified in 2004.

The NACS is anchored on five pillars: prevention of corruption, public engagement, campaign for ethical re-orientation, enforcement and sanctions, and recovery and management of proceeds of crime. The strategy was aimed at removing corruption related factors inhibiting the government's accessibility and capacity to deliver quality service to Nigerians.

Concept of Whistleblowing

Whistleblowing is the act of disclosing information about wrongdoing or misconduct taking place in an organization which could be public or private. The need to blow the whistle, most of the time, is motivated by the desire to make public illegal activities that have negative consequences on the organization. Reporting fraudulent practices through whistleblowing will likely put an end to such happenings if properly handled. A whistleblower, therefore, is an individual who engages in blowing the whistle to expose wrongdoing occurring in an organization. The majority of those who blow the whistle within an organization do so by first reporting to a supervisor or a neutral third party. Information about fraudulent activities can also be communicated to external bodies (media, government, law enforcement agencies) by whistleblowers (Chalouat, *et al.*, 2019).

Most whistleblowers face the risk of revenge as they often pay a serious price for engaging in whistleblowing (Nakitende *et al.*, (2021). Some could have their employment terminated abruptly while others constantly face bullying at work, workload increase and a drastic reduction in work hours (Vandekerckhove, 2016). In some environments, whistleblowers also face death threats. Because of the benefits associated with whistleblowing (combating fraud, avoiding reputational damage, preventing issues from escalating, minimizing losses, raising awareness of the issue and creating open culture), many countries around the world have attempted to regulate whistleblowing and give legal backing to whistleblowers. But the laws adopted in these countries differ from public to private sector whistleblowing.

Whistleblowers do not achieve their aims most of the time. To succeed, they are expected to put out credible and verifiable claims, as well as compelling evidence to support their claims to enable the government or the anti-graft agency to investigate and take necessary actions. While whistleblowers may succeed in some cases, in others, they give false information to mislead government or regulating bodies thereby putting them in bad light before the general public. The term whistleblower was initially used to refer to public servants who exposed all forms of mismanagement in government, profligacy, or fraud but it now covers a whole gamut of activities of any employee, including officers of public or private organizations who revealed acts of misconduct such as extravagant spending, corruption, embezzlement of government or company funds and fraud to the larger society (Kleinig, n.d).

The origin of the word "whistleblowing" dates back to the 19th century but it was Ralph Nader, U.S. civic activist that popularize it. He was said to have coined the phrase in the early 1970s to distinguish it from the negative connotations found in other words such as "informer" and "snitch". Whistleblower is a word associated with the use of a whistle to warn the public about a crime being committed by an individual or group that could affect the generality of the people as well as the violation of the rules in a game. Whistleblower became linked with law enforcement officials in the 19th century because they used the whistle to warn the public or fellow police. Apart from law enforcement, sports referees were also referred to as whistleblowers because they were using the whistle to show foul play (Etymonline.com., n.d; Wordorigins.org. 2021).

Whistleblowers operate under three channels: internal, external and third party. Internal whistleblowers are those who report acts of misconduct on the part of a fellow worker or superior within the organization using hotlines (Ferrell, Fraedrich & Ferrell, 2021). Internal whistleblowing often generates some curious questions but one of the most interesting that often comes to mind is: under what circumstances do people report unacceptable behaviour or react to stop it from festering (Rowe, Wilcox & Gadlin, 2009)? With respect to internal whistleblowing, the reporting mechanism tends to work smoothly in an organization where the complaint systems provide a choice of options for complete confidentiality and not options dictated by the planning and control organization (Rowe, 1993).

In the case of external channels, the whistleblowers report acts of misconduct to bodies outside the organization. Depending on the nature of the information at their disposal those blowing the whistle are likely to report the malfeasance to lawyers, the media, law enforcement officers or watchdog agencies, or government agencies (local, state or federal). External whistleblowing in some cases offers monetary rewards to entice people to blow the whistle. In third party channels, organizations use external agencies to create protected and nameless reporting mechanisms for its staff referred to as a whistleblowing hotline. The organizations also ensure the full protection of the identity of the whistleblower. These services are put in place to notify individuals at the top echelon of the organization of misdemeanor through integration with specialized case management software. This will help the organization to put in place a whistleblowing policy where one is lacking.

Countries with Legal Protection for Whistleblowers

Several countries of the world have put in place laws to strengthen the whistleblowing policy and protect whistleblowers against retaliation from those involved in corrupt practices and other wrongdoings. The laws differ from country to country depending on how the whistleblowing activities are carried out and the mechanisms for reporting the malpractice. Below are select countries that have legal protection for whistleblowers.

Australia

Some states in Australia have enacted laws protecting whistleblowers even though whistleblowers are despised by people (Whistleblowers Australia, n.d.; Caillier, 2015). For providing evidence of Australia's disputed spying operation against the East Timor government in 2004, former Australian intelligence officer (Witness k) faced jail terms if found guilty (Davidson, 2018). An Association for whistleblowers who have been abused for exposing corruption and other wrongdoings has been established in Australia. It is known as whistleblowers Australia (Whistleblowers Australia, n.d.).

Canada

In Canada, whistleblowers are protected by a law known as Public Servants Disclosure Protection Act. The Act empowers the Public Sector Integrity Commissioner (PSIC) to investigate cases of wrongdoings reported to it. The PSIC provides a safe and confidential mechanism that enables public servants and the public at large to reveal or report wrongdoings taking place in the public sector. PSIC also protects or shields public servants who disclosed wrongdoing and those who cooperated in investigations from retaliation (PSIC, n.d, Government of Canada, PSIC, 2014). The PSIC is a permanent and independent body created by the parliament of Canada.

The Public Servants Disclosure Protection Act came into being in 2007 and it is applicable to the federal public sector with about 400,000 workers (Government of Canada, PSIC, 2013) covering government departments, agencies, parent crown corporations, the Royal Canadian Mounted Police and other public sector bodies. Not all the information provided about wrongdoings can be investigated by PSIC. The Act clearly spelt out the jurisdiction of the commissioner with regard to what to investigate or not. After investigating and no wrongdoing was committed, the commissioner was duty-bound to report his findings to the person that disclosed the wrongdoing and to the chief executive of the organization. Where findings of an investigation show a wrongdoing was committed, the PSIC must present a report of its findings to the House of Commons and the Senate.

The Public Servants Disclosure Protection Act also established the Public Servants Disclosure Protection Tribunal (PSDPT) whose duty is to protect public servants by hearing reprisal complaints referred to it by the PSIC. The tribunal in the exercise of its duties can grant remedies in favor of complainants and order disciplinary action against those who take retaliatory actions.

European Union

A "whistleblower Protection Directive" to protect whistleblowers was endorsed by the European Parliament. It contains broad free speech protections for whistleblowers in private and public sectors in all European Union member states. The Directive forbids direct or indirect reprisals against current and former employees, in the private and public sectors. The Directive's protections cover employees, volunteers, civil society organizations and journalists who write stories or reports based on evidence provided. The Directive provides equal rights for whistleblowers in the national security sector who challenge the denial or removal of their security clearances. Whistleblowers are also protected against criminal prosecution and corporate lawsuits for damages resulting from their whistleblowing and provide psychological support for dealing with harassment stress (Government Accountability Project, 2018).

Ireland

The quest of the government of Ireland to have a comprehensive whistleblower protection law began in January 2012 with the introduction of the "Whistleblower Bill" in parliament. The bill covers the public and private sectors. The bill was passed into law in 2014 and it became known as "Protected Disclosures Act" (PDA). The Act covers workers in the public and private sectors, and it also includes contractors, trainees, agency staff, former employees, and job seekers. Different types of wrongdoing which may be reported are listed under the law. The law provides protections for workers from a range of employment actions as well as whistleblowers (Protected Disclosures Act, 2014).

Netherlands

The government of the Netherlands has put in place measures to alleviate the risks of whistleblowing. A body known as the House for Whistleblowers (Huis Voor Klokkenluiders) has been set up to offer advice and support to whistleblowers. Parliament equally passed a proposal in 2016 to establish the house and to protect whistleblowers from severe negative consequences that they might face while blowing the whistle. The Dutch media also provide support to whistleblowers. Some major influential Dutch media outlets were united in their support for the launch of Publeaks on September 9, 2013. Publeaks provides a secure website (www.publeaks.nl) for those who want to leak documents to the media. It was designed to protect whistleblowers. Publeaks operates on the Globaleaks software developed by the Hermes Center for Transparency and Digital Human Rights, which supports whistleblower-oriented technologies globally (Reding *et al.*, 2014).

United Kingdom

The Public Interest Disclosure Act 1998 (PIDA) provides protection for whistleblowers in the United Kingdom. Under the Act, protected disclosures are allowed even if a non-disclosure agreement exists between the employer and employee (former or current). In 2019, a consultation to further restrict confidentiality clauses was held (UK Department for Business, Energy and Industrial Strategy, 2019).

Freedom to Speak Up Review has listed 20 principles to help improve whistleblowers activities in the NHS. They include:

- Culture of raising concerns – to make raising issues a part of the normal routine business of a well-led NHS organization.
- Culture free from bullying – freedom of staff to speak out relies on staff being able to work in a culture that is free from bulling.
- Training – every member of staff should receive training in their trust's approach to raising concerns and in receiving and acting on them.
- Support – all NHS trusts should ensure there is a dedicated person to whom concerns can be easily reported and without formality, a "speak up guardian".
- Support to find alternative employment in the NHS- where a worker who has raised a concern cannot, as a result, continue their role; the NHS should help them seek an alternative job.

Ghana

The legal instrument that protects whistleblowers in Ghana is the Whistleblower Act, 2006 Act 720. The Act was assented to on October 16, 2006. It contains thirty-two sections. Amongst other things, the Act makes provisions for the protection of whistleblowers, police protection for whistleblower and family, protection against civil and criminal action, whistleblower reward fund and the establishment of whistleblower reward fund. Section 3 of the Act specified those to whom disclosures of misconduct (impropriety) are made. A whistleblower who is an employee is shielded from being dismissed, suspended, declared redundant, denied promotion, transferred against the whistleblowers will, etc. If not an employee, a whistleblower is protected against victimization, discrimination, intimidation, or harassment. Upon receipt of an investigation report from a person or institution, the Attorney General takes necessary action. For making a disclosure that leads to the arrest and conviction of an accused person, and the recovery of stolen funds, the whistleblower is rewarded financially from the whistleblower's fund.

Uganda

Those who blow the whistle in Uganda are protected by "The Whistleblowers Protection Act, 2010". The Act was assented to on 22nd April 2010. Part V of the Act precludes whistleblowers from victimization and court action. It provides state protection for whistleblowers and families, court assistance and void employment contracts. For whistleblowers who are employees, it specifically protects them against dismissal, suspension, denial of promotion, demotion, redundancy, harassment, intimidation and threats with regard to any of the mentioned reprisals.

External disclosures of impropriety can be made to (a) the Inspectorate of Government; (b) the Directorate of Public Prosecutions; (c) the Uganda Human Rights Commission; (d) the Directorate for Ethics and Integrity; (e) the Office of the Resident District Commissioner; (f) Parliament of Uganda; (g) the National Environment Management Authority; and (h) the Uganda Police force. The Act provides for a reward system whereby a whistleblower gets up to 5 percent of recovered stolen funds. Whistleblowers who give false information are liable to imprisonment of more than five years or a fine of not more than one hundred and twenty currency points or both if found guilty of making false disclosures.

South Africa

In South Africa, the law that regulates whistleblowing as well as protects whistleblowers was first enacted in 2000 and amended in 2017. The first legislation was known as the Protected Disclosures Act No. 26 of 2000 while the current law in operation is known as Protected Disclosures Amendment Act, No 5 of 2017 (the Amendment Act). It was assented to by former President Jacob Zuma on 31st July 2017.

The aim of the Protected Disclosures Act No 26 of 2000 was to provide procedures and to offer protection from occupational detriment. The Act provides procedures in terms of which any employee may disclose information relating to an offence or wrongdoing in the workplace by his or her employer or fellow employees. The Act provides for the protection of an employee, who made a disclosure in accordance with the procedures provided for by the Act, against any reprisals as a result of such a disclosure.

The Act requires anybody to make a disclosure. The preamble of the act makes it clear that:

- every employer and employee have a responsibility to disclose criminal and other irregular conduct in the workplace; and
- every employer has a responsibility to take all necessary steps to ensure that employees who disclose such information are protected from any reprisals as a result of such disclosure.

Under the PDA, disclosures can be made to the Public Protector or Auditor-General and the disclosures should be matters that are handled by the PP and AG. An employee whistleblower can disclose information to (a) a legal representative (b) his or her employer (c) a minister or a member of the Executive Council of a province (MEC) (d) a specified person or body; or (e) a general disclosure to any other person.

The Protected Disclosures Amendment Act, No 5 of 2017 introduces several changes to the Protected Disclosures Act, No 26 of 2000 (the PDA). The Amendment Act expands the scope of the PDA and introduces new provisions which place additional responsibilities on whistleblowers and their employers. The Amendment Act modifies some definitions and introduces new ones. Occupational detriment definition was extended to include being subjected to a civil claim for the alleged violation of a duty of confidentiality or a confidentiality agreement that arose out of the revealing of a criminal offence or information which shows a considerable level of transgression against the law has taken place, is taking place or is likely to take place (Mohammed & Stansfield, 2017).

The definitions of 'temporary employment service' as well as 'worker' were introduced by the Amendment Act. 'Worker' was defined to include individuals currently or previously employed by the state as well as independent contractors, consultants, agents and those who render services to a client whilst being employed by a 'temporary employment service' (i.e., a labour broker). Another new provision in the Amendment Act is a joint liability. This is a situation where an employer and its client are jointly and severally responsible for those instances where the employer under the express or implied authority or with the knowledge of a client subjects an employee or worker to an occupational detriment. Also introduced by the Amendment Act is a responsibility for employers to (a) authorize appropriate internal procedures for receiving and dealing with information about improprieties; and (b) take reasonable steps to bring the internal procedures to the attention of every employee and worker (Mohammed & Stansfield, 2017).

A new provision in the PDA occasioned by the Amendment is the right to inform an employee of the necessary steps taken once a revelation is made. To this end, employers are mandated, among other requirements, to take a stand within 21 days after receiving the protected disclosure, whether to investigate the matter or refer it to another person or body. Employees who make protected disclosures are expected to do so in good faith. Making false disclosures constitute an offence. If found guilty of giving false information, such a whistleblower (employee); is liable to a fine or imprisonment of two years or both. The Amendment Act also introduced a provision that precludes an employee or worker from being liable to any civil, criminal or disciplinary proceedings for making a disclosure that is forbidden by any other law, oath, contract, practice or agreement demanding his or her to maintain secrecy (Mohammed & Stansfield, 2017).

Nigeria

Currently, there is no law to protect whistleblowers and define the parameters of whistleblowing in Nigeria, even though the whistleblowing policy was introduced in 2016 to strengthen and rejig the anti-corruption campaign of President Mohammadu Buhari's administration. The idea of the policy was to galvanize citizens to take active part in the fight against corruption as they were encouraged to blow the whistle on corruption and all other forms of wrongdoing such as fraud, bribery, looting of government funds etc.

The whistleblowing policy provides that any whistleblower who makes available information about any financial impropriety or stolen funds to the ministry of finance's portal will be rewarded with a portion of the recovered stolen funds (between 2.5 percent and 5 percent).

At the inception of the whistleblowing policy, many Nigerians determined to expose corruption took advantage of it to disclose information about fraud, bribery, looted public funds and assets, financial mismanagement and other forms of gratification or theft to anti-graft agencies. Consequently, large responses were recorded. Billions of supposedly looted funds were discovered, arrests made, and legal cases instituted against suspects (Atabo, 2022).

Figures released by the ministry of finance showed that as of 2021, the whistleblowing policy had fetched the federal government N605 billion in recovered funds. The largest chunk of this sum N540 billion was recovered in 2018 alone. The sum of $174 million was recovered from a multinational oil company operating in Nigeria. Through the policy, the federal government also confiscated 20 houses, a poultry farm, 42 brand new cargo tricycles, four cars, 20 trucks, 10 plots of land, 189 shops, one event center, five LPG plants, one warehouse, 17 vehicles, nine trailer heads, 40 trailer backs and 473 trailers. 68 cases of corruption were reported to the government; out of which 36 were false while the remaining 32 were true and the government moved to seize the cash and assets involved (Chiejina, 2021).

The Minister of Finance, Budget and National Planning, Mrs. Zainab Ahmed said the federal government has recovered more than N700 billion from its whistleblower policy. She stated that the government was able to recover a huge sum of money from the activities of whistleblowers who came forward with actionable claims of corruption. According to her, "*There were recoveries and the cleaning of the Integrated Personnel Payroll Information System (IPPIS); stoppage of non-compliance with the Treasury Single Account (TSA) and violations of the procurement Act 2007*". Giving an update on recovered stolen funds, Attorney General of the Federation (AGF) and Minister of Justice, Abubakar Malami, disclosed recently that the federal government has recovered about $1billion since inception of the President Muhammadu Buhari's administration in 2015. Malami, who revealed that the recovered assets have been deployed to various sectors of the economy, including the government's poverty alleviation schemes, further announced the Federal Executive Council's approval of the new Anti-corruption Strategy Document (2022 to 2026) aimed at boosting the fight against graft in the country (Daka, 2022).

Lessons of Whistleblowing Legislation for Nigeria

The role of whistleblowing in the fight against corruption cannot be overemphasized. Hence a lot of countries deeply troubled by corruption are developing the strategy to combat the scourge of corruption. Most countries of the world, realizing its growing importance, have gone ahead to protect whistleblowers against retaliation through legislation and Nigeria cannot be an exception. As the United Nations Office on Drugs and Crime (UNODC) noted, "*The risk of corruption is significantly heightened in environments where the reporting of wrongdoing is not supported or protected. Public and private sector employees have access to up-to-date information concerning their workplaces' practices and are usually the first to recognize wrongdoings.*" (Omilusi, 2019).

The fight against corruption needs to be stepped up through the enactment of more legislation to prevent and combat corruption. Efforts should be made to quickly pass the pending anti-corruption bills before the National Assembly. Some of them are the Whistleblowers Policy Bill, Witness Protection Bill, and Public Interest Disclosure Bill. The government and citizens must be decisive in the fight against corruption. Like Brazil, Nigeria has its general election in 2023. The citizens must resolve to vote against those with 'operation car wash reputation'[3] to enable Nigeria to wear a new look. In fact, the citizens deserve a new Nigeria.

The importance of whistleblowing in the fight against corruption cannot be underestimated as its impact could be felt in economic recovery, poverty reduction and other areas. Hence governments around the world are using it as a strategy to nip corrupt practices in the bud. When President Muhammadu Buhari's government introduced the whistleblowing policy in 2016, many Nigerians who were determined to assist in fighting corruption jumped at it by exposing all forms of corruption. And so, they voluntarily reported corrupt practices to anti-corruption agencies, particularly the Economic and Financial Crimes Commission (EFCC). The disclosures led to the recovery of stolen funds and assets running into billions of Naira.

However, that initial enthusiasm has waned so much that Nigerians are no longer interested in blowing the whistle. Dr. Kola Shettima, African Director, of the MacArthur Foundation noted recently that the number of whistleblowers in the country had reduced compared to when the policy started. He observed that at the beginning of the policy, many people came out to reveal individuals and institutions that were not doing things right. Rather than the policy achieving the desired results, many Nigerians are now hesitant to expose corrupt practices. Mr. Taiye Abegunde, an analyst and academic averred that instead of the whistle-blowers becoming heroes for exposing corruption, they turn out to become victims for daring to expose corrupt officials. He added that the whistle-blowers were usually persecuted, and intimidated at their places of work, with many losing their jobs.

Atabo (2021) and Ogunshola (2022) document victims of whistleblowing retaliation as follows: Mr. Joseph Akeju, a chief lecturer at the Yaba College of Technology, Lagos was dismissed from work just two weeks before his retirement from public service because he dared to report financial irregularities to the tune of N1.68 billion perpetrated between March 2008 and 2014. To date, his case has not been resolved even with the intervention of the Senate Committee on Public Petitions.

Dr. Murtala Ibrahim, an Internal Auditor with the Federal Mortgage Bank of Nigeria, who exposed corruption in the bank did not bargain for the ill-treatment that followed. He was first transferred to Jalingo in Taraba State and later had his appointment terminated in May 2017. Ibrahim had gone to court to challenge his dismissal from work. Mr. Joseph Ameh, an architect and head of the physical planning division had in 2020 exposed some corrupt practices at the Federal College of Education (Technical) Asaba. Although the Independent Corrupt Practices and other Related Offences Commission found merit in his petition by taking those found culpable in the crime to court, the school sacked him months later. He has since been languishing without a job or any other means of livelihood and all pleas to ICPC to help him get his job back have not received a favourable response.

Mr. Sambo Abdullahi, Head of Internal Audit, Nigerian Bulk Electricity Trading (NBET) Plc had his salaries and other allowances withheld for about three years for daring to blow the whistle on the shady deals of his boss. Abdullahi while recounting his ordeal said "*I went to work for almost three years without pay. During that period, I had no money and could not make ends meet. I had to depend on family and friends to survive. Everybody suffered it; my children felt it, my wife, my mother. There was a day we went out and my son said, dad I would have asked you to buy us shawarma, but we know you do not collect salary. They knew what it meant and unfortunately, I did not prepare for such, because I thought I was doing something good*". Mr. Ntia Thompson, who was Assistant Director at the time he reported fraud against his boss, Mr. Mohammed Kachalla at the Department of Technical Cooperation in Africa (DTCA), an agency of the Federal Ministry of Foreign Affairs was also a victim of whistle-blowing retaliation.

Other victims of whistleblowing retaliation include Jaafar Jaafar and Aaron Kaase. Jaafar Jaafar, an investigative journalist, exposed the video of Abdullahi Ganduje, governor of Kano State, as he was stuffing bales of dollars said to be bribe money allegedly paid by a contractor working for the government. Mr. Aaron Kaase, Chief Information Officer at the Police Service Commission (PSC) blew the whistle on a former chairman of the commission, Mr. Mike Okiro. Kaase was suspended without pay for three years and, in between, was harassed regularly and even had his life threatened. "*The reprisal attack from the person I blew the whistle against was massive because he was using police to harass me*," he said.

These experiences and others not documented tend to impede the blossoming of the whistleblowing policy in Nigeria. Another contributory factor to the slowing down of whistleblowing in the country is the lack of citizens' trust in the government to judiciously manage the recovered looted funds for the general well-being of the society. Many Nigerians, because of the high level of corruption in the country, strongly believe that funds recovered through whistleblowing are re-looted by government officials. And so, some of the questions often asked in the public domain are: why blow the whistle for the benefit of few? What do they use all the recovered monies for? The erroneous belief that the funds are usually re-looted is reinforced by the way the recovered funds are managed by the government. Citizens appear not to have accurate knowledge about what the recoveries are used for as it is often shrouded in secrecy. In the midst of this confusion, corruption continues to thrive and negatively affects development in all areas of human endeavor. There is therefore the need to rejig the whistleblowing policy to achieve its set objectives for the overall benefit of Nigerian society.

SOLUTIONS AND RECOMMENDATIONS

Solutions

The fight against corruption is a collective effort that requires a pragmatic approach. The following solutions are hereby put forward to revive the dying interest of Nigerians in blowing the whistle against corrupt practices.

1. The government, civil society and relevant stakeholders should create awareness about the whistleblowing policy as most Nigerians appear not to have knowledge about the policy and what the country and citizens stand to gain by identifying with the policy.
2. Citizens need to collaborate with the government by raising their voices when necessary to challenge the process and ensure that the right thing is done all the time in order to keep the country on the right track.
3. All local and national media outlets should be deployed to galvanize citizens to take advantage of the policy to help the government in the fight against corruption by blowing the whistle when they see something going wrong. The concomitant effect of successful whistleblowing will save public funds or resources and ensure the public office is not abused for private gain. The fund saved or prevented from being stolen can be used to provide social amenities which can help in addressing development challenges.
4. Government should be open in disclosing recovered stolen funds and how they are applied for the benefit of society. This will help to restore citizens' trust in the government and propel them to continue to blow the whistle against corruption.

Recommendations

The whistleblowing policy is an important tool in the fight against graft in Nigeria. If properly implemented by the government, the policy would add value to the anti-corruption fight. The following recommendations are hereby proposed.

1. For the whistleblowing policy to succeed in Nigeria, there is a need to put in place an enabling law to protect whistleblowers against all forms of retaliation. Because there is no law backing the whistleblowing policy, citizens are not eager to blow the whistle as there is no legal guarantee that if they blow the whistle they are protected. A whistleblower protection is therefore essential in the whole process of whistleblowing.
2. In line with the above, Nigerians, civil society organizations and other progressive groups who are interested in ending the circle of corruption in the country should come up with private bills that would provide the necessary legal framework for whistleblowers to operate without fear or intimidation. The policy at the moment is not working hence whistleblowers are subjected to a series of threats both internally and externally. Protection of whistleblowers will no doubt boost the anti-corruption war of the federal government of Nigeria.
3. There is a need to make whistleblowers anonymous to protect their identity. This will help to minimize the reprisal attacks from the people or institutions they blow the whistle against.

4. Government should establish a whistleblower victims' fund to support those who volunteer credible information. This is necessary because corruption cases usually take a long before they are concluded in Nigeria. It will therefore be unfair to consign the whistleblower to such prolonged suffering with nothing to fall back on.

FUTURE RESEARCH DIRECTIONS

Currently, there is no law in place in Nigeria to protect whistleblowers. However, pressures are mounting for a law to be enacted as the country is long overdue for such legislation, given its corruption status in the world and the fact that some African countries like South Africa, Uganda and Ghana have put in place laws to protect whistleblowers and regulate the whole process of whistleblowing

Apart from enacting a law to protect whistleblowers, Nigerians' waning desire to blow the whistle is information centered. Therefore, a sustained media campaign is required to mobilize Nigerians to identify with the policy. In line with this, this chapter is anchored on the Agenda-Setting theory of the mass media and News Framing theory. The basic idea of Agenda-setting theory is that the news media by their display of news have the power to structure public issues, and can exert some influence on public consciousness, cognition, and behaviour.

Livingston (1992) noted that *"through control of the agenda, the mass media place some emphasis on news stories by size, placement and frequency of appearance of stories"*. Writing about the agenda-setting power of the media, Baran (2012) pointed out that the agenda setting power of the media resides in more than the amount of space or time devoted to a story and its placement in the broadcast or on the page. Also important, he said, is the fact that there is great consistency between media sources across all media in the choice and type of coverage they give an issue or event. This consistency and repetition signal to people the importance of the issue or event.

Another way the mass media could influence its target public is through news framing. Framing is one approach that seeks to understand the way the media influence audience. Fairhurst & Sarr (1996) referred to a frame as *"the way media and media gatekeepers organize and present the events and issues they cover, and the way audience interprets what they are provided"*. In their submission on the way the media organize and present events and issues they cover, Gamson & Modigliani (1989) identified: metaphors, exemplars, catch-phrases, depictions and visual images, among others, as 'framing devices' that condense information and offer a 'media package' of an issue. The most comprehensive empirical approach to framing is offered by Tankard (2001) who suggested a list of 11 framing mechanisms or focal points for identifying and measuring new frames. They are headlines, subheads, photos, photo captions, leads, source selection, quotes selection, full quotes, logos, statistics and charts, and concluding statements and paragraphs.

The media has set agendas to discuss an issue that is of public importance and ensure that they frame their news stories on the issue to elicit the kind of response they desire to have from their target audience. As Soderlund *et al.* (2012) puts it: *"The importance of media framing, of course lies in its ability to influence the way in which various audiences come to gain an understanding of developing events"*. The way journalists usually frame newspaper stories on government policies (such as whistleblowing) could influence the interpretations and meanings the members of the public would attach to the report of the media on the issue.

CONCLUSION

It is clear from the discourse that whistleblowing is proving to be a good strategy to fight corruption. All over the world, corruption retards development and economic growth. Because of the growing commitment to fight corruption to a standstill, many national governments are making efforts to enact laws to protect whistleblowers and define the boundary of whistleblowing. African governments are no exception as countries such as South Africa, Uganda and Ghana have gone ahead to put in place legislation to protect whistleblowers.

Currently, there is no law in Nigeria to protect whistleblowers. And because there is no law, those who attempted to blow the whistle when the policy was introduced suffered reprisal attacks thus forcing many who intend to do so to withdraw. As the citizens withdraw, corruption has continued unabated. And this portends danger for a country that is suffocating under the burden of widespread corruption.

It is time the Nigerian government rejigs the whistleblowing policy via a requisite legal framework to strengthen the anti-corruption fight. The majority of the citizens in the country lack awareness about the policy and its objectives. It is therefore imperative for government to use all available media channels to sensitize the people on the need to identify with the whistleblowing policy. The policy has a lot to achieve for the country if properly implemented.

DECLARATION

The author declares that the manuscript follows ethical standards and there are no potential conflicts of interest with respect to the research, authorship and/or publication of this chapter.

DISCLAIMER

The contents and views of this chapter are expressed by the author in his personal capacity. It is not necessary for the Editor and the Publisher to agree with these viewpoints, and they are not responsible for any duty of care in this regard.

ACKNOWLEDGMENT

The author extends sincere gratitude to

- The Editor and the International Editorial Advisory Board (IEAB) of this book who initially desk reviewed, arranged a rigorous double/triple blind review process, and conducted a thorough, minute, and critical final review before accepting the chapter for publication.
- All anonymous reviewers who provided very constructive feedbacks for thorough revision, improvement, extension, and fine tuning of the chapter.
- All colleagues, assistants and well-wishers who assisted to complete this task.

REFERENCES

Abdul-Ismail, A. (n.d.). *Corruption and its threats to the consolidation of democracy in Nigeria: The sharia perspective*. Bayero University.

Achebe, C. (1984). *The trouble with Nigeria*. Heinemann.

Agbu, O. (2003). Corruption and human trafficking: The Nigerian case. *West Africa Review*, *4*(1), 1–13.

Agenyi, E., & Ameh, I. E. (2009). Corruption in some public sectors: Implications for sustainable socio-economic development in Nigeria. *NASHER Journal*, *7*(1), 128–134.

Ajibewa, A. (2006). Democracy and corruption in Nigeria. In E. O. Ojo (Ed.), *Challenges of Sustainable Democracy in Nigeria*. John Archers.

Aluko, Y. A. (2009). Corruption in Nigeria: Concepts and dimension. In D. U. Enweremadu & E. E. Okafor (Eds.), *Anti-corruption reforms in Nigeria since 1999: Issues, challenges and the way forward*. IFRA.

Andvig, J. C., Fjeldstad, O. H., Weltzien, Å., Amundsen, I., Sissener, T. K., & Søreide, T. (2001). *Corruption. A review of contemporary research*. CRIStin. Retrieved from https://nmbu.brage.unit.no/nmbu-xmlui/handle/11250/2473686

Atabo, A. (2022, January 7). Whistleblowing Policy: The gains, threats, losses and grief. *News Agency of Nigeria*. Retrieved from https://www.corruptionanonymous.org/ whistleblowing-policy-the-gains-threats-losses-and-grief/

Austine, E., Charles, M., & Raymond, A. O. (2013). Corruption in Nigeria: A historical perspective. *Research Humanities and Social Sciences Journal*, *3*, 16–19.

Babalola, A. A. (2019). *The elusive search for nation Nigeria*. Afe Babalola University Press.

Baran, S. J. (2012). *Introduction to mass communication*. McGraw-Hill.

Bello-Imam, L. B. (2004). Corruption and national development. In I. B. Bellow-Imam & M. I. Obadan (Eds.), *Democratic governance and development management in Nigeria's fourth republic 1999-2003*. Centre for Local Government and Rural Development Studies Business.

Caillier, J. G. (2015). Transformational leadership and whistle-blowing attitudes: Is this relationship mediated by organizational commitment and public service motivation? *American Review of Public Administration*, *45*(4), 458–475. doi:10.1177/0275074013515299

Chalouat, I., Carrion-Crespo, C., & Licata, M. (2019). *Law and practice on protecting whistle-blowers in the public and financial services sectors* (Working paper 328). Geneva: International Labor Office. Retrieved from https://www.ilo.org/wcmsp5/groups/public/---ed_dialogue/---sector/documents /publication/wcms_718048.pdf

Chiejina, N. (2021, June 27). Whistleblower policy yields N605b cash, others. *The Nation*. Retrieved from https://thenationonlineng.net/whistleblower-policy-yields-n605bn-cash-others/#:~:text=Whistleblower%20policy%20yields%20N605bn%20cash%2C%20others%20The%20Nation,billion%20in%20recovered%20funds%2C%20The%20Nation%20can%20reveal

ChijiokeUtomi, J. M. (2022, October 14). Nigeria @62: Corruption as war without end. *The Sun*. Retrieved from https://www.sunnewsonline.com/nigeria-at-62-corruption-as-war-without-end/

Chukwuemeka, E. (2006). *Administration and politics in Nigeria: Past, present and issues*. Vinez Communications.

Chukwuemeka, E., Ugwuanyi, B. J., & Ewuim, N. (2012). Curbing corruption in Nigeria: The imperatives of good leadership. *African Research Review*, *6*(3), 338–358. doi:10.4314/afrrev.v6i3.25

Chuta, S. C. (2004). *Corruption in Nigeria*. Afro-Obis.

Crowder, M. (1978). *The story of Nigeria*. Faber and Faber.

Daka, T. (2022, November 22). Federal government says $1b stolen funds recovered since 2015, Okays anti-corruption document. *The Guardian*. Retrieved from https://guardian.ng/news/fg-says-1b-stolen-funds-recovered-since-2015-okays-anti-corruption-document/

Davidson, H. (2018, July 22). Timor-leste activists shocked by Australia's prosecution of spy witness K and lawyer. *The Guardian*. https://www.theguardian.com/world/2018/jul/22/timor-leste-activists-shocked-by-australias-prosecution-of-spy-witness-k-and-lawyer

Derin, K. O. (2007). Leadership, governance and corruption in Nigeria. *Journal of Sustainable Development in Africa*, *9*(3).

Dike, V. E. (2001). *Democracy and political life in Nigeria*. Ahmadu Bello University Press.

Dike, V. E. (2003). *Nigeria and the politics of unreason: A study of the Obasanjo regime*. Adonis and Abbey Publishers.

Dudley, B. J. (1973). *Instability and political order: Politics and Crises in Nigeria*. Ibadan University Press.

Egwemi, V. (Ed.). (2012). *Corruption in Nigeria: Issues, Challenges and possibilities*. Aboki Publishers.

Etymonline.com. (n.d.). *Whistleblower*. Retrieved from https://www.etymonline.com/search?q=whistleblower

Ezeogidi, C. (2020). A historical survey of corruption in Nigeria. SSRN *Electronic Journal*. Retrieved from https://ssrn.com/abstract=3563261 doi:10.2139/ssrn.3563261

Fairhurst, G., & Sarr, R. (1996). *The art of framing*. Jossey-Bass.

Faloore, O. O. (2010). The family and corruption in Nigeria. *Journal of Social and Policy Issues*, *7*(2), 84–89.

Ferrell, O. C., Fraedrich, J., & Ferrell, L. (2021). *Business Ethics: Ethical Decision Making and Cases*. Cengage Learning.

Gamson, W. A., & Modigliani, A. (1989). Media discourse and public opinion on nuclear power: A constructionist approach. *American Journal of Sociology*, *95*(1), 1–37. doi:10.1086/229213

Girling, J. L. S., & Staff, G. J. (1997). *Corruption, capitalism and democracy* (Vol. 11). Routledge.

Government Accountability Project. (2018, 21 November). European parliament panel approves whistleblower protections for all EU countries. *Common Dreams*. Retrieved from https://www.commondreams.org/newswire/2018/11/21/european-parliament-panel-approves-whistleblower-protections-all-eu-countries

Government of Canada. PSIC. (2013, 10 September). *The servants disclosure protection act*. Retrieved from http://www.psic.gc.ca/eng/aboutus/psdpa

Government of Canada. PSIC. (2014). *Background, objectives, scope*. Retrieved from http://www.psic.ge.ca/ eng/content/background-objectives-scope

Igbuzor, O. (2008). *Strategies for winning the anti-corruption war in Nigeria*. Action Aid.

Ikubaje, J. (2004). *Nigeria: Anti-corruption initiatives and the constitution*. Workshop on corruption in Nigeria, organized by Zero Corruption Coalition and the UNDP at Niimah Guest Palace, Kano, Nigeria.

Kazeem, Y. (2016, December 9). An 8 million dollar refugee fund scandal shows Buhari's anti-corruption drive in Nigeria is not going to plan. *Quartz*. Retrieved from https://qz.com/africa/858019/a-new-8m-scam-of-relief-funds-shows-nigerias-buhari-anti-corruption-drive-is-not-going-to-plan

Kleinig, J. (n.d.). *Whistleblower*. Retrieved from https://www.britannica.com/topic/whistleblower

Lash, N. A. (2003). *Corruption and economic development*. Layola University.

Livingston, S. G. (1992). The politics of international agenda-setting: Reagan and North-South relations. *International Studies Quarterly*, *36*(3), 313–329. doi:10.2307/2600775

Mohamed, Z., & Stansfield, G. (2017). *What does the protected disclosures amendment act mean for whistleblowers and employers alike*? Cliffe Dekker Hofmeyr. Retrieved from https://www.lexology.com/library/detail.aspx?g=e9fc5039-f162-4609-bd1d-10e94ffe00da#:~:text=The%20PDA%20provides%20protection%20to%20whistleblowers%20in%20the,places%20further%20obligations%20on%20whistleblowers%20and%20employers%20alike

Nakitende, M. G., Rafay, A., & Waseem, M. (2021). Frauds in Business Organizations: A Comprehensive Overview. In A. Rafay (Ed.), *Handbook of Research on Theory and Practice of Financial Crimes* (pp. 21–38). IGI Global. doi:10.4018/978-1-7998-5567-5.ch002

Nye, J. S. (1967). Corruption and political development: A cost-benefit analysis. *The American Political Science Review*, *61*(2), 417–427. doi:10.2307/1953254

Nzekwe, A. (1994). *Can Nigeria Survive*. Transafrican Links.

Obasanjo, O. (1994). Keynote address. In A. Mahadi, G. A. Kwanashie, & M. Yakubu (Eds.), *Nigeria: The state of the nation and the way forward*. Arewa House.

Ogundiya, I. S. (2009). Political corruption in Nigeria: Theoretical perspectives and some explanations. *The Anthropologist*, *11*(4), 281–292. doi:10.1080/09720073.2009.11891117

Ogundiya, I. S., & Baba, T. K. (2004). Electoral Violence and the prospects of democratic consolidation in Nigeria. Paper presented at the National Conference on Electoral Violence in Nigeria Organized by NPSA at Rock View Hotel, Abuja, Nigeria.

Ogunshola, F. (2022, February 8). Protecting whistle-blowers via requisite legal framework. *New Telegraph*. Retrieved from https://www.newtelegraphng.com/?s=whistle-blowers

Okolie, D. O. (2007). *Nigeria government and politics: The changing scene*. John Jacobs Publishers.

Okonkwo, R. (2005). Corruption in Nigeria. In F. Anyika (Ed.), *African Humanities*. Afro-Orbis.

Oluikpe, N. (2018, December 24). Anti-corruption war: Stakeholders ruminate on role of media. *Daily Independent*.

Omilusi, M. (2019). *Buhari's change and challenges: Democratic transition and governance assessment in Nigeria*. Human & Organizational Resources Development Centre.

Omotola, J. S. (2006). 'Through a glass darkly': Assessing the 'new' war against corruption in Nigeria. *Africa Insight, 36*(3-4), 214-228.

Onyeacholem, G. (2017, August 10). Malami and anti-graft agencies. *Nation (New York, N.Y.)*.

Protected Disclosures Act. (2014). *A new era for whistleblowing in Ireland*. Retrieved from https://www.icsa.org.uk/ireland/knowledge-and-guidance/governance-and-directors/protected-disclosures-act-2014-a-new-era-for-whistleblowing-in-ireland

PSIC. (n.d.). *Tell us. You are protected*. Office of the public sector integrity commissioner of Canada. Retrieved from https://www.psic-ispc.gc.ca/

Rafay, A. (Ed.). (2021a). *Money Laundering and Terrorism Financing in Global Financial Systems*. IGI Global. doi:10.4018/978-1-7998-8758-4

Rafay, A. (Ed.). (2021b). *Handbook of Research on Theory and Practice of Financial Crimes*. IGI Global. doi:10.4018/978-1-7998-5567-5

Rafay, A. (Ed.). (2023). *Concepts and Cases of Illicit and Illegitimate Finance*. IGI Global. doi:10.4018/978-1-6684-8587-3

Reding, A., Gorp, A. V., Cox, K., Walczak, A., Giacomantonio, C., & Hoorens, S. (2014). *Handling ethical problems in counter terrorism: An inventory of methods to support ethical decision making*. Rand Corporation. Retrieved from https://www.rand.org/pubs/research_reports/RR251.html

Rowe, M. (1993). Options and choice for conflict resolution in the workplace. In L. Hall (Ed.), *Negotiation: Strategies for mutual gain*. Sage.

Rowe, M., Wilcox, L., & Gadlin, H. (2009). Dealing with--or Reporting--"Unacceptable" Behavior. *Journal of the International Ombudsman Association, 2*(1), 52-64.

Soderlund, W. C., Briggs, E. D., Najem, T. P., & Roberts, B. C. (2012). *Africa's Deadliest Conflict: Media Coverage of the Humanitarian Disaster in the Congo and the United Nations Response, 1997–2008*. Wilfrid Laurier University Press.

Tankard, J. W. (2001). The empirical approach to the study of media framing. In S. D. Reese, O. H. Gandy, & A. E. Grant (Eds.), *Framing public life: Perspectives on media and our understanding of the social world*. Routledge.

Tanzi, V. (1998). Corruption around the world: Causes, consequences, scope, and cures. *IMF Staff Papers, 45*(4), 559–594. doi:10.2307/3867585

Uju, J. (2002). The military and corruption in Nigeria. In C. O. T. Ugwu (Ed.), *Corruption in Nigeria: Critical perspectives*. Academic Publishing Company.

UK Department for Business, Energy & Industrial Strategy. (2019, March). *Confidentiality clauses: Consultation on measures to prevent misuse in situations of workplace harassment or discrimination*. Retrieved from https://assets.publishing.service.gov.uk /government/uploads /system/uploads/attachment_data/file/783011/confidentiality-clauses-consultation.pdf

Unachukwu, G. C., Ojiakor, N., & Okafor, G. (2003). *Nigeria peoples and culture*. John Jacobs Classic Publishers.

Vandekerckhove, W. (2016). *Whistleblowing and organizational social responsibility: A global assessment*. Routledge. doi:10.4324/9781315547299

Welch, C. E. (1987). The military and the state in Africa: Problems of political transition. In Z. Ergas (Ed.), *The African State in transition*. Springer. doi:10.1007/978-1-349-18886-4_9

Whistleblowers Australia. (n.d.). *How to blow the Whistle?* Retrieved from http://www.whistleblowers.org.au/

Wordorigins.org. (2021). *Whistleblower*. Retrieved from https://www.wordorigins.org/big-list-entries/whistleblower?rq=whistleblower

Yaru, M. A. (2009). Economic perspective of corruption in public sector: A theoretical explanation and lessons for Nigeria. *Ilorin Journal of Business and Social Sciences, 13*(2), 143–153.

ADDITIONAL READING

Boot, E. R. (2019). *The ethics of whistleblowing*. Routledge. doi:10.4324/9780429439001

Johnson, R. A. (2003). *Whistleblowing: When it works-and why*. Lynn Rienner Publishers.

Kohn, S. M. (2011). *The whistleblower's handbook: A step-by-step guide to doing what's right and protecting yourself.* Lyons Press.

Micceli, M. P., & Near, J. P. (1992). *Blowing the whistle: The organizational and legal implications for companies and employees*. Lexington Books.

Micceli, M. P., Near, J. P., & Morehead, T. (2008). *Whistleblowing in Organizations*. Psychology Press.

Mueller, T. (2019). *Crisis of conscience: Whistleblowing in an age of fraud*. Random House.

Stanger, A. (2019). *Whistleblowers: Honesty in America from Washington to Trump*. Yale University Press.

KEY TERMS AND DEFINITIONS

Anti-Graft Agency: Is an agency set up by government to fight corruption. The Independent Corrupt Practices and other Related Offences Commission (ICPC) and the Economic and Financial Crime Commission (EFCC) are the two key anti-corruption agencies in Nigeria. Disclosure: In financial terms, it means the action of making all relevant information about a business available to the public.

Legal Framework: It refers to the set of laws, regulations and rules that apply in a particular country.

Pervasive Corruption: Is widespread corruption that affects all levels of government in a country.

Protection: It means to shield a person from harm.

Whistleblowing Policy: Is an innovative strategy introduced in 2016 by the Nigerian government to tackle the menace of corruption in the country.

ENDNOTES

1. Body language means the actions of a person, in this case, the actions of the President that show that he abhors corruption in all ramifications and that anybody who engages in it will not be in his good books.
2. Rotten to the core means to be highly corrupt. It means that the warrant chief system operated by the colonial masters' stinks with corruption.
3. Operation car wash reputation means a reputation that is unstable, questionable, that cannot be trusted or relied on by anybody.

Chapter 5
Perceived Corruption in the Process of the Entrepreneurial Intention:
An Extension into the Ajzen's Theory of Planned Behaviour

Mohammad Heydari
https://orcid.org/0000-0003-3942-2107
Southwest University, China

Yanan Fan
University of Wrocław, Poland

Xiaoyang Li
Southwest University, China

Kin Keung Lai
Shaanxi Normal University, China

ABSTRACT

Several factors like cognitive attitude, norms, and behavioral control still influence corruption. Ajzen theory states that social and psychological aspects can be antecedents. This research looks into the variables of the theory of planned behavior (TPB) to anticipate the effect of perceived corruption (PC). Considering the primary entrepreneurial deterrent, the dataset is based on 400 Polish graduate students' entrepreneurial intents and behavior who graduated from higher education programs at eight universities in Poland. These three variables were examined for their influence on corrupt perception and behavior. This study explores the attitude and behavior of corruption/fraud by using Ajzen's TPB. This is accomplished by paying closer attention to the impact of cognition attitude (CA), subjective norm (SN), and perceived behavioral control (PBC), which influence the intention to commit corruption. This provides a solid theoretical basis for this research.

DOI: 10.4018/978-1-6684-5007-9.ch005

INTRODUCTION

Since 2010, the social psychology of corruption has become a new field of academic growth. Many theories exist about the causes of corruption, ranging from economic models to cultural explanations. Despite this, the social-psychological reasons for corruption have received comparatively little research, especially at the individual level, as can be seen in a recent paper (Traditional theories of corruption frequently involve assumptions about motives that aren't always correct) (Heydari *et al.*, 2020a,b; Xiaohu *et al.*, 2020). It discovered the power of an alternative theoretical paradigm to describe corrupt behavior: based on TPB theory (Ajzen, 1991; Heydari *et al.*, 2020c). The existing cognitive psychology literature on corruption found that the psychological impact of power, personal gain and loss and loss aversion, self-control, risk rationalization, acceptance, and emotion on the propensity to act corruptly. The previous research literature on the personal characteristics and motivations of corrupt actors has accumulated some data, and a growing number of empirical studies have investigated why an individual may engage in dishonest behavior, especially considering that an individual's tendency to corrupt may depend on the individual's moral identity and the surrounding environment (Ajzen, 1991). However, still do not understand much, such as the interrelation of cognition leading to corrupt action, motivation, volition, and emotion. As a result, this research examines these person-based drivers of human behavior in a particular situational environment, the business context.

In research titled *"both sides of the coin: Corrupt motivations between business employees and public officials"*, Gorsira *et al.* (2018) described the goal of their study as to better understand why business employees and public officials engage in corruption. They used a self-report questionnaire to collect data about personal-level descriptions of corruption. Their findings showed that the most important indicators of the tendency to engage (or not engage) in corruption are as follows: the ethical beliefs that prevent the person from corruption; perceptions of whether their employees approve of and engage in corruption; and the problems experienced in respecting the rules regarding corruption. The mechanism of these outcomes was identical for business colleagues and public governance and, consequently, both sides of corrupt activities. It was found that corruption in both public and private sectors and its active and passive forms originate from the same motives. There is not enough evidence providing robust support for the assumption that corruption can be essentially predicted by economic considerations, i.e., expected costs and advantages. Given the findings that the perceived opportunity and norms to comply with rules are prominent predictors of corruption, this study focuses on the practical implications of developing anti-corruption approaches within the private and public sectors.

Boehm & Lambsdorff (2009) identify several corruption practices as instances of corruption, containing embezzlement, extortion, bribery, nepotism, favoritism, fraud, and conspiracy between businesses to set prices surreptitiously or allocate market share. These illicit practices have logic, economic systems, and reality. Interactions among corrupted parties are buried in a *"black box,"* Most formal economic models ignore transaction costs arising from corrupt behaviors, the institutions involved, or their complexity. Instead, as a distribution issue, corruption is often minimized. There are also variances in the severity of corrupt activities and their monetary value. Low-level corruption, such as that of police personnel, is distinguished from high-level corruption, typically attributed to politicians and business leaders.

The cognitive, emotional, and behavioral aspects, as stated by (Bolivar & Baressi, 1995), are in constant interaction and are periodic, i.e., they may be defined as both antecedents and consequences of acts since they affect the aspect, and hence individual ATT toward objects and circumstances.

Overall, Entrepreneurship is an uncertain process, risky and complicated; for this reason, not everyone can begin a new venture. Although the entrepreneurial process is inherently experimental, past experiences, personal formation, and attitudes may influence entrepreneurial intentions (EI). For instance, based on (Lund, 2016; Estrin *et al.*, 2013), intentions and attitudes can be learned, assessed, and improved about entrepreneurship.

Many scholars referred that skills about entrepreneurship could be learned, as seen by the expanding number of university-based entrepreneurship programs. Further research stressed entrepreneurial intent (EI) to understand better the factors that influence young entrepreneurs' decision-making.

While many studies have been done on how people decide to become entrepreneurs, little research has been done on the factors restricting people from beginning their ventures. Entrepreneurship intention and corruption studies have gained popularity in recent years; however, there is no empirical evidence of its prevalence among students, particularly in Poland. The significance of this kind of study about entrepreneurial inhibitors, more specifically about corruption as an obstacle, can be derived from the purpose of this study in Poland. In Poland, universities are between others expected 'to be the place where practice-based learning takes place intending to produce job creators and address society's problems.' It is crucial to note that corruption and entrepreneurial intention among university students are relatively new in Poland's education system. They provide practice-based ethics training, vocational diplomas, and degrees in entrepreneurial behavior and business. As a result, Polish universities play a critical role in easing the pressures of poverty, inequality, and unemployment. A study by Pihie & Akmaliah posited that universities need to increase their teaching approaches to improve ESE[i] and the desire between students to opt for entrepreneurship as their final career choice (Shapero & Sokol, 1982; Pihie & Akmaliah, 2009).' Entrepreneurial intentions are frequently used as a proxy for entrepreneurial action, and the formation of entrepreneurial intentions is a popular topic in entrepreneurship research. On the other hand, entrepreneurial intentions may not always translate into action.

The present research investigates the perceived corruption (PC), the primary entrepreneurial inhibitor (Shin, 2015), on students' EI and behavior. Several factors influence corruption, namely cognitive attitude, norms, and behavioral control (Shin, 2015), by adopting Ajzen's TPB (1991), stating that social and psychological aspects can be antecedents. Current research examines TPB factors as anticipant the effect of PC, considered the main impediment to entrepreneurship on graduate students' [EI, & EB]. In addition, these three variables were examined for their impact on corrupt perception and behavior (Shin, 2015). This study explores the behavior and cognitive attitude of corruption/fraud by utilizing the TPB. This is accomplished by focusing on the impact of cognitive attitude (CA), subjective norm (SN), and individual or group behavior control, all of which impact the intent to commit corruption. Therefore, the study contends that to better understand the impact of corruption on entrepreneurial intents (EI), it is essential to find out how corruption perception (PC) is mediated by the theory of planned behavior three-pronged pattern of entrepreneurial CN, SN, PBC; (Ajzen, 1991). This produces a solid theoretical basis for this study (see the recent longitudinal study by Estrin *et al.*, 2013). According to Ajzen, all factors that may affect behavior indirectly affect behavior performance through entrepreneurial intentions. The entrepreneurial intent (EI) is the result of the combined effect of the individual's own *"attitude," external "subjective norm,"* and *"perceived behavioral control."*

This study combines Ajzen's (1991) theory of planned behavior with an institutional embeddedness logic to investigate the impact of corruption on creating entrepreneurial ambitions. Corruption perceptions are modeled as a background factor mediated by Ajzen's (1991) classic intention antecedents (CA, SN, and PBC). The experience indicates that the strategy acknowledges that all entrepreneurial conduct is embedded and cannot be separated from its institutional framework. It follows Boehm and Lambsdorff's request for a more in-depth analysis of the role of institutions in the development of EI (Boehm & Lambsdorff, 2009). This is the focus of investigation in this study. This study has chosen the TPB because its prediction power is widely recognized in past studies (Kautonen *et al.*, 2013; 2015).

RESEARCH MODEL: ANTECEDENTS OF CORRUPTION

Ajzen's TPB (1991) stipulates that a person's intention to engage in a specific behavior tends to depend on three factors: CAB, SN, and PBC, and that the person's behavioral intentions tend to influence their actual behavior. In the extended version of TPB, moral obligation is considered an antecedent to planned behavior.

Several studies have used TPB to predict intentions regarding tax behavior. It is recognized in the literature that there are many challenges in exploring the actual immoral behavior, including how to locate perpetrators, gain access, and deal with information censorship. Consequently, scholars have resorted to utilizing intended actions rather than actual behavior to study unethical behavior.

This study uses Ajzen's TPB to explain how the formation of entrepreneurial intents (EI) can be affected by corruption. Tested thoroughly for the expected causality direction (Gollwitzer & Brandstätter, 1997), TPB has proven to be a reliable model for predicting any deliberate behavior (Kautonen *et al.*, 2013; 2015). The hypothesis of planned conduct has been thoroughly examined in various cultural contexts, including post-socialist ones. As a result, it offers a soundly robust theoretical foundation for this research.

Based on the TPB, an individual's behavior is preceded by their desire to take a specific action. The intent reflects how willing people are to *"give it a shot"* and how much effort they intend to put in to carry out the habit. The intention is influenced by the individual's attitude (ATT) toward the behavior's outcome, the perceived SNs (i.e., normative institutions concerning the behavior and its outcome), and the PBC over the action. Thus, according to TPB, any intention or planned behavior can be predicted by three independent determinants. The inclination to respond to the planned behavior with some degree of favorability or unfavourability is referred to as attitude (ATT). Norms indicate the person's sense that one has to conform to other people's expectations about doing or not doing a specific action. PBC refers to the degree to which people believe they can perform and control a specific activity. This antecedent concerns the consideration of what information, opportunities, skills, and other sources needed to carry out the behavior are available, and also what potential difficulties or barriers must be overcome.

The TPB predicts that having a favorable ATT toward an entrepreneurial activity, having a positive perception of critical peer support, and feeling that one may overcome the hurdles facing that activity are all positively associated with a stronger intention to start that activity. Thus, the effects of all other potential determinants of intention are indirect and mediated by these three antecedents (Ajzen, 1991), which are referred to as *"background factors."* Background influences only impact entrepreneurial intent if the individual perceives and values them. In the TPB, these factors are governed by the person's beliefs, which reflect their information about a given issue or behavior. Beliefs are formed through daily interactions with the real world and are not intrinsic. Although a person's opinions may be incorrect or biased, this has no bearing on the forecast and explanation of the purpose. What matters is what they say. In light of this, the study proposes a conceptual model where corruption perception (as a manifestation of corruption-related beliefs) influences entrepreneurial intent via all three intention antecedents (CA, SN, and PBC).

Attitudes can mediate corruption perceptions through the subjective cost-benefit analysis of entrepreneurship. This is linked to finding prospective business opportunities, evaluating their projected benefits and expenses, and determining whether to pursue them. On the one hand, a person's attitude toward an entrepreneurial venture may become more positive upon the realization that the corrupt environment facilitates the outcomes they expect from that venture (e.g., more income, less workload, more flexibility, higher personal satisfaction), bolstering their original goal. On the other hand, concerns about the implications of engaging in corruption (e.g., being discovered bribing or abandoning moral ideals) can make potential founders develop a negative ATT toward entrepreneurial ventures, weakening their intention. This is congruent with Collier's (2002) model of corruption as an institutional choice, which encompasses both external (structural) and internal (agency) domains. The inner domain represents the agent's (in this case, the prospective entrepreneur's) rational decision-making process according to cost-benefit analysis. The external domain is the institutional (rule) framework that influences an agent's inner decision-making. Material source elements in the external domain also influence agent information about predicted costs and benefits, which may be a precursor for corrupt behavior.

A more active research society demonstrates the growing interest in theoretical modeling for simulation in this domain. Over the last decade, there has been an enhancement in conferences and journal papers on conceptual modeling and an edited book on the topic.

Figure 1. Conceptual research model

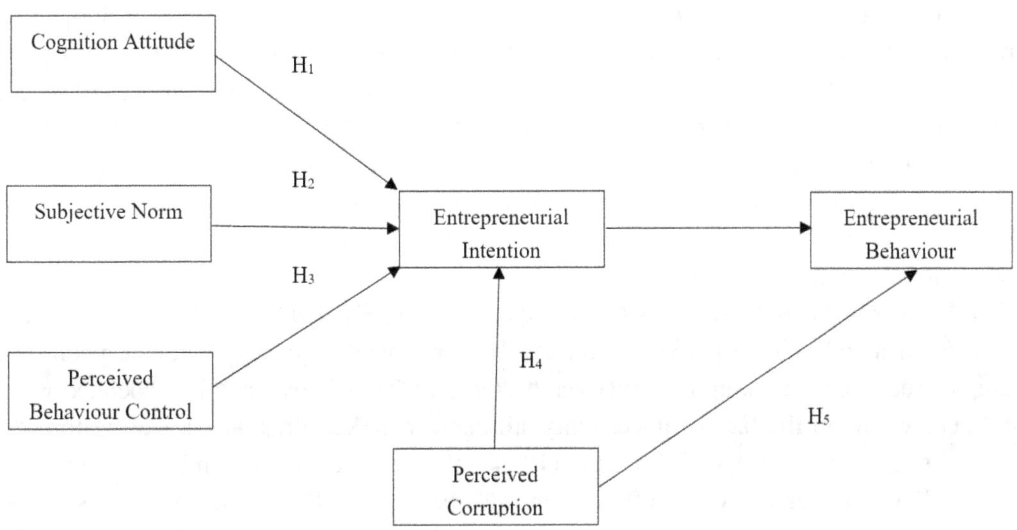

Hypothesized Model. This model indicates (a) the linkage and paths between CA = Cognition Attitude, SN = Subjective Norm, PBC = Perceived Behavioral Control, EI = Entrepreneurial Intention; and (b) PC = Perceived Corruption, on EI = Entrepreneurial Intention; and (c) PC = Perceived Corruption, on EB = Entrepreneurial Behavior.

LITERATURE REVIEW AND HYPOTHESIS

The primary goal of this study was to examine students' entrepreneurial intention utilizing a modified version of Ajzen's (1991) TPB and the PC. This study surveyed Polish society, students who had graduated from higher education programs at eight different universities, and other entrepreneurs who had no ethical training in using these teaching methods. Demographic variables/students and entrepreneurs' characteristics of CA, SN, PBC, and PC, specifically ATT toward entrepreneurial BI and EB.

The personal desirability of completing the behavior is represented by this construct (Everett, 2007). Individual expectations and ideas about the behavior's outcomes are crucial to ATT. This construct allows us to assess people's expectations about their capacity to achieve anything in the sample (Ajzen,1985). It refers to the extent to which an individual views the behavior in question favorably. Individuals establish ATTs about a specific behavior by linking it with the most likely consequence. The more desirable the outcomes, the stronger the intent will be to conduct the behavior. In the instance of EI, the desirability of launching a new business might be regarded as the attitude toward the behavior. An optimistic expectation of success is often associated with beginning one's business in the entrepreneurial context. The following theory can be stated, according to the referenced authors:

H_1. The Cognitive Attitude Toward Behavior (CAB) Is Positively Connected with Entrepreneurial Intention (EI).

Normative beliefs (NB) or perceived social norms is a construct that allows us to comprehend the significance of one's perceptions of performing a specific behavior (Ajzen,1985). For instance, think about what your family expects about whether being a doctor, an accountant, or an entrepreneur is desirable. On the other hand, these NB are dependent on the degree of the drive to follow them (Ajzen,1985). Subjective Norm can influence business purposes in a variety of ways. The impact of Subjective Norm on entrepreneurial intent has been studied, but the results have been equivocal. For North American students, Krueger (2007) discovered that the impacts of social support are unrelated to EI. A comparative study (Autio & Arcs, 2010; Liñán & Chen, 2009) discovered that social support is poorly connected with EI in American students, but the inverse is right in students in Scandinavian countries.

Social support shall be an essential element that significantly impacts entrepreneurial intention in contexts with more uncertainty. Students who receive more support can become entrepreneurs. According to other literature, the following hypothesis can be stated:

H_2. The Subjective Norm (SN) Is Positively Connected with Entrepreneurial Intention (EI).

PBC refers to an individual's perceived self-efficacy or capability in carrying out a specific behavior (for example, becoming an entrepreneur) (Everett *et al.*, 2007). Self-efficacy is associated with taking risks and persevering in the face of uncertainty, aiming for higher aims, and lowering threat rigidity and learned helplessness. Krueger & Dickson (1994) referred that This notion is critical because situational controllability is linked to self-efficacy and self-perception. Despite its usefulness in predicting certain behaviors, entrepreneurship academics frequently ignore self-efficacy (Zhao *et al.*, 2005). Some scholars have linked self-efficacy to recognizing opportunities and taking risks (Sánchez, 2009) as well as professional choices (Krueger & Dickson, 1994). It can provide the following hypothesis based on more literature:

H_3. Perceived Behavioral Control (PBC) Is Positively Connected to Entrepreneurial Intention (EI).

The TPB was combined with the perception of corruption. According to some scholars (Gaglio & Katz, 2001), PC is an outside element that inhibits entrepreneurial effort. Corruption is a social ailment and a business and governmental issue (Foo MD, 2011; Gielnik *et al.*, 2012). It contains all behaviors that take advantage of public positions and solutions, prioritizing personal gain over public benefit. It can manifest itself in a variety of areas, including economics (trade policy and privatization), law (the rule of law, judicial independence), transnational elements, administrative, bureaucratic, and civil liberties, and press freedoms (Grichnik *et al.*, 2010). A powerful computer might demotivate people and make them hesitant to start their own business. People with strong personal principles who choose not to be self-employed, or entrepreneurs might avoid the challenges caused by compromised systems.

Corruption is a common occurrence in Poland (Davis, 2009). Corruption is a serious issue within the public section, with certain corporate activities delaying economic growth. Poland's high level of corruption is well-known throughout the EU; the 2017 TI[i] Survey ranked Poland 36th out of 180 countries in terms of PC. This information is crucial since a high PC level can stifle entrepreneurial activities (Melgar *et al.*, 2010). Because the playing field is not leveled due to high levels of corruption, it is difficult for new businesses to succeed. It is even more difficult for new entrepreneurs to decide not to launch a new endeavor. In light of the preceding statement, it can formulate the following hypotheses:

H_4. Corruption Perception (PC) Strongly Negatively Impacts Students' Intention to Be Entrepreneurs (EI).

H_5. Corruption Perception (PC) Strongly Negatively Impacts Students' Entrepreneurial Behavior (EB).

METHODOLOGY

Considering that modern empirical studies often utilize survey tools and services such as Survey Gizmo, Survey Monkey, and Key Survey, this dissertation is carried out with Common Method Variance (CMV) considered. Using a single survey as the source of both dependent and independent data in a tool may pose the problem of bias due to the use of a single data collection method. Moreover, the design of the survey tool itself can encourage responders to be biased in their responses. The purpose of CMV is to control and factor in this bias. The effects of this bias have been a subject of debate since the 1950s and cannot be ignored as they can inject significant errors into findings.

In checking for CMV, the goal is to determine whether there is such bias and to what extent. There are several analytical methods for assessing how much data can be affected by biases due to the survey tool or methodology. Here, this research describes three commonly used methods of CMV estimation. Also, as a second method, this dissertation mainly analyzed based on structural equation (SEM). In this way, the reliability and standardization of the analysis results are enhanced through two kinds of demonstration methods.

The sampling process of this research was stratified sampling, whereby 400 graduates of eight universities were recruited. The survey population comprised entrepreneurs who graduated from universities and other entrepreneurs with no formal education. Creswell & Creswell (2017) recommends stratified random sampling to improve approximate precision and narrow confidence intervals. Probability sampling designs are efficient because (a) the results can be generalized to the population under study and (b) approximate what is true, considering the population can be carried out from a smaller number of people. The students' data were included in the first section. The TPB dimensions were covered in the second part utilizing 45 various questions, including 11 for the subjective norm (SN), 8 for perceived behavioral control (PBC), 11 questions for cognitive attitude (CA), 3 for perceived corruption (PC), 3 for entrepreneurial Behavior (EB), and 9 for entrepreneurial intentions (EI). The corruption perception (PC) between students was covered in the third section through three questions. A five-point Likert Scale set was used to quantify all the questions, ranking 5 for strongly agree to 1 for strongly disagree. SPSS and Warp PLS were used in this work to analyze the data. Anderson & Gerbing study (1988) conducted a CFA to assess the model capability and utilized SEM to evaluate the causal associations.

Moreover, this research carried out the Heterotrait-Monotrait ratio of correlations (HTMT) to analyze the discriminant validity of (PLS-SEM & PLS-PM)[i], the crucial building block model evaluation. This study analyzed quality indices and model GFI and conducted the R-square. This test is extensively utilized for analyzing the model's adequacy. The results reveal the model's capability to reflect the covariance and variance of the data based on (Anderson & Gerbing, 1988).

DATA ANALYSIS AND RESULTS

Adequacy and Suitability of Sampling

The Kaiser-Meyer-Olkin (KMO)

To test how suited your data is for Factor Analysis, the Bartlett sphericity test is used (see table 1). Its purpose is to reject the H_0 that the same matrix (i.e., a matrix whose diagonal elements are one and all non-diagonal elements are zero) is correct in society. In other words, Bartlett's test tests the hypothesis that the observed correlation matrix belongs to a society with uncorrelated variables. For the factor model to be valuable and meaningful, the variables need to be correlated. If the hypothesis that the variables are not related; Does not reject, the application of the factor model will be questioned and should be reconsidered. In the present study, the characteristic of the Bartlett sphericity test (80.48) is significant at the level of less than 0.01, which indicates that the data correlation matrix is not zero in the population so that the fact-finding operation can be justified.

Table 1. KMO and Bartlett sphericity test results

KMO		**0.555**
Bartlett's Test	*Chi-Square*	80.484
	Df	15
	Sig.	.001

The extracted factors were transferred based on conventional methods (see table 2)

Table 2. Component matrix[a]

	Component					
	Perceived Corruption	Subjective Norm	Perceived Behavioral	Cognition Attitude	Entrepreneurial Behavior	Entrepreneurial Intention
Q1	.281	.309	-.203	-.137	-.185	-.281
Q2	.772	.050	-.216	.183	-.097	-.095
Q3	.468	-.027	.581	-.250	-.113	.209
Q4	.733	-.032	-.162	.163	.115	.121
Q5	.530	-.132	-.153	-.122	.228	.171
Q6	.493	-.001	-.073	-.306	.166	.152
Q7	.370	-.071	-.343	-.294	.120	.084
Q8	.183	.189	-.297	-.299	.312	-.150
Q9	.003	.202	-.314	-.162	.250	.040
Q10	.014	.112	.043	-.045	.632	.043
Q11	.002	.268	.291	-.006	.370	.204
Q12	-.056	.264	.063	.163	.344	.163
Q13	.066	.360	.219	.222	.385	.246
Q14	-.024	.696	.257	.116	-.052	.202
Q15	-.159	.692	-.027	-.012	-.132	.269
Q16	-.005	.661	.136	.004	-.007	.024
Q17	-.106	.754	-.107	-.034	-.026	.220
Q18	.148	.646	-.016	.138	-.271	-.061
Q19	.013	.592	.126	.027	.041	-.392
Q20	.168	-.196	.414	.655	.133	-.132
Q21	.055	-.120	.245	.631	.148	-.087
Q22	.151	-.211	.355	.668	.093	-.152
Q23	.152	.195	.126	.171	-.250	-.084
Q24	.202	.120	.106	.106	-.075	.309
Q25	-.037	.085	-.215	.202	-.172	.270
Q26	-.098	-.039	-.143	-.024	-.185	.484
Q27	.156	.046	-.218	.431	.175	.351
Q28	-.039	.747	-.097	.031	.064	.269
Q29	.100	.637	-.006	.051	-.203	-.206
Q30	.004	.628	.111	.057	.099	-.418
Q31	.279	.396	-.142	-.077	-.098	-.342
Q32	.798	.014	-.115	.083	-.161	-.253
Q33	.460	-.035	.736	-.304	-.182	.000
Q34	.798	-.073	-.179	.036	.154	.134
Q35	.823	.034	-.239	.131	-.087	-.064
Q36	.506	.001	.648	-.327	-.074	.212

Continued on following page

Table 2. Continued

	Component					
	Perceived Corruption	**Subjective Norm**	**Perceived Behavioral**	**Cognition Attitude**	**Entrepreneurial Behavior**	**Entrepreneurial Intention**
Q37	.134	.082	.024	.035	.388	-.122
Q38	.006	.089	.154	-.234	.533	-.261
Q39	.082	-.030	-.036	-.219	.252	-.128
Q40	-.125	.014	.123	-.237	.466	-.162
Q41	.060	.048	-.084	-.072	-.009	.013
Q42	.029	.037	.230	.131	.363	-.013
Q43	.460	-.035	.736	-.304	-.182	.000
Q44	.798	-.073	-.179	.036	.154	.134
Q45	.823	.034	-.239	.131	-.087	-.064

Extraction Method: Principal Component Analysis (PCA).

The resulting structure matrix after 24 rotations is shown in Table 3. This table is the Matrix of six factors extracted by the PCA method after rotation.

Table 3. Rotated component matrix[a]

	Component					
	Perceived Corruption	Subjective Norm	Perceived Behavioral	Cognition Attitude	Entrepreneurial Behavior	Entrepreneurial Intention
Q1	.271	.428**	-.021	-.183	-.232	.057
Q2	.795**	.182	.037	.107	-.116	-.073
Q3	.204	-.025	.790**	.020	.094	-.029
Q4	.770**	-.027	.063	.078	.119	-.035
Q5	.562**	-.208	.098	-.150	.124	.105
Q6	.466**	-.086	.228	-.293	.107	.137
Q7	.442**	-.133	-.034	-.377	-.034	.100
Q8*	.250	.118	-.151	-.353	.049	.375
Q9*	.106	.070	-.241	-.317	.168	.163
Q10	.049	-.081	-.080	-.026	.446**	.450
Q11	-.069	.078	.174	.024	.510**	.183
Q12	-.028	.096	-.096	.070	.463**	.101
Q13	.040	.164	.048	.151	.615**	.086
Q14	-.128	.573**	.166	-.003	.454**	-.172
Q15	-.176	.528**	-.029	-.263	.375	-.271
Q16	-.083	.582**	.086	-.088	.309	-.012
Q17	-.097	.573**	-.099	-.308	.413	-.168
Q18	.100	.688**	.012	-.022	.089	-.209
Q19	-.067	.666**	.003	.062	.046	.263
Q20	.111	-.064	.086	.815**	.116	.029
Q21	.059	-.038	-.079	.686**	.154	-.008
Q22	.112	-.064	.034	.806**	.066	.000
Q23*	.082	.303	.122	.174	-.068	-.165
Q24*	.161	.044	.174	.028	.237	-.252
Q25*	.052	.025	-.189	-.033	.110	-.381
Q26*	-.044	-.183	-.023	-.223	.155	-.436
Q27	.296	-.090	-.277	.163	.392**	-.246
Q28	-.021	.538**	-.105	-.256	.508**	-.150
Q29	.043	.704**	.000	-.046	.018	-.046
Q30	-.063	.693**	-.043	.081	.082	.308
Q31	.257	.513**	-.028	-.106	-.160	.143
Q32	.763**	.223	.158	.121	-.274	.023
Q33	.124	.064	.916**	.102	-.066	.084
Q34	.827**	-.086	.118	-.023	.103	.027
Q35	.847**	.153	.061	.051	-.114	-.068
Q36	.210	-.012	.879**	-.017	.125	.033

Continued on following page

Table 3. Continued

	Component					
	Perceived Corruption	**Subjective Norm**	**Perceived Behavioral**	**Cognition Attitude**	**Entrepreneurial Behavior**	**Entrepreneurial Intention**
Q37*	.149	.034	-.055	.079	.194	.349
Q38	-.037	.023	.057	-.046	.165	.636**
Q39	.083	-.058	.014	-.137	.002	.428**
Q40	-.147	-.076	.020	-.083	.155	.521**
Q41*	.073	.035	-.015	-.108	-.008	.000
Q42	-.004	-.032	.057	.222	.288	.260
Q43	.124	.064	.916**	.102	-.066	.084
Q44	.827**	-.086	.118	-.023	.103	.027
Q45	.847**	.153	.061	.051	-.114	-.068

Extraction Method: Principal Component Analysis (PCA).
Rotation Method: Varimax with Kaiser Normalization.

1. Rotation converged in 25 iterations.
2. (*) Low load factor
3. (**) Strong load factor

This section presents all inferential statistics concerning the models.
Test of normality of survey variables:
The normality of data was measured utilizing Kolmogorov-Smirnov (K-S); (see table 4):

Table 4. Questionnaire variables normality

Result	Sig.	K-S statistic	Variable
Unusual	0.000	2.907	EB
Unusual	0.011	1.607	EI
Unusual	0.000	2.302	CA
Unusual	0.002	1.884	PBC
Unusual	0.009	1.647	SN
Unusual	0.000	3.051	PC

As the above table shows, the significance statistic of the K-S test was less than 0.05, confirming the alternative hypothesis (H_1) that all variables of this statistical sample have an unusual distribution. Since all survey variables were found to have an unusual distribution, it was decided to use Smart PLS software to examine the conceptual model, carry out structural equation modelling, and assess the measurement models.

To determine whether a structural equation model appropriately describes the target phenomenon, it is necessary to examine three criteria.

1. GOF[1] of the measurement model
2. GOF of the structural model
3. GOF of the final model

GOF of the Measurement Model

One of the most commonly used methods for selecting and evaluating measurement models for conceptual modeling is the four-step process described by Fizan *et al.* (2018).

A measurement model is an entire model section that includes a variable with questions about that variable. As shown below, there are seven measurement models for the six research variables in the research model. As seen in the figure, the *model indicates measurement items: observables, connected via each variable (Fig 2.)*

Figure 2. Fitting the hypothesized model

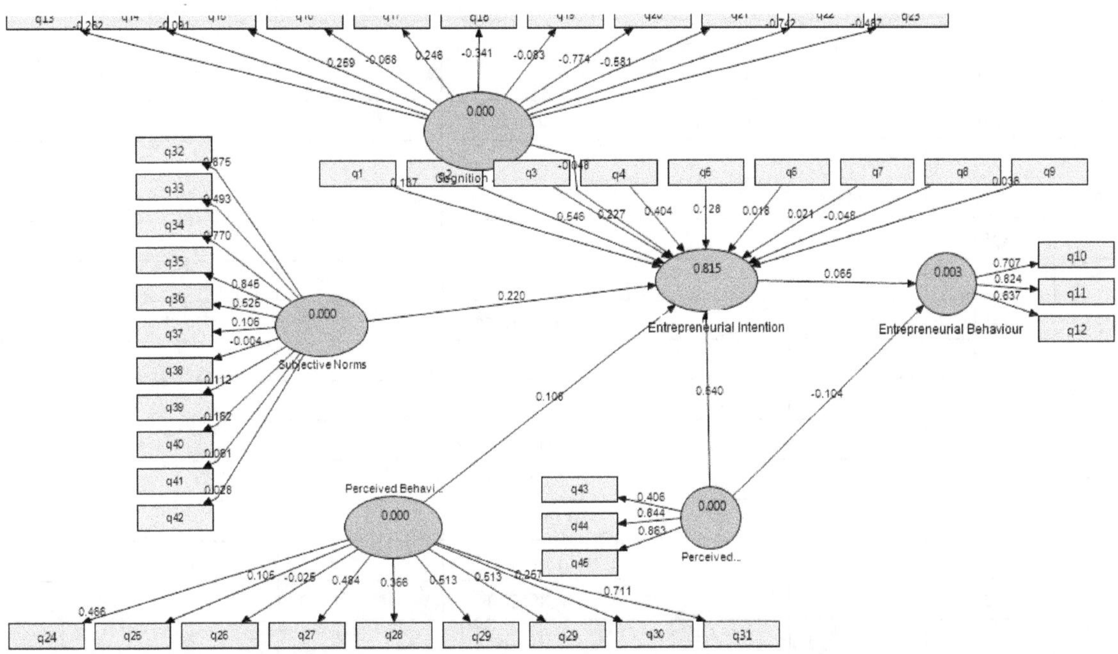

Therefore, to analyze the overall model, this research needs to examine five existing measurement models. Three reliability aspects, divergent validity, and convergent validity, are utilized to evaluate models' fitness.

Factor Loadings Coefficients

Factor loads are counted by counting the correlation value of a variable's questions via that construct. Suppose this value is equal to or more than 0.4. In that case, it indicates the variance among the variable, and their questions are more than the error variance of that construct. The reliability of the case for that measurement model is acceptable. This research examines each question's factor loadings coefficients connected with the six main variables in the research model.

The critical point here is that if the researcher has encountered values less than 0.4 after calculating the factor loadings (table 5) between the variable and its questions (Fig 3.), it should correct that question or remove it from the research model.

Table 5. Factor loadings coefficients

	Questions	EB	EI	CA	PBC	SN	PC
	Q1		0.381026				
	Q2		1.122050				
	Q3		0.587364				
	Q4		0.881602				
EI	Q5		0.546320				
	Q6		0.478621				
	Q7		0.329447				
	Q8		0.137446 **				
	Q9		-0.008894 **				
	Q10	-0.829329					
EB	Q11	-0.648766					
	Q12	-1.102862					
	Q13			-0.359651			
	Q14			-0.176712 **			
	Q15			0.264880 **			
	Q16			-0.120121 **			
	Q17			0.270686 **			
CA	Q18			-0.422360			
	Q19			-0.110666 **			
	Q20			-1.021725			
	Q21			-0.856740			
	Q22			-1.034183			
	Q23			-0.645906			
	Q24				0.648230		
	Q25				0.186294 **		
	Q26				0.046363 **		
	Q27				0.839263		
PBC	Q28				0.476327		
	Q29				0.617153		
	Q29				0.617153		
	Q30				0.298341		
	Q31				0.753486		

Continued on following page

Table 5. Continued

	Questions	EB	EI	CA	PBC	SN	PC
SN	Q32					0.87191	
	Q33					0.503461	
	Q34					0.759297	
	Q35					0.846790	
	Q36					0.539147	
	Q37					0.104416 **	
	Q38					-0.000651 **	
	Q39					0.108282 **	
	Q40					-0.160875 **	
	Q41					0.059940 **	
	Q42					0.032577 **	
PC	Q43						0.419121
	Q44						0.833235
	Q45						0.868145

Notice. The questions with (**) should be eliminated because they are ** <0.3.

After examining the factor loadings and eliminating the questions with factor loadings less than 0.3, this study re-fitting the model and examine the indices. As you can see, all factor loadings value is more than 0.3 for all the questions.

Figure 3. Fitting the adjusted model

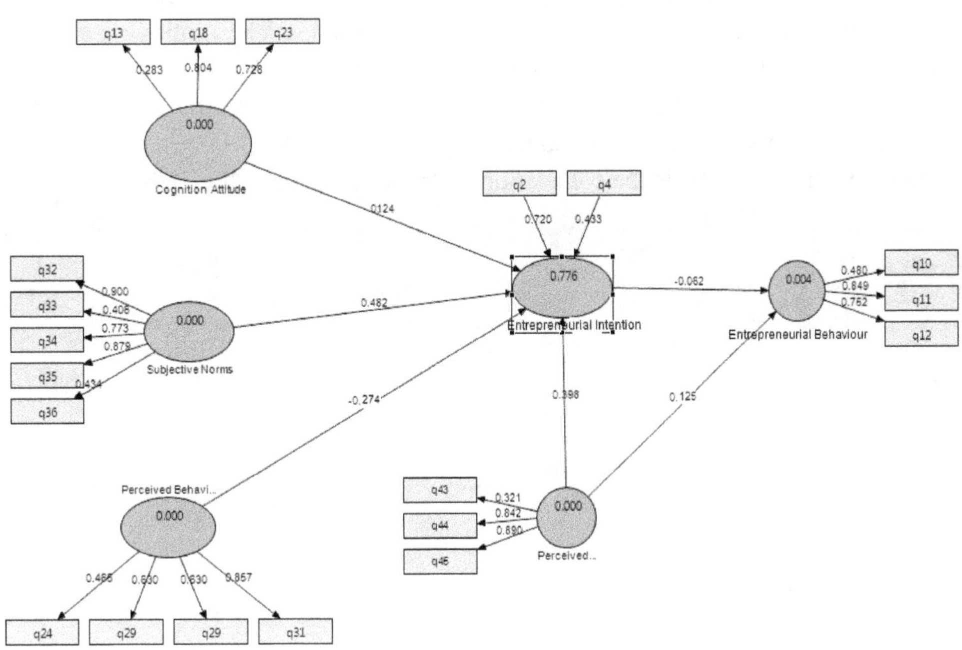

Composite Reliability and Cronbach's Alpha

As (table 6) indicates, the values corresponding to these criteria, Cronbach's alpha, and the reliability of the composite variables in all five variables were higher than 0.6, indicating good model reliability.

Table 6. Reliability of indicators

Variables	Cronbach's alpha	Composite Reliability
EB	0.720	0.745
EI	0.725	0.695
CA	0.745	0.712
PBC	0.813	0.754
SN	0.789	0.815
PC	0.719	0.775

Divergent Validity

Divergent validity is the third criterion for evaluating the suitability of measurement models covering two issues:

Comparison of one variable's correlation with its items versus its variable's correlation with other variables.

Investigation.

Another essential criterion identified by divergent validity is the level of relationship a variable has with its questions compared to that variable's relation with other variables. The admissible divergent validity indicates that a variable in the model interacts more via its questions than with other variables. Divergent validity is permissible when the AVE[2] level for every variable is higher than the variance shared between that variable and the other variables in the model.

The following matrix (table 7) is the correlation matrix of the research variables:

Table 7. Examination of correlation of sub-indexes with index

	Entrepreneurial Behavior	Entrepreneurial Intention	Cognition Attitude	Perceived Corruption	Perceived Behavioral	Subjective Norm
Entrepreneurial Behavior	0.703112					
Entrepreneurial Intention	-0.059624	1.000000				
Cognition Attitude	0.090374	0.184404	0.739877			
Perceived Corruption	-0.051272	0.870081	0.124341	0.73102		
Perceived Behavioral	0.138057	0.211011	0.464365	0.208387	0.739647	
Subjective Norm	-0.080333	0.873297	0.144835	0.970797	0.242408	0.723265

The Fornell-Larcker (1981) method of divergent validity proposes a matrix similar to the matrix above, except that the matrix's original diameter contains the R^2 value of AVE for each of the six variables.

As can be seen in the above table (7), the average variance's square-root value concluded that every variable is greater than the two variables' correlation value.

Divergent Validity by Fornell-Larcker (1981) Method

As shown in the above table (7), the values of the R^2 value of average variance extracted from the Latent variables in the current research located in the houses of the original diameter of the matrix were more significant than the correlation between those arranged in the lower and left leading diameter houses. Therefore, it can be stated that in the research, the variables (Latent Variables) in the model interact more with their indicators than with other variables. In other words, the divergent validity of the model is reasonable.

Table 8. Discriminant validity

	Entrepreneurial Behavior	Entrepreneurial Intention	Cognition Attitude	Perceived Behavioral	Subjective Norm
Entrepreneurial Behavior	0.705	0.00	0.00	0.00	0.00
Entrepreneurial Intention	0.601	0.753	0.00	0.00	0.00
Cognition Attitude	0.602	0.617	0.644	0.00	0.00
Perceived Behavioral	0.719	0.30	0.606	0.644	0.00
Subjective Norm	0.605	0.683	0.722	0.729	0.649

As shown in the table above (table 8), each variable's square root value is greater than the two variables' correlation value.

HTMT Analysis

The Heterotrait-Monotrait is an evaluation of similarity among latent variables. If the Heterotrait-Monotrait is smaller than one, discriminant validity can be regarded as established. In many practical situations, a threshold of [Heterotrait-Monotrait (HTMT) Value < 0.85] reliably distinguishes among those pairs of latent variables that are discriminant valid and those that are not. MCS[3] provides evidence for the Heterotrait-Monotrait's good classification performance.

In a well-cited work by Fornell-Larcker (1981) on SEM, it is stated to verify discriminant validity, the variance accounted for by the latent variable in its related indicator variables should be higher than the variance shared between those variables and other constructs in the same model. This requirement can be checked by comparing the AVE from each construct with its squared correlations with other constructs in the model. *"[t]his comparison harkens back to the tests of correlations in multi-trait multi-method matrices, and the logic is quite similar."*

The average variance extracted illustrates the average variance explained by a construct relative to its overall variance in its indicator variables. The average variance extracted for construct ξ_j is illustrated as:

$$\mathrm{AVE}\xi_j = \frac{\sum_{K=1}^{K_j} \lambda_{jk}^2}{\sum_{K=1}^{K_j} \lambda_{jk}^2 + \Theta_{jk}}, \tag{1}$$

Where λ_{jk} denotes the loading and Θ_{jk} denotes the error variance of the kth indicator $(k = 1,\ldots,K_j)$ of the construct ξ_j. K_j is the number of indicators for the construct ξ_j. If indexes are standardized (i.e., have a variance of 1 and a mean of 0), equation (1) can be simplified to

$$\mathrm{AVE}\xi_j = \frac{1}{K_j}\sum_{K=1}^{K_j} \lambda_{jk}^2, \tag{2}$$

AVE is therefore equivalent to the mean reliability value of the indicators. Defining r_{ij} the correlation coefficient between the construct scores of constructs ξ_i and ξ_j r_{ij}^2 (squared inter-construct correlation) will indicate the proportion of the variance shared between constructs ξ_i and ξ_j. On this basis, the Fornell-Larcker criterion (1981) stipulates that discriminant validity is established if the following inequality is true:

$$\mathrm{AVE}\xi_j \succ \max r_{ij}^2 \qquad \forall_i \neq j. \tag{3}$$

Considering the common use of inter-construct correlations in publications, it is common to use the following distinct notation for discriminant validity:

$$\sqrt{\text{AVE}\xi_j} \succ \max\left|r_{ij}\right| \qquad \forall_i \neq j. \tag{4}$$

From a conceptual perspective, using the Fornell-Larcker (1981) criterion has its own limitations. For instance, variance-based structural equation modelling algorithms are very likely to overestimate indicator loadings. This problem originates from how the method treats constructs. In variance-based structural equation modelling approaches, such as generalized structured components or PLS, composites of indicator variables are commonly used as replacements for the underlying constructs.

After the elimination of the impact of the actual construct, the residual error variance should be a pure random error based on the reflecting measurement model:

$$\varepsilon_{jk} = \mathrm{x}_{jk} - \lambda_{jk}\xi_j, \qquad \varepsilon_{jk} \perp \xi_j, \qquad \forall_i. \tag{5}$$

This suggests that the correlation between an index's error term and another construct is significant. Thus, it is impossible to assume that ε_{jk} it is a pure random error, and it is necessary to acknowledge that part of the measurement error is systematic. If this systematic error is due to another construct, one can conclude that the indicator does not indiscriminately measure its focal construct ξ_j and the other construct ξ_i, which means the discriminant validity hypothesis must be rejected. The working principle of the significance test of partial cross-loadings is shown in Figure 4-b (Henseler *et al.*, 2015).

Figure 4. Using the cross-loadings

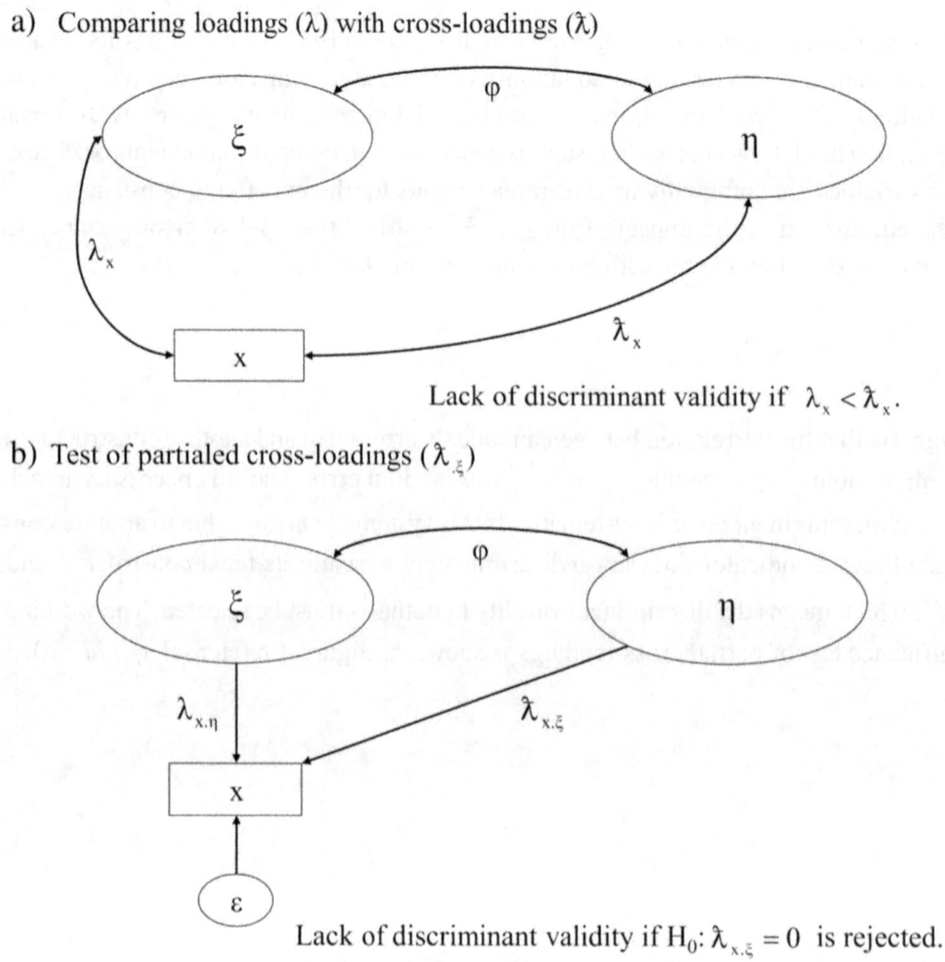

When it comes to determining discriminant validity, traditional algorithms have unacceptably low sensitivity, necessitating the development of a new criterion. In the next section of this chapter, this research will derive such a criterion from the multitrait-multimethod matrix, which allows for systematic discriminant validity assessment in order to establish (or reject) construct validity. Surprisingly, this approach has not been used much in variance-based structural equation modelling

The MTMM matrix[4] analysis provides evidence of discriminant validity if the HTMT[5] algorithm correlations are larger than the HTMT algorithm correlations. The correlations between indicators in the same construct are more robust than those between indicators evaluating distinct phenomena, implying that a construct is empirically unique and a phenomenon of relevance that other measures in the algorithm do not capture.

The purpose of examining the HTMT, which is the mean of HTMT algorithm correlations (i.e., correlations of indicators across constructs evaluating distinct phenomena) compared to the mean of monotrait-heater method correlations (i.e., the correlations of indicators within the same construct).

Hence, the approach involves building two HTMT submatrices and using the geometric mean of their average correlations. Thus, the HTMT of constructs ξ_i and ξ_j indicators, K_i and K_j can be written as:

$$\text{HTMT}_{ij} = \underbrace{\frac{1}{K_i K_j}\sum_{g=1}^{K_i}\sum_{h=1}^{K_j} r_{ig,jh}}_{\text{Average heterotrait-heteromethod}} \div \underbrace{\left(\frac{2}{K_i\left(K_i-1\right)}\cdot\sum_{g=1}^{K_{i-1}}\sum_{h=g+1}^{K_i} r_{ig,ih}\cdot\frac{2}{K_j\left(K_j-1\right)}\sum_{g=1}^{K_{j-1}}\sum_{h=g+1}^{K_j} r_{jg,jh}\right)^{\frac{1}{2}}}_{\substack{\text{Geometric mean of the average monotrait-heteromethod} \\ \text{correlation of construct } \xi_i \text{ and the average} \\ \text{HTMT correlation of construct } \xi_j}}. \quad (6)$$

In essence, the HTMT approach estimates the correlation among the constructs ξ_i and ξ_j parallels the dis-attenuated construct score correlation.

Significance Coefficients (t-values)

As shown in Figure (5), the T-values obtained for four of the six relationships considered for the variables based on research hypotheses are statistically significant (>1.96), which confirms the existence of these four relationships and indicates the appropriate fitness of the model.

Figure 5. GOF of the SEM according to t-values

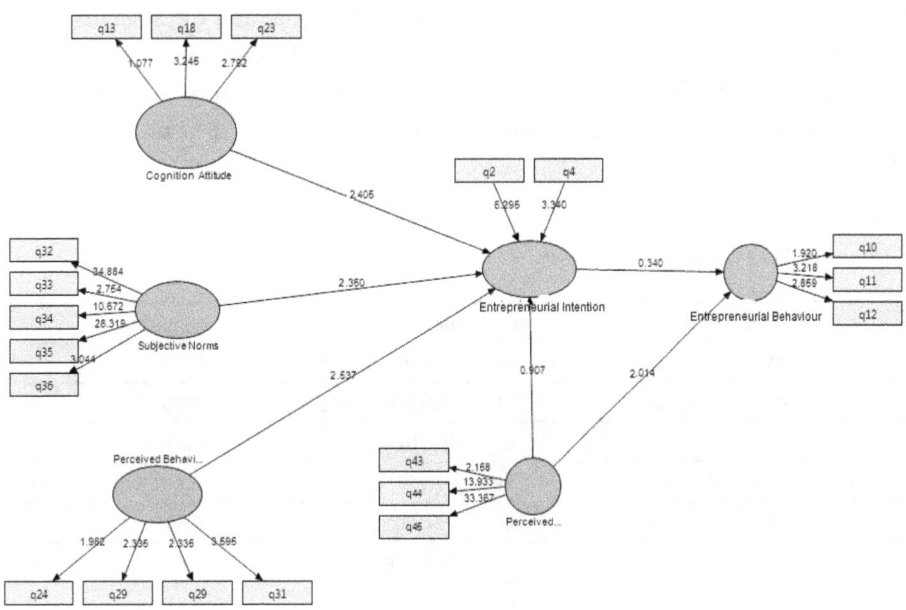

R Squared (R^2) Criterion

This criterion can be used to investigate the fitness of the structural model in relation to endogenous (dependent) variables. R-squared is a measure of the impact of an independent variable on the dependent variable. The thresholds commonly considered for differentiating weak, moderate, and robust relationships are 0.19, 0.33, and 0.67, respectively. Finally, the ideal R^2 value for exogenous or independent variables is zero (Table 9).

Table 9. Analysis of R^2 according to communality

Variables	R Square	Communality
Entrepreneurial Behavior	0.602058	0.494368
Entrepreneurial Intention	0.777782	0.529502
Average	0.68992	0.511935

As the above table shows, the R^2 values obtained for the dependent variables indicate a moderate or robust relationship, confirming the suitability of the structural equations.

GOF of the Final Model

The final model is a combination of both the measurement model and the structural model. Once the acceptable fitness of this model is established, the assessment of the model's GOF will be complete.

The GOF index concerns the general part of SEM, which means it must be used to check the fitness of the model as a whole once the appropriate fitness of the model's measurement part and structural part is established (Table 10).

Table 10. Fitness results for the final model

Index	Ideal value	Acceptable value	Result in the model	Result
GFI[6]	$.95 \leq GFI \leq 1.00$	$.80 \leq GFI < .95$	0.845	Acceptable
AGFI[7]	$.90 \leq AGFI \leq 1.00$	$.80 \leq AGFI < .95$	0.810	Acceptable
RMR[8]	$0 \leq RMR \leq .05$	$0 < RMR \leq .10$	0.035	Acceptable
CFI[9]	$.97 \leq CFI \leq 1.00$	$.90 \leq CFI < .97$	0.840	Acceptable
NFI[10]	$.90 \leq NFI \leq 1.00$	$.80 \leq NFI < .90$	0.823	Acceptable
RMSEA[11]	$0 \leq RMSEA \leq .05$	$.05 < RMSEA \leq .08$	0.039	Acceptable
PGFI[12]	$.60 \leq PGFI \leq 1.00$	$.50 \leq PGFI < .60$	0.811	Ideal
PNFI[13]	$.60 \leq PNFI \leq 1.00$	$.50 \leq PNFI < .60$	0.795	Ideal

$$GOF = \sqrt{0.512 \times 0.690} = 0.594 \quad (7)$$

GFI values of 0.01, 0.25, and 0.36 are thresholds for differentiating weak, moderate, and robust fitness. Thus, the GFI value obtained for the final model (0.594) indicates the goodness of fit of this model (Table 6).

According to (Ali *et al.* 2018; Hair *et al.* 2019), for several years, covariance-based SEM (CB-SEM) had been a leading approach to analyses of the complicated inter-relationships between the latent and observed variables. Therefore, before 2010, far more papers published in social science journals were using CB-SEM rather than PLS-SEM. However, several studies reported achieving considerably better with PLS-SEM than with CB-SEM. For GFI, as a comparative index, values of more than 0.7 indicate that the model properly fits the data. The GFI value obtained for the model of this study was 0.845, which signifies the good fitness of the model.

It is common to use the residual matrix to assess the general fit (the model as a whole) as well as the partial fit (inter-variable correlation). RMR of the model was determined to be 0.035, which is acceptable for a quantitative model.

For CFI, values between 0.9 and 0.97 can be regarded as acceptable. The CFI value obtained for the model was 0.840, which signifies good fitness.

Similar to RMR, RMSEA is a measure computed based on the residual matrix analysis. For a model to be considered acceptably fit, it must have an RMSEA of 0.035 or lower. RMSEA values of more than 0.1 indicate the poor fitness of the model. The RMSEA value obtained for the model of this study was 0.039, which suggests that the model has acceptable fitness.

Exploratory Factor Analysis (EFA)

To test this hypothesis, the Bartlett sphericity test is used. Its purpose is to reject the H_0 that the same matrix (i.e., a matrix whose diagonal elements are one and all non-diagonal elements are zero) is correct in society. In other words, Bartlett's test tests the assumption that the observed correlation matrix belongs to a society with uncorrelated variables. For the factor model to be valuable and meaningful, the variables need to be correlated. If the hypothesis that the variables are not related; Does not reject, the application of the factor model will be questioned and should be reconsidered. In the present study, the characteristic of the Bartlett sphericity test (80.48) is significant at a level lower than 0.01, which indicates that the data correlation matrix is not zero in the population, so the fact-finding operation can be justified.

It is observed that the lowest number of subscriptions is equal to 0.175 and belongs to question number 23, and the highest number of subscriptions, equal to 0.880, belongs to question number 33.

Figure 6. Scree Plot

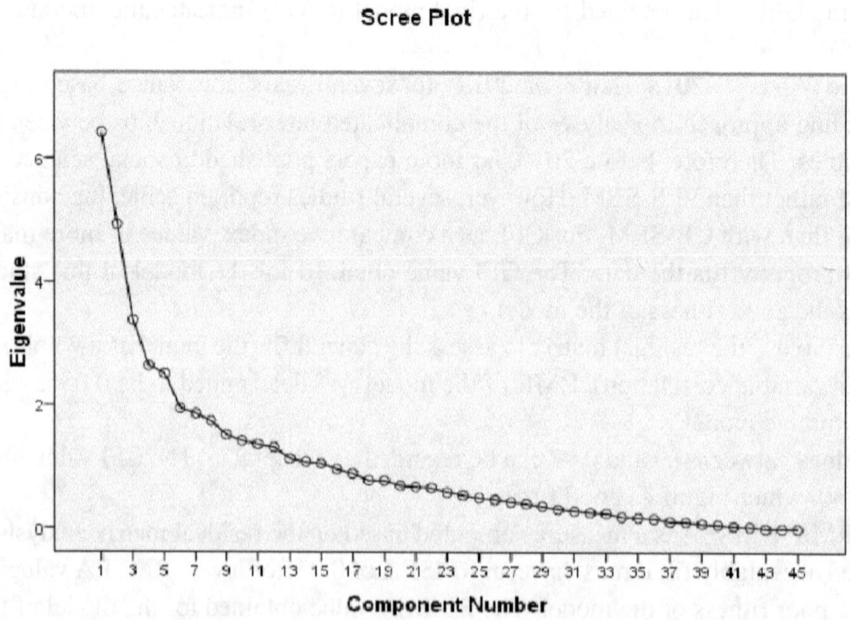

This test has been criticized in the past for being subjective. Scree plots might include several *"elbows,"* making it difficult to decide how many elements or components to keep, rendering the test inaccurate. Different statistical tools can create different plots from the same data because there is no standard for scaling the x and y axes.

The test has also been chastised for providing insufficient factors or components for factor retention. The (CNG scree test)[14] has been proposed as a more objective variant of the screen test [see fig 6].

The eigenvalue, the density percentage of the factors, and the percentage of variance described are presented in (table 11). In the next stage, the rate of explanation of the common variance between the variables for these six factors together is 48.5 percent of the total variance of the variables.

Table 11. The percentage of compression, percentage of variance explained, and eigenvalue of the six factors of the questionnaire

After Rotate			Before Rotate			Variable
Eigenvalue	**Variance Percentage**	**Compression Percentage**	**Eigenvalue**	**Variance Percentage**	**Compression Percentage**	
5.973	13.273	13.273	6.423	14.273	14.273	Perceived Corruption
4.352	9.671	22.945	4.930	10.956	25.229	Subjective Norm
3.575	7.943	30.888	3.374	7.499	32.727	Perceived Behavioral
2.846	6.324	37.212	2.635	5.856	38.583	Cognition Attitude
2.726	6.058	43.270	2.505	5.566	44.149	Entrepreneurial Behavior
2.343	5.207	48.477	1.947	4.327	48.477	Entrepreneurial Intention

Extraction Method: PCA[15]
Rotation Method: Varimax with Kaiser Normalisation.

– Questions 8, 9, 23, 24, 25, 26, 37, and 41 are not included in any index.
– Question 28 consists of two factors.
– Other questions are relatively good and normal, and there is no special complexity.
– The largest factor load in the structure matrix is related to question 46 and factor 0.916.
– Based on the factor structure matrix, a set of questions jointly related to a factored form a subscale.

Confirmatory Factor Analysis (CFA)

CFA proposes an SEM-based measurement paradigm. It has something to do with exploratory factor analysis (latent variables are defined factors, and item weights are factor loadings). However, it is free of some exploratory factor analysis for bias study constraints. Instead of using the correlation matrix, it uses the means and Cov()[16](Heydari *et al.*, 2021a,b). As a result, both non-uniform and uniform bias can be detected.

To be regarded as necessary, your variable should have a rotated factor loading (fig 7) of at least |0.4| (meaning +. 4 or –. 4) onto one of the factors. Some researchers utilize considerably stricter criteria, such as a |0.7| cut-off.

Figure 7. Path coefficient and factor load between research variables

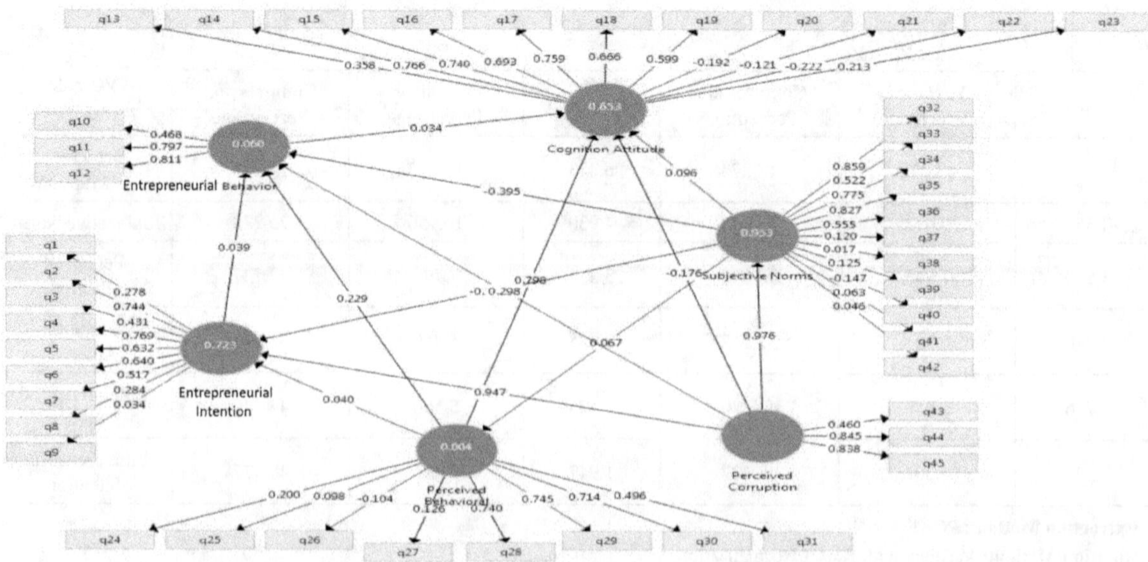

Our conceptual model analysis the factor load coefficients of each of the questions linked to each variable (see fig 8):

Figure 8. T-Value results among research variables

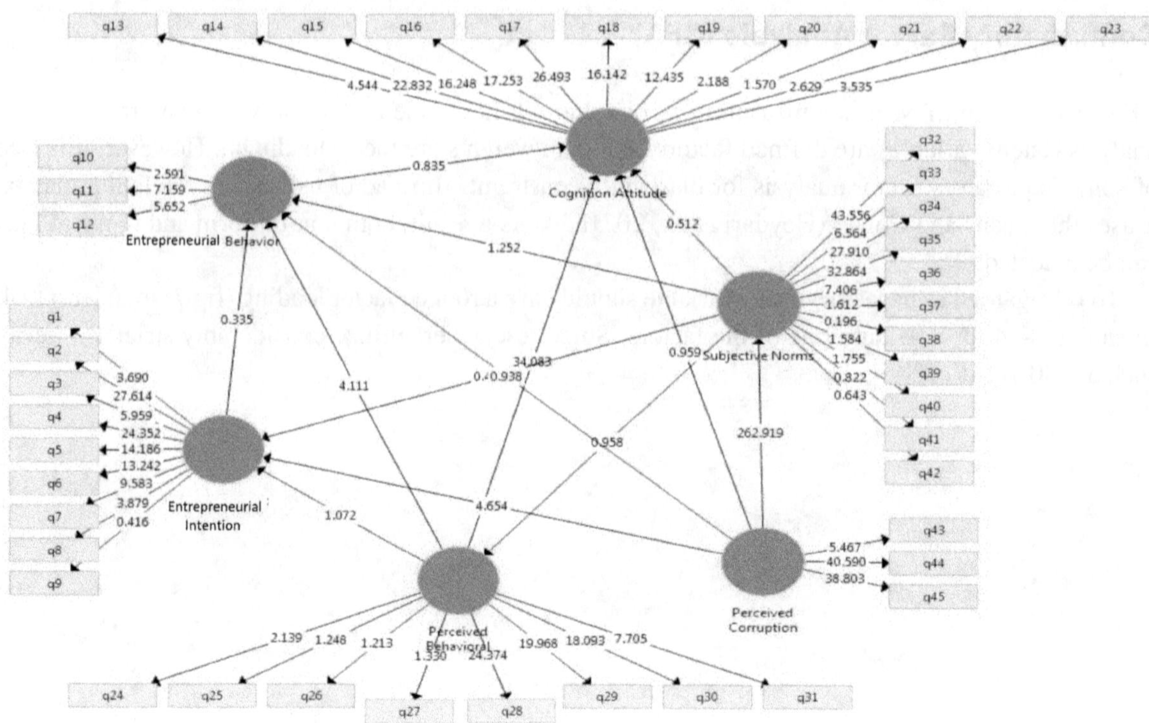

The appropriateness of the factor load coefficients criterion has a value of 0.4. All 45-factor loading coefficients of the questions in the preceding table are greater than 0.4, showing that this criterion is adequate.

If, after running the model, the analysis encounters questions with factor loads less than 0.4, now should delete that question so that the examination of other criteria is not affected. Here the operating loads of any of the questions are not less than 0.4.

As can be seen, the factor load of all variables in predicting the relevant items in the fitted FA model had a significant difference with zero at the confidence level of 0.95.

DISCUSSION AND CONCLUSION

Hypothesis Testing

The outcomes based on the hypotheses are presented in this section. The main hypothesis (H1) was tested, indicating that the hypothesized model's covariance matrix is identical to the empirical covariance matrix. According to Ajzen's TPB (1991), the hypothesized measurement model demonstrates how latent variables represented by circles interact with observables (indicators) represented by rectangles. The lines on the model represent a direct relationship between the variables that are hypothesized. The latent variable predicts the model's rectangle indicators in Figure (3).

Table 12. Hypothesis test

Hypothesis	Variable	Path Coefficient	T-VALUE	Sig.	Result
H1	Cognition Attitude ⟶ Entrepreneurial Intention	0.124	2.41	0.001	Accept
H2	Subjective Norm ⟶ Entrepreneurial Intention	0.482	2.35	0.001	Accept
H3	Perceived Behavioral Control ⟶ Entrepreneurial Intention	-0.274	2.53	0.001	Accept
H4	Corruption perception ⟶ Entrepreneurial Intention	0.398	0.907	0.427	Reject
H5	Corruption perception ⟶ Entrepreneurial Behavior	0.125	2.014	0.001	Accept

H1. The cognitive attitude toward behavior (CAB) is positively connected with entrepreneurial intention (EI)

According to the results of (table 12), Cognition Attitude directly affects Entrepreneurial Intent at a 95% confidence level (significance level is lower than 0.05, and T-Value is more than 1.96); its intensity is 0.124. As a result, the hypothesis is confirmed.

CAB has a negligible impact on EI (b = 0.124 & T-Value > 1.96). Personal perception to perform the behavior does not strongly affect students' EI. The outcomes of the present research concur with Davidsson

(1995) but not with Douglas and Shepherd (2002). According to Phan *et al.* (2002), cognitive attitude is a better predictor of self-employment and entrepreneurship inclination. Even though there is a poor link between cognitive attitude and entrepreneurial desire, Polish students have a high EI. Another research shows that the cognitive attitude has a low path coefficient, making it a poor predictor. The fundamental explanation for this is that students' attitudes reflect their inclination toward self-employment; therefore, they may want to try their luck and start self-employed in a challenging situation (Cohen *et al.*, 2010). As a result, hypothesis 1 is completely supported.

H2. The subjective norm (SN) is positively connected with entrepreneurial intention (EI)

According to the results of (table 12), Subjective Norm directly affects Entrepreneurial Intention at a 95% confidence level (significance level is lower than 0.05, & T-Value is more than 1.96); its intensity is 0.482. As a result, the hypothesis is confirmed.

Concerning the SNs, the outcomes of the present research indicate a strong and statistically significant connection with EI (b = 0.482 with T-Value > 1.96). Subjective Norm is the main factor that describes the students' EI. These results do not agree with the results from Turker and Selcuk (2009), based on which social assistance (Heydari *et al.*, 2016; 2020) has little effect on EI. These disparate results could be explained by the fact that social pressure is exerted by persons whom students consider significant in their life in Poland, perhaps more so than in many other nations. The results demonstrate that Polish students place a high weight on what their family members (i.e., their parents) think about starting a business. Students in Polish society may become entrepreneurs if they believe they will receive strong societal backing. This arises because students may experience *"fear of failure,"* which can be eased in part by the social group's support. As a result, hypothesis 2 is accepted.

H3. Perceived behavioral control (PBC) is positively connected to entrepreneurial intention (EI)

According to the results in (table 12), PBC has a reversed impact on EI at a 95% confidence level and has a reversed effect (significance level is less than 0.05, & T-Value is more than 1.96), and its intensity is -0.274. As a result, the hypothesis is confirmed.

It is found that perceived behavioral control has a positive reversed relationship with EI (b = -0.274 & T-Value > 1.96). Based on these findings, the pupils have a strong belief in their abilities to achieve a predetermined goal. Furthermore, Polish students have a positive sense of their own self-efficacy and believe that they can become entrepreneurs. Perceived behavioral control is linked to commitment measures such as behavioral expectations, according to other empirical data (Armitage & Conner, 2001; Gollwitzer & Sheeran, 2006; Dreher & Gassebner, 2013). Hypothesis 3 has been accepted.

H4. Corruption perception (PC) strongly negatively impacts students' intention to be entrepreneurs (EI)

According to the results in (table 12), Corruption Perception does not affect Entrepreneurial Intention at a 95% confidence level (significance level is more than 0.05, and T-Value is lower than 1.96); its intensity is 0.398. As a result, the hypothesis is rejected.

Concerning perceived corruption (PC), the outcomes of the present research show there is not a strong and statistically relevant relation with Entrepreneurial Intent (EI) (b = 0.398 & T-Value < 1.96). These results are in the reversed position of (Estrin *et al.* 2013; Melgar *et al.* 2010) that corruption can inhibit Entrepreneurial Intent. Also, the outcomes of the present research agree with the general idea that Polish students do not have any limitations in their work choices by *"external variables."* Hypothesis 4 is not supported.

H5. Corruption perception (PC) strongly negatively impacts students' entrepreneurial behavior (EB)

According to the results of (table 12), Corruption Perception directly affects Entrepreneurial Behavior at a 95% confidence level (significance level is lower than 0.05, & T-Value is more than 1.96), and its intensity is 0.125. As a result, the hypothesis is confirmed.

Finally, concerning PC, the outcomes of the present research indicate the existence of a robust and statistically significant relationship with EB (b = 0.125 with T-Value > 1.96). These outcomes reinforce the position of (Estrin *et al.* 2013; Melgar *et al.* 2010) that Corruption may act as a deterrent to EB. Indeed, the outcomes of the present research show that the PC significantly reduces entrepreneurial behavior, so it is possible to state that corruption significantly damages entrepreneurial activity (Dreher & Gassebner, 2013; Heydari & Lai, 2019; Heydari *et al.*, 2019, Heydari *et al.*, 2020 a-f, Heydari *et al.*, 2021 a,b). Also, it is possible to state that there is a lower intent to start as an entrepreneur with a higher level of corruption perception. This statement is compliant with the results of (Cohen *et al.* 2010; Azmat & Samaratunge 2009). As a result, hypothesis 5 is completely supported.

Hypothesis Regression Analysis

The coefficient of determination $\left(R^2\right)$ counted in the table shows the percentage of changes in the dependent variable, expressed by the assumed independent variable.

Table (13) shows regression analysis, and in this table, the value of F and P statistics confirms the significance of the regression model for all of the hypotheses $\left(P - value \prec 0.05\right)$.; also, the value $\left(R^2\right)$ for all of the variables can display changes in the BI variable (See table 13, and Figs 9-13).

Table 13. Regression analysis

R^2	F-Test / P-Value	Y-Intercept / P-Value	Slope / P-Value	Durbin-Watson (DW)	Variable	Hypothesis
0.223	20.88	2.22	0.315	1.91	Cognition Attitude → Entrepreneurial Intention	H1
	0.001	0.001	0.001			
0.195	3.58	2.66	0.160	1.98	Subjective Norm → Entrepreneurial Intention	H2
	0.049	0.001	0.001			
0.165	11.11	2.41	0.248	2.14	Perceived Behavioral Control → Entrepreneurial Intention	H3
	0.049	0.001	0.001			
0.381	3.41	1.41	0.137	2.54	Corruption Perception → Entrepreneurial Intention	H4
	0.042	0.024	0.001			
0.692	366.53	1.58	0.496	1.84	Corruption Perception → Entrepreneurial Behavior	H5
	0.001	0.001	0.001			

Figure 9. Regression analysis for the first hypothesis

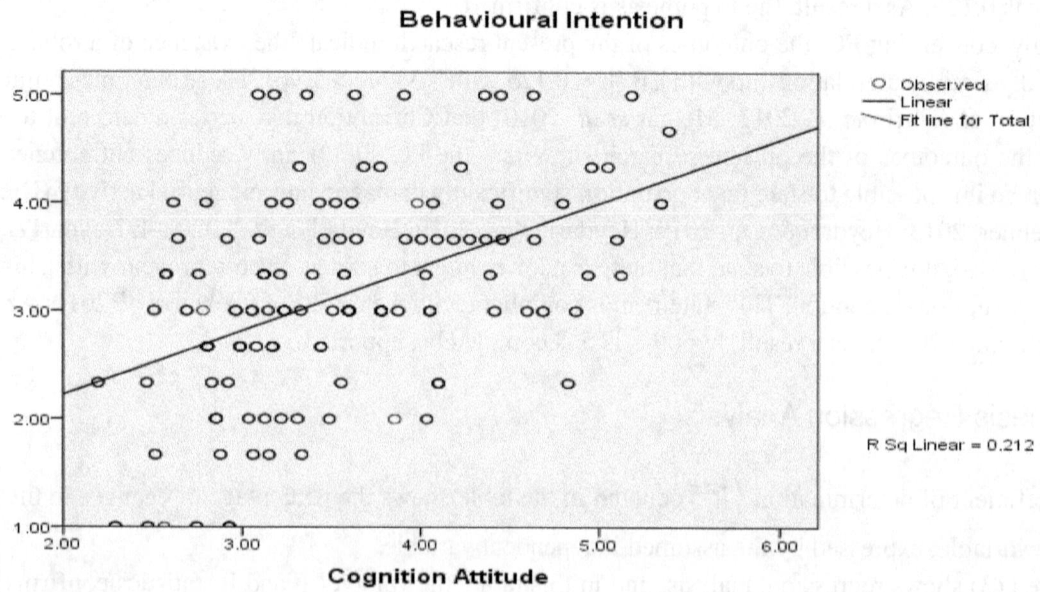

Figure 10. Regression analysis for the second hypothesis

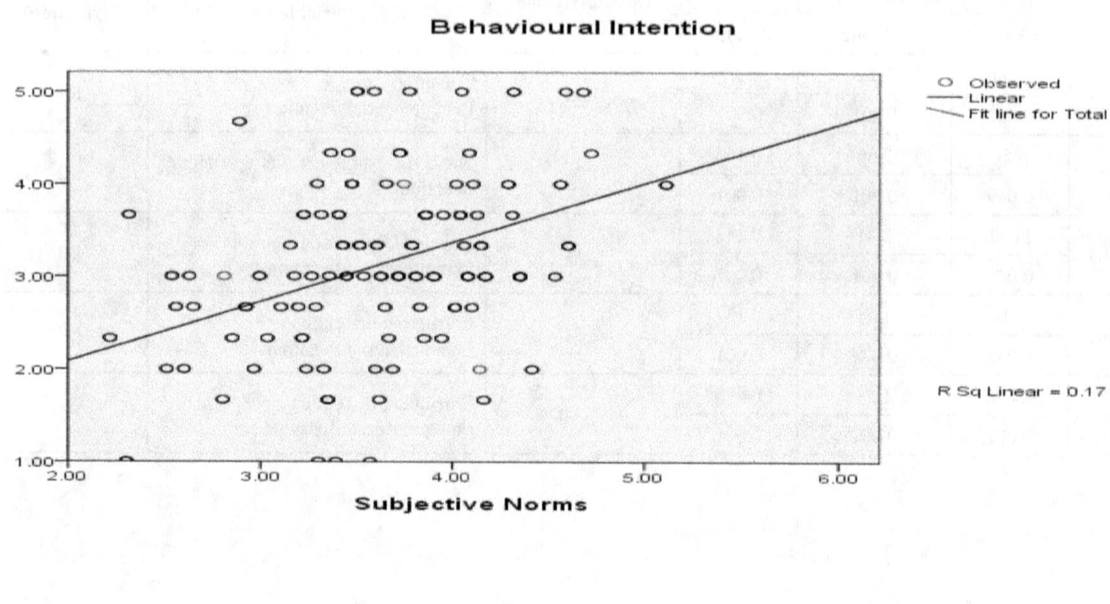

Figure 11. Regression analysis for the third hypothesis

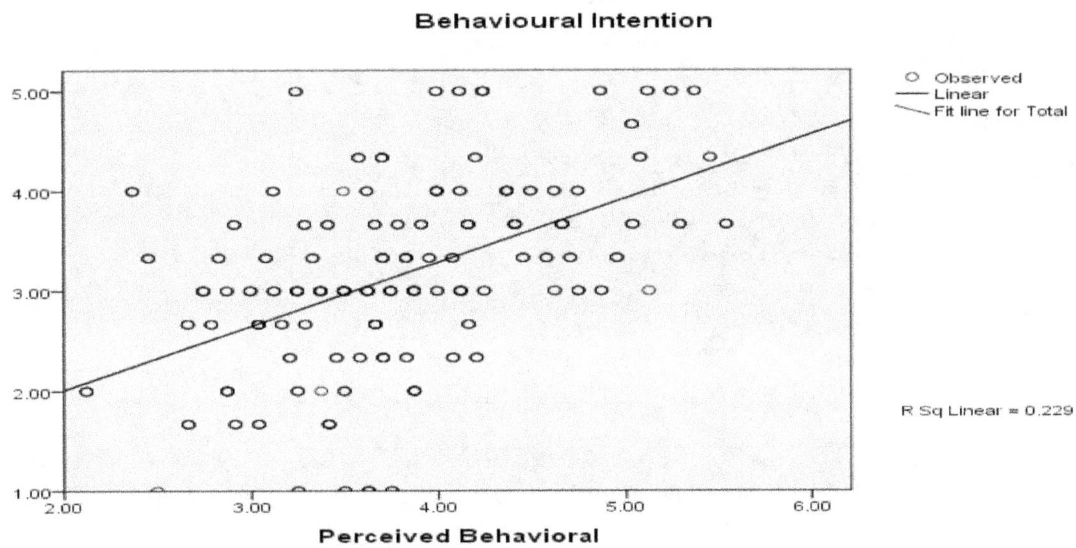

Figure 12. Regression analysis for the fourth hypothesis

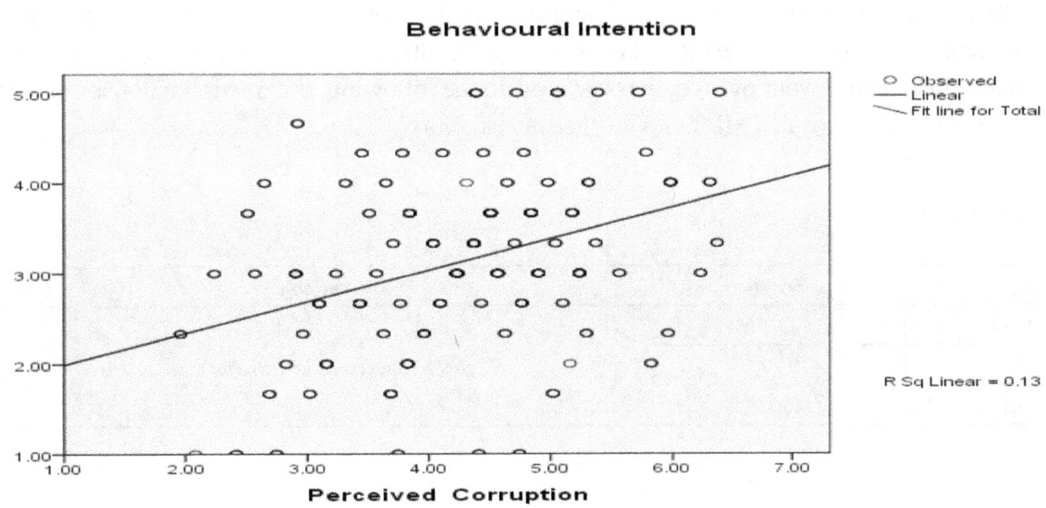

Figure 13. Regression analysis for the fifth hypothesis

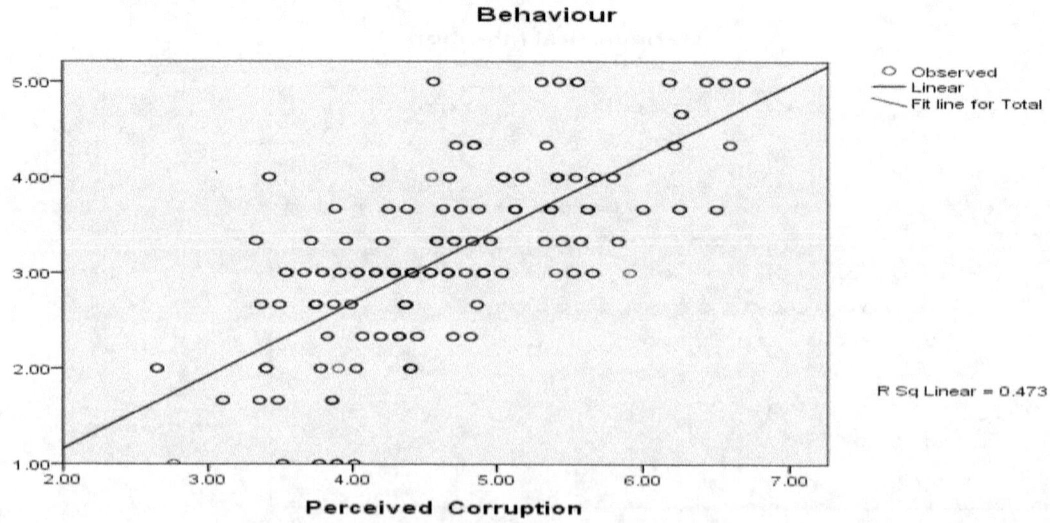

Hypothesis ANOVA Analysis

This test is designed to compare the mean of a variable in more than two independent groups.

As can be seen in the table (14), the significance level obtained for the variable is compared with the value of 0.05. Considering that this value is 0.001 for the variable and is less than the desired error coefficient (0.05), the *null* hypothesis that the importance is the same among the groups regarding this variable is rejected. Becomes. As a result, the mean is significantly different between age groups, ethics training groups, and creating your own business groups. In the following, this section will use Duncan's new multiple range test (Duncan's MRT) for further investigation.

Table 14. ANOVA Test

Sig.	F-Test	Variable
0.001	15.2	Entrepreneurial Behavior
0.001	10.74	
0.001	13.41	

Table 15. Duncan's MRT for comparison of respondents' age with entrepreneurial behavior

Sig.=0.05			Age
1	**2**	**3**	
3.180			Between 25 to 35
		3.837	Between 35 to 45
		3.912	Between 45 to 55
	3.41		More than 55
0.001	0.001	0.001	Sig

According to the table above (15), Duncan's MRT test has classified the age index into three groups. Entrepreneurial behavior rate is in 3 groups; the highest values are in the age group between 35 to 45 years and 45 to 55 years. As a result, age affects entrepreneurial behavior.

Table 16. Duncan's MRT for comparison of respondents' ethics training with entrepreneurial behavior

Sig.=0.05			Ethics Training
1	**2**	**3**	
2.95			1 to 2 years
	3.11		3 to 5 years
	3.24		6 to 10 years
		3.57	11 to 15 years
		3.85	More than 15 years
0.001	0.001	0.001	Sig

According to the table above (16), Duncan's MRT test has classified the age index into three groups. Entrepreneurial behavior rate is in 3 groups; the highest value is in the group of behavioral training duration between 11 to 15 years and more than 15 years. As a result, the duration of respondents' behavioral training is effective for entrepreneurial behavior.

Table 17. Duncan's MRT for comparison of respondents' creating your own business with entrepreneurial behavior

Sig.=0.05			Creating your Own Business
1	**2**	**3**	
2.91			I don't establish any business
3.08			Less than 3 months
	3.25		3 – 20 months
	3.38		20 – 42 months
		3.65	More than 42 months
0.001	0.001	0.001	Sig

According to the table above (17), Duncan's MRT test has classified the age index into three groups. Entrepreneurial behavior rate is in 3 groups; the highest value is in the group of behavioral training duration between 11 to 15 years and more than 15 years. As a result, respondents' time to start a new business affects entrepreneurial behavior.

DISCUSSION ON FINDINGS

Existing research tends to show that intention can successfully predict behavior. The psychological literature also tells us that intention explains behavior better than other factors, especially when the behavior is rare and hard to detect. The intention is a powerful predictor of actual behavior. Meta-analysis shows that intention can successfully predict behavior, and attitude can predict intention. Other researchers have argued that intent is the single best predictor of planning behavior (EB is typical of planning behavior) and that attitude influences behavior through intention. However, entrepreneurial intent is a complex variable, different from the simple psychological variables mentioned in psychology. The emergence of entrepreneurial intention to develop entrepreneurial behavior is a complicated process that is affected by a variety of elements. Entrepreneurial intention is only an essential factor in its expansion into the behavior, but EI does not necessarily lead to EB. This has some basis in psychology. According to the cognitive dissonance theory of the famous social psychologist Festinger, people's attitudes and behavior are consistent under normal circumstances (Heydari *et al.*, 2020a-f). Still, sometimes the attitude and behavior are inconsistent, resulting in cognitive dissonance. This is called the deviation theory of entrepreneurial intent and entrepreneurial behavior. The process from entrepreneurial intent to entrepreneurial behavior is a psychological and behavioral process during which there will be deviations.

Furthermore, this kind of maladjustment phenomenon is closely related to the internal and external factors in its development process. In the study of Polish students, based on the questionnaire answers, before considering the definitions and discussion (entrepreneurial intention), the research did not see you have any relationship with the perception of corruption; this may be based on the general due to the internal variables, the polish society students in choosing a job without any limitation. Nevertheless, once they start thinking about starting a business and doing some research and preparation, they find several external constraints that can discourage their intent to begin a new venture and make it fail. One of the fundamental factors is the perceived corruption of the would-be entrepreneur. This study demonstrates that Polish students' PC significantly decreases their entrepreneurial behavior, so it can be claimed that corruption significantly damages entrepreneurial activity in an area. It can also be said that the higher the perception of corruption, the lower the EB. This statement is consistent with Azmat & Samaratunge's (2010) and Cohen *et al.* (2010) findings.

Promoting the actual occurrence of entrepreneurship is a need for entrepreneurship theory research and the need for national strategy practice to encourage global entrepreneurship development. Although many potential entrepreneurs have prepared for entrepreneurship but have not engaged in entrepreneurial behavior, the deviation between entrepreneurial intention and entrepreneurial behavior indicates many internal and external variables in transforming entrepreneurial intention into entrepreneurial behavior. The need to analyze the pre-factors of entrepreneurial intention, the factors that affect entrepreneurial decision-making, the process links of entrepreneurial decision-making, and the non-decision-making factors (such as personality characteristics) that affect entrepreneurial behavior and analyze it from the perspective of entrepreneurship details of the inhibitory factors and variables in the process from intention generation to the triggering of entrepreneurial behavior.

Small-scale or micro-corruption occurs in small dimensions within the social frameworks and customs. For example, they were exchanging inappropriate gifts or using personal communication for profit *(Another example uses the word rather than the exchange of gifts (Favoritism)* favor*ing family, friends or specific groups, etc., which is the leader's purpose the* organization, *government, or military. The question often asks from those kinds of people is:* ***Why are you doing this? You realise that this is to the detriment of some and for the benefit of the person or persons you are targeting.*** *However, the answer is more interesting.* ***If I do not, who does?*** *In dictatorial or growing societies, such cases are often abundant). This type of corruption is particularly evident in developing countries where public servants live well below poverty (Baumol, 1996; Gámez Gutiérrez et al., 2017).* Big-scale or macro-corruption occurs at the highest levels of government and requires the overthrow of the legislative, political, and economic system. Corruption generally occurs in dictatorial governments and governments that lack the proper laws to prevent corruption. System of government in many countries, including branches, legislative, executive, and judicial independence, which operate independently and according to the rule, must keep them out of corruption. Systematic corruption (or endemic corruption) occurs primarily because of a weakness in an organization or process. It can be seen as opposed to corruption, where only a few employees or agents are involved in corruption.

RESEARCH CONTRIBUTIONS

According to the TBP model of Ajzen, this research takes the antecedent variables of entrepreneurial intention as the background, introduces the corruption variables according to entrepreneurial cognition, constructs a conceptual model according to the perception of corruption, and uses the mediating effect model to conduct an empirical study on the influence of the PC in the entrepreneurial cognition on entrepreneurial intention (Ajzen,1985).

Ajzen's TPB shows that entrepreneurial intent can be explained by three antecedent variables: the ATTs towards entrepreneurial behavior, the perception of SN, and the PBC, also known as self-efficacy. In examining these three antecedent variables, it is found a phenomenon that these variables in Azjen's TPB study did not consider (this phenomenon is called *unfair play:* To avoid wasting time and effort, High levels of PC can deter people from starting their own businesses. This occurrence raises an important issue: corruption can decrease entrepreneurial intent (EI), weakening a state or region's economy and limiting students' employment opportunities. Scholars and practitioners must thoroughly understand the restrictions depicted by entrepreneurial inhibitors to mitigate the negative influence on potential entrepreneurs' behavior and choices). To study these restraining factors more comprehensively, it is reviewed the research on antecedent variables of entrepreneurial intentions conducted by domestic and foreign scholars after Ajzen (Ajzen,1985).

These studies can be summarized. Depression and emotional burnout are important antecedent variables. Pollack *et al.* (2012) examined the mediating role of depression in the linkage between economic stress and entrepreneurial withdrawal. Sardeshmukh *et al.* (2012) found that emotional burnout mediated job stress and entrepreneurial withdrawal (intention). Secondly, the perception of entrepreneurial pressure is also a critical antecedent variable. Shepherd *et al.* (2013) found in their research that entrepreneurs' entrepreneurial cognition and attitude towards entrepreneurship are inevitably related to their entrepreneurial behaviors. Therefore, while entrepreneurs' cognition of entrepreneurial pressure affects their entrepreneurial behaviors, it also profoundly impacts their attitude towards entrepreneurship (Manstead *et al.*, 1983). Wu *et al.* (2021) believe that entrepreneurial pressure is a vital antecedent variable that encourages entrepreneurial exit intentions. The negative effect of entrepreneurial passion mediates the positive impact of entrepreneurial pressure on entrepreneurial exit intention, which means entrepreneurial pressure inhibits entrepreneurial passion.

In contrast, suppressed entrepreneurial passion strengthens entrepreneurial exit intention. Third, Zhao *et al.* (2020) take four types of venture capital as antecedent variables to study the impact of four types of venture capital on entrepreneurial intention. Among the four types of venture capital, psychological capital is far higher than economic, human, and social capital, and psychological capital has the most significant impact on EI. On the one hand, psychological capital directly affects college students' entrepreneurial intention. It affects the entrepreneurial willingness of college students through the intermediary effect of human capital, traditional economic capital, and social capital. All entrepreneurial capital is built on psychological capital. Fourth, Wu *et al.* (2021) believe that the entrepreneurial exit process is highly situation dependent. Entrepreneurs' cognition, emotion, and behavior towards entrepreneurship will undoubtedly be affected by the entrepreneurial situation (Baumol, 1996).

In addition, Wu *et al.* (2021) believe that the impacting factors of EI can be divided into the following four categories: the first is psychological traits, including the big five personality traits, such as ambiguity tolerance, desire for achievement, risk tolerance, perceived desirability, impromptu tendency, action tendency, internal control points, enthusiasm and openness to change. The second is demographic characteristics, including gender, age, and education. Psychological factors and demographic characteristics constitute individual characteristics. The third is the perceived desirability, including attitudes, cultural factors, and values. The fourth is the feasibility perception, including self-efficacy perception, behavior control perception, skill structure, entrepreneurial knowledge, skills, and experience. The perceived desirability and the feasibility perception constitute individual cognition. In addition, family tradition, entrepreneurial education, role model, social norm perception, social capital, and social network also influence individual cognition and thus affect entrepreneurial intention (Manstead *et al.*, 1983).

However, the previous scholars mentioned above did not specifically mention corruption in analyzing antecedent variables affecting entrepreneurial behavior. Therefore, this study attempts to introduce the perception of corruption as an antecedent variable to empirically study the influence of corruption in entrepreneurial cognitive theory on EI and entrepreneurial behavior. The primary considerations for making this decision are: First, corruption (external factors) and personal characteristic risk aversion affect the entrepreneurial intention. Costa & Mainardes (2016) found that risk aversion reduced the probability of individuals' entrepreneurial intent by 6.67%. For every one-unit SD. Enhance the corruption perception level, the likelihood of individuals' EI decreases by 0.96%. Secondly, the perception of corruption has a mediating effect on attitudes, social norms, and behavioral control. Finally, scholars proposed that the increased level of corruption would significantly inhibit entrepreneurial activities, and there was a dual-threshold effect on financial development. In China's low-level financial development regions, the negative impact of corruption on entrepreneurship is very significant. Still, with the improvement of financial development, this negative effect is significantly reduced or even not noticeable. Lai Min *et al.* (2016) believes that the higher the government's supervision of corruption, the more conducive to stabilizing enterprise expectations and stimulating enterprise innovation and entrepreneurship. Institutional environments, such as corruption management, have a more significant impact on innovation in high-income countries. Huang *et al.* (2022) believe that anticorruption can significantly promote regional entrepreneurial activities and increase start-ups. The reason lies in that anticorruption can promote entrepreneurship through three influential channels: considerably improving local governments' administrative efficiency, the degree of marketization, and market confidence. Based on the above, this paper takes the antecedent variable corruption as the background factor, constructs a conceptual model around the perception of corruption, and uses the mediating effect model to empirically research the influence of corruption in entrepreneurial cognition on entrepreneurial intent. Therefore, introducing corruption and its empirical research is essential to this paper.

On the one hand, this paper analyzes the interaction between motivation, will, emotion, cognition, and other factors and a specific situation (business situation) based on cognitive psychology. On the other hand, it further studies how the interaction between the two leads to corrupt behavior. In conclusion, this paper has not only theoretical guiding value for public and private sectors to formulate anti-corruption strategies but also has great significance for university educators, business decision-makers, governments, and scholars to cultivate, develop and encourage students' entrepreneurial intention and spirit, and encourage them to start businesses in the future.

From the aspect of research direction, this study has made many essential contributions to corruption, especially between entrepreneurs. First, being different from previous studies that focus on bribery, this research finds the determinants of corruption from entrepreneurs' perspective as bribery recipients. Only an investigation of both parties engaged in corrupt arrangements can better understand corruption and thus enable us to combat it effectively. Secondly, compared with previous studies, this is a more detailed examination of the institutional factors of corruption. In general, institutional investigations into corruption are rare. Few recent institutional studies on corruption have investigated the restrictive effects of formal institutions (e.g., barriers to market access, trade barriers, and industrial policies for new and multinational corporations) on corruption (e.g., Koppl, & Minniti, 2003; Stevenson, & Jarillo, 2007; Douglas, 2017). Other studies have concentrated on transaction cost considerations associated with the arrangement and execution of corrupt transactions (McGrath, & MacMillan, 2000; Lee *et al.*, 2004; Akinola & Mendes, 2008). However, this study is unique. It examines the connection between corruption and the efficiency of formal institutions in each country and the relationship between informal institutions and trust, which are considered an integral part of entrepreneurial decision-making. Doing so made it clear that entrepreneurs must be analyzed as rooted in the social context (Akinola, & Mendes, 2008), guided and promoted through their position in the social network with family, friends, and state bureaucrats.

If an entrepreneur has a high degree of special trust in state officials to keep their promises, he will likely engage in corruption. Thus, reducing Gerring corruption requires policy measures that may destabilize corrupt agreements, for example, by fostering the opportunism of corrupt contracts in the context of public bureaucrats or entrepreneurs. For instance, Lambsdorff and Nell proposed a legal method to destabilize corrupt transactions based on the asymmetric design of imposing legal sanctions (Lambsdorff, & Nell, 2006). It indicates that regular rotation of public administration staff might be another measure to prevent corruption since it would undermine the special trust established among bureaucrats and people in business. Although change is more costly than influence, creating a more favorable social environment is also necessary. The possibility that entrepreneurs in transition countries engage in corruption is associated with culturally limited and deep-rooted SN who justify *"if other people's illegal practices can, so can I"* (Widmalm, 2008).

The likelihood of engaging in other types of violations, such as failure to pay tariffs, disregard for trade laws, and protracted participation in the unofficial (shadow) economy, is also closely related to the likelihood of engaging in corrupt transactions. There is also a connection between corruption and social networks established through family and friends. Although theoretically, the connection between corruption and institutions is still underdeveloped, it seems to positively link with institutions close to the outside world (Siggelkow,2001; Sarasvathy, 2001; Simon, 2013). Such systems reduce transaction costs associated with discovering contract partners and initiating and executing corrupt transactions. As a result, they also provide a breeding ground for corruption. It is worth noting that *"path dependence"* (Brazeal, 1993) may help to describe the current level of corruption in a country (Xiaohu *et al.*, 2020). If a country has a high initial level of corruption, it may be *"locked"* into this equilibrium and have difficulty getting into another country with a lower level of corruption. Given the prevalence of informal institutions that support corruption, the challenge for policymakers is to find mechanisms to coordinate the transition from one country to another (Köbis, 2018). In the long run, entrenched societies can be changed through education and training, the building and promoting of civil society, and reliable mass media. Government officials and businessmen must be convinced of corruption's social and economic costs through sustained public campaigns. Ultimately, improving effective anticorruption reform requires attention to the formal and informal institutions in each country that provide the environment in which businesses and entrepreneurs can flourish.

Furthermore, while many studies describe how people decide to start as entrepreneurs, there is a paucity of literature on the factors that discourage them, including corruption. Even while perceptions of corruption differ greatly from actual levels of corruption, the latter can influence the former. Therefore, strong perceptions of corruption are enough to undermine the economy (the growth of institutional instability and the deterioration of relationships between individuals, institutions, and states). Additionally, the definition of corruption depends on social and cultural factors, as do perceptions of corruption.

From the perspective of research objects and research subjects, and through careful comparison of previous international literature and theoretical reviews, the contribution of this study was consistent with Davidsson's (1995) but different from Douglas & Shepherd (2002). Attitude (ATT) was found to be a stronger predictor of interest in self-employment and entrepreneurship by Phan *et al.* (2002). Although the correlation between attitude and entrepreneurial intention (EI) is weak, Polish students still have a robust entrepreneurial intention. Other studies have shown that a low path coefficient of attitude is regarded as a poor predictor. The primary cause for this is that students' preferences for self-employment are incorporated into their attitudes, so they may be more willing to try their luck and become self-employed (Manstead *et al.*, 1983).

Subjective norm is the main factor reflecting students' EI. These results are inconsistent with the conclusion of Turker & Selcuk (2009), who argue that social support has little effect on EI and EB. One possible description for these different results is that the Polish students perceived essential people in their lives to exert much social pressure, perhaps more so than people in many other countries. The results suggest that Polish students attach great importance to the views of those close to them (i.e., their family members) about engaging in entrepreneurial activity. If Polish students feel socially solid support, they can become entrepreneurs. This is because students develop a *"fear of failure,"* which can be mitigated to some extent by support from social groups. Based on the outcomes of the present research, students have a good perception ability to achieve the preset goal. More specifically, the Polish students had a good perception of their self-efficacy. In their view, they can become entrepreneurs. Other empirical evidence (Marshall, 1890; McCLELLAND, 1969; Kirzner, 1982; Hayek, 2012; Moriano *et al.*, 2012) showed that perceptual, behavioral control is closely related to commitment measures such as behavioral expectations, such as behavioral expectations.

Finally, the results also reveal two messages: on the one hand, this study shows there is no solid statistical correlation between perceived corruption (PC) and entrepreneurial intention. These results contradict the views of (Estrin *et al.* 2013; Melgar *et al.* 2010), which suggest that corruption may inhibit entrepreneurial intent. Moreover, the contribution of this study is consistent with the general idea that Polish students are not restricted by *"external variables"* in their choice of work. On the other hand, the results show a strong statistical correlation between perceived corruption (CORR) and entrepreneurial behavior. These outcomes reinforce the position of (Estrin *et al.* 2013; Melgar *et al.* 2010) that corruption may inhibit entrepreneurial behavior. The results show that perceptions of corruption significantly reduce entrepreneurial behavior, so it can be argued that corruption severely undermines entrepreneurial activity in a region (Manstead *et al.*, 1983). In addition, it can also be said that the higher the perception of corruption, the lower the willingness to start as an entrepreneur. This view is consistent with Azmat & Samaratunge (2009) findings and Cohen *et al.* (2010). However, most existing literature assumes that entrepreneurial intent necessarily leads to entrepreneurial behavior. If a factor (here, the research considers perceptions of corruption) strongly correlates with entrepreneurial behavior, then that factor is also associated with entrepreneurial intentions. However, the opposite is found, which raises the question: Why do perceptions of corruption have a robust negative effect on entrepreneurial behavior but not the entrepreneurial intention? To explain the reasons behind this unique phenomenon it must start with a theoretical discussion of entrepreneurial intent, entrepreneurial behavior, and perceptions of corruption and try to find a reasonable explanation.

LIMITATIONS

Over 2,000 empirical research have utilized the theory of planned behavior in attempts to predict and/or change behavior in a variety of domains. Investigators have encountered various issues in applying the theory, sometimes turning to me for assistance. In this section, the effort is to provide a brief analysis of the limitations and boundaries of TPB.

Criticism

There has been plenty of criticism leveled at the theory of planned behavior. The trade-off between parSimony and validity has been called into question; is a theory of all volitional behavior based on only four explanatory concepts sufficiently elaborated? For example, the theory has been criticized for focusing solely on rational reasoning and ignoring unconscious influences on behavior and the role of emotions beyond expected effective outcomes. Furthermore, the TPB's static explanatory nature makes it difficult to comprehend the evidenced effects of behavior on cognitions and future behavior.

Validity

The main issue with the theory of planned behavior is not that it does not explain enough variation in behavior. The main problem is that some of the theory's assertions are demonstrably false. The mediation assumptions in the theory of planned behavior contradict the evidence. For example, beliefs, rather than intentions, frequently predict behavior. The bold sufficiency hypothesis, which assumes that all theory-external influences on behavior are mediated through the theory of planned behavior, is empirically and conceptually indefensible and has been proven false. When the theory of planned behavior predictors is controlled for, there is consistent evidence that age, socioeconomic status, physical health, mental health, and environment features predict objectively evaluated physical activity.

Utility

The theory of planned behavior may be a useful falsehood, so the question is whether it is useful. In the 1970s, the TRA proved extremely useful in demonstrating that behavior was not simply a reflection of attitudes, as previous theories had suggested. It proposed new explanatory measures (intention and SN) and new research designs and contributed to the advancement of knowledge. Three decades later, the concept of planned behavior has outlived its usefulness. It does not help practitioners improve beneficial interventions. It does not lend itself well to laboratory tests. It does not provide explanatory hypotheses that are significantly different from other prevalent theories, limiting the ability to conduct comparative experimental tests of two plausible competing hypotheses against each other.

Hypothetical Bias

In general, intentions are skewed toward what is socially desirable. Because the beliefs readily accessible in memory when intentions are evaluated differ significantly from those readily accessible in the behavioral context, this hypothetical bias grows. People's behavioral, normative, and control beliefs about a socially desirable behavior are more favorable when the behavior is considered in the abstract rather than when confronted with engaging in the behavior.

There is No Standard Survey

There is no such thing as a standard theory of planned behavior questionnaire. To be sure, traditional methods and procedures for developing reliable and valid measures of the theory of planned behavior constructs have been developed. To summarize, first, a study is conducted to elicit behavioral, normative, and control beliefs from the research population. The most frequently expressed beliefs are chosen. Second, the study is used to create items with good psychometric properties to assess AB, SN, PBC, and intention, as well as to identify indicators of actual behavioral control where possible. Third, the main study will administer a questionnaire containing the formative research items. Although other scale types are possible, seven-point bipolar adjective scales are commonly used. Finally, interest behavior is observed.

DECLARATION

The authors declare that the manuscript follows ethical standards and there are no potential conflicts of interest with respect to the research, authorship and/or publication of this chapter.

DISCLAIMER

The contents and views of this chapter are expressed by the authors in their personal capacities. It is not necessary for the Editor and the Publisher to agree with these viewpoints, and they are not responsible for any duty of care in this regard.

This Chapter is extracted from the unpublished doctoral dissertation titled "A cognitive basis perceived corruption and attitudes towards entrepreneurial intention" by Mohammad Heydari. The thesis was submitted to the School of Economics and Management, Nanjing University of Science and Technology, Nanjing, Jiangsu, China in 2020 to fulfill doctoral degree requirements

ACKNOWLEDGMENT

The authors extend sincere gratitude to:

- The Editor and International Editorial Advisory Board (IEAB) of this book who initially desk reviewed, arranged a rigorous double/triple blind review process, and conducted a thorough, minute and critical final review before accepting the chapter for publication.
- All anonymous reviewers who provided very constructive feedbacks for thorough revision, improvement, extension and fine-tuning of the chapter.
- All colleagues, assistants and well-wishers who assisted to complete this task.

REFERENCES

Ajzen, I. (1985). From Intentions to Actions: A Theory of Planned Behavior. In Action Control. SSSP Springer Series in Social Psychology. Berlin: Springer. doi:10.1007/978-3-642-69746-3_2

Ajzen, I. (1991). The theory of planned behavior. *Organizational Behavior and Human Decision Processes, 50*(2), 179–211. doi:10.1016/0749-5978(91)90020-T

Akinola, M., & Mendes, W. B. (2008). The dark side of creativity: Biological vulnerability and negative emotions lead to greater artistic creativity. *Personality and Social Psychology Bulletin, 34*(12), 1677–1686. doi:10.1177/0146167208323933 PMID:18832338

Ali, F., Rasoolimanesh, S. M., Sarstedt, M., Ringle, C. M., & Ryu, K. (2018). An assessment of the use of partial least squares structural equation modeling (PLS-SEM) in hospitality research. *International Journal of Contemporary Hospitality Management, 30*(1), 514–538. doi:10.1108/IJCHM-10-2016-0568

Anderson, J. C., & Gerbing, D. W. (1988). Structural equation modeling in practice: A review and recommended two-step approach. *Psychological Bulletin, 103*(3), 411–423. doi:10.1037/0033-2909.103.3.411

Armitage, C. J., & Conner, M. (2001). Efficacy of the theory of planned behavior: A meta-analytic review. *British Journal of Social Psychology, 40*(4), 471–499. doi:10.1348/014466601164939 PMID:11795063

Autio, E., & Acs, Z. (2010). Intellectual property protection and the formation of entrepreneurial growth aspirations. *Strategic Entrepreneurship Journal, 4*(3), 234–251. doi:10.1002ej.93

Azmat, F., & Samaratunge, R. (2009). Responsible entrepreneurship in developing countries: Understanding the realities and complexities. *Journal of Business Ethics*, *90*(3), 437–452. doi:10.100710551-009-0054-8

Baumol, W. J. (1996). Entrepreneurship: Productive, unproductive, and destructive. *Journal of Business Venturing*, *11*(1), 3–22. doi:10.1016/0883-9026(94)00014-X

Boehm, F., & Lambsdorff, J. G. (2009). Corrupción y anticorrupción: Una perspectiva neo-institucional. *Revista de Economia Institucional*, *11*(21), 45–72.

Bolivar, V. J., & Baressi, J. (1995). Giving meaning to movement: A developmental study. *Ecological Psychology*, *7*(2), 71–97. doi:10.120715326969eco0702_1

Brazeal, D. V. (1993). Organizing for internally developed corporate ventures. *Journal of Business Venturing*, *8*(1), 75–90. doi:10.1016/0883-9026(93)90012-T

Cohen, J., Krishnamoorthy, G., & Wright, A. (2010). Corporate governance in the post-Sarbanes-Oxley era: Auditors' experiences. *Contemporary Accounting Research*, *27*(3), 751–786. doi:10.1111/j.1911-3846.2010.01026.x

Collier, M. W. (2002). Explaining corruption: An institutional choice approach. *Crime, Law, and Social Change*, *38*(1), 1–32. doi:10.1023/A:1019802614530

Costa, L. D. A., & Mainardes, E. W. (2016). The role of corruption and risk aversion in entrepreneurial intentions. *Applied Economics Letters*, *23*(4), 290–293. doi:10.1080/13504851.2015.1071462

Creswell, J. W., & Creswell, J. D. (2017). *Research design: Qualitative, quantitative, and mixed methods approaches*. Sage.

Davidsson, P. (1995). Culture, structure and regional levels of entrepreneurship. *Entrepreneurship and Regional Development*, *7*(1), 41–62. doi:10.1080/08985629500000003

Davis, M. A. (2009). Understanding the relationship between mood and creativity: A meta-analysis. *Organizational Behavior and Human Decision Processes*, *108*(1), 25–38. doi:10.1016/j.obhdp.2008.04.001

Douglas, E. (2017). Perceptions: Looking at the world through entrepreneurial lenses. In *Revisiting the Entrepreneurial Mind* (pp. 41–59). Springer. doi:10.1007/978-3-319-45544-0_4

Douglas, E. J., & Shepherd, D. A. (2002). Self-employment as a career choice: Attitudes, entrepreneurial intentions, and utility maximization. *Entrepreneurship Theory and Practice*, *26*(3), 81–90. doi:10.1177/104225870202600305

Dreher, A., & Gassebner, M. (2013). Greasing the wheels? The impact of regulations and corruption on firm entry. *Public Choice*, *155*(3), 413–432. doi:10.100711127-011-9871-2

Estrin, S., Korosteleva, J., & Mickiewicz, T. (2013). Which institutions encourage entrepreneurial growth aspirations? *Journal of Business Venturing*, *28*(4), 564–580. doi:10.1016/j.jbusvent.2012.05.001

Everett, J., Neu, D., & Rahaman, A. S. (2007). Accounting and the global fight against corruption. *Accounting, Organizations and Society*, *32*(6), 513–542. doi:10.1016/j.aos.2006.07.002

Foo, M. D. (2011). Emotions and entrepreneurial opportunity evaluation. *Entrepreneurship Theory and Practice*, *35*(2), 375–393. doi:10.1111/j.1540-6520.2009.00357.x

Fornell, C., & Larcker, D. F. (1981). Evaluating structural equation models with unobservable variables and measurement error. *JMR, Journal of Marketing Research*, *18*(1), 39–50. doi:10.1177/002224378101800104

Gaglio, C. M., & Katz, J. A. (2001). The psychological basis of opportunity identification: Entrepreneurial alertness. *Small Business Economics*, *16*(2), 95–111. doi:10.1023/A:1011132102464

Gámez Gutiérrez, J., Saiz-Álvarez, J. M., & Gil Ángel, G. (2017). A cognitive, emotional and behavioral assessment of Colombian entrepreneurs attitudes toward corruption. *Revista Universidad y Empresa*, *19*(33), 9–51. doi:10.12804/revistas.urosario.edu.co/empresa/a.4682

Gielnik, M. M., Frese, M., Graf, J. M., & Kampschulte, A. (2012). Creativity in the opportunity identification process and the moderating effect of diversity of information. *Journal of Business Venturing*, *27*(5), 559–576. doi:10.1016/j.jbusvent.2011.10.003

Gollwitzer, P. M., & Brandstätter, V. (1997). Implementation intentions and effective goal pursuit. *Journal of Personality and Social Psychology*, *73*(1), 186–199. doi:10.1037/0022-3514.73.1.186

Gollwitzer, P. M., & Sheeran, P. (2006). Implementation intentions and goal achievement: A meta-analysis of effects and processes. *Advances in Experimental Social Psychology*, *38*, 69–119. doi:10.1016/S0065-2601(06)38002-1

Gorsira, M., Denkers, A., & Huisman, W. (2018). Both sides of the coin: Motives for corruption among public officials and business employees. *Journal of Business Ethics*, *151*(1), 179–194. doi:10.100710551-016-3219-2

Grichnik, D., Smeja, A., & Welpe, I. (2010). The importance of being emotional: How do emotions affect entrepreneurial opportunity evaluation and exploitation? *Journal of Economic Behavior & Organization*, *76*(1), 15–29. doi:10.1016/j.jebo.2010.02.010

Hair, J. F., Risher, J. J., Sarstedt, M., & Ringle, C. M. (2019). When to use and how to report the results of PLS-SEM. *European Business Review*, *31*(1), 2–24. doi:10.1108/EBR-11-2018-0203

Hayek, M. (2012). Control beliefs and positive psychological capital: Can nascent entrepreneurs discriminate between what can and cannot be controlled? *Journal of Management Research, 12*(1), 3–13.

Henseler, J., Ringle, C. M., & Sarstedt, M. (2015). A new criterion for assessing discriminant validity in variance-based structural equation modeling. *Journal of the Academy of Marketing Science*, *43*(1), 115–135. doi:10.100711747-014-0403-8

Heydari, M., Lai, K. K., & Xiaohu, Z. (2020a). *Risk Management in Public-Private Partnerships*. Routledge. doi:10.4324/9781003112051

Heydari, M., Lai, K. K., & Xiaohu, Z. (2021a). *Corruption, Infrastructure Management and Public–Private Partnership: Optimizing through Mathematical Models*. Routledge. doi:10.4324/9781003177258

Heydari, M., Saeidi, M., & Danai, H. (2016). Examine the relationship between leadership style (based on likert theory) with job satisfaction of teachers in Shahed high schools for girls in Tehran in the academic year 2014-2015. *Mediterranean Journal of Social Sciences, 7*(2), 224–224.

Heydari, M., Xiaohu, Z., Keung, L. K., & Shang, Y. (2020b). Entrepreneurial intentions and behavior as the creation of business: Based on the theory of planned behavior extension evidence from Polish universities and entrepreneurs. *Propósitos y Representaciones, 8*(SPE2), e674.

Heydari, M., Xiaohu, Z., Lai, K. K., & Wang, S. B. (2019). Social-Psychology and Situational Elements Affecting Individual Social Behavior. *Journal of Hotel and Business Management*, *8*(2), 1–9.

Heydari, M., Xiaohu, Z., Lai, K. K., & Yuxi, Z. (2020c). Evaluation of organizational performance strategies. *Proceedings of the National Aviation University*, *82*, 77–93. doi:10.18372/2306-1472.82.14615

Heydari, M., Xiaohu, Z., Lai, K. K., & Yuxi, Z. (2021b). How might entrepreneurial activities affect behavior and emotions? *Proceedings of the National Aviation University*, *87*(2), 65–77. doi:10.18372/2306-1472.87.15722

Heydari, M., Xiaohu, Z., Saeidi, M., Lai, K. K., Shang, Y., & Yuxi, Z. (2020f). Analysis of the role of social support-cognitive psychology and emotional process approach. *European Journal of Translational Myology*, *30*(3), 1–17. doi:10.4081/ejtm.2020.8975 PMID:33117505

Heydari, M., Xiaohu, Z., Saeidi, M., Lai, K. K., & Yuxi, Z. (2020d). Entrepreneurship process as the creation of business by engaging family members: Based on the perceived emotion. *REICE: Revista Electrónica de Investigación en Ciencias Económicas*, *8*(15), 210–241. doi:10.5377/reice.v8i15.9955

Heydari, M., Xiaohu, Z., Saeidi, M., Lai, K. K., & Yuxi, Z. (2020e). Entrepreneurial cognition and effect on neuro entrepreneurship. *Gelpat Caderno Suplementar*, *3*, 1–27.

Heydari, M. D., & Lai, K. K. (2019). The effect employee commitment on service performance through a mediating function of organizational citizenship behavior using servqual and collaborative filtering modeling: Evidence from China's hospitality industry. *Journal of Tourism & Hospitality (Los Angeles, Calif.)*, *8*(2), 1–10.

Huang, L., Ma, M., & Wang, X. (2022). Clan culture and risk-taking of Chinese enterprises. *China Economic Review*, *72*, 101763. doi:10.1016/j.chieco.2022.101763

Kautonen, T., Van Gelderen, M., & Fink, M. (2015). Robustness of the theory of planned behavior in predicting entrepreneurial intentions and actions. *Entrepreneurship Theory and Practice*, *39*(3), 655–674. doi:10.1111/etap.12056

Kautonen, T., Van Gelderen, M., & Tornikoski, E. T. (2013). Predicting entrepreneurial behavior: A test of the theory of planned behavior. *Applied Economics*, *45*(6), 697–707. doi:10.1080/00036846.2011.610750

Kirzner, I. M. (1982). The theory of entrepreneurship in economic growth. Encyclopedia of Entrepreneurship, 272, 276.

Köbis, N. C. (2018). *The social psychology of corruption*. Vrije Universiteit.

Koppl, R., & Minniti, M. (2003). Market processes and entrepreneurial studies. In *Handbook of Entrepreneurship Research* (pp. 81–102). Springer.

Krueger, N. Jr, & Dickson, P. R. (1994). How believing in ourselves increases risk taking: Perceived self-efficacy and opportunity recognition. *Decision Sciences, 25*(3), 385–400. doi:10.1111/j.1540-5915.1994.tb01849.x

Krueger, N. F. (2007). The cognitive infrastructure of opportunity emergence. In *Entrepreneurship* (pp. 185–206). Springer.

Lai, M. M., Lein, S. Y., Lau, S. H., & Lai, M. L. (2016). Modeling age-friendly environment, active aging, and social connectedness in an emerging Asian economy. *Journal of Aging Research, 2016*, 2052380. doi:10.1155/2016/2052380 PMID:27293889

Lambsdorff, J. G., & Nell, M. (2006). Corruption: Where we stand and where to go. In M. Kreutner (Ed.), *The Corruption Monster: Ethik, Politik und Korruption*. Czernin.

Lee, S. Y., Florida, R., & Acs, Z. (2004). Creativity and entrepreneurship: A regional analysis of new firm formation. *Regional Studies, 38*(8), 879–891. doi:10.1080/0034340042000280910

Liñán, F., & Chen, Y. W. (2009). Development and cross–cultural application of a specific instrument to measure entrepreneurial intentions. *Entrepreneurship Theory and Practice, 33*(3), 593–617. doi:10.1111/j.1540-6520.2009.00318.x

Lund, K. (2016). *Facilitating corporate entrepreneurial behavior: A study of corporate entrepreneurial behavior in corporate banking*. Turun Yliopisto.

Manstead, A. S., Proffitt, C., & Smart, J. L. (1983). Predicting and understanding mothers' infant-feeding intentions and behavior: Testing the theory of reasoned action. *Journal of Personality and Social Psychology, 44*(4), 657–671. doi:10.1037/0022-3514.44.4.657 PMID:6842361

Marshall, A. (1890). *Principles of Economics: an introductory volume, book 4, ch. 6, version numérique.* McMaster University, Archive for the History of Economic Thought.

McClelland, D. C., & Winter, D. G. (1969). *Motivating Economic Achievement.* FreePress.

McGrath, R. G., & MacMillan, I. C. (2000). *The entrepreneurial mindset: Strategies for continuously creating opportunity in an age of uncertainty* (Vol. 284). Harvard Business Press.

Melgar, N., Rossi, M., & Smith, T. W. (2010). The perception of corruption in a cross-country perspective: Why are some individuals more perceptive than others? *Economia Aplicada, 14*(2), 183–198. doi:10.1590/S1413-80502010000200004

Moriano, J. A., Gorgievski, M., Laguna, M., Stephan, U., & Zarafshani, K. (2012). A cross-cultural approach to understanding entrepreneurial intention. *Journal of Career Development, 39*(2), 162–185. doi:10.1177/0894845310384481

Phan, P. H., Wong, P. K., & Wang, C. K. (2002). Antecedents to entrepreneurship among university students in Singapore: Beliefs, attitudes and background. *Journal of Enterprising Culture, 10*(02), 151–174. doi:10.1142/S0218495802000189

Pihie, Z. A. L., & Akmaliah, Z. (2009). Entrepreneurship as a career choice: An analysis of entrepreneurial self-efficacy and intention of university students. *European Journal of Soil Science*, *9*(2), 338–349.

Pollack, J. M., Vanepps, E. M., & Hayes, A. F. (2012). The moderating role of social ties on entrepreneurs' depressed affect and withdrawal intentions in response to economic stress. *Journal of Organizational Behavior*, *33*(6), 789–810. doi:10.1002/job.1794

Sánchez, J. C. (2009). Social learning and entrepreneurial intentions: A comparative study between Mexico, Spain and Portugal. *Revista Latinoamericana de Psicología*, *41*(1), 109–119.

Sarasvathy, S. D. (2001). Causation and effectuation: Toward a theoretical shift from economic inevitability to entrepreneurial contingency. *Academy of Management Review*, *26*(2), 243–263. doi:10.2307/259121

Sardeshmukh, S. R., Sharma, D., & Golden, T. D. (2012). Impact of telework on exhaustion and job engagement: A job demands and job resources model. *New Technology, Work and Employment*, *27*(3), 193–207. doi:10.1111/j.1468-005X.2012.00284.x

Shapero, A., & Sokol, L. (1982). *The social dimensions of entrepreneurship*. University of Illinois at Urbana-Champaign's Academy for Entrepreneurial Leadership Historical Research Reference in Entrepreneurship.

Shepherd, D. A., Patzelt, H., & Baron, R. A. (2013). I care about nature, but…: Disengaging values in assessing opportunities that cause harm. *Academy of Management Journal*, *56*(5), 1251–1273. doi:10.5465/amj.2011.0776

Shin, H. (2015). The Relationship between the Arab Spring Revolutions and Entrepreneurial Inhibitors, Enablers, and Activity in North Africa. In *Economics: Concepts, Methodologies, Tools, and Applications* (pp. 921–937). IGI Global. doi:10.4018/978-1-4666-8468-3.ch050

Siggelkow, N. (2001). Change in the presence of fit: The rise, the fall, and the renaissance of Liz Claiborne. *Academy of Management Journal*, *44*(4), 838–857. doi:10.2307/3069418

Simon, H. A. (2013). *Administrative Behavior*. Simon and Schuster.

Stevenson, H. H., & Jarillo, J. C. (2007). A paradigm of entrepreneurship: Entrepreneurial management. In *Entrepreneurship* (pp. 155–170). Springer.

Turker, D., & Selcuk, S. S. (2009). Which factors affect entrepreneurial intention of university students? *Journal of European Industrial Training*, *33*(2), 142–159. doi:10.1108/03090590910939049

Widmalm, S. (2008). *Decentralisation, corruption and social capital: from India to the West*. SAGE. doi:10.4135/9788132100263

Wu, T., Wang, D., Wang, R., Zhao, B., Tang, M., Zhang, S., & Nie, L. (2021). Pressure drops axial distribution uniformity of the particle bed in the radial bed. *Korean Journal of Chemical Engineering*, *38*(8), 1578–1591. doi:10.100711814-021-0818-0

Xiaohu, Z., Heydari, M., Lai, K. K., & Yuxi, Z. (2020). Analysis and Modeling of Corruption among Entrepreneurs. *REICE: Revista Electrónica de Investigación en Ciencias Económicas*, *8*(16), 262–311. doi:10.5377/reice.v8i16.10699

Zhao, H., Seibert, S. E., & Hills, G. E. (2005). The mediating role of self-efficacy in the development of entrepreneurial intentions. *The Journal of Applied Psychology*, *90*(6), 1265–1272. doi:10.1037/0021-9010.90.6.1265 PMID:16316279

Zhao, J., Wei, G., Chen, K. H., & Yien, J. M. (2020). Psychological Capital and university students' entrepreneurial intention in China: Mediation effect of entrepreneurial capitals. *Frontiers in Psychology*, *10*, 2984. doi:10.3389/fpsyg.2019.02984 PMID:32038375

KEY TERMS AND DEFINITIONS

Cognitive Attitude (CA): A person's attitude is a psychological construct, a mental and emotional entity that resides in or defines them. This research uses (CA) for cognitive attitude and (ATT) for attitude.

Corruption: Is the misuse of entrusted power for personal benefit, including bribery.

Entrepreneurial Behavior (EB): Desire to begin a new business.

Entrepreneurial Intentions (EI): A person's willingness to engage in a specific behavior. It is a direct cause of behaviors.

Fraud: Any intentional act or omission intended to deceive others that causes harm to the victim or benefits the offender.

Perceived Behavioral Control (PBC): A person's perception of the difficulty of engaging in a specific behavior.

Subjective Norm (SN): An individual's viewpoint on a specific behavior that is influenced by the views of others (e.g., teachers, parents, spouse, friends).

Theory of Planned Behavior (TPB): Planned behavior is a model for predicting and understanding human behavior. It asserts that behavioral intentions, determined by a combination of three factors: ATT toward the behavior, SNs, and PBC, immediately determine behaviors.

ENDNOTES

1 Goodness of Fit (GOF)
2 Average Variance Extracted (AVE)
3 Monte Carlo Simulations
4 Multitrait-multimethod matrix (MTMM)
5 Heterotrait-Monotrait ratio of correlations
6 Goodness of Fit Index
7 Adjusted Goodness-of-Fit Index
8 Root Mean square Residual
9 Comparative Fit Index
10 Normed Fit Index
11 Root Mean Square Error of Approximation
12 Parsimonious Goodness-Of-Fit Index
13 Parsimonious Normed Fit Index
14 Cattell–Nelson–Gorsuch scree test
15 Principal Component Analysis (PCA)
16 Variance-covariance matrix

Chapter 6
Economic Growth, Financial Development and Bank Failure:
The Case of Corruption in Nigeria

Shafiu Ibrahim Abdullahi
https://orcid.org/0000-0003-3471-4493
Bayero University, Kano, Nigeria

Mukhtar Shuaibu
Kebbi State Polytechnic, Dakingari, Nigeria

Mustapha Yusufu
Federal College of Education, Yola Adamawa State Nigeria, Nigeria

Kamal Kabiru Shehu
Federal University of Kashere, Nigeria

Abdul Rafay
https://orcid.org/0000-0002-0285-5980
University of Management and Technology, Pakistan

ABSTRACT

Corruption is one of the main causes of inefficiency and poor productivity. This chapter looks at the relationship between banking failure, corruption, financial development, and economic growth in Nigeria during the period from 1989 to 2019. The work uses the autoregressive distributed lag (ARDL) cointegration and error correction model and the Granger causality test for the analysis of data. The results of the empirical analyses show a negative relationship between corruption and both financial development and economic growth. This shows that corruption is bad for both the financial sector and the economy. The result also shows that corruption is a good reason for causing bank failures in Nigeria. Hence, for financial development and economic growth, corruption must be reduced as much as possible if not eliminated. It is recommended to put the fight against all forms of corruption in Nigeria in top gear.

DOI: 10.4018/978-1-6684-5007-9.ch006

INTRODUCTION

Nigeria has witnessed the rise of E-commerce and internet fraud concurrently. The evolution of the internet has provided cover for all kinds of real-world criminals to transfer their offline workspaces to the net. Internet related financial crimes in Nigeria today is only second to public sector corruption and it continues to grow at a faster rate. Due to the bad habits of few Nigerian online criminals, Nigeria is now one of the countries that are associated with online fraud around the world. But other forms of corruption are not left out; they have continued to serve as serious threats to Nigeria's economic growth and development. Corruption is one of the main causes of bank failure in Nigeria. Between 1997 to 2002 about 34 banks collapsed in Nigeria (Ndulue, 2003). In 1997 alone, 26 banks were liquidated (Yuguda, 1997). According to a study, fraud and embezzlement are linked with corporate failure in Nigeria (Dogarawa, 2007). Corruption has become endemic in Nigeria, as in many other African countries (Abdullahi, 2007). But the Nigerian government through the Economic and Financial Crime Commission (EFCC) has been doing a good job of curtailing this menace through investigation, prosecution, effective monitoring, and collaborations with sister agencies from the US, EU and elsewhere. According to Transparency International (TI) corruption is the abuse of entrusted power for private gain (TI, 2006). Corruption and poverty reinforce one another; corruption results in poverty when money means for people's welfare are looted or when it increases the cost of doing business, thus causing a decrease in investment (Abdullahi, 2007). Corruption caused inefficiency and poor productivity and in the financial sector, the banking crisis is most associated with the lack of transparency. Financial sector transparency together with tighter regulation and adherence to principles that ensure adequate banking supervision are the parameters that indicate good banking practices (TI, 2006). According to a Shirley (1996), bureaucracy helps corruption. One worrying variable connected with rising crimes in Nigeria is unemployment (Mukhtar and Abdullahi, 2020).

According to some studies, during the global financial crisis of 2009, financial institutions collapsed due to reckless lending practices (Abdullahi, 2019; Deman, 2009). The world of finance is full of crooks and thieves from Michael Milken of Drexel to Kenneth Lay of Enron who created ingenious ways of stealing shareholders' money. In Nigeria, the history of the Nigerian corporate and financial industry is full of chief executive officers (CEOs) and other top executives who connive to steal people's money. Some of the recent notorious corporate failure cases that were tried in the Nigerian courts include Cecelia Ibru of Oceanic Bank and Erastus Akhingbola of Intercontinental bank PLC who was accused of stealing the money of the banks they controlled that later led to the bankruptcy of these banks. The banking crisis of 2009 led to the creation of the Assets Management Corporation of Nigeria (AMCON) to manage the assets of failed banks and other corporations that collapsed during the crisis period. During the period, the Nigerian government used trillions of Naira of public money to bail out these banks. All these helps to show the extent to which corruption and mismanagement have gone into killing the Nigerian economy. Banks in Africa and around the world have helped boosted corruption by helping corrupt politicians and others to stash their ill-gotten wealth. Around the world, ethical banking such as Islamic banking has been associated with a reduction in corruption in the system (Uddin, Chowdhury & Islam, 2017). The modern banking system faced the main challenge of having to make a profit in midst of tight regulatory requirements enforced by regulators in order to achieve market discipline (Abdullahi, 2019). At the macro level, a sound and the robust financial system makes it difficult for corruption to linger. On the other hand, a sound macroeconomic policy reduces corruption and promotes economic growth.

This chapter aims to analyze the relationships between corruption, bank failure, financial development and economic growth in Nigeria. But the specific objectives of the work are to measure the effects of corruption and banking failure on economic growth as well as to measure the effects of corruption and banking failure on financial development. The chapter noted the direction of causality, such as who causes who between corruption and bank failure, economic growth and bank failure or corruption and economic growth. Does education or the absence of it contribute to affecting economic growth and financial development in unison with corruption and bank failure? The work uses the Autoregressive Distributed Lag (ARDL) cointegration and Error correction model and the Granger causality method for the analyses of the data. The results of the empirical analyses show negative relationships between corruption and both financial development and economic growth. This shows that corruption is bad for both the financial sector and the economy. The result also shows that corruption is a good candidate for causing bank failures in Nigeria. The chapter is divided into an introduction, empirical literature review, conceptual and theoretical framework, data and methodology, results and discussion, and conclusion and recommendations.

EMPIRICAL LITERATURE REVIEW

Sharma (2021) has examined the effects of corruption and political instability and violence on the financial sector development around the world. The study considers the period from 1996 to 2015. The results show that corruption has a negative effect on financial sector development. The results further show corruption is more financial development-reducing when its level is very high. Praoyao and Eugene (2018) look at how institutional factors affected financial development in 29 African countries during the period from 2000 to 2014. They used the econometric method of pool mean group to analyze the data. The result shows that corruption is positively correlated with financial development. Liu, Li, & Guo (2020) studied the impacts of corruption on firms' access to bank loans in China. The authors used data collected by the World Bank based on survey data of 2,848 enterprises. Their findings show low level of corruption increases access to bank loans for firms, while a high level of corruption stops firms from obtaining bank loans. Mild level corruption may serve as a suboptimal choice. Uddin *et al.* (2017) examined the impact of socioeconomic factors on the performance of banks in Bangladesh. The paper used static and dynamic GMM model for the analysis. The study found that socio-economic factors especially corruption has a negative effect on banks' profitability. Funmi *et al.* (2018) examined the effects of bank fraud on economic growth in Nigeria using multiple linear regression models. Banking failure was also analysed to determine the impact of banking fraud on the economy. The result shows that bank fraud has a negative effect on economic growth. Boudriga, Taktak & Jellouli (2009) in a cross-country study on the determinants of nonperforming loans found that a higher capital adequacy ratio and prudent provisioning policy reduced the level of non-performing loans. They also noted that regulatory devices do not significantly reduce nonperforming loans for countries with weak institutions, corrupt environments, and poor democratic systems. They recommended that the effective way to reduce bad loans is through strengthening the legal system and boosting transparency and democracy.

AlBassam (2013) tried to confirm whether a strong relationship exists between governance and economic growth during times of crisis and non-crisis periods. The result is mixed, with crisis having unnoticeable effects on the relationship and level of country development as another important variable in explaining the relation. Evans (2020) analyzes the relationship between fiscal discipline, financial development and economic growth in Nigeria during the period from 1980 to 2017. Specifically, the study examined the effects of fiscal discipline in the form of policy uncertainty, corruption, budgeting reforms, fiscal policy sustainability and crowding out on financial development and economic growth. The author used the ARDL cointegration method for the analysis; the findings show that policy uncertainty, corruption and fiscal deficits have a negative relationship with financial development and economic growth. Mathew *et al.* (2013) studied the correlation between corruption and economic growth in Nigeria using ordinary least squares (OLS) and Granger causality methods of analysis. The outcome of the study shows that corruption slows economic growth. Abiloro *et al.* (2019) also studied the relationship between corruption, inequality and this time around economic development in Nigeria. They used the OLS technique to analyze the data covering the period from 1999 to 2017. They discovered that both corruption and inequality have a negative effect on economic development. Aliyu and Elijah (2008) examined the relationship between corruption and economic growth in Nigeria (1986-2007) and noted that corruption has a direct effect on economic growth as well as indirect through variables such as Government Capital Expenditure, Human Capital Development and Total employment. Their paper employed Engle-Granger cointegration and error correction mechanism (ECM) for data analysis.

Siaplay (2020) examined the effects of corruption on economic growth and income distribution in West Africa. The results reveal that decreasing corruption increase economic growth. Corruption and income inequality were also positively correlated. The study observes that corruption generates lower economic growth and exacerbates income inequality. Ahmad, Ullah, & Arfeen (2012) used a panel data model to analyze the relationship between corruption and economic growth around the world; data was collected for the period 1984 to 2009 for 71 countries. The result shows that a decrease in corruption raised economic growth. Work by Shuaibu *et al.* (2021) shows that public debt and by extension mismanagement was responsible for a high rate of unemployment in Nigeria between 1985 to 2020. In a study on the relationship between governance and economic development in Organisation for Islamic Cooperation (OIC) countries, Azam (2016) found that corruption and inflation have negative effects on economic growth in member countries, and external debt was also found to have a negative effect on economic growth. The work is based on panel data from 20 Organisation for Islamic Cooperation (OIC) member countries for the period 1986 to 2012. Adegoke *et al.* (2018) examined the determinants of financial development in West African countries during the period from 2000 to 2015. The authors used a panel data model for estimating the data, the result shows that the rule of law and political stability positively affect financial development while trade openness and interest rate negatively affected it. Garba *et al.* (2016) in a study on institutions, natural resources, and economic growth in Nigeria during the period 1960-2014 found that institutions and natural resources have a significant positive effect on economic growth. The methods of analysis employed for the work are cointegration and vector error correction models.

CONCEPTUAL AND THEORETICAL FRAMEWORKS

Financial Development and Economic Growth

The financial sector comprises of tools, institutions, and markets, as well as the legal and regulatory framework that allows financial transactions to be completed. Among other functions, financial development involves reducing costs and learning processes within a financial system. This way of reducing the costs of receiving information, imposition of contracts and making of transactions is increased through financial contracts, markets, and intermediaries. Diverse forms of groupings of information, enforcement, and transaction costs in combination with different legal, control, and tax systems have driven distinct financial contracts, markets, and intermediaries across nations and entire history. It is generally known that financial development is a multidimensional concept and constitutes a possibly important mechanism for long-term economic growth. Financial development plays a key role in the development and growth of an economy. The successes and efficiency realized in performing these roles, particularly the intermediation between the excess and shortfall units of an economy, are in the end determined by the level of development of the financial system. Functions of the financial system include providing information about investments opportunities and distribution of capital, Monitoring investments and enforcement of corporate governance standards after the provision of finance, enabling trading, diversification, and management of risk, Assembling and distribution of savings and recording auspicious exchange of goods and services.

Financial sector development plays a vigorous part in the economic development process of nations. It inspires economic growth through capital accumulation and technological development by raising the rate of savings mobilization, providing investment information, facilitating the inflows of external capital, as well as enhancing the allocation of capital. Nations with well-established financial systems tend to develop faster over long periods, and various evidence suggests that this effect is fundamental; financial development is not just an outcome of economic growth it contributes to this growth. Moreover, it lessens poverty and inequality by enlarging access to finance for the poor and susceptible groups; enabling risk management by increasing their susceptibility to shocks and growth in investment and productivity that result in larger income generation. Financial sector progress aids the growth of small and medium enterprises (SMEs) by giving them access to finance. SMEs are usually labor intensive and generate more jobs than large firms. They play a vital role in economic development, particularly in developing economies such as Nigeria. Financial sector growth goes beyond having financial intermediaries and grows in financial infrastructures. It involves having sound policies for the command and supervision of all important entities connected with it. The worldwide financial crises have highlighted the calamitous consequences of having a weak financial sector and poor policies to regulate them. Financial crises have shown the potentially calamitous consequences of having feeble financial sector policies and their influence on economic outcomes.

Empirical measurement of financial growth is vital to the development of the financial sector and to properly comprehend the influence of financial development on economic growth and poverty reduction. In practice, though, it is tough to measure financial growth as it is an enormous concept and has several magnitudes. Practical work done so far is mostly based on standard quantitative gauges, using long time series data and for a broad range of nations. Prominent indicators include the proportion of financial institutions to gross domestic product (GDP), the relation of liquid liabilities to GDP and the proportion of deposits to GDP. However, since the financial sector of a nation encompasses a diversity of financial institutions, markets and products, the above procedures provide just a rough estimate and do not include all the aspects of financial development. The World Bank's Global Financial Growth Report has developed a comprehensive yet comparatively modest framework to measure financial development in the world. This framework recognizes four sets of proxy variables characterizing a well-functioning financial system: financial depth, access, efficiency, and stability. These four measures are then measured against the two key components of the financial sector, i.e., the financial institutions and markets.

Corruption and Financial Crimes

Activities such as skimming (using a disguised card reader to electronically capture card information or phishing (using email to trick people into revealing sensitive accounts or card information) are being used by online fraudsters to commit financial crimes of various degrees (Sullivan, 2010). Online fraudsters also penetrate computer systems to steal information. Hackers, scammers, and those who engage in fraudulent social engineering have become some of the most prominent computer fraudsters. In the US and other developed parts of the world, more money is stolen from banks by data breaches than by robbery (Sullivan, 2010). Corruption in developing countries affects the poor more than it affects the rich. Corruption increases where there is a positive stimulus such as poor regulation, mismanagement, and an inefficient legal system. In a general context, as an economic phenomenon corruption gives disutility instead of utility. Thus, under normal circumstances given it negative effect and presumed disutility, demand for corruption shall be low relative to supply. But this is not the case in most circumstances. Only where the moral fabric is low and poverty is widespread, corruption is greater than supply. The supply of corruption is directly related to the positive stimulus.

Corruption, financial indiscipline, and mismanagement have been the cancerous viruses bedeviling the progress and operational efficiency of institutions in Nigeria. The prime aim of establishing anti-graft agencies such as the Economic and Financial Crimes Commission (EFCC) and Independent Corrupt Practices and Other Related Offences Commission (ICPC) is to act as watchdogs that sniff out all illegal financial dealings taking place in different sectors within the Nigerian economy. They are backed by law to arrest, investigate and prosecute all those involved in corrupt acts. They are meant to stop all acts of serial abuse of public offices, fraud and embezzlement of the commonwealth. Many corruptions related offences have been linked to high-profile Nigerians; ranging from former presidents, ex-vice presidents, current and former governors, current and former ministers, heads of government agencies and heads of private corporations. According to Orjiude (2021), eight banks lost 1.9 billion Naira to fraud in 2020. Orjiude (2022) again reported that four of Nigerian banks had lost 1.77 billion Naira to fraud involving bank workers and consumers in 2021 alone. The Economic and Financial Crimes Commission (EFCC) had also accused Nigerian banks of aiding corruption. According to EFCC, in a bid to protect people suspected of financial crimes from an official investigation, banks in Nigeria deliberately provided inadequate information, in some cases completely hide information from anti-corruption agencies (Tukur, 2012). Financial Times (2016) also reported that three Nigerian banks' chief executive officers (CEOs) were questioned by EFCC in 2016 in cases related to corrupt dealings. EFCC (in October of 2009) made a public showcase of notorious corruption cases valued at over one trillion Naira; where ex-governors, ex-ministers, and serving members of the Nigerian national assembly were involved.

Other high-profile corruption cases were successfully executed by the commissions. These include that of former Nigerian Police Inspector General Mustapha Tafa Balogun who was forced to retire from the Nigerian Police in January 2005 due to corruption allegations. He was later arrested and charged for stealing public funds worth more than one hundred and twenty million Dollars. Unfortunately, he was only detained for a period of six months. In addition, the commission collected thirty thousand Dollars from him and confiscated his belongings worth one hundred and fifty million Dollars. A former governor of Bayelsa State, Diepreye Alamieyeseigha was also caught and convicted of money laundering by a court. He was subsequently impeached from office in 2004 and imprisoned for two years. Timipreye Sylva was another governor of Bayelsa State who was charged with misappropriation of public money close to five billion Naira. A former Comptroller-General of Nigeria Customs Service from 2009 to

2015, Abdullahi Dikko Inde was charged with money corruption worth forty billion Naira by EFCC. His property worth two billion Naira was confiscated. He also returned one billion Naira to the government. Musiliu Babatunde Obanikoro, an ex-senator, former high commissioner, and former minister was in 2014 accused (together with his two sons) of financial fraud worth about four billion seven hundred million Naira. He was reported to have returned one hundred million Naira to the government. James Ibori (Delta State governor, 1999-2007) was arrested in Dubai, UAE and extradited to the United Kingdom over corruption charges that also involved his wife, her sister, and a mistress. He pleaded guilty to stealing fifty million Pound Sterling. He was imprisoned in the United Kingdom, but later released and returned to Nigeria in 2017.

Failure of Governance

Under agency theory, it is postulated that hired managers do not have the same objectives as owners of a business venture. This separation between ownership and management allows managers to engage in acts that are detrimental to the interest of owners; such acts include fraud and various other types of mismanagement. Because public corporations generated funds from the public to function and operate, they assume an obligation of public trust to act in a way that safeguards the public interest and make full and fair public disclosure of corporate information, including financial results (Yuguda, 2012). The following are the major tenets of corporate governance: accountability, efficiency and effectiveness, integrity and fairness, probity, responsibility and transparency. Good governance reduces poverty when it reduces corruption (Shirley, 1996). Disclosure of revenue payment by firms is found to have a positive correlation with best corporate performance (TI, 2006). Financial liberalization in developing countries and these nations' inability to manage the process have been blamed for causing banking failure during the crisis period (Mishkin, 2013). Risky lending and weak credit culture have been blamed for banking failure. So also, politicians and other powerful people use regulatory loopholes to exploit banks they have access to.

Mishkin (2013) has defined the financial market as "*a market in which funds are transferred from people who have an excess of available funds to people who have a shortage*". The financial market has an important role to play in channeling investment to where it is needed; where the financial market is hampered economic growth is equally affected. From period-to-period nations or global financial system experience a crisis that is generally known as a financial crisis. Financial crises according to Mishkin (2013) are "*major disruptions in the financial market that are characterized by sharp declines in asset prices and the failures of many financial and nonfinancial firms*". Banking failures, defaults and bankruptcies are some of the consequences of financial crises. The problem of adverse selection and moral hazard is at the heart of banking failures in developing countries of the world. The problem of asymmetric information in financial markets is the causal agent of the problem of adverse selection and moral hazard. The inefficiencies that resulted from the problem of asymmetric information led to the financial crisis and the subsequent collapse of the financial firms. The poor condition of balance sheets and the difficult banking environment lead some banks into insolvency with net worth becoming negative. As a result of banks' inability to pay depositors and other creditors, they collapse and become failed entities.

THEORETICAL FRAMES

One of the main guiding theoretical frameworks for this work is the traditional production function, Y = f(K,L) and the neoclassical growth models. Solow's (1956) neoclassical model is based on the production function:

$$Y = F\left(K,L\right)$$

Where Y = output/economic growth, K = capital, L = labour. demand for goods and services in the Solow'd model comes from consumption and investment. Output per worker y is divided between consumption per worker c and investment per worker i:

$$Y = c + i$$

Solow assumes that each year people save a percentage *s* of their income and consume a percentage (*1-s*).

$$c = \left(1 - s\right)y \tag{3}$$

A saving rate is a number between zero and one. Under Solow's model investment equals saving, the model shows that the saving rate is a key determinant of capital stock in an economy. Higher saving also leads to faster economic growth in the model.

The other guiding frameworks are the money-saving-investment functions that underpin the modern financial system. Here the money market equilibrium is:

$$M/P = L\left(i,Y\right) \tag{4}$$

Where equation (4) is the equilibrium point at which money supply equals money demand. Where M = quantity of money, p = price, i = interest rate, y = income. The interest rate that equilibrates the money market is:

$$i = \left(e/f\right)y - \left(1/f\right)m / p \tag{5}$$

Where e and f are numbers greater than zero. The value of e determines how much demand for money rises when income rises. F determines how much demand for money falls when interest rises (Mankiw, 2007). Investment is also influenced by general consumption spending in an economy.

$$C_t = \varphi Y_{t-1} \tag{6}$$

$$I_t = \propto \left(C_t - C_{t-1}\right) \tag{7}$$

Where $\varphi = MPC, \propto = the accelarator$, C_t = consumption at time t, Y_t = income at time t, I_t = investment at time t.

$$I_t = \propto \varphi\left(Y_{t-1} - Y_{t-2}\right) \tag{8}$$

DATA AND METHODOLOGY

Data

The data used for the study is secondary data sourced from the National Bureau of Statistics, Central Bank of Nigeria, Transparency International and World Bank. Data is collected for the period 1989 to 2019 for the following variables corruption level (TI index), bank failure, financial development and economic growth. Control variables were introduced (inequality, unemployment, Population Growth, per capita income, political stability index, gender, interest rate, trade openness and environmental quality) in order to minimize omitted variable bias. Both unemployment and inequality are sometimes considered likely candidates in forcing a certain set of people (especially the financial constraint) into corruption. Gender and population growth are also good candidates on the list of relevant variables in models dealing with corruption. Political stability is measured as 1 if a democratically elected government is in power, and 0 if a military dictator is in power.

Models

The work looks at the relationship between economic growth, corruption rate, banking failure and financial development. The work has two models: model 1 measures the effects of corruption and banking failure on economic growth; while model 2 measures the effects of corruption and banking failure on financial development.

Model 1

$$EG = \partial_1 CI + \partial_2 BF + \partial_3 PG + \partial_4 PS + \partial_5 GD + \partial_6 EQ + \mu$$

Where EG is economic growth, CI is corruption index, BF represents bank failure, PG population growth, PS political stability, GD gender, EQ environmental quality.

Model 2

$$FD = \delta_1 CI + \delta_2 BF + \delta_3 IR + \delta_4 IE + \delta_5 UE + \delta_6 PI + \delta_7 GD + \delta_8 TO + \varepsilon$$

Where FD is financial development, IR is the interest rate, IE is inequality, UE represents unemployment, PI is per capita income, GD is for gender, TO for trade openness.

Method of Analysis

The methods of analysis used for the study are Autoregressive Distributed Lag (ARDL) error correction model (ECM) and Granger causality analysis. Diagnostic tests that include stationary tests are conducted. To forecast whether one variable is useful for predicting another variable the test of Granger causality is frequently used. Clive Granger (1969) who invented the procedure has argued that economic causality could be tested by measuring the ability to predict the future values of a variable using prior values of another variable. Pesaran and Shin (1999) were credited with pioneering the use of the ARDL method. Further development of the ARDL model was published by Pesaran, Shin and Smith (2001). Over the years, the ARDL model has received wide acclaim among empirical economists due to its flexibility and ease of usage. ARDL has the advantage of tolerating different lags in different variables. ARDL can be used whether a series is I(0), I(1) or fractionally integrated. In the case of series I(2) the integration order invalidates the F-Statistics and all the critical values. The Error correction model of the ARDL integrates both the short run and long run equilibrium. ARDL is of the form:

$$\varnothing(L) y_t = \varphi + \theta_1(L) x_{1t} + \theta_2(L) x_{2t} + \theta_k(L) x_{kt} + \mu_t ()$$

Manipulating the lag operator L to each part of a vector, $L^k y = y_{t-k}$, hence it is better to characterize the lag polynomial $\Phi(L,p)$ and the vector polynomial $\beta(L,q)$. An EC_t is the error correction term which is of the form:

$$EC_t = \varepsilon_t = y_t - \sum_{i-1}^{k} \theta_t x_{it} - \omega' W_t \qquad (10)$$

Empirically, the ARDL is of the form:

$$\Delta X_t = \delta_{0i} + \sum_{i=1}^{k} \alpha_i \Delta X_{t-1} + \sum_{i=1}^{k} \alpha_2 \Delta Y_{t-i} + \ldots \sum_{i=1}^{k} \alpha_2 \Delta Z_{t-1} + \delta_1 X_{t-1} + \delta_2 Y_{t-1} + \ldots \delta_i Z_{t-1} + v_{1t}$$

$$\Delta Y_t = \delta_{0i} + \sum_{i=1}^{k} \alpha_i \Delta Y_{t-1} + \sum_{i=1}^{k} \alpha_2 \Delta X_{t-i} + \ldots \sum_{i=1}^{k} \alpha_2 \Delta Z_{t-1} + \delta_1 Y_{t-1} + \delta_2 X_{t-1} + \ldots \delta_i Z_{t-1} + v_{1t}$$

$$\Delta Z_t = \delta_{0i} + \sum_{i=1}^{k} \alpha_i \Delta Z_{t-1} + \sum_{i=1}^{k} \alpha_2 \Delta X_{t-i} + \ldots \sum_{i=1}^{k} \alpha_2 \Delta W_{t-1} + \delta_1 Z_{t-1} + \delta_2 X_{t-1} + \ldots \delta_i W_{t-1} + v_{1t}$$

The combined hypotheses to be tested for the ARDL bound testing are as follows:

$$H_0 : \delta_2 = \delta_3 = \delta_4 = \delta_i = 0$$

$$H_1 : \delta_2 \neq 0, i = 4,5,7, \ldots$$

The F-Statistics test is used to test for cointegration by quantifying the significance of the lagged levels of the time series variables.

RESULTS AND DISCUSSIONS

Summary Statistics

The summary statistics shows mean, median, maximum, minimum, standard deviation, skewness, kurtosis and Jarque Bera for the variables data used for the study, see appendix 1.

Stationarity Tests:

The results of the unit root tests conducted show a mixture of stationarity at a level and at the first difference for the various variables in the study. This satisfies the condition for using the ARDL cointegration and error correction model. Hence, we proceed with the testing of the ARDL model.

Results of Causality Tests

The summary of the results of Granger causality tests conducted shows that corruption Granger cause bank failure, inequality caused bank failure and bank failure cause inequality, interest rate cause bank failure and bank failure cause interest, political stability Granger cause bank failure and vice versa, trade openness Granger cause bank failure and vice versa, unemployment Granger cause bank failure and bank failure Granger cause unemployment, corruption cause inequality and interest rate cause corruption. Other two ways causalities include corruption and population growth, corruption and trade openness, corruption and unemployment, environmental quality and financial development, gender and financial development, inequality and financial development, interest rate and financial development, political stability and financial development, trade openness and financial development, and unemployment and financial development. Two ways causality also include between interest rate and environment quality, interest rate and inequality, per capita income and interest rate, political stability and interest rate, unemployment and interest rate; while inequality Granger cause political stability,

ARDL Analyses Results

Model 1

The results of the analysis show that there is a negative though the statistically insignificant relationship between bank failure and economic growth. Lagged value of corruption also shows a negative and statistically significant relationship with economic growth. In addition, population growth has a negative and statistically significant relationship with economic growth. But gender, environmental quality and political stability are not statistically significant. The results of the Error correction regression show that there is a 54% adjustment to restore equilibrium for model 1 (see table 3). The result of the bound testing shows no cointegration at 5% to 1% levels. The negative relationship between corruption and economic growth is also found in the works of Evans (2020); Mathew, *et al.* (2013); Abiloro, *et al.* (2019); Siaplay (2020); Ahmad, *et al.* (2012); and Azam (2016).

Table 1. ARDL regression results

Variable	Coefficient	Std. Error	t-Statistic	Prob.*
EG(-1)	0.884059	0.246900	3.580636	0.0038
EG(-2)	-0.432445	0.253474	-1.706072	0.1137
CI	61839280	1.22E+09	0.050757	0.9604
CI(-1)	3.17E+09	1.06E+09	2.990938	0.0113
CI(-2)	-2.22E+09	1.00E+09	-2.208900	0.0474
BF	-1.65E+09	1.50E+09	-1.094623	0.2952
PG	-4.29E+12	1.41E+12	-3.049546	0.0101
PG(-1)	4.84E+12	1.57E+12	3.082945	0.0095
PS	3.22E+09	6.68E+10	0.048206	0.9623
PS(-1)	-6.99E+10	5.86E+10	-1.193746	0.2556
GD	-6.50E+12	3.57E+12	-1.819678	0.0938
GD(-1)	8.63E+10	3.69E+12	0.023417	0.9817
GD(-2)	-8.35E+12	3.29E+12	-2.537419	0.0261
EQ	5.58E+08	8.26E+08	0.675415	0.5122
EQ(-1)	-1.64E+09	7.75E+08	-2.120271	0.0555
EQ(-2)	-1.47E+09	1.08E+09	-1.366249	0.1969
C	1.41E+13	6.19E+12	2.283644	0.0414

Table 2. Error correction result

Variable	Coefficient	Std. Error	t-Statistic	Prob.
CointEq(-1)*	-0.548387	0.105559	-5.195049	0.0002

Table 3. Bound testing resul

F-Bounds Test		Null Hypothesis: No levels relationship		
Test Statistic	Value	Signif.	I(0)	I(1)
F-statistic	2.130674	10%	1.99	2.94
K	6	5%	2.27	3.28
		2.5%	2.55	3.61
		1%	2.88	3.99

Model 2

For model 2 the results show that there is a negative relationship between financial development and corruption, bank failure is also negatively related to financial development though it is not statistically significant. Lagged value of interest rate (IR) is negatively related to financial development, while inequality (IE) and per capita income (PI) are positively related to financial development. The results of the Error correction regression show that there is an 84% adjustment to restore equilibrium for model 2 (see table 6), while the result of the bound testing shows cointegration at 10% and 5% levels. The finding of a negative relationship between corruption and financial development is in line with the findings of Sharma (2021); Evans (2020); Adegoke, *et al.* (2018); but contradicts the finding of Praoyao and Eugene (2018).

Table 4. ARDL regression results

Variable	Coefficient	Std. Error	t-Statistic	Prob.*
FD(-1)	0.495814	0.182002	2.724218	0.0157
FD(-2)	-0.341160	0.157486	-2.166287	0.0468
CI	-0.000605	0.000284	-2.131890	0.0500
BF	-0.000592	0.000454	-1.301669	0.2127
IR	-0.001607	0.001083	-1.483574	0.1586
IR(-1)	-0.003811	0.001139	-3.345435	0.0044
IE	0.003264	0.001271	2.569023	0.0214
IE(-1)	-0.004432	0.001393	-3.182107	0.0062
UE	0.000700	0.002353	0.297709	0.7700
PI	3.39E-05	1.30E-05	2.609582	0.0197
PI(-1)	-2.56E-05	1.34E-05	-1.905614	0.0760
GD	-1.253043	0.715717	-1.750751	0.1004
TO	-8.56E-05	0.000388	-0.220845	0.8282
C	1.681119	0.768767	2.186774	0.0450

Table 5. Error correction regression result

Variable	Coefficient	Std. Error	t-Statistic	Prob.
CointEq(-1)*	-0.845346	0.114674	-7.371742	0.0000

Table 6. Bound testing result

F-Bounds Test		Null Hypothesis: No levels relationship	
Value	Signif.	I(0)	I(1)
3.396411	10%	1.85	2.85
8	5%	2.11	3.15
	2.5%	2.33	3.42
	1%	2.62	3.77

IMPLICATIONS

The finding of a negative relationship between corruption and financial development indicates that corruption is detrimental to financial development and to boost financial development corruption must be curtailed. This further validates the calls for governments around the world to take seriously the fight against financial fraud, embezzlement, corruption and related acts harmful to the financial sector and the entire economy (Nakitende *et al.*, 2021). The negative relationship between interest rate and financial development is a pointer to the unfavorable nature of the various interest regimes that have existed during the study period. The implication of any negative effect of bank failure on economic growth is that the collapse of banks in Nigeria during past decades has great toll on Nigeria's economic growth and may have caused retardation in the actual economic growth. The negative effect of corruption on economic growth has also been buttressed by the study. By implication, corruption can rightly be blamed as one of the main causes of the economic underdevelopment of Nigeria. The results of the Granger causality test also indicate that corruption and the presence or absence of political stability might have been responsible for bank failure in Nigeria.

CONCLUSION AND RECOMMENDATIONS

The findings of this work show that corruption is bad for both the financial sector and the entire economy of Nigeria. It also shows that corruption is a likely candidate for causing banking failure in Nigeria. The chapter cited previous cases of corruption in Nigeria and how they have helped in ruining the image of the country and its economy. Hence, for success in the financial sector and the entire economy corruption must be reduced. Thus, this work recommends putting the fight against corruption in top gear. Banking sector corruption has been linked to the collapse of Nigerian banks between 1990 to 2010. In the 1990s, a failed banks tribunal was set up by the federal government of Nigeria to adjudge over the rampant cases of Nigerian banks that collapsed between the late 1980s and early 1990s. For developing countries such as Nigeria, the war against corruption whether in the real world or in the cyber world shall be a must (a sort of do-or-die affair); as the saying goes, if you don't stop (kill) corruption, corruption will stop (kill) you. For mismanagement in the banking sector to reduce, authorities must take the war against financial mismanagement in the sector as a top priority in their schedules, instead of paying overdue attention to higher profits and increase in bank revenue; because a reduction in the level of financial mismanagement both higher profit and higher revenue can be realized. Transparency in the affairs of government and private corporations shall also be enhanced, as it is linked with reducing corruption. Cases of corruption brought before Nigerian courts must be allowed to reach their logical conclusions without interference by those in the position of authority. The agencies in Nigeria responsible for the war against corruption shall be empowered and given all the support they need to succeed in their primary assignments. Punitive measures shall be put in place to serve as punishment for the crime of corruption and as deterrence to those that may want to engage in the practice.

The building of a sound and transparent financial system shall be seen as an important goal in the fight against corruption in Nigeria. This is because over the years financial institutions have served as channels in the transmission of corrupt money and as incubators of corruption themselves. An inefficient banking system is more inclined to corruption than an efficient system; hence, Nigerian monetary authorities shall endeavor to establish a sound and efficient banking system as an antidote to corruption in the country. With no iota of doubt, the root causes and the subsequent challenges of the aforementioned corruption cases, have strongly affected every aspect of the Nigerian economy negatively. Therefore, there is an urgent need to carefully study this phenomenon and come up with lasting solutions. The immunity clause in the Nigerian constitution of 1999 covers the incumbent President and Vice President, Governors and their deputies against arrest, detention and prosecution. This has emboldened corrupt public officeholders to steal and plunder the wealth of the nation and should therefore be reviewed and modified to meet the needs of the majority of Nigerians. There is also the problem of delays and slow movements of court proceedings that resulted from an inadequate number of courts and judges. The Nigerian authorities shall provide emergency courts that specialized in the judgment of money laundering, corruption and other finance related offences with immediate effect. Corruption has negative social, political and economic effects that bring about the environmental crisis, widen inequality and social stratification, bankrupt government and increase poverty level.

The fight against corruption and money laundering shall be given wide coverage by the government at various levels and settings. In order to inculcate the spirit of discipline and vigilance and checkmate the menace of financial crimes and mismanagement in the wider society. In the sphere of ensuring transparency and accountability, no single individual at whatever level shall be allowed into the management of public funds once his name is linked to corruption. This shall be the rule right from the grassroots level; whether in nomination or election. Assets declaration as overseen by the Code of Conduct Bureau shall be given the utmost importance on the assumption of duty of civil servants; and the process of checks and continued supervision shall be administered at regular time intervals.

DECLARATION

The authors declare that the manuscript follows ethical standards and there are no potential conflicts of interest with respect to the research, authorship and/or publication of this chapter.

DISCLAIMER

The contents and views of this chapter are expressed by the authors in their personal capacities. It is not necessary for the Editor and the Publisher to agree with these viewpoints, and they are not responsible for any duty of care in this regard.

ACKNOWLEDGMENT

The authors extend sincere gratitude to

- The Editor and the International Editorial Advisory Board (IEAB) of this book who initially desk reviewed, arranged a rigorous double/triple blind review process, and conducted a thorough, minute, and critical final review before accepting the chapter for publication.
- All anonymous reviewers who provided very constructive feedbacks for thorough revision, improvement, extension, and fine tuning of the chapter.
- All colleagues, assistants and well-wishers who assisted to complete this task.

REFERENCES

Abdullahi, S. I. (2007). Essay on Corruption. Unpublished monograph, Kano Nigeria.

Abdullahi, S. I. (2019). Risk management and corporate governance: an Islamic perspective. In T. Azid, A. A. Alnodl, & M. A. Qureshi (Eds.), *Research in Corporate and Shariah Governance in the Muslim World: Theory and Practice*. Emerald.

Abiloro, T. O., Olawole, A., & Adeniran, T. E. (2019). Corruption, income inequality, and economic development in Nigeria. *International Journal of Academic Research in Accounting, Finance and Management Sciences*, *9*(4), 304–319.

Adegoke, A. O., Donga, M., Idi, A., & Abdullahi, B. (2018). An examination of drivers of financial development: Evidence in west African countries. *Pakistan Journal of Humanities and Social Sciences*, *6*(1), 132–143. doi:10.52131/pjhss.2018.0601.0038

Ahmad, E., Ullah, M. A., & Arfeen, M. I. (2012). Does corruption affect economic growth? *Latin American Journal of Economics*, *49*(2), 277–305. doi:10.7764/LAJE.49.2.277

AlBassam, B. A. (2013). The relationship between governance and economic growth during times of crisis. *European Journal of Sustainable Development*, *2*(4), 1–18. doi:10.14207/ejsd.2013.v2n2p1

Aliyu, S. U. R., & Elijah, A. O. (2008). *Corruption and Economic Growth in Nigeria: 1986–2007*. MPRA Paper No. 12504. Retrieved from https://mpra.ub.uni-muenchen.de/12504/

Azam, M. (2016). Does governance and foreign capital inflows affect economic development in OIC countries? *Journal of Economic Cooperation and Development*, *37*(4), 21–50.

Boudriga, A., Taktak, N. B., & Jellouli, S. (2009). Banking supervision and nonperforming loans: A cross-country analysis. *Journal of Financial Economic Policy*, *1*(4), 286–318. doi:10.1108/17576380911050043

Deman, S. (2009). *A strategic approach to global financial crises*. Retrieved from https://www.researchgate.net/publication/273448060_A_Strategic_Approach_to_Global_Financial_Crises

Dogarawa, A. B. (2007). Corporate failure: Accounting and auditing resolution. *Journal of Social and Management Sciences*, *12*(December), 120–127.

Evans, O. (2020). Fiscal discipline, financial development & economic growth in Nigeria. In C. I. Nwaogwugwu (Ed.), *Dynamics of Fiscal and Monetary Policies in ECOWAS Countries*. University of Lagos Press.

Financial Times. (2016, May 10). *Three Nigerian bank CEOs questioned in anti-corruption drive*. Retrieved from https://www.ft.com/content/fa964f22-16ae-11e6-9d98-00386a18e39d

Funmi, P. A., Omotayo, F. I., Isaac, O. I., & Olukayode, O. (2018). Bank fraud and its effect on Nigerian economy- a study of selected quoted banks. *European Journal of Accounting. Auditing and Finance Research*, *6*(8), 104–120.

Garba, T., Bello, U., Abdullahi, H., & Abubakar, M. (2016). Institutions, natural resources and economic growth: An application of co-integration with structural break on Nigerian dataset. *Central Bank of Nigeria Economic and Financial Review*, *54*(4), 1–27.

Granger, C. W. J. (1969). Investigating causal relations by econometric models and cross-spectral methods. *Econometrica*, *37*(3), 424–438. doi:10.2307/1912791

Liu, P., Li, H., & Guo, H. (2020). The impact of corruption on firms' access to bank loans: Evidence from China. *Economic Research-Ekonomska Istraživanja*, *33*(1), 1963–1984. doi:10.1080/1331677X.2020.1768427

Mankiw, N. G. (2007). *Macroeconomics*. Worth publishers.

Mathew, R. E., Barnabas, O., Lawal, A. I., & Joseph, I. O. (2013). Analysis of corruption and economic growth in Nigeria. *Afro Asian Journal of Social Sciences*, *4*(4), 1–19.

Mishkin, F. S. (2013). *The Economics of Money, Banking and Financial Markets*. Pearson.

Mukhtar, S., & Abdullahi, S. I. (2020). Do poverty, unemployment and sexual violence explain suicide rate in Nigeria: What the data says. *Journal of Conflict Resolution and Social Issues*, *1*(1), 72–80.

Nakitende, M. G., Rafay, A., & Waseem, M. (2021). Frauds in Business Organizations: A Comprehensive Overview. In A. Rafay (Ed.), *Handbook of Research on Theory and Practice of Financial Crimes* (pp. 21–38). IGI Global., doi:10.4018/978-1-7998-5567-5.ch002

Ndulue, J. (2003). Bank failure: Causes and prevention. *International Journal of Economic and Development Issues*, *3*(1), 162–178.

Orjiude, A. (2021, August 22). Eight banks lose N1.9bn to fraud in one year. *Punch.* Retrieved from https://punchng.com/eight-banks-lose-n1-9bn-to-fraud-in-one-year/

Orjiude, A. (2022, March 31). Four banks lost N1.77bn to fraud in 2021. *Punch.* Retrieved from https://punchng.com/four-banks-lost-n1-77bn-to-fraud-in-2021-says-report/

Pesaran, M. H., & Shin, Y. (1999). An autoregressive distributed lag modelling approach to cointegration analysis. In S. Strøm (Ed.), *Econometrics and Economic Theory in the 20th Century: The Ragnar Frisch Centennial Symposium*. Cambridge University Press. 10.1017/CCOL521633230.011

Pesaran, M. H., Shin, Y., & Smith, R. J. (2001). Bounds testing approaches to the analysis of level relationships. *Journal of Applied Econometrics*, *16*(3), 289–326. doi:10.1002/jae.616

Praoyao, S., & Eugene, K. (2018). Institutions and financial development in African countries: An empirical analysis. *Business. Management and Economics Research*, *4*(5), 43–50.

Sharma, C. (2021). Does corruption sand the wheels of financial sector development? Evidence from global panel data. *Journal of Financial Management. Markets and Institutions*, *9*(2), 1–32.

Shirley, M. (1996). *Bureaucrat in business: the economics and policies of government ownership.* The World Bank. Retrieved from https://documents.worldbank.org /en/publication/documents-reports/documentdetail/867101468780298811/bureaucrats-in-business-the-economics-and-politics-of-government-ownership#:~:text=Bureaucrats%20in%20 business%20%3A%20the%20economics%20and%20politics,also%20assesses%20why%20so%20few%20countries%20are%20reforming

Shuaibu, M., Muhammad, H. M., Abdullahi, S. I., & Gwazawa, U. G. (2021). Impact of public debt on inflation and unemployment in Nigeria: An ARDL vector error correction model. *Noble International Journal of Economics and Financial Research*, *6*(5), 91–98. doi:10.51550/nijefr65.91.98

Siaplay, M. (2020). Rent-seeking in West Africa – How corruption affects economic growth and income inequality. *West African Financial and Economic Review*, *20*(12), 1–24.

Solow, R. (1956). A contribution to the theory of economic growth. *The Quarterly Journal of Economics*, *70*(1), 65–94. doi:10.2307/1884513

Sullivan, R. J. (2010). The changing nature of US card payment fraud: Industry and public policy options. *FRBKC Economic Review*, *95*(2), 101–133.

TI. (2006). *International global corruption report.* Transparency International.

Tukur, S. (2012, September 10). Nigerian banks aid corruption-EFCC. *Premium Times*. Retrieved from https://www.premiumtimesng.com/business/99682-nigerian-banks-aid-corruption-efcc.html

Uddin, A., Chowdhury, M. A. F., & Islam, N. (2017). Do socio-economic factors matter for the financial development of a Muslim country? A study in Bangladesh banking sector. *International Journal of Business and Society*, *18*(1), 59–78.

Yuguda, I. (2012). Effective corporate governance for economic development in Nigeria. *Management in Nigeria*, *48*(1), 6–17.

APPENDIX 1

Summary Statistics

	BF	CI	EG	FD	EQ	GD	IR	IE	PG	PI	PS	TO	UE
Mean	1.709677	122.7419	2.23E+11	0.187742	75.66935	1.038710	19.40355	43.01613	2.577419	1408.774	0.677419	37.17774	4.313226
Median	0.000000	130.0000	1.36E+11	0.190000	77.90000	1.030000	18.18000	43.00000	2.580000	1007.870	1.000000	37.02000	3.760000
Maximum	27.00000	152.0000	5.68E+11	0.270000	130.3700	1.060000	31.65000	51.90000	2.680000	3222.690	1.000000	53.28000	8.390000
Minimum	0.000000	90.00000	4.95E+10	0.120000	33.74000	1.030000	15.14000	35.10000	2.490000	467.8500	0.000000	20.72000	3.540000
Std. Dev.	5.380171	20.45478	1.79E+11	0.039892	33.54967	0.011178	3.562424	5.568908	0.069569	927.6583	0.475191	8.420759	1.447684
Skewness	3.824570	-0.193457	0.486348	-0.071110	0.239375	0.838871	1.563201	0.224820	0.105731	0.434071	-0.759072	-0.008899	2.210175
Kurtosis	17.50943	1.531872	1.655354	2.168569	1.666952	2.208390	5.723523	2.203453	1.536300	1.662745	1.576190	2.565328	6.116259
Jarque-Bera	347.5009	2.977425	3.557523	0.919026	2.591367	4.445221	22.20629	1.080689	2.825047	3.283314	5.595494	0.244456	37.78198
Probability	0.000000	0.225663	0.168847	0.631591	0.273711	0.108326	0.000015	0.582547	0.243528	0.193659	0.060947	0.884947	0.000000
Sum	53.00000	3805.000	6.90E+12	5.820000	2345.750	32.20000	601.5100	1333.500	79.90000	43671.99	21.00000	1152.510	133.7100
Sum Sq. Dev.	868.3871	12551.94	9.62E+23	0.047742	33767.41	0.003748	380.7259	930.3819	0.145194	25816498	6.774194	2127.276	62.87368

Section 2
Fraud in the Financial Sector

Chapter 7
Principles-Based Accounting Standards:
A Slippery Slope to Financial Reporting Fraud

Clement Chiahemba M. Ajekwe
https://orcid.org/0000-0001-9617-6438
Benue State University, Nigeria

ABSTRACT

Principles-based accounting standards (PBS) are imbued with high levels of flexibility that enable any company to apply accounting policies that suit its unique circumstances. The use of PBS necessarily leaves much room for extensive use of the 'ingredients or elements of accounting flexibility' including, estimates, multiple measurement types, and professional judgments to select accounting policies and make decisions around 'materiality'. By invoking these flexibilities, entities can manipulate financial numbers and perpetuate improper acts that significantly impact the fairness of published general-purpose financial statements particularly the financial position and financial performance. This chapter concluded that while flexibility embedded in PBS is inevitable and necessary in financial reporting, its unintended consequence is to facilitate aggressive optimistic or pessimistic (as opposed to neutral) reporting practices. The flexibilities inherently pervasive in PBS can constitute the slippery slope through which fraudulent actions and reporting could be perpetuated.

INTRODUCTION

With the globalisation and internationalisation of financial and capital markets, there has been a need and call for the adoption of a single financial reporting language, i.e., a set of accounting standards, for use worldwide. Relevant literature identifies two main types of accounting standards: principles- and rule-based standards (Agoglia *et al.*, 2011; Cohen *et al.*, 2011; Peytcheva & Wright, 2011; Jamal & Tan, 2010; Segovia *et al.*, 2009). Principles-based standards (PBS) are epitomised by the International

DOI: 10.4018/978-1-6684-5007-9.ch007

Financial Reporting Standards (IFRS) and the generally accepted accounting principles (GAAP) by the USA represent the rules-based standards (RBS). The rule-based standards require strict compliance with specific accounting rules and detailed implementation guidance (Nelson, 2003); hence they (the RBS) may not be readily suitable for worldwide application. The principles-based standards, unlike the RBS, can be adopted and implemented worldwide, in a variety of legal and cultural contexts, by companies that vary considerably in size, ownership structure, capital structure, political jurisdictions, and financial reporting sophistication (Schipper, 2005).

PBS derive from and are consistent with a framework, formally referred to as the *Conceptual Framework for Financial Reporting* (subsequently, *Conceptual Framework, 2018)* issued by the International Accounting Standards Board (IASB), the standard-setting body of the IFRS Foundation that was established in 2001 as an independent, public interest organisation (IFRS, 2018;). As stated in its Mission Statement, the IASB is committed to developing a single set of high-quality, global accounting Standards that provide high-quality, transparent and comparable information in general-purpose financial statements (IASB, 2015).

"Our mission is to develop IFRS that brings transparency, accountability and efficiency to financial markets around the world. Our work serves the public interest by fostering trust, growth and long-term financial stability within the global economy." (IASB, 2015)

As the name suggests, principles-based standards are generic, they only provide principles and are flexible, allowing preparers of financial statements to apply judgment in the recording and reporting of transactions in a manner that provides a faithful representation of the underlying economic consequences of the relevant transactions and events (*Conceptual Framework, 2018*: chapter 2). PBS have the following characteristics:

1. each standard is drafted in clear, concise and plain language, consistent with the objectives set in the overarching, coherent *Conceptual Framework (2018)* that unifies the accounting system as a whole;
2. each standard states its accounting/financial reporting objective(s); financial statement preparers apply their judgment to decide how to fulfil the objective(s) contained in the particular standard that responds to users' needs for clarity and transparency;
3. information from PBS is specifically defined and framed by the substantive objective(s) built into each pertinent standard in a manner that faithfully reflects the economic consequences of transactions, other events and conditions, and not merely their legal form.
4. each standard clearly articulates the class of transactions to which they apply and so preparers have a structure within which to make their judgements in determining the appropriate accounting for the company's transactions (Ajekwe, 2022; Sunder, 2010; PwC, 2008; SEC, 2003; Rooijen, 2002; Herdman, 2002; Parfet, 2000; Brown, Collins & Thornton, 1993).

PBS are supported and adopted worldwide; approximately 120 nations and reporting jurisdictions permit or require IFRS for listed companies and approximately 90 countries have fully conformed to IFRS as promulgated by the IASB and include a statement acknowledging such conformity in audit reports (AICPA, 2022; Khan *et al.*, 2020). It is articulated that how PBS are not a comprehensive code of rigid rules that override the exercise of an informed judgment, emplaning that each reporting accountant must apply his/her professional judgment with integrity to determine whether a company's financial statements are a fair representation of the financial position, performance and cash flows of the reporting economic entity. Moreover, the ability to exercise professional judgment is the hallmark of a professional accountant as well as a key skill for preparers, auditors, and regulators of financial statements (Ajekwe, 2022).

The problem this chapter addresses is the unintended consequences of the high levels of flexibility in PBS. Principles-based standards allow for a lot of flexibility in implementing the principles contained in the various accounting standards. Arising from these flexibilities, entities have the freedom to report the economic consequences of transactions other events and conditions in a manner that reflects the underlying economics of transactions more accurately than under RBS (Fang *et al.*, 2018). However, with the flexibilities PBS allow, particularly in high-tech industries and others that have complex operational practices as exist in the contemporary business environment, PBS can provide levers for managers to engage in intentionally misleading accounting and reporting practices that may escalate over time and become fraudulent. For example, revenue might be inflated; expenses might be decreased or increased within and possibly outside the limits allowed by PBS in order to meet pre-determined desirable profit levels or other thresholds, such as to avoid losing bonus payments or ensuring increases in share prices. In effect, with the flexibility, latitude, and judgmental discretions allowed in PBS, entities may cross the figurative line that divides 'aggressive' but allowable accounting policies and fraudulent unacceptable accounting policies. In other words, the dividing line between the two actions (i.e., engaging in an aggressive but acceptable accounting & fraudulent unacceptable accounting) may become blurred and less clear-cut; more importantly, the line between them only emerges, over time, as the situation deteriorates significantly (ICAEW, 2022; Rafay, 2021).

This chapter contributes to accounting, auditing and corporate governance literature by providing insight into the role of PBS in financial reporting. The chapter acknowledges the role of flexibility, embedded in PBS, as being essential in making good professional judgements. At the same time, the chapter is concerned about the improper use to which the PBS can be applied in facilitating improper accounting and misreporting practices through the slippery slope of the flexibility embedded in the PBS. In other words, the chapter presents PBS (and the flexibility that comes with them) as a "*double-edged sword*"; that can be used to facilitate the application of good professional judgement and as a weapon to execute improper financial actions/reporting.

The rest of the chapter is organised as follows: the next section discusses the concept and role of flexibility in PBS. Section 3 links financial reporting fraud and the concept of a slippery slope. Section 4 accesses how the flexibility embedded in PBS can facilitate financial reporting fraud; section 5 summarises the chapter.

FLEXIBILITY IN PBS-BASED ACCOUNTING

The concept of flexibility in principles-based accounting standards is both robust and compelling. The flexibility affords those who prepare financial statements the flexibility to select accounting policies, including the use of (i) estimates, (ii) multiple measurement types, (iii) professional judgment to recognise or de-recognise accounting elements when preparing and presenting financial statements. In addition, flexibility allows managers to make measurement and presentation decisions around the concept of 'materiality' (Ajekwe, 2021). Flexibility in PBS is compelling and necessary because it provides the mechanism for coping with changing circumstances and variations across companies and industries (Ajekwe, 2017; Mulford & Comiskey, 2002).

Being generic and flexible, PBS are suitable for application in different legal and cultural environments, by companies of various sizes, ownership and capital structures (Rafay, Sadiq & Ajmal, 2016), within different political jurisdictions, and financial reporting sophistication (Schipper, 2005). In addition, PBS permit honest managers, while exercising professional judgment, to appropriately reflect the underlying economic consequences on a firm's performance, financial position, and cash flows. Furthermore, flexibility promotes the use of private knowledge that is peculiar to a specific business firm and its opportunities in selecting accounting policies, reporting methods, estimates, and disclosures that match the firms' business economics, thereby increasing the value of accounting as a form of communication (Ajekwe, 2021). So central is the concept of flexibility in financial reporting under PBS that the *Conceptual Framework* boldly states that 'to a large extent, financial statements that conform to the IFRS are (flexible) based on estimates, judgments, and models rather than exact depictions of reality' (*Conceptual Framework for Financial Reporting*, 2018: Chapter 1: The objectives of general-purpose financial reporting).

By itself, flexibility in accounting should not cause financial misreporting or other improprieties because of the several management control agents and other control mechanisms, including the board of directors, corporate ethics, audit committee oversight, capable internal and external auditing, and public accountability, *etc.*; these control agents and mechanisms should constrain any improper reporting behaviour within organisations (Parfet, 2000). However, instituting these mechanisms will not always function as intended; financial misreporting will not always be stopped. For example, auditing being an imperfect practice (Baglioni & Colombo, 2011) sometimes fails to constrain opportunistic behaviour within an organisation. The management of an entity can sometimes override controls (Tillman & Indergaard, 2007) and "out manoeuvre" auditors through the exploitative exercise of discretions and judgements necessary for implementing PBS-based standards to deceive users, particularly investors and creditors. Managers can weaponize the flexibility embedded in PBS, to play financial number game and create illusions in financial statements (Levitt, 1998; Ramzan *et al.*, 2020) through the 'slippery slope' of improper accounting choices, egregious estimates, and other judgemental indiscretions that do not accurately reflect the underlying economics of the reporting firms. Indeed, there is a genuine concern that companies will exploit the flexibilities allowed in PBS and use them as weapons and opportunities to intentionally misreport the effect of a firm's transactions to be able to report the achievement of pre-determined preferred performance targets and financial position (Palepu *et al.*, 1996; Fields *et al.*, 2001).

SLIPPERY SLOPE TO FINANCIAL REPORTING FRAUD

Apart from the use of improper accounting choices, egregious estimates, judgmental indiscretions, *etc.*, the term 'slippery slope' also refers to a situation in which a relatively insignificant first event leads to a significant event which, in turn, leads to a more significant event and so on until some ultimate, most significant event is reached (Bennett, 2021). In this chapter, the term 'slippery slope' also refers to a situation where 'immaterial' indiscretions in reporting accounting numbers escalate over time into larger violations that materially misstate financial reports, such as where managers make initial insignificant 'earnings management' adjustment(s)[1] that build up over time to eventually represent significant misleading financial numbers. The process by which flexibility in accounting follows a slippery slope to becoming a fraudulent action follows these approximate steps as explained by Senogles and Glowka (2013) and Schrand and Zechman (2012):

1. Management starts off making an "*innocuous accrual*" to plug "*a small gap*" in earnings without any intention to commit fraud; management genuinely believes that selecting a particular accrual policy (which may be characterised as being 'aggressive' but permissible) is in the best interest of everyone involved: management, employees, customers, creditors, and owners – to manage a short-term challenge, so that the firm's stakeholders do not 'misinterpret' the current weak performance as a sign of a future adverse performance.
2. If the desired target performance is not met in spite of the nudging attempts over several reporting periods, more aggressive accounting accruals are deployed to plug the earnings gap.
3. If the target performance is still not met, management may begin to feel that more extreme actions are the only way out of the threatening bad situation (Schrand & Zechman, 2012).
4. Like the proverbial frog being heated slowly in water, accounting numbers are gently 'massaged' and 'nudged' progressively; both management and auditors only realise, after the fact, that the effect of the nudging and massaging actions has crossed the line from aggressive but acceptable earnings management actions to unacceptable fraudulent accounting.
5. Once fraudulent reporting[2] has taken root in the organisation, managers' beliefs about its appropriateness, haven being incubated, nurtured, and socialised into its organisational culture; financial reporting games become as normalised as they escalate without control, as if down a steep slippery slope of fraud (Levitt, 1998; Suh *et al.*, 2020).

Beasley *et al.* (2010) also propose a similar pathway through the tempting slippery slope to fraud which often starts like a 'trickle', i.e., it often starts as a small patch of earnings management and rarely as a conscious plan. It is so small that the perpetrators of the fraudulent behaviour believe they are doing nothing more than legitimately managing the image of the company and/or merely exploring the flexibility allowed in the accounting standards. Over several reporting periods, the small indiscretions begin to take on the semblance of unacceptable behaviour sliding down a steep slippery slope and metamorphizing into fraudulent actions (Young, 2000)

The idea that fraudulent financial reporting under a PBS-based accounting regime follows a slippery slope is due to the continuum pathway overlap that begins with an innocuous 'adjusting accrual', through aggressive accounting and finally into fraud (Ajekwe, 2017, 2021, 2022; Dechow & Skinner, 2000). Managers have the flexibility discretions to select accounting policies: they determine policies for revenue recognition, expected lives of non-current assets, and their salvage values; they account for obligations of post-employment pension benefits and determine the level of credit losses of account receivables, including asset impairments, *etc*. Managers also affect changes to depreciation or inventory valuation methods; they effectively and legitimately influence the financial outcomes of entities. Through these discretionary actions, managers make incremental adjustment(s) to fill perceived performance gap(s). If the perceived gap(s) is/are not bridged within the targeted period, then, the company moves to make estimates or judgments and accruals forcefully and aggressively to the outer limits of allowed flexibilities. At this stage, management actions constitute aggressive accounting. With continued 'pushing of the envelope', a line is crossed when the accounting practices employed move beyond the within-flexibility boundaries. This is usually only known with hindsight. Beyond a point, a line is crossed after which the resulting financial statements are not a fair representation of the subject company's financial results and financial position because of material misstatements, omissions, or improper disclosures. At this stage, if a reader of these financial statements has used them to his or her detriment, and/or the statements are adjudged to be fraudulent by an administrative, civil, or criminal proceeding (such as that of the Securities and Exchange Commission or a court), then the misreporting constitutes fraudulent reporting.

It should be noted that a very thin line separates aggressive accounting, which may be tolerated and fraudulent financial reporting, which is not acceptable. Several reasons/factors have been adduced for this:

1. Both aggressive and fraudulent accounting have the same elements; they are intended to deceive or mislead the users of financial reports. Both are deliberate management actions with the objective of reaping private gains, potentially causing material loss or damage to the users that rely on the false information. Erickson *et al.* (2006) and Dechow and Skinner (2000) explain and indicate that acceptable aggressive accounting as being within the provisions of accounting standards and fraudulent reporting as being outside the provisions of accounting standards.
2. By themselves, accounting policies do not indicate clear limits beyond which a policy might be considered fraudulent. For example, an estimate of expenses may be fraudulent if the estimated amount is extreme, but allowable if it is reasonable and within the spirit of accounting standards (Rosner, 2003). PBS do not tell managers specifically what is normal and what is extreme; managers must use their judgment to determine this. Regulators have stressed that they would go after companies that engaged in "*practices that appear to manage earnings*". Without clearly distinguishing between earnings managed in the ordinary course of business and earnings fraudulently managed in a deliberate attempt to deceive the financial community, it is difficult to determine whether the registrants have infringed the regulations or not. Therefore, in between legitimate, and fraudulent accounting are judgments that push the limits of accounting standards that may result in unacceptable reporting misbehaviour.
3. Aggressive accounting techniques do not necessarily constitute fraudulent action; however, it may be the start of a slippery slope where acceptable earnings management practices slide into unacceptable misreporting.

The International Standards on Auditing (ISA) 240 identifies two types of misstatements caused by fraudulent actions as improper financial reporting and misappropriation of assets. This chapter focuses on fraudulent financial reporting that is often hidden away in estimates and other judgmental techniques/practices that intentionally alter account balances thereby achieving fraudulent outcomes (ICAEW, 2022). Fraudulent financial reporting is usually motivated by dishonesty and personal gain, such as the quest to protect bonuses; alternatively, it may originate from organisational pressure to meet financial targets and the fear that missing these targets will be unforgivable. Financial reporting fraud is usually orchestrated by the top echelons of the firm who often put inordinate pressure on subordinates to achieve results that are impossible without resorting to extreme 'financial engineering' actions. Subordinates may not initially realise that they are a party to the commission of fraud; rather, they see themselves as simply doing what is expected of them to 'make their numbers' or responding to the directives of their superior(s) as is expected of them.

PRINCIPLES-BASED STANDARDS AND FINANCIAL REPORTING FRAUD[3]

Managers can influence accounting numbers through the use of the flexibility available in PBS. While preparing financial statements, accountants are permitted, indeed, mandated to use estimates, professional judgements, multiple measurement types, and to recognise and/or de-recognise elements of accounting as well as to adopt accounting policies and to make decisions around the concept of materiality. These five actions constitute the 'ingredients or elements of flexibility in accounting' and are discussed *ad seriatim:*

Estimates

Estimates are the reported amounts of assets and liabilities and related revenues and expenses in any period where such amounts cannot be measured with precision and certainty. Apart from cash in local currency, almost all assets and liability amounts recognised in financial statements today reflect some estimates of the future (Barth, 2006); it can be said, therefore, that financial statements are a collection of estimates. However, making estimates implies a certain level of subjectivity; two different estimates for an item can result in presenting different accounting pictures regarding the financial position and performance of a company (Sacer *et al.*, 2016; Ajekwe, 2021, 2022). It is obvious therefore that, estimates have a significant effect on the carrying amounts of assets, liabilities, and related revenues and expenses. Indeed, as the level of complexity and subjectivity of judgments around estimates increases, not only the inherent level of precision in the financial statements decreases but there is also the likelihood that materially different amounts would be reported under different conditions or using different assumptions. Financial statements can, therefore, be distorted and manipulated through the use of accounting estimates to inflate, deflate or smooth the reported financial performance of an entity.

If accounting estimates can be used to distort or manipulate financial statements, then the number of estimates permitted or mandated in PBS that guide or determine the preparation of financial statements is important.

Almost all accounting standards allow or mandate the use of estimates; when an electronic keyword search for the word 'estimate' (and its derivatives: 'estimated', 'estimating', & 'estimation(s)') is conducted on a digital copy of the IFRS issued by IASB, over a thousand 'hits' are obtained. Regarding the definition and nature of 'estimates', (i) IAS 8: *Accounting Policies, Changes in Accounting Estimates and Errors* defines accounting estimates as "*monetary amounts in financial statements that are subject to measurement uncertainty*"; (ii) the International Standards on Auditing (ISA) 540 (paragraphs 2–4) explain that an accounting estimate is "*an approximation of the amount of an item in the absence of a precise means of measurement*". ISA 540 further explains:

- The nature and reliability of information available to management to support the making of an accounting estimate vary widely, affecting the associated degree of estimation uncertainty which, in turn, affects the risks of material misstatement of the estimates, including their susceptibility to unintentional or intentional management bias (a euphemism for intentional distortion).
- Typical examples of situations where accounting estimates, other than fair value accounting estimates, may be required include: (i) Allowance for doubtful account receivables (IFRS 9); (ii) Inventory obsolescence (IAS 2); (iii) Warranty obligations (IFRS 15); (iv) The method of depreciation or asset useful life (IAS 16); (v) Provision against the carrying amount of an investment where there is uncertainty regarding its recoverability (IAS 36). Other situations include (vi)

Outcomes of long-term contracts (IFRS 15), (vii) Costs arising from litigation settlements and judgments (IAS 37), *etc.*

Because accounting estimates provide relevant information in financial statements for users to base their economic decisions; it follows, therefore, that the large number of estimates found in PBS (such as the IFRS) creates opportunities for making a lot of accounting estimates in financial statements. Considering the nature of accounting estimates, there is a veritable risk that estimates can be used to intentionally distort and manipulate accounting numbers reported in financial statements.

Professional Judgment

The process of preparing a company's financial statements is essentially interpretive, i.e., a translation of economic reality into an accounting framework as defined by a set of standards (SEC, 2003). This interpretive process necessarily involves judgment. By changing the focus of professional judgment to the objectives of the accounting standard, PBS allow accounting professionals to operationalise accounting treatments in a manner that best fulfil the objective of each standard, thereby best capturing the underlying economic reality. Thus, PBS provide management with the latitude to exercise professional judgment in determining the most appropriate accounting and disclosure choices for a particular transaction (Sunder, 2010; Rooijen, 2002; Herdman, 2002; Parfet, 2000; Brown *et al.*, 1992).

Professional judgment refers to the appropriate level of discretion the accounting professional exercises in applying accounting standard(s) to specific situations based on his/her accumulated knowledge, experience, objectivity, and the relevant facts and circumstances within the stated accounting objective(s) of the applicable accounting standard(s). Professional judgment is a combination of relevant knowledge, experience, objectivity, and integrity in choosing between accounting alternatives (Cormier & Magnan, 2005; Gibbins & Mason, 1988). Judgments occur in a setting of uncertainty, in complex or novel transactions and/or risk and could, therefore, differ between knowledgeable, experienced, and objective persons. Such differences do not, in themselves, suggest that one judgment is wrong and the other is correct. Consequently, two financial statements prepared by different accountants could reach different conclusions and report differently on similar circumstances (Wüstemann & Wüstemann, 2010). The differences may arise because of (i) judgments made in the selection of accounting policies among options offered by the relevant standard(s), and (ii) differences in other management judgements exercised. As noted by Roberts *et al.* (2008), whenever accounting standards permit more than one alternative treatment for the same event, different individuals and different companies are likely to produce different figures that would not necessarily suggest that one is correct and the other is wrong or that one is fraudulent and the other is not. Because PBS require extensive use of professional judgments is evident from IAS 1: *Presentation of Financial Statements* (paragraph 123) which indicates examples of situations requiring the use of professional judgment:

1. Whether substantially all the significant risks and rewards of ownership of assets are transferred;
2. Whether, in substance, particular sales of goods are financing arrangements and thus do not give rise to revenue;
3. Whether to consolidate an investee company;
4. Whether a company is acting as principal or agent;

5. Whether the terms of a financial asset give rise to cash flows that are solely payments of principal and interest on the principal loan amount outstanding.

Other situations mentioned in other accounting standards where professional judgment is exercisable depending on the circumstances, so long as it is disclosed and explained, include:

1. Changing the depreciation method from an accelerated method to a more conservative straight-line method and vice versa (IAS 16; IAS 40);
2. Reviewing the useful lives or the estimates of the salvage value of assets (IAS 16);
3. Determining whether/when assets have become impaired, and are required to be reserved against or written off (IAS 36; IAS: 16; IFRS 9);
4. Determining the appropriate allowance required for credit losses (uncollectable accounts receivables) (IFRS 7);
5. Choosing an appropriate method of inventory valuation (FIFO, AVCO, or specific identification (IAS 2);
6. Determining whether a decline in the market value of an investment is temporary, or permanent (IAS 28; IAS 40; IFRS 9),
7. Estimating the write-downs required for investments (IAS 28), and
8. Reporting interests of a company in other entities as well as the effects of those interests on the financial position, financial performance, and cash flows of the reporting entity (IFRS 12).

In situations such as these, management can hide under the auspices of professional judgment requirements to take decisions that materially alter account balances, especially where there is an urgency to meet pre-determined performance targets. Yielding to pressure to meet pre-determined targets and using improper or intentionally flawed judgment clearly distorts financial statements and works against the interests of financial statement users.

Measurements

The *Conceptual Framework* (2018, chapter 6) mandates flexibility of measurement in financial reports. Revaluation of intangible assets, property, plant, and equipment (PPE), investment property, and inventories in certain industries is allowed (ICAEW, 2006; Rafay, Yasser & Khalid, 2019). IFRS also requires the measurement at the fair value of certain categories of financial instruments and biological assets. In particular, the IASB's principles of measurement in accounting are:

1. The objective of measurement is to contribute to the faithful representation of relevant information about:
   (i) The resources of an entity, claims against the entity, and changes in resources and claims; and
   (ii) How efficiently and effectively an entity's management and governing board have discharged their responsibilities in the use of the entity's resources.
2. A single measurement basis for all assets and liabilities may not provide the most relevant information for users of financial statements.

3. When selecting which measurement to use for a particular item, the IASB urges preparers to consider what information that measurement will produce in the statement of financial position and the income statement and other comprehensive income.
4. The relevance of a particular measurement will depend on how investors, creditors, and other lenders are likely to assess how an asset or a liability of that type will contribute to future cash flows. Consequently, the selection of measurement for a particular asset should depend on how that asset contributes to future cash flows, and for a particular liability, should depend on how the entity will settle or fulfil that liability.
5. The number of different measurements used should be the smallest number necessary to provide relevant information. Unnecessary measurement changes should be avoided, and necessary measurement changes should be explained.
6. The benefits of a particular measurement to users of financial statements need to be sufficient to justify the cost.

The IASB's *Conceptual Framework for Financial Reporting (2018, Chapter 6)* mandates **historical costs** and **current values** as the bases that should be employed to measure assets and liabilities and the related income and expenses in financial statements, as follows:

Historical Cost

Measure provides monetary information about assets, liabilities, and related income and expense, using information derived, at least in part, from the price of the transaction or other event that gave rise to them. The historical cost of assets and liabilities are updated over time.

1. in the case of an asset, by depreciation or amortisation, payments received that extinguish part or the entire asset, impairments and accrual of interest to reflect any financing component of the asset;
2. in the case of a liability, by fulfilment of part or all the liability, extending the liability and accrual of interest to reflect any financing component of the liability.
3. in the case of financial assets or financial liabilities, by subsequent changes, such as the accrual of interest, the impairment of a financial asset and receipts or payments

Current Value

Measures provide monetary information about assets, liabilities and related income and expense, using information updated to reflect conditions at the measurement date. Because of the updated current values of assets and liabilities reflect changes since the previous measurement date, in estimates of cash flows and other factors reflected in those current values. Current value measurement bases are three, being: (a) **Fair value,** (b) **Value in use** for assets/ **fulfilment value** for liabilities, and (c) **Current cost**. Current value measurement bases are explained as follows:

Fair Value

The price that would be received to sell an asset, or paid to transfer a liability, in an orderly transaction between market participants at the measurement date. Fair value reflects the perspective of market participants—participants in a market to which the entity has access. The asset or liability is measured using the same assumptions that market participants would use when pricing the asset or liability if those market participants act in their economic best interest.

Value in Use and Fulfilment Value

Value in use is the present value of the cash flows or other economic benefits that an entity expects to derive from the use of an asset and from its ultimate disposal. Fulfilment value is the present value of the cash, or other economic resources, that an entity expects to be obliged to transfer as it fulfils a liability. Those amounts of cash or other economic resources include not only the amounts to be transferred to the liability counterparty but also the amounts that the entity expects to be obliged to transfer to other parties to enable it to fulfil the liability.

Value in use and fulfilment value cannot be observed directly and must be determined using future cash-flow techniques; they do not include transaction costs incurred on acquiring an asset or taking on a liability. However, value in use and fulfilment value include the present value of any transaction costs an entity expects to incur on the ultimate disposal of the asset or on fulfilling the liability. Value in use and fulfilment value reflect entity-specific assumptions rather than assumptions by market participants as the case with fair value measurement. In practice, there may sometimes be little difference between the assumptions that market participants would use and those that an entity itself uses.

Current Cost

Current cost of an asset is the cost of an equivalent asset at the measurement date, comprising the consideration that would be paid at the measurement date plus the transaction costs that would be incurred at that date. The current cost of a liability is the consideration that would be received for an equivalent liability at the measurement date minus the transaction costs that would be incurred at that date. Current cost, like historical cost, is an entry value: it reflects prices in the market in which the entity would acquire the asset or would incur the liability. Hence, it is different from fair value, value in use and fulfilment value, which are exit values. However, unlike historical cost, current cost reflects conditions at the measurement date.

In some cases, current cost cannot be determined directly by observing prices in an active market and must be determined indirectly by other means. For example, if prices are available only for new assets, the current cost of a used asset might need to be estimated by adjusting the current price of a new asset to reflect the current age and condition of the asset held by the entity.

It should be apparent that financial reporting attempts to use different measurement types to measure inherently abstract and debatable concepts such as income, and net assets; and it has particular features that make it, to some extent, inevitably subjective, and even arbitrary. It is worth noting that differences in measurement bases do not result from differences specified in the *Conceptual Framework*. Rather, they result from conventions and differences in practice that have evolved over time. When viewed in terms of the *Conceptual Framework,* therefore, these differences cause financial statements to be internally inconsistent. Not only is the use of multiple measurement types conceptually unappealing but it also creates difficulties for financial statement users. Measuring financial statement amounts in different ways complicates the interpretation of accounting summary amounts such as the income and the financial position statements (Barth, 2006).

Therefore, under existing requirements, the amount presented as total net assets has little meaning because it is an aggregation of items measured using different measurement types. Not only are the measurement requirements varied, but they can also be equally confusing to the extent that within an entity's accounts, the same elements may be measured differently. For example:

1. Plant and equipment may be measured on different bases (i.e., on a historical cost model or current value model);
2. Non-current assets are valued at different bases (e.g., plant and equipment can be measured at historical cost or at current cost; biological assets must be carried at fair value);
3. Liabilities are measured on different bases (e.g., pension scheme assets must be discounted, deferred tax liabilities must not (Rafay & Ajmal, 2014);
4. Fair value can be measured in different ways (determined directly by observing prices in an active market; sometimes, determined indirectly using other measurement techniques, e.g., cash-flow-based measurement techniques); and
5. The effects of inflation are treated in different ways (sometimes reflecting the changing value of money, sometimes not).

It should be apparent that measurement types in financial reporting are not something to which there are immutably right and wrong answers and therefore, may constitute avenues and opportunities for managers, who have cause to do so, to massage accounting numbers, to play the financial numbers game with measurement types; to create illusions regarding reported accounting numbers and to render the resultant financial statements misleading and open to fraudulent reporting.

Accounting Policy Choices

An accounting policy is a specific rule or principle that an entity has chosen to apply to the transaction(s), other events, or conditions when preparing and presenting financial statements. It encompasses everything, from the recognition and measurement of assets and liabilities to presentation and disclosures in financial statements. Managers are required to fully disclose their accounting policies so that users can better interpret a company's financial statements. PBS requirements for accounting policies are that:

6. Where an IFRS specifically applies to a transaction, other event, or condition, the accounting policy applied to that item is determined by applying that standard and selecting accounting policy choice(s) alternatives/elections in IFRS[4] adjudged to be the most appropriate among the options offered in that Standard (IAS 8:7)
7. In the absence of an IFRS that specifically applies to a transaction, other event, or condition, preparers of financial statements are entitled to use their judgments in developing and applying an accounting policy that results in relevant and reliable information (IAS 8: 10–11). In making that judgement, preparers refer to and consider the applicability of, in descending order: (a) the requirements in IFRS dealing with similar and related issues; and (b) the definitions, recognition/de-recognition criteria and measurement concepts for assets, liabilities, income, and expenses in the *Conceptual Framework*.
8. Preparers of financial statements may also refer to the definitions, recognition criteria or measurement concepts in the *Conceptual Framework* if both: (a) no IFRS specifically applies to a transaction,

other event or condition; and (b) no IFRS deals with similar and related issues. In such situations, preparers of financial statements might refer to the requirements in an IFRS for some issues and to concepts in the *Conceptual Framework* for other issues, including consideration of the most recent pronouncements of IASB, other judgments by other standard-setting bodies, such as the USA-based Financial Accounting Standards Board (FASB), recognised literature and accepted industry practices. Management may consider these and other sources to the extent they do not conflict with the *Conceptual Framework* or with the requirements in IFRS dealing with similar and related issues (IAS 8:12).

Thus, managers have a lot of latitude in making accounting policy choices under the PBS. It is possible, in the light of these provisions, for management to select those accounting principles which benefit management the most, but which may be to the detriment of the other users of financial statements. For example, a company that is likely to miss its performance target but is optimistic about future performance may select aggressive accounting policies so as to meet the current year's performance target. In general, the adoption of aggressive accounting policies, while enabling the reporting of better performance, i.e., higher profits in earlier years, tend to reverse and report lower performance in later years. If a firm's performance actually declines in subsequent periods, the aggressive accounting policies adopted earlier will naturally escalate the reversal of the high performance that had been reported in earlier years. Under this scenario, management will have no other alternative to extricate itself from the threatening self-inflicted predicament than to intentionally manipulate accounting policies to falsely paint an improved financial picture, or conversely, mask a deteriorating financial picture of performance in the latter year(s). Hence, under these circumstances, PBS becomes a weapon that facilitates the preparation of distorted, misleading, non-transparent, and unreliable financial reports.

Materiality

The concept of materiality is of crucial importance in the preparation and presentation of financial statements. It impacts many decisions, such as how an entity should recognise or de-recognise, measure, and disclose specific transactions and information in the financial statements; whether misstatements require correction, and whether assets and liabilities or items of income or expense should be presented separately. Reflecting on its importance to the financial reporting process, the IFRS makes several references to the application of materiality with emphasis on whether an item 'could influence the economic decisions that users make' (IAS 1:7).

Accounting regulations apply different rules, approaches and requirements for material and immaterial items. For example, IAS 8: *Accounting Policies, Changes in Accounting Estimates and Errors* requires that accounting policies specified by the IFRS need not be applied when the effect of applying them is immaterial. Similarly, IAS 37: *Provisions, Contingent Liabilities and Contingent Assets* only require material contingent assets and liabilities to be disclosed.

Levitt (1998) supports the invocation of materiality in helping to build flexibility in financial reporting but observes that materiality is often abused to falsify earnings performance to pre-determined desirable levels. Flexibility relating to materiality is based on the idea that some items may be so insignificant that they are not worth measuring with exact precision. Indeed, the enforcement goal of financial reporting by regulators is to promote transparent, timely, and reliable financial statements. Financial statements of a company need not, and as a practical matter, cannot be perfectly accurate down to the last penny

(Brennan & Gray, 2005). The p reparation of financial statements, being a complex process, requires the exercise of professional judgment, the use of estimates, *etc.* In recognition of this fact, financial reporting regulators do not mandate perfection in financial reporting; rather, they require that financial statements be accurate in 'all material respects' (IAS 1). Materiality recognises that some discrepancies are so minor, that they have no reporting significance.

Companies are known to abuse this flexibility built into financial reporting by intentionally not recording 'small amounts' within a defined percentage ceiling; auditors are persuaded not to scrutinise such 'small amounts' because they are immaterial. Management will excuse these errors by arguing that their effect on the bottom line is so small as not to matter. These 'small errors' build up and can mislead the stock market and other stakeholders. The quote below from the November 9, 2001, edition of *The New York Times* in relation to the Enron audit illustrates this point:

"The remainder of the earnings reductions of $92 million from 1997 through 2000 came from what Enron called 'prior year proposed audit adjustment and reclassifications,' which appear to have been previously recommended by Arthur Andersen, Enron's auditors, but not made because the auditors were persuaded the amounts were immaterial." (Oppel & Sorkin, 2001).

Invariably, the items disclosed in financial statements are often determined by their materiality. Thus, the content of financial statements is, in part, a result of judgments exercised around materiality. Therefore, materiality could be used as an avenue to record small and intentional misstatements in the financial statements; the cumulative effect of the 'small misstatements' would be to tilt to fraudulent reporting, misleading users of financial statements.

SUMMARY

Flexibility gives PBS its importance and suitability for application in different legal and cultural contexts, by companies of various sizes, with various ownership and capital structures (Nosheen *et al.*, 2016) in different political jurisdictions and financial reporting sophistication. Flexibility enables any company to apply, adopt or adapt accounting policies and methods that suit the company's unique circumstances and that communicate useful information to financial statement users for making economic decisions. Without flexibility, it would be imperative to have in place a 'rulebook' that would be so incredibly detailed to capture all possible conceivable transactions and scenarios in companies this would be too cumbersome to be of any value. PBS provide generic guidance and give reporting accountants the flexibility to present reports that are in sync with the firm's economics. By its nature, flexibility enables managers to use estimates, professional judgments and to take discretionary decisions around materiality. These are subjectivities that require assumptions about matters that are highly uncertain, and which can vary widely to the extent that a slight change in the assumptions and any of the flexibility elements could have a large impact on reported financial outcomes. This situation prompts regulators to require companies to disclose their critical accounting judgments and major sources of estimation uncertainties that significantly impact financial results in published financial statements (Ajekwe & Ibiamke, 2019).

On the other hand, the amount of flexibility available in PBS can provide levers for managers to engage in aggressively optimistic accounting and reporting practices which may, with time, go beyond acceptable limits and slide into the realm of fraud. There is veritable concern that the flexibility, latitude and discretions embedded in PBS could constitute a slippery slope for incrementally desperate earnings management accruals, improper accounting choices, egregious estimates and judgmental indiscretions that do not accurately reflect the firms' underlying economics. In particular, PBS can provide the levers with which (i) financial illusions could be created, (ii) games could be played with financial numbers, (iii) financial statements could be distorted intentionally, and (iv) a false picture of a company's financial performance and financial position could be painted.

DECLARATION

The author declares that the manuscript follows ethical standards and there are no potential conflicts of interest with respect to the research, authorship and/or publication of this chapter.

DISCLAIMER

The contents and views of this chapter are expressed by the author in his personal capacity. It is not necessary for the Editor and the Publisher to agree with these viewpoints, and they are not responsible for any duty of care in this regard.

ACKNOWLEDGMENT

The author extends sincere gratitude to

- The Editor and the International Editorial Advisory Board (IEAB) of this book who initially desk reviewed, arranged a rigorous double/triple blind review process, and conducted a thorough, minute, and critical final review before accepting the chapter for publication.
- All anonymous reviewers who provided very constructive feedbacks for thorough revision, improvement, extension, and fine tuning of the chapter.
- All colleagues, assistants and well-wishers who assisted to complete this task.

REFERENCES

Agoglia, C. P., Doupnik, T. P. S., & Tsakumis, G. T. (2011). Principles-based versus rules-based accounting standards: The influence of standard precision and audit committee strength on financial reporting decisions. *The Accounting Review*, *86*(3), 747–767. doi:10.2308/accr.00000045

AICPA. (2022). *Updates*. Retrieved from https://www.ifrs.com/updates/aicpa/ifrs_faq.html#q3

AjekweC. (2017). Accounting Flexibility: Slippery Slope to Fraud? Retrieved from https://ssrn.com/abstract=2972726 doi:10.2139/ssrn.2972726

Ajekwe, C. (2021). Impact of Flexibility in Accounting on Financial Reporting. *European Journal of Accounting, Auditing and Finance Research*, *9*(3), 74–87.

Ajekwe, C. (2022). Application of professional judgement in international financial reporting standard. *European Journal of Accounting, Auditing and Finance Research, 10*(7), 17–30.

Ajekwe, C., & Ibiamke, A. (2019). Disclosure of critical accounting judgments and key sources of estimation uncertainty in the financial statements of companies in Nigeria. *Journal of Finance and Accounting, 7*(1), 22–31. doi:10.11648/j.jfa.20190701.14

Baglioni, A., & Colombo, L. (2011). The effects of imperfect auditing on managerial compensation. *International Review of Economics & Finance, 20*(4), 542–548. doi:10.1016/j.iref.2010.10.001

Barth, M. E. (2006). Including estimates of future in today's financial statements. *Accounting Horizons, 20*(3), 271–285. doi:10.2308/acch.2006.20.3.271

Beasley, M. S., Hermanson, D. R., Carcello, J. V., & Neal, T. L. (2010). Fraudulent Financial Reporting: 1997–2007: An analysis of U.S. public companies. *Association Sections, Divisions, Boards, Teams*, 453. Retrieved from https://egrove.olemiss.edu/cgi/viewcontent.cgi?article=1534&context=aicpa_assoc

Bennett, B. (2021). *Logically fallacious: The ultimate collection of over 300 logical fallacies*. Archieboy Holdings, LLC.

Brennan, N., & Gray, S. J. (2005). The impact of materiality: Accounting's best kept secret. *Asian Academy of Management Journal of Accounting and Finance, 1*, 1–31.

Brown, G., Collins, R., & Thornton, D. (1993). Professional Judgment and Accounting Standards. *Accounting, Organizations and Society, 8*(4), 275–289. doi:10.1016/0361-3682(93)90017-Z

Cohen, J. R., Krishnamoorthy, G., Peytcheva, M., & Wright, A. M. (2011). *The impact of regulatory enforcement and principles-based accounting on auditors' judgments to curb aggressive reporting* (Working paper). Boston College, Northeastern University, and Lehigh University.

Cormier, D., & Magnan, M. L. (2005). From accounting to 'forecounting'. *Canadian Accounting Perspectives, 4*(2), 243–255. doi:10.1506/4CDJ-M98H-FH0Q-KQ1M

Dechow, P. M., & Skinner, D. J. (2000). Earnings management: Reconciling the views of accounting academics, practitioners, and regulators. *Accounting Horizons, 14*(2), 235–250. doi:10.2308/acch.2000.14.2.235

Erickson, M., Hanlon, M., & Maydew, E. (2006). Is there a link between executive equity incentives and accounting fraud? *Journal of Accounting Research, 44*(1), 113–143. doi:10.1111/j.1475-679X.2006.00194.x

Fang, L., Pittman, J., Zhang, Y., & Zhao, Y. (2018). *Accounting standard precision, corporate governance, and accounting restatements*. Retrieved from https://www.fox.temple.edu/wp-content/uploads/2018/01/Zhang-Yinqi-Accounting-Standard-Precision-Corporate-Governance-and-Accounting-Restatements.pdf

Fields, T. D., Lys, T. Z., & Vincent, L. (2001). Empirical research on accounting choice. *Journal of Accounting and Economics, 31*(1-3), 255–307. doi:10.1016/S0165-4101(01)00028-3

Gibbins, M., & Mason, A.K. (1988). *Professional judgment in financial reporting*. CICA Research Study.

Herdman, R. (2002). *Critical accounting and critical disclosures.* Speech by SEC Chief Accountant at Financial Executives International — San Diego on January 24, 2002. Retrieved from https://www.sec.gov/news/speech/spch537.htm

IASB. (2015). *IFRS Mission Statement*. International Accounting Standard Board. Retrieved from https://www.ifrs.org/content/dam/ifrs/about-us/our-history/2015-mission-statement.pdf?la=en

ICAEW. (2006). *Measurement in Financial Reporting*. The Institute of Chartered Accountants in England & Wales. Retrieved from www.icaew.co.uk/bettermarkets

ICAEW. (2022). *Fraudulent financial reporting: Fresh thinking.* The Institute of Chartered Accountants of England and Wales. Retrieved from https://www.icaew.com/technical/thought-leadership/full-collection/audit-and-assurance-thought-leadership/fraudulent-financial-reporting-fresh-thinking#:~:text=Fraudulent%20financial%20reporting%3A%20fresh%20thinking%20In%20this%20essay%2C,maximise%20the%20likelihood%20of%20identifying%20fraudulent%20financial%20reporting

IFRS. (2018). *Conceptual Framework for Financial Reporting 2018*. IFRS Foundation. Retrieved from https://www.ifrs.org/

Jamal, K., & Tan, H. (2010). Joint effects of principles-based versus rules-based standards and auditor type in constraining financial managers' aggressive reporting. *The Accounting Review*, *85*(4), 1325–1346. doi:10.2308/accr.2010.85.4.1325

Khan, N., Rafay, A., & Shakeel, A. (2020). Attributes of Internal Audit and Prevention, Detection and Assessment of Fraud in Pakistan. *Lahore Journal of Business*, *9*(1), 33–58. doi:10.35536/ljb.2020.v9.i1.a2

Levitt, A. (1998). *The 'numbers game'*. Speech delivered at New York University Law and Business Centre. Retrieved from http://www.sec.gov

Mulford, C. W., & Comiskey, E. E. (2002). *The financial numbers game: detecting creative accounting practices*. John Wiley and Sons Inc.

Nelson, M. W. (2003). Behavioural evidence on the effect of principles- and rules-based standards. *Accounting Horizons*, *17*(1), 91–104. doi:10.2308/acch.2003.17.1.91

Nosheen, S., Sadiq, R., & Rafay, A. (2016). The Primacy of Innovation in Strategic Financial Management-Understanding the Impact of Innovation and Performance on Capital Structure. *Proceedings of the 2016 IEEE International Conference on Management of Innovation and Technology (ICMIT)*. 10.1109/ICMIT.2016.7605048

Oppel, R. A., & Sorkin, A. R. (2001, November 9). Enron admits to overstating profits by about $ 600 million. *The New York Times*. Retrieved from https://www.nytimes.com/2001/11/09/business/enron-admits-to-overstating-profits-by-about-600-million.html

Palepu, K. G., Bernard, V. L., & Healy, P. M. (1996). *Business analysis and valuation using financial statements*. South-Western Publishing Company.

Parfet, W. (2000). Accounting subjectivity and earnings management: A preparer's perspective. *Accounting Horizons, 14*(4), 481–488. doi:10.2308/acch.2000.14.4.481

Peytcheva, M., & Wright, A. M. (2011). *The impact of principles versus rules-based accounting standards on auditor's process accountability, epistemic motivation, and reporting decisions* (Working Paper). Lehigh University and North-Eastern University.

PwC. (2008). *Principles-based Accounting Standards*. PriceWaterhouseCoopers. Retrieved from https://pwc.blogs.com/corporatereporting/files/principlesbased_accounting_standards.pdf

Rafay, A. (Ed.). (2021). *Handbook of Research on Theory and Practice of Financial Crimes*. IGI Global. doi:10.4018/978-1-7998-5567-5

Rafay, A., & Ajmal, M. M. (2014). Earnings Management through Deferred Taxes Recognized under IAS 12: Evidence from Pakistan. *Lahore Journal of Business, 3*(1), 1–19. doi:10.35536/ljb.2014.v3.i1.a1

Rafay, A., Sadiq, R., & Ajmal, M. M. (2016). The Effect of IAS-24 Disclosures on Governance Mechanisms and Ownership Structures in Pakistan. *Lahore Journal of Business, 5*(1), 15–36. doi:10.35536/ljb.2016.v5.i1.a2

Rafay, A., Yasser, F., & Khalid, Z. (2019). Revaluation of Non-Current Assets under IAS-16: Possibility of any Managerial inducement - Evidence from a South Asian Economy. *DLSU Business and Economics Review, 29*(1), 93–105.

Ramzan, M., Ahmad, I., & Rafay, A. (2020). Is Auditor independence influenced by Non-audit services? A stakeholder's viewpoint. *Pakistan Journal of Commerce and Social Sciences, 14*(1), 388–408.

Roberts, C., Weetman, P., & Gordon, P. (2008). *International corporate reporting: A comparative approach* (4th ed.). Pearson Education Limited.

Rooijen, J. G. van. (2002). *Flexibility in financial accounting income strategies and earnings management in the Netherlands*. Retrieved from http://hdl.handle.net/11245/1.209698

Rosner, R. (2003). Earnings manipulation in failing firms. *Contemporary Accounting Research, 20*(2), 361–408. doi:10.1506/8EVN-9KRB-3AE4-EE81

Sacer, I. M., Malis, S. S., & Pavic, I. (2016). The Impact of accounting estimates on financial position and business performance–case of non-current intangible and tangible assets. *Procedia Economics and Finance, 39*, 399–411. doi:10.1016/S2212-5671(16)30341-0

Schipper, K. (2005). The introduction of international accounting standards in Europe: Implications for international convergence. *European Accounting Review, 14*(1), 101–126. doi:10.1080/0963818042000338013

Schrand, C. M., & Zechman, S. C. (2012). Executive overconfidence and the slippery slope to financial misreporting. *Journal of Accounting and Economics, 53*(1–2), 311–329. doi:10.1016/j.jacceco.2011.09.001

SEC. (2003). *Study Pursuant to Section 108(d) of the Sarbanes-Oxley Act of 2002 on the Adoption by the United States Financial Reporting System of a Principles-Based Accounting System*. Securities and Exchange Commission. Retrieved from https://www.sec.gov/news/studies/principlesbasedstand.htm

Segovia, J., Arnold, V., & Sutton, S. G. (2009). Do principles- vs. rules-based standards have a differential impact on U.S. auditors' decisions? *Advances in Accounting Behavioural Research, 12, 61–84.* doi:10.1108/S1475-1488(2009)0000012006

Senogles, G., & Glowka, M. (2013). *Aggressive accounting versus fraudulent accounting*. Retrieved from https://www.financierworldwide.com/aggressive-accounting-vs-fraudulent-accounting/

Suh, I., Sweeney, J. T., Linke, K., & Wall, J. M. (2020). Boiling the Frog Slowly: The Immersion of C-Suite Financial Executives into Fraud. *Journal of Business Ethics*, *162*(3), 645–673. doi:10.100710551-018-3982-3

Sunder, S. (2010). Adverse effects of uniform written reporting standards on accounting practice, education, and research. *Journal of Accounting and Public Policy*, *29*(2), 99–114. doi:10.1016/j.jaccpubpol.2009.10.011

Tillman, R., & Indergaard, M. (2007). *Control Overrides in Financial Statement Fraud: A Report to the Institute for Fraud Prevention.* Retrieved from https://www.researchgate.net/profile/Robert-Tillman-2/publication/241868976

Wüstemann, J., & Wüstemann, S. (2010). Why consistency of accounting standards matters: A contribution to the rules-versus-principles debate in financial reporting. *Abacus*, *46*(1), 1–27. doi:10.1111/j.1467-6281.2010.00304.x

Young, M. R. (2000). *Accounting irregularities and financial fraud.* Harcourt Inc.

ENDNOTES

1. Most financial statement fraud schemes start with 'earnings management' or other 'accrual' techniques that do not involve outright violations of accounting standards. The techniques may involve, for example, the choice of aggressive accounting policies that ensure attainment of targets without being fraudulent. Often, earnings management entails 'cookie jar accounting' that 'stores' profits during good years and 'releases' the stored profits' in not so good years (Mulford & Comiskey, 2002)
2. Technically, it must be shown that a reader of financial statements that contain material misstatements has used those statements to his or her detriment, moreover, accounting practices are not held to be fraudulent until so adjudged by an administrative, civil or criminal proceeding such as the Securities and Exchange Commission or a court (Mulford & Comiskey, 2002)
3. This section draws extensively from *The Conceptual Framework for Financial Reporting* (2018) and the identified IASB standards (i.e., IFRS/1AS)
4. A discussion of the various accounting policy choices / elections available in IFRS and considerations of the bases on which those choices can be exercised is outside the scope of this chapter.

Chapter 8
Impression Management in Accounting:
Evolution and Trends

Fábio Albuquerque
https://orcid.org/0000-0001-8877-9634
Instituto Politécnico de Lisboa, Portugal

Vinícius Stoltzemburg
Instituto Politécnico de Lisboa, Portugal

António Cariano
https://orcid.org/0000-0003-2469-4126
Instituto Politécnico de Lisboa, Portugal

ABSTRACT

Several ways or tactics can be used by entities to manage disclosed information, undermining its transparency and mitigating its credibility. Even though accounting literature has covered a wide range of IM strategies and investigation lines since the seminal research from the last decade of the 20th century, this chapter demonstrates that IM remains relevant since it can be assessed and adapted from the perspective of trending accounting topics. A textual analysis tool is complementary used to assess papers gathered from the Scopus database by 27th August 2022. Based on the findings, seminal papers were mainly concerned with analyzing the graphs and messages reported to manipulate or obfuscate the information provided to stakeholders. Papers were initially focused on mandatory (financial) information but soon expanded to include voluntary (non-financial) information, as well as enriching the sources, contents, and types of analysis. Future research may focus on stakeholders' perspectives and include small and medium entities, not-for-profit organizations, and the public sector.

DOI: 10.4018/978-1-6684-5007-9.ch008

INTRODUCTION

Traditionally, as stressed by Falschlunger, *et al.* (2015) financial reporting is one of the most important types of entity communication, providing information on the past, the present, the entity's economic activity and its perspectives. Also, it is an opportunity for entities to legitimate themselves and their activities (Dhanani & Kennedy, 2022). Increasingly, different types of accounting narratives have been included or separately disclosed as complementary and relevant information to stakeholders (Clatworthy & Jones, 2003; Tauringana & Mangena, 2014). Therefore, entities' disclosures have been "*a longstanding pre-occupation of accounting researchers and policymakers*" (Leung *et al.*, 2015).

Furthermore, along with technological developments, the reporting of entities has also undergone several changes in recent decades (Rafay, 2019), covering a wide range of forms of dissemination that include, in addition to financial reporting, non-financial or sustainability reporting and, more recently, integrated reporting (Barkemeyer *et al.*, 2014; Pitrakkos & Maroun, 2020). As mentioned by Hamza and Jarboui (2022), society has been increasingly concerned regarding environmental, social, and governance issues, which consequently sheds light on the entities' corporate social responsibility activities from the investors' perspective, as a piece of relevant information for the decision-making process.

The evolution of disclosures entails new challenges related to the content of the information since "*increasing the amount of information being disclosed does not necessarily imply an improvement in the quality of the disclosure about underlying activities*" (Sahyoun & Magnan, 2020). Therefore, due to the lack of specific rules guiding a significant part of entities' disclosures, the credibility of corporate narratives and their characteristics still represent matters of increasing relevance as a guarantee of reporting usefulness, which includes aspects such as the narratives' length, tone, and readability (El-Sayed *et al.*, 2021; Rafay, 2022).

Furthermore, literature has evidenced that, consciously biased or not, managers provide a different view of reality when reporting the entities' past performances and perspectives (Schleicher, 2012), also using mechanisms to improve the entities' self-images to their shareholders (Yang & Liu, 2017). This resource is particularly used in turbulent times, such as the latest global financial crisis of 2008-2009 (Khanna & Irvine, 2018). The concerns about the quality, which impacts the overall reporting usefulness, are relevant since there are strategies available to the preparers that go towards conveying a dissimilar message of reality in the reporting provided by them (Melloni *et al.*, 2017). On the other hand, auditors and stakeholders are also increasingly able to carry out a more careful analysis of information (Ramzan *et al.*, 2020; Khan *et al.*, 2020), either due to the increase in information available via websites and social media or by the emergence of new technological tools that allow a rapid and consistent analysis of the financial and non-financial information reported (Perkiss *et al.*, 2021), despite they are still underexplored (Corazza *et al.*, 2020).

Several ways or tactics can be used by entities to manage users' perceptions, through the different tools available that allow entities to manage the disclosed information, undermining its transparency and mitigating its quality and credibility (Diouf & Boiral, 2017; Rafay & Farid, 2018). Those strategies are recognized in the literature as impression management (IM) strategies, which can be defined, in an attempt to summarize the literature on this topic in accounting, as the behavior assumed by management to strategically select and manipulate, through different mechanisms, the reported information, which can be graphically or textually described, about the managers or entities' image and/or figures to influence and, consequently, distort the users' perceptions on their different aspects, such as managers characteristics and entities' accountability, historical performance and perspectives (Beattie & Jones, 1999; Godfrey *et al.*, 2003; Clatworthy & Jones, 2006; Merkl-Davies & Brennan, 2007, 2011; Merkl-Davies *et al.*, 2011).

To sum up, the information provided by entities may be affected using IM, which can influence stakeholders' decision-making processes. It is therefore increasingly important for stakeholders to distinguish reliable from misleading information. IM can be performed by different strategies (Sandberg & Holmlund, 2015). As proposed by Merkl-Davies and Brennan, (2007), those strategies are traditionally divided into two major areas of analysis, namely the concealment and obfuscation strategies, which will be further detailed in the next section.

Merkl-Davies and Brennan (2011) provide evidence that research on this topic covers a wide range of topics and subjects since a variety of human actions can be influenced by IM strategies. Therefore, it is a topic of interest in a variety of fields other than accounting, such as social and human sciences, anthropology, communication, law, linguistics, management (including marketing and labor relations), and sociology, as well as medical sciences (psychology and sports).

This chapter proposes for its scope the use of IM strategies with possible impacts, directly or indirectly, on the accounting area to provide an overview of the literature on this subject since the seminal papers from the latest research found. Consequently, an Evolutive analysis of the literature is provided in this chapter. Papers included on the Scopus database by 27 August 2022 are selected as the source of information. Textual analysis is used as a complementary tool to assess the information gathered.

This chapter intends to contribute to the literature by providing an outline of the investigations on this topic, offering a synthesis of the papers related to this subject, including the evolutive analysis and the trending topics for future avenues. The research by Merkl-Davies and Brennan (2007) already presents an important literature review on this subject, given its significant impact since its publication. This work was subsequently complemented by other more specific literature reviews, such as the work by Beattie and Jones (2008) on the use of graphs. The purpose of this research, however, is neither to provide specific outputs nor to compare the findings from the papers with a critical perspective of analysis. It is instead committed to assessing the papers in the scope of this chapter to provide a summary of existing investigations, identifying specific elements such as traditional and new themes proposed by their authors, the topics covered by them, and their contributions.

Despite proposing a different perspective, this chapter provides an overall update on this work, which is useful for researchers around the world. In addition, its relevance can also be justified by the changes accounting has undergone, as it has been influenced by a variety of issues including new regulatory matters, stakeholder needs, and technological advancements.

As regards its practical and social impacts, the relevance of this topic can be justified by the possible effects on the entities' financial and non-financial reporting, which may be avoided by having a better understanding of possible IM strategies used by entities, as well as their sources, tactics, and patterns. Different users can benefit from this, including capital providers and other stakeholders whose decision-making process relies on accounting information. Additionally, it is relevant to those who, in some way, are responsible for ensuring the quality of the information provided by entities, such as standard-setting bodies, auditors, governments, and supervisory agencies.

In addition to this Introduction, this chapter is divided into three further sections. In the second section (Background), the main aspects of IM strategies in accounting are discussed. The third section (Literature analysis) summarizes the papers selected for the analysis purpose, as outlined in this chapter. The fourth section (Conclusions) provides the main conclusions along with recommendations for future research related to the topic.

BACKGROUND

In a business context, and particularly related to the entities reporting, IM refers to the behavior assumed by the management to select, make available, and strategically present their narratives, including the use of graphs, to distort the users' perceptions about the entity, influencing the users' impressions on its performance and perspectives (Godfrey *et al.*, 2003).

Merkl-Davies and Brennan (2007) categorized seven IM strategies under two groups of behavior: concealment and attribution. Figure 1 summarizes the different strategies associated with the two categories above mentioned.

Figure 1. Synthesis of IM strategies

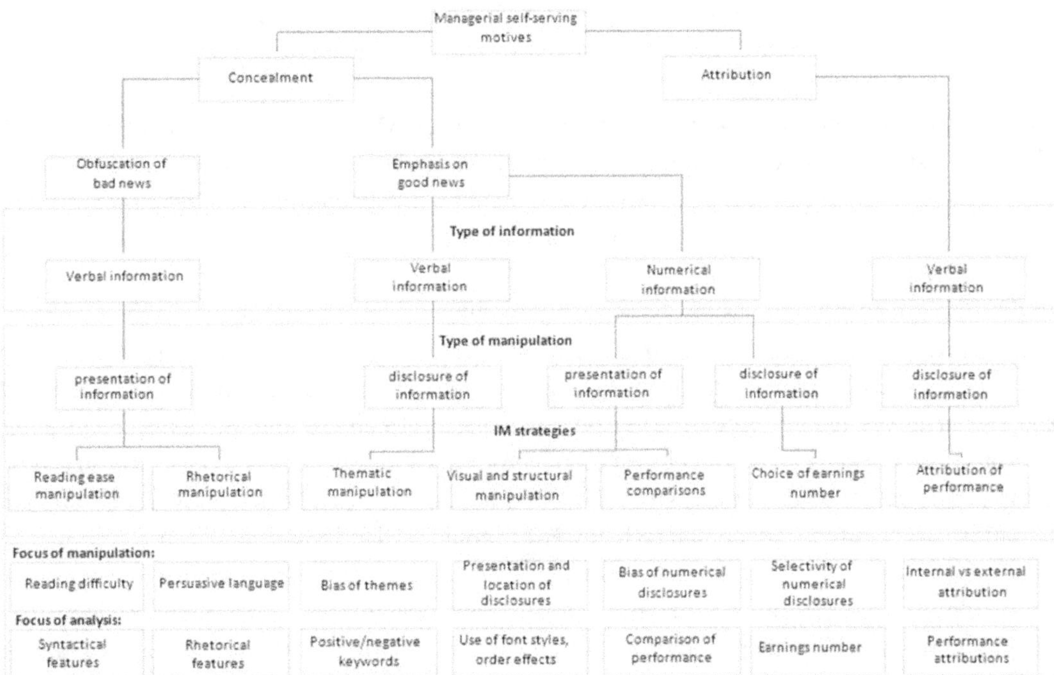

These categories are consistent with the proposition that disclosers can introduce bias into the communication process, by using ambiguity and responsibility avoidance (Cho *et al.*, 2010).

According to Merkl-Davies and Brennan (2007), the concealment strategy covers two techniques, summarized in a set of strategies that aims to obscure or obfuscate bad news and emphasize good news.

In the first case (**obfuscation of bad news**), it is commonly used strategies associated with information **readability** (i.e., making the text more difficult to read) and rhetorical manipulation (i.e., using persuasive language). These strategies are carried out, in both cases, through verbal manipulation of the information presented. In the second case (**emphasis on good news**), four strategies were identified either through verbal, numerical or graphical manipulation, as follows:

1. **Thematic manipulation**, which emphasizes positive words or positive financial performance, being a verbal manipulation of the disclosed information. Thus, it analyses the positive and negative expressions used in the writing process;
2. **Visual and structural manipulation**, which emphasizes the visual aspect and the strategic ordering of verbal or numerical information. This strategy can be used to emphasize information through, for example, the use of colours, repetitions, and reinforcements (Leung *et al.*, 2015);
3. **Performance comparisons**, which involve choosing benchmarks that portray the current financial performance as best as possible. Leung *et al.* (2015) state that this strategy is used as a mechanism to highlight moments of positive performance.
4. **Choice of figures** with a positive and relevant impact, for instance, when the entity selects a given result to portray a more favourable financial performance. Allen *et al.* (2007) understands that the choice of specific results, namely those associated with earnings, is also an IM strategy since it can make investors' judgments less refined, which can be performed, for instance, through a strategic presentation of those figures in the press releases and other accounting narratives.

Following, the **attribution strategy** is also classified as an IM strategy, corresponding to the attribution of certain results to different factors through verbal manipulation in the way information is disclosed (Merkl-Davies & Brennan, 2007). The strategy associated with attribution is selfish, assuming that the entities' positive results are attributed to internal factors, whilst negative results are attributed to external circumstances (Aerts, 2005).

Readability can be broadly defined as the ease of reading and understanding, and, therefore, syntactic manipulation in narratives presupposes that the management deliberately uses a language that is more difficult to read to hide negative performance (El-Sayed *et al.,* 2021). Through literature, the importance of corporate narratives' readability can be reasoned to make an effective communication of value-relevant information (Fisher *et al.*, 2020). The obfuscation hypothesis and broader IM theory are consistent with the opinion that executives draft negative reports that are unnecessarily difficult to read while making positive information easier to understand (Riley & Luippold, 2015; Demaline, 2020).

Also, El-Sayed *et al.* (2021) reported that simple (more readable) disclosures improve non-professional investors' judgment of the entities' future performance. The readability of disclosures made by management is a topic that has been repeatedly studied in recent years. Most of the works associated with this subject have attempted to assess the readability of the entities reporting, particularly the financial report and its components, including the letters to shareholders (for instance, Sydserff & Weetman, 2002; Aerts & Yan, 2017). More recently, the research has been also considering the pieces of non-financial reporting in this field (for instance, Fisher *et al.*, 2020).

The manipulation carried out by the management, namely the concealment of events in the disclosures made, is a strategy adopted when managers have incentives to hide information whenever the entity's performance is not favorable (Merkl-Davies & Brennan, 2007; Rafay, Sadiq & Ajmal, 2016). While complexity and tone of language can be influential to investors, a more subtle linguistic style can also influence the meaning of a message, namely by simply altering the use of predicates (verbs versus adjectives/nouns), which may change the interpretation of a given narrative (Riley & Luippold, 2015).

Demaline (2020) states an important consequence of the use of this strategy, stressing that complexity and usefulness of financial information are inversely related, as the obfuscation hypothesis of IM theory is in line with the view that managers release bad news that is unnecessarily difficult to understand. Melloni *et al.* (2017) have concluded, for instance, that even in sustainability reports, entities have provided foggier reports, consistent with the IM use, suggesting that entities with low social performance adopt those strategies more based on syntactical reading ease manipulation and thematic content manipulation, especially focusing on "fine-tuning" environmental, social and governance topics coverage.

Rhetorical manipulation can be classified as the use of language to persuade or influence others (Merkl-Davies & Brennan, 2007). Through its use, the management makes strategic linguistic choices to persuade or impress readers (Brennan *et al.*, 2010). Merkl-Davies and Brennan (2007) believe that rhetorical manipulation uses persuasive language as a proxy for obfuscation.

The different writing styles are mechanisms by which meaning can be conveyed to the audience and add a sense-giving layer to the content of words, giving a rational, credible, and persuasive sense to the messages (Aerts & Yan, 2017). The studies carried out by Aerts (1994) and Clatworthy and Jones (2003), for instance, identified that entities with negative results tend to communicate using accounting terminologies, while positive results are explained by explicit statements of cause and effect. Schleicher (2012) found vagueness as one of the predominant IM strategies used by entities as an important signal for future financial performance.

Thematic manipulation emphasizes positive performances in the narratives, using a verbal manipulation of the information disclosed using positive expressions (Merkl-Davies & Brennan, 2007).

Studies focusing on thematic manipulation presuppose that managers seek to hide bad news, either through non-disclosure or through less emphatic dissemination when compared to positive news (Brennan *et al.*, 2010; Cho *et al.*, 2010; Melloni *et al.*, 2017). Thematic manipulation is based on the Pollyanna principle, which means that positive and affirmative words and subjects are remembered more frequently than negative ones (Merkl-Davies & Brennan, 2007).

The empirical studies developed in this line using accounting narratives indicate that managers seek to present themselves or the entities' performance in the best possible way. Clatworthy and Jones (2003), for instance, identified that entities with positive performances are more likely to focus on good news, instead of bad news, having found that declining financial performance entities do not discuss, nor do they analyze the nature and reasons for poor performance and, at best (at worst) they discuss good and bad news equally (focus on good news). Aligned with this finding, Schleicher and Walker (2010) evidenced that entities with riskier business or forecast analysts provide a more positive tone, oppositely to those with declining earnings.

Visual manipulation, in turn, is mostly evidenced using graphs, which are powerful tools that affect the reader's perceptions and decision-making processes, playing an important role in shaping users' judgments regarding the entities' future performance and prospects (Beattie & Jones, 2000a, 2002, 2008; Cho *et al.*, 2012; Dilla and Janvrin, 2010; El-Sayed *et al.*, 2021). This IM strategy occurs when entities display strategically selected information or present information in such a way that it distorts readers' perception of the entities' true performance (Godfrey *et al.*, 2003).

Falschlunger *et al.* (2015) stated that graphs inserted in annual reports have a long tradition of being prepared and selected to give a more favorable view of the performance of the entities. This can be explained by the several possibilities available for designing and developing them in a way to portray the entities' image and performance favorably, as they are beyond the scope of auditors and the absence of regulations to guide their disclosure can be considered as a part of the impression management process (Beattie & Jones, 2002, 2008).

Beattie and Jones (1999) provide several examples of practical evidence of possible uses of IM strategies associated with graphic distortion, as shown in Figure 2.

Figure 2. Visual and structural manipulation

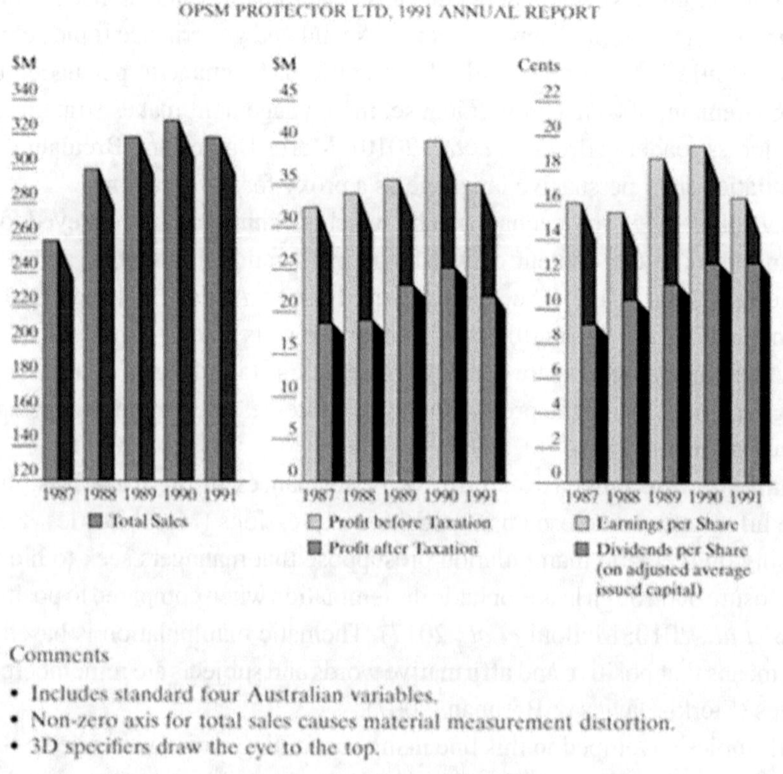

In recent research, El-Sayed *et al.* (2021) identified three main types of graph manipulations that can be used by entities to bias users' perceptions and provide a favorable impression about the entities' prospects: graph selectivity, graphic distortion, and presentational enhancement. The authors recommended market participants, especially non-professional investors, should be aware of management control over certain non-verbal communications as there is a strong possibility that these graphics are strategically used to bias the investors' judgments (El-Sayed *et al.*, 2021).

Selectivity and performance comparison are strategies implemented by management to select the metrics that portray the entity at its best performance (Brennan *et al.*, 2009) since the perceptions of the entities' performance can be manipulated using previously selected information and variables and how they are specifically presented to users (Merkl-Davies & Brennan, 2007). As part of an IM strategy, selectivity involves 'omitting' or 'including' certain items of information, which can be achieved either by manipulating the presentation of narrative disclosures (selectivity as regards the information presented) or by omitting narrative disclosure (selectivity as regards the information content) (Leung *et al.*, 2015; Melloni *et al.*, 2017).

Furthermore, the selection of key figures and the most suitable variables to provide comparisons regarding the entities' performance is a recurrent IM strategy in their accounting narratives (Brennan *et al.*, 2009), which can be used to either accentuate an increasing tendency or implicitly hide a negative one (Clatworthy & Jones, 2006; Schleicher, 2012).

Finally, the **attribution strategy** assumes that management acts selfishly, where it seeks to attribute positive results to internal factors while negative results are associated with external factors (Merkl-Davies & Brennan, 2007; Brennan *et al.*, 2009; Edgar *et al.* 2018). The performance attributions may also be a consequence of managerial retrospective sense-making, which involves managers retrospectively assigning causes to the entities' events and actions (Aerts, 2005).

The attribution strategy was studied on several occasions in the context of accounting narratives (Aerts, 1994; Clatworthy & Jones, 2003; Riley & Luippold, 2015). In general, such studies identified a tendency to attribute positive effects or results to internal factors (i.e., actions of the organization itself, such as entity strategy, decisions, know-how, and human resource potential, among others) and negative results in the case of external events or random factors (current market status, inflation, market prices, government policy, among others).

LITERATURE ANALYSIS

This section presents a summary of the literature on the use of IM strategies in the accounting area, based on the papers selected for this purpose. It is divided into three subsections. The first provides the basic methodological aspects surrounding the analysis proposed for this chapter, including those related to the scope defined for this chapter and the textual analysis performed. The second one presents an overview of the papers gathered. Finally, the third subsection intends to complement the previous one, presenting a more in-depth analysis of those papers as regards their characteristics, such as the themes under assessment, as well as the sources, samples, and research methods used.

Methodological Notes

The findings from this chapter are based on the papers gathered on the Scopus database by 27 August 2022. No restrictions were applied as regards the date of the release of the papers and, therefore, the analysis is comprised of seminal papers and the latest research, providing an Evolutive analysis of literature on this field. The expression "impression management" was used as the key search term in the abstracts of the papers selected. The search was also restricted to papers published in journals in the English language and, finally, in the "Business, Accounting and Management Area", as only the main areas can be selected. Considering that those papers still covered generic research on IM, a secondary filter was applied to only identify the journals considered by Scopus as within the accounting area, more specifically. At the end of this process, 117 papers were gathered for assessment.

The information regarding the number of citations by each paper is used as a proxy for their impact on the literature in this field.

A textual analysis tool (the {L}exos) is also used, particularly to identify the most frequent words found in the abstract of the papers gathered, which will be performed as a complementary analysis in the third subsection. As usual in these processes, some of the most frequent words have no meaning for research purposes. As such, those words must be classified as "stop words" and, subsequently, removed from the analysis. The {L}exos has no automatic process, requesting users to identify those words. Therefore, a judgment must be made to exclude them. For this research, the most common abbreviations were excluded, such as articles, adverbs (mostly, conjunctive adverbs), determiners, numbers, prepositions, pronouns, and the verb "to be" and "to have" in their different forms, and modal verbs. On the other hand, adjectives and some adverbs were kept, as they could express different feelings of students as regards the topics on NFI. Finally, the expression "impression management" was also eliminated since it comprises the key searching terms.

Besides a global overview of the papers selected, some analysis provides a breakdown of four distinct periods: from 1990 (the first paper found is from 1991) to 1999, from 2000 to 2009, from 2010 to 2019, and, finally, from 2020 to 2022. The first two periods include those that would expectedly be the seminal papers in the different investigation lines on the IM strategies, which are followed by the consolidation period of research in this field. The last period was particularly selected to identify the trending topics on IM strategies in accounting, despite being shorter than the previous ones. Then, some analysis should take this element into account.

Table 1 presents a summary of the papers selected by period and their textual characteristics.

Table 1. Summary of the textual characteristics of papers selected by period

Period	Number of papers	Number of terms occurring once	Total number of terms	Distinct number of terms	Vocabulary Density
1990-1999	3	131	231	161	0.697
2000-2009	18	557	1,632	830	0.509
2010-2019	64	1,256	6,662	2,361	0.354
2020-2022	32	975	3,632	1,593	0.439
Global	387	1,759	12,156	3,474	0.286

A review of the papers selected is presented in the following subsection.

Overview of Papers Selected

Figure 3 indicates the number of papers (NoP), citations (NoC), and the average citations by period.

Figure 3. Summary of the number of papers and citations by period

For the first ten-year's period (from 1990 to 1999), only three papers were identified. However, the average citation in this period is, even so, higher than the number obtained for the period between 2010 and 2019 (consolidation period), despite the comparison should consider the lower number of years between the current and the release year for the papers included in this last period. For this reason, it is also difficult to assess by now the number of citations for the last period (from 2020 to 2022), which has the minimum difference for the same gap.

The second ten-year period (from 2000 to 2009) presents the highest average citation, despite the number of papers significantly lower than the one identified for the subsequent period (from 2010 to 2019), which has four times more releases.

Notwithstanding, the average citation observed from 1990 to 1999 is significantly influenced by the Merkl-Davies and Brennan (2007) paper, the most cited paper, with 916 citations, followed by the second one by Cho *et al.* (2010), with 405 citations, published in the period from 2000 to 2009. However, the previous conclusion remains valid even after excluding those relevant papers from the analysis (both or the most cited one).

IM research remains relevant for the last periods, as evidenced by the number of papers for the past three years (2020 to 2022), which is equal to half of what was found in the previous ten years (2000 to 2019). It is probably too early, however, to provide conclusions on the relevance based on the number of citations for the latest periods. Despite that, it seems by now that the growth rate has a tendency for deceleration over the period under assessment.

Table 2, in Appendix 1, provides information on the number of papers and citations by period and accounting journals.

As it can be seen in that table, the *Accounting, Auditing and Accountability Journal* appears as the journal with the highest number of both papers (30) and citations (1,537), of which seven papers present more than 100 citations (Beattie & Jones, 2002; Sydserff & Weetman, 2002; Ogden & Clarke, 2005; Clatworthy & Jones, 2006; Brennan *et al.*, 2009; Merkl-Davies *et al.*, 2011; Diouf & Boiral, 2017), mostly from the period between 2000 and 2009. Notwithstanding, the most recent between them (Diouf & Boiral, 2017) is also the most cited, having the information from sustainability reports as a source.

Following, the Journal of Accounting Literature has the second highest number of citations with only two papers published, which is explained by the relevant impact of two literature reviews released in the period between 2000 and 2009. The first was released by Merkl-Davies and Brennan (2007), already mentioned as the most cited paper in the set of research found on IM strategies in accounting (916). Then, it was followed by Beattie's and Jones's (2002) research, which provided a synthesis of the literature on IM studies that used graphs as an object of analysis.

Finally, *Accounting, Organization and Society,* and *Accounting and Business Research* emerged as the third and fourth ones, respectively.

The first released eight papers over the period, with 886 citations, five out of eight with more than 100 citations (Aerts, 1994, 2005; Cho *et al.*, 2010; García Osma, 2011; Solomon *et al.*, 2013) and mostly covering the first years of the third period under assessment (from 2010 to 2019). Among these papers, the research previously mentioned by Cho *et al.* (2010) needs to be highlighted, with 405 citations (the second most cited paper).

Then, the second journal mentioned released more papers (10) with a lower impact on literature, since only two have reached more than 100 citations, namely Clatworthy and Jones (2003) and Merkl-Davies and Brennan (2011), with 209 and 130 citations, respectively. Again, the work developed by Merkl-Davies and Brennan (2011) is not classified as empirical research. Instead, it proposed a conceptual framework of IM, based on the concepts of rationality and motivation, using theories and empirical research from psychology/behavioral finance, sociology, and critical accounting.

Commonly, all the papers previously mentioned, except the more theoretical papers published by Merkl-Davies and Brennan (2007, 2011), assessed accounting narratives (disclosures) on either concealment or attributional strategies within the literature on IM.

Other important journals (considering the number of papers and/or citations), which published either seminal or recent papers on this topic, include the following: *Accounting Forum, Critical Perspectives on Accounting, Abacus, Contemporary Accounting Research, Journal of International Accounting, Auditing and Taxation,* and *Journal of Applied Accounting Research.* All those journals are ranked in the first (mostly) or second quartile of the Scopus database.

It is worthwhile to mention that the number of journals with publications on this topic has been increasing, including relevant journals such as the *Journal of Accounting and Public Policy*, *British Accounting Review*, and *European Accounting Review,* to cite some of them ranked in the first quartile of the Scopus database.

Following, Table 3, in Appendix 2, provides information on the papers by period and number of citations, including those with 10 citations at a minimum.

As it is shown from the figures provided in that table, besides the papers previously mentioned, five journals also published papers with more than or equal to 100 citations. All of them are ranked in the first quartile of Scopus, with a single exception (Abacus), which is ranked in the second one.

Amongst those papers, it can be found the works developed by Jeacle (2008), published in *Critical Perspectives on Accounting,* on the weight of the stigma of the accounting stereotype (144 citations). Following, three out of five were developed using sustainability or integrated reporting as the source, namely Melloni *et al.* (2017), in the *Journal of Accounting and Public Policy,* Higgins and Walker (2012), in *Accounting Forum*, and, finally, Cho *et al.* (2012), in *Sustainability Accounting, Management and Policy Journal.*

Interestingly, the work by Cho *et al.* (2012) is also the only amongst the set of the most cited (more than or equal to 100 citations) that uses graph analysis as the specific content to assess the use of IM strategies. Finally, the research by Godfrey *et al.* (2003), published in *Abacus*, fulfills the set of the most cited papers, covering the accounting narratives and using financial reports as the main data source.

By period, it is interesting to note that the already mentioned paper by Aerts (1994), on accounting narratives, is the only one with more than or equal to 100 citations (exactly 100 citations, in this case) included in the first period of analysis (from 1990 to 1999), which was published in *Accounting Organizations and Society*. As regards the impact of the literature in this period, the previous research followed by Neu (1999), on the accounting profession, with 86 citations and also published in *Critical Perspectives on Accounting*, similar to Jeacle's (2008) work. Finally, it appears the seminal paper on the analysis of graphical manipulation, which was published by Beattie and Jones (1999) in *Abacus*, with less than 50 citations (46).

Further, as previously indicated, the second period (from 2000 to 2009) has a lower number of papers and citations in comparison with the third one (from 2010 to 2019). On the other hand, it has a higher average citation, which remains valid even after excluding from the analysis the most cited paper in this period, namely the research by Merkl-Davies and Brennan (2007).

Finally, Table 4, in Appendix 3, provides information on the authors by the number of papers and citations, including those with 10 citations at a minimum.

As this table shows, six authors present three papers on the topic of IM (Hossain, D. M.; Jeacle, I.; Mather, P.; Ramsay, A.; Merkl-Davies, D. M.; Patten, D.M.). Following, five authors published between four and 10 papers (the maximum number), namely Parker, L.D. (four papers), Aerts, W., Beattie, V.A., and Cho, C.H. (five papers), and Brennan, N.M. (7 papers). Jones, M.J. is the author with the maximum number of research (12 papers).

Looking at the papers published by these authors, a diversified set of topics and research characteristics can be found within the scope of IM strategies. However, similarities can be also found in some cases, for instance, the graphical analysis in the papers jointly published by Mather, P. and Ramsay, A. and Beattie, V. and Jones, M. J., as well as the use of non-financial information in the research by Hossain. All papers published by Beattie, V. had Jones, M. J. as co-author. The same is applied to Merkl-Davies, D. M., which always had Brennan, N. M. as co-author. Finally, all papers that had Patten, D. M. as a co-author also had Cho, C. H. as an author or also as a co-author.

As regards the paper released over the period under assessment, the longest periods of published works can be found between 1999 and 2008, for the works together developed by Beattie, V. and Jones, M. J. The research by Mather, P., and Ramsay, A. together was published between 2000 and 2007, while the work by Patten, D.M. was published together with Cho, C.H. between 2010 and 2017. Different works by Cho, C.H. were also published in this period. Finally, Merkl-Davies, D. M. and Brennan, N.M. published between 2007 and 2011, while the research by Jeacle, I. was published between 2008 and 2014. Furthermore, Aerts, W. and Brennan, N. M. are the authors with the highest gap between the oldest and latest research on IM (1994 *versus* 2017 and 2007 *versus* 2021, respectively). Finally, Parker, L. D. and Hossain, D. M. have been publishing on this topic only from 2015 onwards, with the first (last) work released in 2015 (2022) and 2016 (2020), respectively.

Considering the average citation for authors with, at least, three papers on the topic of IM, half of the twelve before mentioned have more than 100 citations, namely Merkl-Davies, D. M. (394) and Brennan, N. M. (195), Patten, D. M. (181), Cho, C. H. (112), as well as Beattie, V. (104). These figures are particularly influenced by a couple of works published by them, included in the set of the most cited ones namely: Merkl-Davies and Brennan (2007), with 916 citations; Cho *et al.* (2010), with 405 citations, Beattie and Jones (2002, 2008), with 213 and 170, respectively.

Following, five of these authors had between 50 and 100 citations on average, which include Jones, M. J. (82), Jeacle, I. (71), Aerts, W. (58), Mather, P., and Ramsay, A. (both with 55 citations). Finally, Parker, L. D. (29), and Hossain, D. M. (19) had the lowest level of citations among these authors.

Furthermore, it is also relevant to stress that 21 authors had more than 100 citations with a single work, such as Roberts, R.W. (405 citations), as co-author with Cho C. H. and Patten D.M. in the second most cited paper, as well as Diouf, D. and Boiral, O. (153 citations), who have reached together the fourth most cited paper under assessment in this chapter.

Finally, Clatworthy, M., always having Jones, M. J. as a co-author, published two papers in 2003 and 2006 on the scope of IM strategies in accounting. These papers have reached 209 and 136 citations since then, respectively, which means 173 citations on average. All other authors with two recorded works had less than 100 citations on average, and only two obtained between 50 and 100 citations in this group (Guillamon-Saorin, E. and Weetman, P.).

Analysis of Papers Selected by Themes and Other Characteristics

As detailed in the previous section, IM can be evidenced by different strategies. Traditionally, those strategies can be grouped into two are of analysis, following Merkl-Davies and Brennan (2007).

The first group includes the set of concealment strategies, with a more prominent number of papers identified as it is also more diverse in terms of types of manipulation included in this context (for instance, Aerts, 1994; Beattie & Jones, 2000; Ogden & Clarke, 2005; Brennan *et al.*, 2010; Jones, 2011; Aerts & Cheng, 2011; Merkl-Davies *et al.*, 2011; Guillamon-Saorin *et al.*, 2012; Schleicher, 2012; Leung *et al.*, 2015; Riley & Luippold, 2015; Adler *et al.*, 2017; Diouf & Boiral, 2017; Melloni *et al.*, 2017; Hamza & Jarboui, 2022). The second one is related to the attribution strategy, which has been more neglected by literature (for instance, Aerts, 1994; Clatworthy & Jones, 2003; Aerts, 2005; Riley & Luippold, 2015; Nègre *et al.*, 2017).

Two main sets of data are commonly the focus of those papers to assess the information bias or manipulation. The first one is related to the purposeful manipulation, choice or distortion of the figures presented by graphs, more prominent in the previous years (for instance, Beattie & Jones, 1999, 2000a, 2000b, 2002, 2008; Matter *et al.*, 2000; Godfrey *et al.*, 2003; Mather & Ramsay, 2007; Jones, 2011; Cho *et al.*, 2012; Falschlunger *et al.*, 2015; Jones *et al.*, 2018; El-Sayed *et al.*, 2021). Then, with a higher number of investigations and, also, with the highest impact in the literature, the second one relates to the analysis of accounting narratives (for instance, Clatworthy & Jones, 2003, 2006; Aerts, 2005; Cho *et al.*, 2010, 2012; Zhang & Aerts, 2015; Al-Sayani *et al.*, 2020; Demaline, 2019, 2020; Fisher *et al.*, 2020; El-Sayed *et al.*, 2021; Jugnandan & Willows, 2022; Abou-El-Sood & El-Sayed, 2022; Hamza & Jarboui, 2022; Kayed & Meqbel, 2022).

A wide range of documents that integrates the set of entities' reporting can be used to disseminate IM strategies. These include several pieces of information that traditionally make part of the financial and non-financial reports – in their separate or consolidated format and their annual or interim periodicity – as well as all supplementary documents usually designated as accounting narratives that may be included or not in those reports.

Documents sometimes mentioned, in general, as managers' narratives, such as CEO's, presidents', or chairpersons' letters or reports, as well as letters or reports to shareholders or stockholders, represent one of the sources mostly used by researchers to investigate IM strategies (for instance, Godfrey *et al.*, 2003; Clatworthy & Jones, 2006; Mather & Ramsay, 2007; Hadro *et al.*, 2017; Al-Sayani *et al.*, 2020).

Then, financial information other than financial statements (for instance, Dilla & Janvrin, 2010; Yekini *et al.*, 2016) and financial statements, including the notes to the financial statement (for instance, Zeller *et al.*, 2012; Tauringana & Mangena, 2014) are also used for this purpose. Following, prospectuses, press releases, and conference calls (for instance, Mather *et al.*, 2000; Brennan *et al.*, 2010; Aerts & Cheng, 2011; Guillamon-Saorin *et al.*, 2012; Kayed & Meqbel, 2022) comprise a further source of information used by researchers.

Further, to the same extent of its increasing relevance, the analysis of IM through the different ways and formats for disclosing non-financial or ESG information, such as sustainability or integrated reports (for instance, Higgins & Walker, 2012; Haji & Hossain, 2016; Diouf & Boiral, 2017; Melloni *et al.*, 2017; McNally & Maroun, 2018; Pitrakkos & Maroun, 2020; Hamza & Jarboui, 2022; Jugnandan & Willows, 2022) has been also growing.

Associated with IM as an investigation line, legitimacy theory is frequently used as the basis for those papers (for instance, Ogden & Clarke, 2005; Higginson *et al.*, 2006; Samkin & Schneider, 2010; Cho *et al.*, 2012; Holm & Zaman, 2012; Conway *et al.*, 2015; Soobaroyen & Mahadeo; 2016; Nègre *et al.*, 2017; Chong *et al.*, 2019; Martins *et al.*, 2019; Courtois & Gendron, 2020; Hossain *et al.*, 2020; Moussa *et al.*, 2021; Dhanani & Kennedy, 2022), being followed by the agency theory (for instance, Aerts & Cheng, 2011; Jones *et al.*, 2018; Al-Sayani *et al.*, 2020; Abou-El-Sood & El-Sayed, 2022).

Other theoretical supports can be found, particularly from 2020 onwards, such as the political cost theories (Dilla & Janvrin, 2010), psychology/behavioural finance (Merkl-Davies & Brennan, 2007, 2011) theories of surveillance and interaction ritual (Abraham & Bamber, 2017), entrepreneurship perspective (Abeysekera, 2020), resource-based theory (Abeysekera, 2020), image restoration theory (Corazza *et al.*, 2020), multi-disciplinary theoretical understanding of boundary setting (Miles & Ringham, 2020), stakeholder theory (Moussa *et al.*, 2021). Some studies also propose the assessment of possible links between IM and earnings management practices (Godfrey *et al.*, 2003; Aerts & Cheng, 2011; Sahyoun & Magnan, 2020; Abou-El-Sood & El-Sayed, 2022; Kayed & Meqbel, 2022).

Geographically, most of the papers on IM assess entities from developed countries individually or as a multi-country analysis, such as European countries, and, more particularly, Anglo-Saxon countries, which includes the United States, United Kingdom, Australia, and New Zealand (for instance, Beattie & Jones, 1999, 2000a, 2000b; Mather *et al.*, 2000; Clatworthy & Jones, 2003, 2006; Godfrey *et al.*, 2003; Mather & Ramsay, 2007; Dilla & Janvrin, 2010; Aerts & Cheng, 2011; Merkl-Davies *et al.*, 2011; Andon & Free, 2014; Conway *et al.*, 2015; Adler *et al.*, 2017; Khanna & Irvine, 2018; Chong *et al.*, 2019; Demaline, 2019, 2020; Chang & Stone, 2021; Hamza & Jarboui, 2022; Kayed & Meqbel, 2022).

Notwithstanding, it has been emerging literature that covers entities from developing countries, such as Bangladesh, China, Malaysia, Mauritius, South Africa, and Sri Lanka (for instance, Shafer, 2009; Aerts & Cheng, 2011; Haji & Hossain, 2016; McNally & Maroun, 2018; Ahmad & Hossain, 2019; Hossain *et al.*, 2020; Kumarasinghe & Samkin, 2020; Zhao & Atkins, 2021).

Larger and, particularly, listed entities are prominently used by researchers, indicating a relevant research gap in what concerns small and medium entities, especially for those non-listed. Research on not-for-profit organizations and government sectors has been emerging, despite still being limited (for instance, Higginson *et al.*, 2006; Conway *et al.*, 2015; Khanna & Irvine, 2018; Chang & Stone, 2021; Dhanani & Kennedy, 2022).

Finally, most of the papers use mixed (qualitative and quantitative) methods, based on content and/or discourse analysis as techniques and, subsequently, statistical methods (mostly, regression analysis) for data assessment, following the seminal papers on IM strategies (for instance, the research by Beattie & Jones, 1999, 2000a, 2000b; Clatworthy & Jones, 2003, 2006; Merkl-Davies & Brennan, 2007).

Nevertheless, it has been increasingly the papers that exclusively propose theoretical and/or qualitative approaches for data analysis, which include surveys and interviews, to discuss this topic (for instance, Haji & Hossain, 2016; Abraham & Bamber, 2017; Corrigan & Rixon, 2017; Parker & Warren, 2017; Martins *et al.*, 2019; Westermann *et al.*, 2019; Corazza *et al.*, 2020; Nyagadza *et al.*, 2020; Dhanani & Kennedy, 2022). Besides that, it should be mentioned that the conceptual framework proposed by Merkl-Davies and Brennan (2011), is included in the selected group of papers that have reached more than 100 citations.

Following the previous analysis, Figures 4 to 8 present two distinct interactions of {L}exos, which produced word clouds (whole period and by period) as an auxiliary tool to identify the most frequent words included in the abstract of papers selected.

Figure 4 indicates the most common words for the whole period.

Figure 4. Word clouds (for the whole period)

From Figure 4 above, it can be initially highlighted, as regards the nature of information assessed in the literature, the emergence of words such as “sustainability”, “environmental”, “social” and “nature”, which are associated with non-financial information, together with more traditional ways of companies reporting, evidenced by the word “financial”. Both are associated with words such as “report”, “reporting” and “annual”.

Following, the words “graph” or “graphs” and, on the other hand, “narrative” or “narratives”, “tone”, “textual” and “discourses” (despite some not being evidenced in the figure above) indicate the focus of analysis within the companies reporting, with a prevalence over the second group of analysis (accounting narratives). The words “earnings” and/or “performance” indicate the common variable assessed by the authors to justify the use of IM strategies or “practices”.

Finally, regarding the sample, words such as “listed” and “public” evidence the major use of these types of entities, particularly listed companies.

Figure 5 indicates the most common words for the period between 1990 and 1999.

Figure 5. Word clouds (from 1990 to 1999)

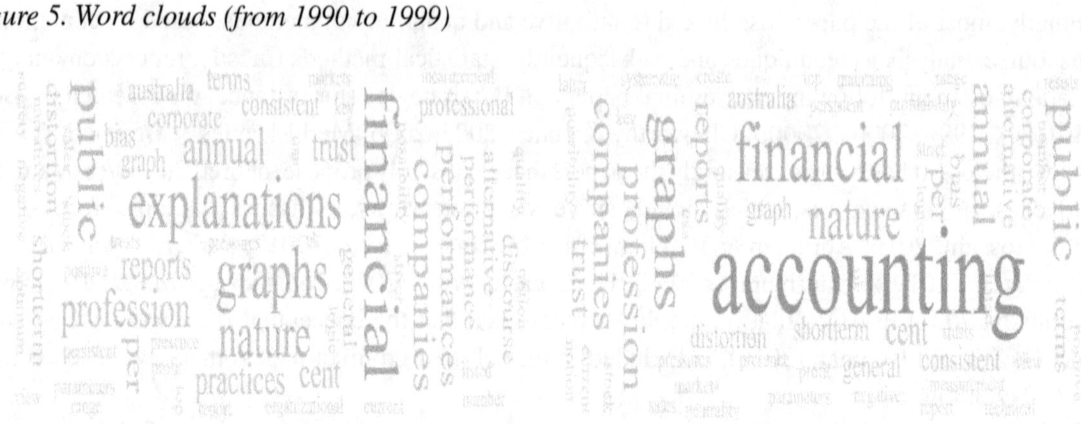

Figure 5 above is particularly relevant to stress the absence of the non-financial information assessment for this specific period.

The diversified focus of the only three seminal papers gathered for this period is also evidenced by the words "accounting" and "explanations" (Aerts, 1994), "public", "accounting" (also), and "profession" (Neu, 1991), as well as "graph" or "graphs", "percent", and "distortion" (Beattie & Jones, 1999).

Figure 6 indicates, in turn, the most common words for the period between 2000 and 2009.

Figure 6. Word clouds (from 2000 to 2009)

For the period summarized in Figure 6 above, the increasing number of papers evidenced the two major lines of investigation associated with the use of graphical analysis and accounting narratives from companies' disclosures.

Financial information also continues to be the main source. However, more diversified pieces of information appear, such as "prospectuses", "CEO"' and "managers".

Furthermore, the use of theoretical background evidenced by "legitimacy" theory, and the different IM strategies, are shown, for instance, by "selectivity". Words such as "climate", "ethical", and "water" indicate the emergence of these themes as a novelty.

Following, Figure 7 provides the same analysis for the period between 2010 and 2019.

Figure 7. Word clouds (from 2010 to 2019)

In Figure 7 above, which summarises the period between 2010 and 2019, words such as "voluntary", "social", "environmental", "sustainability", "integrated", and "biodiversity" are significantly used in comparison with the previous period, indicating the strength in the use of those themes, despite not as a novelty.

Additionally, the use of graphics for assessing IM strategies is significantly reduced in comparison with accounting "narratives", "tone", "rhetorical", "content", and "disclosures", which are mostly the focus of analysis in the papers from this period.

Again, new pieces of information continue to be evident, such as "press", "releases", "media", and "visual". Finally, the words "audit", "external", "auditors", and "risk" indicate the emergence of the assessment analysis of these aspects in the literature on IM strategies.

Finally, Figure 8 presents the most common words for the latest period, from 2020 onwards.

Figure 8. Word clouds (from 2020 to 2022)

Figure 8 above, which summarizes the latest period, indicates a continuity of previous findings regarding aspects such as the types of information, as both financial and non-financial contents are used, the latter evidenced by different words such as "sustainability", "CSR", "social", "gender", "nature", "power", and "SASRS", as well as new sources, and pieces of data are used by the authors, evidenced by words such as "call" or "calls", "non GAAP", and "SEC". The auditing perspective also keeps its relevance in the literature, as it can be seen from words such as "assurance" and "audit".

Furthermore, new topics also emerge, with a profusion of different words such as "users" and "stakeholders", which indicates a more diversified set of perspectives for analysis.

To sum up, the previous analysis indicates the consolidation of the traditional analysis that has emerged since 1990. Notwithstanding, from 2010 onwards, and particularly clearer since 2015, new lines of investigation have been emerging, proposing diversified sources, contents, as well as types of analysis where IM strategies may appear, for instance:

- Using different pieces of entities' information, such as media coverage (media prints) to promote favorable viewpoints and interpretations, possibly impacting auditors' judgments (Andon & Free, 2014), as well as the inclusion of photographs to depict corporate social responsibility (Chong *et al.*, 2019);

- Through other innovative ways available to entities for releasing information to their stakeholders, such as the IM strategies used by entities in their messages reported on new social media, such as Twitter (Yekini *et al.*, 2015);
- Exploring the effects of IM strategies from different subjects, such as the stakeholder perspective proposed by Cardoso *et al.* (2018);
- Assessing the influence of subjects other than managers within the entity, such as the impact of the audit committee to mitigate IM strategies (Al-Sayani *et al.*, 2020);
- Exploring innovative content other than the traditional ones in accounting, such as disclosures related to gender (Hossain *et al.*, 2020), carbon emissions (Pitrakkos & Maroun, 2020), water (Fialho *et al.*, 2020) and child labor and unsustainable farming practice (Perkiss *et al.*, 2021);
- Using different sources of analysis other than reporting companies, for instance, the audit proposals presented by audit firms to their clients, which can be used as marketing tools to balance the potentially conflicting values of professionalism (Chang & Stone, 2021);
- Through different perspectives of analysis, such as the qualitative research performed by Kumarasinghe and Samkin (2020), which evidenced the techniques used by charismatic historic leaders to portray their leadership, and also found similarities between them and contemporary leaders, as well as the research by Parker and Warren (2017), which assessed the accountant professional role, identity, values, and image to face professional stereotypes;
- Using innovative techniques to assess the impact of the information from the users' perspectives, such as the eye-tracking experiments proposed by Cho *et al.* (2017), as well as by using machine learning associated with more traditional textual analysis tools, as proposed by Corazza *et al.* (2020).

Following the analysis performed in this subsection, the next section presents the conclusions from the literature review proposed for this chapter as well as its contributions to future investigations on the matters related to IM strategies.

CONCLUSION AND FUTURE RESEARCH DIRECTIONS

As identified in this chapter, several IM strategies can be used by the entities' managers to present a different view on their own or the entities' images and figures reported. These possible misrepresentations of reality can change the user's decision-making based on the analysis of the entity's accountability, its past, present, and perspectives, and, therefore, the risks and opportunities that can be assessed through this information.

Literature has found that those strategies are often used, deliberately or unintentionally, through the different ways available to entities to communicate with their stakeholders. Data provided by entities may have different uses from the stakeholders' perspectives, depending on several aspects such as the data characteristics (nature, format, details available, source, periodicity, etc.) and the objectives behind the interest defined (perceived usefulness) by each type of stakeholder. Therefore, the identification and proper knowledge of IM strategies used by entities may be relevant to a different set of accounting information users.

The findings from this chapter show that seminal papers were particularly focused on the analysis of the graphs and the message reported to manipulate or obfuscate the information provided to stakeholders on the entities' performance and perspectives. Initially, papers were especially dedicated to mandatory (financial) information, being quickly evolved into the analysis of voluntary (non-financial) reports, also enriching the sources of analysis, the tools and techniques used, as well as the topics under assessment.

Therefore, despite the different IM strategies and investigation lines that literature in accounting has been covering since the seminal research from the last decade of the 20th century, this theme remains relevant as long as it can be assessed and adapted from the perspective of the trending topics in accounting. The gender-related disclosure analysis proposed by Hossain *et al.* (2020) is an example of a topic that can be inserted and, therefore, may represent an innovative investigation even in the traditional research on IM strategies.

As some latest research provides evidence, the emergence of non-financial reporting, social media, technologies, and innovative information management systems as research sources may be mentioned as examples of sources for future avenues on this subject. The use of new technological tools, such as big data analysis, machine learning, and other artificial intelligence tools may also represent new boundaries for developing different methods and techniques to assess either the use or the impact of IM strategies by entities. The eye-tracking experiments performed by Cho *et al.* (2017) and the machine learning tool used by Corazza *et al* (2020) represent two interesting examples in this context.

Furthermore, few studies assess the cognitive effects of IM strategies from the stakeholders' perspective, such as investors and analysts, to take into consideration the subjective processes that are behind the information analysis, as proposed, for instance, by Cardoso *et al.* (2018). Experimental studies using subjective and psychological interpretations and impacts can provide significant inputs to the literature in this field.

The scope of this chapter has been restricted to the accounting field and papers with the IM as an expression explicitly included in their abstracts, which can be seen as its main limitations. Also, as observed during the process of gathering and assessing the papers for the literature review, IM research has been associated with a multiplicity of topics within several areas of social and human sciences. Consequently, the inputs from those papers can provide interesting insights for new research in accounting and, therefore, should be also considered by researchers in accounting. Also, the assessment of papers published in journals with a traditional background on innovative research, such as *Critical Perspectives on Accounting*, could be useful (see, for instance, the work by Jeacle (2008) on the accounting stereotype).

Finally, regarding the samples used for research on the information disclosed by entities that can make use of IM strategies, it is worthwhile to mention that most studies on this topic were based on entities from developed countries, larger companies (and, particularly, listed companies), and for-profit private sector entities. Then, there are still different geographies other than developed countries, small and medium entities, and either not-for-profit organizations or government entities that can be included in the scope of analysis of future research.

This chapter summarizes the themes and other specific characteristics of the papers selected for its scope, without presenting specific findings. However, its contribution can be useful to a wide audience, which includes not only researchers, but also regulators, financial and non-financial standard-setting bodies and users, auditors, and other stakeholders who are interested in the knowledge and identification of different sources and methods from which entities can use IM strategies.

DECLARATION

The authors declare that the manuscript follows ethical standards and there are no potential conflicts of interest with respect to the research, authorship and/or publication of this chapter.

DISCLAIMER

The contents and views of this chapter are expressed by the authors in their personal capacities. It is not necessary for the Editor and the Publisher to agree with these viewpoints, and they are not responsible for any duty of care in this regard.

ACKNOWLEDGMENT

The authors extend sincere gratitude to

- The Instituto Politécnico de Lisboa (IPL/2022/REPUKRAINE _ISCAL) for valuable support.
- The Editor and the International Editorial Advisory Board (IEAB) of this book who initially desk reviewed, arranged a rigorous double/triple blind review process, and conducted a thorough, minute, and critical final review before accepting the chapter for publication.
- All anonymous reviewers who provided very constructive feedbacks for thorough revision, improvement, extension, and fine tuning of the chapter.
- All colleagues, assistants and well-wishers who assisted to complete this task.

REFERENCES

Abeysekera, I. (2020). Intangibles disclosure on entrepreneurial small businesses' websites to influence stakeholders' impressions. *Australian Accounting Review*, *30*(1), 22–32. doi:10.1111/auar.12277

Abou-El-Sood, H., & El-Sayed, D. (2022). Abnormal disclosure tone, earnings management and earnings quality. *Journal of Applied Accounting Research*, *23*(2), 402–433. doi:10.1108/JAAR-07-2020-0139

Abraham, S., & Bamber, M. (2017). The Q&A: Under surveillance. *Accounting, Organizations and Society*, *58*, 15–31. doi:10.1016/j.aos.2017.04.001

Adler, R., Mansi, M., Pandey, R., & Stringer, C. (2017). United Nations decade on biodiversity: A study of the reporting practices of the Australian mining industry. *Accounting, Auditing & Accountability Journal*, *30*(8), 1711–1745. doi:10.1108/AAAJ-04-2015-2028

Aerts, W. (1994). On the use of accounting logic as an explanatory category in narrative accounting disclosures. *Accounting, Organizations and Society*, *19*(4-5), 337–353. doi:10.1016/0361-3682(94)90001-9

Aerts, W. (2005). Picking up the pieces: Impression management in the retrospective attributional framing of accounting outcomes. *Accounting, Organizations and Society*, *30*(6), 493–517. doi:10.1016/j.aos.2004.07.001

Aerts, W., & Cheng, P. (2011). Causal disclosures on earnings and earnings management in an IPO setting. *Journal of Accounting and Public Policy*, *30*(5), 431–459. doi:10.1016/j.jaccpubpol.2011.03.006

Aerts, W., & Yan, B. (2017). Rhetorical impression management in the letter to shareholders and institutional setting: A metadiscourse perspective. *Accounting, Auditing & Accountability Journal*, *30*(2), 404–432. doi:10.1108/AAAJ-01-2015-1916

Ahmad, N. N. N., & Hossain, D. M. (2019). Exploring the meaning of climate change discourses: An impression management exercise? *Accounting Research Journal*, *32*(2), 113–128. doi:10.1108/ARJ-07-2016-0085

Al-Sayani, Y. M., Mohamad Nor, M. N., & Amran, N. A. (2020). The influence of audit committee characteristics on impression management in chairman statement: Evidence from Malaysia. *Cogent Business and Management*, *7*(1), 1774250. doi:10.1080/23311975.2020.1774250

Allen, R., Helms, M., Takeda, M., & White, C. (2007). Porter's generic strategies: An exploratory study of their use in Japan. *The Journal of Business Strategy*, *24*(1), 69–90. doi:10.54155/jbs.24.1.69-90

Andon, P., & Free, C. (2014). Media coverage of accounting: The NRL salary cap crisis. *Accounting, Auditing & Accountability Journal*, *27*(1), 15–47. doi:10.1108/AAAJ-02-2012-00936

Barkemeyer, R., Comyns, B., Figge, F., & Napolitano, G. (2014). CEO statements in sustainability reports: Substantive information or background noise? *Accounting Forum*, *38*(4), 241–257. doi:10.1016/j.accfor.2014.07.002

Beattie, V., & Jones, M. (2002). Measurement distortion of graphs in corporate reports: An experimental study. *Accounting, Auditing & Accountability Journal*, *15*(4), 546–564. doi:10.1108/09513570210440595

Beattie, V., & Jones, M. (2008). Corporate reporting using graphs: A review and synthesis. *Journal of Accounting Literature*, *27*, 71–110.

Beattie, V., & Jones, M. J. (1999). Australian financial graphs: An empirical study. *Abacus*, *35*(1), 46–76. doi:10.1111/1467-6281.00034

Beattie, V., & Jones, M. J. (2000a). Changing graph use in corporate annual reports: A time-series analysis. *Contemporary Accounting Research*, *17*(2), 213–226. doi:10.1506/AAT8-3CGL-3J94-PH4F

Beattie, V., & Jones, M. J. (2000b). Impression management: The case of inter-country financial graphs. *Journal of International Accounting, Auditing & Taxation*, *9*(2), 159–183. doi:10.1016/S1061-9518(00)00030-6

Brennan, N. M., Daly, C. A., & Harrington, C. S. (2010). Rhetoric, argument and impression management in hostile takeover defence documents. *The British Accounting Review*, *42*(4), 253–268. doi:10.1016/j.bar.2010.07.008

Brennan, N. M., Guillamon-Saorin, E., & Pierce, A. (2009). Impression management: Developing and illustrating a scheme of analysis for narrative disclosures - A methodological note. *Accounting, Auditing & Accountability Journal*, *22*(5), 789–832. doi:10.1108/09513570910966379

Brivot, M., Cho, C. H., & Kuhn, J. R. (2015). Marketing or parrhesia: A longitudinal study of AICPA's shifting languages in times of turbulence. *Critical Perspectives on Accounting*, *31*, 23–43. doi:10.1016/j.cpa.2015.04.001

Bujaki, M., & McConomy, B. (2012). Metaphor in Nortel's letters to shareholders 1997-2006. *Accounting, Auditing & Accountability Journal*, *25*(7), 1113–1139. doi:10.1108/09513571211263211

Cardoso, R. L., Leite, R. O., & Aquino, A. C. B. (2018). The effect of cognitive reflection on the efficacy of impression management: An experimental analysis with financial analysts. *Accounting, Auditing & Accountability Journal*, *31*(6), 1668–1690. doi:10.1108/AAAJ-10-2016-2731

Chang, Y.-T., & Stone, D. N. (2021). Impression management in public sector audit proposals: Language and fees. *European Accounting Review*, 1–33. doi:10.1080/09638180.2021.1969260

Cho, C. H., Hageman, A. M., & Jérôme, T. (2017). Eye-tracking experiments in social and environmental accounting research. *Social and Environmental Accountability Journal*, *37*(3), 155–173. doi:10.1080/0969160X.2017.1350588

Cho, C. H., Michelon, G., & Patten, D. M. (2012). Enhancement and obfuscation through the use of graphs in sustainability reports: An international comparison. *Sustainability Accounting. Management and Policy Journal*, *3*(1), 74–88. doi:10.1108/20408021211223561

Cho, C. H., Roberts, R. W., & Patten, D. M. (2010). The language of US corporate environmental disclosure. *Accounting, Organizations and Society*, *35*(4), 431–443. doi:10.1016/j.aos.2009.10.002

Chong, S., & Rahman, A. (2020). Web-based impression management? Salient features for CSR disclosure prominence. *Sustainability Accounting, Management and Policy Journal*, *11*(1), 99–136. doi:10.1108/SAMPJ-08-2018-0221

Clatworthy, M., & Jones, M. J. (2003). Financial reporting of good news and bad news: Evidence from accounting narratives. *Accounting and Business Research*, *33*(3), 171–185. doi:10.1080/00014788.2003.9729645

Clatworthy, M., & Jones, M. J. (2006). Differential patterns of textual characteristics and company performance in the chairman's statement. *Accounting, Auditing & Accountability Journal*, *19*(4), 493–511. doi:10.1108/09513570610679100

Compernolle, T. (2018). Communication of the external auditor with the audit committee: Managing impressions to deal with multiple accountability relationships. *Accounting, Auditing & Accountability Journal*, *31*(3), 900–924. doi:10.1108/AAAJ-05-2013-1356

Conway, S. L., O'Keefe, P. A., & Hrasky, S. (2015). Legitimacy, accountability and impression management in NGOs: The Indian ocean tsunami. *Accounting, Auditing & Accountability Journal*, *28*(7), 1075–1098. doi:10.1108/AAAJ-04-2012-01007

Cooper, S., & Slack, R. (2015). Reporting practice, impression management and company performance: A longitudinal and comparative analysis of water leakage disclosure. *Accounting and Business Research*, *45*(6-7), 801–840. doi:10.1080/00014788.2015.1081554

Corazza, L., Truant, E., Scagnelli, S. D., & Mio, C. (2020). Sustainability reporting after the costa concordia disaster: A multi-theory study on legitimacy, impression management and image restoration. *Accounting, Auditing & Accountability Journal, 33*(8), 1909–1941. doi:10.1108/AAAJ-05-2018-3488

Corrigan, L. T., & Rixon, D. (2017). A dramaturgical accounting of Cooperative performance indicators. *Qualitative Research in Accounting & Management, 14*(1), 60–80. doi:10.1108/QRAM-08-2016-0060

Courtois, C., & Gendron, Y. (2020). The show must go on! legitimization processes surrounding certified fraud examiners' claim to expertise. *European Accounting Review, 29*(3), 437–465. doi:10.1080/09638180.2019.1643753

Davison, J. (2015). Visualising accounting: An interdisciplinary review and synthesis. *Accounting and Business Research, 45*(2), 121–165. doi:10.1080/00014788.2014.987203

Demaline, C. (2019). Disclosure characteristics of firms being investigated by the SEC. *Journal of Corporate Accounting & Finance, 30*(4), 11–24. doi:10.1002/jcaf.22412

Demaline, C. (2020). Disclosure readability of firms investigated for books-and-records infractions: An impression management perspective. *Journal of Financial Reporting and Accounting, 18*(1), 131–145. doi:10.1108/JFRA-10-2018-0094

Dhanani, A., & Kennedy, D. (2022). Envisioning legitimacy: Visual dimensions of NGO annual reports. *Accounting, Auditing & Accountability Journal*. Advance online publication. doi:10.1108/AAAJ-01-2020-4377

Dilla, W. N., & Janvrin, D. J. (2010). Voluntary Disclosure in Annual Reports: The Association between magnitude and direction of change in corporate financial performance and graph Use. *Accounting Horizons, 24*(2), 257–278. doi:10.2308/acch.2010.24.2.257

Diouf, D., & Boiral, O. (2017). The quality of sustainability reports and impression management: A stakeholder perspective. *Accounting, Auditing & Accountability Journal, 30*(3), 643–667. doi:10.1108/AAAJ-04-2015-2044

Edgar, V. C., Beck, M., & Brennan, N. M. (2018). Impression management in annual report narratives: The case of the UK private finance initiative. *Accounting, Auditing & Accountability Journal, 31*(6), 1566–1592. doi:10.1108/AAAJ-10-2016-2733

El-Sayed, D., Adel, E., Elmougy, O., Fawzy, N., Hatem, N., & Elhakey, F. (2021). The influence of narrative disclosure readability, information ordering and graphical representations on non-professional investors' judgment: Evidence from an emerging market. *Journal of Applied Accounting Research, 22*(1), 138–167. doi:10.1108/JAAR-06-2020-0115

Evans, L., & Pierpoint, J. (2015). Framing the magdalen: Sentimental narratives and impression management in charity annual reporting. *Accounting and Business Research, 45*(6–7), 661–690. doi:10.1080/00014788.2015.1039931

Falschlunger, L. M., Eisl, C., Losbichler, H., & Greil, A. M. (2015). Impression management in annual reports of the largest European companies: A longitudinal study on graphical representations. *Journal of Applied Accounting Research, 16*(3), 383–399. doi:10.1108/JAAR-10-2014-0109

Fialho, A., Morais, A., & Costa, R. P. (2020). Impression management strategies and water disclosures – the case of CDP A-list. *Meditari Accountancy Research, 29*(3), 568–585. doi:10.1108/MEDAR-08-2019-0542

Fisher, R., van Staden, C. J., & Richards, G. (2020). Watch that tone: An investigation of the use and stylistic consequences of tone in corporate accountability disclosures. *Accounting, Auditing & Accountability Journal, 33*(1), 77–105. doi:10.1108/AAAJ-10-2016-2745

García Osma, B., & Guillamón-Saorín, E. (2011). Corporate governance and impression management in annual results press releases. *Accounting, Organizations and Society, 36*(4-5), 187–208. doi:10.1016/j.aos.2011.03.005

Godfrey, J., Mather, P., & Ramsay, A. (2003). Earnings and impression management in financial reports: The case of CEO changes. *Abacus, 39*(1), 95–123. doi:10.1111/1467-6281.00122

Guillamon-Saorin, E., Osma, B. G., & Jones, M. J. (2012). Opportunistic disclosure in press release headlines. *Accounting and Business Research, 42*(2), 143–168. doi:10.1080/00014788.2012.632575

Hadro, D., Klimczak, K. M., & Pauka, M. (2017). Impression management in letters to shareholders: Evidence from Poland. *Accounting in Europe, 14*(3), 305–330. doi:10.1080/17449480.2017.1378428

Haji, A. A., & Hossain, D. M. (2016). Exploring the implications of integrated reporting on organisational reporting practice: Evidence from highly regarded integrated reporters. *Qualitative Research in Accounting & Management, 13*(4), 415–444. doi:10.1108/QRAM-07-2015-0065

Hamza, S., & Jarboui, A. (2022). CSR or social impression management? Tone management in CSR reports. *Journal of Financial Reporting and Accounting, 20*(3-4), 599–617. doi:10.1108/JFRA-04-2020-0115

Higgins, C., & Walker, R. (2012). Ethos, logos, pathos: Strategies of persuasion in social/environmental reports. *Accounting Forum, 36*(3), 194–208. doi:10.1016/j.accfor.2012.02.003

Higginson, N., Simmons, C., & Warsame, H. (2006). Environmental disclosure and legitimation in the annual report - evidence from the joint solutions project. *Journal of Applied Accounting Research, 8*(2), 3–23. doi:10.1108/96754260680001048

Holm, C., & Zaman, M. (2012). Regulating audit quality: Restoring trust and legitimacy. *Accounting Forum, 36*(1), 51–61. doi:10.1016/j.accfor.2011.11.004

Hossain, D. M., Alam, M. S., Mazumder, M. M. M., & Amin, A. (2020). Gender-related discourses in corporate annual reports: An exploratory study on the Bangladeshi companies. *Journal of Accounting and Organizational Change, 17*(3), 394–415. doi:10.1108/JAOC-01-2020-0006

Hrasky, S., & Jones, M. J. (2016). Lake pedder: Accounting, environmental decision-making, nature and impression management. *Accounting Forum, 40*(4), 285–299. doi:10.1016/j.accfor.2016.06.005

Jeacle, I. (2008). Beyond the boring grey: The construction of the colourful accountant. *Critical Perspectives on Accounting, 19*(8), 1296–1320. doi:10.1016/j.cpa.2007.02.008

Jeacle, I. (2014). "And the BAFTA goes to [...]": The assurance role of the auditor in the film awards ceremony. *Accounting, Auditing & Accountability Journal, 27*(5), 778–808. doi:10.1108/AAAJ-03-2013-1252

Jeacle, I., & Carter, C. (2012). Fashioning the popular masses: Accounting as mediator between creativity and control. *Accounting, Auditing & Accountability Journal, 25*(4), 719–751. doi:10.1108/09513571211225114

Jones, M. J. (2011). The nature, use and impression management of graphs in social and environmental accounting. *Accounting Forum, 35*(2), 75–89. doi:10.1016/j.accfor.2011.03.002

Jones, M. J., Melis, A., Gaia, S., & Aresu, S. (2018). Does graphical reporting improve risk disclosure? Evidence from European banks. *Journal of Applied Accounting Research, 19*(1), 161–180. doi:10.1108/JAAR-07-2016-0068

Jugnandan, S., & Willows, G. D. (2022). "It's a long story…" – impression management in South African corporate reporting. *Accounting Research Journal, 35*(5), 581–597. doi:10.1108/ARJ-07-2021-0209

Kayed, S., & Meqbel, R. (2022). (in press). Earnings management and tone management: Evidence from FTSE 350 companies. *Journal of Financial Reporting and Accounting*. Advance online publication. doi:10.1108/JFRA-10-2021-0373

Khan, N., Rafay, A., & Shakeel, A. (2020). Attributes of Internal Audit and Prevention, Detection and Assessment of Fraud in Pakistan. *Lahore Journal of Business, 9*(1), 33–58. doi:10.35536/ljb.2020.v9.i1.a2

Khanna, K., & Irvine, H. (2018). Communicating the impact of the global financial crisis in annual reports: A study of Australian NGOs. *Australian Accounting Review, 28*(1), 109–126. doi:10.1111/auar.12162

Kumarasinghe, S., & Samkin, G. (2020). Impression management and ancient Ceylonese rulers. *Accounting History, 25*(1), 5–26. doi:10.1177/1032373218802892

Lau, C. M., & Martin-Sardesai, A. V. (2012). The role of organisational concern for workplace fairness in the choice of a performance measurement system. *The British Accounting Review, 44*(3), 157–172. doi:10.1016/j.bar.2012.07.006

Leung, S., Parker, L., & Courtis, J. (2015). Impression management through minimal narrative disclosure in annual reports. *The British Accounting Review, 47*(3), 275–289. doi:10.1016/j.bar.2015.04.002

Leventis, S., & Weetman, P. (2004). Impression management: Dual language reporting and voluntary disclosure. *Accounting Forum, 28*(3), 307–328. doi:10.1016/j.accfor.2004.07.004

Martins, A., Gomes, D., Oliveira, L., & Ribeiro, J. L. (2019). Telling a success story through the president's letter. *Qualitative Research in Accounting & Management, 16*(3), 403–433. doi:10.1108/QRAM-03-2018-0018

Mather, P., & Ramsay, A. (2007). Do board characteristics influence impression management through graph selectivity around CEO changes? *Australian Accounting Review, 17*(42), 84–95. doi:10.1111/j.1835-2561.2007.tb00446.x

Mather, P., Ramsay, A., & Steen, A. (2000). The use and representational faithfulness of graphs in Australian IPO prospectuses. *Accounting, Auditing & Accountability Journal, 13*(1), 65–83. doi:10.1108/09513570010316144

McNally, M. A., & Maroun, W. (2018). It is not always bad news: Illustrating the potential of integrated reporting using a case study in the eco-tourism industry. *Accounting, Auditing & Accountability Journal, 31*(5), 1319–1348. doi:10.1108/AAAJ-05-2016-2577

Melloni, G., Caglio, A., & Perego, P. (2017). Saying more with less? Disclosure conciseness, completeness and balance in integrated reports. *Journal of Accounting and Public Policy, 36*(3), 220–238. doi:10.1016/j.jaccpubpol.2017.03.001

Merkl-Davies, D. M., & Brennan, N. M. (2007). Discretionary disclosure strategies in corporate narratives: Incremental information or impression management? *Journal of Accounting Literature, 27*, 116–196. https://ssrn.com/abstract=1089447

Merkl-Davies, D. M., & Brennan, N. M. (2011). A conceptual framework of impression management: New insights from psychology, sociology and critical perspectives. *Accounting and Business Research, 41*(5), 415–437. doi:10.1080/00014788.2011.574222

Merkl-Davies, D. M., Brennan, N. M., & McLeay, S. J. (2011). Impression management and retrospective sense-making in corporate narratives: A social psychology perspective. *Accounting, Auditing & Accountability Journal, 24*(3), 315–344. doi:10.1108/09513571111124036

Miles, S., & Ringham, K. (2020). The boundary of sustainability reporting: Evidence from the FTSE100. *Accounting, Auditing & Accountability Journal, 33*(2), 357–390. doi:10.1108/AAAJ-05-2018-3478

Moreno, A., Jones, M. J., & Quinn, M. (2019). A longitudinal study of the textual characteristics in the chairman's statements of Guinness: An impression management perspective. *Accounting, Auditing & Accountability Journal, 32*(6), 1714–1741. doi:10.1108/AAAJ-01-2018-3308

Moussa, T., Kotb, A., & Helfaya, A. (2021). An empirical investigation of U.K. environmental targets disclosure: The role of environmental governance and performance. *European Accounting Review*, 1–35. doi:10.1080/09638180.2021.1890173

Nègre, E., Verdier, M. A., Cho, C. H., & Patten, D. M. (2017). Disclosure strategies and investor reactions to downsizing announcements: A legitimacy perspective. *Journal of Accounting and Public Policy, 36*(3), 239–257. doi:10.1016/j.jaccpubpol.2017.03.003

Neu, D. (1991). Trust, impression management and the public accounting profession. *Critical Perspectives on Accounting, 2*(3), 295–313. doi:10.1016/1045-2354(91)90015-6

Neu, D. (1999). "Discovering" indigenous peoples: Accounting and the machinery of empire. *The Accounting Historians Journal, 26*(1), 53–82. doi:10.2308/0148-4184.26.1.53

Nyagadza, B., Kadembo, E. M., & Makasi, A. (2020). Exploring internal stakeholders' emotional attachment & corporate brand perceptions through corporate storytelling for branding. *Cogent Business and Management, 7*(1), 1816254. doi:10.1080/23311975.2020.1816254

Ogden, S., & Clarke, J. (2005). Customer disclosures, impression management and the construction of legitimacy: Corporate reports in the UK privatised water industry. *Accounting, Auditing & Accountability Journal, 18*(3), 313–345. doi:10.1108/09513570510600729

Parker, L. D. (2016). From scientific to activity based office management: A mirage of Change. *Journal of Accounting & Organizational Change*, *12*(2), 177–202. doi:10.1108/JAOC-01-2015-0007

Parker, L. D., & Schmitz, J. (2022). The reinvented accounting firm office: Impression management for efficiency, client relations and cost control. *Accounting, Organizations and Society*, *98*, 101306. doi:10.1016/j.aos.2021.101306

Parker, L. D., & Warren, S. (2017). The presentation of the self and professional identity: Countering the accountant's stereotype. *Accounting, Auditing & Accountability Journal*, *30*(8), 1895–1924. doi:10.1108/AAAJ-09-2016-2720

Perkiss, S., Bernardi, C., Dumay, J., & Haslam, J. (2021). A sticky chocolate problem: Impression management and counter accounts in the shaping of corporate image. *Critical Perspectives on Accounting*, *81*, 102229. doi:10.1016/j.cpa.2020.102229

Pitrakkos, P., & Maroun, W. (2020). Evaluating the quality of carbon disclosures. *Sustainability Accounting. Management and Policy Journal*, *11*(3), 553–589. doi:10.1108/SAMPJ-03-2018-0081

Rafay, A. (Ed.). (2019). *FinTech as a Disruptive Technology for Financial Institutions*. IGI Global. doi:10.4018/978-1-5225-7805-5

Rafay, A. (2022). Related Party Disclosures in Financial Reporting for Islamic Banks. *Journal of Islamic Accounting and Business Research*, *13*(7), 997–1017. doi:10.1108/JIABR-03-2020-0066

Rafay, A., & Farid, S. (2018). Shariah Supervisory Board Report (SSBR) in Islamic Banks: An experimental study of Investors' perception and behaviour. *International Journal of Islamic and Middle Eastern Finance and Management*, *11*(2), 274–296. doi:10.1108/IMEFM-07-2017-0180

Rafay, A., Sadiq, R., & Ajmal, M. M. (2016). The Effect of IAS-24 Disclosures on Governance Mechanisms and Ownership Structures in Pakistan. *Lahore Journal of Business*, *5*(1), 15–36. doi:10.35536/ljb.2016.v5.i1.a2

Ramzan, M., Ahmad, I., & Rafay, A. (2020). Is Auditor independence influenced by Non-audit services? A stakeholder's viewpoint. *Pakistan Journal of Commerce and Social Sciences*, *14*(1), 388–408.

Riley, T. J., & Luippold, B. L. (2015). Managing investors' perception through strategic word choices in financial narratives. *Journal of Corporate Accounting & Finance*, *26*(5), 57–62. doi:10.1002/jcaf.22064

Sahyoun, N., & Magnan, M. (2020). The association between voluntary disclosure in audit committee reports and banks' earnings management. *Managerial Auditing Journal*, *35*(6), 795–817. doi:10.1108/MAJ-05-2019-2279

Samkin, G., & Schneider, A. (2010). Accountability, narrative reporting and legitimation: The case of a New Zealand public benefit entity. *Accounting, Auditing & Accountability Journal*, *23*(2), 256–289. doi:10.1108/09513571011023219

Sandberg, M., & Holmlund, M. (2015). Impression management tactics in sustainability reporting. *Social Responsibility Journal*, *11*(4), 677–689. doi:10.1108/SRJ-12-2013-0152

Schleicher, T. (2012). When is good news really good news? *Accounting and Business Research*, *42*(5), 547–573. doi:10.1080/00014788.2012.685275

Schleicher, T., & Walker, M. (2010). Bias in the tone of forward-looking narratives. *Accounting and Business Research*, *40*(4), 371–390. doi:10.1080/00014788.2010.9995318

Shafer, W. E. (2009). Ethical climate, organizational-professional conflict and organizational commitment: A study of Chinese auditors. *Accounting, Auditing & Accountability Journal*, *22*(7), 1087–1110. doi:10.1108/09513570910987385

Sheldon, M. D., & Jenkins, J. G. (2020). The influence of firm performance and (level of) assurance on the believability of management's environmental report. *Accounting, Auditing & Accountability Journal*, *33*(3), 501–528. doi:10.1108/AAAJ-11-2018-3726

Solomon, J. F., Solomon, A., Joseph, N. L., & Norton, S. D. (2013). Impression management, myth creation and fabrication in private social and environmental reporting: Insights from Erving Goffman. *Accounting, Organizations and Society*, *38*(3), 195–213. doi:10.1016/j.aos.2013.01.001

Soobaroyen, T., & Mahadeo, J. D. (2016). Community disclosures in a developing country: Insights from a neo-pluralist perspective. *Accounting, Auditing & Accountability Journal*, *29*(3), 452–482. doi:10.1108/AAAJ-08-2014-1810

Sydserff, R., & Weetman, P. (2002). Developments in content analysis: A transitivity index and DICTION scores. *Accounting, Auditing & Accountability Journal*, *15*(4), 523–545. doi:10.1108/09513570210440586

Tauringana, V., & Mangena, M. (2014). Board structure and supplementary commentary on the primary financial statements. *Journal of Applied Accounting Research*, *15*(3), 273–290. doi:10.1108/JAAR-11-2013-0090

Westermann, K. D., Cohen, J., & Trompeter, G. (2019). PCAOB inspections: Public accounting firms on "trial". *Contemporary Accounting Research*, *36*(2), 694–731. doi:10.1111/1911-3846.12454

Yang, J. H., & Liu, S. (2017). Accounting narratives and impression management on social media. *Accounting and Business Research*, *47*(6), 673–694. doi:10.1080/00014788.2017.1322936

Yekini, L. S., Wisniewski, T. P., & Millo, Y. (2016). Market reaction to the positiveness of annual report narratives. *The British Accounting Review*, *48*(4), 415–430. doi:10.1016/j.bar.2015.12.001

Zeng, X., Momin, M., & Nurunnabi, M. (2022). Photo disclosure in human rights issues by fortune companies: An impression management perspective. *Sustainability Accounting. Management and Policy Journal*, *13*(3), 568–599. doi:10.1108/SAMPJ-06-2019-0243

Zhang, S., & Aerts, W. (2015). Management's performance justification and failure to meet earnings thresholds. *Accounting and Business Research*, *45*(6-7), 841–868. doi:10.1080/00014788.2015.1048771

Zhao, L., & Atkins, J. (2021). Assessing the emancipatory nature of Chinese extinction accounting. *Social and Environmental Accountability Journal*, *41*(1-2), 8–36. doi:10.1080/0969160X.2021.1889386

ADDITIONAL READING

García-Sánchez, I. M., & Araújo-Bernardo, C. A. (2020). What colour is the corporate social responsibility report? Structural visual rhetoric, impression management strategies, and stakeholder engagement. *Corporate Social Responsibility and Environmental Management*, *27*(2), 1117–1142. doi:10.1002/csr.1869

Lee, G., Cho, S. Y., Arthurs, J., & Lee, E. K. (2020). Celebrity CEO, identity threat, and impression management: Impact of celebrity status on corporate social responsibility. *Journal of Business Research*, *111*, 69–84. doi:10.1016/j.jbusres.2020.01.015

Martins, A., Gomes, D., & Branco, M. C. (2020). Managing corporate social and environmental disclosure: An accountability vs. impression management framework. *Sustainability*, *13*(1), 296. doi:10.3390u13010296

Moreno, A., & Jones, M. J. (2022). Impression management in corporate annual reports during the global financial crisis. *European Management Journal*, *40*(4), 503–517. doi:10.1016/j.emj.2021.08.007

Sezer, O. (2022). Impression (mis) management: When what you say is not what they hear. *Current Opinion in Psychology*, *44*, 31–37. doi:10.1016/j.copsyc.2021.08.025 PMID:34555683

Sun, Y., Fang, S., & Zhang, Z. J. (2021). Impression management strategies on enterprise social media platforms: An affordance perspective. *International Journal of Information Management*, *60*, 102359. doi:10.1016/j.ijinfomgt.2021.102359

APPENDIX 1. NUMBER OF PAPERS AND CITATIONS BY PERIOD AND ACCOUNTING JOURNALS

Table 2.

	1990-1999			2000-2009			2010-2019			2020-2022			Total		
Journal	**P**	**C**	**%**	**P**	**C**	**%**	**P**	**C**	**%**	**P**	**C**	**%**	**P**	**C**	**%**
Acc, Aud & Accty J				6	550	12	18	722	13	5	52	18	29	1,324	25
J of Acc Literature				1	916	21							1	916	17
Acc, Org & Society	1	100	22	1	130	3	4	651	12	2	5	2	8	886	16
Acc &Bus Res				1	209	5	9	416	7				10	625	12
Acc Forum				1	26	1	5	291	5	1	9	3	7	326	6
C Persp on Acc	1	86	19	1	144	3	1	14	0	1	13	5	4	257	5
J of Acc & Public Policy							3	181	3				3	181	3
Abacus	1	46	10	1	124	3							2	170	3
British Acc Review							4	148	3				4	148	3
Acc & the Pub Interest							1	112	2				1	112	2
Cont Acc Res				1	39	1	1	62	1				2	101	2
Qual Res in Acc & Man							3	59	1				3	59	1
J of Int Acc, Aud &Tax				1	52	1				1	2	1	2	54	1
J of App Acc Res				1	5	0	3	31	1	2	3	1	6	39	1
J of Acc & Org Change							1	26	0	1	1	0	2	27	1
Australian Acc Review				1	14	0	1	8	0	1	3	1	3	25	0
Sus Acc, Man & Policy J										1	20	7	1	20	0
Acc in Europe							1	17	0				1	17	0
Pacific Acc Review							2	17	0				2	17	0
Acc Horizons							1	16	0				1	16	0
Cogent Bus and Man										2	10	3	2	10	0
Man Aud J										1	10	3	1	10	0
Acc History							1	9	0	1	0	0	2	9	0
J of Corp Acc &Finance							2	8	0				2	8	0
Social and Env Accty J							1	2	0	2	5	2	3	7	0
European Acc Review										4	5	2	4	5	0
J of Fin Rep & Acc										3	5	2	3	5	0
Acc Res J							1	4	0	1	0	0	2	4	0
Ac of Acc and Fin Studies J							1	3	0				1	3	0
Meditari Acccy Res										1	1	0	1	1	0
Acc										1	0	0	1	0	0
Acc and Finance										1	0	0	1	0	0

Notes: P = Number of papers; C = Number of citations; % = paper citation over total citations; Acc, Aud & Accty J = Accounting, Auditing and Accountability Journal; J of Acc Literature = Journal of Accounting Literature; Acc, Org & Society = Accounting, Organizations and Society; Acc &Bus Res = Accounting and Business Research; Acc Forum = Accounting Forum; C Persp on Acc = Critical Perspectives on Accounting; J of Acc & Public Policy = Journal of Accounting and Public Policy; Abacus = Abacus; British Acc Review = British Accounting Review; Acc & the Pub Interest = Accounting and the Public Interest; Cont Acc Res = Contemporary Accounting Research; Qual Res in Acc & Man = Qualitative Research in Accounting and Management; J of Int Acc, Aud &Tax = Journal of International Accounting, Auditing and Taxation; J of App Acc Res = Journal of Applied Accounting Research; J of Acc & Org Change = Journal of Accounting and Organizational Change; Australian Acc Review = Australian Accounting Review; Sus Acc, Man & Policy J = Sustainability Accounting, Management and Policy Journal; Acc in Europe = Accounting in Europe; Pacific Acc Review = Pacific Accounting Review; Acc Horizons = Accounting Horizons; Cogent Bus and Man = Cogent Business and Management; Man Aud J = Managerial Auditing Journal; Acc History = Accounting History; J of Corp Acc &Finance = Journal of Corporate Accounting and Finance; Social and Env Accty J = Social and Environmental Accountability Journal; European Acc Review = European Accounting Review; J of Fin Rep & Acc = Journal of Financial Reporting and Accounting; Acc Res J = Accounting Research Journal; Ac of Acc and Fin Studies J = Academy of Accounting and Financial Studies Journal; Meditari Acccy Res = Meditari Accountancy Research; Acc = Accounting; Acc and Finance = Accounting and Finance

APPENDIX 2. PAPERS BY PERIOD AND NUMBER OF CITATIONS (TEN AT A MINIMUM)

Table 3.

Papers	1990-1999	2000-2009	2010-2019	2020-2022
Merkl-Davies & Brennan (2007)		916		
Cho *et al.* (2010)			405	
Clatworthy & Jones (2003)		209		
Diouf & Boiral (2017)			153	
Jeacle (2008)		144		
Brennan *et al.* (2009)		138		
Merkl-Davies *et al.* (2011)			137	
Clatworthy *et al.* (2006)		136		
Melloni *et al.* (2017)			131	
Aerts (2005)		130		
Higgins *et al.* (2011)			130	
Solomon *et al.* (2013)			128	
Godfrey *et al.* (2003)		124		
Cho *et al.* (2012)			112	
García Osma *et al.* (2011)			104	
Ogden & Clarke (2005)		103		
Sydserff & Weetman (2002)		102		
Aerts (1994)	100			
Beattie & Jones (2000)		91		
Neu (1991)	86			
Schleicher & Walker (2010)			81	
Samkin & Schneider (2010)			80	
Davison (2015)			68	
Leung *et al.* (2015)			67	
Westermann *et al.* (2019)			62	
Haji & Hossain (2016); Jones (2011)			52	
Barkemeyer *et al.* (2014)			47	
Beattie & Jones (1999)	46			
Holm & Zaman (2012)			46	
Jeacle & Carter (2012)			45	
Shafer (2009)		45		
McNally & Maroun (2018)			37	
Yekini *et al.* (2016)			36	

Continued on following page

Table 3. Continued

Papers	1990-1999	2000-2009	2010-2019	2020-2022
Adler *et al.* (2017); Guillamon-Saorin *et al.* (2012)			35	
Conway *et al.* (2015)			34	
Cooper & Slack (2015); Soobaroyen & Mahadeo (2016); Yang & Liu (2017)			33	
Aerts & Yan (2017)			31	
Leventis & Weetman (2004); Mather *et al.* (2000)		26		
Brennan *et al.* (2010); Nègre & (2017); Parker (2016)			26	
Jeacle (2014)			25	
Aerts & Cheng (2011); Andon & Free (2014)			24	
Falschlunger *et al.* (2015); Parker & Warren (2017)			21	
Pitrakkos & Maroun (2020)				20
Fisher *et al.* (2020)				19
Lau & Martin-Sardesai (2012)			19	
Hadro *et al.* (2017)			17	
Dilla & Janvrin (2010); Hrasky & Jones (2016)			16	
Bujaki & McConomy (2012)			15	
Abraham & Bamber (2017); Brivot *et al.* (2015); Compernolle (2018); Moreno *et al.* (2019); Schleicher (2012)			14	
Corazza *et al.* (2020)				14
Mather P., Ramsay A. (2007)		14		
Edgar *et al.* (2018)			13	
Perkiss *et al.* (2021)				13
Evans & Pierpoint (2015); Zhang & Aerts (2015)			11	
Sheldon & Jenkins (2020)				11
Sahyoun & Magnan (2020)				10

APPENDIX 3. AUTHORS BY NUMBER OF PAPERS AND CITATIONS (TEN AT A MINIMUM)

Table 4.

Authors	P	C	Av.	Authors	P	C	Av.	Authors	P	C	Av.
Roberts, R.W.	1	405	405	Barkemeyer, R.	1	47	47	Greil, A.M.	1	21	21
Merkl-Davies, D.M.	3	1,183	394	Comyns, B.	1	47	47	Losbichler, H.	1	21	21
Brennan, N.M.	7	1,365	195	Figge, F.	1	47	47	Warren, S.	1	21	21
Patten, D.M.	3	543	181	Napolitano, G.	1	47	47	Maroun,, W.	1	20	20
Clatworthy, M.	2	345	173	Holm, C.	1	46	46	Pitrakkos,, P.	1	20	20
Boiral, O.	1	153	153	Zaman, M.	1	46	46	Yan, B.	2	40	20
Diouf, D.	1	153	153	Beattie, V.	3	137	46	Fisher, R.	1	19	19
Pierce, A.	1	138	138	Carter, C.	1	45	45	Hossain, D.M.	3	57	19
McLeay, S.J.	1	137	137	Shafer, W.E.	1	45	45	Lau, C.M.	1	19	19
Caglio, A.	1	131	131	Samkin, G.	2	80	40	Martin-Sardesai, A.V.	1	19	19
Melloni, G.	1	131	131	Davison, J.	2	77	39	Richards, G.	1	19	19
Perego, P.	1	131	131	Maroun, W.	1	37	37	van, Staden, C.J.	1	19	19
Higgins, C.	1	130	130	McNally, M.-A.	1	37	37	Hadro, D.	1	17	17
Walker, R.	1	130	130	Momin, M.	1	36	36	Klimczak, K.M.	1	17	17
Joseph, N.L.	1	128	128	Nurunnabi, M.	1	36	36	Pauka, M.	1	17	17
Norton, S.D.	1	128	128	Zeng, X.	1	36	36	Dilla, W.N.	1	16	16
Solomon, A.	1	128	128	Adler, R.	1	35	35	Janvrin, D.J.	1	16	16
Solomon, J.F.	1	128	128	Mansi, M.	1	35	35	Bujaki, M.	1	15	15
Godfrey, J.	1	124	124	Osma, B.G.	1	35	35	McConomy, B.	1	15	15
Michelon, G.	1	112	112	Pandey, R.	1	35	35	Abraham, S.	1	14	14
Cho, C.H.	5	559	112	Stringer, C.	1	35	35	Bamber, M.	1	14	14
García, Osma, B.	1	104	104	Conway, S.L.	1	34	34	Brivot, M.	1	14	14
Guillamón-Saorín, E.	1	104	104	O'Keefe, P.A.	1	34	34	Compernolle, T.	1	14	14
Clarke, J.	1	103	103	Cooper, S.	1	33	33	Corazza, L.	1	14	14
Ogden, S.	1	103	103	Mahadeo, J.D.	1	33	33	Kuhn, J.R.	1	14	14
Sydserff, R.	1	102	102	Millo, Y.	1	33	33	Mio, C.	1	14	14
Guillamon-Saorin, E.	2	173	87	Slack, R.	1	33	33	Moreno, A.	1	14	14
Neu, D.	1	86	86	Soobaroyen, T.	1	33	33	Quinn, M.	1	14	14
Walker, M.	1	81	81	Wisniewski, T.P.	1	33	33	Scagnelli, S.D.	1	14	14
Schneider, A.	1	80	80	Yekini, L.S.	1	33	33	Truant, E.	1	14	14
Jeacle, I.	3	214	71	Parker, L.D.	4	114	29	Beck, M.	1	13	13
Courtis, J.	1	67	67	Daly, C.A.	1	26	26	Bernardi, C.	1	13	13
Leung, S.	1	67	67	Harrington, C.S.	1	26	26	Dumay, J.	1	13	13

Continued on following page

Table 4. Continued

Authors	P	C	Av.	Authors	P	C	Av.	Authors	P	C	Av.
Weetman, P.	2	128	64	Leventis, S.	1	26	26	Edgar, V.C.	1	13	13
Cohen, J.	1	62	62	Nègre, E.	1	26	26	Haslam, J.	1	13	13
Trompeter, G.	1	62	62	Steen, A.	1	26	26	Perkiss, S.	1	13	13
Westermann, K.D.	1	62	62	Verdier, M.-A.	1	26	26	Chen,, H.	1	11	11
Jones, M.J.	10	606	61	Hrasky, S.	2	50	25	Evans, L.	1	11	11
Aerts, W.	5	288	58	Andon, P.	1	24	24	Jenkins, J.G.	1	11	11
Mather, P.	3	164	55	Cheng, P.	1	24	24	Pierpoint, J.	1	11	11
Ramsay, A.	3	164	55	Free, C.	1	24	24	Sheldon, M.D.	1	11	11
Haji, A.A.	1	52	52	Eisl, C.	1	21	21	Magnan,, M	1	10	10
Schleicher, T.	2	95	48	Falschlunger, L.M.	1	21	21	Sahyoun,, N.	1	10	10

Chapter 9
Enterprise Risk Management and Shadow Banking Systems:
The Case of European Union

Stefano de Nichilo
https://orcid.org/0000-0003-4542-2365
University of Cagliari, Italy

ABSTRACT

Banking regulations are beneficial to limit bank' portfolios against excessive risk-taking. The introduction of enterprise risk management (ERM) allows banks to enhance their capabilities to identify risks accurately and manage them to minimize unexpected costs or losses. During the last few years, the European Court of Auditors highlighted the importance of "special reports" that examine the economy, efficiency, and effectiveness of EU spending. This European institutional focus argues that shadow banking improves welfare because it provides a channel to escape excessive regulation that is asymmetrically more valuable for banks or European paying agencies with access to efficient investment opportunities. Performance audits, alongside traditional financial and compliance audits, allow the EU to understand, validate, and reform their own policies and programs. This study contributes theoretically and empirically regarding the fraud and management bad practice of agile marketing concepts in the context of digital transformation and international business.

INTRODUCTION

The fraud and scandals that occur in dynamic and highly competitive business environments shed light on traditional risk management deficiencies (DeNichilo, 2021b & 2022, Nakitende *et al.*, 2021). This situation has pushed experts towards designing robust risk management practices, which consider a more coordinated and broader approach, resulting in the development of new enterprise risk management (ERM) frameworks (Hoerner & Stephenson, 2012). The increasing responsibilities toward stakeholders have pressured companies into adopting ERM frameworks, one of which, the Committee of Sponsoring

DOI: 10.4018/978-1-6684-5007-9.ch009

Organizations of the Treadway Commission (COSO, 2004) framework, is regarded as the main reference worldwide (Anderson & Dekker, 2014).

This chapter examines the developments of ERM, the COSO framework and the problems experienced by firms during implementation (Mendez & Bactler, 2011). Risk identification practices are described by outlining the stages of risk assessment and risk response. A discussion is presented on how the crisis impacted ERM and how ERM mitigated the crisis, whit the last paragraph briefly concluding the paper (Balint, Bauer & Knill, 2008).

In recent decades, significant attention has been dedicated to risk management advances in the accounting and management literature. Academics and practitioners have experienced a crucial shift from the traditional method of managing risks, called "risk silo management", to more integrated management of all risks, known as enterprise risk management. Risk silo management represents a fragmented and narrowly focused approach (Caiden, 1998).

Firstly, a fragmented approach to risk management implies that the numerous organizational units inside the same firm manage interdependent operational, financial, and technical risks in isolation. As the aggregation of risks in such an environment could make delivering results difficult, a firm is unable to conduct an integrated risk analysis. This methodology leads to the potential misalignment of business strategy with risk appetite at the aggregate level resulting in a lack of awareness of and accountability for the risks borne across the company (Hagen, Zucchela & Ghauri, 2018). *Secondly*, an ad hoc approach means that the execution of risk management is employed sporadically, which contrast with the routine and systematic controls that are typical of the best management accounting procedures. *Thirdly*, a narrowly focused approach implies that risk management is geared towards protecting mainly tangible assets while ignoring intangible assets, employees' capabilities, and entity brands.

Heightened concerns about risk management, due to financial reporting scandals, have cast serious doubt on its ability to manage risks adequately. Furthermore, nowadays, shareholders and bondholders place growing importance on poor results, a lack of transparency and reputational losses. To provide a framework that could respond to past calls for enhanced risk management, the COSO represents the most important and recognized standard of reference for ERM.

Due to the above-mentioned traditional risk management limitations, the COSO framework is widely implemented in practice. The framework defines ERM as "*a process, effected by an entity's board of directors, management and other personnel, applied in strategy setting and across the enterprise, designed to identify potential events that may affect the entity, and manage risk to be within its risk appetite, to provide reasonable assurance regarding the achievement of entity objectives*" (Ansoff, 1975). ERM incorporates risk management. Moreover, COSO supports the view that ERM is an ongoing activity and applicable worldwide. It was developed by a professional group made up of distinguished members from different backgrounds, such as accounting professors, partners of accounting firms, managers, and board members, and was promoted by five major professional associations in the US. The COSO framework supports a three-dimensional model that consists of eight components represented by horizontal rows, with four objectives represented by the vertical columns and four units displayed in the last dimension of the cube. This depiction clearly emphasizes two features: the strategic contribution and integration of the ERM system.

Unfortunately, not all organizations are adopting ERM. Previous studies indicate that firms experience problems during the transition from risk management to ERM. Particularly, Prison and Turnbull (2011) find that boards have limited access and are not informed about firm risk management strategy, while Viscelli, Hermanson and Beasley (2017), by interviewing ERM champions, report that the lack of organizational culture, leadership and management of key risks was the main reason why the integration of ERM and strategy was limited.

In the end, Tekathen and Dechow (2013) assert that the framework emphasizes the importance of the alignment of the processes that people within firms utilize to communicate risks efficiently to the top of the company, to align risks and strategy, but the ways in which risk management processes should be implemented are unclear.

The case study concerning a "Special Report in European Shadow Bank System" organization highlighted great difficulties encountered during the integration of risk information at an enterprise-wide level, which impeded the firm in managing risk holistically.

Figure 1. Chain of accountability of European special reports

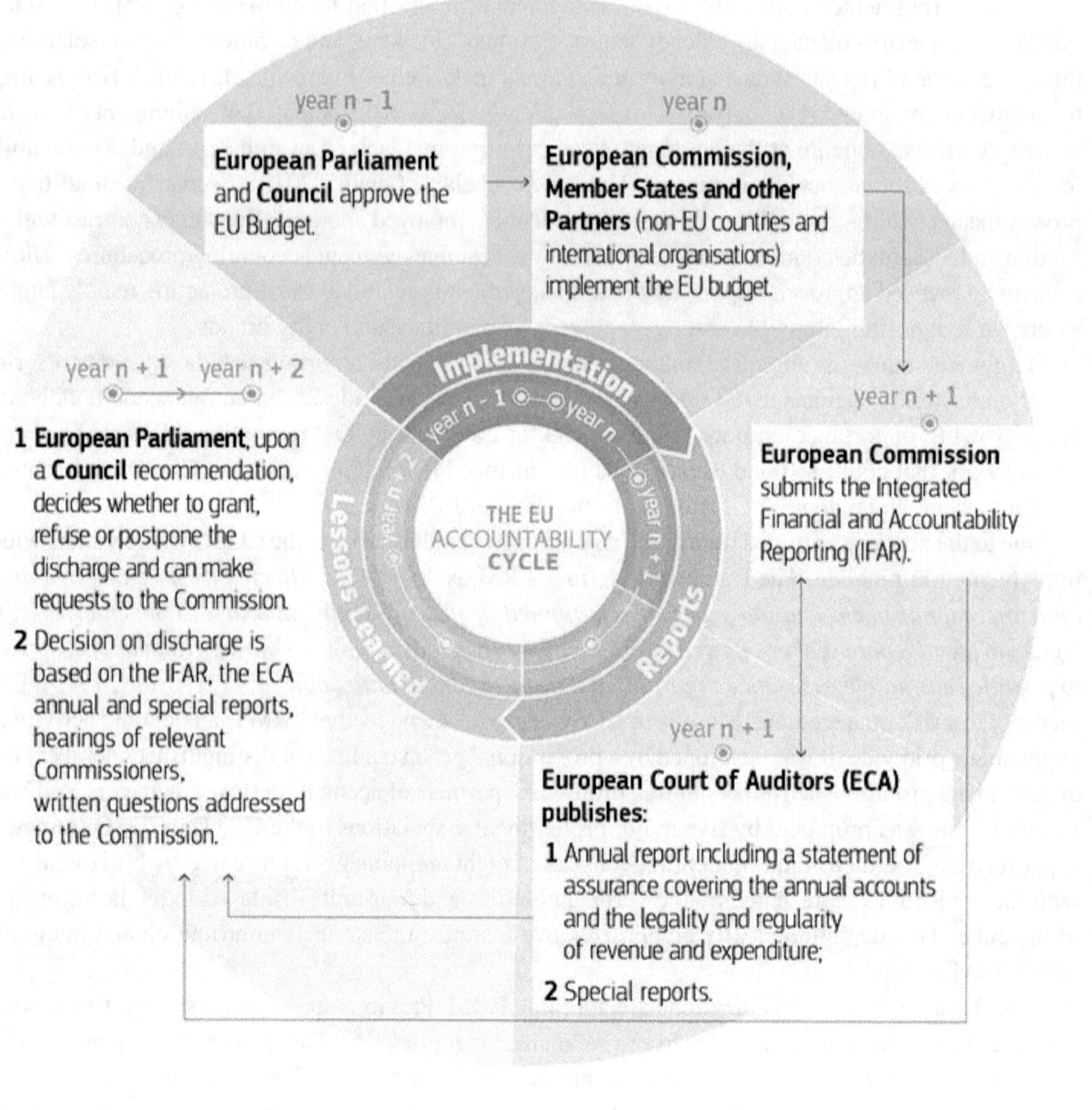

Moreover, there are further reasons that could limit proper ERM implementation.

Firstly, ERM is not "one size fits all". Consequently, tailoring ERM to a firm's unique risks, industry, structure, and culture could be challenging, mainly during the first stages of ERM implementation. *Secondly*, the financial crisis of 2008 could have discouraged firms from implementing ERM programmers because of a lack of sufficient financial resources with which to invest (Ashby, 1956). *Thirdly*, any ERM initiative needs to be continuously improved in the long term. This implies fatigue and time, as risk managers should always be looking for ways of improving risk management practices, given that what works for an organization in one moment may not work in the future. Furthermore, to ensure an efficient review of firm risks, the ERM program is on demand, instead of developing as a one-time project. *Fourthly*, practitioners have not used terminology consistently across risk management processes to facilitate an efficient communication flow.

Consequently, the above-mentioned qualitative research reveals that an appropriate application of ERM is far from what could be considered a full implementation. Recently, in response to this need for guidance, the COSO published an exposure draft, which reflects its proposed revision of its framework, in which it clarified the importance of ERM both for future strategic planning and for entity performance. The most significant change, according to the COSO, concerns a more comprehensive examination of the role of culture and ethical values in ERM and more detailed analysis for facilitating the integration of ERM into strategy.

In conclusion, this study seeks to identify the key theoretical dimension of the Agile Marketing Capability in the European Shadow Bank system and provide empirical guidelines needed to facilitate its implementation. Our findings in current theoretical and empirical research on agility concept in the context of digital transformation and international marketing management.

LITERATURE REVIEW

In many contexts, corporate governance codes represent an important motivator for risk management and internal control practices, requiring the board to maintain a sound system of internal control, such as the UK Corporate Governance Code, the French AFEP- MEDEF Code and the Italian Corporate Governance Code.

However, while the codes simply prescribe companies to review the effectiveness of risk and control processes, those that are willing to implement robust ERM practices should adopt appropriate ERM frameworks. Particularly, effective ERM implementation requires firms to employ risk identification processes that are robust, representing one of the basic components found in most ERM frameworks.

Risk identification constitutes the third component of the COSO framework, which consist of determining the new, emerging and changing risks that are likely to affect any project. This represents the basis of risk assessment and risk control. Furthermore, rating agencies, such as Standard & Poor's, have begun to consider firms' ERM practices and consider different aspects of risk control, including risk identification activities, when formulating the credit rating of all firms (Rafay *et al.*, 2018).

ERM frameworks are not specific to any industry or country. Since there is no single recipe for optimal ERM implementation, the level of ERM implementation and practice significantly depends on firm characteristics as well, larger, multinational corporations are expected to support highly developed and well-resourced ERM systems. The top management team is entrusted with the selection of the most appropriate technique or combination of techniques to effectively manage risks holistically and support the organization by considering entity size, culture industry and regulation.

Risk identification techniques may be utilized at the firm level, as well as for assessing risk at the business unit or process level. Risk identification can be conducted by employing different techniques.

Questionnaires, Surveys, and Brainstorming

A firm may submit a risk questionnaire to business unit staff, which requires them to list external and internal risks that could cause unwanted events. Regarding external risks, questions may concern economic, regulatory, and environmental risks; the internal risks may prompt questions related to customers, suppliers, personnel, and products (Chaffey, 2010). Companies may even survey external parties, such as customers and suppliers, who know the market in which the business operates and can provide an objective, independent view.

Questionnaires and survey are crucial when firms need to produce information about unresolved or changing issues regarding certain risks (Eckstein *et al.*, 2015). For instance, a firm may decide to analyze the changing trends in social factors and the external environment by using a broad-based survey (Bock, Opsahl, George & Gann, 2012). In the end, a brainstorming session can be used to generate a list of risks, assess these risks, and find possible solutions. In turn, management can benefit from the views of knowledgeable and experienced personnel, with different backgrounds and levels or units in the enterprise. Firms often identify a facilitator to manage the session and assist participants (Chen, Wang, Nervo & Benitez-Amado & Kou, 2015).

Strengths/Weaknesses/Opportunities/SWOT Analysis

SWOT analysis is based on classifying the capabilities of the firm in four respects: strengths, weaknesses, opportunities, and threats (DeNichilo, 2020c). It is used to formulate strategy at the firm level. It is a technique used to examine strengths and weaknesses, which represent internal factors, such as a firm's human, financial and reputational resources, while opportunities and threats represent external factors, which include changes in technology (Rafay, 2019), markets, and legislation (Melis, 2004). While internal factors can come under managerial control, very little control can be exerted over threats and opportunities.

Loss Event Data Tracking

The risk identification technique focused on past events (DeNichilo, 2013). It enables firms to compare data collected internally against external data. Sources of external data include newspaper articles, financial statements, public findings, and consortia created in certain industries with the aim of sharing internal data (Jednak & Jednak, 2019). Firms normally utilize an external database, available on a subscription basis, from outside providers to acquire external data. (Van der Meer & Edelenbos, 2006). This technique is different from other tools, since it allows firms to obtain valuable data and information regarding events that have occurred in the industry involving peers and competitors (Rafay & Gilani, 2016). Furthermore, the company can even compare the data on one department or division with those of other departments or divisions in order to assess a specific risk in terms of likelihood and impact

(Griffin, Colella & Goparaju, 2000). Conclusively, loss event data tracking is useful for identifying trends and root causes of events (March & Olsen, 1996).

Scenario Analysis

A company uses scenario analysis to evaluate the impacts of possible future events by considering diverse plausible scenarios (Melis & Gaia, 2011). Sometimes, each scenario is associated with a probability of occurrence and an average loss estimate (Ellinas & Suleiman, 2008). One of the main advantages of risk scenario analysis is that it helps organizations to overcome resistance when discussing relevant catastrophic events, which are rare, or events that have not previously occurred (Cortese & Del Carlo, 2008). External data are of fundamental importance in scenario analysis, as they are a valuable source of background information on what could happen and how a given situation might be handled (Rolle, 2010). Consequently, this event identification technique looks to the past as well as the future.

Event Inventories

A list containing genetic or industry risks is provided to participants, as a starting point, for two main reasons: to identify risks relevant to the company in question and to simulate a discussion on risk among management (Harber, Marx& De Jager, 2020). The list is generated either by an entity, based on previous risk identification processes, or by an external consulting firm (Woham, 2015).

Escalation Triggers

Managers set thresholds, depending on a firm's risk appetite, with the aim of monitoring data about events that deserve management attention (DeNichilo, 2020a). When the predefined limits are exceeded, managers are notified to take the necessary actions to accept or mitigate risk (Ernst & Young, 2013).

Outcome of a Risk Identification Process

A list of risks would be the output of a risk identification process, which should be updated periodically because of the dynamic and complex environment where companies operate. Once risks are identified, the organizations categorize similar risks together (Power & Gendron, 2015). Moreover, while some discovered risks can be managed at a lower level organizationally, the ones that are linked to strategy should be monitored by senior management immediately (Van Wolleghem, 2022).

METHODOLOGY: QUALITATIVE RESEARCH OF THE EUROPEAN SHADOW BANK SYSTEM

Qualitative research identifies three distinct subgroups of the European Shadow Banking System. These are: (A) the government-sponsored shadow banking sub-system; (B) the "internal" shadow banking sub-system; and (C) the "external" shadow banking sub-system (Grewal & Tansuhaj, 2001).

The Government-Sponsored Shadow Banking Sub-System (Lending to Nonbanking Financial Institutions)

The seeds of the European Shadow Banking System were sown nearly 30 years ago, with the creation the government-sponsored enterprises (GSE) (Lagoarde-Segot & Paranque, 2017). The GSEs have dramatically changed the way banks fund themselves and conduct lending (AGEA, PwC Audit Reports 2011-2013). The funding "utility" functions performed by the GSEs for banks and the way they funded themselves were the models for what we refer today to as the wholesale funding market (AGEA, PwC Special Report 2014).

The "Internal" Shadow Banking Sub-System (Interbank Payment)

The principal drivers of the growth of the European Shadow Banking System have been the transformation of the largest banks since the early-1990s from low return on equity (ROE) utilities that originate loans and hold and fund them until maturity with deposits, to high ROE entities that originate loans in order to warehouse and later securitize and distribute them, or retain securitized loans through off-financial statement asset management vehicles (Manes Rossi, Brusca & Condor, 2020). The transformation of banks occurred within the legal framework of financial holding companies, which through the acquisition of broker-dealers and asset managers, allowed large banks to transform their traditional process of hold-to-maturity, spread-banking to a more profitable process of originate-to-distribute, fee-banking (DeNichilo, 2011).

Banks' portfolio management started to decide which assets were retained and which assets were sold and charged originators (Rafay *et al.*, 2017) both internal and external) the replacement cost of financial statements for warehoused assets. Modern banks "rent" their financial statements and set their "rents" based on the replacement cost of their financial statements (AGEA, E&Y Up Grade Procedure Services 2014).

The "External" Shadow Banking Sub-System (Off-Balance Sheet)

The mixture of bank and markets-based credit intermediation process that emerged was also practiced by some European banks and was later adopted by diversified broker-dealers and turned a range of independent, specialist non-banks into an interconnected network of financial entities that operated completely external to banks and the official safety net extended to banks, hence the term "external" shadow banking sub-system (AGEA, E&Y Financial Letters 2019).

Special reports (table 1) must continuously rethink their business model (Barrales-Molina, Martinez-Lopez & Gazquez-Abad, 2014), offering, and processes to stay in tune with the digital transformation characterized by technological progress (Asseraf, Lages & Shoham, 2019), digital communication, and shifting customer demand and to integrate technology with marketing communication strategies to satisfy customer needs (Barkema, Baum & Mannix, 2002).

Table 1. Checklist of internal controls for special reports on European shadow bank system (Objective: 30% – 60% of PM; Estimated Error > 5% of Payments; Projected Error < 10% of the Reported Expenditure)

Range of Performance Materiality	1- 10% PM	1- 30% PM	Over 60% PM
Level	Hard	Medium	Soft
Usefulness	Audit	Advisory	Reporting
Significance of Risk:			
Risk Materiality	High	Medium	Low
Relevance	Big	Medium	Small
Coverage	Over	In line	Under
General Controls: Umbrella Themes			
Smart and Inclusive Growth	Innovative	Inclusive	Growth
Sustainable Growth-Natural Resources	Agricultural	Commerce	Industrial
Security and Citizenship	Participation	Collaboration	Only Vote
Administration	Labor	Finance	Service
Other	Exclusive	Customization	Unique
Multilevel Cooperation:			
Media Pressure	Legal	Structural	Weak
Application Controls: CAVR			
Completeness	Not All	All	Overall
Accuracy	Adequacy	Precision	Accurate
Validity	Flexibility	Competitiveness	Adaptation
Restricted Access	Accessibility	Timeliness	Cycle Time
Shadow Bank System:			
A) The Government-Sponsored	Utility Functions		
B) The "Internal"	ROE (Return On Equity)		
C) The "External"	Ritual or Abuse of Right		

RESULT OF THE AUDIT INVESTIGATION[1]

Among the main causes of the accumulation of private debt (Okonjo, 2021) were the intensity and persistence of severe macroeconomic imbalances within countries and between major economies; the expansive stance of monetary policies (Rafay & Farid, 2019), also justified by a low inflation context, which produced an abundant supply of liquidity and credit; the uncontrolled acceleration of financial innovation in forms that made distribution and distribution opaque the extent of the risks, to which the transition of banks from the "originate and hold" model to the "originate to distribute" model contributed; under these circumstances, the surge in the default rate on worst-quality mortgages in the United States was the spark which lit a colossal fire, extending to the credit system (with the failure of many banks, until the liquidation of Lehman Brothers in September 2008) and then to the entire financial system international and the global economy (Birindelli *et al.*, 2020). Faced with the explosion and spread of the crisis, many governments intervened massively to rescue financial institutions, causing a sharp and rapid surge in the deficit and public debt with European Shadow Bank Systems (Ahlström, & Monciardini, 2022). So, the automatic effects of the crisis on tax revenues and some expenses contributed to the worsening of public accounts.

This work advances the field of dynamic marketing capabilities in special reports by defining a new capability: the Agile Marketing Capability of the European Shadow Bank System Carè, Rania & De Lisa, 2020) (Table 2 and 3).

Table 2. Dynamic marketing capabilities of internal control

Application Controls	General Controls
Prevent, detect, and correct transaction errors and fraud in application programs. These are concerned with the accuracy, completeness, validity and authorization of data captured, stored, transmitted to the other system, and reported.	Make sure an organization's control environment is stable and well managed. Examples include security; IT infrastructure; and software acquisition, development, and maintenance controls.

Table 3. Internal control assertions: CAVR

Internal Control Assertions	Evidence of controls	Test	Types of Internal controls
Completeness	Controls to ensure financial transactions and data are completed.	Control totals and sequencing.	Manual Semi-Manual Automated
Accuracy	Controls to ensure financial transactions and data are accurate.	Logic tests and checksums.	Manual Semi-Manual Automated
Validity	Controls to ensure financial transactions and data are valid.	Maintain record trail and electronic signature.	Manual Semi-Manual Automated
Restricted Access	Controls to ensure restricted access to data and financial transactions.	Passwords, asset tags, locks and approval forms.	Manual Semi-Manual Automated

In sum (Table 4 and 5), the study findings support a framework that identifies the key dimension of the Agile Marketing Capability; continual improvement pace, customer-oriented responsiveness, high flexibility, and people collaboration (Teece, Peteraf, & Leih, 2016).

Table 4. Correlation matrix between control assertions and audits assertion for transaction-level. number of observations: 100% of AGEA debt register practices year 2014 (number of observation 4.887 practices)

Control Assertions	Audit Assertion for Transaction-level				
CAVR	**Accuracy**	**Classification**	**Completeness**	**Cut-off**	**Occurrence**
Completeness	0.05	0.1	1	0.8	0.05
Accuracy	0.8	0.05	0	0.05	0.1
Validity	0.05	0.8	0	0.1	0.05
Restricted Access	0.1	0.05	0	0.05	0.8

Audit Assertion for Transaction-level	Audit Evidence
Accuracy	The assertion is that the full amounts of all transactions were recorded, without error.
Classification	The assertion is that all transactions have been recorded within the correct accounts in the general ledger.
Completeness	The assertion is that all business events to which the company was subjected were recorded.
Cut-off	The assertion is that all transactions were recorded within the correct reporting period.
Occurrence	The assertion is that recorded business transactions took place.

Table 5. Key dimension of the agile marketing capability. Number of observations: 100% of AGEA debt register practices year 2014 (Number of observation 4.887 practices)

Item	Weighted Average	First Quartile	Median	Third Quartile	Std. Dev./ Max	Min	Max
1	2.33	0.77	2.01	2.31	0.22	0.22	3.33
2	1.33	0.54	1.05	1.34	0.33	0.12	4.35
Significance of Risk: Materiality							
3	3.33	1.22	3.34	4.23	0.45	0.15	5.55
4	4.33	1.55	3.77	4.31	0.55	0.11	7.33
5	5.70	2.55	4.77	6.21	0.66	0.05	5.34
General Controls: Umbrella Themes							
6	5.33	2.77	3.33	6.33	0.33	0.23	7.22
7	7.29	3.77	4.24	7.22	0.77	0.55	14.51
8	8.29	4.88	5.77	8.22	0.66	0.77	12.44
9	9.10	5.99	6.22	10.02	0.99	1.01	17.9
10	5.22	2.22	3.44	5.21	0.32	0.51	7.22
Multilevel Cooperation: Media Pressure							
11	7.23	3.79	4.77	8.22	0.67	1.66	12.11
Application Controls: CAVR							
12	6.23	1.88	4.56	6.24	0.22	1.77	8.29
13	7.33	3.99	4.55	8.33	0.55	1.88	9.99
14	5.55	1.75	2.77	5.25	0.33	0.55	8.88
15	6.99	3.77	4.88	6.88	0.67	1.57	7.59

CONCLUSION

One of the main objectives of ERM is to help firms delivered the entity's performance and create, protect, and enhance value for its shareholders. Consequently, during economic downturns, high-quality ERM programs should protect companies against a loss of resources. Nevertheless, difficulties faced by same companies during the financial crisis of 2008 have cast some doubt on the efficacy of ERM practices (Barton, 1993).

Indeed, there is a small number of recent studies that deals with how ERM mitigated the crisis. Fraser, Simkins and Narvaez (2014), underline that, before the crisis, the absence of an enterprise-wide dimension of risks led firms to underestimate their exposure to toxic asset. Particularity, the authors highlight that failed firms, due to excessive risk-taking behavior, which caused the 2008 crisis, hired chief risk officers, without giving them real powers. Nair *et al.* (2014) theorized that firms with superior ERM systems experienced competitive advantages during periods of the financial crisis in 2008. Drawing on a dynamic capabilities' framework, the authors found that companies with more highly developed ERM experienced a lower negative impact on their market price during the crisis and benefited from higher profitability after it. Consequently, ERM capabilities led investors to move toward less risky stocks during the downturn. Furthermore, such firms responded quickly to the crisis, yielding superior profitability later. Baxter *et al.* (2013) found a positive relationship between higher ERM ratings and market value only after the crisis. They evidenced that investors valued ERM in the post-crisis period, since it signaled to the market firms' future ability to mitigate risks effectively.

In the end, Ellul and Yerramilli (2013) reported that institutions with stronger risk controls in place before the beginning of the financial crisis experienced a lower tail risk during the crisis period. Furthermore, firms characterized by more developed risk controls enjoyed higher performance and annual returns exclusively during the crisis period. Since corporate boards were deficient in terms of managing risk before 2008, ERM has emerged as an important function inside companies in response to increased uncertainty in the aftermath of the financial crisis. Gendron, Brivot, and Guénin-Paravicini (2016) reinforced this argument, underlining that ERM's credibility has remained unaffected by corporate scandals following led to incompetence, negligence, and drawbacks about controls and procedures among those responsible for its functioning.

An international survey, conducted by Ernst & Young (2013), which involved the financial services industry, found that firms have been working in the aftermath of the global crisis to increase risk culture. Respondent noted a consistent tone at the top concerning the development of risk management competences and improved communication as important factors in strengthening risk culture. A further area that deserves considerable improvement, according to many respondents, is the lack of adequate risk data and system. Despite significant investments having been made in the recent years in the area, the improvement of management accounting systems for ERM continues to be a challenge for many firms.

The growing attention on ERM has resulted in broadening the role and the responsibilities of chief risk officers, whose decisions are now considered at a strategic level. Since the crisis, chief risk officers have also enhanced the link with chief executive officers. In recent decades, regulators, numerous governance-related organizations, and credit rating agencies have confirmed the importance of adopting sound risk management practices (Argyris, 1980). Moreover, the recent financial crisis has contributed to an increase in stakeholder' expectations regarding risk management, although there was a clear failure to achieve the key objectives in such circumstance. Nowadays, ERM is a prerequisite for managing risks associated with firm's activity because the accounting profession considers such risk management apparatus to be of value in dynamic environments where risks are always presented and changing (Sposato, 2010).

Risk identification and risk assessment activities impact heavily on the achievement of an entity's strategy and business objectives. Deficiencies in identifying and assessing risks may lead to a failure in selecting and deploying risk responses, which, in turn, influences, the enterprise risk profile.

In conclusion the need for an orderly reduction of excessive private and public debt with European Shadow Bank Systems (table 6) was clearly anticipated by Spaventa (2008); on the problems encountered and on the few steps forward made in this area (DeNichilo 2020b). Under the traditional originate-and-hold model, the lending bank retains the credits in its assets, and hedges the risk with capital. With the originate-to-distribute model, on the other hand, credit risk is transferred, using the most varied and ever-changing techniques of securitization and creation of "derivative" credits (Köhler, Ratzinger-Sakel & Theis, 2020).

However, the problems of public debt are of a very special nature, they are different from the rest of the world shadow bank systems (Buchak, Matvos, Piskorski & Seru, 2018). The split between responsibility for money and exchange, assigned to the center, and that of fiscal and debt policies, which remain on the periphery, deprives sovereign states of an important piece of their sovereignty, a lender of last resort that provides markets with an implicit debt guarantee (Dörry, & Schulz, 2018).

Table 6. Capability overall conclusion of policy investigations template

Overall Error	**% Performance Materiality**	**Tolerance**	**Effective Error**	**Adjusted Error**	**Opinion**
Projected Error (Call)	30% - 60% Medium Risk	<10%	1.33%	7.55%	Accepted
Estimated Error (Put)	30% - 60% Medium Risk	>5%	6.77%	4.5%	Rejected
Overall Consistency Test	% Performance Materiality	Tolerance	Effective Error	Adjusted Error	Opinion
Rho di Spearman	30% - 60% Medium Risk	5.23%	4.25%	5.25%	Accepted
Tau di Kendal	30% - 60% Medium Risk	4.33%	5.25%	5.66%	Rejected
Internal Consistency Test	% Performance Materiality	Tolerance	Effective Error	Adjusted Error	Opinion
Likert's Interquartile Gap Test	30% - 60% Medium Risk	<2	1.77	1.66	Accepted

These insights (DeNichilo, 2021a) would help managers and practitioners in employing agile features in their marketing strategies and operations (Lee *et al.*, 2015). Future studies could also develop scales for measuring Agile Marketing Capability of European Shadow Bank System (Ravichardran, 2018). and use survey instrument to validate our findings (Rixen, 2013). It would be interesting to understand the relationship between the identified dimension and their underlying nature, as well as develop a proper procedure (Lu & Ramamurthy, 2011).

DECLARATION

The author declares that the manuscript follows ethical standards and there are no potential conflicts of interest with respect to the research, authorship and/or publication of this chapter.

DISCLAIMER

The contents and views of this chapter are expressed by the author in his personal capacity. It is not necessary for the Editor and the Publisher to agree with these viewpoints, and they are not responsible for any duty of care in this regard.

ACKNOWLEDGMENT

The author extends sincere gratitude to

- The Editor and the International Editorial Advisory Board (IEAB) of this book who initially desk reviewed, arranged a rigorous double/triple blind review process, and conducted a thorough, minute, and critical final review before accepting the chapter for publication.
- All anonymous reviewers who provided very constructive feedbacks for thorough revision, improvement, extension, and fine tuning of the chapter.
- All colleagues, assistants and well-wishers who assisted to complete this task.

REFERENCES

AGEA, E&Y Up Grade Procedure Services. (2014). AGEA.

AGEA. PwC Special Report. (2014). AGEA.

AGEA, E&Y Financial Letters. (2019). AGEA.

AGEA, PwC Audit Reports 2011-2013. (n.d.). AGEA.

Ahlström, H., & Monciardini, D. (2022). The regulatory dynamics of sustainable finance: Paradoxical success and limitations of EU reforms. *Journal of Business Ethics, 177*(1), 193–212. doi:10.100710551-021-04763-x PMID:33642657

Anderson, S. W., & Dekker, H. C. (2014). The role of management controls in transforming firm boundaries and sustaining hybrid organizational forms. *Foundations and Trends® in Accounting, 8*(2), 75–141.

Ansoff, H. I. (1975). Managing strategic surprise by response to weak signals. *California Management Review, 18*(2), 21–33. doi:10.2307/41164635

Argyris, C. (1980). Making the undiscussable and its undiscussability discussable. *Public Administration Review, 40*(3), 205–213. doi:10.2307/975372

Ashby, W. R. (1956). *An introduction to Cybernetics*. Chapaman & Hall. doi:10.5962/bhl.title.5851

Asseraf, Y., Lages, L. F., & Shoham, A. (2019). Assessing the drivers and impact of international marketing agility. *International Marketing Review, 36*(2), 289–315. doi:10.1108/IMR-12-2017-0267

Balint, T., Bauer, M. W., & Knill, C. (2008). Bureaucratic change in the European administrative space: The case of the European Commission. *West European Politics, 31*(4), 677–700. doi:10.1080/01402380801905967

Barkema, H. G., Baum, J. A., & Mannix, E. A. (2002). Management challenges in new time. *Academy of Management Journal, 45*(5), 916–930. doi:10.2307/3069322

Barrales-Molina, V., Martinez-Lopez, F. J., & Gazquez-Abad, J. C. (2014). Dynamic marketing capabilities: Toward an integrative framework. *International Journal of Management Reviews, 16*(4), 397–416. doi:10.1111/ijmr.12026

Barton, L. (1993). *Crisis in Organizations: Managing and communication in the heat of chaos*. South-Western Publishing Company.

Baxter, R., Bedard, J. C., Hoitash, R., & Yezegel, A. (2013). Enterprise risk management program quality: Determinants, value relevance and the financial crisis. *Contemporary Accounting Research, 30*(4), 1264–1295. doi:10.1111/j.1911-3846.2012.01194.x

Birindelli, G., Trotta, A., Chiappini, H., & Rizzello, A. (2020). Environmental impact investments in Europe: Where are we headed? In *Contemporary Issues in Sustainable Finance* (pp. 151–175). Palgrave Macmillan. doi:10.1007/978-3-030-40248-8_7

Bock, A. J., Opsahl, T., George, G., & Gann, D. M. (2012). The effects of culture and structure on strategic flexibility during business model innovation. *Journal of Management Studies, 49*(2), 279–305. doi:10.1111/j.1467-6486.2011.01030.x

Buchak, G., Matvos, G., Piskorski, T., & Seru, A. (2018). Fintech, regulatory arbitrage, and the rise of shadow banks. *Journal of Financial Economics, 130*(3), 453–483. doi:10.1016/j.jfineco.2018.03.011

Caiden, N. (1998). Public service professionalism for performance measurement and evaluation. *Public Budgeting & Finance, 18*(2), 35–52. doi:10.1046/j.0275-1100.1998.01133.x

Carè, R., Rania, F., & De Lisa, R. (2020). Critical success factors, motivations, and risks in social impact bonds. *Sustainability, 12*(18), 7291. doi:10.3390u12187291

Chaffey, D. (2010). Applying organizational capability models to assess the maturity of digital-marketing governance. *Journal of Marketing Management, 26*(3-4), 187–196. doi:10.1080/02672571003612192

Chen, Y., Wang, Y., Nervo, S., Benitez-Amado, J., & Kou, G. (2015). IT capabilities and product innovation performance: The roles of corporate entrepreneurship and competitive intensity. *Information & Management, 52*(6), 643–657. doi:10.1016/j.im.2015.05.003

Cortese, G., & Del Carlo, A. (2008). *La selezione del personale. Dalla ricerca all'inserimento in azienda: come scegliere il candidato migliore*. Raffaello Cortina Editore.

COSO. (2004). *Enterprise Risk Management: Aligning Risk with Strategy and Performance. Committee of sponsoring organizations of the Treadway Commission*. AICPA.

DeNichilo, N. (2013). *Le Metodologie innovative di reclutamento*. Tesi Magistrale Università degli studi Roma Tre.

DeNichilo, S. (2020a). *Public Choice in European Affairs: Measuring Election Model. European Journal of Social Impact and Circular Economy*. University of Turin.

DeNichilo, S. (2020b). Shadow Bank System in European Affairs: Measuring Capability (Discussion paper). European Association for Banking and Financial Law.

DeNichilo, S. (2020c). How Do Earnings Management Practices Distract International Environmental Funds? Empirical Evidence of European Development Funds in Italy. *GeoProgress Journal*, *7*(1), 87–101.

DeNichilo, S. (2021a). *Management Accounting in European Finance for Smart Tourism and Sustainable Destination: How Organizations Deficiency?* University of Turin.

DeNichilo, S. (2021b), Management Accounting in European Affairs: a Memorandum Methodology for Formalize Audit Evidence. *Corporate Governance and Research & Development Studies, 1*, 153-171.

DeNichilo, S. (2022). *How to resolve audit matters in European Affairs? Introduction to a sustainable management accounting under IAS 37*. University of Turin.

DeNichilo, S. & Pedone, A. (2009). *The efficiency of the tax systems in Europe*. Università degli studi La Sapienza di Roma.

DeNichilo, S. & Regogliosi, C. (2011). *L'internal auditing in un organismo di diritto pubblico: il caso Agea*. Università degli studi Roma Tre.

Dörry, S., & Schulz, C. (2018). Green financing, interrupted. Potential directions for sustainable finance in Luxembourg. *Local Environment*, *23*(7), 717–733. doi:10.1080/13549839.2018.1428792

Eckstein, D., Goellner, M., Blome, C., & Henke, M. (2015). The performance impact of supply chain agility and supply chain adaptability: The moderating effect of product complexity. *International Journal of Production Research*, *53*(10), 3028–3046. doi:10.1080/00207543.2014.970707

Ellinas, A., & Suleiman, E. (2008). The Reforming the Commission: Between modernization and bureaucratization. *Journal of European Public Policy*, *15*(5), 708–725. doi:10.1080/13501760802133179

Ellul, A., & Yerramilli, V. (2013). Stronger risk controls, lower risk: Evidence from U.S. bank holding companies. *The Journal of Finance*, *68*(5), 1757–1803. doi:10.1111/jofi.12057

Ernst & Young. (2013). *Remarking financial services: risk management five years after the crisis. A survey of major financial institutions*. EY & Institute of International Finance. Retrieved from https://www.iif.com/portals/0/files/private/EY-Remaking_financial_services_Executive_ Summary_1.pdf

Fraser, J. R., Simkins, B., & Narvaez, K. (2014). *Implementing Enterprise Risk Management: Case studies and best practices*. John Wiley & Sons.

Gendron, Y., Brivot, M., & Guénin-Paravicini, H. (2016). The construction of risk management credibility within corporate boardrooms. *European Accounting Review*, *25*(3), 549–578. doi:10.1080/09638180.2015.1064008

Grewal, R., & Tansuhaj, P. (2001). Building organizational capabilities for managing economic crisis: The role of market orientation and strategic flexibility. *Journal of Marketing, 65*(2), 67–80. doi:10.1509/jmkg.65.2.67.18259

Griffin, A. E., Colella, A., & Goparaju, S. (2000). Newcomer and organizational socialization tactics: An interactionist perspective. *Human Resource Management Review, 10*(4), 453–474. doi:10.1016/S1053-4822(00)00036-X

Hagen, B., Zucchela, A., & Ghauri, P. N. (2018). From fragile to agile: Marketing as a key driver of entrepreneurial internationalization. *International Marketing Review, 36*(2), 260–288. doi:10.1108/IMR-01-2018-0023

Harber, M., Marx, B., & De Jager, P. (2020). The perceived financial effects of mandatory audit firm rotation. *Journal of International Financial Management & Accounting, 31*(2), 215–234. doi:10.1111/jifm.12115

Hoerner, J., & Stephenson, P. (2012). Theoretical perspectives on approaches to policy evaluation in the EU: The case of cohesion policy. *Public Administration, 90*(3), 699–715. doi:10.1111/j.1467-9299.2011.02013.x

Jednak, D., & Jednak, S. (2019). Socially responsible financial markets. In *Financing Sustainable Development* (pp. 103–125). Palgrave Macmillan. doi:10.1007/978-3-030-16522-2_5

Köhler, A., Ratzinger-Sakel, N., & Theis, J. (2020). The effects of key audit matters on the auditor's report's communicative value: Experimental evidence from investment professionals and non-professional investors. *Accounting in Europe, 17*(2), 105–128. doi:10.1080/17449480.2020.1726420

Lagoarde-Segot, T., & Paranque, B. (2017). Sustainability and the reconstruction of academic finance. *Research in International Business and Finance, 39*(B), 657–662.

Lee, O. K., Sambamurthy, V., Lim, K. H., & Wei, K. K. (2015). How does IT ambidexterity impact organizational agility? *Information Systems Research, 26*(2), 398–417. doi:10.1287/isre.2015.0577

Lu, Y., & Ramamurthy, K. (2011). Understanding the link between information technology capability and organizational agility: An empirical examination. *Management Information Systems Quarterly, 35*(4), 931–954. doi:10.2307/41409967

Manes Rossi, F., Brusca, I., & Condor, V. (2021). In the pursuit of harmonization: Comparing the audit systems of European local governments. *Public Money & Management, 41*(8), 604–614. doi:10.1080/09540962.2020.1772549

March, J. G., & Olsen, J. P. (1996). Institutional perspectives on political institutions. *Governance: An International Journal of Policy, Administration and Institutions, 9*(3), 247–264. doi:10.1111/j.1468-0491.1996.tb00242.x

Melis, A. (2004). On the role of the board of statutory auditors in Italian listed companies. *Corporate Governance, 12*(1), 74–84. doi:10.1111/j.1467-8683.2004.00344.x

Melis, A., & Gaia, S. (2011). Corporate governance in Italy: Normative developments vs. actual practices. In *Handbook on International Corporate Governance*. Edward Elgar Publishing. doi:10.4337/9781849808293.00010

Mendez, C., & Bachtler, J. (2011). Administrative reform and unintended consequences: An assessment of the EU Cohesion policy 'audit explosion'. *Journal of European Public Policy, 18*(5), 746–765. doi:10.1080/13501763.2011.586802

Nair, A., Rustambekov, E., McShane, M., & Fainshmidt, S. (2014). Enterprise risk management as a dynamic capability: A test of its effectiveness during a crisis. *Managerial and Decision Economics, 35*(8), 555–566. doi:10.1002/mde.2641

Nakitende, M. G., Rafay, A., & Waseem, M. (2021). Frauds in Business Organizations: A Comprehensive Overview. In A. Rafay (Ed.), *Handbook of Research on Theory and Practice of Financial Crimes* (pp. 21–38). IGI Global. doi:10.4018/978-1-7998-5567-5.ch002

Okonjo, J. (2021). International financial regulation and sustainable finance. In *Encyclopedia of Law and Development*. Edward Elgar Publishing. doi:10.4337/9781788117975.00044

Pirson, M., & Turnbull, S. (2011). Corporate governance, risk management, and the financial crisis: An information processing view. *Corporate Governance, 19*(5), 459–470. doi:10.1111/j.1467-8683.2011.00860.x

Power, M. K., & Gendron, Y. (2015). Qualitative research in auditing: A methodological roadmap. *Auditing, 34*(2), 147–165. doi:10.2308/ajpt-10423

Rafay, A. (Ed.). (2019). *FinTech as a Disruptive Technology for Financial Institutions*. IGI Global. doi:10.4018/978-1-5225-7805-5

Rafay, A., Chen, Y., Naeem, M. A. B., & Ijaz, M. (2018). Analyzing the impact of Credit Ratings on Firm Performance and Stock Returns: An Evidence from Taiwan. *Indian Economic Review, 22*(3), 767–786. doi:10.22059/ier.2018.67452

Rafay, A., & Farid, S. (2019). Islamic Banking System: A Credit Channel of Monetary Policy – Evidence from an Emerging Economy. *Economic Research-Ekonomska Istrazivanja, 32*(1), 742–754. doi:10.1080/1331677X.2019.1579662

Rafay, A., Mohsan, T., & Sadiq, R. (2017). Structural Mix of Credit Portfolios in Islamic Banking System: Evidence from a South Asian Economy. In D. Mutum, M. M. Butt, & M. Rashid (Eds.), *Advances in Islamic Finance, Marketing, and Management: An Asian Perspective* (pp. 185–210). Emerald Group Publishing Limited. doi:10.1108/978-1-78635-899-820161010

Ravichardran, T. (2018). Exploring the relationship between IT competence, innovation capacity and organizational agility. *The Journal of Strategic Information Systems, 27*(1), 22–42. doi:10.1016/j.jsis.2017.07.002

Rixen, T. (2013). Why reregulation after the crisis is feeble: Shadow banking, offshore financial centers, and jurisdictional competition. *Regulation & Governance, 7*(4), 435–459. doi:10.1111/rego.12024

Rolle, L. (2010). *Risorse umane e benchmarking. Prassi eccellenti in aziende innovative*. Franco Angeli.

Spaventa, L. (2008). *Una crisi della nuova finanza*. Giuffrè Editore.

Sposato, P. (2010). *Valutazione e selezione del personale. Come scegliere e valorizzare il tuo staff ideale*. Bruno Editore.

Teece, D., Peteraf, M., & Leih, S. (2016). Dynamic capabilities and organizational agility: Risk, uncertainty, and strategy in the innovation economy. *California Management Review*, *58*(4), 13–35. doi:10.1525/cmr.2016.58.4.13

Tekathen, M., & Dechow, N. (2013). Enterprise risk management and continuous realignment in the pursuit of accountability: A German case. *Management Accounting Research*, *24*(2), 100–121. doi:10.1016/j.mar.2013.04.005

Van Der Meer, F. B., & Edelenbos, J. (2006). Evaluation in multi-actor policy processes: Accountability, learning and co-operation. *Evaluation*, *12*(2), 201–218. doi:10.1177/1356389006066972

Van Wolleghem, P. G. (2022). Does administrative capacity matter? The absorption of the European Fund for the integration of migrants. *Policy Studies*, *43*(4), 640–658. doi:10.1080/01442872.2020.1770209

Viscelli, T. R., Hermanson, D. R., & Beasley, M. S. (2017). The integration of ERM and strategy: Implications for corporate governance. *Accounting Horizons*, *31*(2), 69–82. doi:10.2308/acch-51692

Woham, W. M. (2015). Supervisory control of discrete-event systems. Lecture Notes. Department of electrical and computer engineering. University of Toronto.

ENDNOTE

1 Theme of the essay by Professor Ernesto Longobardi and Professor Antonio Pedone "*Public debt in the euro area after the crisis: restructuring hypotheses, insolvency proceedings, (weak) prospects for fiscal union*", in A. Di Maio and U. Marani (edited by), Economic policies and international crisis, L'Asino d'ora Edizioni, Rome 2017, pp. 99-125. For a broader examination of the same theme, see Longobardi-Pedone and DeNichilo (2009).

Chapter 10
Insurance Fraud and Financial Performance:
The Case of Tanzania

Pendo Shukrani Kasoga
https://orcid.org/0000-0001-6634-3020
The University of Dodoma, Tanzania

Amani Gration Tegambwage
https://orcid.org/0000-0002-9529-4712
The University of Dodoma, Tanzania

ABSTRACT

Insurance fraud has been identified as a significant risk that undermines investor and customer trust. This chapter examines the effect of insurance fraud on the financial performance of the insurance industry of Tanzania. A standardized questionnaire was used to conduct a survey of 119 insurance companies and brokers. The data were analyzed using the multiple regression technique. The findings reveal that policyholder fraud, internal fraud, and intermediary fraud have a negative effect on the financial performance of insurance companies and brokers. Fraudulent documents, customers demanding significant compensation relative to the actual damage, a fake accident, weak internal control, employee dishonesty, poor staff compensation, ineffective supervision, and the inability to detect fraud were the causes of insurance fraud. In order to reduce insurance frauds, it is suggested to (1) thoroughly evaluate claims, (2) establish a transparent anti-fraud bureau, (3) use information technology for effective internal audit, and (4) implement a comprehensive internal fraud policy.

INTRODUCTION

The insurance industry plays a vital role in economic growth by facilitating trade and commerce, capital formation, financial security, and funding development initiatives (Kiptoo *et al.*, 2021). Even though it serves a crucial function, the insurance industry has been performing poorly on a global scale (Zhu *et*

DOI: 10.4018/978-1-6684-5007-9.ch010

al., 2021). Over the past decades, financial fraud has brought shocking losses to the global economy, threatening the efficiency and stability of capital markets (Li *et al.,* 2021; Rafay, 2021a). For instance, in the United States of America, underwriting losses, declining premiums, and a general reduction in net income have been reported by insurers (IRA, 2021). The IRA (2020) revealed that the low interest rate environment had a severe impact on the insurance sector in Europe, resulting in poor investment returns. The continent of Africa has experienced underwriting losses and return volatility in every nation (Re, 2016). Insurance penetration is also low, with an average of 3% compared to a global average of 6%. Furthermore, over time, the premium of life insurance in Africa has remained unchanged (Re, 2016).

Globally, the performance of insurance firms has been negatively influenced by the onset of pandemics like the most recent COVID-19 (Farooq *et al.,* 2021).). The sector is facing more difficulties as a result of COVID-19, such as operational restrictions, financial distress, and regulatory obstacles (Baumann, 2020). The performance of insurance companies has been negatively impacted by COVID-19, which has adversely impacted investment returns in many nations, particularly in developing countries (Farooq *et al.,* 2021). In China, the impact of COVID-19 has led to a decrease in insurance premium income, lowered the growth rate of premiums, and decreased insurance depth and insurance density (Wang *et al.,* 2020). In Tanzania, COVID-19 has adversely impacted insurance firms through decreased returns from funds invested in capital markets, a decrease in premiums, and an increase in claims in some insurance classes like medical (IRA, 2021).

Fraud in the insurance industry has been identified as a significant risk that undermines investor and customer trust, harms the reputation of individual insurers and the industry as a whole, and has a detrimental influence on economic growth (ACFE, 2022). Since it depletes the funds required to cover legitimate claims, insurance fraud makes business conditions even more challenging. Insurance fraud is a significant levy on every policyholder at a time of economic pressure, inflation, and other pressures (Insurance Outlook Report, 2022).

Insurance fraud has grown in complexity and frequency over time, and it is now the second most common financial crime after tax evasion (Bastürk, 2020). Insurance fraud and the fight against it have been high on the global insurance service industry's agenda (Patil & Godbole, 2018). Due to a rise in fraud claims and auto theft, the Special Investigative Unit was created in the USA in 1980 (Ghezzi, 1983). Conceptual studies were conducted in Canada, particularly following the advent of scams in the sector of health insurance (Dionne, 1984). In the late 1980s, fraud in England became a concern that was taken into consideration in the travel, automobile, housing, and business sectors (Clarke, 1989). In Tanzania, the Tanzania Insurance Regulatory Authority (TIRA) is collaborating with other parties to prevent fraud and other misconduct in the insurance industry (TIRA, 2022).

The number of empirical studies on insurance fraud in the insurance service business around the world has been increasing in recent years (Amiram *et al.,* 2018; Daudi & Shandika, 2021; Gomes *et al.,* 2021; Goswami *et al.,* 2022; Jung & Kim, 2021; Karpoff, 2020; Kiptoo *et al.,* 2021). This is the outcome of massive losses attributed to insurance fraud on the global insurance markets, which are in the billions of dollars, hurting insurance firms' growth and the financial well-being of both insured and uninsured people (Bastürk, 2020; Loveday & Jung, 2021). Insurance fraud is a continuing danger, according to the Insurance Outlook Report (2020). Similarly, Button *et al.* (2017) state that insurance fraud is a significant economic issue for the insurance industry as well as national economies.

In Tanzania, fraudulent claims have been growing within the insurance service industry, posing a hazard to all members of society (Daudi & Shandika, 2021). These researchers point out that the Tanzanian insurance industry has remained small in terms of insurance service providers and customers due to fraud and other financial malpractices. Despite the establishment of the TIRA in 2009 to monitor the performance of the insurance industry in Tanzania, the industry has been increasingly vulnerable to fraud (Daudi & Shandika, 2021). They hypothesize that this situation may be responsible for the poor performance of Tanzanian insurance service providers, such as insurance companies and brokers.

Little empirical research has been done on the consequences of insurance fraud on the financial performance of insurance service providers, particularly in developing countries (e.g., Frimpong *et al.*, 2016). These researchers found that insurance fraud negatively affects the financial performance of insurance companies in Ghana. These researchers, however, rely on data from insurance companies and ignore the role of insurance brokers. Frimpong *et al.* (2016), for example, employ a sample size of 39 insurance companies, which may not accurately reflect the opinions of all insurance service providers. According to Frimpong *et al.* (2016), Gomes *et al.* (2021), Jung and Kim (2021), and Yusuf (2011), insurance fraud is a context-specific phenomenon. As such, these researchers recommend further research in other developing countries like Tanzania. This was crucial because there isn't a universal consensus over how insurance fraud affects the financial performance of the insurance service industry (Otiso, 2021). Thus, the effect of insurance fraud on the financial performance of Tanzania's insurance service providers, i.e., insurance companies and brokers, was examined in this chapter.

The chapter also examines the causes of insurance fraud as well as measures that are being taken to combat it in Tanzania. This was important because previous studies did not identify all of the causes of insurance fraud (Wolfe & Hermanson, 2004). Thus, more in-depth research into the causes of insurance fraud and the strategies employed to combat it is required. The findings of this chapter will aid practitioners and policymakers in enhancing Tanzania's efforts to fight insurance fraud.

LITERATURE REVIEW

Definitions of Fraud and Insurance Fraud

Fraud is defined as a purposeful trick or deception used to acquire an unfair and unneeded advantage over others (Derrig, 2002; Rafay, 2021b). The definition of fraud given by Derrig (2002) incorporates four criminal law principles: (i) it must be a clear and deliberate activity; (ii) it must be illegal; (iii) financial gain must be acquired; and (iv) it must be a false statement. They further elaborate that if all four principles are present, a person can be charged with fraud. There will be no successful prosecution if one or more of these is absent. Without the full range of four elements, there is noncriminal coverage, which is called abuse and moral hazard. Abuse is considered as noncriminal fraud attempts, unintended mistakes, suspected damages, and a problem with the company (Derrig, 2002; Rafay, 2023)

The Insurance Fraud Handbook (2018) points out that for the insurance policy to be valid, conditions that did not previously exist must not emerge. For example, buying accident insurance after an accident has taken place does not count as insurance for the accident in question, and if the accident had resulted in injuries, the injured party would not be covered. Insurance fraud takes place when individuals try to gain an unfair financial advantage by violating the terms of the insurance policy (IAIS, 2011). Those involved in an insurance transaction can commit insurance fraud at different stages and may include (Insurance Fraud Handbook, 2018):

- People applying for insurance

- Policyholders;
- Third parties that stand to be affected by the policy;
- Professionals provide services to different parties involved in the process.

According to the Utah Insurance Department (2022), fraud is defined as the use of deception to obtain undue benefits while avoiding obligations, resulting in a loss to the opposing party. As per the International Association of Insurance Supervisors (IAIS), insurance fraud is defined as an act or omission intended to obtain a dishonest advantage for the fraudster or for the benefit of others (IAIS, 2007). The misappropriation of assets and/or insider trading; deliberate misrepresentation, suppression, or non-disclosure of one or more material facts relevant to a financial decision or transaction; and abuse of responsibility, a position of trust, or a fiduciary relationship are all examples of how this can happen (IAIS, 2007). Park (2014) defined insurance fraud as the act of claiming insurance reimbursement by lying to the insurer about the occurrence, cause, or specifics of an insurance incident. Insurance fraud, according to Derrig (2002), is a criminal crime that involves earning financial gain from an insurer or an insured by misrepresentation of facts or falsified evidence. Insurance fraud is defined by ACFE (2022) as any illegal act involving deception, concealment, or a violation of trust.

This study uses IAIS's (2007) well-known definition of insurance fraud from the literature. Insurance fraud is defined as an act or omission intended to obtain a dishonest advantage for the fraudster or for the benefit of others. This can happen as a result of asset misappropriation, insider trading, deliberate misrepresentation, concealment, or non-disclosure of one or more material facts important to a financial decision or transaction and abuse of a position of trust or fiduciary relationship.

Types of Insurance Fraud

In the insurance literature, insurance fraud has been classified as internal fraud, policyholder fraud, and intermediary fraud (Yusuf, 2010, 2011; Todd *et al.,* 2000). Yusuf (2010, 2011) and Todd *et al.* (2000) pointed out that internal fraud is done by employees, and the fraud that exists within the insurance industry is committed by the insurance service providers. External parties or stakeholders, who are directly tied to the insurer, can also commit insurance fraud (Yusuf, 2011). This takes the form of a policyholder or consumer fraud, which is when a person defrauds an insurer by gaining erroneous coverage or payment through the acquisition of an insurance policy or the execution of a claim (Yusuf, 2010; Derrig, 2002).

Moreover, insurance intermediaries (independent brokers or independent insurance agents) also perpetrate intermediary fraud against the insurer or policyholders (IAIS, 2007). External fraud is further separated into two types: fraud committed by consumers or policyholders against insurance service providers (policyholder fraud) and fraud conducted by independent brokers or agents against insurers (independent broker or agent fraud) (intermediary fraud). However, the classifications of Bastürk (2020), Frimpong *et al.* (2016), and Pao *et al.* (2014) are used in this work. They divide insurance fraud into policyholder fraud, internal fraud, and intermediary fraud.

Social Costs of Insurance Fraud

According to the Insurance Fraud Handbook (2018), fraud costs the insurance sector between 80 billion and 110 billion dollars annually. Furthermore, Patil and Godbole (2018) noted that around 10% of every dollar made in the insurance sector is lost to fraud. They also noted that due to losses in this industry, the cost of the insured's insurance has been rising every year. Insurance fraud typically does not happen until the amounts increase and it is only realized that there is a large-scale fraud in its final stages (Insurance Fraud Handbook, 2018). They advise that in order to identify and stop these frauds, personnel must be trained and given proper equipment.

Hassan and Abraham (2013) found out that insurance fraud occurs as a result of changes in technologies, economic, and social systems. They point out that it is difficult to define the scope of total job losses that result from fraudulent activities because fraud is a dynamic process. They further point out that if industries solve a particular type of fraud, and put obstacles to prevent it from re-occurring, another type of fraud will occur. In this context, the insurance industry looks for technological solutions that can resolve the problem of fraud actively and regenerate the industry (Morley *et al.*, 2006). Accordingly, the insurance industry provides significant social and economic benefits, but it should be kept in mind that insurance also has social costs that include (Morley *et al.*, 2006):

- Fraudulent claims;
- Exaggerated claims;

In line with the scope of the present study, this chapter examines the effects of policyholder fraud, internal fraud, and intermediary fraud on the financial performance of insurance companies. Further, the chapter examines the causes of insurance fraud as well as measures that are being taken to prevent it in Tanzania.

Fraudulent Claims

According to Morley *et al.* (2006), when false claims are made, the cost of insurance increases. Examples of fraudulent claims are as indicated below:

- False health insurance claims are filed with the intention of receiving compensation.
- False claims of slips are made by individuals requesting compensation.
- False death scenarios are used by dishonest policyholders who have purchased life insurance from insurance companies.
- People fabricate or exaggerate car accident claims in an effort to receive compensation.
- Insurance companies receive reports of fake crimes, thefts, or vandalism.

The payment of such fraudulent claims ultimately increases the premiums of all policyholders, and these costs are transferred directly to society (Çetin, 2015).

Exaggerated Claims

As per Bastürk (2020), exaggerated or inflated claims can also lead to an increase in insurance costs. Examples of exaggerated claims are as indicated below:

- Policyholders may overstate the value or quantity of the items seized from their homes or places of employment.

- Policyholders may exaggerate the damage sustained in an auto accident in order to get the insurer to pay the deductibles.
- People who were formerly disabled may claim to be disabled after recovering in order to continue receiving disability benefits.
- The claimant's attorneys may request a liability claim that is higher than the actual economic loss.

Exaggerated insurance claims are seen to be a significant social cost of insurance, and as a result, rates must be raised. In the end, insurance holders would see a decrease in their income and savings that may be used to purchase other goods and services (Çetin, 2015), the healthcare industry is put in a risky position (Akpınar & Kasapbas, 2019), price increases for consumer goods (as the cost of health and commercial insurance for businesses increases), (Insurance Fraud Handbook, 2018), and job losses as a result of insurance company failure (Pešout & Andrle, 2011).

In light of this, IAIS (2011) noted that insurance service providers should be proactive in deterring fraudsters as part of good corporate governance, understand the dangers of fraud to their business, and be aware of the many types and repercussions of fraud. They emphasize that insurance firms should think about how to effectively, and economically decrease the risks posed by insured, intermediary, or organized fraudsters through procedures or controls. They claimed that risk should be considered when insurance firms determine their mission, strategy, and goals.

According to Ngai *et al.* (2011), Financial Fraud Detection (FFD) is essential for preventing the negative effects of financial fraud. With the help of FFD, decision-makers may identify bogus financial data from real data, uncover fake behaviors and actions, and create effective measures to lessen the impact of fraud.

Bose and Mahapatra (2001) uncover that data mining is usually used to reveal the hidden truths behind enormous amounts of data. They also emphasized that data mining plays a significant part in FFD. Turban *et al.* (2007) describes data mining as a process that employs mathematical, artificial intelligence, machine learning, and statistical methods to extract and discover relevant information from big databases.

Additionally, Patil and Godbole (2018) found out that in order to identify and analyze fraudulent activities, data mining techniques have become more widely used in almost every institution and organization recently. They make the point that, depending on the requirements and data types of an organization, machine learning offers a wide variety of methods and algorithms to handle various types of problems. They continue by pointing out that machine learning models use previous data to create predictions based on historical information extrapolated from the data, are updated with fresh data, and continue to learn as new data comes in.

Additionally, the majority of prior studies have shown that techniques for organizing and selecting databases, fuzzy clustering, simple regression, and probit models have begun to be employed in the investigation of fraud activities (Brockett *et al.,* 2002; Derrig, 2002).

The explanations provided above show that fraud is an important problem that affects the insurance industry, and this adds to the importance of investigating the effect of insurance fraud on the financial performance of Tanzania's insurance service providers.

THEORETICAL REVIEW

Fraud Triangle

Cressey (1971) established the fraud triangle theory to describe the elements that drive people to commit fraud. The fraud triangle is a useful paradigm for analyzing the fraudulent activities of actors in the insurance industry.

The components of the fraud triangle are as follows:

- Opportunities to conduct fraud: The possibility of committing fraud, concealing it, and evading punishment motivate people to commit fraud against insurance service providers (Brockner *et al.,* 1986). Weak internal controls, as well as a failure to penalize violators, are the factors that increase the opportunity to commit insurance fraud (Cressey, 1971).
- Insurance fraud motivation, incentive, or pressure: This is when an individual (employee, consumer, or intermediary) is pressured or enticed to commit fraud against insurance service providers. Workplace pressures, financial pressures, vices, and other pressures, such as a desire for material possessions that mirror their more affluent counterparts, contribute to insurance fraud (Anand *et al.,* 2004).
- Rationalizations for Fraud: People use their own subjective feelings or views to explain the fraud they commit against insurance service providers (Cressey, 1971). The absence of empathy or indifference shown by criminals, which stems from a succession of justifications or explanations to absolve themselves of the guilt resulting from the deviant activity, is a common feature of insurance fraud and all white-collar crime (Derrig, 2002; IAIS, 2007).

The fraud triangle theory is related to this study because it explains some of the factors that drive people to commit fraud (Nakitende *et al.*, 2021). According to researchers, the aspects indicated by the theory are not exhaustive, and the fraud triangle should be modified to form either a fraud diamond or a fraud pentagon (Wolfe & Hermanson, 2004). According to Wolfe and Hermanson (2004), the ability is derived from a person's position or job within an organization and combined with intellectual and cognitive traits and abilities, allows a potential offender to perceive a fraud opportunity and make it into a reality. Raval (2013) proposes a more in-depth investigation of the reasons for fraud among insurance service providers. He provides a series of arguments in a predictive manner for future investigation, claiming that insurance fraud is a human behavior and context-specific phenomenon. As a result, this study adds to the literature by addressing the reasons for insurance fraud in Tanzania as well as the steps being taken to counteract it.

Adam's Equity Theory

According to Adams (1963, 1965), fairness refers to people's awareness of and comparisons to other people's situations. They add that people would try to keep things fair by comparing the inputs and outputs that other people bring to and receive from the same action. People may regard the situation as fair as long as the ratio between these inputs and outputs is equal. According to his theory, customers can expect to pay the same price for the same advantages in the same transactions. People would be unhappy if they perceived that others were receiving more advantages for their contributions, and this could lead to an unfair impression (Brockner *et al.,* 1986; Lopes & Fletcher, 2004).

Adam's equity theory is relevant in the study of insurance fraud because it highlights consumer fairness as an important matter for insurance service providers to address. Unfair treatment by insurance service providers (e.g., an unfair deductible amount) may encourage customers to commit insurance fraud (Tseng & Kuo, 2014). By evaluating the inputs and outputs that other people contribute to and gain from the same conduct, people will try to uphold fairness. Insurance fraud is more likely to be seen as acceptable behavior by consumers who feel unfairly treated by insurance firms (Tseng & Kuo, 2014). Therefore, customers' dissatisfaction with insurance providers may motivate them to engage in and support insurance fraud (Brinkmann, 2005; Miyazaki, 2009).

According to Miyazaki (2009), deductible amounts have an impact on policyholders' opinions on whether claim padding is acceptable. As per Tseng and Kuo (2014), policyholders may compare deductible premium ratios with those of other insurance service providers, and the perceived unfairness of the ratios may further contribute to their acceptance of certain actions such as cheating or claim padding. They further pointed out that the deductible amount over the insurance premium situation may affect policyholders' decision-making in insurance fraud. As a result, clients' bad views against insurance service providers may be a motivator for them to commit and accept insurance fraud (Brinkmann, 2005; Miyazaki, 2009).

TIRA and the War Against Frauds

The Tanzania Insurance Regulatory Authority is a government organization tasked with monitoring insurance services in the country, as established by the Insurance Act No. 10 of 2009. TIRA has been working to combat insurance fraud since its inception, in accordance with Section 161 of the Insurance Act. According to Otiso (2021), the incidence of insurance fraud boosts insurance premiums, puts pressure on insurance firms' financial soundness, and reduces access. As per the ACFE (2022), the average company loses 5% of its annual revenue to fraud every year, resulting in a median loss of $117,000 before it is discovered. Individuals committing occupational fraud against their companies is not a new notion, but it is apparent that the pandemic has given fraudsters new chances. They advise businesses to learn how fraud is perpetrated in their field, build effective tools for early detection, and have a plan in place to respond when occupational fraud is discovered.

Therefore, it is important to strengthen the fight against fraudulent practices and money laundering in the insurance sector, particularly through proper detection and appropriate reporting (Yildrim & Rafay, 2021). In this regard TIRA has signed a Memorandum of Understanding (MOU) with the East African Insurance Supervisors Association (EAISA), the Insurance Regulatory Authority (Uganda), the Insurance Regulatory Authority (Kenya), the Agence de Regulation et de Controle des Assurances (Burundi), and the National Bank of Rwanda (Rwanda). Nonetheless, despite TIRA's efforts to combat fraudulent activities and oversee the insurance industry's performance in Tanzania, the business has become increasingly prone to fraud (Daudi & Shandika, 2021).

In addition, prior research has found that the insurance business has long been notorious for having a high level of fraud (ACFE, 2022; Daudi & Shandika, 2021; Otiso, 2021). Insurance fraud, on the other hand, has been given little scholarly scrutiny. According to Button *et al.* (2017), there are several global studies on various types of fraud done by individuals and/or organizations in various industries, but little research has been done on insurance fraud. As a result, there is still a paucity of literature in this field of insurance fraud, which necessitates further research. Therefore, it is necessary to investigate the impact of insurance fraud on the financial performance of Tanzania's insurance service providers, as well as the causes of insurance fraud and the steps being taken to counteract it in Tanzania.

METHODOLOGY

Research Design

For the purpose of testing the hypotheses concerning the relationship between insurance fraud and the financial performance of the insurance service providers, this study was conducted as an analytic cross-sectional survey design. This design is appropriate because the study involves the collection of data from a population at a specific point in time with the goal of receiving maximum insight from survey research (Hair *et al.*, 2019).

Population and Sample Size

As per the TIRA report (2022), there are 27 insurance companies, 99 insurance brokers, 17 locally accredited reinsurance companies, and 39 locally accredited reinsurance brokers. The study population was drawn from all of the TIRA-registered insurance companies and brokers in Tanzania. One manager responsible for claims and underwritings from each of the insurance companies and insurance brokers as of 2021 was purposively selected as a respondent to match the secondary data (financial statements for 2021) for the analysis.

Data Gathering Instruments and Procedures

A survey questionnaire was used to collect primary data from managers in charge of claims and underwriting at each of the insurance companies and brokers. The questionnaire was adapted from Frimpong *et al.* (2016) to include open-ended questions to explore the reasons for insurance fraud and the actions taken by the insurance service providers to combat fraud. Secondary data (annual financial statements as at 2021) of insurance companies and brokers was obtained from TIRA. A pilot study was conducted with 30 respondents to check the clarity of the language used. This stage resulted in no significant amendments.

The research assistants distributed 126 questionnaires by hand, with 119 valid questionnaires returned (a 94.4 percent response rate). 94.4 percent represent insurance companies and brokers who accepted and completed the questionnaires, while 5.6 percent represent those who refused to complete the questionnaires. According to Creswell (2019), a response rate of more than 50% for research is sufficient for analysis and presenting findings for making inferences.

Method of Data Analysis

To investigate the association between financial performance and insurance fraud variables, the multiple regression model below was employed.

$$ROA_i = \alpha_0 + \beta_1 PHF_i + \beta_2 INF_i + \beta_3 IRF_i + \beta_4 OLC_i + \beta_5 NY_i + \varepsilon_i$$

ROA_i = return on assets as of 2021 for insurance company/ broker i

PHF_i = policyholder fraud as of 2021 for insurance company/ broker i
INF_i = internal fraud as of 2021 for insurance company/ broker i;
IRF_i = intermediary fraud as of 2021 for insurance company/ broker i;
$OLCi$ = the percentage of owner's capital to the total long-term capital of insurance company/ broker i;
$NOYi$ = number of years an insurance company/ broker i has been in operations as of 2021;
α_0 = intercept
ε_i = error term
βs are the coefficients for every independent variable.

The dependent variable (financial performance) was measured by return on assets (ROA). This is the most common indicator of performance in the insurance industry, which is measured by monitoring profitability levels (Garba & Abubakar, 2014). ROA was calculated as follows (Anderson and Reeb, 2003):

$$ROA = \frac{\text{Net income}}{\text{Total Assets}}$$

Policyholder fraud, internal fraud, and intermediary fraud are the main independent variables in this chapter, which were generated using fraud indicators from the insurance fraud literature (Bastürk, 2020; Frimpong *et al.,* 2016; Pao *et al.,* 2014). They are represented by the effects they pose on the financial performance of insurance companies. These effects were developed from fraud indicators in insurance fraud. These effects, as shown in Table 1, are ranked on the Likert scale (Likert, 1952) ranging from 1 to 5, to get the views or perceptions of insurers on the effects of insurance fraud on their financial performance. Several researchers (Carifio & Perla, 2007; Frimpong *et al.,* 2016) have employed this technique and believe that applying it in parametric tests is statistically valid. The following variables were included in the model as control variables to ensure robustness and reduce specification bias: the OLC_i, which was calculated as the percentage of shareholders' or owners' equity to total long-term capital of the insurance companies/ brokers; and NOY_i, which was measured as the number of years insurance companies/brokers. These variables have also been utilized as control variables in previous research (Frimpong *et al.,* 2016).

Table 1. Effects of the independent variables

Policyholder fraud	Internal fraud	Intermediary fraud
Huge amounts are paid for inflated claims	Increased costs of operations	Reputational risk/damage
Less revenue from the insurance premium	Breach of ethical standards	Decline market share

RESULTS

Descriptive Statistics

Table 2 shows the descriptive data for policyholder fraud, internal fraud, intermediary fraud, owner's capital to the total long-term capital, number of years an insurance company/broker, and the return on assets.

Table 2. Descriptive statistics

Variables	Mean	SD	Minimum	Maximum	Skewness	Kurtosis	Cronbach's alpha
ROA	0.19	0.23	0.01	0.81	1.01	1.77	
PHF	3.67	0.96	2.00	5.00	-0.32	-0.82	0.823
INF	3.92	0.80	2.00	5.00	-0.33	-0.41	0.741
IRF	3.86	0.81	2.00	5.00	-0.04	-0.90	0.831
OLC	0.61	0.17	0.30	0.85	-0.21	-1.21	
NOY	7.75	9.45	2.00	58.00	3.36	15.46	

Table 2 shows that the return on assets has a lot of variation. Insurance companies and insurance brokers in the sample had returns on assets ranging from 0.01 to 0.81, with a mean of 0.19 and a standard deviation of 0.23. According to Ibendahl (2018), a return on assets of 5% or higher is good. The higher the return on assets, the more efficient the company is at generating profits (Kasoga, 2020). In terms of policyholder fraud, internal fraud, and intermediary fraud, the mean was 3.67, 3.92, and 3.86, respectively, with a minimum of 2.00 and a maximum of 5.00. These findings imply that policyholder fraud, internal fraud, and intermediary fraud are all prevalent in Tanzanian insurance companies and brokers. The average owner's capital to total long-term capital ratio was 0.61, implying that insurance companies and brokers in Tanzania had an average owner's capital to total long-term capital ratio of 61 percent. The average number of years was 7.75 years, with a minimum of 2 years and a maximum of 58 years.

The Cronbach's alpha coefficients (α) for policyholder fraud, internal fraud, and intermediary fraud were greater than the required standard of 0.6 (Hair *et al.*, 2019). This indicates that the study methods, measures, and research procedures were constant and steady, resulting in predictable, repeatable, and accurate outcomes (Creswell, 2019). Furthermore, the skewness and kurtosis measurements were within acceptable limits (Hair *et al.*, 2019). Specifically, skewness values are not less than -1 nor more than +1, and kurtosis values are not less than -2 nor more than +2, indicating that the sample has a normal distribution (Table 2).

Correlation Results

The correlations between the dependent and independent variables are shown in Table 3. As shown in Table 3, variables were unrelated to one another, with a correlation of less than 0.8. These findings imply that there is no problem of multicollinearity among independent variables. According to Field (2009), a correlation of independent variables of more than 0.8 is cause for concern. In addition, the tolerance value and variance inflation factor for each predictor were examined to evaluate the degree of multicollinearity among the explanatory measurement constructs (Hair *et al.*, 2019). All of the predictors' tolerance values are higher than the recommended value of 0.2, and the VIF values are lower than the typical cut-off criterion of 10 (Table 4), indicating that the variables are not significantly associated (Hair *et al.*, 2019).

Table 3. Correlation matrix

VARIABLES	ROA	PHF	INF	IRF	OLC	NOY
ROA	1					
PHF	-0.045**	1				
INF	-0.143**	0.051	1			
IRF	-0.061*	0.267*	-0.030	1		
OLC	0.005**	-0.015	-0.015	0.025	1	
NOY	0.049	0.109	0.186**	0.075	0.145	1

**, * imply significance < 0.01 levels, and 0.05 levels (2-tailed) respectively

The findings of Table 3 also show that there is a negative correlation between policyholder fraud, internal fraud, intermediary fraud, and the return on assets ($r = -0.045$, $p< 0.01$; $r = -0.143$, $p< 0.01$; -0.061, $p< 0.05$ respectively). These findings imply that policyholder fraud, internal fraud, and intermediary fraud have a negative effect on the financial performance of insurance companies and insurance brokers. The findings also show that there is a positive correlation between OLC, the number of years of insurance companies/brokers and the return on assets ($r = 0.005$, $p< 0.01$; $r = 0.049$, $p>0.05$ respectively). These findings suggest a positive and significant relationship between the owner's capital to the total long-term capital and return on assets and an insignificant relationship between the number of years insurance companies and insurance brokers have been in operation and the financial performance.

Multiple Regression Results

The results of the multiple regression analyses are shown in Table 4. Generally, the independent variables explain 42 percent of the variation in the return on assets. The findings revealed that the value of Durbin Watson statistics was within the range ($1.5 < d < 2.5$) implying the absence of an autocorrelation problem in the data (Field, 2009). The values of F-statistics were statistically significant ($p<0.01$) implying that the variables fit the model well.

Table 4. Multiple regression results

Variables	Coefficient	Standard error	t-statists	p-value	Collinearity Statistics	
					Tolerance	Variance inflation factor
Intercept	0.357	0.180	1.984	0.00		
PHF	-0.048*	0.023	-0.499	0.01	0.913	1.095
INF	-0.153*	0.026	-1.616	0.03	0.959	1.043
IRF	-0.075*	0.027	-0.782	0.04	0.925	1.082
OLC	0.011**	0.122	0.122	0.00	0.977	1.023
NOY	0.080	0.070	-0.831	0.408	0.929	1.076
$R = .71$, $R^2 = .53$, Adj.$R^2 = .42$, Durbin-Watson = 0.854, F = 127.41, Sig. 0.00						

Dependent variable: ROA

Note: **, * imply significance < 0.01 levels, and 0.05 levels (2-tailed) respectively

Table 4 shows that policyholder, internal, and intermediary fraud all have significant negative ($p<0.05$) effects on the return on assets ($\beta = -0.048$, $\beta = -0.153$, $\beta = -0.075$, respectively). Nonetheless, the effect of OLC on the return on assets was found to be positive and significant ($\beta = 0.011$, $p<0.01$). The effect of the number of years of insurance companies/brokers on the return on assets was found to be insignificant ($\beta = 0.080$, $p>0.05$).

Causes of Insurance Fraud

Table 5 summarizes the results of the causes of policyholder insurance fraud in Tanzania. The majority (40%) of respondents responded to the submission of fraudulent documents such as application forms, claim forms, and receipts. Then, it was followed by customers demanding significant compensation relative to the actual damage (33%). Fake accidents were the third most common cause of policyholder fraud (27%).

Table 5. Causes of policyholder insurance fraud in Tanzania

Causes of policyholder insurance fraud	Frequency	Percentage
Total number of respondents = 119		
Submission of fake documents	48	40
Customers demand huge compensation compared to the actual damage.	39	33
Fake accidents	32	27

Table 6 summarizes the results of the causes of internal insurance fraud in Tanzania. Weak internal control (55%) was cited by the majority of respondents as the main cause of internal fraud (Table 6). Then, it was followed by the dishonesty of employees (30%). Finally, 15% of respondents indicated that poor staff compensation was a cause of internal insurance fraud.

Table 6. Causes of internal insurance fraud in Tanzania

Causes	Frequency	Percentage
Total number of respondents = 119		
Weak internal control	65	55
Dishonest of employees	36	30
Low salaries to employees	18	15

Table 7 summarizes the results of the causes of intermediary fraud in Tanzania. The majority of respondents (61%) identified ineffective supervision as the leading cause of intermediary insurance fraud in Tanzania. Respondents also cited a lack of ability to detect fraud as a cause of intermediary fraud (39%).

Table 7. Causes of intermediary fraud in Tanzania

Causes	Frequency	Percentage
Total number of respondents = 119		
Ineffective supervision	72	61
Incompetence in detecting fraud	47	39

Efforts to Combat Insurance Fraud in Tanzania

Table 8 summarizes the results of the efforts used to combat insurance fraud in Tanzania. The table demonstrates that thorough claims evaluation (32%) was regarded as the most important tool to combat insurance fraud in Tanzania. Then it was followed by the use of the bureau of anti-fraud (23%), the use of internal and external auditors (15%), having an effective internal audit unit (12%), the use of information technology (10%), and having an internal fraud policy that is both transparent and rigorous (8%).

Table 8. Measures to combat insurance fraud in Tanzania

Measures	Frequency	Percentage
Total number of respondents = 119		
Extensive claims evaluation	38	32
Bureau of anti-fraud	27	23
Use of internal and external auditors	18	15
Effective internal audit unit	14	12
The use of information technology	12	10
Internal fraud policy that is both transparent and rigorous	10	8

DISCUSSION OF RESULTS

The effect of insurance fraud on the financial performance of the insurance service industry in Tanzania is examined in this chapter. The findings reveal that the effects of policyholder fraud, internal fraud, intermediary fraud, and the return on assets were negative and significant (Table 4). These findings imply that a unit change in policyholder fraud, internal fraud, and intermediary fraud would result in a decrease in financial performance by 0.048, 0.153, and 0.075 respectively (Table 4). These findings are consistent with those of Frimpong *et al.* (2016) and Irungu (2016), who found that policyholder fraud, internal fraud, and intermediary fraud negatively influence the return on assets. However, the findings of this study conflict with those of Irungu (2016), who investigated the relationship between fraud and the financial performance of insurance companies in Kenya. The study findings indicated a strong positive relationship between the amount of fraud and the return on assets.

However, the effect of the percentage of shareholders/owners' equity on the total long-term capital of the insurance companies/brokers on the return on assets was found to be positive and significant (Table 4). This finding implies that a unit change in the owner's capital to the total long-term capital would lead to a 0.011 increase in the financial performance of the insurance companies and brokers in Tanzania. On the other hand, the effect of the number of years of insurance companies or brokers on the return on assets was insignificant (Table 4). This finding suggests that there are no significant effects between the years of insurance companies' or brokers' operations and the financial performance of insurance companies or brokers in Tanzania.

With regard to the causes of insurance fraud in Tanzania, the findings reveal that the submission of fraudulent documents, such as application forms, claim forms, and receipts are the leading cause of policyholder insurance fraud in Tanzania. Then, it was followed by customers demanding significant compensation relative to the actual damage (Table 5). These situations happen most often when customers wish to generate some more cash and exaggerate costs by overcharging the insurer. The third cause of policyholder fraud was fake accidents (Table 5). This includes any instances in which a driver purposefully or strategically causes a collision with another vehicle in order to obtain a fraudulent insurance claim. The specifics of the occurrence are frequently exaggerated or twisted in order to place blame on the innocent driver. Sometimes, this can also happen when personnel of insurance companies or brokers coordinate with customers on what to write on claim forms and also provide official support to justify the fraud. These findings concur with ACFE (2022), Tseng and Kuo (2014), Pao *et al.* (2014), and Otiso (2021) on the reasons leading to policyholder insurance fraud.

In terms of internal insurance fraud, weak internal control was identified by the majority of respondents as the main cause of internal fraud (Table 6). When insurance companies or brokers fail to implement effective internal controls, such as risk assessment, internal audit, employee training, and a thorough analysis of departmental financial reports, this can happen. Then, it was followed by the dishonesty of employees. When employees are dissatisfied with their jobs, the management of the company, or the working circumstances, they commit fraud. These findings are consistent with the triangle theory established by Cressey (1971) that weak internal controls, financial pressures, and a desire for material possessions, as well as a failure to penalize violators, increase the opportunity to commit insurance fraud.

Finally, respondents indicated that poor staff compensation was a concern (Table 6). This finding implies that employees' financial stress causes this to happen. This may be explained by the fact that Tanzania's economy has grown slowly in recent years as a result of the global economic slowdown brought on by COVID-19 and the wars in Ukraine and Russia. Workers have been subjected to uncontrollable suffering as a result of the current economic scenario. Workers' earnings remain unchanged, while other costs continue to rise on a daily basis, putting financial strain on family members and dependents. Workers turn to unethical and thieving methods to achieve their financial necessities. As a result, staff or management conspires with policyholders or middlemen to scam insurance firms out of huge amounts of money. Because of their massive tasks of inspecting financial statements, claims audits, and then fraud, most insurance firms' internal audit units are weak and ineffective. As a result, they have less time to devote to detecting and combating insurance fraud. Employees are able to steal, conceal, and misrepresent some insurance contracts. These findings concur with Morley *et al.* (2006), Omar *et al.* (2016), Tseng and Su (2013), and Yusuf (2011) on the reasons leading to internal insurance fraud.

With regard to intermediary insurance fraud, the findings of this study show that the majority of respondents identified ineffective supervision as the leading cause of intermediary insurance fraud in Tanzania (Table 7). This occurs when some intermediaries manipulate the payment systems in their favor. Intermediary fraud is difficult to detect, according to Yusuf (2011), because intermediaries sit in a position of trust between insurance purchasers and insurers, and the intermediary operates far from the insurer or the insured. They frequently keep some of the information obtained from either the insured or the insurer and benefit from it. It was then followed by a lack of ability to detect fraud (Table 7). This occurs as a result of insufficient training provided to insurance brokers and agents, who are unable to detect and combat fraudulent dealings. These findings are consistent with Morley *et al.* (2006) and Omar *et al.* (2016) on the reasons leading to intermediary insurance fraud.

With respect to the measures to fight insurance fraud in Tanzania, the findings of this study show that thorough claims evaluation was regarded as the most important tool to combat insurance fraud in Tanzania (Table 8). Then it was followed by the use of the bureau of anti-fraud, the use of internal and external auditors, having an effective internal audit unit, the use of information technology, and finally, an internal fraud policy that is both transparent and rigorous (Table 8). These findings are consistent with Otiso (2021), who found that effective verification of the claims data leads to a claim being acknowledged and settled. They further uncover that having proper software and employing highly qualified and experienced fraud-fighting personnel who are well compensated are critical in combating insurance fraud. Internal fraud units that are well-established will also aid in the fight against insurance fraud. These findings suggest that internal and external auditors play an important role in the fight against insurance fraud. Mahyoro and Kasoga (2021) point out that the internal auditor gives management assurance that the control functions are appropriate and operational. They further demonstrate that internal auditors identify system flaws and make recommendations on how to fix them. On the other hand, external auditors execute annual audits to ensure that internal control systems are effective, efficient, and adequate (Mahyoro and Kasoga, 2021). Thus, these findings suggest that despite the insurance industry's using both internal and external auditors, their efforts have not helped in combating insurance fraud. This can be explained partly by the fact that management rarely implements their recommendations.

CONCLUSION AND RECOMMENDATIONS

This chapter examines the effect of insurance fraud on the financial performance of the Tanzania insurance service industry. According to the findings of this study, policyholder insurance fraud, internal insurance fraud, and intermediary insurance fraud all have a negative effect on the financial performance of insurance companies and brokers in Tanzania. These findings suggest that an increase in policyholder insurance fraud, internal insurance fraud, and intermediary insurance fraud will lower Tanzanian insurance companies' and brokers' financial performance.

The percentage of shareholders' or owners' equity to the total long-term capital of insurance companies or brokers has a positive and significant effect on the financial performance of insurance companies or brokers. This shows that increasing the proportion of owner's capital in total long-term capital would improve the financial performance of Tanzanian insurance companies and brokers. The relationship between the number of years an insurance company or broker has been in business and its financial performance was insignificant, implying that the number of years an insurance company or broker has been in business has no bearing on the financial performance of insurance companies or brokers in Tanzania.

Furthermore, insurance fraud in Tanzania was found to be caused by the submission of fraudulent documents, customers demanding significant compensation relative to the actual damage, a fake accident, weak internal control, employee dishonesty, poor staff compensation, ineffective supervision, and the inability to detect fraud. The findings reveal the importance of claims evaluation besides employing an anti-fraud bureau, employing effective internal and external auditors' recommendations, effective internal audit unit and employing information technology in internal fraud policy (Khan *et al.*, 2020).

This chapter contributes to the body of knowledge by examining the effect of insurance fraud on the financial performance of Tanzania's insurance service industry. This was significant because, while insurance fraud is a context-specific issue, there is no worldwide agreement on the impact of insurance fraud on the financial performance of the insurance service industry (Otiso, 2021). Prior studies, on the other hand, have relied on data from insurance companies and have overlooked the role of insurance brokers, which may not truly reflect the views of all insurance service providers. In addition, the study contributes to the body of knowledge by addressing the causes of insurance fraud in Tanzania as well as the actions used to combat it. This was significant since earlier research had shed light on some of the reasons that motivate people to defraud others. However, previous studies did not identify all of the causes of insurance fraud (Wolfe & Hermanson, 2004). As a result, Raval (2013) advises more in-depth research on the causes of insurance fraud and the strategies employed to combat it.

In terms of the chapter's practical implications, TIRA, Tanzania's regulatory organization, should host a stakeholder summit on insurance fraud where all stakeholders can discuss the impact of insurance fraud on insurance service delivery and the role of each stakeholder in combating the threat. In addition, the government should establish an insurance fraud bureau that will launch a public awareness campaign on the dangers of insurance fraud and assist society in developing a culture of integrity and anti-fraud attitudes.

In addition, policymakers are encouraged to establish approaches and regulations to reduce insurance fraud in the insurance service industry. This would not only help to reduce insurance fraud, but it would also help the insurance industry in Tanzania improve its financial performance.

This research has certain drawbacks. First, the study relied solely on one-year data and used cross-sectional data (single point estimate). In future studies, panel data or longitudinal data could be used to gain more insight into this issue. Second, it took place in Tanzania, which limits the applicability of the findings to other contexts. As a result, comparable studies should be conducted in a variety of settings so that a more thorough picture may be documented as an addition to the insurance fraud literature.

DECLARATION

The authors declare that the manuscript follows ethical standards and there are no potential conflicts of interest with respect to the research, authorship and/or publication of this chapter.

DISCLAIMER

The contents and views of this chapter are expressed by the authors in their personal capacities. It is not necessary for the Editor and the Publisher to agree with these viewpoints, and they are not responsible for any duty of care in this regard.

ACKNOWLEDGMENT

The authors extend sincere gratitude to

• The Editor and the International Editorial Advisory Board (IEAB) of this book who initially desk reviewed, arranged a rigorous double/triple blind review process, and conducted a thorough, minute, and critical final review before accepting the chapter for publication.

• All anonymous reviewers who provided very constructive feedbacks for thorough revision, improvement, extension, and fine tuning of the chapter.

• All colleagues, assistants and well-wishers who assisted to complete this task.

REFERENCES

ACFE. (2022). *Association of certified fraud examiners report to the Nations: Fraud trends and key takeaways*. Retrieved from https://www.acfe.com/-/media/files/acfe/pdfs/2012-report-to-nations.ashx

Adams, J. S. (1963). Toward an understanding of inequity. *Journal of Abnormal and Social Psychology*, *67*(5), 422–436. doi:10.1037/h0040968 PMID:14081885

Adams, J. S. (1965). Inequity in social exchange. In L. Berkowitz (Ed.). Advances in Experimental Social Psychology. Academic Press. doi:10.1016/S0065-2601(08)60108-2

Akpınar, E., & Kasapbas, I. M. C. (2019). Association analysis between pharmacies and pharmaceutical companies in healthcare insurance systems. *Haliç University Journal of Science*, *2*(1), 35–47.

Amiram, D., Bozanic, Z., Cox, J. D., Dupont, Q., Karpoff, J. M., & Sloan, R. (2018). Financial reporting fraud and other forms of misconduct: A multidisciplinary review of the literature. *Review of Accounting Studies*, *23*(2), 732–783. doi:10.100711142-017-9435-x

Anand, V., Blake, E. A., & Joshi, M. (2004). Business as usual: The acceptance and perpetuation of corruption. *The Academy of Management Executive*, *18*(2), 39–53. doi:10.5465/ame.2004.13837437

Anderson, R. C., & Reeb, D. M. (2003). Founding family ownership and firm performance: Evidence from the S&P 500. *The Journal of Finance*, *58*(3), 1301–1328. doi:10.1111/1540-6261.00567

Bastürk, F. H. (2020). Insurance Fraud: The Case in Turkey. In S. Grima, E. Boztepe, & P. J. Baldacchino (Eds.), *Contemporary Issues in Audit Management and Forensic Accounting*. Emerald. doi:10.1108/S1569-375920200000102009

Baumann, N. (2020). *Understanding COVID-19's impact on the insurance sector*. Deloitte. Retrieved from https://www2.deloitte.com/global/en/pages/about-deloitte/articles/covid- 19/understandingcovid-19-s-impact-on-the- insurance-sector-.html

Bose, I., & Mahapatra, R. K. (2001). Business data mining – A machine learning perspective. *Information & Management*, *39*(3), 211–225. doi:10.1016/S0378-7206(01)00091-X

Brinkmann, J. (2005). Understanding insurance customer dishonesty: Outline of a situational approach. *Journal of Business Ethics*, *61*(2), 183–197. doi:10.100710551-005-0278-1

Brockett, P. L., Derrig, R. A., Golden, L. L., Levine, A., & Alpert, M. (2002). Fraud classification using principal component analysis of RIDITs. *The Journal of Risk and Insurance*, *69*(3), 341–373. doi:10.1111/1539-6975.00027

Brockner, J., Greenberg, J., Brockner, A., Bortz, J., Davy, J., & Carter, C. (1986). Layoffs, equity theory, and work performance: Further evidence of the impact of survivor guilt. *Academy of Management Journal*, *29*(2), 373–384. doi:10.2307/256193

Button, M., Brooks, G., Lewis, C., & Aleem, A. (2017). Just about everybody doing the business? Explaining 'cash-for-crash' insurance fraud in the United Kingdom. *Australian and New Zealand Journal of Criminology*, *50*(2), 176–194. doi:10.1177/0004865816638910

Carifio, J., & Perla, R. (2007). Ten common misunderstandings, misconceptions, persistent myths and urban legends about Likert scale and Likert response formats and their antidotes. *Journal of Social Sciences*, *3*(3), 106–116. doi:10.3844/jssp.2007.106.116

Çetin, M. (2015). Risk yönetimi ve sigortacilik ilkeleri, sigorta ve riziko (Vol. 2). In Principles of risk management and insurance (Vol. 12). Pearson.

Clarke, M. (1989). Insurance fraud. *British Journal of Criminology*, *29*(1), 1–20. doi:10.1093/oxfordjournals.bjc.a047785

Cressey, D. R. (1971). *Other Peoples' Money: A Study in the Social Psychology of Embezzlement*. Wadsworth Publishing.

Creswell, W. J. (2019). Research Design: Qualitative, Quantitative, and Mixed Methods Approaches. *Sage (Atlanta, Ga.)*.

Daudi, F., & Shindika, S. E. (2021). Reckoning frauds in Tanzania's insurance services: An ethical perspective. *International Journal of Innovative Science and Research Technology*, *6*(3), 99–104.

Derrig, A. R. (2002). Insurance fraud. *The Journal of Risk and Insurance*, *69*(3), 271–287. doi:10.1111/1539-6975.00026

Dionne, G. (1984). The effects of insurance on the possibilities of fraud. *The Geneva Papers on Risk and Insurance. Issues and Practice*, *9*(3), 304–321. doi:10.1057/gpp.1984.18

Farooq, U., Nasir, A., & Quddoos, M. U. (2021). The impact of COVID-19 pandemic on abnormal returns of insurance firms: A cross-country evidence. *Applied Economics*, *53*(31), 3658–3678. doi:10.1080/00036846.2021.1884839

Field, A. (2009). *Discovering statistics using SPSS* (3rd ed.). SAGE.

Frimpong, A. I., Andoh, C., & Ofosu-Hene, D. E. (2016). Causes, effects and deterrence of insurance fraud: Evidence from Ghana. *Journal of Financial Crime*, *23*(4), 678–699. doi:10.1108/JFC-11-2015-0062

Garba, T., & Abubakar, B. A. (2014). Corporate board diversity and financial performance of insurance companies in Nigeria: An application of panel data approach. *Asian Economic and Financial Review*, *4*(2), 257–277.

Ghezzi, S. G. (1983). A private network of social control: Insurance investigation units. *Social Problems*, *30*(5), 521–531. doi:10.2307/800269

Gill, K. M., Woolley, A., & Gill, M. (2005). Insurance fraud: The business as a victim? In M. Gill (Ed.), *Crime at work* (Vol. 1). Springer. doi:10.1007/978-1-349-23551-3_6

Gomes, C., Jin, Z., & Yang, H. (2021). Insurance fraud detection with unsupervised deep learning. *The Journal of Risk and Insurance*, *88*(3), 591–624. doi:10.1111/jori.12359

Goswami, Y., Kannan Asokan, K., & Arunasalam, K. (2022). Impact of frauds on the Financial Performance of Insurance Companies in India. *International Journal of Early Childhood Special Education*, *14*(3), 7490–7499.

Hair, J. F., Risher, J. J., Sarstedt, M., & Ringle, C. M. (2019). When to use and How to Report the Results of PLS-SEM. *European Business Review*, *31*(1), 2–24. doi:10.1108/EBR-11-2018-0203

Hassan, A. I. K., & Abraham, A. (2013). Computational intelligence models for insurance fraud detection: A review of a decade of research. *Journal of Network and Innovative Computing*, *1*, 341–347.

IAIS. (2007). *Report on the survey on preventing, detecting and remedying fraud in insurance.* Basel: International Association of Insurance Supervisors. Retrieved from www.iaisweb.org/

IAIS. (2011). *Deterring, Preventing, Detecting, Reporting and Remedying Fraud in Insurance.* Basel: International Association of Insurance Supervisors. Retrieved from https://www.iaisweb.org/page/supervisory-material/application-papers/file/58019/application-paper-on-the-regulationand-supervision-ofcaptive-insurers

Ibendahl, G. (2018). *Comparing the financial ratios ROA and ROE.* Kansas State University Department of Agricultural Economics. Retrieved from https://agmanager.info /sites/default/files/pdf/ROA-ROE_2018_Ibendahl.pdf

Insurance Fraud Handbook. (2018). *Association of Certified Fraud Examiners.* Retrieved from https://www.acfe.com/uploadedFiles/ACFE_Website/Content/documents/Insurance-Fraud-Handbook.pdf

IRA. (2020). *Insurance industry annual report.* Insurance Regulatory Authority. Retrieved from https://www.ira.go.ke/index.php/publications/statistical-reports/annual-reports

IRA. (2021). *Insurance industry annual report.* Insurance Regulatory Authority. Retrieved from https://www.ira.go.ke/index.php/publications/statistical-reports/annual-reports

Irungu, M. J. (2016). *Relationship between Fraud and Financial Performance of Insurance Companies in Kenya* [Unpublished MSC (Finance) Project]. University of Nairobi. Retrieved from http://erepository.uonbi.ac.ke/handle/11295/98963?show=full

Jung, J., & Kim, J. B. (2021). Insurance fraud in Korea, its seriousness, and policy implications. Front. *Frontiers in Public Health*, *9*, 791820. doi:10.3389/fpubh.2021.791820 PMID:34869196

Karpoff, J. M. (2020). The future of financial fraud. *Journal of Corporate Finance*, *66*(1), 101694.

Kasoga, P. S. (2020). Does investing in intellectual capital improve financial performance? Panel evidence from firms listed in Tanzania DSE. *Cogent Economics and Finance*, *8*(1), 1–26. doi:10.1080/23322039.2020.1802815

Khan, N., Rafay, A., & Shakeel, A. (2020). Attributes of Internal Audit and Prevention, Detection and Assessment of Fraud in Pakistan. *Lahore Journal of Business*, *9*(1), 33–58. doi:10.35536/ljb.2020.v9.i1.a2

Kiptoo, K., Kariuki, S. N., & Ocharo, K. N. (2021). Risk management and financial performance of insurance firms in Kenya. *Cogent Business & Management*, *8*(1), 1–17. doi:10.1080/23311975.2021.1997246

Li, C., Lou, C., Luo, D., & Kai, X. (2021). Chinese corporate distress prediction using LASSO: The role of earnings management. *International Review of Financial Analysis*, *76*(C), 101776. doi:10.1016/j.irfa.2021.101776

Likert, R. A. (1952). A technique for the development of attitude scales. *Educational and Psychological Measurement*, *12*(2), 313–315.

Lopes, J., & Fletcher, C. (2004). Fairness of impression management in employment interviews: A cross-country study of the role of equity and Machiavellianism. *Social Behavior and Personality*, *32*(8), 747–768. doi:10.2224bp.2004.32.8.747

Loveday, B., & Jung, J. (2021). A current and future challenge to contemporary policing: the changing profile of crime and the police response. examples of policing fraud in two police jurisdictions: England and Wales and South Korea. *Policing. Journal of Policy Practice*, *15*(3), 1633–1650.

Mahyoro, A. K., & Kasoga, P. S. (2021). Attributes of the internal audit function and effectiveness of internal audit services: Evidence from local government authorities in Tanzania. *Managerial Auditing Journal*, *36*(7), 999–1023. doi:10.1108/MAJ-12-2020-2929

Maina, B. W. (2016). *The Effects of Financial Fraud and Liquidity on Financial Performance of Insurance Companies in Kenya* [Unpublished MBA Project]. University of Nairobi. Retrieved from http://erepository.uonbi.ac.ke/bitstream/handle/11295/99055/maina_The%20Effects%20of%20Financial%20Fraud%20and%20Liquidity%20on%20Financial%20Perform

Miyazaki, A. D. (2009). Perceived ethicality of insurance claim fraud: Do higher deductibles lead to lower ethical standards? *Journal of Business Ethics*, *87*(4), 589–598. doi:10.100710551-008-9960-4

Morley, N. J., Ball, L. J., & Ormerod, T. C. (2006). How the detection of insurance fraud succeeds and fails. *Psychology, Crime & Law*, *12*(2), 163–180. doi:10.1080/10683160512331316325

Nakitende, M. G., Rafay, A., & Waseem, M. (2021). Frauds in Business Organizations: A Comprehensive Overview. In A. Rafay (Ed.), *Handbook of Research on Theory and Practice of Financial Crimes* (pp. 21–38). IGI Global. doi:10.4018/978-1-7998-5567-5.ch002

Ngai, E. W., Hu, Y., Wong, Y. H., Chen, Y., & Sun, X. (2011). The application of data mining techniques in financial fraud detection: A classification framework and an academic review of literature. *Decision Support Systems*, *50*(3), 559–569. doi:10.1016/j.dss.2010.08.006

Omar, M., Nawawi, A., & Salin, A. S. A. P. (2016). The causes, impact and prevention of employee fraud: A case study of an automotive company. *Journal of Financial Crime*, *23*(4), 1012–1027. doi:10.1108/JFC-04-2015-0020

Otiso, N. H. (2021). The effects of fraud on performance of insurance industry: A critical review of literature. *International Journal of Management and Social Sciences*, *9*(2), 60–76.

Pao, T. I., Tzeng, L. Y., & Wang, C. W. (2014). Typhoons and opportunistic fraud: Claim patterns of automobile theft insurance in Taiwan. *The Journal of Risk and Insurance*, *8*(1), 91–112. doi:10.1111/j.1539-6975.2012.01498.x

Park, Y. (2014). A study on the strategies for reducing insurance crime. *Korean Police Studies Review*, *13*, 61–90.

Patil, K. S., & Godbole, A. (2018). A survey on machine learning techniques for insurance fraud prediction. *Helix*, *8*(6), 4358–4363. doi:10.29042/2018-4358-4363

Pešout, P., & Andrle, M. (2011). Insurance fraud management as an integrated part of business intelligence framework. World Academy of Science, Engineering and Technology. *International Journal of Industrial and Systems Engineering*, *5*(11), 1387–1392.

Rafay, A. (Ed.). (2021a). *Money Laundering and Terrorism Financing in Global Financial Systems*. IGI Global. doi:10.4018/978-1-7998-8758-4

Rafay, A. (Ed.). (2021b). *Handbook of Research on Theory and Practice of Financial Crimes*. IGI Global. doi:10.4018/978-1-7998-5567-5

Rafay, A. (Ed.). (2023). *Concepts and Cases of Illicit and Illegitimate Finance*. IGI Global. doi:10.4018/978-1-6684-8587-3

Raval, V. (2013). Human disposition and the fraud cycle. *International Journal of Applied Behavioral Economics*, *2*(1), 1–16. doi:10.4018/ijabe.2013010101

Re, S. (2016). World insurance in 2015: Steady growth amid regional disparities. *Sigma*, *3*(1), 1–50.

Report, I. O. (2020). *The East Africa Insurance Outlook Report 2019/2020*. Deloitte. Retrieved from https://www2.deloitte.com/content/dam/Deloitte/ke/Documents/financialservices/ea_insurance_outlook_report_2019.pdf

Report, I. O. (2021). *The East Africa Insurance Outlook Report 2020/2021*. Deloitte. Retrieved from https://www2.deloitte.com/content/dam/Deloitte/ke/Documents/financialservices/ea_insurance_outlook_report_2020.pdf

TIRA. (2022). *Tanzania insurance quarterly performance for the three months period from 1st January to 31st March, 2022*. Tanzania Insurance Regulatory Authority. Retrieved from https://www.tira.go.tz

Todd, J. D., Welch, S. T., Welch, O. J., & Holmes, S. A. (2000). The nature and characteristics of insurance agent fraud. *CPCU Journal*, *53*(3), 152–167.

Tseng, L. M., & Kuo, C. L. (2014). Customers' attitudes towards insurance frauds: An application of Adam's equity theory. *Geneva Papers on Risk & Insurance*, *41*(11), 1038–1054. doi:10.1108/IJSE-08-2012-0142

Tseng, L. M., & Su, W. P. (2013). Customer orientation, social consensus and insurance salespeople's tolerance of customer insurance frauds. *International Journal of Bank Marketing*, *31*(1), 38–55. doi:10.1108/02652321311292047

Turban, E., Sharda, R., Delen, D., & Efraim, T. (2007). *Decision support and business intelligence systems*. Pearson Education.

Utah Insurance Department. (2022). *What is insurance fraud?* Retrieved from https://insurance. utah. gov/agent/fraud/what.php

Wang, Y., Zhang, D., Wang, X., & Fu, Q. (2020). How does COVID-19 affect China's insurance market? *Emerging Markets Finance & Trade*, *56*(10), 2350–2362. doi:10.1080/1540496X.2020.1791074

Wolfe, D. T., & Hermanson, D. R. (2004). The fraud diamond: Considering the four elements of Fraud. *The CPA Journal*, 38–42.

Yildrim, I., & Rafay, A. (2021). Anti-Money Laundering in the Insurance Sector: The Turkish Case. In A. Rafay (Ed.), *Money Laundering and Terrorism Financing in Global Financial Systems* (pp. 108–127). IGI Global. doi:10.4018/978-1-7998-8758-4.ch005

Yusuf, O. T. (2010). Brokers and the control of post contractual opportunism in the Nigerian insurance market. *Journal of Financial Crime*, *17*(2), 223–239. doi:10.1108/13590791011033917

Yusuf, O. T. (2011). Brokers' incentives and conflicts of interest in the control of opportunism. *The Journal of Risk Finance*, *12*(3), 168–218. doi:10.1108/15265941111136923

Zhu, X., Ao, X., Qin, Z., Chang, Y., Liu, Y., He, Q., & Li, J. (2021). Intelligent financial fraud detection practices in post-pandemic era. *The Innovation*, *2*(4), 1–11. doi:10.1016/j.xinn.2021.100176 PMID:34806059

ADDITIONAL READING

Button, M., Blackbourn, D., Lewis, D., & Shepherd, D. (2015). Uncovering the hidden cost of staff fraud: An assessment of 45 cases in the UK. *Journal of Financial Crime*, *22*(2), 170–183. doi:10.1108/JFC-11-2013-0070

Hoyt, R. E., Mustard, D. B., & Powell, L. S. (2006). The effectiveness of state legislation in mitigating moral hazard: Evidence from automobile insurance. *The Journal of Law & Economics*, *49*(2), 427–450. doi:10.1086/501092

Lesch, W. C., & Brinkmann, J. (2011). Consumer insurance fraud/abuse as a co-creation and co-responsibility: A new paradigm. *Journal of Business Ethics*, *103*(1), 17–32. doi:10.100710551-012-1226-5

Lindberg, D. L., & Seifert, D. L. (2016). Micro-insurance, Fraud, and Fraud Controls. *Journal of Forensic and Investigative Accounting*, *8*(1), 29–35.

Chapter 11
Base Erosion and Profit Shifting (BEPS) in International Taxation System:
The Case of Mauritius in the Light of OECD/G20 Initiatives

Ambareen Beebeejaun
University of Mauritius, Mauritius

Rajendra Parsad Gunputh
University of Mauritius, Mauritius

Abdul Rafay
https://orcid.org/0000-0002-0285-5980
University of Management and Technology, Pakistan

ABSTRACT

The aftermath of the 2008 global financial crisis has led to the emergence of the OECD/G20 Base Erosion and Profit Shifting (BEPS) initiative developed in 2013. This project provides several actions plans to establish coherence and transparency and also to prevent malpractices in the international taxation system. Being a member of the OECD, Mauritius joined the inclusive framework on BEPS in 2016. This research assesses the adoption of the BEPS standards by Mauritius on Controlled Foreign Corporations (CFCs), transfer pricing, and on country-by-country (CbC) reporting. The purpose of this study is to identify any convergence and divergence between BEPS standards and the corresponding implementation measures in Mauritius. To achieve this research objective, the study has adopted the black letter approach by analyzing existing laws. A critical analysis is conducted about the implementation measures by Mauritius and assessing their implications on the domestic and the international taxation systems.

DOI: 10.4018/978-1-6684-5007-9.ch011

INTRODUCTION

Emerging trends in free trade and globalization have rendered the international taxation system obsolete which was designed a century ago. This is mainly because these rules enabled base erosion and profit shifting (BEPS)[1] opportunities. This has reduced the confidence of governments and the public in the international taxation frameworks.

In 2013, the OECD member countries and the G20 leaders discussed the means and ways to tackle BEPS issues at the international level. This was the first serious attempt to enhance trust in the international taxation system by streamlining cross-border transactions and new trading methods. In this regard, a comprehensive package comprised of 15 action plans on BEPS was designed. The purpose was to implement recommendations locally and through international agreements in a harmonized manner to ensure the formation of an appropriate monitoring and transparency framework. In addition to attributing taxing rights to countries where economic activities take place, the BEPS action plans aim to (1) facilitate the information sharing process across countries and revenue authorities, (2) minimize the incidence of double taxation (3) suggest dispute resolution procedures that are more efficient in terms of time and cost, and (4) set up mechanisms to monitor the BEPS action plans implementation process.

Xu (2018) has classified the 15 BEPS action plans into five main categories which are:

Category 1:

- Taxation rules for the digitalized economy (Action 1)

Category 2:

- Rules to prevent double taxation namely recommendations on hybrid mismatch agreements (Action 2)
- Controlled Foreign Corporation (CFC)[2] rules (Action 3)
- Policies on interest deductions (Action 4)
- Minimizing harmful tax practices (Action 5) and
- Prevention of treaty abuses (Action 6)

Category 3:

- Suggestions to align economic value creation to taxation which includes rules on the permanent establishment (Action 7)
- Recommendations on transfer pricing[3] of intangibles, risks and capital and high-risk transactions (Actions 8, 9 and 10),

Category 4:

- Rules for information sharing and dispute resolution namely BEPS data analysis (Action 11)
- Compulsory disclosures (Action 12)
- Country-by-Country (CbC) reporting[4] (Action 13) and
- Mutual agreement procedure (Action 14) and

Category 5:

- Implementation and monitoring of BEPS actions plan through the multilateral instruments (Action 15)

Mauritius is a developing country located in the Indian Ocean. The Gross Domestic Product (GDP) of Mauritius is USD 13 billion as of 31st December 2021 (Statistics Mauritius, 2022). Since the country's independence in 1968, Mauritius has transitioned from a poor sugar economy into one of the most remarkable flourishing economies in Africa. This economic development is attributed mainly to a long history of political stability and good governance in addition to the growing corporate, ICT and tourism sectors. As of 31st December 2021, the tertiary economic sector comprises 65% of the entire Mauritian economy as compared to the 19% and 16% secondary and primary sectors respectively (EDB, 2022). Moreover, as part of the tertiary economic sector, the financial services sector of Mauritius accounted for 14% of the GDP for the year 2021 (EDP, 2022).

Mauritius joined the inclusive framework on BEPS in 2016 with a view to participating in the OCED/G20 BEPS project (OECD, 2016). Mauritius is actively involved in implementing BEPS action plans although it is not feasible to adopt all the 15 standards at one go. To this effect, it is noted that the Mauritius government has placed much emphasis on adopting some particular BEPS action plans which would relieve the country of the alleged reputation of acting as a simple post-box in the international services sector (Beebeejaun, 2019). This is because the country is often accused of siphoning billions of funds from least developed countries or developing countries, especially from the African continent to transform itself into a thriving financial center (Fitzgibbon, 2019). Consequently, much priority is being given to the implementation of BEPS action plans on rules concerning CFC (Action 3), transfer pricing (Actions 8, 9, and 10) and on CbC reporting (Action 13) with the view to minimizing instances of tax avoidance in the form of base erosion and profit shifting from other countries.

In addition to BEPS action plans, Mauritius has its own set of local legislation tackling BEPS issues. This legislation consists of special anti-avoidance rules and general anti-avoidance rules embedded in the Mauritius Income Tax Act 1995. The special anti-avoidance rules (Section 84–89 of the Mauritius Income Tax Act) include policies regarding excessive remuneration or share of profits, benefits to shareholders, excessive management expenses, and rights over income retained. Moreover, the general anti-avoidance rules are provided for under Section 90 of the said Act which sets out a series of transactions that are designed to avoid liability to income tax. Furthermore, to strengthen the existing anti-avoidance taxation framework, Mauritius has implemented various measures during the years 2018–2020.

The main purpose of this chapter is to critically assess the initiatives undertaken by the Mauritius government and to identify any convergence and divergence between these measures and the corresponding BEPS standards on rules relating to CFC, transfer pricing and CbC reporting. These three topics of BEPS standards have been identified for the subject matter of this research primarily because Mauritius has recently enacted laws on CFC and CbC reporting. In order to consolidate its image as a reputable international financial center. These enactments will also restrict the maneuvers of multinational companies (MNCs) to avoid paying their share of taxes in the parent country which is often a developed one having high tax rates. Additionally, Mauritius is also planning to establish extensive and substantive rules on transfer pricing in addition to the existing legal provision on the arm's length principle (ALP)[5] in order to foster a fair taxation environment concerning MNCs (MFEPD, 2019a). It is therefore imperative to assess the extent to which Mauritius has followed and implemented BEPS standards in its legislation relating to these three main areas. To achieve this research objective, the study has adopted the black letter approach by analyzing existing laws on the subject matter. A critical and comparative analysis is conducted on the implementation measures undertaken by the Mauritian authorities against the respective BEPS standards.

Limited literature is available and this study will be one of the initial academic writings on the adherence to some specific OECD/G20 BEPS standards by Mauritius. The study is carried out with the aim of combining a large amount of empirical, theoretical and factual information that can be of use to various stakeholders.

BEPS ACTION 3 AND IMPLEMENTATION BY MAURITIUS

The Formation of Effective CfC Rules

Some three decades back, governments were not really bothered about profit-shifting trends by MNCs. However, the consequence of these practices reveals that corporate bodies are hiding their large profits in some other regions of the world to pay no or less tax. In this regard, various techniques are being used to exploit loopholes in legislation to transfer profits to countries that have low corporate tax rates. Consequently, this led to a loss of governmental revenues. A study by Garcia-Bernardo and Jansky (2021) concluded that the scale of profit shifting across the globe is around USD 1 trillion while an amount of USD 200-300 billion of tax revenue is lost with these practices.

It becomes necessary for countries to adopt anti-avoidance rules like legislation for CFCs. In a nutshell, CFC rules aim at taxing the income of foreign subsidiaries or associates irrespective of whether it is repatriated or not, especially if this income is purported to be shifted profits. In fact, CFC rules target mostly passive income in a low-tax jurisdiction which is being generated by a subsidiary located in that country from *inter alia* patents, royalties, or trademarks. Prettl and von Hagen (2022) consider this type of subsidiary as a vessel to amass profits while eroding the income originating from the country's right to taxation. As such, a CFC rule will be effective to enable the revenue authority of a multinational parent company to tax the income of its foreign subsidiary even if this amount is not remitted to the parent company. Recognizing the vital role of CFC rules, the OCED earmarked these rules as a standard to tackle Base Erosion Profit Shifting (BEPS). By exploring the impact of CFC legislation on passive income generated in other foreign jurisdictions, Prettl (2018) and Clifford (2019) support the effectiveness of CFC rules to curb profit-shifting behavior by MNCs.

BEPS Action 3 targets MNCs that have subsidiaries or affiliates in different countries and a centralized head office in another jurisdiction that coordinates global management (Petutschnig & Resenig, 2019). It is a common practice for MNCs to avoid paying taxes in the country in which they are operating and where the revenue is generated by setting up offshore structures and shifting profits to these structures. In this way, the country of operation is deprived of tax revenue which undoubtedly would be of use for its own economic activities.

BEPS Action 3 provides for an explicit legal framework that encompasses all types of CFCs including MNCs. A CFC is defined as a foreign company that is either directly or indirectly controlled by a resident taxpayer (OECD, 2020). In this regard, the term "control" is determined using various criteria such as *inter alia* voting rights including legal control based on the percentage of ownership rights in the foreign company or *de facto* control by looking at the decision-making process of the foreign company (Beebeejaun, 2019). In contrast, a corporation is classified as a CFC if it carries out its main revenue-generating activities in a low-tax country (Karhunen, Ledyaeva & Brouthers, 2021). Some other scholars rely on the taxation test also known as the substance activity test that is in place in the country of operation (Kofler *et al.*, 2020). Therefore, to align the interpretation issues across countries, BEPS Action 3 has put forward suggestions in the form of building blocks regarding the drafting of efficient CFC rules. The purpose was to harmonize across countries the definition of CFC and CFC income, the computation of CFC income and it's repartitioning to shareholders, the treatment of CFC income, and rules to eliminate double taxation. As a result of this initiative, CFC rules were finalized by 49 OECD/G20 countries in mid-2019 (OECD, 2020).

Fundamentally, BEPS Action 3 recommends that the principles for determining an entity as a CFC, should be clearly elaborated in the domestic laws of the relevant countries. *Firstly*, it is suggested that a broad definition is attributed to those entities that may fall under the status of a CFC in a way that will also encompass transparent entities such as partnerships and permanent establishments (OECD, 2015a). *Secondly*, the CFC rules have to explicitly ascertain the existence of a control relationship. In essence, BEPS Action 3 strongly recommends that both a legal and an economic control test has to be applied to figure out if a foreign entity is under the significant influence of a resident corporation. In this respect, it follows that 4 main types of control tests are advocated by the OECD namely:

1) *the legal control* which refers to the voting rights held by the resident company in the foreign entity. Indeed, legal control is established if the prescribed amount of share ownership in the foreign entity is met which is usually 50% or a lesser percentage as may be determined by the relevant countries.
2) **the economic control test** assesses the entitlement of the resident company to profits, assets and capital in the foreign company. In other words, economic control is established if the resident company receives dividends, capital gains upon disposal of shares held, or surplus assets in the case of the foreign company's winding up or dissolution.
3) **the de facto control** considers the decision-making power of the foreign entity. That is, it is imperative to find out who takes the strategic decisions of the entity and thus influences its daily activities. This implies that the de facto control test requires an analysis of dominating influence over a corporation on a case-by-case basis. However, determination of this type of control is often difficult for revenue authorities.
4) **control based on consolidation,** as the name suggests, looks at whether the accounts of the foreign company are consolidated in the accounts of the resident company as per the principles of International Financial Reporting Standards (IFRS).

In addition to the control requirement, BEPS Action 3 makes it imperative for CFC rules to provide for an elaborated definition of "CFC income" that will be attributable to the taxable income of the resident company. In this regard, specific rules for defining CFC income may be categorized in terms of dividends, interest, insurance income, royalties and intellectual property income, or sales/services income. The main concern with these types of income is that they are more likely to be geographically mobile and hence raise greater concerns for profit shifting. Another method to determine the CFC income is to define the income of the foreign entity that is in excess of a certain prescribed amount as the attributable income of the resident corporation. Lastly, BEPS Action 3 suggests two approaches to determine CFC income: the transactional approach and the entity approaches. While *the entity approach* looks at those activities that will not give rise to any attributable income, *the transactional approach* investigates each source of income generation to conclude if the income generated is attributable or not.

Moreover, closely associated with the definition of CFC income, BEPS Action 3 provides recommendations on the computation of CFC income. In particular, it is suggested that the offsetting of CFC losses should be limited to profits of the same CFC or against profits of other CFCs in the same jurisdiction. Additionally, in order to harmonize the computation of CFC income, BEPS Action 3 recommends the use of IFRS principles if the country in question does not have any specific legislation in this regard.

Keeping in view the CFC rules put forward by BEPS Action 3, it is vital to figure out the extent to which Mauritius, being a signatory member of the BEPS project and a member of the OECD, has converged or diverged from BEPS Action 3. The following section will compare the endeavors undertaken by the Mauritius government against BEPS Action 3.

Implementation of BEPS Action 3 by Mauritius

Since 2019, CFC rules have been introduced in the Mauritius Income Tax Act and have come into effect in respect of the year of assessment commenced on July 01, 2020, and for each subsequent year of assessment thereafter (MFEPD, 2019b). This legislative amendment comprises inclusion of a new subsection under the existing Section 90 of the Mauritius Income Tax Act which is entitled "*transactions designed to avoid liability to income tax*". Section 90 deals with general anti-avoidance rules while Sections 84 – 89 of the said Act refer to some specific anti-avoidance rules. Section 90 provides for a list of instances whereby tax authorities have the power to assess the tax liability of the taxpayer and may even counteract a tax benefit obtained by the taxpayer by having engaged in these prescribed transactions. For this purpose, "tax benefit" is defined as the avoidance or postponement of the liability to pay income tax or the reduction in the amount thereof, while a "transaction" is defined as any operation or scheme irrespective of whether enforceable or not by legal proceedings.

Consequently, the Mauritius legislator has included CFC rules under the general anti-avoidance legal provision by inserting Section 90A in the Mauritius Income Tax Act. CFCs are defined as companies that are located outside Mauritius but are owned and controlled by a Mauritius resident. This implies that 50% or more of the total CFC's shares or participating rights must be held directly or indirectly by a Mauritius resident company. A permanent establishment is also considered to meet the 50% threshold control. Accordingly, the new Section 90A empowers the Mauritius Revenue Authority (MRA) to tax the non-distributed income of a CFC if it arises from non-genuine transactions with a view to obtaining a tax benefit (MRA, 2020). Furthermore, Section 90A reiterates the definition of a tax benefit as the avoidance or postponement of the liability to pay tax or reduce the tax amount. Hence, income to be taxed from the CFC will be included in the taxable amount of the Mauritius resident company but is limited to the amounts derived from the involvement of assets and risks linked to the significant activities carried out by the controlling Mauritius resident company. Subsequently, this tax amount from the CFC will reduce the taxable dividend income received from the same CFC even if the latter is located in a jurisdiction with which Mauritius has a tax treaty. However, this rule will not apply to a CFC if:

1) its accounting profits are less than EUR 750,000 (USD 783,000), and non-trading income is less than EUR 75,000 (USD 78,300);
2) its accounting profits amount to less than 10 percent of its operating costs for the tax period; or

3) the tax rate in the country of residence of the CFC is more than 50 percent of the tax rate in Mauritius.

The main distinction between Section 90 and Section 90A of the Mauritius Income Tax Act is that the former section governs transactions giving rise to tax liability due in Mauritius only whereas Section 90A concerns schemes that involve not only Mauritius but also aim at eroding other countries' tax bases. In fact, CFC rules are designed to tax entities located in low or no tax areas generating passive income and with little economic substance. Nevertheless, it is quite early to decipher the impact of the CFC rules on the Mauritian global business sector, especially in the context of the difficult economic situation entailed by Covid-19.

The Divergences Between Mauritius CFC Rules and BEPS Action 3

In view of the foregoing discussion about the CFC legal provision of Mauritius, some convergences and divergences are noted for and against the OECD/G20 BEPS Action 3. Regarding the definition of CFCs, BEPS Action 3 suggests that CFCs should be broadly defined so as to encompass transparent entities and permanent establishments. While permanent establishments are included in the legal definition of a CFC under Mauritius laws, transparent entities (also known as pass-through entities or fiscally transparent entities) are excluded from the definition of a CFC under the Mauritius Income Tax Act. A transparent entity is a legal entity that allows income to go directly to investors or owners since the income of this entity is treated as the income of the respective investors or owners (Parada, 2020). The idea behind the setting up of a transparent entity is to avoid dividend tax or double taxation since only the owners are taxed on the income received from the entity. As such, the absence of a transparent entity in the definition of a CFC may lead to a situation where the Mauritius resident company incorporates a foreign subsidiary in the form of a fiscally transparent entity in another jurisdiction. This subsidiary generates passive income but the MRA will not be able to tax this income as it is considered as income of the investors or owners, a category that does not form part of a CFC under Mauritius laws. Additionally, in terms of participating rights, the Mauritius legal definition of a CFC sets the threshold at 50% or above in a foreign company to establish control. Nevertheless, BEPS Action 3 explicitly suggests for at least two types of tests in the form of legal and economic control to ascertain the existence of a significant influence by the resident company in the CFC. Consequently, there can arise a situation where a Mauritius company incorporates a foreign subsidiary with less than 50% of share ownership but the directors of the same Mauritius Company sit on the board of the foreign subsidiary and they are able to take decisions of that company abroad. The existence of this type of significant influence is in line with the concept of CFC established by the OECD (2015) which unfortunately has not been catered for by the Mauritius legislator when drafting CFC rules (MRA, 2020). This loophole in turn provides a leeway for Mauritius resident companies not to declare CFC income for taxation. Although the resident entities may not be holding ownership rights of more than 50% in the CFC, they may still control this CFC's strategic decision-making process.

Another discrepancy noted between Mauritius CFC rules and BEPS Action 3 refers to the absence of the definition and computation of CFC income. Indeed, it is imperative to define which part of the CFC's income is attributable or not since only the non-distributed income of the CFC forms part of the chargeable income of the Mauritian resident company. Similarly, no legal provision is given on the offsetting of CFC losses against profits. In order to avoid double taxation, BEPS Action 3 recommends the deduction of foreign tax credit by the CFC in its country of residence of the parent company as well as the exemption of dividends and capital gains on income that have already been taxed in the domestic country of the CFC. However, these legal provisions have not been catered for in Mauritius laws which may give rise to double taxation of the CFC income in the country. Eventually, the absence of double taxation anti-avoidance provision on CFC income may in turn be detrimental to international trade and may affect the economic growth of Mauritius coupled with a reduction in the trust and confidence of the investors.

The Convergence Between Mauritius CFC Rules and BEPS Action 3

It is noted that Mauritius laws have adopted the minimum threshold recommendation of BEPS Action 3 based on a prescribed amount of the accounting profits, non-trading income of the CFC, the proportion to operation costs and the tax rate of the CFC in its domestic country. Essentially, CFCs who have accounting income of less than EUR 750,000 and non-trading income of less than EUR 75,000 are exempted from CFC rules in Mauritius in an income year. In addition, this exemption also applies to CFCs whose accounting profits are less than 10% of their operating costs for the tax year and to those CFCs whose tax rate in their domestic country exceeds the tax rate of Mauritius by more than 50%. While these minimum thresholds and exemptions may give rise to various maneuvers to fit into the respective categories of CFC rules exemptions, BEPS Action 3 has suggested that the country in question establishes the appropriate anti-avoidance safeguards. In this attempt, Mauritius laws have restricted (1) the operating costs of the CFC by excluding the cost of goods sold outside the country where the entity is resident for tax purposes and (2) the payments to associated enterprises when computing the proportion of accounting profits to operating costs of the CFC (MRA, 2020).

While CFC rules have taken some time to be implemented in Mauritius, the inclusion of these rules in the Mauritius Income Tax Act somehow demonstrates the positive attitude of Mauritius towards BEPS Action Plans. The country used CFC rules as a means to strengthen its own anti-avoidance legal framework.

With the increasing foreign direct investment flows in Mauritius, it becomes vital to adopt other BEPS measures to counter global tax avoidance. In this regard, the next section will look at the OECD/G20 recommendations on transfer pricing and the corresponding Mauritius transfer pricing rules.

BEPS ACTIONS 8 – 10 AND IMPLEMENTATION BY MAURITIUS

The Formation of Transfer Pricing Rules

Another tax base erosion technique commonly practiced by MNCs is to determine prices in related-party transactions in a manner that shifts profits to low-tax jurisdictions and losses to high-tax countries. Hence, to regulate the determination of transfer prices, the OECD promulgated the ALP back in the year 1970 which requires that the amount charged by one related party in a particular transaction needs to be the same as if the parties to that same transaction are not related. In fact, the practice of determining transfer prices in related-party transactions is known as transfer pricing. Terms such as “abusive transfer pricing”, “transfer mispricing” or “transfer pricing manipulation” are used where transfer prices are not according to ALP, are above market rates, or do not conform with domestic laws or internationally applicable norms.

Abusive transfer pricing has caused several tax authorities to raise serious concerns. Transfer pricing techniques have adverse consequences on countries where the MNCs operate. Melnychenko, Pugachevska & Kasianok (2014) Klassen (2017) and White (2020) argue that by shifting income to another country, the tax revenue of the host governments of the MNCs is consequently reduced. Moreover, local shareholders are penalized through a loss of profits available for distribution. Furthermore, there is a wide spectrum of negative effects arising from transfer pricing manipulations to the host country where the MNC branch, subsidiary, or permanent establishment is based and these have been identified as, *inter alia*:

- low remuneration to local staff because of distorted operating results;
- poor balance of payment situation; and
- a reduction in the market competition since low-profit levels act as a deterrent for other local businesses to engage in the respective field (Lo, 2020).

In essence, the aforementioned studies and the harmful effects of transfer pricing manipulation indicate that the international transfer pricing problem will need to be curbed effectively so as to maximize revenue collection in developing countries. As such, studies conducted by Beebeejaun (2019) and Lohse and Riedel (2013) indicate that the tightening of transfer pricing legislation is capable of dissuading multinationals to engage in transfer pricing abuses. For instance, Marques and Pinho (2016) found that transfer pricing penalties reduce profit-shifting behaviors by around 50% on average. Consequently, to ensure that transfer pricing rules are correctly applied, the OECD/G20 countries have come up with BEPS Actions 8 – 10 with the aim to align the transfer pricing outcomes with economic activity and value creation (OECD, 2015b).

In the context of transfer pricing, BEPS Action Plans to focus on three main areas, notably, transfer pricing of intangibles (Action 8), a contractual allocation of risks, functions, and assets (Action 9) and high-risk areas which involve the structuring of transactions that promote BEPS (Action 10). The purpose behind these standards is mainly to prevent the allocation of risks and excessive capital to only one or two members within the group of companies. In other words, BEPS Actions 8 – 10 ensure that inappropriate returns are not restricted to only one entity within the group simply because it has provided capital or assumed risks. The idea is to align returns with economic activities and value creation. Moreover, BEPS Actions emphasize the conduct of an appropriate comparability analysis during the process of pricing goods or services when trading between related parties. This assessment involves the identification of commercial or financial relations between related parties and then comparing the conditions and circumstances of these controlled transactions with similar conditions and circumstances between independent enterprises. Several factors are considered during this comparability analysis such as the contractual terms of the transaction, the functions of each entity within the group of companies, an analysis, assumption and allocation of risks, characteristics of goods/services involved in the related party transaction, economic circumstances, business strategies, governmental policies amongst others. Thereafter, to determine the arm's length transfer price, the OECD transfer pricing methods are used on the comparable price ascertained to arrive at an appropriate price.

In order to prevent malpractices in the context of transfer pricing, the OECD/G20 countries have suggested appropriate BEPS safeguards when making use of Cost Contribution Agreements (CCA)[6]. An under or overvaluation of these contributions and benefits is likely to shift profits from jurisdictions where value is created through the structuring of economic activities. Consequently, it is fundamental to ensure that the conditions established under a CCA between related parties are at arm's length with similar conditions in transactions involving independent entities. Accordingly, the valuation of each entity's contribution and sharing of risks has to be in line with what independent parties would expect under comparable circumstances in proportion to their share of total benefits derived from the arrangement.

Coupled with detailed guidance on transfer pricing of intangibles and CCAs, BEPS Action 10 recommends countries develop transfer pricing rules in a manner that would avoid BEPS in cross-border commodity transactions between associated enterprises. As such, it is suggested that the Comparable Uncontrolled Price method be used to determine the transfer price of commodities traded between associated enterprises. Also, BEPS Action 10 suggests that transfer pricing rules include a definition of the pricing date for commodity transactions so as to prevent taxpayers to use the most advantageous quoted price in contracts.

BEPS Action 10 also provides some more clarity on the pricing of intra-group services provided by one member within a group of companies to another entity within the same group. These forms of payment may be categorized into management fees, consultancy fees, and head office expenses. Indeed, it has been noted in the past that intra-group payments were being made with the main idea of shifting profits to low-tax jurisdictions. Hence, BEPS Action 10 has come up with two main recommendations in this context, mainly (1) to analyze whether intra-group services have in fact been provided and (2) whether the payment made for these services is in line with the ALP. For this purpose, a benefit test is conducted to ascertain whether the intra-group services from one entity to another related party have increased the latter's economic and commercial value to enhance and maintain its business position.

Transfer Pricing Rules in Mauritius

Undeniably, the government of Mauritius has taken various initiatives to foster a favorable climate in the country that is conducive to foreign direct investments, including but not limited to competitive tax rates, tax holidays, and ease of bureaucracy for setting up business structures amongst others. Multinational enterprises also establish their offices in the country because of some inherent facilities that the country offers in terms of cheap labor, good infrastructure, network, and communication amongst others. As a result, the country has witnessed an increase in foreign entities as well as multinational companies being established locally. This rise in economic activities, in turn, suggests that there is an increase in related party transactions or transactions between associated enterprises which necessitate the requirement to regulate transfer prices of goods/services traded amongst these associated enterprises and related parties.

Essentially, being a member of the OECD, Mauritius has enacted the ALP in its domestic laws more precisely under Section 75 of the Mauritius Income Tax Act. This legal provision requires some entities to transact at the arm's length price in their dealings with related parties located outside of Mauritius. The entities concerned by Section 75 are the ones whose business or income-earning activity carried on in Mauritius are:

1. controlled by a non-resident.
2. carried on by a non-resident company; or
3. carried on by a company in which more than one-half of the shares are held by or on behalf of a non-resident.

Section 75(2) of the Mauritius Income Tax Act allows the Director General of the Mauritius Revenue Authority (MRA) to adjust the taxable profits of the relevant entities if he determines that in his opinion, prices are not concluded at arm's length with the related party. Apart from the aforementioned provision, no further guidance is provided for in respect of the application of transfer pricing rules of Mauritius in either regulation, code, or circular letter. Furthermore, no information is provided on the acceptable forms of transfer pricing methods, the conditions regarding the comparability analysis, the transfer pricing of intangibles and high risks areas that promote profit-shifting behaviors. Additionally, the laws of Mauritius do not specify the types of documents that are required to be kept and maintained for transfer pricing purposes which are usually required during a tax assessment. Lack of transparency creates uncertainties in the manner in which taxpayers handle their related party transactions and there is always a fear that taxpayers are charged with a higher tax liability than that forecasted in the event that the MRA considers the transfer prices as not meeting the ALP. Besides, from the perspective of the MRA, having an inadequate transfer pricing framework will lead to MNCs over-pricing imports and underpricing exports such that profits are reduced and there is less avenue for tax collection, which is definitely an opportunity cost for the Mauritius government could have used the tax foregone for the development purposes. However, Section 75(3) of the Mauritius Income Tax Act empowers the Minister of Finance and Economic Development to enact regulations concerning transfer pricing.

Besides the above-mentioned legal provisions, there is no substantive and extensive domestic regulations in the country regarding the ALP. Accordingly, it is noted that the term "control" is not defined under Mauritius laws for the purposes of Section 75 of the Mauritius Income Tax Act and in this respect, the requirement to transact at arm's length with related parties applies only to those entities in which more than 50% of ownership interests are owned by non-resident companies. Consequently, it follows that the Mauritius Revenue Authority does not consider any type of *de facto* or economic control when assessing related party transactions. This lack of consideration provides flexibility for related parties and MNCs to engage in transfer pricing in a manner that would shift profits to low-tax jurisdictions (MRA, 2019).

In addition to the domestic legal source, at the international level, Mauritius relies on the provisions of the Double Taxation Anti-Avoidance Agreements (DTAAs)[7] concluded with other countries to require related parties to transact at arm's length. While the country has concluded as of date 46 DTAAs with several countries such as Australia, Croatia, France, the United Kingdom, and Zimbabwe amongst others, some other 21 tax treaties are being negotiated with countries such as Algeria, Burkina Faso, Saudi Arabia, Senegal, Spain amongst others (MRA, 2022). In fact, these DTAAs are based on the OECD Model Tax Convention on Income and Capital. Article 9 of the same convention provides for the ALP as the legal source for transfer pricing regarding related party transactions between the contracting states (MFEPD, 2019b). A reading of Article 9 of the OECD Model Tax Convention which is entitled "associated enterprises" reveals that it is mandatory for an entity of a signatory country that participates directly or indirectly in the "management, control or capital" of an entity of the other signatory state, to transact according to ALP. However, there is no further explanation in the OECD Model Tax Convention to define participation in the "management, control or capital" of an enterprise. Consequently, reference is made to the domestic laws of the contracting parties but if these laws are also silent on the relevant parameters, then the stakeholders concerned are faced with a severe dilemma as to whether their transactions fall under the ambit of Article 9 of the respective DTAAs.

Further to the above analysis, it is noted that despite the mushrooming of foreign entities and MNCs in Mauritius, the country has neither come up with a complete set of regulations on transfer pricing rules nor has it implemented BEPS Action 8 – 10 as of date. Concerning issues of uncertainty and lack of transparency in the context of transfer pricing, the best way to eliminate or reduce these problems is to establish and issue detailed rules to identify related party transactions. It is also necessary to explicitly put in place the control requirements, the acceptable methods of calculating the transfer price, the definition of high-risk transactions, the framework for the treatment of intangibles in related party dealings, and on enforcement mechanisms as well.

BEPS ACTION 13 AND IMPLEMENTATION BY MAURITIUS

Apart from OECD BEPS Action 8 – 10, another relevant OECD/G20 countries' recommendation closely related to transfer pricing, is the BEPS Action 13 which concerns the CbC reporting.

The Formation of Effective Rules on Transfer Pricing Documentation

One of the main characteristics of a multinational group is that its headquarter is located in one jurisdiction while subsidiaries and affiliates of the group are situated in some other parts of the world. This structuring in turn gives rise to intra-group transactions among entities of the same multinational group. Subsequently, it becomes necessary to keep and maintain the appropriate documentation to reflect related party transactions in a manner that would ensure transparency for tax authorities. Thus, BEPS Action 13 has been recommended by the OECD/G20 countries to provide for standards regarding transfer pricing documentation and a template report for CbC reporting.

In order to harmonize CbC reporting legislation across countries, BEPS Action 13 suggests that multinational enterprises should keep a master file that will include some high-level information regarding business operations and transfer pricing policies. This master file has to be made available to all concerned tax administrators. Thereafter, a local file has to be maintained which comprises of information relating to intra-group transactions, the amounts involved in these transactions and the application of transfer pricing policies in respect of these transactions. A CbC reporting legislation based on BEPS Action 13 requires all multinationals to file annually with the tax authority of each country in which it is operating, some information on revenue, profit before income tax, amount of income tax paid or accrued, number of employees, share capital, retained earnings and tangible assets as well as the type of business activities.

Furthermore, BEPS Action 13 has come up with a new Chapter V of the OECD Transfer Pricing Guidelines which has replaced the previous Chapter V of the same guidelines which are relevant to transfer pricing documentation. In particular, the old Chapter V emphasized reasonableness in documenting transfer pricing transactions without stating the types of documents or information that have to be kept and maintained which often led to uncertainty and lack of transparency among tax authorities across borders. In contrast, the new Chapter V of the OECD Transfer Pricing Guidelines provides detailed information on the assessment of the ALP, transfer pricing risk assessment and transfer pricing auditing. Nevertheless, in an attempt to alleviate compliance issues by multinationals, BEPS Action 13 has come up with a more soft and lenient approach concerning the application of the said Chapter V. For instance, BEPS Action 13 highlights that the request for documentation by tax authorities should not overburden taxpayers in a way that would imply highly excessive costs and burdens in producing documentation. Additionally, flexibility is provided to taxpayers in terms of deadlines, materiality, frequency of documentation updates, and language amongst others.

It has been concluded by various academic studies that an appropriate CbC legislation results in a reduction in corporate tax avoidance behaviors. For instance, Longhorn (2015) assessed the importance of CbC reporting by multinationals in each jurisdiction. Based on the critical analysis conducted by the researcher, it was found that a CbC report is in line with the corporate reporting system and information disclosed in a CbC satisfies the needs of various stakeholders including but not limited to shareholders, and governments, and tax authorities. The researcher admitted that the multilateral exchange of CbC reports across countries helps developing countries to access/analyze the necessary data more efficiently, for the purpose of tax imposition to prevent BEPS. Furthermore, Thiart and Nel (2018) emphasized the importance of the proper drafting of laws on CbC reporting at the domestic level. The researchers assessed the ambiguities faced by the companies listed on Johannesburg Stock Exchange concerning the CbC filing requirements. The results depicted some incoherence in the South African CbC Regulations about the categories of a multinational group and the revenue threshold applicable for a company to mandatorily file its report. Consequently, the study found a low level of compliance with the filing of CbC reports.

Implementation of BEPS Action 13 by Mauritius

The Mauritius legislator has enacted an income tax regulation under Section 76 of the Mauritius Income Tax Act which enables the Ministry of Finance and Economic Development to enter into arrangements with the governments of other countries to exchange tax information and also, to give the force of law to such arrangement (MRA, 2020). Accordingly, in 2018, Mauritius signed the Multilateral Convention on Administrative Assistance in Tax Matters (MCAA)[8]. The Income Tax (Country-by-Country Reporting) Regulations were also implemented in 2018 in order to attribute legal and binding obligations entailed by the MCAA to multinational companies that are headquartered in Mauritius.

The Convergence Between Mauritius Transfer Pricing Documentation and BEPS Action 13

In essence, the CbC Regulations in Mauritius require the ultimate parent entity of a multinational group that is resident for tax purposes in Mauritius to file with the MRA, a CbC report for its respective fiscal year. The term "group" is defined in the definition section of the CbC Regulations refer to a collection of enterprises related through ownership or control that is required to prepare consolidated financial statements for financial reporting purposes under the applicable accounting principles and whose annual consolidated group revenue is more than EUR 750 million (USD 784 Million) in the preceding fiscal year.

Additionally, Section 5 of the CbC Regulations mentions the information that has to be provided in the CbC report which includes information on revenue, profit or loss before income tax, income tax paid and accrued, share capital, tangible assets, accumulated earnings and number of employees. The timeline for filing the CbC report is within 12 months from the last day of the reporting fiscal year of the multinational group and failure to do so will entail a fine not exceeding MUR 5,000 (USD 110) and an imprisonment term not exceeding 6 months. Moreover, the CbC Regulations have emphasized the need to maintain the secrecy of information from CbC reporting by imposing an obligation on the Director-General (DG) of the MRA. The DG MRA should keep the information contained in a CbC report confidential to the same extent if such information were provided to him under the provisions of the multilateral Convention on Mutual Assistance in Tax Matters.

Nevertheless, even if a multinational does not have its parent company in Mauritius, it is still possible to elect a surrogate parent in Mauritius to file a CbC report with the MRA if, for some reasons (like the absence of proper CbC rules), the parent company has not been able to file this report in the headquartered country. Accordingly, the MRA may share this report with the tax authority under the relevant and applicable tax information exchange agreements.

The Divergence Between Mauritius Transfer Pricing Documentation and BEPS Action 13

To sum up, the recommendations of the OECD/G20 countries under BEPS Action 13 require a multinational group to keep a master file, and a local file and to file CbC reports with the tax authorities. In this context, while Mauritius has established the appropriate legal and regulatory framework concerning CbC reporting, the requirement to keep and maintain the master and local files is still missing in the law. Subsequently, multinational companies based in Mauritius have to comply with the general record-keeping requirement set out in Section 153 of the Mauritius Income Tax Act. More specifically, Section 153(1) of the said Act requires taxpayers, for each transaction, to keep proper books, registers, accounts, records such as receipts, invoices and vouchers, contracts and records of all acts to determine gross income and allowable deductions. The timeline for keeping these records is 5 years from the date of completion of the transaction. However, particularities of information pertaining to transfer pricing transactions are not explicitly mentioned in the law. So, multinational companies in Mauritius do not have to keep and maintain information that is usually contained in the master and local files as suggested by Chapter V of the OECD Transfer Pricing Guidelines. As a result, the absence of this legal obligation may create uncertainty regarding the correct application of the ALP by multinational companies. It is therefore advisable for Mauritius lawmakers to precise the specific types of transfer pricing documents that have to be provided by multinational enterprises located in the country to meet the expectations of the MRA while assessing the determination of the arm's length transfer price and identifying high-risk transfer pricing transactions which may lead to BEPS.

DISCUSSION OF RESULTS AND RECOMMENDATIONS

While Mauritius has joined the inclusive framework of OECD BEPS Actions, this participation not only provides the country with an opportunity to contribute to the establishment of modern, sophisticated and more adapted international tax rules but also gives Mauritius the chance to review and improve its existing taxation framework. Fundamentally, this research compares the implementation by Mauritius against BEPS Action Plans on CFC rules, transfer pricing, and CbC reporting, the three areas in respect of which the Mauritian government has given much attention in recent years.

It is noted that Mauritius has adopted a positive attitude towards the aforesaid OECD/G20 countries' recommendations by firstly incorporating CFC rules under Section 90A of the Mauritius Income Tax Act and enacting specific CbC Regulations. Nevertheless, some discrepancies have been noted regarding CFC rules, basically in terms of the limited definition of a CFC provided for in the Mauritius Income Tax Act. There is a lack of precision regarding the definition of "control" in the context of a CFC and the absence of computation guidelines on CFC income. In particular, a situation where the key person of the Mauritian company sits on the board of the foreign company and these persons participate in the decision-making process of the foreign company without the 50% shareholding, is not regulated by the CFC rules. Indeed, all these subject matters need to be clarified such that both businesses and the revenue authority are on the same line concerning the interpretation of legal terminologies and this will prevent or reduce the occurrence of potential conflicts. Similarly, in terms of transfer pricing rules, while Mauritius has adopted the ALP in its domestic legislation under Section 75 of the Income Tax Act, there is no substantive and extensive rule regarding the definition of "control", the specific types of transfer pricing documentation that have to be kept and maintained, the acceptable forms of transfer pricing methods, the valuation of intangible assets under cost contribution agreement, the proper repartitioning of risks and participation across entities in the multinational group. All of these discrepancies create issues of uncertainty and lack of transparency among investors and businesses.

Additionally, it has been observed that while Mauritius has implemented BEPS Action 13 by enacting the CbC Regulations, the requirement to maintain a master and a local file for each multinational group has not yet been incorporated into the domestic legislation. Also, the CbC Regulations do not cater for instances whereby the revenue authority of another jurisdiction believes that the information reported by the reporting entity comprises of errors. Nothing is mentioned about the relevant course of action to be undertaken. In order to avoid confusion, this particular aspect needs to be catered for in the CbC Regulations of Mauritius.

CONCLUSION

This study has been conducted to evaluate the extent to which Mauritius has adopted the BEPS standards on CFC rules, transfer pricing, and CbC reporting. The comparative and critical analysis approach used by the researchers reveals that the intention of the Mauritian legislator to align the domestic laws with international standards has been witnessed through the enactment of the new law. However, there still remains some divergences between Mauritian legislation and the corresponding BEPS standards on each subject of this study. Eventually, these discrepancies against the OCED/G20 standards which are considered loopholes in Mauritius law are likely to create an expectation gap, especially during the course of a transfer pricing audit between the MRA and multinational taxpayers based in Mauritius. As such, Mauritius needs to clarify rules on CFC, transfer pricing and reporting of multinational group's particularities so as to be able to integrate into and benefit from the world economy more effectively.

In the future, it will be a research area of great interest to assess the effectiveness of the CFC rules and CbC reporting regulations that have recently been enacted by the Mauritian government. It is quite early to assess the impacts; however, some positive outcomes are expected in the years to come.

DECLARATION

The authors declare that the manuscript follows ethical standards and there are no potential conflicts of interest with respect to the research, authorship and/or publication of this chapter.

DISCLAIMER

ACKNOWLEDGMENT

The authors extend sincere gratitude to

- The Editor and the International Editorial Advisory Board (IEAB) of this book who initially desk reviewed, arranged a rigorous double/triple blind review process, and conducted a thorough, minute, and critical final review before accepting the chapter for publication.
- All anonymous reviewers who provided very constructive feedbacks for thorough revision, improvement, extension, and fine tuning of the chapter.
- All colleagues, assistants and well-wishers who assisted to complete this task.

REFERENCES

Beebeejaun, A. (2019). The fight against international transfer pricing abuses: A recommendation for Mauritius. *International Journal of Law and Management*, *61*(1), 205–231. doi:10.1108/IJLMA-05-2018-0083

Clifford, S. (2019). Taxing multinationals beyond borders: Financial and locational responses to CFC rules. *Journal of Public Economics*, *173*, 44–71. doi:10.1016/j.jpubeco.2019.01.010

EDB. (2022). *Budget Highlights 2022/2023*. Economic Development Board, Mauritius. Retrieved from https://www.edbmauritius.org/edb-budget-corner

Fitzgibbon, W. (2019, July 23). *Treasure Island: Leak reveals how Mauritius siphons tax from poor nations to benefit elites*. International Consortium of Investigative Journalists. Retrieved from https://www.icij.org/investigations/mauritius-leaks/treasure-island-leak-reveals-how-mauritius-siphons-tax-from-poor-nations-to-benefit-elites/

Garcia-Bernardo, J., & Jansky, P. (2021). *Profit Shifting of Multinational Corporations Worldwide* (IES Working Papers 14/2021). IES FSV. Charles University.

Karhunen, P., Ledyaeva, S., & Brouthers, K. D. (2021). Capital Round-Tripping: Determinants of Emerging Market Firm Investments into Offshore Financial Centers and Their Ethical Implications. *Journal of Business Ethics*, 1–21. doi:10.100710551-021-04908-y

Klassen, J., Lisowsky, P., & Mescall, D. (2017). Transfer pricing: Strategies, practices and tax minimization. *Contemporary Accounting Research*, *34*(1), 455–493. doi:10.1111/1911-3846.12239

Kofler, G., Krever, R., Lang, M., & Staringer, C. (2020). *Controlled Foreign Company Legislation*. IBFD.

Lo, W. Y. (2020). *International Transfer Pricing in a developing economy context: Perspectives from the taxpayers and the tax authorities* [PhD Thesis]. Lingnan University. Retrieved from https://scholars.ln.edu.hk/en/studentTheses/international-transfer-pricing-in-a-developing-economy-context-pe

Lohse, T., & Riedel, N. (2013). *Do transfer pricing laws limit international income shifting? Evidence from European Multinationals* (CESifo Working Paper Series No. 4404). Retrieved from https://www.cesifo.org/en/publikationen/2013/working-paper/do-transfer-pricing-laws-limit-international-income-shifting

Longhorn, M. (2015). *Country-by-Country Reporting: A Critical Analysis* [Master's Thesis]. Queensland University of Technology. https://eprints.qut.edu.au/84604/4/Monique_Longhorn_Thesis.pdf

Marques, M., & Pinho, C. (2016). Is transfer pricing strictness deterring profit shifting within multinationals? Empirical evidence from Europe. *Accounting and Business Research, 46*(7), 703–730. doi:10.1080/00014788.2015.1135782

Melnychenko, R., Pugachevska, K., & Kasianok, K. (2014). Tax control of transfer pricing. *Investment Management and Financial Innovations, 14*(4), 40–49. doi:10.21511/imfi.14(4).2017.05

MFEPD. (2019a). *Budget Speech 2019: Embracing a brighter future together as a nation.* Ministry of Finance, Economic Planning and Development, Mauritius. Retrieved from https://mof.govmu.org/Documents/Documents/2019/2019_20budget speech.pdf

MFEPD. (2019b). *Annual Report 2019/2020.* Ministry of Finance, Economic Planning and Development, Mauritius. Retrieved from https://mof.govmu.org/Documents/Annual%20Report/MOFED_Annual_Report%20-%20FY%202020-2021.pdf

MRA. (2019). *Guidelines for the Appropriate Use of Information contained in CbC Reports.* Mauritius Revenue Authority. Retrieved from https://www.mra.mu/download/GuideCBCR.pdf

MRA. (2020). Article. *MRA Technical Journal, 2,* 1-67. Retrieved from https://www.mra.mu/download/MRATechnicalJournal.pdf

MRA. (2022). *Double Taxation Avoidance Agreements.* Mauritius Revenue Authority. Retrieved from https://www.mra.mu/index.php/taxes-duties/international-taxation/double-taxation-agreements

OECD. (2015a). *Designing Effective CFC Rules, Action 3- 2015 Final Report.* Organisation for Economic Co-operation and Development. Retrieved from https://www.oecd.org/publications/designing-effective-controlled-foreign-company-rules-action-3-2015-final-report-978926
4241152-en.htm

OECD. (2015b). *Aligning transfer pricing outcomes with value creation, Actions 8-10 Reports.* Organisation for Economic Co-operation and Development. Retrieved from https://www.oecd.org/tax/aligning-transfer-pricing-outcomes-with-value-creation-actions-8-10-2015-final-reports-97892642
41244-en.htm

OECD. (2016). *Macau (China), Mauritius and Ukraine join the inclusive framework on BEPS*. Organisation for Economic Co-operation and Development. Retrieved from https://www.oecd.org/tax/beps/macau-china-mauritius-and-ukraine-join-the-inclusive-framework-on-beps.htm

OECD. (2020). *OECD/G20 Inclusive Framework on BEPS – Progress Report July 2019 – July 2020*. Organisation for Economic Co-operation and Development. Retrieved from https://www.oecd.org/tax/beps/oecd-g20-inclusive-framework-on-beps-progress-report-july-2019-july-2020.htm

Parada, L. (2020). Tax Treaty Entitlement and Fiscally Transparent Entities: Improvements or Unnecessary Complications? In J. Wheeler (Ed.), *The Aftermath of BEPS*. IBFD.

Petutschnig, M., & Resenig, K. (2019, January). Market reactions of multinationals to the OECD BEPS Action Plan. In *Proceedings. Annual Conference on Taxation and Minutes of the Annual Meeting of the National Tax Association* (Vol. 112, pp. 1-31). National Tax Association.

Prettl, A. (2018). *Profit shifting and controlled foreign corporation rules – The thin bridge between corporate tax system*. Retrieved from https://papers.ssrn.com/sol3/papers.cfm ?abstract_id=3102553

Prettl, A., & von Hagen, D. (2022). Multinational ownership patterns and anti-tax avoidance legislation. *International Tax and Public Finance*, 1–70. doi:10.100710797-021-09719-5

Statistics Mauritius. (2022). *National Accounts Estimates (2018 – 2021): December 2021 Issue*. Retrieved from https:// statsmauritius.govmu.org/Pages/Statistics/ESI/National_Accounts/NA/NAE_Dec21.aspx

Thiart, C., & Nel, G. F. (2018). An exploratory study of the effect of country-by-country reporting ambiguities on Johannesburg Stock Exchange-listed companies. *Suid-Afrikaanse Tydskrif vir Ekonomiese en Bestuurswetenskappe*, *21*(1), 1–8. doi:10.4102ajems.v21i1.2129

White, J. (2020, January 30). *Transfer pricing cases to watch in 2020*. Retrieved from https://www.internationaltaxreview.com/article/b1k3znjpb16b3v/transfer-pricing-cases-to-watch-in-2020

Xu, D. (2018). The convergence and divergence between China's implementation and OECD/G20 BEPS minimum standards. *World Tax Journal*, *10*(3), 471–496.

ENDNOTES

1 **Base Erosion and Profit Shifting (BEPS):** Tax planning strategies used by MNCs that exploit gaps and mismatches in tax rules to avoid paying tax.

2 **Controlled Foreign Corporation (CFC):** A foreign company that is either directly or indirectly controlled by a resident taxpayer.

3 **Transfer Pricing:** Prices of goods and services that are exchanged between companies under common control.

4 **Country-by-Country (CbC) Reporting:** The sharing of information with tax administrations in various jurisdiction for use in high level transfer pricing and BEPS risk assessments.

5 **Arm's Length Principle (ALP):** The principle that a price in a transaction between two related parties must be the same as the price agreed in a comparable transaction between two unrelated parties.

6 **Cost Contribution Agreements (CCA):** Special contractual arrangements among business enterprises to share the contributions and risks involved in the joint development, production or the obtaining of intangibles, tangible assets or services with the understanding that such intangibles, tangible assets or services are expected to create benefits for the individual businesses of each of the participants. (OECD, 2015, pp. 12).

7 **Double Taxation Avoidance Agreement (DTAA):** A tax treaty signed between India and another country (or any two/multiple countries) so that taxpayers can avoid paying double taxes on their income earned from the source country as well as the residence country.

8 **Multilateral Convention on Administrative Assistance in Tax Matters (MCAA):** A freestanding multilateral agreement designed to promote international co-operation for a better operation of national tax laws, while respecting the fundamental rights of taxpayers.

Chapter 12
Circular VAT Fraud by Transfer of Tax Liability:
The Case of the EU

Valentina Vinšalek Stipić
https://orcid.org/0000-0001-7065-2918
Veleučilište "Nikola Tesla" u Gospiću, Croatia

ABSTRACT

Tax frauds with fake traders have existed since the 1980s and are certainly not a new phenomenon. Likewise, ways to fight against these frauds have existed since the moment they first appeared. Just as the frauds have evolved over time, so have the proposals for solving them becoming more sophisticated and comprehensive. With the development of the VAT system in the European Union, the methods of fraud are also developing, and over time the EU member states realize that they cannot fight against these frauds alone. The directive on the common system of VAT in 2006 represents the unification and the beginning of the joint fight of the member states of the European Union against these frauds. The EU member states systematically reinforced the measures of the common fraud prevention strategy. One such measure is the transfer of tax liability between the member states of the European Union.

INTRODUCTION

The issue of tax fraud is complex for several reasons, but the first thing that needs to be clarified is the very definition of tax fraud, as well as the definition of what this term is not. When referring to any activities that result in the reduction of government revenue from taxation, it is possible to group them into three main groups: tax avoidance, tax evasion and tax fraud. The concept of tax evasion in its simplest definition represents any attempt to reduce the taxpayer's tax payments in a legal way, for example through the exploitation of loopholes in the law (Kirchler *et al.*, 2003). This definition is very broad in nature and includes a large number of possible tax liability reduction activities. Devereux *et al.* (2012) therefore point out that it is neither possible nor helpful to try to find a single definition of tax evasion and further conclude that it is necessary to break down all evasion activities with the aim

DOI: 10.4018/978-1-6684-5007-9.ch012

of finding appropriate ways to limit such undesirable activities, through the appropriate legislature. It is possible to conclude that although tax evasion activities are of a legal nature, they are also subject to social undesirability because they result in a decrease in state tax revenues. Jelčić *et al.* (2008) define tax avoidance or tax evasion as resistance to paying taxes and a conscious effort to remove or reduce the unwanted effects of taxation. This resistance can be active (intentional) and passive (unintentional), for example by an honest mistake when getting used to a new system. Furthermore, the same author draws a distinction between legal and illegal tax evasion and equates illegal forms with the concept of tax evasion (Rafay & Ajmal, 2014).

Analysis of available statistical data on foreign trade confirms the existence of significant impacts of foreign trade on economic growth and income. A study by Frankel and Romer (1999) identified channels through which trade affects economic growth: a) specialization based on comparative advantages and b) diffusion of technologies through investment activity. As a rule, growth rates are higher in countries with a diversified export structure or that improve the quality of their exports regardless of the level of added value (Henn *et al.*, 2017), or in countries that are deeply integrated into global production and trade processes (Didier & Pinat, 2017). Factor analysis explains numerous components that influence the contemporary restructuring of the export system. This refers to the system of benefits and privileges for exports, which are offered by both exporting and contracting states (Abshari *et al.*, 2021).

For example, VAT tax benefits are an incentive for foreign trade participants to increase their export activity (Ainsworth & Alwohaibi, 2016; Zu *et al.*, 2020). The burden of VAT is borne by the end consumer, the key here is the interaction between the state (represented by its supervisory authorities) and business entities in the tax administration process (de la Feria & Schoeman, 2019). On the one hand, exporters receive state support, while customs formalities are simplified and computerized to the greatest extent possible. On the other hand, the number of disputes related to VAT refunds is increasing every year, the most important of which are disputes that fail to be resolved in pre-criminal proceedings. The European Union is actively discussing different models of combating fraudulent actions of entities that lead to differences in VAT (Van Doesum & Nellen, 2021) three key categories of actors are defined: end consumers, sellers and the tax administration must ensure the bona fide fulfillment of their duties (Poniatowski *et al.*, 2020). The negative impact of VAT fraud, as an illegal activity, creates some of the most dangerous consequences for economies (Fjeldstad *et al.*, 2020; Pouwels, 2021), and such activities could be directly or indirectly involved in the financing of terrorism. The most important instrument to combat VAT fraud is the development of international cooperation (Ding *et al.*, 2021) and the use of modern technologies (Kowal & Przekota, 2021). In recent years, research in the field of VAT application has been more focused on improving the effectiveness of tax control (Mitusova 2021), improving the quality and efficiency of tax administration (Zhirova, 2017) and minimizing the risk of tax fraud and developing methods to reduce the scope of shadow business (Gurdgiev, 2019).

Tax evasion is closely related to the gray economy and such activities have significant economic and social consequences because they directly reduce budget revenues, and thus the quality and availability of public services (Šimurina *et al.*, 2018; Walker-Munro, 2021). It is important to conclude that the result of tax avoidance as form 4 of legal tax evasion is the same as that resulting from illegal tax evasion, which is the reduction of state revenues from taxation, and as such it represents a major problem for the state. Tax frauds with fake traders have existed since the 1980s, and are certainly not a new phenomenon. Likewise, ways to fight against these frauds have existed since the moment they first appeared, and just as the frauds have evolved over time, so have the proposals for solving them becoming more sophisticated and comprehensive. With the development of the VAT system in the European Union, the methods of fraud are also developing, and over time the member states realize that they cannot fight against these frauds alone. The directive on the common system of VAT from 2006 represents the unification and the beginning of the joint fight of the member states of the European Union against these frauds. The EU member states systematically and reinforced the measures of the common fraud prevention strategy. One such measure is the transfer of tax liability between the member states of the European Union. In addition to the above-mentioned problem, the question arises as to what the EU is specifically doing to prevent circular VAT fraud. One of the mechanisms of receipt of circular fraud is the transfer of tax liability between EU member states. This chapter presents an analysis of the advantages of the transfer of tax liability as a mechanism for preventing circular fraud in the EU.

TAX EVASION AND TAX FRAUD

Tax evasion is a deliberate illegal reduction of the taxpayer's tax payments, for example by reporting lower income during the tax return (Kirchler *et al.*, 2003). It is important to emphasize that deliberate actions are considered tax evasion and honest mistakes do not fall under the concept of tax evasion (FindLaw Staff, 2021). For example, according to the Criminal Code of the Republic of Croatia 2011, tax evasion activities are considered to be activities with the aim of not paying a part or the full amount of tax, in which incorrect or incomplete data on income, items or other facts that influence the determination of the amount of tax or customs liability are given, then failure to report income, items or other facts that have an impact on the determination of tax or customs liability, resulting in a reduction or non-determination of tax or customs liability. The law expressly defines tax evasion and its forms and provides for prison sentences for such actions. While payment avoidance activities (legal evasion) are not strictly defined. However, both groups of activities have the same goal and result - the reduction of the taxpayer's tax payments, which results in reduced state revenues from the collection of these same taxes. Kirchler *et al.* (2003) in their study on the above issue surveyed 252 fiscal officers, lawyers and entrepreneurs about scenarios concerning tax avoidance, tax evasion and tax evasion. They concluded that payment evasion was mostly assessed as legal and moral and associated with intelligence and a good idea, while tax evasion was assessed as illegal and immoral – associated with crime. What the researchers noticed is that there is a significant difference in opinions between groups of people, so fiscal officials rated all notions of reducing tax payments as unfair, while entrepreneurs considered avoidance and evasion to be fair (Kirchler *et al.*, 2003). Risk analysis and assessment do not represent a simple approach to the problem of money laundering (Rafay, 2021a), but rather a more difficult path, in which proper judgment is extremely important for the entire system. In order for the risk assessment to be as real as possible, it is necessary to concentrate on the actual risk and try to maximize the benefits for the social community as the basic benefit of introducing this approach and as a measure for risk identification, prevention or reduction (Vinšalek Stipić, 2022). From the aforementioned study, it is possible to conclude that the distinction between legal and illegal reduction of tax liability depends not only on strictly economic aspects, but also on moral ones, and these same moral beliefs differ greatly between groups of people with different knowledge of the tax system, tax laws, and possession different tax interests. Having considered this issue on a deeper level, it becomes clear that it is not enough to simply distinguish between these concepts into what is legal and what is illegal, but these activities are fundamentally determined by the tax behavior of individuals, and various factors can significantly affect the tax revenues of a state. If we take into account the perspective of the state, which is interested in maximizing tax revenues, it is logical that it is, therefore, necessary to maximize the good tax behavior of individuals, that is, to reduce tax avoidance and tax evasion, and all forms of reducing tax payments, regardless of whether they are legal or illegal. However, in the domain of the tax system, there are also those activities that cannot simply be "fixed" by greater financial literacy and are much more serious and "dangerous" for the state than simple tax evasion. Such forms of fraud often concern organized crime on a large scale, and as such it is necessary to define them separately. Business analysis based on risk assessment is a management measure or tool that includes the determination, analysis and management of risks relevant to the truthfulness and credibility of financial statements in accordance with generally accepted accounting methods, considering events inside and outside the company.

The concept of tax fraud is similar to the concept of tax evasion, however, according to the scope of the activity, it includes more participants. The US Internal Revenue Service (IRS) lists the following activities as types of general tax fraud (IRS, 2022):

- deliberate omission or reporting of lower income/profits than actual ones
- reporting higher tax deductions than the actual ones
- keeping double books (accounting fraud)
- false entry in business books
- reporting personal expenses as business expenses
- reporting false deductions
- concealment or transfer of assets and profits

While individuals can be participants in tax frauds, this term most often refers to frauds involving legal entities - companies. In addition to tax evasion, which concerns the omission/reduction of income and/or the increase of deductions, the term tax fraud also includes other forms of intentional fraud with the aim of reducing or completely avoiding paying taxes. The European Union places special emphasis on this issue, and the European Union has numerous specifics regarding the taxation system, especially in the domain of value-added tax. On a general level, the European Union in 2022 estimates that the estimated loss from tax fraud and tax evasion has exceeded €1 trillion, and the main culprits are companies and individuals who participate in fraud, evasion, tax havens and aggressive tax planning with the aim of minimizing tax payments. Tax frauds are numerous and concern all types of taxes and all levels of taxation. The concept of tax fraud is divided into tax evasion and organized fraud. While tax evasion concerns individual or informal fraud and part-time crime, organized fraud implies coordinated and systematic actions with various levels of sophistication and organization with the aim of achieving an illegal tax financial advantage (De la Feria, 2020). Organized fraud is most often manifested at transnational levels, under the leadership of criminal organizations with the aim of exploiting tax systems, most often the value-added tax system, in order to "extract" money from one or more countries. This case is the most common in the domain of Value-added Tax, and in the European Union precisely because of the specificity of the framework of this tax within the European Union, as well as the EU organization itself as a community of a large number of different member states. Therefore, in order to understand the issue of organized tax fraud within the European Union, it is first necessary to understand the framework of the value-added tax system within the Union.

SYSTEM OF TAX ON ADDED VALUE WITHIN THE FRAMEWORK OF THE EUROPEAN UNION

Value-added tax (VAT) belongs to the domain of sales tax, to the group of indirect taxes. It is a form of general and comprehensive net sales tax. It means that this tax is collected at all stages of production and turnover, and only the added value (net) that the seller adds to the inputs before selling them as outputs is taxed (Šimurina *et al.*, 2018). First of all, the definition of value-added tax requires an understanding of the very concept of value-added. Value-added is the value that a producer adds to his inventory of raw materials or goods before selling them on as an improved product or service. In simpler terms, a business entity buys certain inputs, pays wages to workers to work on these inputs, and after selling the final products, it retains a certain portion of the profit. Therefore, the concept of added value can be viewed on the one hand as wages plus profit, or on the other hand as output minus input (Tait, 1988). The subtractive-indirect VAT calculation model is also known as the invoice method or the credit method, and it is this method that is generally used today. The invoicing method or the credit method of VAT calculation is the key to understanding the modern value-added tax system within the European Union, and thus the issue of tax fraud within this system. The unusualness of VAT calculation is evident if we compare it with almost any other tax. Normally, tax is calculated by first finding a tax base, such as profit, and then multiplying a certain tax rate by that base to get the tax amount. In the same way, it is possible to obtain the amount of VAT using one of the direct methods. With the credit method, however, the added value itself, which would serve as the tax base, is never calculated, but the tax rate is multiplied by the individual components of the added value (outputs and inputs), and from an accounting point of view, input tax claims and VAT liabilities arise, which are at the end of the period they are set off to obtain the final obligation to pay this tax (Tait, 1988; Alavuotunki *et al.*, 2019). More precisely, from a technical point of view, the term input tax represents the amount of VAT that the taxpayer paid to his supplier in the price of supplied inputs and that he has the right to deduct from VAT on his output (Benazic, 2016). The credit or invoice method is therefore called the indirect method of VAT calculation. The reasons for using the credit method are manifested, first of all, through several main advantages that it creates. First, the credit method binds the tax liability to the transaction itself, which effectively binds the tax liability to the invoice (Tait, 1988). This fact is of great importance from the legal and technical aspects of value-added taxation. It effectively achieves that it is in the interest of every entrepreneur to receive a valid invoice from his supplier so that he can deduct the paid input tax based on his input invoices (Šimović & Deskar-Škrbić, 2020). This also provides a solid audit trail, which is another advantage of the credit method. Furthermore, the advantage of the credit method is that it allows the use of different VAT rates. Simply put, in the case of the direct calculation method, companies would be forced to distinguish the income from the sale of products with different tax rates, and also the input costs of inputs according to different rates of tax liability, which would create administrative complications while the invoice method solves this problem (Tait, 1988). Finally, the credit method ensures the realization of the basic principle of value-added tax - the principle of neutrality. Neutrality is a property of value-added tax according to which VAT is neutral for the taxpayer due to the possibility of an input tax deduction on incoming invoices, which does not favor any activity over another (Šimurina, 2018). This property of VAT results in a reduction in tax evasion. Logically, since the final amount of VAT is by design passed on to the end customer, companies have less reason to engage in tax evasion and tax evasion activities. However, this system in which companies are given the right to deduct input tax also opens up opportunities for fraud, as is the case with the European Union. In addition to its neutrality and impact on reducing tax evasion, VAT serves as an effective instrument in the fight against the gray economy. The previously mentioned attachment of VAT payment to the invoice implies that input tax cannot be deducted without an input invoice, and thus the invoice serves as proof for tax calculation and as a way of controlling the tax liability. It is in the interest of every taxpayer that VAT is calculated correctly in the previous phase because his future tax liability depends on it, so self-control has been introduced into the entire system, which affects the level of the gray economy. VAT, as a tax that taxes added value, avoids the effect of price inflation, which in turn has more positive effects than other forms of sales tax (Šimurina *et al.*, 2018). Globalization has led to new paradigms and concepts of public finance management. The goal of realizing the concept is to build a free, moral and cohesive society based on universal social inclusion and a market economy (Vinšalek Stipić, 2020).

Understanding the complete issue of VAT requires understanding the calculation of VAT in international traffic. From a theoretical point of view, there are two principles of international value-added taxation: the principle of the country of origin and the principle of the country of destination. According to the principle of the country of origin, VAT is paid in the country where the goods were produced, regardless of the country in which the goods will actually be finally consumed. In this case, all goods exported from a country are taxed with VAT, while all goods imported from abroad are exempt from VAT. In the case of the country of destination principle, VAT is paid in the country where the final consumption of a good occurs, regardless of where it was produced. Contrary to the principle of the country of origin, in this case, exports are exempt from paying VAT, while imports are burdened with VAT (Šimović & Deskar-Škrbić, 2020; Šimurina *et al.*, 2018). In almost all countries that tax added value, the principle of the country of destination is applied, and this is also the case in the European Union, whose goal is that, among other things, all goods have the same tax treatment regardless of the country of origin. Thus, in the end, we can highlight the credit method of VAT calculation and the principle of the country of destination as important factors that enable the occurrence of tax frauds, and before describing the frauds themselves and their functioning mechanisms, it is still necessary to define the specifics of the common VAT system in the European Union.

Directive of the Common System of Value-Added Tax of the European Union

The idea of the European Union as a single market of member states based on the principles of free movement of goods and services, labor and capital is linked to the very beginnings of the union and represents a kind of foundation on which it is based. The realization of this foundation entails a large number of prerequisites, and in the domain of freedom of movement of goods and services, the main prerequisite is certainly the standardization of sales tax. For this purpose, on May 17, 1977, the European Union adopted the Sixth Directive on the harmonization of the laws of the member states regarding sales tax, better known as the Common Value-added Tax System. The sixth directive was the first in a series of subsequent directives by which the European Union tries to harmonize and standardize the VAT system between member countries. With the entry into force of the Sixth Directive[1] in 1977, the member states undertook to harmonize their own laws with the European ones, thus accepting the supranational VAT system as their own. Numerous modifications and additions to the Sixth Directive in the coming years created the need for legislation, and therefore Directive 2006/112/EC[2] on the common system of value-added tax was adopted on November 28, 2006. This directive is a continuation of the former Sixth Directive, and it introduces a kind of framework within which member countries develop their legislation (Šimović & Deskar-Škrbić, 2020). With the aim of making the VAT legislation within the

European Union clearer and more comprehensible, the Directive on the common system of VAT from 2006 replaces the old directives and introduces new rules of the common system of VAT in a simple way. The highlighted key items of this directive are as follows[3]:

1. What is subject to VAT? All payment transactions of the taxpayer (natural and legal persons who supply goods and services when doing business within the EU, and imports by all taxpayers).
2. Which transactions are taxable? Delivery of goods and services within the EU; Acquisition of goods between EU member states; Import of goods into the EU from outside
3. When is VAT calculated? When goods or services are delivered in accordance with the type of transaction. For the acquisition of goods within the EU, it is taxed when the delivery is completed; for import within the EU when the goods are brought to a member state.
4. What amount is taxable? For the supply of goods and services and the acquisition of goods between Member States, the taxable amount includes all payments to the supplier; For the import of goods, the taxable amount represents their value for customs purposes.
5. Standard rate of VAT. In all member states it is at least 15%; The possibility of applying a reduced rate of at least 5% to certain goods or services according to the given list (Annex 3 of the Directive).
6. Permitted exemptions from VAT. Exemptions without the right to deductions (e.g. medical care); Exemptions with the right to deductions (e.g. deliveries of goods between member states or exports of goods to non-EU countries); Exemptions are mostly mandatory, but there are also optional ones
7. Possibility of VAT deduction. The taxpayer may deduct the amount of VAT paid for the acquired goods or services used for taxable transactions in the Member State in which the goods or services were acquired. This input VAT can be deducted from the VAT payable on taxable transactions, e.g. domestic supplies of goods and services.
8. Possibility of general transfer of tax liability - general reverse charge (added in 2018). Countries affected by significant VAT fraud may temporarily apply a general transfer of VAT liability. This includes the transfer of the obligation to pay VAT from the supplier to the customer, only on supplies of goods and services in the own country in the amount of more than EUR 17,500 per transaction.

Transactions between EU member states are taxed according to the already mentioned destination principle. This means that VAT is paid only in the Member State where the goods are consumed, it is paid by the company acquiring the goods. Where the problem arises is the fact that supplies of goods in transactions from one member state to another are exempt from paying VAT, and the companies performing the transactions have the right to deduct input tax. Namely, Directive 91/680/EEC of December 16, 1991, which entered into force on January 1, 1993, created the internal free market of the European Union, which effectively removed barriers to internal trade. The member states adopted the so-called "transitional system" which was originally supposed to be in force for only four years, and according to which intra-community transactions between legal entities are taxable in the destination member state, at the rate and under the conditions of that destination member state (Cindori & Zakarija, 2016; Podlipnik, 2012). These transactions are treated as exports from one member state and imports into another member state, which effectively means that this turnover is taxable with the so-called zero rate, that is, VAT is not paid on such purchases. While in the case of real import and export there is strict control of goods at the borders, intra-community transactions are not physically controlled and there is only document control (Podlipnik, 2012). It is evident from the previous statement that transactions between legal entities within member states (intra-community B2B) are taxable transactions. Therefore, with the aim of creating a free intra-community market, the Directive from 1991 decided that such transactions should be taxed at a zero VAT rate. This means that in such transactions the supplier has the right to deduct input VAT in the country that exports the product/service. The intention of a zero VAT rate is to preserve the principle of further taxation in the country of destination. What happens is that the supplier can now deduct input VAT on the goods supplied in the country of origin. On the other hand, in the country of destination, the buyer has the obligation to calculate VAT on the acquired goods, and at the same time can deduct that amount. No amount of VAT is actually paid in the country of destination when the acquisition takes place, but the country of destination collects VAT only when the next transaction takes place when the acquirer sells the goods to a third party in the same country (Podlipnik, 2012). This is precisely the critical flaw in the European Union's value-added tax system that makes it vulnerable to fraud, especially those involving the disappearing trader, for the reason that the collection of that amount of VAT depends on the company that acquires the goods and has to pay the VAT liability at the time those goods are sold in their own country. For this reason, already with the Directive from 2006, joint strategy measures have been systematically and reinforced for the prevention of fraudulent actions based on the application of VAT legislation (Cindori & Zakarija, 2016). However, in practice, these measures proved to be insufficient.

Value-Added Tax in the Member States of the European Union

The directive on the common system of VAT allows the use of only standard and reduced rates, however, due to numerous exceptions and transitional periods in the EU there are also deviations regarding zero rates, super-reduced rates and transitional or parking rates. Super-reduced rates are applied to the turnover of goods and services to which a reduced VAT rate can be applied. Parking rates are applied to transactions for which the general rate should be applied, and are used in member countries that had introduced VAT before January 1, 1991, and their rate was then below 15%, and thus they were allowed a transitional period. From these different rates and exceptions, another layer of the problem of the VAT system in the European Union is visible, which is the different treatment of individual countries. While the Republic of Croatia and other newer members of the European Union fully respect the framework of the Directive from 2006, countries with reduced parking rates have a privileged position. Taking into account the inherent flaws of the European Union VAT system in terms of the vulnerability of the mechanism itself to tax fraud, and the incomplete compliance of all member states with the current Directive, it can be concluded that the common VAT system in the European Union is far from firmly regulated, a functional and rigid system as it was conceived more than three decades ago. There is clearly a need for a better arrangement of the system itself. From the perspective of defense against tax fraud, it is first of all necessary to define the existing dangers faced by the VAT system in order to be able to understand the advantages and disadvantages of the defense mechanism against them.

TAX FRAUDS IN THE SYSTEM OF VALUE-ADDED TAX IN THE FRAMEWORK OF THE EUROPEAN UNION

The European Commission (2021) report estimates that the European Union lost €134 billion in value-added tax revenue in 2019 as a result of fraud, evasion, evasion, reporting errors and business failures. This means that in 2019, the European Union lost an average of 4,000 euros in revenue every second, and a large part of these losses is related to tax fraud. With the aim of defining the amount of damage caused by tax fraud and the significance of this issue, the European Commission is introducing the concept of the VAT gap. The Commission defines the VAT gap as the difference between the expected VAT revenues (that is, the total VAT tax liability - VTTL) and the amount actually collected, in absolute or percentage value (European Commission, 2021).

Table 1. VAT gap in EU member states in 2019

State	Total revenues from VAT in million EUR	Total liabilities for VAT in million EUR	VAT gap in millions of EUR	VAT gap %
Belgium	31,702	36,146	4,444	12,3%
Bulgaria	5,628	6,136	508	8,3%
Czech Republic	16,931	19,766	2,835	14,3%
Denmark	29,632	32,410	2,778	8,6%
Germany	244,111	267,554	23,443	4,8%
Estonia	2,483	2,599	116	4,5%
Ireland	15,281	17,002	1,721	10,1%
Greece	15,390	20,740	5,350	25,8%
Spain	79,308	85,148	5,840	6,9%
France	173,953	187,811	13,858	7,4%
Croatia	7,419	7,497	77	1,0%
Italy	111,533	141,639	30,106	21,3%
Cyprus	1,943	1,998	54	2,7%
Latvia	2,632	2,869	237	8,3%
Lithuania	3,850	4,898	1,048	21,4%
Luxembourg	3,763	4,030	267	6,6%
Hungary	13,916	15,98	1,483	9,6%
Malta	934	1,221	287	23,5%
Netherlands	58,131	60,791	2,660	4,4%
Austria	30,405	33,301	2,895	8,7%
Poland	42,383	47,762	5,379	11,3%
Portugal	18,786	20,395	1,609	7,9%
Romanian	13,795	21,206	7,411	34,9%
Slavonia	3,888	4,186	298	7,1%
Slovakia	6,830	8,143	1,313	16,1%
Finland	21,974	22,620	646	2,9%
Sweden	43,412	44,009	597	1,4%

The data show a significant disparity in the amount of the VAT gap between member states. The lowest VAT gap in 2019 was recorded by the Republic of Croatia (1%), Sweden (1.4%) and Cyprus (2.7%), while the highest was recorded by Romania (34.9%), Greece (25.8%) and Malta (23.5%). Furthermore, the nominally largest gap was recorded in Italy (EUR 30.1 billion) and Germany (EUR 23.4 billion). Variations in the VAT gap are a reflection of existing differences between member states in the domain of tax compliance, tax fraud, avoidance of payment, bankruptcy and failure of companies and other factors such as the success of tax administrations and administrations in combating fraud and VAT fraud. The reason why this situation is problematic is precisely the fact that VAT revenues make up a significant part of the state budgets of the member states, and thus of the European Union itself (European Commission, 2021). Among other things, it is in the general interest of the European Union as an economic community of countries that its members collect income from their taxes safely and efficiently. Given that certain tax frauds within the European Union require criminal organizations to operate in the territories of several member states at once, tax frauds as a major reason for the VAT gap are becoming a problem that concerns all EU member states. It can be concluded that the problem of tax fraud is a problem that concerns the entire EU, and there is a need for a joint fight against such activities. The effectiveness of value-added tax by its very nature relies on the integrity and trust of a large number of intermediaries who collect and pay VAT along the economic chain (Frunza, 2019). The first and basic weakness of the VAT system is therefore precisely the number of entities that participate in its calculation and collection. What additionally exposes the value-added tax system within the EU to vulnerabilities to tax fraud is precisely its structure prescribed by the Directive on the common system of VAT from 2006, which, among other things, already foresees measures for the common fight against fraud. Transactions carried out between EU member states are taxed with value-added tax according to the destination principle, however, deliveries of goods from one member state to another are exempt from VAT. Since the taxpayers who carry out these transactions have the right to deduct the input tax, the possibility of tax fraud is opened in which money is "extracted" from member states in the form of recognition of claims for input tax on VAT that has never been paid (Cindori & Zakarija, 2016). The structure of the VAT system in the European Union is primarily susceptible to frauds that take advantage of this very mechanism, that is, frauds with the disappearing trader - Missing Trader Intra-Community Fraud (MTIC). Frunza (2019) points out that in order to define fraud in VAT systems, it is necessary to first look at the economy of a country as a combination of the so-called formal economy and informal or gray economy. Within the formal economy, there are economic activities under the jurisdiction of national laws, with measurable and visible results, while the informal or gray economy implies all exchange of goods and services that is carried out outside the parameters of national laws, and its volume cannot be precisely measured, nor can these activities be directly observed. Based on this division, it is possible to create a general framework of fraud in the VAT system, and divide fraud into the following types of activities (Frunza, 2019):

- fraud in the domain of the gray economy (domestic and cross-border transactions of goods and services that do not appear in the VAT system)
- dissimilation of exchange within the formal economy (missing trade fraud)
- accounting fraud
- false representation of goods and services (declaration of certain goods and services in incorrect categories with the aim of reducing the tax liability

Based on these categories, it is possible to separate those frauds that can be solved by changing the VAT structure within the EU from those that will occur in any system. The gray economy is a matter of crime that avoids all rules, and it can hardly be solved strictly by introducing certain economic and accounting measures into the system. The situation is similar with the false representation of taxable goods and services, and with accounting fraud because these frauds do not so much exploit the weaknesses of the system itself as avoid the entire system itself. All of these frauds are illegal in themselves (Rafay, 2021b), and all categories require the intervention of bodies responsible for law enforcement, however, certain types of fraud that are of great harm to the European Union can also be mitigated by the application of certain economic mechanisms. First of all, it is necessary to separate frauds with the disappearing merchant from other categories.

TAX TRANSFER MECHANISM IN THE EUROPEAN UNION AS A MEASURE TO PREVENT CIRCULAR VAT FRAUD

The main methods of combating fraud in the VAT system concern so-called structural solutions, and changes in the structure of the VAT system itself. In particular, according to the 2006 Directive itself, the Council of the EU has the power to allow each member state to introduce special measures deviating from the provisions of the Directive with the aim of preventing tax evasion and fraud in the VAT system. As part of this, Directives 2013/42/EU on the common system of VAT in relation to the rapid response mechanism to VAT fraud, and Directive 2013/43/EU on the common system of VAT in relation to optional and temporary by applying the tax liability transfer mechanism (Cindori & Zakarija, 2016). Transfer of tax liability (reverse charge) is the transfer of the obligation to pay value-added tax from the seller to the buyer. It functions in such a way that during the transaction of goods or services, the supplier does not charge or calculate the amount of VAT, but the buyer, when acquiring goods or services, declares both the input VAT (as input tax) and the supplier's output VAT in the same VAT return. That is, the buyer transfers the supplier's tax liability to himself. Only when selling to the last customer in the series, the output VAT is paid to the competent tax authority (Cindori & Zakarija, 2016; Stiller & Heinemann, 2021). With the aim of preventing MTIC fraud, the idea of applying this method of value-added taxation is to transfer the tax liability to B2B transactions (transactions between legal entities) in order to prevent disappearing merchants from "disappearing" without paying the obligation. This actually turns VAT into a kind of "retail turnover tax" (Stiller & Heinemann, 2021).

The Legal Basis of the Tax Liability Transfer Mechanism and its Application in the European Union

The tax liability transfer mechanism was first introduced within Article 199 of the Directive on the Common VAT System in 2006, according to which it was applied to the performance of construction works, the provision of personnel involved in construction work activities, the delivery of immovable property, and the delivery of used materials, garbage and waste. Four years later, the first extension of the area of transfer of tax liability was enacted by the addition of Article 199a, which extends the application of the mechanism mainly to emissions trading. However, the sectors of telecommunications, trade in microprocessors, perfumes and other high-value goods have already been proposed due to their susceptibility to MTIC fraud. In 2013, the next in a series of extensions of the tax liability transfer mechanism was passed, according to which member states are allowed to apply the mechanism on an optional and temporary basis until 2018, and to a number of products such as mobile phones, high-tech devices and components, gas and electricity supplies energy, telecommunication services, game consoles, tablets, laptops and personal computers, cereals and industrial plants, and finally raw and unfinished materials. Also, for the first time, significant deviations from the current rules of the common VAT system, which certain countries are allowed to use, are allowed for the first time, according to Article 395 of the Directive to apply the mechanism of transfer of tax liability to specific goods and services (De la Feria, 2019). The goods and services approved by the European Commission are mostly those that are the most common targets of MTIC fraud such as mobile phones, microprocessors, high value technology products and light transport and the like. It is interesting to point out the cases of bankruptcy proceedings and food trade in transition countries such as Hungary and Lithuania. Of the possibility of applying the tax liability transfer mechanism provided for in Articles 394 and 395 of the Directive, only a small number of member states have expanded their scope of application to new permitted sectors, namely the following:

- works on real estate: construction, repair, cleaning and maintenance, installation of movable goods, sanitation, electrical network, fire protection system, alarm, telephone, air conditioning equipment, built-in wardrobes, storage, etc.: Belgium
- deliveries of certain types of wood (planks, beams, etc.): Lithuania, Latvia and Romania
- supplies of gas and electricity to a taxable reseller: France
- goods or services acquired from a VAT payer in bankruptcy proceedings: Lithuania

The final step towards the implementation of the transfer of tax liability mechanism as a method of defense against tax fraud came with the introduction of the previously mentioned quick reaction system (Directive 2013/42/EU on the common system of VAT), the QRM mechanism - Quick Reaction Mechanism. According to the QRM mechanism, a member state can, due to the need for urgency, designate a recipient as the person responsible for paying VAT for a certain supply of goods or services. This represents a special measure to combat sudden frauds, especially those of large value that would lead to serious losses for the state budget. It was this QRM mechanism that served as the background for the final introduction of the general transfer of tax liability (Cindori & Zakarija, 2016; De la Feria, 2019). In 2016, a proposal was made to introduce a general reverse charge. In 2018, the general transfer of tax liability was finally approved, and the biggest, and according to some, the only advantage of the new mechanism is manifested in the potential elimination of MTIC fraud, along with the appearance of numerous other shortcomings (the already mentioned conversion of VAT into a kind of sales tax in retail).

Let's quote an example of the application of the tax liability transfer mechanism in the Republic of Croatia. The Republic of Croatia, in contrast to relatively close member states such as Hungary and Romania, and especially to other transition countries such as Slovakia, the Czech Republic and Poland, records an almost negligible VAT gap. In 2019, Croatia recorded the lowest VAT gap in the entire European Union. Furthermore, over the years, circular frauds have not been such a significant problem affecting the Croatian state budget, although a case was discovered in 2019 when 15 natural persons were arrested in the territory of the Republic of Croatia for participating in a circular fraud through companies in Croatia and Slovenia. The reason for this can be simply manifested in the fact that the Republic of Croatia is the last member state of the European Union in terms of chronological accession to the community, and until 2013 it was not even possible to participate in intra-community fraud through legal entities within the Republic of Croatia. There is also the problem of adaptation time to doing business with the EU, and then there are other problems that make it difficult for disappearing traders to do business, such as high bureaucracy, slowness of the system, etc., which make fraud more difficult, for which, among other things, it is crucial to quickly open an entity, quickly collect overpaid

VAT and quickly disappear. Over time, Croatia becomes one more candidate for MTIC fraud, and it is certainly in the interest of the state budget to maintain the record of the member with the lowest VAT gap in the European Union. With the accession to the European Union, numerous provisions from the EU legislation were incorporated into the Croatian legislation, and thus, among other things, the Directive on the Common VAT System with its amendments was incorporated into the Value-added Tax Act. This is the first time that the transfer of tax liability has been introduced into the practice of VAT taxation in Croatia. First, the tax paid on acquisitions of goods within the EU (which are subject to VAT taxation) is taxed using the tax liability transfer mechanism. Secondly, according to the Law, it is prescribed that a taxpayer registered in the VAT system in Croatia must apply the tax liability transfer mechanism when performing the following deliveries:

- construction services, which are considered to be all services related to the construction, putting into use, maintenance, change or removal of a construction object, including cleaning services (the same applies to the assignment of personnel if they perform construction services)
- used material and what cannot be reused in the same form, waste, industrial and non-industrial waste, recycling waste, partially processed waste and certain goods and services
- real estate sold by the executor in the foreclosure procedure
- transfer of quotas of emission units of greenhouse gases according to Art. 3. Directive 2003/87/EC on the establishment of a trading system for greenhouse gas emission quotas in the EU

These provisions of the VAT Act actually directly copy the provisions of the Directive on the Common VAT System from 2006 and affect the same transactions that are listed in the Directive. Given that the construction sector is very large and strong in the Republic of Croatia, the domestic transfer of tax liability in practice almost exclusively concerns only construction services. The foreign transfer of tax liability concerns the acquisition of goods from EU countries, and the net effect on the company is zero since the same amount is reported as a liability for VAT and a claim for input VAT on the same VAT return. What is interesting about the Republic of Croatia is that even after the extension of the Directive and the inclusion of the general transfer of tax liability, Croatia leaves only the mentioned sectors in its legislation, with the exception of the addition of the right to apply the domestic transfer of tax liability to the right to the emission of greenhouse gases, which was considerably susceptible frauds. The Republic of Croatia thus applies the tax liability transfer mechanism to the six categories provided for in Article 199 and 199a of the Directive, and it should be noted that the sectors to which the mechanism is applied make up 3% of the total economy. If they were applied to all sectors, 6% of gross added value would be achieved from the activities to which the mechanism is applied (Benazic, 2016).

The Effects of the Tax Liability Transfer Mechanism on the Prevention of Tax Fraud

Applying the transfer of tax liability to domestic B2B transactions is, according to some scientists, the most radical strategy to combat VAT fraud (Borselli, 2011). The most radical reason that although it theoretically very effectively stops the possibilities of MTIC fraud, it creates numerous other costs for the tax system itself (Borselli, 2011; De la Feria, 2019; Van Brederode & Pfeiffer, 2015). Despite the high relevance of the tax liability transfer mechanism in both economic and political terms, its own effects have not been sufficiently well scientifically researched, and empirical studies mainly focus on specific member states (Stiller & Heinemann, 2021). The question of the real effects of this mechanism on the entire VAT system of the European Union opens up so that we could potentially answer the problem of the final regulation of the EU system. The transfer of tax liability on domestic B2B transactions works as follows: The VAT liability is transferred from the supplier (seller) to the buyer. The buyer calculates VAT on the purchase of his goods/services in his VAT declaration as output VAT, and in the same declaration records the same amount as input VAT (input tax). There is no actual payment to the tax authority. If we take as an example a supply chain of five entities, A to E, in which the last entity (E) is a retailer, we can describe the mechanism as follows. For a sale from entity A to B, entity B will be responsible for reporting entity A's VAT liability and its own input tax on the same return. On the sale from B to C, subject C is responsible, again, for the declaration and obligations for VAT and withholding tax in the same VAT return. The same goes from C to D, and D to E. Only when we get to the entity that carries out retail sales (B2C), the tax authority actually collects the tax, and in this case, entity E has the obligation to pay the amount of VAT to the tax authority after the sale to the final customer. (state). As a consequence of this mechanism, no entity in the series will receive any payment of VAT from the state, whether in domestic or foreign transactions. In simpler terms, the possibility of fraud in the way of demanding the payment of input tax that was not paid by the disappearing merchant in an earlier step disappears completely. It can be seen that during the entire B2B chain of transactions, at no time is the balance of VAT liabilities and input tax receivables in companies that sell to another company different from zero. Only when the goods/services are sold to the final customer (B2C) does the retail company record the VAT liability it pays to the state. In this way, the liability for VAT that the disappearing trader does not pay, and the input tax that the final company fraudulently collects, are eliminated. Also, this shows why VAT is also called retail sales tax within the tax liability transfer mechanism because only retail sales are effectively taxed. The main advantage of using this mechanism can be easily seen. If we have a sector of the economy within which transactions related to fraud are easy and frequent, and significantly damage the state budget, we can implement the transfer of tax liability to that sector and thus eliminate MTIC fraud. The European Union is a community of a large number of member states, and almost every member historically implements the transfer of tax liability to different sectors. Consequently, it is possible to conclude that the introduction of the tax liability transfer mechanism in one member state increases tax fraud in another member state without tax liability transfer. Stiller and Heinemann (2021) confirm this hypothesis through an analysis of the effects of the transfer of tax liability mechanism on asymmetries in international trade and conclude that the introduction of the transfer of tax liability mechanism on laptops, mobile phones, tablets and game consoles in the importing country led to the elimination of MTIC fraud in these products. Furthermore, in his study, he states that reported exports in the exporting country fell by about 25% after the introduction of the transfer of tax liability mechanism in the importing country. This effect of eliminating MTIC fraud is countered by the negative effect of increasing MTIC fraud in countries that do not use the transfer of tax liability mechanism on these goods, by about 15%. It is possible to conclude that the current model of application of the transfer of tax liability mechanism within the EU results in a kind of domino effect, and a uniform, common application of this mechanism is needed. In the period between 2007 and 2019, the loss of VAT from MTIC fraud in transactions of electronic devices amounted to 663 million euros in countries that implemented the mechanism of transfer of tax liability on these products, while in the same period the loss was caused by the transfer of MTIC fraud to countries without this mechanism was 3 to 4 times higher (Stiller & Heinemann, 2021). These data point to the first major problem of the tax liability transfer mechanism within the European Union, which is that it is simply not uniform enough among the member states. The introduction of the general mechanism of transfer of tax liability in 2018 through Directive[4] 2018/2057 amending the Directive on the common system of VAT, countries affected by MTIC fraud are allowed to apply transfer tax obligations on all domestic transactions above the threshold of EUR 17,500 per transaction. This mechanism allows countries affected by MTIC fraud to introduce transfer of tax liabilities on transactions where they lose the most, without seeking permission and waiting for long processes in the European Council. However, this current system of general transfer of tax liability, which was in operation until June 30, 2022, still does not address the aforementioned flaw where the implementation of the transfer of tax liability mechanism in one country, leads to the relocation of MTIC fraud to a country without such a system. The general transfer of tax liability carries with it other disadvantages. First, this system directly increases administrative costs and compliance monitoring costs for companies due to increased reporting, the introduction of separation in processes between B2B and B2C transactions, and separation in business between transactions below and above the value threshold (De la Feria, 2019). The problem at the fundamental level is precisely this transformation of the value-added tax into a retail sales tax. This is a problem due to the very nature of VAT and its advantages over sales tax arising from the characteristics of VAT. VAT is calculated using the credit method, according to which the tax is collected repeatedly along the economic chain, where all B2B transactions charge VAT, but also deduct input tax on VAT paid at the time of purchase, which ensures the basic principle of VAT that it is neutral for business entities. The credit method ensures that buyers of intermediate goods and suppliers have conflicting interests, that is, it is in the buyer's interest to receive a valid invoice with expressed VAT, which ensures better tax behavior and reduces the desire for tax evasion. In the credit method model, the risk of tax evasion and tax evasion spreads over the entire production chain and creates an incentive for traders to ensure that their suppliers provide them with valid invoices in order to be able to deduct input VAT, which actually means that there is a certain self-control in the VAT system (De la Feria, 2019; Šimović & Deskar-Škrbić, 2020; Tait, 1988). On the other hand, sales tax in retail does not have multiple collections like VAT, which actually means that the entire risk of tax evasion is concentrated at the last link of the chain. This, of course, creates a huge risk of tax evasion where there was none before, which essentially means that in order to eliminate MTIC fraud, we remove all the security of VAT collection from a regular business that the system had until now. The main problems arising from the transfer of tax liability to domestic B2B transactions are:

- non-compliance by sectors and member states, since after the implementation of the transfer of tax liability mechanism in one sector and/or country, MTIC fraud can simply move to another sector and/or country where the mechanism has not been implemented
- increasing the risk of tax evasion and tax evasion due to the transformation of VAT into sales tax in retail
- increase in administrative and other costs of compliance with the VAT system

The main advantages of the tax liability transfer mechanism for domestic B2B transactions are:

- elimination of MTIC fraud and consequent losses in state budgets of member states and the European Union
- maintaining and potentially improving the principle of VAT neutrality for B2B companies

The question that consequently arises for the European Union and its members is how to form the VAT system of the future. The current transition system implemented in 1993 is obviously not the final version that it should have been almost three decades ago, and the problems of inconsistency, from the rates themselves (especially the super-reduced and parking rates to which individual states are entitled) and from the different rules on transfer tax obligations for different countries, they effectively do not achieve so many benefits as they violate the basic principles of VAT as a general and comprehensive sales tax, nor do they successfully solve the problems of circular fraud until the system is fully harmonized throughout the European Union (Grasgruber *et al.*, 2013; Stiller & Heinemann, 2021; Šimović & Deskar-Škrbić, 2020).

Other Measures to Prevent Tax Fraud

In the member states, national VAT laws are based on EU legislation, mainly Directive 2006/112/EC on the common system of value-added tax, amending the First and Sixth VAT Directives, as amended. The Directive is binding on each Member State to which it is addressed as to the result to be achieved but allows national authorities to choose the form and methods for achieving such an objective. As a result of this freedom of choice, national VAT laws are not identical. However, in the final analysis, EU legislation is decisive; individual taxpayers can exercise rights from it (Terra & Kajus, 2021). Vanishing trader scams and other forms of tax fraud are serious crimes. As such, they entail certain penalties, most often prison terms. According to a 2020 Europol report, three people were arrested in the territory of the Republic of Hungary after the Hungarian Tax Administration in cooperation with investigators from Croatia and Slovenia discovered a sophisticated circular MTIC fraud that damaged the Republic of Hungary for 1.4 million euros. Those involved in the fraud now face a potential 20 years in prison (Europol, 2020). In the UK, as a member of the EU, huge MTIC frauds have been recorded over the years, there was a case of a criminal organization whose participants were sentenced to nine years in prison, and among other things, a fine of 14 million pounds for the leader of the organization and other fines for the participants (BBC, 2011). Such cases are numerous and generally result in long prison terms and huge fines when discovered, which is the first and foremost deterrent to any crime - legal retribution. On a more technical level, numerous member states have created early warning systems for certain sectors and types of transactions that are at risk of fraud. Given that the disappearing trader must open a business on the market before committing fraud, that is, must obtain a valid VAT number, a risk analysis system that can identify potential fraud early is almost necessary. Such systems are mainly based on software for risk analysis and virtual databases of companies (Borselli, 2011). In addition to such technological solutions, a potential solution is also possible through the improvement of the following (Podlipnik, 2012):

- efficiency of tax inspections
- cooperation between tax authorities in member states
- the imposition of responsibility on persons who participate in fraud and the removal of the possibility of input tax deduction

These solutions, like those previously mentioned, do not require any changes in the current VAT system within the European Union, and member states are able to apply them on an individual level. While technological early warning systems could be grouped in the domain of improving the efficiency of tax inspections, the implementation of organizational measures such as the establishment of special departments dealing with the detection and investigation of MTIC fraud, then more frequent and detailed company checks, training and education of tax officials could also be added here. inspectors, etc. (Podlipnik, 2012). Stronger cooperation between member states is needed, as more frequent use of VIES and other databases could help in the detection of fraud-related transactions. The use of VIES databases, however, eliminates the need for criminals to have their own people inside the customs office who will pass their goods through border controls and thus becomes an instrument of certain other types of fraud, therefore one should be careful in the approach itself (Pashev, 2006). European Council Regulation 904/2010 on administrative cooperation and suppression of fraud in the field of value-added tax prescribes the conditions of cooperation of member states in this area of cooperation, exchange of information and determination of the correctness of transactions. The solution that is interesting to highlight from the Regulation is the introduction of financial incentives in the form of bonuses for tax authorities that help another member state in detecting fraud in the VAT system. Over the years, other amendments have been adopted establishing platforms for the exchange of information (EUROFISC), the establishment of comparative supervision of taxpayers and numerous similar administrative attempts to reduce the problem (Cindori & Zakarija, 2016). A certified tax program called Digital VAT (D-VAT) is also proposed, which, like the VLN system, enables the monitoring of VAT calculations throughout the entire chain, so that it connects the input tax of the recipient with the calculated amount of VAT of the supplier. The application of this system is most useful precisely in the subsequent finding of criminal entities and their capture. There is also a so-called Real Time VAT (RTvat) which enables detailed monitoring of the VAT collection process from the date of invoice to the date of payment (Ainsworth, 2008; Cindori & Zakraija, 2016). Such and similar detection and prevention systems are very useful for the reason that they do not require structural changes within the EU itself, but they certainly entail large implementation costs. An argument can also be made that higher implementation costs represent a better alternative than the damage caused by tax fraud.

With the development of the tax and customs administration system, verification methods were developed for the export operation and for the physical export of goods from the territory of the Union. This prevents taxpayers from obtaining tax benefits in the form of VAT offsets for the fraudulent export of goods. One of these verification methods is the request to submit documents that confirm that the goods have physically crossed the border of the given country and the option for automatic exchange of documents between customs and tax authorities. However, in some cases, the fake export scheme could still be successfully implemented today — but this requires the involvement of the employees of the customs control entities (Sidorova *et al.*, 2021).

The European Union is trying to reduce tax fraud with new measures, although fraud involving disappearing traders has existed since the 1980s, and is certainly not a new phenomenon. Ways to fight against these frauds have existed since the moment they first appeared, and just as the frauds have evolved over time, so have the proposals for solving them becoming more sophisticated and comprehensive. With the development of the VAT system in the European Union, the methods of fraud are also developing, and over time the member states realize that they cannot fight against these frauds alone. The directive on the common system of VAT is also the beginning of the joint fight of the European Union member states against these frauds, and the measures of the common fraud prevention strategy are systematically and reinforced. The complexity of these frauds, however, can hardly be solved without detecting the very weaknesses of the VAT system in the European Union.

CONCLUSION

Tax fraud in the value-added tax system is one of the biggest problems of the European Union. The European Union loses a significant amount of value-added tax revenue each year (€134 billion in 2019 alone) as a result of fraud, tax evasion, tax evasion, filing errors and corporate bankruptcy. Vanishing trader scams or MTIC circular scams make up the largest and most dangerous part of these losses, and unlike activities in the domain of tax avoidance and tax evasion, they differ in that they mainly concern sophisticated international organized crime. Circular scams with the disappearing trader exploit a key flaw in the European Union's value-added tax system, which allows member states to apply a zero VAT rate when performing cross-border transactions within the community, VAT taxation according to the destination principle. Since, according to this principle, VAT is only paid in the member state where the good is consumed, and companies that further sell that product in their home country have the right to deduct input tax due to the credit method of calculating VAT, it happens that a company that imports goods or services from another Member State can now resell the goods within the country and disappear without paying VAT liability, while the downstream company can export the goods or services back to the starting Member State and collect input tax refunds from the tax authority. The value-added tax system within the European Union enables organized crime to steal money directly from the state budgets of the member states and thus damage not only the budgets of the member states but also the quality of public services within the European Union at the expense of all taxpayers. The European Union has recognized the importance of these frauds since the early years of the common VAT system, and with the aim of suppressing them with the new Directive on the common VAT system, the member states are starting a joint systematic fight against fraud with the disappearing trader. Among numerous administrative solutions such as increased cooperation between tax authorities between member countries, and technological achievements such as software solutions and VLN numbers, the most serious and radical solution is manifested through the introduction of a mechanism for the transfer of tax liability on domestic (domestic) transactions between legal entities (B2B). The mechanism for the transfer of tax liability on domestic B2B transactions was first introduced to certain sectors of the economy that the European Union considers being the most affected by fraud, and over the years that list was expanded to include a larger number of sectors and specially identified goods and services until 2018, when introduces the so-called general transfer of tax liability, which allows countries most affected by disappearing trader fraud to apply domestic transfer of tax liability to all domestic transactions above the value threshold of EUR 17,500 per transaction. The use of this mechanism completely eliminates MTIC fraud in the sector in which it is implemented, for the reason that by transferring the VAT liability from the supplier to the customer along the entire chain, the possibility of input tax deduction and disappearing without settling the VAT liability disappears since the tax is no longer collected at each step. but only during the final retail sale. In practice, this mechanism has not succeeded in completely suppressing MTIC fraud in the European Union, and the main reason for this is that the mechanism is not equally and evenly introduced to all sectors and all member states, and therefore the implementation of the transfer of tax liability mechanism on domestic transactions in one sector or member state leads to until the transfer of MTIC fraud to another sector or a member state where the system has not been implemented. The VAT system within the EU needs to be regulated in detail. From the transition system from 1993, which has never been replaced, to the inequality of the member states in the use of the mechanism, the system is fundamentally disordered and thus vulnerable not only to fraud, but also creates dissatisfaction between different members, which seriously undermines the unity of the EU. The EU cannot postpone changes and introduce half-hearted solutions to its problems, so among other things, the problem of tax fraud will not disappear until equal rules for everyone are introduced into the VAT system. In the case of MTIC fraud, domestic transfer of tax liability should be standardized between member states and the sectors to which it applies, and administrative cooperation between member tax authorities should be strengthened.

DECLARATION

The author declares that the manuscript follows ethical standards and there are no potential conflicts of interest with respect to the research, authorship and/or publication of this chapter.

DISCLAIMER

The contents and views of this chapter are expressed by the author in her personal capacity. It is not necessary for the Editor and the Publisher to agree with these viewpoints, and they are not responsible for any duty of care in this regard.

ACKNOWLEDGMENT

The author extends sincere gratitude to:

- The Editor and the International Editorial Advisory Board (IEAB) of this book who initially desk reviewed, arranged a rigorous double/triple blind review process and conducted a thorough, minute and critical final review before accepting the chapter for publication.
- All anonymous reviewers who provided very constructive feedbacks for thorough revision, improvement, extension and fine tuning of the chapter.
- All colleagues, assistants and well-wishers who assisted to complete this task.

REFERENCES

Abshari, Z., Jenkins, G. P., Kuo, C. Y., & Shahee, M. (2021). Progressive taxation versus progressive targeted transfers in the design of a sustainable value-added tax system. *Sustainability*, *13*(20), 11165. doi:10.3390u132011165

Ainsworth, R. T. (2008). *MTIC (Carousel) fraud: Twelve ways forward; two ways' preferred'-has the technology-based administrative solution been rejected?* Boston University School of Law Working Paper, (08–10).

Ainsworth, R. T., & Alwohaibi, M. (2016). GCC VAT: The intra-gulf trade problem. SSRN *Electronic Journal*. Retrieved from https://ssrn.com/abstract=2916252 doi:10.2139/ssrn.2916252

Alavuotunki, K., Haapanen, M., & Pirttilä, J. (2019). The effects of the value-added tax on revenue and inequality. *The Journal of Development Studies*, *55*(4), 490–508. doi:10.1080/00220388.2017.1400015

BBC. (2011). *Gang of 15 jailed for £250m VAT fraud.* Retrieved from https://www.bbc.com/news/uk-england-16262390

Benazic, A. (2016). Primjena mehanizma obrnutog oporezivanja i njegovi učinci na troškove ispunjavanja obveze PDV-a u Europskoj uniji. *Porezni vjesnik, 2.*

Borselli, F. (2011). *Organised VAT Fraud: Features, Magnitude, Policy Perspectives* (Banca d'Italia occasional paper series, no. 106.). Retrieved from https://www.bancaditalia.it/pubblicazioni/qef/2011-0106/QEF_106.pdf

Cindori, S., & Zakarija, A. (2016). Prevencija prijevara u sustavu poreza na dodanu vrijednost u okvirima Europske unije. *Pravni vjesnik, 32*(3–4), 71–90. Retrieved from https://hrcak.srce.hr/179199

de la Feria, R., & Schoeman, A. (2019). Addressing VAT fraud in developing countries: The tax policy-administration symbiosis. *Intertax, 47*(11), 950–967.

Devereux, M. P., Freedman, J., & Vella, J. (2012). Tax avoidance. SSRN *Electronic Journal.* Retrieved from https://www.researchgate.net/publication/350490406_Tax_Avoidance doi:10.2139/ssrn.3754562

Didier, T., & Pinat, M. (2017). *The Nature of trade and growth linkages* (World Bank Policy Research Working Paper 8168). Washington, DC: World Bank.

Ding, K., Xu, H., & Yang, R. (2021). Taxation and enterprise innovation: Evidence from China's value-added tax reform. *Sustainability, 13*(10), 5700. doi:10.3390u13105700

European Comission. (2021). *VAT gap in the EU: Report 2021.* Retrieved from https://taxation-customs.ec.europa.eu/business/vat/vat-gap_en

Europol. (2020). *Three arrested in Hungary in €1.4 million VAT fraud investigation.* Retrieved from https://www.europol.europa.eu/media-press/newsroom/news/3-arrested-in-hungary-in-%E2%82%AC14-million-vat-fraud-investigation

FindLaw Staff. (2021). *Tax Evasion vs Tax Avoidance.* FindLaw. Retrieved from https://www.findlaw.com/tax/tax-problems-audits/tax-evasion-vs-tax-avoidance.htm

Fjeldstad, O. H., Kagoma, C., Mdee, E., Sjursen, I. H., & Somville, V. (2020). The customer is king: Evidence on VAT compliance in Tanzania. *World Development, 128*, 104841. doi:10.1016/j.worlddev.2019.104841

Frankel, J. A., & Romer, D. H. (1999). Does trade cause growth? *The American Economic Review, 89*(3), 379–399. doi:10.1257/aer.89.3.379

Frunza, M. (2019). *Value-added Tax Fraud.* Routledge.

Grasgruber, M., Otavova, M., & Semerad, P. (2013). Impacts of the application of the reverse charge mechanism of the value-added tax. *Acta Universitatis Agriculturae et Silviculturae Mendelianae Brunensis, 61*(7), 2133–2141. doi:10.11118/actaun201361072133

Gurdgiev, C. (2019). OECD-Led tax reforms: A prescription for a less competitive economy. SSRN *Electronic Journal.* Retrieved from https://ssrn.com/abstract=3406260 doi:10.2139/ssrn.3406260

Henn, C., Papageorgiou, C., Romero, J. M., & Spatafora, N. (2017). *Export quality in advanced and developing economies: evidence from a new data set* (World Bank Policy Research Working Paper 8196). Washington, DC: World Bank.

IRS. (2022). *Types of Fraudulent Activities – General Fraud.* Internal Revenue Service. Retrieved from https://www.irs.gov/

Jelčić, B., Lončarić H., Šimović, J., Arbutina, H., & Mijatović, N. (2008). *Financijsko pravo i financijska znanost.* Zagreb: Narodne Novine.

Kirchler, E., Maciejovsky, B., & Schneider, F. (2003). Everyday representations of tax avoidance, tax evasion, and tax flight: Do legal differences matter? *Journal of Economic Psychology, 24*(4), 535–553. doi:10.1016/S0167-4870(02)00164-2

Kowal, A., & Przekota, G. (2021). VAT Efficiency—A discussion on the VAT System in the European Union. *Sustainability, 13*(9), 4768. doi:10.3390u13094768

Mitusova, E. Y. (2021). Prospects of integration of operational control in the system of fiscal control. *Russian Economic Developments, 7*, 49–56.

Pashev, K. (2006). *Fighting VAT Fraud: The Bulgarian Experience* (CSD Working Paper No. WP 0606/2). Retrieved from https://mpra.ub.uni-muenchen.de/998

Podlipnik, J. (2012). Missing trader intra-community and carousel VAT frauds - ECJ and ECTHR case law. *Croatian Yearbook of European Law & Policy, 8*(1), 457–472. Retrieved from https://hrcak.srce.hr/94656

Poniatowski, G., Bonch-Osmolovskiy, M., Durán-Cabré, J. M., Esteller-Moré, A., & Smietanka, A. (2020). *Study and Reports on the VAT Gap in the EU-28 member states: 2019 Final report. CASE No. 500.* Retrieved from https://www.case-research.eu/files/?id_plik=6251

Pouwels, A. (2021). *Missing Trader Intra-Community Fraud.* Affairs Directorate—General for Internal Policies PE 690.462—June 2021, Policy Department for Budgetary. Retrieved from https://www.europarl.europa.eu/RegData/etudes/BRIE/2021/690462/IPOL_BRI(2021)690462_EN.pdf

Rafay, A. (Ed.). (2021a). *Money Laundering and Terrorism Financing in Global Financial Systems.* IGI Global. doi:10.4018/978-1-7998-8758-4

Rafay, A. (Ed.). (2021b). *Handbook of Research on Theory and Practice of Financial Crimes.* IGI Global. doi:10.4018/978-1-7998-5567-5

Rafay, A., & Ajmal, M. M. (2014). Earnings Management through Deferred Taxes Recognized under IAS 12: Evidence from Pakistan. *Lahore Journal of Business*, *3*(1), 1–19. doi:10.35536/ljb.2014.v3.i1.a1

Sidorova, E., Sebechenko, E., Kostyukhin, Y., Boboshko, D., Kostin, A., Kostina, O., & Vikhrova, N. (2021). Formation of a sustainable mechanism of preferential VAT taxation of exports as evidenced by the Russian Federation Practice. *Economies*, *9*(4), 190. doi:10.3390/economies9040190

Šimović, H., & Deskar-Škrbić, M. (2020). *Ekonomika javnog sektora s hrvatskim primjerima*. Arhivanalitika.

Šimurina, N., Dražić Lutilsky, I., Barbić, D., & Dragija Kostić, M. (2018). *Osnove porezne pismenosti*. Zagreb: Narodne Novine.

Stiller, W., & Heinemann, M. (2021). *Do more harm than good? The optional reverse charge mechanism against VAT Fraud*. Retrieved from https://www.researchgate.net/publication/351904988_Do_More_Harm_than_Good_The_Optional_Reverse_Charge_Mechanism_against_VAT_Fraud

Tait, A. (1988). *Value-added Tax – International practice and problems*. International Monetary Fund.

Terra, B., & Kajus, J. (2021). *A Guide to the European VAT Directives*. IBFD.

Van Brederode, R., & Pfeiffer, S. (2015). Combating Carousel Fraud: The General Reverse Charge VAT. *International VAT Monitor*, *26*, 146–157.

Van DoesumA.NellenF. (2021). *VAT in a Day*. Retrieved from https://ssrn.com/abstract=3867201

Vinšalek Stipić, V. (2020). Korporativno upravljanje i ekonomija trećeg puta. *Obrazovanje za poduzetništvo-E4E: znanstveno stručni časopis o obrazovanju za poduzetništvo, 10*(1), 132–146.

Vinšalek Stipić, V. (2022). The concept and importance of social audit for sustainable community development. *BH Ekonomski Forum, 16*(1), 151–165.

Walker-Munro, B. (2021). Tax Enforcement in the Black Economy: Tackling disruptive Challenges. In A. Rafay (Ed.), *Handbook of Research on Theory and Practice of Financial Crimes* (pp. 356–380). IGI Global. doi:10.4018/978-1-7998-5567-5.ch019

ZhirovaG. (2017). *Tax Monitoring Development in Russia*. Regional Authorities, Local Self-Government and Civil Society: Mechanisms of Interaction. Saratov, 2017. C.80–82. Retrieved from https://ssrn.com/abstract=3167060

Zu, Y., Evans, C., & Krever, R. (2020). The VAT Compliance Burden in the UK: A Comparative Assessment. *British Tax Review*, *3*, 354–377.

ADDITIONAL READING

Morić, N. (2013). Obveza plaćanja poreza na dodanu vrijednost. *Porezni vijesnik, 11*, 54–69. Retrieved from https://www.ijf.hr/upload/files/file/PV/2013/11/moric.pdf

ENDNOTES

1 European Council directive 77/388/EEC on the harmonization of laws of the Member States relating to turnover taxes – Common system of value added tax: uniform basis of assessment. (1977). *Official Journal of the European Union, L 145*. Retrieved from https://eur-lex.europa.eu/legal-content/EN/TXT/?uri=celex%3A31977L0388

2 European Council directive 2006/112/EC on the common system of value added tax. (2006). *Official Journal of the European Union, L 347/1*. Retrieved from https://eur-lex.europa.eu/legal-content/EN/TXT/?uri=celex%3A32006L0112

3 EUR-Lex (2021). *The EU's common system of value added tax (VAT)*. Retrieved from EUR-Lex - 32021R0478 - EN - EUR-Lex (europa.eu)

4 European Council Directive. (2018/2057). of 20 December 2018 amending Directive 2006/112/EC on the common system of value added tax as regards the temporary application of a generalised reverse charge mechanism in relation to supplies of goods and services above a certain threshold. (2018). Official Journal of the European Union, L 329. https://eur-lex.europa.eu/legal-content/EN/ALL/?uri=CELEX:32018L2057

Section 3
Fraud and Technology

Chapter 13
Fight Against Corruption Through Technology:
The Case of Morocco

Hicham Sadok
https://orcid.org/0000-0003-4402-0954
Mohammed V University in Rabat, Morocco

ABSTRACT

Corruption secures benefits for those with power, status, money, or protection. Corruption generally manifests itself in the form of a tacit convention that is put in place discreetly, gradually, and cumulatively by feeding itself and secreting its own rules, mechanisms, and intermediaries. In Morocco, social tolerance towards corruption is strong, influenced by a general feeling of impunity and the inequality of citizens under the law. The force of the political discourse displayed, and which is supposed to fight it remains unchanged without notorious effects. However, emerging technologies can serve as a remarkable lever to transform public actions in their fight against corruption through a paperless environment, the reduction of red tape, and highlighting the gray areas where corruption thrives. By focusing on the Moroccan case, this chapter highlights the role that digitalization can have in the moralization of public life by acting on three levers: publishing multiple data, mitigating risks associated with excessive discretion, and creating new public-private partnerships.

INTRODUCTION

Corruption is found with varying intensity in many countries and gives rise to necessarily different analyses. For some, it is marginal, cyclical and seems to be under control thanks to the effective functioning of the institutions in place and the application of the laws in force; while in others it is heavy, structural, and systemic. It deactivates and blocks not only the political and legal control supposed to fight and stem it but also the economic development of the country. According to a former minister of economy and finance in Morocco, corruption costs Morocco annually 7 billion Euros, or nearly 7% of its gross domestic product (GDP) (North Africa Post, 2020). A scourge that plagues Morocco and which

DOI: 10.4018/978-1-6684-5007-9.ch013

is getting worse and worse despite the announcements of the authorities, the launch of several strategies and the establishment of an authority to fight against corruption. Government efforts to tackle it appear ineffective. Transparency International's 2021 Corruption Perceptions Index (CPI) ranks Morocco 87th out of 180 countries on the index. Morocco thus fell seven places compared to 2019. In addition, with a score of 39 out of 100, it lost four points compared to 2019 (Transparency International, 2021). The results of this survey attest to the prevalence of corruption in Morocco, while political discourse continues to show a fierce will to fight it. Hibou and Tozy (2009) sum up this ambivalence perfectly: "*How to interpret the different episodes of a fight against corruption now made visible and even almost routine? Are we in the presence of a pure and simple staging? Or of an instrumentalization of a power still based on the purchase, the exchange of services and corruption?*" Such questions lead to several other questions about the urgency of a political response and about the solutions to be engaged in a visible paradox between the displayed force of its denunciation – at the level of intentions, of taking charge of the phenomenon, and the force of daily corruption. However, if the latter generally consists of an abuse of a power received in the delegation for private ends, to combat it is necessary to remedy the weaknesses of the underlying processes and institutions. Among these essential weaknesses is the main function of our bureaucratic institutions consisting in certifying the authenticity of the information jealously guarded by the administrations (Dimant & Tosato, 2018). In The Castle, the last novel by Franz Kafka, he deplores the fact that bureaucratic organizations exercise "*the tyranny of paper*". Indeed, most of our daily transactions are meticulously listed in ledgers. However, by opting for digital, governments can improve the transparency and efficiency of bloated bureaucracies that often date from another era (Kahn *et al.*, 2018). Leaders around the world advocating for reform have appreciated how technology can help simplify administration (Rafay, 2019) and curb corruption by reducing red tape and illuminating the gray areas where corruption thrives (Banerjee *et al.*, 2012). For Louis Brandeis[1], "*sunlight would be the best disinfectant*".

In this respect, a bubble of expectations is forming on the contributions of digitalization for the generalization of transparency and governments are struggling to catch up. Digitally savvy citizens are much less tolerant of bureaucracy, nepotism and corruption which remain a formidable challenge, although the digital revolution is gradually changing the game (Rafay, 2021b). Today, new technologies allow "corruption hunters" to reveal, prosecute, prevent and even predict questionable practices that could previously be covered with the opacity of paper. As a result, there are heightened and even exaggerated expectations about the potential of digital to improve public service delivery and enhance efficiency and integrity in public action. It is therefore important to reflect on both the promises and the pitfalls of this ongoing revolution to deal with endemic corruption in general and in Morocco in particular (North Africa Post, 2020), by reflecting on the potential of digitalization to change the rules of governance in place. This change in promoting transparency will first require accountability for opening and publishing multiple data (Transparency International, 2021). Second, by mitigating the risks associated with excessive discretion of power (Transparency International, 2021). This is how unlocking the potential of the Blockchain could be an important lever in the fight against corruption (Transparency International, 2021), as well as the creation of new public-private partnerships to transform public services (Transparency Maroc, 2020).

CORRUPTION IN MOROCCO: ALARMING AND WELL-ESTABLISHED FACTS

Different sources, both national and international, report worrying indices, facts and figures regarding the situation of corruption in Morocco. In 2021, the CPI (corruption index perception), published annually by the NGO Transparency International, gave Morocco a score of 39/100 points and placed it in the 87th position out of a total of 180 countries (Transparency International, 2021). A score that ranked it among the countries with "systemic corruption". It thus lost one point and one place compared to 2020, and 7 places compared to 2019. This result confirms the endemic nature of corruption in Morocco and especially its stagnation in this situation for a very long time: in 2012 and 2013, Morocco had a score of 37/100, which rose to 39 in 2014 and fell to 36 in 2015, then to 37 in 2016. A slight improvement was recorded in 2017 and 2018 (with a score of 43/100) before this score fell to 39 in 2021(Transparency International, 2021). Over the last 10 years, Morocco's average score is 39/100, which means that over the past decade, the fight against corruption in Morocco has stalled and it has made no significant progress. Yet the political discourse against corruption is strong, but so is the reality of corruption: we have on the one hand the law made up of rules, laws, norms, and obligations, and on the other a social practice where the possibilities of doing what the laws do not allow are developed. Non-respect for the rule of law tends to increase, with the corollary of the disintegration of social ties. Corruption is becoming commonplace and assumed as normal behavior, to such an extent that some of its acts are practiced in a confident and calm manner. Thus, whole swathes of exchanges are gradually escaping legal constraint and submitting to another normative order producing repeatedly corruptible exchanges, fueling undue gains, distorting the game of competition and equality of opportunity, increasing state spending, and significantly reducing its resources. The areas of law are receding and those of the shadows take their place, feed themselves and permeate the social construct. This anchoring of corruption is done in a rational manner because arbitration in favor of corruption still denotes a form of calculating the rationality of agents (Atia & Herrold, 2018; Becker, 1968). According to this author, the lower the perception of the risk incurred, whether, in terms of detection or sanction, the more deterrence loses its attributes, and the more corruption is accepted and the arbitration in its favor high (Ades & di Tella, 1997; Jain, 2001). The American economist Robert summarized the factors favoring corruption by the famous equation $C = M + D - A$, *"Corruption is equal to the sum of monopoly and power (discretion), which must be subtract responsibility (accountability)"* (Robert, 1991). In other words, the state's monopoly over public policy-making, combined with the authority of bureaucrats over public services, creates conditions conducive to corruption when it is neither controlled by transparency requirements nor hampered by accountability mechanisms (Ades & Di Tella, 1999). John Waterbury wrote forty-five years ago, that in Morocco *"corruption floats free and is manipulated, guided, planned and desired"*. (Waterbury, 1973)

In 2020, a survey carried out on behalf of the association Transparency Morocco, among a sample of 400 companies, revealed that only 10% of them participated regularly in public procurement and nearly 60% considered that the corresponding procedures are "complex, costly and tainted with corruption". In addition, 53% of respondents consider that "action by public authorities" against corruption is "very ineffective" and 19% consider it "ineffective" (Transparency maroc, 2020).

The Economic and Social Council, a constitutional institution, also presented a study on public procurement and corruption. In this report (Conseil Economique et Social, 2012), implicit reference is made to the lack of transparency, the absence of calls for tenders for certain orders, the non-existence of a joint appeal committee and the risks of conflicts of interest which could taint certain markets.

For its part, the Observatory of Corruption set up by Transparency Morocco, lists that during the year 2021 the sectoral distribution of corruption cases reported by the Moroccan press interested in descending order local communities 34%, housing-urban planning-real estate 14%, health 7%, police 6%, justice 5%, private sector 5%, trade and industry 4%, customs 3% and education 3% (Conseil Economique et Social, 2012).

As for the Court of Auditors, another constitutional institution, one of whose functions is to prevent the risks incurred by public management, its annual reports are full of proven cases of corruption and other forms of embezzlement, misuse of corporate assets, contracts that do not comply with the legislation in force, recurring malfunctions and shortcomings in the management of public orders and contracts, lack of traceability in the accounts, multiple forms of conflicts of interest and squandering of public funds in a number of state agencies, establishments and services (Cour des comptes, 2021).

The Moroccan factors for this anchoring of corruption are numerous: high level of social tolerance and corrupt behavior of actors, failing institutional mechanisms to combat it, weak prevention and absence of deterrence over time, the existence of a discretionary economic public power, predominance informational asymmetry and low probability of sanction (Banhamza, 2016; Brachet, 1992).

In these circumstances, corruption remains a formidable challenge, although the digital revolution is gradually changing the situation. Today, new technologies make it possible to reveal, prosecute, prevent, and even predict dubious practices that could previously be covered by the opacity of administrative machinery. The middle class – a growing, younger, more urban, and increasingly tech-savvy class – is now able to shed light on facts of corruption. It requires a better allocation of resources as well as an improvement in services. In terms of integrity and efficiency, its expectations are higher vis-à-vis the public sector, and the gap continues to widen between these increasingly strong aspirations and the insufficient capacities of the government to obtain results. This is also a root cause of the crisis of confidence in institutions that we observe in Morocco. However, this distrust can be overcome thanks to digitalization, thus allowing access to data is now considered a solution to be implemented to improve the delivery of public services and strengthen efficiency and integrity within public action.

OPENING AND PUBLICATION OF DATA

The ongoing digital revolution is an opportunity to reshape the way public services work. It also makes it possible to meet expectations and restore confidence in these services. The process of digitizing red tape is admittedly complex, as government agencies tend to work in silos, lacking interoperability frameworks to better communicate with each other. That said the greatest challenge of digitization remains political in nature, rooted in the political economy of data governance in the public sector (Klitgaard, 1991).

Thus, the opening and analysis of a mass of data can encourage transparency and improve the efficiency of the administration. More than 2.5 trillion bytes of data are produced every day (Barrenechea, 2019), and governments are increasingly releasing their own data to meet their open government commitments.

This abundance of data, coupled with rapidly improving access and analytical capabilities, is creating a new form of transparency that helps improve governance. Three elements are considered as prerequisites that will contribute to this virtuous process:

1. First, the data must be open, then published, and finally disseminated at an appropriate time to feed the thinking of those interested and/or developing public policies. This data allows political par-

ties, civil parties, civil rights defenders, and oversight institutions to hold governments to account in more effective ways than in the past. In recent years, as part of their open government agenda, some administrations in some countries have published their data on online portals integrating an increasing number of databases. According to the Open Data Index, which measures the degree of openness of data on a global scale, Taiwan, Australia, Great Britain, France and Finland are the countries that have made the most progress in this area (Global Open Data Index, 2016). By putting public data online, leaders are incentivizing public officials to improve the quality of that data, especially in subnational governments and administrations. For example, in 2016, the Colombian government suspended transfers to 125 municipalities that had not provided it with quality public expenditure data on time, as required by law.

To be usable, data published to the public must be easily understandable. Some administrations in some Latin American countries have begun to use advanced techniques in the field of publication and data processing. Thus, with the aim of establishing fiscal transparency, the Mexican Ministry of Finance has enriched open budget data through a latest-generation computer portal (De la Mora & Garduño, 2017), which notably presents data on public procurement, payments for public works and subnational transfers. Mexico City has become the first city to publish data on its public markets by displaying all related data. This approach concerns more than 1,400 contracts under the supervision of 19 public institutions and managed in collaboration with 231 service providers (De la Mora & Garduño, 2017).

In this quest for transparency, come emerging countries such as Mexico and Paraguay use georeferencing technologies to ensure the control and monitoring of investments, especially those concerning infrastructure, deemed to be the most vulnerable to corruption (Kahn *et al.*, 2018). The Development Bank of Brazil also uses these technologies to monitor the progress of projects financed by the Amazon Fund (BNDES, 2020), while the MapaRegalias portal launched by the Colombian government allows the monitoring of public investments financed through mining royalties (Lauletta *et al.*, 2019). And in order to further strengthen transparency and limit corruption in Colombia, some start-ups, such as Datasketch, use the information published to issue alerts (Datasketch, 2019). Also in Mexico City, and thanks to the Torre de Control portal, the Poder project revealed that almost 70% of the contracts related to the construction project of a new international airport had been awarded without a call for tenders. It also made it possible to have more information on the nature of the service providers and the value of their contracts in the total market value (Santiso, 2019). These kinds of initiatives and the creation of these platforms imply that changes are underway in terms of data governance and information management to implement them within bureaucracies that are accustomed to operating in silos and keeping jealously their data.

2. Beyond the sharing and publication of data, the latter must be used effectively when developing public policies. More and more governments offer free access to their databases, but unfortunately, these data are rarely downloaded by the parties supposed to be concerned. The trend is that they are most often used by civil servants to compensate for the lack of exchanges within their organizations or between the different administrations. The idea of implementing digitalization for the open government will be implemented gradually through, first, the process of publishing and opening data to the public, which mainly aims to reach a certain threshold of transparency, then, a second phase will be juxtaposed with an objective of applying the principle of responsibility for the publication of data with the final objective of improving services. The challenge is no longer just to publish

useful data in a timely manner, but to know how to use this data effectively to develop policies and enforce accountability. Often, it is associations, civil parties, start-ups and committed researchers who take advantage of new technologies and especially open data. This accessibility sheds light on obscure practices and trends. It is these actors, through their reports and their activism, who urge the public authorities to find ways to improve resource allocation and service delivery.

Moving forward in this project of moralization through the implementation of digitalization requires a real dialogue between data scientists and political decision-makers to better understand the challenges to be met by bureaucracies. In other words, we need to build partnerships and collaborations between those who identify the problems and those who propose digital solutions. This includes integrating digital specialists within government departments and agencies. This kind of alliance is already made in France, or by the establishment of an agency dedicated to digital transformation that works cross-functionally with the various administrations, as is the case in the United Kingdom.

3. The effective exploitation of the data cannot be effective with regard to the enormous quantity of data produced by the administrations. In order to better understand the government machine, improve its performance and bridge the gap between the objectives of public policies and their implementation, it would be necessary to cross-check data drawn from different databases. For example, the implementation of this strategy has enabled the Public Expenditure Observatory of the Brazilian Ministry of Transparency to detect irregularities in its social benefit programs (Graft *et al.*, 2016). The government was thus able to respond to realize significant savings and modify its benefit allocation policies.

Tax and customs authorities are increasingly using artificial intelligence and predictive analytics to detect fraud and prevent tax evasion (Walker-Munro, 2021; Rafay & Ajmal, 2014). Indeed, the tax services are pioneers in the use of data analysis to simulate the effects of tax and legislative reforms on the State budget and also on the behavior of the taxpayer. In 2019, the US Internal Revenue Service - the agency of the US federal government that collects income tax - prevented the payment of refunds in more than two million cases of identity theft or tax evasion. That's about one in every hundred refunds, or a total of over $15 billion (FBI, 2014).

In the UK, tax authorities use land records, credit card transactions, tax records data and social media analysis to detect fraudulent or hidden activity. The Connect system device mixes data from various sources, from the administration or from companies, which makes it possible to profile and access all the income of each taxpayer, to highlight inconsistencies and therefore to open investigations to collect amounts due (Sanghrajka, 2020). Thanks to this digital system, which cost 100 million pounds sterling in 2008, this investment enabled the tax authorities in the UK to recover 3 billion pounds (Sanghrajka, 2020). Its predictive algorithm also makes it possible to identify in the future people likely to practice tax evasion, and thus to define preventive actions, such as sending letters to remind implicitly people at risk of their omissions or let them know directly the consequences resulting from false declarations.

Several countries have started to actively promote the reuse of open government data for further digitization in both the public and private sectors. Since 2009, Spain has encouraged the reuse of open public data for private purposes through the Aporta initiative (Garcia & Maldonado, 2012). In Mexico, the federal government encourages the use of public data by the private sector through the Labora program (OECD, 2016b). These strategies work with and thanks to start-ups, which brew a large amount of data and act as intermediaries to produce information that is easily understood by the public. They exploit the information drawn from the data collected on the bases to which the government offers free access, to create value for public information which, more and more often, is transformed into economic value.

ADMINISTRATIVE RELIEF PROCEDURES

Digitization can serve as an effective strategy to limit the discretionary power of certain officials, who misuse it and may go so far as to ask for bribes. Automating administrative procedures and digitizing public services can reduce the risk of human-made misuse and tampering. Petty corruption has disastrous effects on public confidence in the administration. This form of corruption is often widespread in developing countries. According to the organization Transparency Morocco, in 2019, one in three Moroccan citizens had to pay a bribe (Guessous, 2020). It is customary to say that corruption greases bureaucratic wheels.

Indeed, the automation of administrative procedures and the digitization of public services can lay the foundations for an administration that is both more efficient and transparent. It makes services more agile, faster and smarter, while producing new data to better understand the internal mechanisms of the state machine (Santiso, 2019). However, the process of digitizing administrative procedures remains complex, with government agencies tending to work in silos and lacking interoperability frameworks. But the biggest challenge of digitization is of a political nature: the whole issue is to know who has an interest or not in this digital transformation and who owns, controls, shares and guarantees the security of data.

Making the bureaucracy nimbler and more open has a direct impact on public trust in government, as it improves the level of citizen satisfaction with public services. France has developed its digital services through an integrated portal that brings together all the services offered by the government (République Française, 2015). This approach allows citizens to access all public services through a one-stop shop. Uruguay plans to offer online access to all of its public services this year. In Morocco, there is almost no administrative procedure that can be carried out entirely online. The task of administrative digitization is technically easy, but not culturally: the introduction of digital services often encounters resistance from interest groups who fear losing the advantages, power and interest of employment (El Mesbahi, 2013).

However, the digitization of Byzantine administrative procedures will have no interest if it has not been preceded by a simplification, a reassessment of their relevance and their costs. Bureaucrats are often the first victims of the administrative maze in terms of the operational efficiency of the tasks required of them, and in terms of the level of productivity of the organization they represent. Moreover, the digitization of public services can only be effective if the public services themselves are redesigned. It is necessary to reconsider the logic of the legislation at the origin of the bureaucratic procedures. The adoption of smarter legislation, therefore, goes hand in hand with administrative simplification. This objective is a challenge in itself: the programs for digital transformation and better legislation are not always mutually reinforcing, as they are often carried out by separate government entities, whose concerns and objectives diverge.

In Portugal, the Simplex program – whose results are promising – includes a multitude of measures aimed at redefining administrative procedures by involving civil society and civil servants (ePortugal, 2020). These targeted initiatives include various measures, ranging from simplifying the formalities for obtaining identity documents, vehicle registration and business registration, to facilitating the payment of taxes thanks to pre-completed declarations and passing through the registration of deaths and births.

These innovations are not only based on the very latest technologies, but they also use the results of behavioral science research to put the citizen back at the center of administration.

Administrative modernization through digitalization is not just a technological issue. It is also about changing behaviors and values, taking advantage of new technologies and information extracted from the mass of data created and assembled, with the idea of making bureaucracies more agile and responsive. It is only gradually that digital public services are entering a new phase of reform aimed at anticipating citizens' needs and offering proactive services (pre-filled forms, interactions, suggestions, sending instant notifications by email or SMS, etc.). Originally, the digital transformation of the administration prioritized e-government and the automation of public services for economic reasons aimed at reducing costs. However, over the past ten years, it has moved into a second phase of transformation – digital in nature and open by default – which puts citizens back at the heart of public interventions. This process is now entering the third phase of reform, in favor of an agile, responsive, smarter government, based on data analysis and, henceforth, artificial intelligence.

In this myriad of technologies serving as support for a digital transformation, the Blockchain would be an innovative technology that could serve as an anti-corruption remedy. Indeed, some key features of distributed ledger technology can help curb corruption, including in the areas of protecting identities, tracking funds, recording assets, and awarding contracts. Given its decentralized nature, the immutability of its records and the traceability of its transactions, this technology can represent an automatic audit trail. A growing number of proofs of concept and pilot projects are emerging in areas such as identity, land, and property titles, as documented by New York University's GovLab and the Center for Stanford Social Innovation (NYU, 2022).

BLOCKCHAIN: PROMISING POTENTIAL TO BE UNLOCKED

Although many people associate blockchain technology only with cryptocurrency transactions, it can still be used to record any type of exchange, for example, real estate sales, paperwork, identification of identities or the chain of supply. In terms of development, blockchain is still in its infancy. According to Forbes magazine, and already in 2017, only 0.5% of the world's population used the blockchain, while more than 50% of the population had access to the Internet (del Castillo & Schifrin, 2022). And just like the Internet, it is almost certain that there will be an explosion of users and users over time; Victor Hugo said, "*Nothing is more powerful than an idea whose time has come*".

This blockchain technology has two distinct characteristics that make it a powerful tool against fraud and corruption:

First, it ensures an unprecedented level of information security and the integrity of the records it manages, guaranteeing their authenticity. It eliminates opportunities for tampering and the risks associated with moral failings or circumstances when handling data or carrying responsibility.

Second, blockchain provides a transparent and decentralized system to record a sequence of transactions. It creates an immutable trace allowing full traceability of each transaction. It thus provides unwavering audit support to identify suspicious activity or wrongdoing by leaving enough digital clues to identify bad actors. In this regard, three proposals for blockchain applications in the fight against fraud and corruption can be put forward. This is the control of transactions carried out for the execution of public contracts, registration and transactions of goods, and identity verification. These three applications of blockchain technology to establish transparency will be briefly developed:

1) Current government payment systems and cash transfers in public procurement processes are particularly vulnerable to corruption. They have multiple points of human discretion that make them susceptible to fraud and tampering and therefore create opportunities for corruption. Limiting the physical interaction between citizens and officials, the business and the manager will reduce opportunities for positional rent-seeking. Every year, according to the OECD, about $9.5 trillion is spent on public sector contracts and major public investment projects. Corruption is estimated to account for 10% of the total cost of doing business globally and up to 25% of the cost of public investment and procurement contracts in developing countries (OECD, 2016a). The World Bank estimates that businesses and individuals pay $1 trillion in bribes every year, which is 2% of the global GDP[2]. Thus, blockchain technology-enabled solutions now provide end-to-end moralization and transparency in public contracts, allowing the detection of cartels, bid-rigging, and ghost suppliers. Blockchain could add critical value to public procurement through the delivery of goods and services, by locking down critical information at every stage of the supply chain that can be monitored, tracked, and audited. Moreover, these "smart contracts", which are still in the experimental stage, would allow the automatic exchange of real assets to be programmed in an unalterable blockchain, which would run autonomously according to programmed conditions. This would reduce the possibility of manipulating the process and will increase the speed of transactions.
2) The registration of assets and land titles in reliable and secure registers could greatly contribute to eradicating expropriation, land predation and fraud in developing countries which are rampant (Nakitende *et al.*, 2021) and affect the people, often vulnerable, who own property and subsistence land, but not yet properly registered in the land registry. By proceeding with this registration, financial institutions and banks can finance projects carried out by vulnerable owners as collateral for these assets, and thus release the "dead" capital (Soto, 2003). Sweden is testing a blockchain-based land registry to make details of real estate transactions visible to all interested parties. Georgia has started registering land titles using blockchain. This technology is also being tested to create business records and provide reliable information on ultimate beneficial ownership. It thus enables effective monitoring for financial regulators, law enforcement and tax authorities. In the United States, the State of Delaware has launched an initiative that will allow companies to use the blockchain for the registration and transfer of ownership of shares.
3) Blockchain can also help improve identity verification conditions for any type of relationship related to public services. It would thus be to verify in the form of a single register the services and aid likely to be granted to everyone. This digital application for developing countries makes it possible to better target and manages the allocation of public resources for the fight against poverty and vulnerability, with a double concern for integrity in declarations and equity in the collection of subsidies. India has taken a step forward by already providing a unique digital identity to its citizens using biometric technology under the Aadhaar program. Estonia runs a national digital identity system where personal information is stored on a distributed ledger that an individual controls.

However, early experiences also suggest that blockchain-based solutions will not work in all institutional settings, and several prerequisites need to be met. These include that existing data must be open and accurate, records must be digitized, and the digital identity system must be trusted. There must also be sufficient connectivity, a technology-aware population, and existing technical support services. Unfortunately, this is not yet the ideal situation in many developing countries, where they often must concentrate on "the essentials". This is why, to paraphrase Allen Schick, most developing countries in their digitalization process should not, from the outset, try New Zealand's reforms by skipping critical stages of institutional digital development (Schick, 1998).

TRANSFORMING THE ADMINISTRATION AND ACCELERATING INNOVATION

Digitization and new technologies challenge the state monopoly in certain areas and promote public-private partnerships. Blockchain is a game changer due to its integrity and decentralized nature. In the old systems, data, assets, and transactions were managed by centralized state institutions. Today, thanks to the blockchain, these elements can be managed by decentralized groups of autonomous entities capable of certifying information, encrypting data, and administering the service. Blockchain, therefore, has the potential to enable private entities to participate in the decentralized provision of public services, which the central state administration has traditionally monopolized. By allowing easy access, and above all by restoring trust, the blockchain is able to reinvent the administration in a more honest and transparent way, and can, on the occasion, introduces a public service approach in an innovative way.

Innovation labs launched by the government or in partnership with private actors can be used to incubate and accelerate innovations in the public sector. Colombia inaugurated a new Public Innovation Lab in December 2018, while Chile's State Services Innovation Lab is incubating projects to increase the agility of public services. Portugal, for its part, created its innovation laboratory in the same direction in 2017. All its initiatives jointly exploit digital technologies and behavioral data to find new solutions to old problems. Public innovation labs provide a space for the emergence of a new type of public-private partnerships to reinvent government by incubating private sector solutions to address public sector challenges.

Governments can therefore collaborate with private companies and start-ups to uncover invisible practices and trends or improve public services. According to the consulting firm Gartner, administrations spend each year more than 400 billion dollars to finance digital technologies (Gartner, 2022). Private-public partnerships can help governments become more agile, open, and innovative. They can also offer effective solutions to those who wish to have a digitalization and data analysis service but struggle to recruit data scientists and have the skills for implementation.

Thus, and to circumvent this handicap, private companies and start-ups working with the public sector to improve the government machine in what is called GovTech. More and more leaders are realizing the transformative potential of these GovTechs vis-à-vis corruption within the administration and are establishing new public-private partnerships to fight against it, and for some countries, accelerate the process of digital transformation in public services. In November 2018, the city of Paris hosted the world's first-ever GovTech Summit. This event reflects the dynamism of public entrepreneurs and startups that imagine the government of tomorrow in certain advanced countries such as the United Kingdom, France, and Canada. In 2017, the British government created a "GovTech catalyst" with a specific fund. Government officials can use it to flag a problem that will be analyzed by private companies and start-ups, and whose solutions can then be incubated. The idea is to encourage people to think differently and to innovate the functioning of administrations, improve public services and reduce transaction costs.

CONCLUSION

Some experiences around the world have shown that the approaches anti-corruption through the implementation of digitalization have had more success than global political discourses of moralization. This last approach was not very effective in the case of Morocco. However, it seems that the approach of developing and encouraging the all-digital at the level of the civil service can mitigate the level of systemic corruption such as that which is rife in Morocco. Corruption in developing countries is not the cause of underdevelopment, but the consequence of a mode of global political and economic management that has shaped the feeling of impunity for a very long time.

However, digital eruption and new technologies are not only disrupting our lives but also transforming the public actions of governments. The latter, by becoming more digitally appropriate and adopting digital innovations, are not only fighting corruption but also modernizing bureaucracy and rebuilding the relationship with citizens, whose expectations are growing in terms of quality, speed and of integrity. This process of digitization will inevitably go through the opening and publication of data, accountability and rendering of accounts, the effective use of data, the adaptation of laws, the implementation of appropriate applications and the encouragement of public-private partnerships for the implementation of adapted technologies, and the installation of good applications in the service of the administration and the taxpayers.

However, if digitalization has tremendous potential for moralizing and modernizing public action, governments must still protect themselves against the new threats of the digital world. The digital shift exposes people to piracy and falsification, even as citizens are becoming more and more sensitive to the protection of their personal data. Social media algorithms and the dissemination of false information can contribute to polarizing debates and influence the conduct of good procedures. In short, the digital revolution brings hope, but it should not be approached with naivety.

DECLARATION

The author declares that the manuscript follows ethical standards and there are no potential conflicts of interest with respect to the research, authorship and/or publication of this chapter.

DISCLAIMER

The contents and views of this chapter are expressed by the author in his personal capacity. It is not necessary for the Editor and the Publisher to agree with these viewpoints, and they are not responsible for any duty of care in this regard.

ACKNOWLEDGMENT

The author extends sincere gratitude to

• The Editor and the International Editorial Advisory Board (IEAB) of this book who initially desk reviewed, arranged a rigorous double/triple blind review process, and conducted a thorough, minute, and critical final review before accepting the chapter for publication.

• All anonymous reviewers who provided very constructive feedbacks for thorough revision, improvement, extension, and fine tuning of the chapter.

• All colleagues, assistants and well-wishers who assisted to complete this task.

REFERENCES

Ades, A., & di Tella, R. (1997). The New economics of corruption: A survey and some new results. *Political Studies*, *45*(3), 496–515. doi:10.1111/1467-9248.00093

Ades, A., & Di Tella, R. (1999). Rents, competition, and Corruption. *The American Economic Review*, *89*(4), 982–993. doi:10.1257/aer.89.4.982

Atia, M., & Herrold, C. E. (2018). Governing through patronage: The rise of NGOs and the fall of civil society in Palestine and Morocco. *Voluntas*, *29*(5), 1044–1054. doi:10.100711266-018-9953-6

Banerjee, A., Mullainathan, S., & Hanna, R. (2012). *Corruption* (w17968). National Bureau of Economic Research. doi:10.3386/w17968

Banhamza, M. (2016, February 3). *EU/Morocco trade: How can a David engage in a win-win situation with a Goliath?* Retrieved from https://politheor.net/eumorocco-trade-how-can-a-david-engage-in-a-win-win-situation-with-a-goliath/

Barrenechea, M. (2019, January 24). Les données ont une pierre angulaire: La confiance. *Globb Security. FR*. Retrieved from http://globbsecurity.fr/les-donnees-ont-une-pierre-angulaire-la-confiance-45128/

Becker, G. S. (1968). Crime and punishment: An economic approach. *Journal of Political Economy*, *76*(2), 169–217. doi:10.1086/259394

BNDES. (2020). *Amazon fund*. Rio de Janeiro: The Brazilian Development Bank. Retrieved from https://www.bndes.gov.br/SiteBNDES/bndes/bndes_en/Institucional/Social_ and_Environmental_Responsibility/amazon_fund.html

Brachet, P. (1992). *Corruption & sous-développement au Maroc*. L'Harmattan.

Conseil Economique et Social. (2012). *La commande publique Levier stratégique de développement* [Public procurement Strategic lever for development verification]. Retrieved from https://www.cese.ma/media/2020/10/Avis-La-commande-publique-levier-strat%C3%A9gique-de-d%C3%A9veloppement-%C3%A9conomique-et-social.pdf

Cour des comptes. (2021). *Rapport relatif à l'audit des comptes des partis politiques et à la vérification de la sincérité de leurs dépenses au titre du soutien public: Année 2020* [Report on the audit of the accounts of political parties and the verification of the sincerity of their expenditure for public support: Year 2020]. Retrieved from https://www.courdescomptes.ma/fr/Page-27/publications

Datasketch. (2019). *Welcome to open government—Datasketch Newsletter Open Gov #0*. Retrieved from https://www.datasketch.co/newsletter/open-government/issue-0-welcome/

De la Mora, D., & Garduño, J. (2017). The Road to Budget Transparency in Mexico. *International Budget Partnership*. Retrieved from https://internationalbudget.org/publications/road-to-budget-transparency-in-mexico/

de Soto, H. (2003). *The mystery of capital: Why capitalism triumphs in the West and fails everywhere else*. BasicBooks.

del Castillo, M., & Schifrin, M. (Eds.). (2022). *Forbes Blockchain 50 2022*. Retrieved from https://www.forbes.com/sites/michaeldelcastillo/2022/02/08/forbes-blockchain-50-2022/?sh=b20678331c6c

Dimant, E., & Tosato, G. (2018). Causes and effects of corruption: What has past decade's empirical research taught us? A survey. *Journal of Economic Surveys*, *32*(2), 335–356. doi:10.1111/joes.12198

El Mesbahi, K. (2013). La prévention de la corruption au Maroc, entre discours et réalité [Corruption prevention in Morocco, between rhetoric and reality]. *Pouvoirs*, *145*(2), 83–97. doi:10.3917/pouv.145.0083

ePortugal. (2020). *Government announces Simplex programme 2020-21*. Retrieved from https://eportugal.gov.pt/en/noticias/governo-apresenta-programa-simplex-2020-21

FBI. (2014). Investigating tax refund fraud. *Federal Bureau of Investigation*. Retrieved from https://www.fbi.gov/news/stories/investigating-tax-refund-fraud

Garcia, E. G., & Maldonado, S. L. S. (2012). Reuse of public sector information in Spain: A solid foundation for a promising future. *Textos Universitaris de Biblioteconomia I Documentació, 29*.

Gartner. (2022). *Gartner forecasts worldwide public cloud end-user spending to reach nearly $500 billion in 2022*. Retrieved from https://www.gartner.com/en/newsroom/press-releases/2022-04-19-gartner-forecasts-worldwide-public-cloud-end-user-spending-to-reach-nearly-500-billion-in-2022

Global Open Data Index. (2016). *Place overview*. Open Knowledge Foundation. Retrieved from http://index.okfn.org/place.html

Graft, A., Verhulst, S., & Young, A. (2016, January). *Brazil's open budget transparency portal. Making public how public money is spent*. Omidyar Network. Retrieved from https://odimpact.org/files/case-study-brazil.pdf

Guessous, H. (2020, January 23). Morocco loses 7 places in 2019 corruption perceptions index. *Morocco World News*. Retrieved from https://www.moroccoworldnews.com/2020/01/291922/morocco-corruption-index

Hibou, B., & Tozy, M. (2009). La lutte contre la corruption au Maroc: Vers une pluralisation des modes de gouvernement? [The fight against corruption in Morocco: towards a pluralization of modes of government?]. *Droit Social*, *72*(2), 339–357. https://doi.org/10.3917/drs.072.0339

Jain, A. K. (2001). Corruption: A Review. *Journal of Economic Surveys*, *15*(1), 71–121. https://doi.org/10.1111/1467-6419.00133

Kahn, T., Baron, A., & Vieyra, J. C. (2018, November). *Digital Technologies for Transparency in Public Investment: New Tools to Empower Citizens and Governments* (Discussion Paper No. IDB-DP-634). Inter-American Development Bank. doi:10.18235/0001418

Klitgaard, R. (1991). *Controlling corruption*. University of California Press.

Lauletta, M., Rossi, M. A., Vieyra, J. C., & Arisi, D. (2019, November). *Monitoring Public Investment: The Impact of MapaRegalías in Colombia*. Inter-American Development Bank. doi:10.18235/0002014

Nakitende, M. G., Rafay, A., & Waseem, M. (2021). Frauds in Business Organizations: A Comprehensive Overview. In A. Rafay (Ed.), *Handbook of Research on Theory and Practice of Financial Crimes* (pp. 21–38). IGI Global. doi:10.4018/978-1-7998-5567-5.ch002

North Africa Post. (2020, September 16). *Corruption costs Moroccan economy up to 7% of GDP annually – Finance Minister.* Retrieved from https://northafricapost.com/43844-corruption-costs-moroccan-economy-up-to-7-of-gdp-annually-finance-minister.html

NYU. (2022). *The Governance Lab (The GovLab)*. NYU Tandon School of Engineering. Retrieved from https://engineering.nyu.edu/research-innovation/centers/governance-lab-govlab

OECD. (2016a). *Preventing corruption in public procurement*. Paris: The Organisation for Economic Co-operation and Development. Retrieved from https://www.oecd.org/gov/ethics/Corruption-Public-Procurement-Brochure.pdf

OECD. (2016b). *Open government data review of Mexico: data reuse for public sector impact and innovation*. Paris: The Organisation for Economic Co-operation and Development. Retrieved from https://www.oecd.org/gov/digital-government/open-government-data-review-of-mexico-9789264259270-en.htm

Rafay, A. (Ed.). (2019). *FinTech as a Disruptive Technology for Financial Institutions*. IGI Global. doi:10.4018/978-1-5225-7805-5

Rafay, A. (Ed.). (2021). *Handbook of Research on Theory and Practice of Financial Crimes*. IGI Global. doi:10.4018/978-1-7998-5567-5

Rafay, A., & Ajmal, M. M. (2014). Earnings Management through Deferred Taxes Recognized under IAS 12: Evidence from Pakistan. *Lahore Journal of Business*, *3*(1), 1–19.

Raman, R. (2018). *Global corruption: People pay $1 trillion in bribes every year*. Raman Media Network. Retrieved from https://www.ramanmedianetwork.com/global-corruption-people-pay-1-trillion-in-bribes-every-year/

République Française. (2015). *Bienvenue sur le site officiel d'information et de démarches administratives* [Welcome to the official website for information and administrative procedures]. Retrieved from https://www.service-public.fr/

Sanghrajka, J. (2020). HMRC's Connect computer and investigations. *Taxation*. Retrieved from https://www.taxation.co.uk/articles/hmrc-s-connect-computer-and-investigations

Santiso, C. (2019). Révolution numérique et transformation de l'action publique [Digital revolution and transformation of public action]. *Politique Etrangere*, 2, 129–142. https://doi.org/10.3917/pe.192.0129

Schick, A. (1998). Why Most Developing Countries Should Not Try New Zealand's Reforms. *The World Bank Research Observer*, *13*(1), 123–131. https://documents1.worldbank.org/curated/en/597171468289000828/pdf/766180JRN0WBRO00Box374385B00PUBLIC0.pdf

Transparency International. (2021). *Corruption perceptions index*. Retrieved from https://www.transparency.org/en/cpi/2021

Transparency Maroc. (2020). *Rapport moral*. Retrieved from https://transparencymaroc.ma/transparency-maroc-lance-son-rapport-moral-au-titre-de-lannee-2020/

Walker-Munro, B. (2021). Tax Enforcement in the Black Economy: Tackling disruptive Challenges. In A. Rafay (Ed.), *Handbook of Research on Theory and Practice of Financial Crimes* (pp. 356–380). IGI Global. doi:10.4018/978-1-7998-5567-5.ch019

Waterbury, J. (1973). Endemic and planned corruption in a monarchical regime. *World Politics*, *25*(4), 533–555. https://doi.org/10.2307/2009951

ENDNOTES

1 Former Justice of the Supreme Court of the United States (1856-1941).

2 For more information see the World Bank website: https://www.worldbank.org/en/events/2021/01/27/finding-fraud#:~:text=Finding%20Fraud%20Event%20Replay&text=According%20to%20the%20United%20Nations,percent%20of%20annual%20global%20GDP.

Chapter 14
Financial Cybercrimes During COVID-19 Pandemic:
The Case of Africa

Usman Sambo
Yobe State University Damaturu, Nigeria

Babayo Sule
Federal University of Kashere, Nigeria

Misbahu Ibrahim Zamfara
Gombe State University, Nigeria

Marie G. Nakitende
Uganda Martyrs University, Uganda

ABSTRACT

The COVID-19 pandemic has influenced and altered the daily routine of the masses around the globe. The pandemic has far-reaching economic, political, social, and cultural implications on the African continent. Although Africa witnessed low levels of infections and deaths as compared to other continents, African socio-economic life was affected tremendously. This scenario facilitated the increased social media usage for source information, communication, and socializing in Africa. The study examined how COVID-19 caused increased social media use in Africa and the corresponding cybersecurity threats. Documented sources were used for data sourcing while empirical data analysis was used to discuss the ideas. The study revealed that COVID-19 significantly increased the number of social media users in Africa and has a correlation with cybersecurity threats and cybercrimes. The study observed that there is a need to secure African cyberspace due to the significant increase in social media activities.

DOI: 10.4018/978-1-6684-5007-9.ch014

INTRODUCTION

The novel Corona Virus popularly known as 'COVID-19' was declared a global pandemic in March 2019 by the World Health Organization (WHO) after the nature and the level of devastation of the disease became uncontrollable (Osler, 2019). The mysterious disease emanated from the industrial city of Wuhan in China in December 2019 and quickly spread to other parts of the world at the speed of light (Zizek, 2020). The pandemic has so far infected millions of people across the world, killed hundreds of thousands, grounded all economic activities and it has affected and influenced political decisions and policy responses by world governments, international organizations and agencies and all global key players in the affected sectors particularly the health sector (Rosberg & Knell, 2020 and Hochberg, 2020). Africa is one of the continents that are affected by COVID-19 pestilence in the early months of 2020. The nature and trend of devastation in Africa are softer than in American and European countries in terms of incidences of infection and deaths but the African economy which is vulnerable in comparison with its American and European counterparts is where the virus hit hard (Hruby, 2020 and Samaddar, 2020).

In the wake of the COVID-19 epidemic, many world countries witnessed their daily livelihood activities abruptly halted. Hence, the scramble for alternative strategies commenced. One of the plausible methods of operation to keep the world going and to engage the various stakeholders actively in responding to countering the virus is the use of digital means (Kredens, 2020). The global revolution in internet service and the explosion of the digital economy linked the world to an era of globalization unprecedented in the history of mankind (Buchanan, 2016). Internet and the digital revolution compelled all for devising means of securing personal details and private data and information. This was the foundation for Cybersecurity. Cybersecurity is necessary because of increased Cybercrimes by hackers, fraudsters and other groups that target individuals and critical national infrastructure (Antonucci, 2017). Currently, there are over 4 billion internet users in the world and nearly 5 billion smartphone users all over the world (Kemp, 2020). Internet spread across Africa rapidly in the 21st century. Almost all African countries are connected today. Cybersecurity is the protection of vital and private data including financial information and big data from unauthorized intrusion. Users of computers, smartphones and the internet are vulnerable and exposed to Cybercriminals once their information is uploaded online. Thus, modern computers, phones and digital gadgets are protected against hackers through effective Cybersecurity by individuals, organizations, businesses and governments (Kshetri, 2019; Rafay, 2023).

The spread of COVID-19 in African countries led to the adoption of the option of the use of the internet for various purposes such as official government meetings, seminars, webinars, conferences, e-learning for pupils and students in tertiary institutions and for private use by individuals as a repercussion of lockdown which kept millions of people at home (KPMG, 2020). Internet usage increased and this implied that the activities of hackers and Cybercriminals will also be intensified. With the increased internet usage and Cybercrimes, Cybersecurity is necessary to avoid losses of information on private finances, attacks on critical national infrastructures by criminals and attacking of vital information on health data such as progress on the treatment and prevention of the deadly COVID-19. Unfortunately, African countries are mostly weak in terms of the strengths of Cybersecurity and the protection of the digital sector. The Global Cybersecurity Index (2018) reported an abysmal performance by most African countries in terms of Cybersecurity index. This study examined practically how the outbreak of COVID-19 led to increased internet usage in Africa and by extension, the role and impact of Cybersecurity in responding to the explosion to protect private and official users. In doing so, the chapter analyzed the following: COVID-19: a global pandemic; the emergence of COVID-19 pandemic in Africa; discourses on internet revolution and Cybersecurity; Cybersecurity in Africa, COVID-19, internet usage and Cybersecurity in Africa and the practical implication for policy making in the conclusion part.

COVID-19: THE OUTBREAK OF A GLOBAL PANDEMIC

The Corona Virus pandemic outbreak devastated and shocked the world in awe because of the pattern in which it quickly spread, the level of casualties and the terrific effects that it has on the economy (Fagih & Forouharfar, 2022). The virus which is related to breathing difficulty usually transmits through interaction which earned it the status of a communicable disease. Severe fever and acute respiratory difficulties ensued which finally weakened the immunity system of the affected patients and hence, eventual death. Several efforts (Wang *et al.*, 2020; He *et al.*, 2020; Chen *et al.*, 2020; Liang, 2020; Grant *et al.*, 2020; Joseph & Ashkan, 2020) from the perspectives of medical sciences were made to respond to proffering an alternative treatment for the virus but it defies all scientific medical responses. COVID-19 is not the first time that the world is facing a global pandemic (Hosseini-Nezhad *et al.*, 2022). 100 year earlier, a similar pandemic known as the Spanish Flu devastated the world in which it was reported that 1/3rd of the world's population was infected with over 50 million deaths from the pandemic (Live Science, 2020; Jarus, 2020).

COVID-19 continues to spread worldwide. The John Hopkins University National Public Health Agencies reported as of 22nd March 2022 that the virus had spread to 188 countries with 473,341,149 total infections and 6,108,827 deaths worldwide with 409,492,504 recoveries and 57,739,818. The US is the largest number of cases with over 2.5 cases making it 25% of the global world. The country also has the world's highest death toll which is trailed by Brazil and UK. In China, where the virus emanated from, 85,000 cases were confirmed with a 4,600 death toll. South Africa and Egypt are the most affected countries in Africa in terms of reported incidences and deaths. In essence, the top ten countries that are most affected by cases of infection and deaths are presented below.

Table 1. Top ten countries with the highest cases and death toll from COVID-19

S/No.	Countries	Total Cases	Deaths	Active Cases
1.	US	81,460,646	999,451	17,166,299
2.	India	43,010,971	516,574	23,882
3.	Brazil	29,641,848	657,363	770,390
4.	France	24,161,339	141,085	1,321,033
5.	UK	20,413,731	163,929	1,549,720
6.	Germany	19,017,693	127,739	3,985,854
7.	Russia	17,637,795	365,373	925,622
8.	Turkey	14,708,850	97,347	268,732
9.	Italy	13,992,092	158,101	1,200,607
10.	Spain	11,378,784	102,053	569,562

It should be noted that the official figures are tentative. Numerous asymptomatic cases are not tested. In some cases, like Africa, a low level of the test is hindering officials from ascertaining the exact figure or near-accurate incidences. The COVID-19 pandemic has already entered its second stage of spread. Some countries that successfully contained the disease are now recording a second rise including Iran, Algeria, Israel, US and China, added the report (Damooei, 2022). The rapid spread of COVID-19 was made possible in a world that becomes complex, interwoven and interconnected with the fastest means of transportation such as planes, rapid boats, and fast track rails. International travel in a globalized world collapsed national boundaries to a larger extent (Choudhary *et al.* 2022). Thus, the spread of communicable diseases in one remote area in the world has the potentials of permeating the globe within a short period of time. Considering the havoc caused by the Spanish Flu, when world interconnectivity was far below the current trend, global key players and stakeholders in the health sector and other related fields became curious, terrified and braced for a possible worse situation. Currently, global politics are in interplay with the world powers such as China and US shifting blames and pointing accusing fingers at each other. For the first time, the US turned its back on WHO due to perceived mishandling of the case and its spread. The global economy is gradually and persistently collapsing while all social movements and activities were halted totally or partially. Although the global and local lockdowns are being relaxed, still there is no insight into the specific period in which the pandemic would be overcome for normalcy to be restored.

EMERGENCE OF COVID-19 PANDEMIC IN AFRICA

Before the outbreak of COVID-19 in Africa, the Continent had witnessed various pandemics and in essence, it has been battling deadly diseases for several decades. The HIV/AIDS pandemic broke out worldwide, but Africa became the most severe hit. Currently, over 80% of individuals living with HIV are obtained in Africa with about 64% of them living in Sub-Saharan Africa. HIV/AIDS killed millions worldwide, particularly in Africa where the cases were rampant. The H1N1 Bird Flu in 2010 also affected Africa sharply. However, the Ebola outbreak in 2014 hit Africa harder leading to the deaths of thousands and infections of hundreds of thousands. The recent COVID-19 pandemic quickly spread in Africa courtesy of global connections. When the pandemic emerged in China and spread to other European, Asian and American countries, millions of Africans were abroad for various human endeavors. These returnees were believed to have been the main source of the arrival of the disease in Africa. At the start of COVID-19, only two African countries recorded confirmed cases in February 2020. Within a week, the virus spread to over a dozen countries. As of 27th June 2020, over 44 African countries recorded confirmed cases. Since the first recorded outbreak case, the WHO has been assisting African countries with test kits, training some selected health personnel, and strengthening community surveillance. WHO has issued guidelines to African countries which are regularly updated as events are unfolding (WHO, 2020). Additionally, the African countries in their respective domain embarked on various policy responses ranging from healthcare, economic measures, palliatives, quarantine, lockdown, the establishment of isolation centers and fiscal adjustments (African Arguments, 2020).

In Africa, at the time of completing this chapter, the incidences of the virus stand at 11,591,000 representing 2.62% of the total global infections, total reported confirmed cases, 251,000 deaths and 178, 524 recoveries. The pattern of the distribution differs from one country to another. While many countries did not register any cases up to May, some have registered confirmed cases as early as February and

March. In May, every African country recorded a case with the last being Lesotho. The major countries that are affected are South Africa, Egypt, Nigeria and others. The following table indicated the top ten countries with the highest incidence of COVID-19 as of 22nd March 2022.

Table 2. African countries with the highest recorded cases of COVID-19

S/No.	Country	Cases	Position	Region
1.	South Africa	3,677,686	1	South Africa
2.	Morocco	1,161,290	2	North Africa
3.	Tunisia	999,441	3	North Africa
4.	Libya	496,778	4	North Africa
5.	Egypt	486,381	5	North Africa
6.	Ethiopia	468,786	6	East Africa
7.	Kenya	323,002	7	East Africa
8.	Zambia	313,203	8	South Africa
9.	Reunion	302,162	9	Central Africa
10.	Algeria	6265,079	10	North Africa

The Africa Centre for Disease Control (ACDC), under the auspice of the African Union, joined the bandwagon of the stakeholders in combating the spread of infectious disease. The ACDC collaborated with WHO and all African countries in providing support and guidelines for the prevention and curbing of the spread of COVID-19. For instance, ACDC presented some stages of prevention to African countries as a guideline including the unequivocal pronouncement that there is no vaccine currently for the treatment of the disease. However, the Centre suggests the following as best health practices for prevention: washing hands regularly, taking all prescribed vaccines, using influenza vaccines, covering your cough, staying at home, using facemasks, using hand sanitizers and practicing social distancing (Africa CDC, 2020). One major obstacle to the countering and prevention of COVID-19 in Africa is the political and socioeconomic settings of most countries on the Continent. This study observed that the African economy is backward and is not flourishing in the era of globalization typical of its counterparts in Asia, South America, and Eastern Europe. The long-protracted mis-governance by the African elites and the long exacerbated external control of the economy impoverished the subjects of the continent leading to a loss of hope in the government. While other countries in America, Europe and Asia are providing meaningful palliatives to their citizens, in Africa, the lockdown was introduced without adequate palliatives or bailouts that will stimulate economic growth. This has affected the informal sector which employs more than 70% of Africans. Containing the virus and its spread is making it difficult for the African authorities because of people's attitudes and perceptions toward the virus itself and their lack of confidence in the government (Campbell & McCaslin, 2020 and Hruby, 2020). Lockdown was not effective, violated and sabotaged by securities through bribery, debilitating hunger pushed people out of their homes in search of survival, failure to extend the palliatives to reach the needy and the perceived corruption scandal in personal enrichment using COVID-19 funds are all issues that surrounded the African response to COVID-19 pandemic (Onwujekwe, Orjiakor & Agwu, 2020). Nevertheless, despite the challenges, the intervention of WHO, financial support from the European Union (EU), the World

Bank and soft loans from the International Monetary Fund (IMF) are helping in arresting the rapid spread of the disease as expected.

COVID-19 has several challenges to health, economy, social and political aspects in Africa. COVID-19 has claimed over 200,000 lives in Africa. Additionally, the pandemic is interrupting basic health services delivery. The situation is further aggravating health conditions in Africa by stagnating the progress achieved in rolling back Human Immunodeficiency Virus/ Acquired Human Immuno Deficiency Syndrome (HIV/AIDS), Tuberculosis (TB), and Malaria. These diseases are considered among the major causes of ill-related deaths in Africa and the number of deaths from these diseases due to negligence in countering COVID-19 increased significantly by around 5% (Holtz, 2021). From 2020 and beyond, access to healthcare services dropped tremendously across more than 24 African countries as reported by the Global Fund (Holtz, 2021).

Apart from health risks, COVID-19 affected the African economies by lowering trade and investment from big partners such as China, America and European states. The demand for African goods, especially, raw materials from America, China and Europe sharply fall affecting domestic, intra and inter-African trade. Jobs were lost while new ones could not be created. The overall productivity declined. Agriculture was drastically halted or declined because of lockdowns and travel bans (OECD, 2020). It is estimated that COVID-19 will drop the African GDP by 1.4% with smaller economies facing a contraction of 7.8% resulting from export adjustments, the decline in tax revenue and the resources allocated in responding to the crisis. Overall, Africa is projected to lose 5% in revenue with total exports accumulated to have contracted by 17% (Gondwe, 2020).

COVID-19 affected the social segment in Africa by increasing the scorch of poverty. For instance, extreme poverty in Western Africa increased by 3% in 2021. The proportion of people in West Africa living with less than $1.90 a day increased from 2.3 percent in 2020 to 2.9 percent in 2021 (Gouro, 2022). The debt burden of countries in the region worsened because of slow economic growth that hinders repayment and compelled increased borrowing. The worsening economic condition has negatively influenced the food security and nutrition mode of men, women, and children in Africa. Around 25 million people in West Africa are unable to meet their basic food needs in the region, an increase of 34% compared to 2020. The situation is most severe in conflict-affected areas such as the Lake Chad Basin and the Sahel region (Gouro, 2022). COVID-19 is also affecting African security and human rights according to UNECA (2020). Most of the African regions are beleaguered by perennial conflicts and wars and the outbreak of COVID-19 may push further for aggressive clashes. This has been witnessed in Nigeria where banditry escalated during lockdown and travel ban and the intensified insurgents' attacks in West Africa, Mozambique, East Africa, and Central African states. The concern for human rights abuse is justified because the enforcement of lockdown is heralded with brutalities, bribery, and assault by security personnel (Sambo & Sule, 2021).

INTERNET REVOLUTION AND CYBERSECURITY: GLOBAL AND AFRICAN PERSPECTIVE

The revolution in science and technology in the early 19th century set the foundation for future discoveries in the world of mankind. By the 1960s, during the Cold War ideological battle, a new development emerged which is the explosion of communication and information technology. Computers were innovated which enabled the storage, transfer and sharing of big data, unprecedented in the history of the world. This development was progressively followed by the discovery of internet services. This era set the foundation for quick and easy spread as well as dissemination of information on a global scale in a minute (Franda, 2001). Internet is a technological breakthrough that secured the leverage for transferring and communicating large data within a blink of an eye from one computer to another and from one source to another such as email, mobile phones, satellite channels and other online destinations (Rafay, 2021a). By the 1970s and 1980s, the internet explosion was mostly regulated by government officials and organizations. By 1990, the internet became permeated and spread among personal and private users worldwide.

Businesses flourished online and e-commerce become considerably an important GDP combination especially in technologically-advanced countries (Tyner, 2009). In the modern world, the internet has succeeded in becoming a global addiction for billions of users worldwide. Life was made easier and communication became possible in a short time (Johnson, 2009). Internet communication in the world revolutionized various aspects of living in the world. For instance, technologies for health and medicine are simplified and disseminated quickly and easily using internet access (Sharif *et al.* 2018). Internet revolution succeeded further in proving and protecting intellectualism and copyright through plagiarism tests and other measures of enforcing compliance for originality in the sciences, social sciences and humanities (Gross and Harmon, 2016). Additionally, internet communication enabled digital democracy and the organization of party activities and politics through digital means (Gerbaudo, 2019). Tiwari & Buse (2020, p.1) emphasizes that innovation is better managed in the digital world today even though there are challenges of insecurity in Cyberspace. In essence, a study (Rahouma *et al.* 2020) suggested that the internet has graduated from official work to social internet in the 21st century owing to the gravity of private users.

The increasing number of internet users in the world is appreciative but so also the rising number of Cybercrimes (Rafay, 2021b). The Global Web Index (2020) reported in the second quarter of 2020 in April a tremendous rise in the use of the internet and social media worldwide. The report pegged the world population at 7.77 billion, 5.6 billion are reported as using mobile phones, and 4.57 billion are using the internet with 3.81 billion social media users. The global digital growth according to the report increased by +128 million mobile users in 2019, 301 million internet users and an increase of 304 million active social media users. The report interestingly suggested that people are considering spending more time on their digital devices resulting from the effects of lockdown which was the repercussions of the Corona Virus pandemic globally. The report also observed a big jump in digital activity in the wake of COVID-19, a significant increase in social media use, pronto adoption and utilization of e-commerce, an increase in the time spent on social media watching the news and playing games and some fresh opportunities for digital advertisers (Kemp, 2020). The top 20 users of the internet in the world according to countries' classification consist of China (850,000,000), India (560,000,000), United States (313,322,868), Indonesia (171,260,000), Brazil (149,057,635), Nigeria (126,078,999), Japan (118,626,672), Russia (116,353,942), Bangladesh (94,199,000), Mexico (88,000,000), Germany (79,127,551), Philippines (79,000,000), Turkey (69,107,183), Vietnam (68,541,344), United Kingdom (63,544,106), Iran (67,602,731), France (60,421,689), Thailand (57,000,000), Italy (54,798,299) and Egypt (49,231,493). These figures indicated two vital signs. One shows that the use of the internet is heralded population of a country and economic buoyancy. Africa is one of the continents that are witnessing rapid and significant internet penetration recently. However, current data indicated that Africa is the world region with the lowest penetration as shown in the table below.

Figure 1. Regional internet users distribution in the world in 2022 Q1

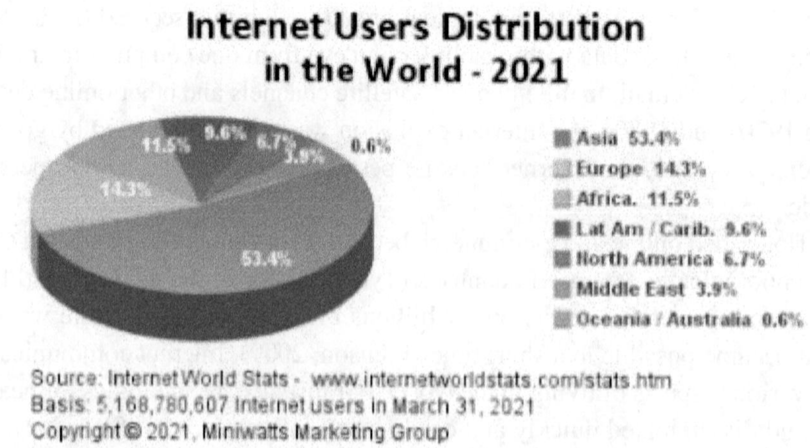

The penetration increased in the first quarter of 2022 from that of 2021 as shown below.

Figure 2. World internet usage and population statistics 2020 year Q1 estimates

WORLD INTERNET USAGE AND POPULATION STATISTICS 2022 Year-Q1 Estimates						
World Regions	Population (2022 Est.)	Population % of World	Internet Users 31 Dec 2021	Penetration Rate (% Pop.)	Growth 2000-2022	Internet World %
Africa	1,394,588,547	17.6 %	601,327,461	43.1 %	13,220 %	11.5 %
Asia	4,350,826,899	54.8 %	2,790,150,527	64.1 %	2,341 %	53.1 %
Europe	841,319,704	10.6 %	743,602,636	88.4 %	608 %	14.2 %
Latin America / Carib.	663,520,324	8.4 %	533,171,730	80.4 %	2,851 %	10.1 %
North America	372,555,585	4.7 %	347,916,694	93.4 %	222 %	6.6 %
Middle East	268,302,801	3.4 %	205,019,130	76.4 %	6,141 %	3.9 %
Oceania / Australia	43,602,955	0.5 %	30,549,185	70.1 %	301 %	0.6 %
WORLD TOTAL	7,934,716,815	100.0 %	5,251,737,363	66.2 %	1,355 %	100.0 %

By 2022, the more global populations increasingly frequented digital Cyberspace as shown in the figure below.

Figure 3. Countries with the largest digital populations in the world as of January 2022 in millions

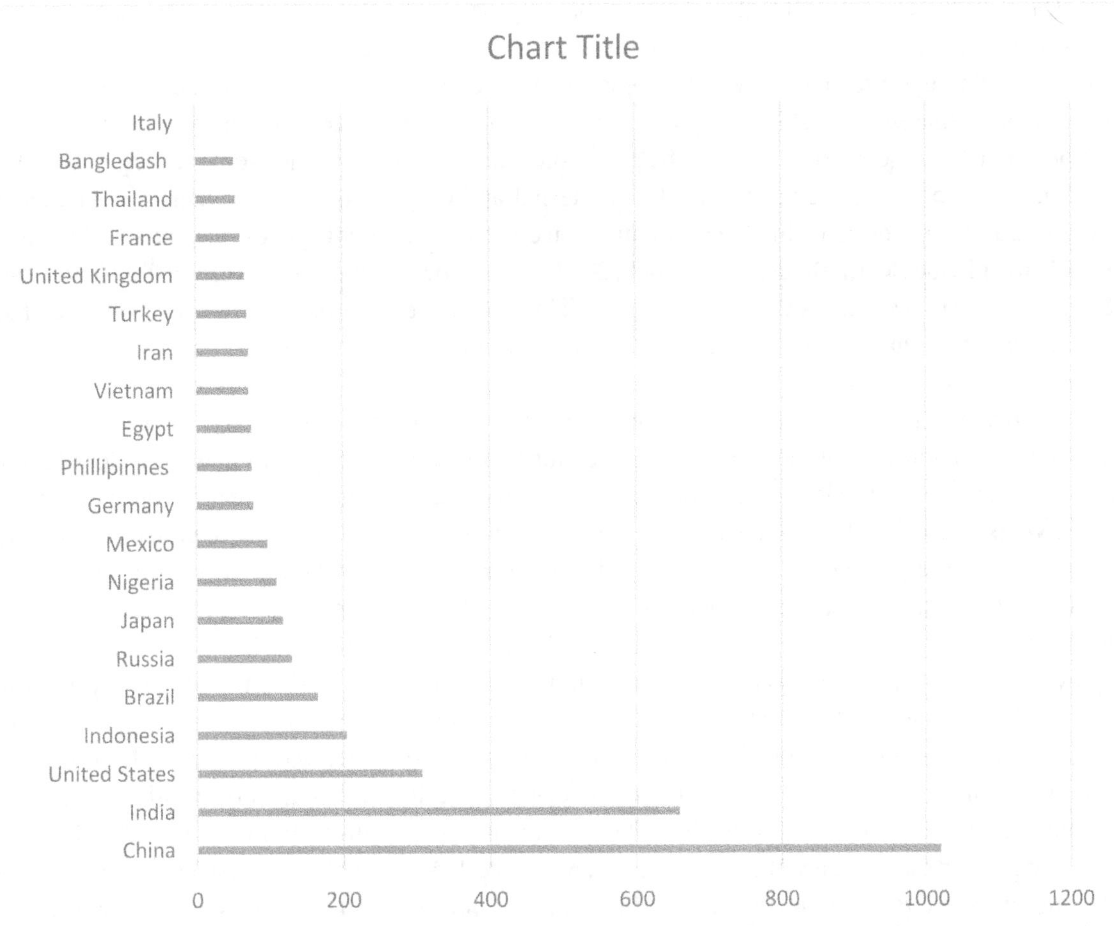

Thus, digital penetration globally indicates two recurring patterns. The number population by country and economic prosperity. The countries with the highest population in the world recorded a high digital presence in millions while other countries in Europe with economic prosperity followed immediately such as the UK, France, Germany, and Italy. This is, however, notwithstanding, to showcase that the European states of the UK, Germany, France, and Italy are not among the most populous globally even if they surpassed many less developed populous countries such as Pakistan in digital presence and penetration. One of the factors noted in the report by Statista (2022) that facilitates digital penetration is the outbreak of COVID-19 pushed a significant percentage of the global population toward the digital arena.

Thus, while Africa, the area of focus in this study, is still the lowest in terms of internet penetration, the percentage growth in usage in 2020 of 11, 567% in the first quarter of 2020 indicates that there is a correlation between the increased usage and the emergence of COVID-19 as discussed in the later sections of this chapter. Fundamentally, the overall world statistic is pointing toward an important phenomenon and a subject matter of great interest, Cybersecurity. Any increase in internet usage, digital activities and social media usage means an increase in the activities of Cybercriminals, fraudsters, and interlopers. Hence, it is germane here to link this section with the concept and dimension of Cybersecurity. Buzan & Hansen (2009) argue that in the post-Cold War, the global security paradigm has shifted to non-traditional security challenges such as political progress, social cohesion, economic prosperity, social issues such as poverty, disease, unemployment, and environmental issues such as climate change and hazards. These are further joined by recent developments such as cyber war and terrorism. Thus, state, and individual security should pay much concern to these non-traditional perspectives.

Cybersecurity is a security concept in the post-Cold war era which signifies some strategies and steps by nation-states to secure their countries from internal and external threats of cyber war. The use of Cyberspace and the internet in digital communication created a vulnerable position for attacks by Cybercriminals worldwide (Rittinghouse & Hancock, 2003). The Cybercriminals were responsible for the theft of $1 trillion world over in cash and stolen assets. This poses a terrible danger for users of Cyberspace including private, organizations and governments. That amount was a total of confirmed cases as of 2013, from 2013 to 2020, the incidences of Cybercrimes keep on rising. Recently, the Global Web Index (2020) confirmed a loss of over $2 trillion from hackers. Cybersecurity is necessary because critical and vital information and data of individuals, organizations, businesses and governments are stored online which made them vulnerable to unauthorized anonymous fellows to hack or steal (Touhill & Touhill, 2014). Cybersecurity involves a set of activities and strategic defensive modes for the protection of digital information and the prevention of unauthorized intrusion from criminals and hostile states who may target cash or critical national infrastructures (Bayuk *et al.* 2012). These strategies of protection require policies, programs, and laws to protect unauthorized access to individuals' information, organizations and governments' data (Meeuwisse, 2015). The strategies should also include the identification of the areas of vulnerabilities to strengthen them against attacks from unscrupulous elements (Fischer, 2009).

Cybersecurity emanated in the 1960s when the mainframe computer was innovated. In those days, chains, guardsmen, and gates were the main sources of security for computers. While managers of computers at that time were aware of the risks and threats to computers, the level of technology and information stored did not reach the level of industry standard. As technology advanced in the 1970s and 1980s, minicomputers were manufactured which enabled portability. This process posed more danger and risk to computer security. The period was accompanied by the internet revolution which further exposed computers to vulnerability and risks of viruses and stealing of information (Heintze & Thielborger, 2016). Still, in those periods, little attention was paid to computers and Cybersecurity because the world was sharply affected by the Cold War and traditional security debates. The nuclear threats cornered the attention of the world in an angle of a uni-linear thought of the security architecture globally. With the demise of the Cold War, the world redirected its attention to the information and communication sector which converted the world into a digital arena for financial and governmental transactions. This scenario set the foundation for policies, programs, and laws on Cybersecurity by different world countries and relevant international organizations (Rafay, 2019). Cybersecurity is now one of the emerging markets in the world to the extent that its growth is overtaking the global economy. For instance, in the European Union alone, 825, 000 professionals are expected to be engaged until 2025 and at the global level, it was estimated at 1.8 million. The financial implications comprise trillions of dollars from the proceeds (White Paper Cybersecurity Trends, 2019).

Cybercrime necessitated the improvement in Cybersecurity. There is no doubt that the internet and digital explosion facilitated economic growth, learning, e-governance, e-commerce, and social relativity. But it also comes with security challenges for individuals, organizations and governments (Beissel, 2016). Cybercrime started historically in the 1980s during the Cold War when the important subject of hacking by criminals involved useful data on nuclear proliferation, intelligence gathering and espionage on governments (Kshetri, 2019). Many world countries are registering losses financially and in big data from hackers on all the continents of the world including Africa (Mordi, 2019). Cybercrime is believed to have generated money worth $1 trillion in 2013, $1.5 trillion in 2018 and $2 trillion in 2020 across the world. This consisted of money stolen from many websites of organizations and hacking of vital data. The annual total amount realized from Cybercrimes consists of illegal online transactions worth $860 billion, trade secrets and IP thefts $500 billion, data trading worth $160 billion, crime-ware $1.6 billion and ransomware $1 billion. The US alone reported a cyber-fraud of $25 billion in 2010 only and AUS $94 million in 2015 in Australia. The major data breaches recently in 2018 included Yahoo $3 billion, Under Armour $150 million, eBay $145, EQUIFAX $110 million, Facebook 87 million, JP Morgan Chase $76 million, PlayStation $77 million, UBER 57.6 million and THE HOME DEPOT $56 million (Nohe, 2018). Africa lost $3.5 billion in 2017 to Cybercrimes in which Nigeria took the largest share of $645 million (Kshetri, 2019) with Nigeria alone losing about $800 (N288 billion) collectively to Cyberattacks in 2018 (Azeez, 2019). This figure from Nigeria is not surprising. The FBI reported Nigeria in 2018 as the third country after the United States and the United Kingdom with the highest incidences of Cybercrime owing to rampant hacking and fraud from criminals (FBI, 2018). ISACA reported that Cybercrime is still increasing in 2020 and the distribution of the pattern of crimes revealed that 22% are Cybercriminals, 19% are hackers, 11% are malicious insiders and 10% are non-malicious insiders and 9% are nation-states attacks and 8% hacktivists. The attack methods are mainly through social engineering (15%), advanced persistent threats (10%) and ransomware and unpatched system (9%) (ISACA, 2020).

The top ten countries in the world in terms of best performance in Cybersecurity are the United Kingdom, United States, France, Lithuania, Estonia, Singapore, Spain, Malaysia, Norway and Canada. In the list, the top ten countries in the middle which exhibited some efforts in Cybersecurity include Uzbekistan, Moldova, Ukraine, Azerbaijan, Cyprus, South Africa, Nigeria, Philippines, Serbia, and Tanzania. African countries are working hard as indicated in this middle group which comprises three promising countries. In the worst performing or bottom performance, the following countries made the list: Gabon, Palestine, Senegal, Sudan, Gambia, Ethiopia, Malawi, Iraq, Tajikistan and Algeria. These statistics indicated that Africa is the least in terms of Cybersecurity and hence, it may fall as the worse victim to cyber-attacks (Kshetri, 2019 and Mordi, 2019).

INTERNET AND CYBERSECURITY IN AFRICA

The internet revolution in Africa is not comparable with global progress. While the world especially America and the European continents has been utilizing the internet for over three decades for businesses, governance, election and learning, Africa is slowly but gradually catching up. Technology is, of course, occupying a significant space in the developing economies in the 21st century as businesses are moving digital and e-commerce is dominating transactions. Cybersecurity is facing threats in developing countries emanating from weak cyber laws and irregular Cybersecurity. Trust in the digital economy and Cyberspace is still low in these countries in comparison with advanced economies of the world (Shalhoub & Al Qasimi, 2010). Africa is facing challenges in Cybersecurity because of weak protection and high risk of vulnerabilities and an increasing Cybercrime which is flourishing in the continent more than in any other in the world. For instance, Symantec Corporation reported in 2013 that Cybercrime is increasing in Africa more than any region in the world and Cybersecurity experts reported that 80% of personal computers on the African continent are affected by viruses and other malicious software. The report further indicated that targeted attacks in Africa in 2012 increased by 42%. Additionally, it was observed that the internet and digital space are aiding terrorism in Africa through undetected communication by armed groups such as Al Shabab in Somalia and Boko Haram in Nigeria. The low level of security provisions to guarantee and safeguard the risk of a data breach, lack of technical know-how in terms of Cybersecurity, failure to establish a legal framework for Cybersecurity to combat Cybercrime and low level of utilization of ICTs all tantamount to challenges of Cybersecurity in Africa (UNECA, 2013). Therefore, African countries are advised to scale up strategies in preventing and countering Cybercrimes through a multi-dimensional approach in collaboration with local and international stakeholders.

Cybersecurity must receive much attention in Africa because the number of internet penetration is increasing higher since 2010. For instance, in the first quarter of 2020, the percentage of internet penetration in Africa reached 39.3%. This is significant even though, the rest of the world recorded 62.9% with a global average of penetration of 58.8%. Countries with high penetration percentage in 2020 consist of Kenya (87.2%), Libya (74.2%), Seychelles (72.5%), Mauritius (67%), Tunisia (66.8%), Morocco (64.3%), Cape Verde (63.3%), Mali (61.6%), Nigeria (61.2%), Gabon (58.8%), Senegal (58.2%), Algeria (58.0%), Zimbabwe (56.5%), South Africa (55%), Djibouti (55.5%), Zambia (53.7%) and Namibia (53%) (Internet World Stats, 2020). This sample is taken only from countries in the report who meet up the criteria of 50% penetration and above in this study. Africa recorded 11.5% global internet penetration in the first quarter of 2020 as against the rest of the world with 88.5% penetration. By 2022, internet penetration in Africa increased significantly due to extra time spent in digital Cyberspace emanating from the effects of COVBID-19 pandemics that drastically minimized physical appearance. This significant change is presented in figure 4.

Figure 4. share of internet users in Africa as of January 2022, by country by percentage (%)

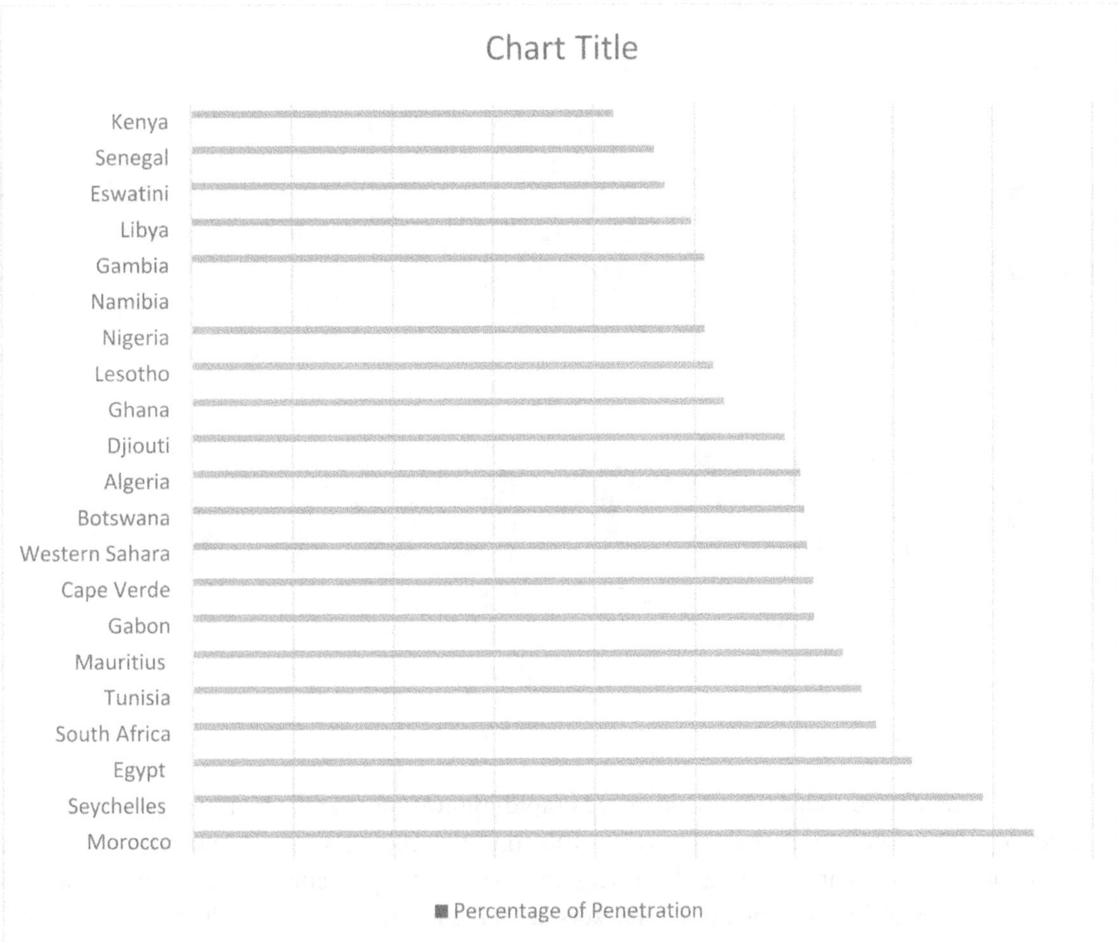

While the above figure indicates the top twenty African countries with a high number of digital penetrations by percentage. The figure below shows the number of internet users by country based on population.

Figure 5. Number of internet users in selected countries in Africa as of January 2022, by country (in millions)

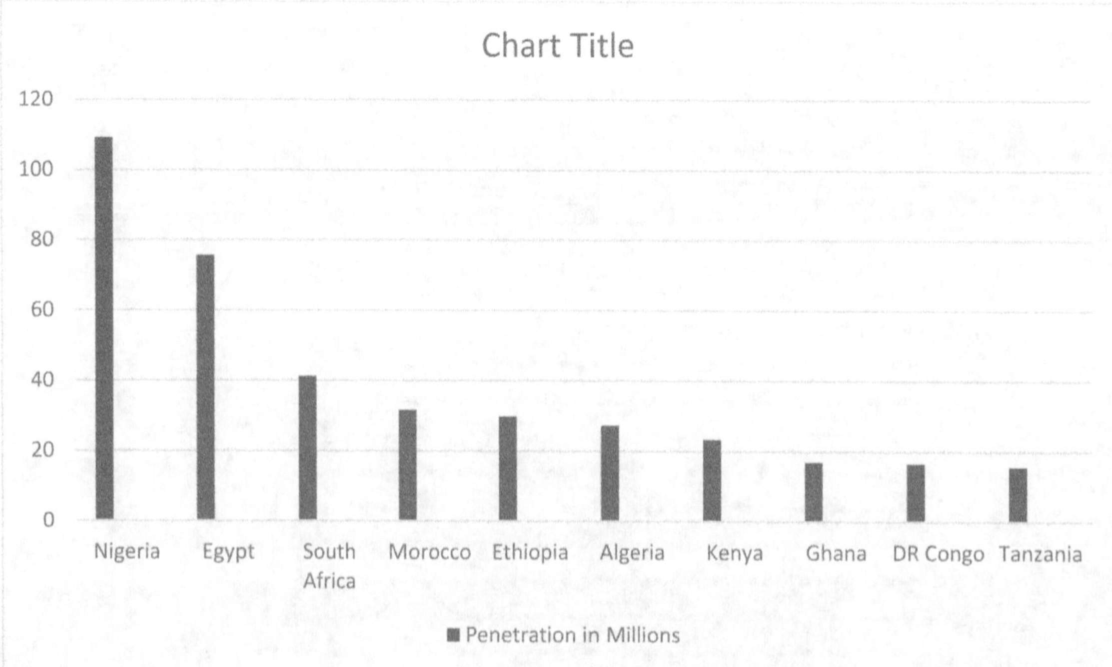

The above statistics revealed why Africa needs rapid improvement and a strategic approach toward Cybersecurity. Cybersecurity is the process of protecting the entry point and exit point of data and information in African computers, digital services and the internet particularly when it was discovered that recent activities of Cybercriminals and hackers are targeting Africa more than any other continent (Mordi, 2019). Cybersecurity in Africa, like other world regions, is battling with the legal issues of privacy, anonymity and weak regulations in punishing criminals (Kshetri, 2019). Kshetri (2019) further predicted that by 2022, over a billion people in Africa will have internet access. Furthermore, the study above observed that African economies and governance are tilting towards digital space which is providing leverage for Cybercriminals to attack. This necessitated intensified Cybersecurity. But not all African countries are showing commitment to Cybersecurity.

Cybersecurity in Africa is not strong yet to the extent that the Secretary-General of the International Telecommunications Unit, Hamadoun Toure, recognized Africa as the haven for Cybercriminals at the moment. The African Union Commission in collaboration with Symantec 2016 reported that 30 out of 54 African countries lacked specific legal provisions to fight Cybercrimes and utilize fully their digital space. The report relied on five major trends: social media, Scams, and Email threats, Smartphones and the Internet, Business Email Scams, the Rise of Ransomware, Crypto locker and Vulnerabilities. Africa requires a national risk plan, an effective Cybersecurity policy, programs for prevention, protection and immediate response to crimes and government policy and expenditure (Mathe, 2019). The 2018 Global Cybersecurity Index disclosed a low level of Cybersecurity performance for African countries as indicated below.

The Global Cybersecurity Index Report 2018 mentioned that Mauritius, Kenya and Rwanda are the top three performers in 2018 in terms of Cybersecurity. Their performances were measured based on legal provisions, technical support, organizational, capacity building and operation. The findings are presented in the chart below.

Figure 6. top three scores in the African region according to the five pillars of global cybersecurity index

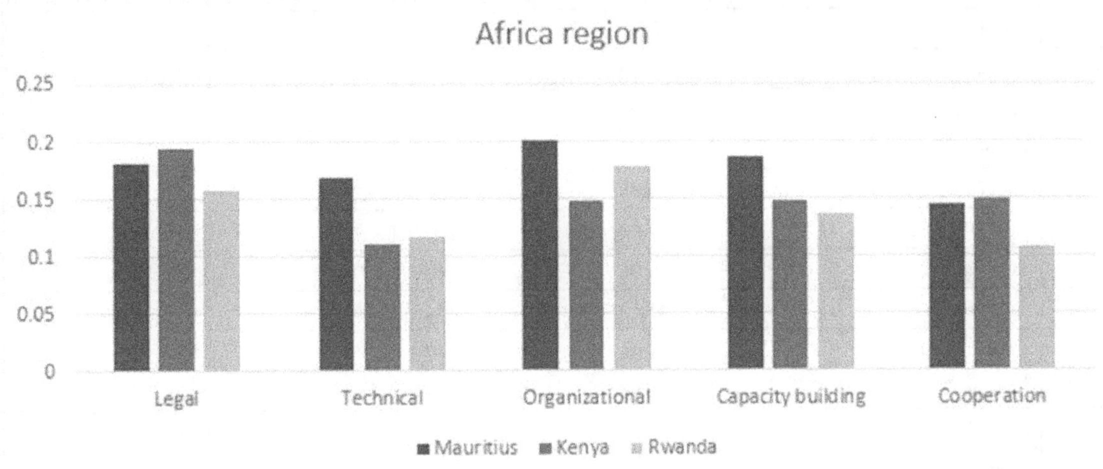

The overall performance of the African countries for the member states including their scores and ranks is presented in table 4 below for further details.

Table 4. African region, performance by countries, scores, regional and global ranking

S/No.	Member State	Overall Score	Regional Rank	Global Rank
1.	Mauritius	96.89	1	17
2.	Tanzania	90.58	2	37
3.	Ghana	86.69	3	43
4.	Nigeria	84.76	4	47
5.	Kenya	81.7	5	51
6.	Benin	80.06	6	56
7.	Rwanda	79.95	7	57
8.	South Africa	78.46	8	59
9.	Uganda	69.98	9	72
10.	Zambia	68.88	10	73
11.	Cote D' Ivoire	67.82	11	75
12.	Botswana	53.06	12	88
13.	Cameroon	45.63	13	93
14.	Chad	44.44	14	95
15.	Burkina Faso	39.98	15	96
16.	Malawi	36.83	16	97
17.	Zimbabwe	36.49	17	98
18.	Senegal	35.85	18	100
19.	Togo	33.19	19	105
20.	Gambia	32.12	20	107
21.	Ethiopia	27.74	21	115
22.	Sierra Leone	25.31	22	121
23.	Mozambique	24.18	23	123
24.	Madagascar	23.33	24	124
25.	Mozambique	0.158	25	132
26.	Guinea	20.53	26	130
27.	Eswatini	18.23	27	135
28.	Cape Verde	17.74	28	136
29.	Sao Tome and Principe	15.24	29	141
30.	Congo Zaire	14.72	30	143
31.	Seychelles	13.23	31	149
32.	Angola	12.99	32	151
33.	Namibia	11.47	33	155
34.	Niger	11.38	34	156
35.	Gabon	11.36	35	157
36.	Mali	10.14	36	160
37.	Guinea Bissau	9.85	37	161
38.	Liberia	9.72	38	162

Continued on following page

Table 4. Continued

S/No.	Member State	Overall Score	Regional Rank	Global Rank
39.	Lesotho	9.08	39	164
40.	South Sudan	5.75	40	169
41.	DR Congo	5.3	41	170
42.	Central African Republic	3.24	42	176
43.	Burundi	1.73	43	179
44.	Eritrea	1.73	43	179
45.	Equatorial Guinea	1.46	44	180

In comparison with other countries in other regions, most African countries displayed a low level of Cybersecurity which is perhaps, the main reason why the Secretary-General of ITU identified the region in 2019 as the most vulnerable and insecure Cyberspace in the world where the Cybercriminals exhibited their business undeterred with impunity. The above figures disclosed why Cybersecurity is an area of concern in Africa. Policies and regulations should be initiated. Even the top performers like Nigeria established Cybersecurity laws recently only in 2015.

COVID-19, INCREASED INTERNET USAGE AND CYBERSECURITY IN AFRICA

The COVID-19 pandemic has successfully altered the style of living in the world for many months now. Governmental activities are now shifted more to e-governance than ever before. Digital activities increased rapidly through online shopping. The digital economy become a plausible alternative for individuals, organizational and governmental operations. E-learning took over schools in most parts of the world. Additionally, social media usage worldwide skyrocketed in the first and second quarters of 2020. Overall, increased internet usage emerged which its attendant consequences of the risk of cyber fraud and Cybercrimes. A survey conducted by PEW Research Centre in the United States which sampled 32 countries in the world confirmed a high rise in internet usage. The study reported increased use of the internet worldwide using the threshold of the selected countries. The report further realized that the increased in usage cuts across all sex, age groups and other social compositions even though, the youth are reported to have used the internet more during the COVID-19 lockdown (Schumacher & Kent, 2020).

In another report, it was discovered that COVID-19 is influencing the use of the internet and social media across the world. COVID-19 has affected African life in many ramifications. The continent with a vulnerable economy, fragile democratic settings and weak political structures, exacerbating insecurity and socioeconomic challenges found itself affected more by the consequences of COVID-19 than the virus itself. The level of infection and deaths are considerably low in comparison with other parts of the world especially America, Europe and Asia. But the dependent nature of the African economy and politics on the global system affected the gamut of life entirely in the continent. Kemp (2020) reported a general pattern and trend of increased social media usage in Africa and the world. For instance, the report concluded that there are big jumps in digital activity, particularly in the countries that witnessed strict lockdowns during COVID-19. There is also significant social media usage in the wake of COVID-19, accelerated adoption of e-commerce, an increased amount of time spent on the internet and social media and a blossoming opportunity for digital advertisers (Kemp, 2020). The African internet economy is projected to be tantamount to approximately $180 billion by 2025 (an increase of 56% from the current value) (Onyango, 2022). The current estimated is $115 billion according to Oluwole (2022a). The report observed that people are now spending more time on the internet and social media in the COVID-19 era than before. The statistics revealed that 76% of the studied area spent more time on smartphones and mobiles, 45% on computer laptops, 32% on the desktop computers, 22% on tablet devices, 34% on media streaming devices, 17% on the game, 11% on smart speakers and 6.3% on smart watch (Kemp, 2020). The report further observed that more people are rushing to register for streamlining applications such as Zoom and other related ones. Additionally, the report identified increased digital activities during the period of the COVID-19 outbreak. 57% are now watching more shows and films on streaming services, 47% is spending longer time using social media, 46% are spending a longer time on messenger services, 39% is listening to more music streaming services, 36% are spending more time on mobile apps, 35% are spending more time playing computer or video games, 15% is creating and uploading games and 14% is listening to more podcast (Kemp, 2020). Internet penetration in 2022 in Africa after the outbreak of COVID-19 shows an increasing performance as indicated in the table below of selected top ten users.

Table 5. Internet usage and population statistics for top fifteen countries in Africa in 2022

S/No.	Country	Population	GDP Per Capita	Internet Users (%)	Facebook Users (%)
1	Morocco	37,626,752	$3,204	29,889,581 (84.1%)	24,953,100 (66.3%)
2	Seychelles	99,334	$17,448	78,100 (79%)	78,100 (79%)
3	Egypt	105,530,371	$3,569	54,741,493 (71.9%)	54,574,100 (70.2%)
4	South Africa	60,536,375	$6,001	38,195,165 (68.2%)	29,375,100 (50.5%)
5	Tunisia	12,020,966	$3,317	8,345,100 (66.7%)	8,602,900 (71.6%)
6	Mauritius	1,275,150	$8,628	1,027,900 (64.9%)	1,027,900 (64.9%)
7	Gabon	2,313,754	$6,882	1,367,641 (62%)	872,600 (37.7%)
8	Cape Verde	565,751	$3,064	352,120 (61.9%)	332,000 (58.7%)
9	Western Sahara	622,105	$1,585	380,000 (61.3%)	380,000 (61.3%)
10	Botswana	2,429,926	$6,405	1,247,000 (61%)	1,223,600 50.4%)
11	Algeria	45,150,879	$3,307	37,836,425 (60.6%)	28,575,400 (51.3%)
12	Djibouti	1,011,573	$3,426	548,832 (59%)	165,700 (16.4%)
13	Ghana	32,154,245	$2,206	14,767,818 (53%)	9,163,200 (28.5%)
14	Lesotho	2,169,819	$875	682,990 (51.9%)	553,900 (48.7%)
15	Nigeria	214,758,624	$2,229	144,949,194 (51%)	34,608,200 (37%)

Additional statistics covered by the report above indicated that social media usage surged during COVID-19 time. For instance, 35% reported watching more news coverage, 25% watched more films and shows from their devices, 24% used more messenger services, 23% is spending more time using social media and 19% watched more TV broadcasts and TV channels. By age group, social media usage increased during COVID-19 lockdown in the following distribution; 58% (16-24 years), 50% (25-34 years), 42% (35-42 years), 34%(45-54%) and 32%(55-64 years). The increased social media usage during COVID-19 by some selected countries revealed that in the Philippines, it has a 64% increase, 58% in Brazil, 55% in India, South Africa 50%, China 49%, Spain 47%, New Zealand 47%, Italy 45%, Canada 43%, Singapore 39%, UK 38%, Australia 38%, USA 36%, Ireland 35%, France 34%, Germany 26% and Japan 23% while the global average internet increased usage was pegged at 47% by the report (Kemp, 2020). It should be observed that most of the countries with the highest increase in internet and social media usage are those that are severely affected by the incidences of COVID-19.

In Africa for instance, South Africa recorded the highest increase in correlation with the highest COVID-19 cases in the continent. The social media stats in Africa in 2022 reveals that Facebook has the highest number of users at 86.55%, followed by YouTube at 7.14%, followed by Twitter at 2.76%, followed by Instagram at 1.7%, followed by Pinterest at 1.56% and LinkedIn at 0.11% (Kemp, 2020). Social media penetration in Africa by region in 2022 shows that North Africa has advanced above other regions as illustrated in the figure below.

Figure 7. Social media penetration in Africa in 2022, by region

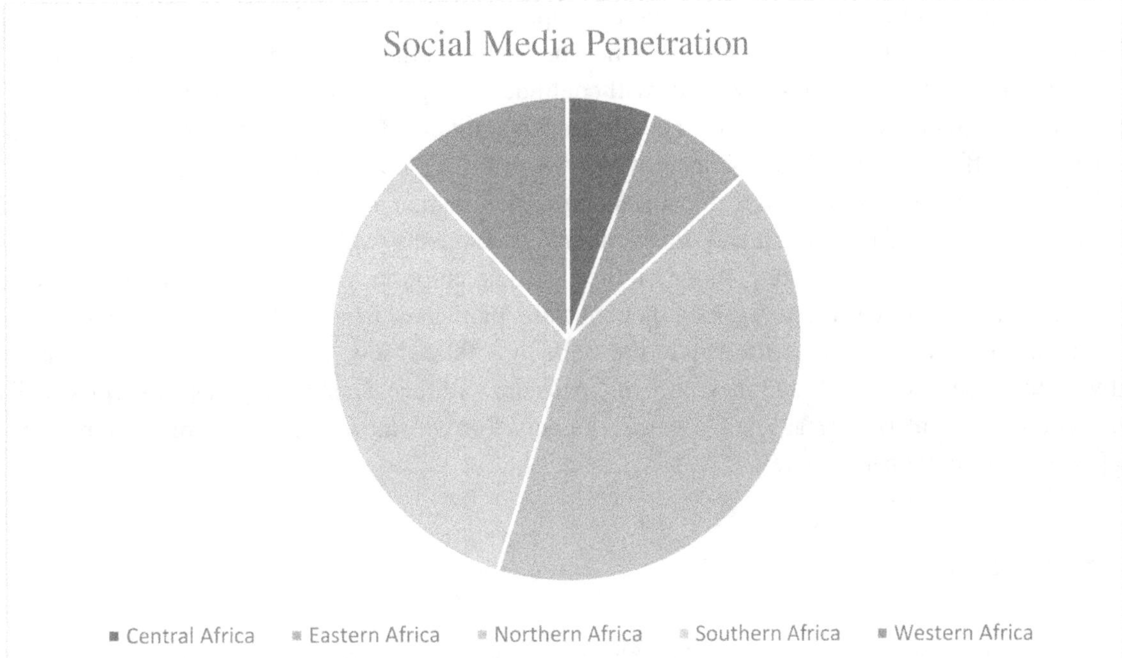

The increase in social media usage in Africa in the wake of COVID-19 from 2020 to 2022 indicates a significant 12% rise in users (Ovuorie, 2022). Ovuorie (2022) further notes that Africans are taking to WhatsApp, Facebook, and Twitter in ever greater numbers to voice their opinions. This according to him, is gingered by the impacts of COVID-19. Social restrictions and lockdowns compelled Africans to resort to social media as an alternative means of physical socializing and sourcing of information. Nigeria tops the list of internet users in 2022 (Oluwole, 2022a) and social media users in Africa with the average user spending 3 hours and 42 minutes on social networks every day (Oluwole, 2022b).

While the African continent recorded an increase in internet and social media usage, there are many factors why the continent is still low relatively among the global regions. One of these reasons is the internet shutdown by some African governments. Ethiopia is one of the countries that are under an internet shutdown, and this has prompted Human Rights Watch to make a call for an immediate lift of the ban to enable a rapid report of the critical health situation (Human Rights Watch, 2020). Another obstacle to internet access and social media usage in Africa is the relatively high cost of data. In most African countries, mobile operators are observed to have been charging around 30% to 50% more on data than in other regions. However, big operators such as MTN, Airtel and Telkom are slashing data prices to ease the lockdown for mobile users and that has been positively influencing the reported increased usage above (Akinpelu, 2020). Hutchings (2020) further observed that lack of internet access is making the lockdown more difficult for Africans.

From the above statistics, the internet and social media may continue to attract more users in Africa. The trend may continue even in the post-COVID-19 era. This will release a new passion for data usage and digital utilization. Since the African performance in Cybersecurity is weak as reported by Global Cybersecurity Index (2021), there is a possibility that a high-security risk in African Cyberspace will emerge soon. Currently, the report identified Africa as the most vulnerable and as rightly observed by Kshetri (2019), most African countries lack a comprehensive policy and program on Cybersecurity especially protection and rapid response. It is thus, possible that the increased internet and social media usage in Africa in the wake of COVID-19 will continue to surge and it will create another dimension of conflict or insecurity for the already bedeviled continent which is presently facing a series of armed conflicts in different parts of the continent. Once the criminals developed the sophistication that this study anticipates they already have, the attacks on critical national infrastructures such as the power sector, governments' data, payroll and organizations' accounts as well as individuals can be targeted. The authors can report in this study based on their participant observation a receipt of emails and text messages severally from fraudsters asking them to claim palliatives from COVID-19 intervention funds in and outside Africa. This is just the tip of the iceberg. A further investigation that will focus specifically on the aspects of emails and messages of fraudsters will reveal a shocking bag of surprises. This study is limited to internet usage and Cybersecurity only. Further studies may be required on the subject matter from different perspectives.

CONCLUSION

This study presented practical implications for policymaking for all African stakeholders in the field of COVID-19 and Cybersecurity. Despite taking several measures to counter the spread of the disease, the study reported that the virus is further spreading. Possibly, Africa should learn to live with it while taking measures but there is a need to cater to the repercussions such as the surge in internet usage and social media. This is because the increased number of internet user will have a direct impact on Cybersecurity and it has been concluded from this work that African Cybersecurity is weak and vulnerable.

Any increase in digital usage will further escalate the risks of Cybersecurity. Thus, Africa should see this era as an opportunity to catch up with its counterparts in America, Europe, and Asia in terms of digital utilization and effective workable Cybersecurity. Countries in Africa should emulate the likes of Nigeria and South Africa which have recently introduced Cybersecurity laws. Weak legal enforcement, irregular policies and programs on Cybersecurity and low financing will all be tantamount to increasing Cybercrimes which are perceived as rising undetected on the continent. People in Africa will continue to utilize the internet more and indeed, the world may never be the same in the post-COVID-19 eras when official meetings, learning, meetings and commercial activities would all be taken into the arena of digital space more than ever in the history of this globe. This phenomenon or recent development would be accompanied by an increase in cyber frauds, cyber hacking and Cybercrime that must be contained. That is where another security risk looms for Africa and it must be arrested now.

DECLARATION

The authors declare that the manuscript follows ethical standards and there are no potential conflicts of interest with respect to the research, authorship and/or publication of this chapter.

DISCLAIMER

The contents and views of this chapter are expressed by the authors in their personal capacities. It is not necessary for the Editor and the Publisher to agree with these viewpoints and they are not responsible for any duty of care in this regard.

ACKNOWLEDGMENT

The authors extend sincere gratitude to:

- The Editor and International Editorial Advisory Board (IEAB) of this book who initially desk reviewed, arranged a rigorous double/triple blind review process, and conducted a thorough, minute, and critical final review before accepting the chapter for publication.
- All anonymous reviewers who provided very constructive feedbacks for thorough revision, improvement, extension and finetuning of the chapter.
- All colleagues, assistants and well-wishers who assisted to complete this task.

REFERENCES

Africa, C. D. C. (2020). *Corona virus disease 2019 (COVID-19)*. African Union. Retrieved from https://africacdc.org/COVID-19/

Africa News. (2022). *Africa COVID-19 stats*. Retrieved from https://www.africanews.com/2020/06/29/coronavirus-in-africa-breakdown-of-infected-virus-free -countries/

African Arguments. (2020). *Corona virus in Africa tracker: How many COVID-19 cases*. Retrieved from https://africanarguments.org/2020/06/29/coronavirus-in-africa-tracker-how-many-cases-and -where-latest/

Akinpelu, O. (2020). COVID-19: How MTN, Telkom, Airtel and Safaricom are helping users cope with self-isolation. *Textnet.ng*. Retrieved from https://technext.ng/2020/03/26/COVID-19-how-mtn-telkom-airtel-and-safaricom-are-helping-users-cope-with-self-isolation/

Antonucci, D. (2017). *The Cyber Risk Handbook: Creating and measuring effective Cybersecurity capabilities*. John Wiley & Sons. doi:10.1002/9781119309741

Azeez, O. (2019). Cybercrime cost Nigeria n288bn in 2018. *Business a.m.* Retrieved from https://www.businessamlive.com/cyber-crime-cost-nigeria-n288bn-in-2018/

Bayuk, J. L., Healey, J., Rohmeyer, P., Sachs, M. H., Schmidt, J., & Weiss, J. (2012). *Cybersecurity policy guidebook*. John Wiley & Sons. doi:10.1002/9781118241530

BBC News. (2022). *Corona Virus: Tracking the Global Outbreak*. Retrieved from https://www.bbc.com/news/world-51235105

Beissel, S. (2016). *Cybersecurity investments: Decision support under economic aspects*. Springer. doi:10.1007/978-3-319-30460-1

Buchanan, B. (2016). *The Cybersecurity dilemma: Hacking, trust and fear between nations*. Oxford University Press.

Buzan, B., & Hansen, L. (2009). *The Evolution of international security studies*. Cambridge University Press. doi:10.1017/CBO9780511817762

Campbell, J., & McCaslin, J. (2020). How Nigeria has responded to COVID-19 so far. *Council on Foreign Relations*. Retrieved from https://www.cfr.org/blog/how-nigeria-has-responded-COVID-19-so-far

Chen, Z., Hu, J., Zhang, Z., Jiang, S., Han, S., Yan, D., Zhuang, R., Hu, B., & Zhang, Z. (2020). *Efficacy of hydroxychloroquine in patients with COVID-19: Results of a randomized clinical trial*. Renmin Hospital of Wuhan University.

Choudhary, A., Ranjan, J. K., Sharma, P., & Asthana, H. S. (2022). Incorporating the outcomes of COVID-19 with other recent pandemic outbreaks on healthcare workers: A systematic review and meta-analysis. In N. Fagih & A. Forouharfar (Eds.), *Socioeconomic Dynamics of the COVID-19 Crisis: Global, Regional and Local Perspectives* (pp. 327–350). Springer. doi:10.1007/978-3-030-89996-7_15

Damooei, J. (2022). Lessons from COVID-19 and its impacts on reallocation of resources: a cross-country comparison in search of a global perspective. In N. Fagih & A. Forouharfar (Eds.), *Socioeconomic Dynamics of the COVID-19 Crisis: Global, Regional and Local Perspectives* (pp. 127–174). Springer. doi:10.1007/978-3-030-89996-7_7

Donovan, D. (2022). *Map tracks coronavirus outbreak in near real time*. National Public Health Agencies. John Hopkins University. Retrieved from https://hub.jhu.edu/2020/01/23/coronavirus-outbreak-mapping-tool-649-em1-art1-dtd-health/

Fagih, N., & Forouharfar, A. (2022). An Introduction to Socioeconomic Dynamics of the COVID-19 Crisis: Global, Regional and Local Perspectives. In N. Fagih & A. Forouharfar (Eds.), *Socioeconomic Dynamics of the COVID-19 Crisis: Global, Regional and Local Perspectives* (pp. 1–18). Springer. doi:10.1007/978-3-030-89996-7_1

Fawzy, L., & Dworski, L. (2011). *Emerging business online: Global markets and the power of b2b internet marketing*. Pearson Education Limited.

FBI. (2018). *Cybercrime Statistics: Top ten countries in the world.* Internet Crime Complaint Centre, Federal Bureau of Investigation (FBI). Retrieved from https://www.ic3.gov/default.aspx

Fischer, E. A. (2009). *Creating a national framework for Cybersecurity. An analysis of issues and options.* Nova Science Publishers.

Franda, M. (2001). *Governing the internet: Emergence of an international regime.* Lynne Rienner Publishers. doi:10.1515/9781626373556

Galal, S. (August 22, 2022). Social media penetration in Africa in 2022 by region. *Statista*. Retrieved from https://www.Statista.com/statistics/1190628/social-media-penetration-in-africa-by-region/#

Gerbaudo, P. (2019). *The Digital party: Political organisation and online democracy.* Pluto Press.

Global Cybersecurity Index. (2021). *Global Cybersecurity Index*. ITU Publications. Retrieved from https://www.itu.int/en/ITU-D/Cybersecurity/Pages/global-Cybersecurity-index.aspx

Gondwe, G. (2020). *Assessing the impact of COVID-19 on Africa's economic development.* UNCTAD. Retrieved from https://unctad.org/webflyer/assessing-impact-COVID-19-africas-economic-development

Gouro, T. (2022). Extreme poverty rises in West Africa due to COVID-19 pandemic. *Relief Web*. Retrieved from https://reliefweb.int/report/world/extreme-poverty-rises-west-africa-due-COVID-19-pandemic

Grant, W. B., Lahore, H., McDonnell, S. L., Baggerly, C. A., French, C. B., Aliano, J. L., & Bhattoa, H. P. (2020). Evidence that vitamin D supplementation could reduce risk of influenza and covid-19 infections and deaths. *Nutrients*, *12*(4), 988. doi:10.3390/nu12040988 PMID:32252338

Gross, A. G., & Harmon, J. E. (2016). *The Internet in the sciences and the humanities.* Oxford University Press.

He, G., Pan, Y., & Tanaka, T. (2020). The short-term impacts of COVID-19 lockdown on urban air pollution in China. *Nature Sustainability, 3*(12), 1005–1011. doi:10.103841893-020-0581-y

Heintze, H., & Thielborger, P. (2016). *From cold war to cyber war: The evolution of the international law of peace and armed conflict over the last 25 years*. Springer. doi:10.1007/978-3-319-19087-7

Hochberg, M. E. (2020). *Importance of suppression and mitigation measures in managing COVID-19 outbreaks*. doi:10.1101/2020.03.31.20048835

Holtz, L. (2021). *COVID-19's Impact on overall health care services in Africa*. Brookings Institution.

Hosseini-Nezhad, S., Safdar, S., Hosseini-Nezhad, P., & Luu, L. A. N. (2022). Psychological perspective on COVID-19. In N. Fagih & A. Forouharfar (Eds.), *Socioeconomic Dynamics of the COVID-19 Crisis: Global, Regional and Local Perspectives* (pp. 291–326). Springer. doi:10.1007/978-3-030-89996-7_14

Hruby, A. (2020). A rough road ahead for Nigeria. *Atlantic Council*. Retrieved from https://www.atlanticcouncil.org/blogs/africasource/a-rough-road-ahead-for-nigeria/

Human Rights Watch. (2020). End internet shutdowns to manage COVID-19. *Human Rights Watch*. Retrieved from https://www.hrw.org/news/2020/03/31/end-internet-shutdowns-manage-COVID-19

Internet World Stats. (2022). *Usage and population statistics: Internet penetration in Africa*. Retrieved from https://www.internetworldstats.com/stats1.htm

ISACA. (2020). *Cybersecurity by the numbers: Increased attacks, rampant under reporting and the power of a fully staffed team*. Retrieved from https://www.ISACA.org/go/state-of-Cybersecurity-2020

Jarus, O. (2020). 20 of the worst epidemics and pandemics in history. *LiveScience*. Retrieved from https://www.livescience.com/worst-epidemics-and-pandemics-in-history.html

Johnson, N. F. (2009). *The ultiplicities of internet addiction: The misrecognition of leisure and learning*. Ashgate Publishing Company.

Joseph, T., & Ashkan, M. (2020). *International pulmonologists consensus on COVID-19*. Amrita Institute of Medical Sciences.

Kamer, L. (2022a). Number of internet users in selected countries. *Statista*. Retrieved from https://www.Statista.com/statistics/505883/number-of-internet-users-in-african-countries/

Kamer, L. (2022b). Internet penetration in Africa. *Statista*. Retrieved from https://www.Statista.com/statistics/1124283/internet-penetration-in-africa-by-country/

Kemp, S. (2020a). *Digital 2020: April 2020 snapshots*. Retrieved from https://datareportal.com/reports/digital-2020-april-global-statshot

Kemp, S. (2020b). Digital trends 2020: Every single stat you need to know about the internet. *Global Web Index*. Retrieved from https://thenextweb.com/podium/2020/01/30/digital-trends-2020-every-single-stat-you-need-to-know-about-the-internet/

KPMG. (2020). Government and institution measures in response to COVID-19. *KPMG*. Retrieved from https://home.kpmg/xx/en/home/insights/2020/04/nigeria-government-and-institution-measures-in-response-to-covid.html

Kredens, M. (2020). The Virus of desire. The life of passion. A COVID-19 Self-Help Erotic Book. Grupa Szeroka: Szeroka Street Publishing House.

Kshetri, N. (2019). Cybercrime and Cybersecurity in Africa. *Journal of Global Information Technology Management*, *22*(2), 77–81. doi:10.1080/1097198X.2019.1603527

Liang, T. (2020). *Handbook of COVID-19 prevention and treatment. Zhejiang*. Zhejiang University of Medicine.

Live Science. (2020). *Spanish Flu: The deadliest pandemic in history*. Retrieved from https://www.livescience.com/spanish-flu.html

Mathe, A. (2019). The misunderstood world of Cybersecurity in Africa. *Policy Centre for the New South*. Retrieved from https://www.policycenter.ma/opinion/misunderstood-world-Cybersecurity-africa

Meeuwisse, R. (2015). *Cybersecurity for beginners*. Icutrain Ltd.

Mordi, M. (2019). Is Nigeria really the headquarters of Cybercrime in the world? *The Guardian*. Retrieved from https://guardian.ng/news/is-nigeria-really-the-headquarters-of-Cybercrime-in-the-world/

Nohe, P. (2018). Re-Hashed: 2018 *Cybercrime Statistics: A closer look at the "Web of Profit*. Retrieved from https://www.thesslstore.com/blog/2018-Cybercrime-statistics/#:~:text=Re-Hashed%3A%202018%20Cybercrime%20Statistics%3A%20A%20closer%20look%20at,profitability%20to%20be%20in%20excess%20of%20%241.5%20trillion.

OECD. (2020). *COVID-19 in Africa: Regional Socio-economic Implications and Policy Priorities*. Organisation for Economic Cooperation and Development.

Oluwole, B. (2022). Nigerians are the most addicted social media users in Africa - See how other countries rank. *Business Insider Africa*. Retrieved from https://africa.businessinsider.com/local/lifestyle/nigerians-are-the-most-addicted-social-media-users-in-africa-see-how-other-countries/7d93c98

Oluwole, B. (2022). Top 10 African countries with the highest number of internet users in 2022. *Business Insider Africa*. Retrieved from https://africa.businessinsider.com/local/markets/top-10-african-countries-with-the-highest-number-of-internet-users-in-2022/zm280z1

Onwujekwe, O., Orjiakor, C., & Agwu, P. (2020). Coronavirus: corruption in health care could get in the way of Nigeria's response. *The Conversation*. Retrieved from https://theconversation.com/coronavirus-corruption-in-health-care-could-get-in-the-way-of-nigerias-response-136913

Onyango, S. (2022). Piling into a future $180 billion African internet economy. *Techcabal*. Retrieved from https://Techcabal.com/2022/03/09/piling-into-a-future-180-billion-african-internet-economy/

Osler, S. (2020). *Coronavirus Outbreak: All the secrets revealed about the COVID-19 pandemic: A complete rational guide of its evolution, expansion, symptoms and first defense*. Independently Published.

Ovuorie, T. (2022). Increased social media use puts African leaders on edge. *DW*. Retrieved from https://www.dw.com/en/increased-social-media-use-puts-african-leaders-on-edge/a-61303854

Rahouma, K. H., Hamed, R., Aly, M., & Hamed, H. M. (2020). Challenges and solutions of using the social internet of things in healthcare and medical solutions. In A. E. Hassanien, R. Bhatnagar, N. M. Khalifa, & M. H. N. Taha (Eds.), *Towards Social Internet of Things (SIOT): Enabling Technologies, Architectures and Applications. Emerging Technologies for Connected and Smart Social Objects* (pp. 13–31). Springer. doi:10.1007/978-3-030-24513-9_2

Rittinghouse, J. W., & Hancock, W. M. (2003). *Cybersecurity Operations Handbook*. Elsevier.

Rosberg, A. G., & Knell, R. G. (2020). *How will this continue? Modelling interactions between the COVID-19 pandemic and policy responses*. Queen Mary University of London. doi:10.1101/2020.03.30.20047597

Samaddar, R. (2020). Introduction: Borders of an epidemic. In R. Samaddar (Ed.), *Borders of an Epidemic: COVID-19 and Migrant Workers*. Mahanirban Calcutta Research Group.

Schumacher, S., & Kent, N. (2020). 8 charts on internet use around the world as countries grapple with COVID-19. *Pew Research Centre*. Retrieved from https://www.pewresearch.org/fact-tank/2020/04/02/8-charts-on-internet-use-around-the-world-as-countries-grapple-with-COVID-19/

Shalhoub, Z. K., & Al Qasimi, S. L. (2010). *Cyber law and cyber security in developing and emerging economies*. Oxford University Press. doi:10.4337/9781849803380

Sharif, M., Ansari, G. J., Yamin, M., & Fernandes, S. L. (2018). Reviews of the implications of vr/ar healthcare applications. In L. Dac-Nihuong, V. L. Chung, G. T. Jolanda, & N. N. Gia (Eds.), *Emerging Technologies for Health and Medicine* (pp. 3–15). Wiley. doi:10.1002/9781119509875.ch1

Statista Research Department. (2022). *Countries with the highest number of internet users*. Retrieved from https://www.statista.com/statistics/262966/number-of-internet-users-in-selected-countries/

Tiwari, R., & Buse, S. (2020). *Managing innovation in a global and digital world: Meeting societal challenges and enhancing competitiveness*. Springer. doi:10.1007/978-3-658-27241-8

Touhill, G. J., & Touhill, C. J. (2014). *Cybersecurity for executives: A practical guide*. John Wiley & Sons. doi:10.1002/9781118908785

Tyner, K. (2009). *Literacy in a digital world: Teaching and learning in the age of information*. Taylor & Francis.

UNECA. (2013). Tackling the challenges of Cybersecurity in Africa. *United Nations Economic Commission for Africa*. Retrieved from https://archive.uneca.org/publications/tackling-challenges-Cybersecurity-africa

UNECA. (2020). *Policy Brief: Impact of COVID-19 in Africa. United Nations Economic Commission for Africa*. Retrieved from https://archive.uneca.org/publications/policy-brief-impact-COVID-19-africa

Wang, L., Wang, Y., Ye, D., & Liu, Q. (2020). A review of the 2019 novel coronavirus (COVID-19) based on current evidence. *International Journal of Antimicrobial Agents*, *55*(6), 105948. doi:10.1016/j.ijantimicag.2020.105948 PMID:32201353

White Paper. (2020). Cybersecurity trends 2019. *Eleven Paths*. Retrieved from https://www.elevenpaths.com/news-events/trend-reports/index.html

World Health Organization. (2020). African countries move from COVID-19 readiness to response as many confirm cases. *WHO Africa*. Retrieved from https://www.afro.who.int/health-topics/coronavirus-COVID-19

Zizek, S. (2020). *Pandemic COVID-19 shakes the world*. OR Books. doi:10.2307/j.ctv16t6n4q

Rafay, A. (Ed.). (2019). *FinTech as a Disruptive Technology for Financial Institutions*. IGI Global. doi:10.4018/978-1-5225-7805-5

Rafay, A. (Ed.). (2021a). *Money Laundering and Terrorism Financing in Global Financial Systems*. IGI Global. doi:10.4018/978-1-7998-8758-4

Rafay, A. (Ed.). (2021b). *Handbook of Research on Theory and Practice of Financial Crimes*. IGI Global. doi:10.4018/978-1-7998-5567-5

Rafay, A. (Ed.). (2023). *Concepts and Cases of Illicit and Illegitimate Finance*. IGI Global. doi:10.4018/978-1-6684-8587-3

Chapter 15
Mobile Money Frauds in the African Continent

Adam Salifu
University of Professional Studies, Accra, Ghana

ABSTRACT

During the last decade, the mobile telecommunication industry has witnessed rapid growth in developing countries, which has facilitated access to cheap and reliable financial services for rural dwellers and the unbanked population. This chapter examines mobile money fraud in developing countries by tracing the evolution of mobile money services, exploring the nature and forms of mobile money fraud and its effects on service providers and users as well as the strategies for minimizing mobile money fraud. The chapter contends that while it may not be possible to completely eliminate mobile money fraud, some key strategies such as collective action, strong regulatory frameworks, and standardization of mobile money transaction processes are important in reducing the phenomenon. The chapter argues that as technology continues to improve, so will the provision of mobile money services, which will result in new forms of fraud. The chapter, therefore, proposes the need for continuous monitoring of mobile money fraud in order to design and implement effective fraud mitigation measures.

INTRODUCTION

Before the introduction of mobile telecommunication and the subsequent use of mobile phones to provide financial services, financial inclusion was a major challenge globally, particularly in the developing world. In the last decade, many countries in the developing world have witnessed improved financial inclusion (Buku & Mazer, 2017), partly because of the rapid growth of the mobile telecommunication industry in both rural and urban areas (Rafay & Khan, 2018). Growth in the mobile telecommunication industry has facilitated access to cheap and reliable financial services for rural dwellers, the informal sector and the unbanked population. This achievement underscores Goals 5, 8 and 17 of the Sustainable Development Goals (SDGs), which emphasize the use of technology to improve access to financial services (Rafay, 2022).

DOI: 10.4018/978-1-6684-5007-9.ch015

At the onset of the COVID-19 pandemic in 2020, it became apparent that mobile-based technology, especially mobile money services would play pivotal roles in providing safe and non-contact ways to pay for food, electricity and other basic needs as well as keeping people connected and delivering vital financial support in many parts of the developing world. With more than $2 billion in mobile money transactions every day and more than 1.2 billion registered mobile users around the world, mobile money services have become a part of a new daily routine for millions of people (Andersson & Naghavi, 2021). In less than two decades, mobile money services have radically transformed the lives of many people in Asia, Sub-Saharan Africa, Latin America and the Caribbeans (Andersson & Naghavi, 2021; Lepoutre & Oguntoye, 2018). Mobile money services have helped in making people more productive with their time and money as well as taking advantage of the socio-economic opportunities around their environment (Andersson & Naghavi, 2021; Lepoutre & Oguntoye, 2018). Mobile money operations have also become the channel through which the unbanked population joins the formal banking systems (Akomea-Frimpong *et al.*, 2019).

Financial transactions that are associated with mobile phone technology have been referred to variously as mobile money, mobile transfers (m-transfer), mobile banking (m-banking), mobile finance (m-finance) and mobile payment (m-payment) (Boamah & Murshid, 2019). While m-transfer, m-banking, m-finance and m-payment have often been attributed to a banking practice in which customers link their mobile phones to their traditional bank accounts, mobile money concerns with the use of mobile phones to make financial transactions without necessarily opening a traditional bank account. In many developing countries, mobile money is rapidly becoming the most convenient and easy-to-use alternative for financial transactions (Andersson & Naghavi, 2021). This is even more so as most of the traditional banks have incorporated mobile money services into their mainstream services.

The focus of this chapter is on mobile money, that is, the ability to use a mobile phone handset to save, send and receive money as well as make payment for goods and services without necessarily operating a bank account (Boamah & Murshid, 2019; INTERPOL, 2020). In other words, the chapter views mobile money as an electronic wallet service, available in many countries that allow users of mobile phones to store, send and receive money on their phones without necessarily operating bank accounts. It is important to note, however, that mobile money services have increasingly been linked to financial institutions such as banks and microfinance institutions. As a result of the interconnectedness between mobile money services and financial institutions, the Mobile Communications Association (GSMA) – a group that represents the interests of mobile network operators worldwide – views mobile money services as those that involve m-transfer, m-banking, m-finance and m-payment (Andersson & Naghavi, 2021). Nevertheless, available data suggest that in many parts of the developing world, people who use mobile money do not usually operate a traditional bank account partly because the banks are not readily accessible to them (Andersson & Naghavi, 2021).

The rapid growth of mobile money services unfortunately offers criminals the opportunity to defraud users in a variety of ways. Put differently, the provision and use of mobile money services have become a conduit for fraud and other criminal activities (Buku and Mazer, 2017; Akomea-Frimpong *et al.*, 2019). In many African countries, the occurrences of mobile money fraud have become commonplace in both rural and urban areas, which has led to substantial financial losses to organizations and individuals (Chatain *et al.*, 2011; Buku and Mazer, 2017; Akomea-Frimpong *et al.*, 2019). In addition, deaths related to mobile money fraud have been reported (Chatain *et al.*, 2011). Fraud is commonly understood as dishonesty and deception deliberately practiced for unfair or unlawful gain (Nakitende *et al.*, 2021). For purposes of this chapter, it is considered as the misrepresentation, concealment, or omission of the truth for deception or manipulation to the financial detriment of an individual or organization (Botchey, Qin, & Hughes-Lartey, 2020; David-West, Iheanachor, & Umukoro, 2019; Khan *et al.*, 2020). Mobile money fraud is, therefore, an intentional act perpetuated by scammers or fraudsters to gain undue advantage over mobile money subscribers, providers and agents (Akomea-Frimpong *et al.*, 2019; Merritt, 2011). The activities of mobile money fraud are well-thought by the perpetrator to take advantage of weaknesses in the mobile money supply chain (Maurer, 2015).

This chapter examines the nature and forms of mobile money fraud as well as its effects on service providers and users alike. This type of analysis is important in helping relevant stakeholders understand the nature and forms of mobile money fraud as well as taking steps to make mobile money services safe, reliable, and sustainable. In particular, understanding the nature and forms of mobile money fraud will help mobile money providers to build robust systems, thereby making it difficult for fraudsters to penetrate.

The rest of the chapter is organized as follows. The section that follows traces the evolution of mobile money fraud. It also provides a global and regional overview of the growth of the mobile money industry. Next, the nature and forms of mobile money fraud are explored. The chapter then examines the negative effects of mobile money fraud and some strategies for reducing or eliminating mobile fraud such as regulations, communication and experience sharing. The chapter concludes with highlights of the key issues discussed and future research direction.

EVOLUTION AND OVERVIEW OF MOBILE MONEY SERVICES

The beginning of mobile money in the context of using a phone handset to undertake money transactions without a bank account is often traced to Kenya (Afawubo *et al.*, 2020; Botchey *et al.*, 2020; David-West *et al.*, 2019; Lepoutre & Oguntoye, 2018). In 2007, Safaricom and Vodafone introduced the first mobile money service, dubbed, M-PESA (M for mobile, PESA for money in Swahili), which remains one of the most successful mobile money service platforms in Africa to date. It started as a public/private sector initiative after Vodafone (UK-based telephone company) won funds from the Financial Deepening Challenge Fund competition established by the UK Government's Department for International Development to encourage private sector companies to engage in innovative projects so as to deepen the provision of financial services in emerging economies. M-PESA was first envisioned as a mobile-based micro-financing application to extend financial access to the unbanked population in East Africa but was later redesigned to serve as mobile money platform when it became apparent that users were using it to perform general money transfers rather than just for microloans purposes alone (Afawubo *et al.*, 2020; Botchey *et al.*, 2020; David-West *et al.*, 2019; Lepoutre & Oguntoye, 2018). With this new platform, users were required to register their mobile phone numbers at authorized M-PESA outlets. M-PESA then provided registered users electronic payment and money storage system that they could access through mobile handsets. With the M-PESA platform, users could deposit to and withdraw cash from their mobile money accounts (wallets) by exchanging cash for electronic credit by visiting agents (Lepoutre and Oguntoye, 2018; David-West, Iheanachor and Umukoro, 2019; Afawubo *et al.*, 2020). The M-PESA platform developed quickly to allow users not only to send and receive money but also became a powerful platform for undertaking a range of mobile-enabled financial services such as bill payments, savings, purchase of air-time and other goods and services (Lepoutre and Oguntoye, 2018; David-West, Iheanachor and Umukoro, 2019; Afawubo *et al.*, 2020).

In view of the above, it was clear to many that the M-PESA platform brought financial services closer to a majority of people, especially the poor, who hitherto had no access to financial services. Owing to the advantages of the M-PESA platform, it rapidly spread to many parts of the developing world. In Africa, for instance, the mobile money service has spread rapidly throughout the continent with well over 153 mobile money services in 45 African countries (INTERPOL, 2020). Currently, mobile money services are no longer provided by only mobile telecommunication service providers but also by a wide range of financial institutions such as bank, credits institutions and government agencies. Bank-led, mobile network operator-led and hybrid models are functioning in several parts of the developing world. Top mobile telecommunication service providers that provide mobile money services in many parts of the developing world include M-PESA, M-Pitesan, Orange, Airtel, and MTN, Vodafone and Tigo. All banks in the countries now provide mobile money services. Some of the popular non-bank providers include Opay, Palm pay, Zee Pay, Paytm, gpay and phonepe.

The number of transactions that a mobile money account holder can perform is growing rapidly partly because of the heightened collaboration among several stakeholders in the mobile money market. Currently, a mobile money account holder can perform a wide range of transactions, which could be person-to-person (e.g., transferring money to another mobile money user, receiving international remittances, airtime top-up), person-to-business (e.g., paying for products and services, making online payment, loan disbursement and repayment), government-to-persons (e.g., tax collection, paying salaries, allowances and subsidies), and NGO-to-person (e.g., aid disbursement). While the other forms of transactions are gaining momentum, it must be noted that person-to-person transactions are currently the most common in developing countries (INTERPOL, 2020).

Table 1 presents key terminologies that are commonly used in the provision of mobile money services. The Personal Identification Number (PIN) is particularly important in all mobile money transactions, and it is one area that criminals target in defrauding users.

Table 1. Key terminologies

Term	Description
Registration	All customers are required to register with a mobile money service provider in order to use the service
Cash-in	The process of funding a mobile money account through either a financial institution or agent
Cash-out	It is simply the withdrawal of cash from a mobile money account through a financial institution or agent
Personal Identification Number (PIN)	It is the unique four digits secret code needed by customers to perform every transaction on mobile money account
P2P	Person-to-person transaction
P2B	Person-to-business transaction
G2P	Government-to-person transaction

There are various models of mobile money service delivery. However, a typical mobile money platform always involves several stakeholders who play distinct roles and derive numerous benefits from the whole mobile money ecosystem. Table 2 presents and describes some of the key stakeholders in the mobile money industry. Among the stakeholders, mobile money users remain one of the key targets for fraudsters, as they are at the centre of mobile money transactions.

Table 2. Key stakeholders in the mobile money industry

Key Stakeholder	Description
Mobile Money Users	They use mobile money services to accomplish their needs such as sending and receiving money, paying bills, and purchasing goods and services.
Mobile Network Operators (MNOs)	MNOs provide mobile money services. Today MNOs provide these services in partnership with banks and other financial service providers. The MNOs use their existing mobile phone service customer base as well as agents and merchants to provide mobile services.
Bank/financial Institutions	They deliver mobile money services in partnership with MNOs. They particularly promote the exchange of money between mobile money users and MNOs as well as leveraging mobile money platforms to reach out to new customers in traditionally underserved areas at much lower costs.
Regulatory institutions	They set up and monitor the regulatory framework under which mobile money services should be provided. Key regulators in many countries include the Central banks for regulating the financial sector and telecommunication regulators for the communication sector.
Agents	Agents provide a wide range of mobile money services to mobile money users including registering new users, educating users on products and services, supporting users in their transactions (cash-in and cash-out), and selling products such as phones and airtime. An agent may serve several mobile money service providers. Agents earn commissions on various transactions carried out by mobile money users.
Third parties: Merchandise and service providers	They accept mobile money payments in exchange for various products and services or use mobile money as a means of delivering their services. They include merchants, retailers, microfinance institutions, insurance providers, large-scale disbursers and bill issuers.
Equipment manufacturers and platform providers	These include a wide array of stakeholders like network equipment providers, mobile phone makers as well as application suppliers. With increases in mobile money users, they also make equipment to manage increased network capacity.

Globally, the use of mobile financial services (MFS) has witnessed rapid growth since the mid-2000s, partly because of their convenience and easy access (Akomea-Frimpong *et al.*, 2019). In 2020 alone, the number of registered mobile money accounts grew by 12.7% globally with an estimate of about 1.21 billion mobile money accounts (see Table 3). Transaction values also grew across the board as more money circulated and was cashed-in and cashed-out than ever before. For the first time, the global value of daily transactions exceeded $2 billion dollars and is expected to surpass $3 billion a day by the end of 2022 (Andersson & Naghavi, 2021).

Table 3. Global overview of mobile money services in 2020

Activity	Quantity	% increase from 2019
Registered Accounts	1.2 billion	13
Transaction Volume	41 billion	15
Transaction value (US$)	767 billion	22
Registered Agents	9.1 billion	14
Mobile money deployment	310 in 96 countries	

Between 2019 and 2020, the number of registered mobile money accounts increased by 12% in Sub-Saharan Africa, 5% in South Asia, 9% in Middle East and North Africa, 38% in Latin America and the Caribbean, 6% in Europe and Central Asia and 24% in East Asia and Pacific (Andersson & Naghavi, 2021). In the same period, transaction volume increased by 15% in Sub-Saharan Africa, 8% in South Asia, 35% in Latin America and the Caribbean, 15% in Europe and Central Asia and 26% in East Asia and the Pacific and decreased by -63% in the Middle East and North Africa (Andersson & Naghavi, 2021). Similarly, transaction value (US$) increased by 23% in Sub-Saharan Africa, 10% in South Asia, 26% in the Middle East and North Africa, 30% in Latin America and the Caribbean, 13% in Europe and Central Asia and 34% in East Asia and Pacific.

Table 4 below provides a summary of recently available statistics by region on registered mobile money accounts as well as transaction volumes and values (Andersson & Naghavi, 2021). Sub-Saharan Africa has the highest registered accounts, transaction volumes and transaction values, suggesting that mobile money services are critical and more relevant in this region. Europe and Central Asia have the least registered accounts, transaction volume and transaction values.

Table 4. Overview of mobile money services in 2020, by region

Region	Registered Accounts	Transaction Volume	Transaction Value (US$)
Global	1.2 billion	41.4 billion	767 billion
East Asia and Pacific	243 million	5.4 billion	111 billion
Europe and Central Asia	21 million	234 million	4.0 billion
Latin America and the Caribbean	39 million	701 million	19.8 billion
Middle East and North Africa	56 million	146 million	10.5 billion
South Asia	305 million	7.5 billion	131 billion
Sub-Saharan Africa	548 million	27.4 billion	490 billion

As shown in Figure 1 below, the value of mobile money transactions processed has witnessed significant growth from 2015 to 2020. With a daily transaction value of US$ 2.1 billion in 2020, it is estimated that the value will increase to US$ 3 billion by the end of 2022. It must be emphasised that as the volume of transactions increases, the activities of mobile money fraudsters are more likely to increase as well.

Figure 1. Global total mobile money value processed per day (2015-2020)

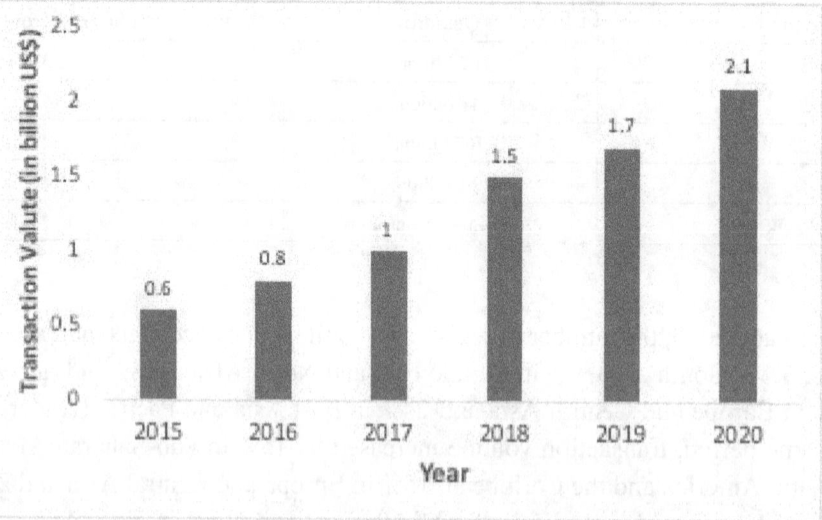

In Africa, mobile money services witnessed growth in different regions from 2019 to 2020. For registered mobile money accounts, there was a 19% increase in West Africa, 24% in Southern Africa, 16% in North Africa, 2% in Central Africa and 9% in East Africa. In terms of transaction volume, there was an increase of 29% in West Africa, 43% in Southern Africa, 29% in North Africa, 30% in Central Africa and 10% in East Africa. Regarding transaction value (US$), there was an increase of 46% in West Africa, 24% in Southern Africa, 37% in North Africa, 23% in Central Africa and 11% in East Africa (Andersson & Naghavi, 2021).

Figure 2. Mobile money accounts in Africa by region, 2021 (in millions)

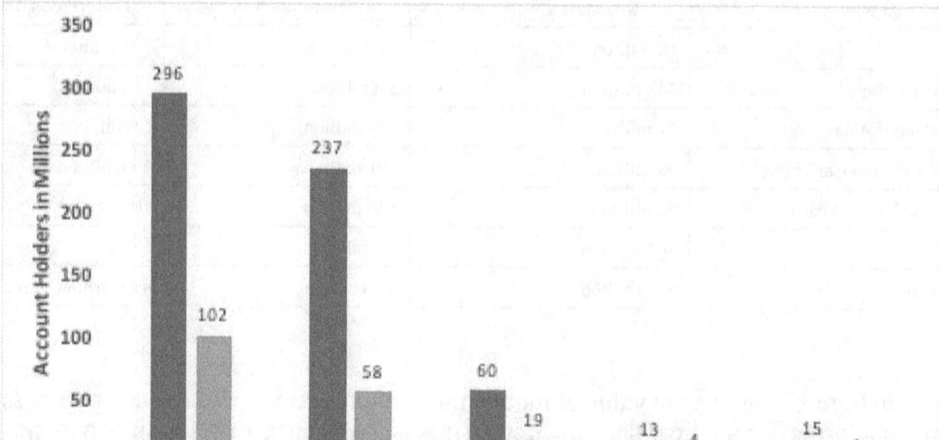

While it is no more in doubt that mobile money is more dominant in Africa as compared to other parts of the developing world, in Africa, East and West Africa have experienced higher penetration of the services than other parts of Africa (see Figure 2). The reasons for the low penetration of mobile money services in some parts of Africa and other developing countries are beyond the scope of this chapter. The remainder of the chapter now focuses on mobile money fraud. The next section explores the nature and forms of mobile money fraud.

NATURE AND FORMS OF MOBILE MONEY FRAUD

Mobile money fraud is on the rise, especially in Africa (Andersson & Naghavi, 2021; Lepoutre & Oguntoye, 2018). In 2015, the number of mobile money fraud cases stood at 53% of the entire mobile money transactions in Uganda, 42% in Tanzania, 23% in Ghana, and 12% in Kenya (Busuulwa, 2016). Arguably, the occurrence and prevalence of mobile money fraud will depend on the nature and longevity of mobile money products. New products are more likely to be susceptible to fraud compared to products that have long been deployed.

In Africa, some have estimated that about $4 billion was lost in the activities of mobile money fraud in 2020 alone (Fitzhenry, 2022). The amount of money lost in the activities of fraudulent mobile money activities is expected to rise over time as the fraudsters are using more sophisticated methods to defraud subscribers, agents and providers.

The rise in mobile money fraud is often attributed to the rapid growth in the number of registered mobile money accounts as well as increases in daily transaction volumes and values. Rapid growth in mobile money accounts and transactions will present criminals with the opportunity to exploit weaknesses in the provision of mobile money services. Fraudulent practices typically involve a highly organized network of perpetrators, who could be subscribers, non-subscribers, agents and even employees of mobile money providers. The activities of fraudsters are targeted at all three key stakeholders: subscribers, agents and mobile money providers, although subscribers remain the primary target.

It is important to note that mobile money fraud can take place when depositing funds into an account (cash in), transferring funds across different accounts (paying for bills and services) and withdrawing funds from an account (cash-out).

Several authors have categorized Mobile money fraud differently, summarized in Table 5 and explained in detail as follows.

Table 5. Categories of mobile money fraud

Author(s)	Categories of Mobile money fraud
INTERPOL (2020)	Transactional, Channel and Internal fraud
Buku and Mazer (2017)	Consumer-based fraud, agent-based fraud, internal fraud
Akomea-Frimpong *et al.* (2019)	Subscribers' fraud, employee and agents' fraud and systems' fraud
INTERPOL (2020)	Consumer-driven fraud, Agent driven fraud, Business partners-driven fraud, System Administration fraud, and Mobile Financial service provider fraud

As shown in Table 5, INTERPOL (2020) categorised mobile money fraud into three: transactional, channel and internal. Transactional fraud is described as one in which fraudsters gather personal data (especially the PIN) through phone calls and SMS to facilitate unauthorised access to users' mobile money accounts. Channel fraud occurs when mobile money agents abuse their position by transferring funding to their personal accounts or a known person without the knowledge of their clients; they may also split the cash in transactions into smaller payments in order to increase their commission or register non-existent clients to increase their registration commission. Finally, internal fraud occurs within mobile money service providers in which employees access customers' data to develop fraudulent financial behaviour and practices (INTERPOL, 2020).

Buku and Mazer (2017) also categorised mobile money fraud into three: Consumer-based fraud, agent-based fraud, and internal fraud. They defined consumer-based fraud as the kind of fraud that is perpetrated against consumers; agent-based fraud as the type perpetrated against agents; and internal fraud as one that is perpetrated by employees of mobile service providers. Among these three, consumer and agent-based fraud are relatively high in most parts of developing countries (Buku & Mazer, 2017).

Similarly, Akomea-Frimpong *et al.* (2019) identified three kinds of mobile money fraud: subscribers' fraud, employee and agents' fraud and systems' fraud. According to them, subscribers' fraud occurs when mobile money subscribers use deceptive means to defraud other mobile money subscribers as well as mobile money operators and agents through the stealing of SIM cards, PINs and other relevant information. They explained that employee and agents' fraud occur when employees and staff of mobile money providers manipulate subscribers' transactions to their advantage. In some cases, employees of the mobile money providers assist the agents to defraud the subscribers, which may involve creating fake mobile money accounts to defraud them. Finally, systems' fraud is one in which criminals take advantage of underlying weaknesses that exist in the mobile money system to deceive subscribers, agents and even the service providers themselves (Akomea-Frimpong *et al.*, 2019).

INTERPOL (2020) further identified five types of mobile money fraud, which are summarised in Table 6 and explained as follows.

Table 6. Typologies of mobile money fraud

Fraud type	Nature and forms	Examples
Consumer-driven fraud	• Consumer defrauding agents • Consumer defrauding consumers • Consumer defrauding business partners	• Unauthorised access to agents' transaction tools • Unauthorised PIN access • Impersonation of business organisations
Agent driven fraud	• Agent defrauding consumers • Agent defrauding Mobile Financial service operators • Agent employees Defrauding agents • Fraud by paster Agents	• Unauthorised access to customers' transaction PIN • Registration of customers with fake details • Under-reporting of cash balances • Unauthorized withdrawals from agent accounts
Business partners-driven fraud	• Employees of B2C and C2B Organisations Defrauding Businesses • Businesses Defrauding Mobile Money Operators	• Illegal reversal of customer payments to the business • Collusion to apply lower tariffs
System Administration fraud	• Manipulation of the system by administrators • Unauthorised access to the system	• Creation of fake/ non-existent users • Abuse of passwords
Mobile Financial service provider fraud	• Finance Fraud • Contact Centre and Operational Support Fraud • Sales and Channel Facing Team	• Theft of mobile money provider's revenue • Unauthorised access to customer payment records • Unauthorised access to agent transactional data

Consumer-driven fraud is the most common type of fraud, which originates mainly from the consumers or users of mobile money services. With this type of fraud, a consumer can defraud other consumers, agents of mobile money services, or even business partners. Fraudsters employ a variety of strategies such as deceit, impersonation and hijacking of users' accounts through unauthorized access. For instance, fraudsters can send false mobile money transaction notifications to consumers and then follow up with calls claiming that they are employees of the mobile money service providers. Unknowing some of the consumers, they will release their PINs to the callers. Once they have access to the accounts, funds are transferred immediately into their accounts leaving the consumers with an empty mobile money wallet. In some instances, the fraudsters will first send a mobile money transaction notification to mobile money users and ring them immediately to say they have made wrong transactions and will request that the money be returned to them. Users who are not diligent or ignorant and have enough money in their mobile money wallets will transfer their own money to the fraudsters unknowingly.

Agent-driven fraud is the type where mobile money agents defraud mobile money consumers, mobile money service providers and other agents using a wide range of strategies such as unauthorised access to customers' mobile money accounts, registering fake or ghost users on to mobile money services and unauthorized withdrawal from other agents' accounts.

Similarly, business partner-driven fraud occurs within business partnership networks. The partnership networks could be consumer-to-business (C2B), business-to-consumer (B2C) or merchant originated. This type of fraud can be committed in several ways including fraudulent transactions through the manipulation of the interfaces between small businesses and financial institutions; undertaking unauthorized transactions in the name of a business and swapping of SIM numbers to gain access to funds illegally.

With system administration fraud, employees or ex-employees use their access to mobile money systems to commit fraud. They may, for example, identify opportunities that will enable them to create fake accounts in order to transfer money to unauthorized destinations. Financial service provider fraud is similar to administration fraud. The only difference is that it is perpetuated by other employees within the service provider beyond the system administrators.

In spite of the various kinds of fraud identified by several authors, the most usual form of fraud in many developing countries is subscriber driven. Put differently, among the three main stakeholders (mobile money providers, agents and subscribers), the activities of fraudsters focus on subscribers. Table 7, therefore, presents the most common fraud cases that are often experienced by mobile money subscribers.

Table 7. Most common mobile fraud cases

Fraud case	Description
Anonymous phone call	This is when the fraudsters call subscribers to deceive them to return money that has been wrongly transferred into their mobile money accounts.
Anonymous SMS	This is when the fraudsters send subscribers SMS to deceive them to return money that has been wrongly transferred into their accounts.
False Promotion	Subscribers are deceived that they are winners of ongoing promotions and need to provide personal details of their mobile money account details and in the process, they are defrauded.
Delivery Services	Subscribers are deceived to pay for the delivery services for goods sent by a relative or friend from abroad before the goods are delivered to them.
The Staff of the Mobile money provider	This involves calling subscribers to explain the best way of performing mobile money transactions. This enables fraudsters to collect vital information such as the PIN from the subscribers.
Family emergency	A subscriber receives a call from someone who claims to know the subscriber. The caller will mention some names of your friends and relatives to convince you that he/she knows you. The caller will then ask you to send money to him/her to solve an urgent problem that one of your friends or relative is facing.

THE EFFECTS OF MOBILE MONEY FRAUD

With the high potential of promoting financial inclusion, the activities of fraudsters in the mobile money sector have far-reaching negative implications in several ways for subscribers, agents and mobile money service providers alike (Buku and Mazer, 2017; Akomea-Frimpong *et al.*, 2019).

Mobile money fraud has implications for the growth of subscribers. Some subscribers have withdrawn from the use of mobile money services because of the risk of losing their money through fraud (Mudiri, n.d.-a). Subscribers will want to be associated with a mobile money sector that is secure and can deliver services timely and efficiently.

Similarly, some mobile money agents have also been kicked out of business because of high levels of mobile money fraud (Buku and Mazer, 2017). At the same time, potential mobile money agents are discouraged from investing in the mobile money sector for fear of losses.

In addition, mobile money fraud affects the credibility of mobile money service providers (Buku and Mazer, 2017; Akomea-Frimpong *et al.*, 2019). It has been reported that the credibility of a leading mobile money service provider in East Africa was badly dented due to the high incidence of mobile money fraud among its staff (INTERPOL, 2020). It should be noted that when the image of one mobile money provider is dented, it has implications for other providers –users may associate fraud with all mobile money providers.

With an increased interconnectedness among mobile money service providers and other financial organisations, particularly the deployment of mobile money services in the payment of goods and services, a high incidence of fraud will limit the patronage of mobile money services by businesses and users. The mobile money industry has seen significant innovation within the last decade, especially opening up several platforms to perform varied financial transactions. The rise in mobile money fraud has the potential of frustrating the innovation drive, as businesses and individuals are less likely to connect to the mobile money platform if the risk of losing money is high.

Last but not least, the cost of managing mobile money fraud is expensive. With prominent levels of fraud, service providers will have to spend more money to make their systems safe and secure. Unfortunately, maintaining safer and less risky mobile money platforms will undoubtedly increase the transaction cost of providing these services, which may be passed on to consumers of mobile services.

STRATEGIES TO REDUCE MOBILE MONEY FRAUD

In discussing the strategies to eliminate or minimise the incidence of mobile money fraud, it is important to highlight the factors that facilitate it: weak regulatory framework, lenient registration systems, non-standardized transaction processes, insecure mobile money platforms, poor communication and awareness of consumers and poor mechanisms for reporting fraud, among others (Andersson & Naghavi, 2021; Buku & Mazer, 2017; INTERPOL, 2020).

To begin with, when appropriate regulatory and supervisory frameworks do not exist, they create avenues for fraud. Central banks have the responsibility to formulate and implement regulatory frameworks that control the activities of mobile money providers and their stakeholders (INTERPOL, 2020). Aspects of a regulatory framework may include customer identification; agents' eligibility; transactions and balance limits. In many developing countries even when they exist, their implementations are very weak (INTERPOL, 2020), as some mobile money providers have indicated that the regulatory frameworks are not enough to help them address the numerous risks associated with providing services to their clients (Andersson & Naghavi, 2021; Buku & Mazer, 2017; INTERPOL, 2020). Weak regulatory frameworks may not only stifle innovation but also make it difficult for regulators to monitor the activities of mobile money fraud in the sector, which can, for example, lead to the proliferation of unlicensed money transfer agencies or unregulated money transfer products. In many countries, the problem of the weak regulatory framework is further compounded by poorly equipped law enforcement agencies to adjudicate fraud cases. Countries must therefore institute effective regulatory frameworks that ensure the compliance of mobile money providers and all relevant stakeholders. At the same time, disciplinary measures should be instituted for those who fail to comply. In Ghana, for example, the Electronic Payments regulations were launched in 2015 to help provide a framework for the activities of mobile money providers (Bank of Ghana, 2015, Sections 26-28). To help minimize the activities of mobile money fraud, Ghana in 2022, made the National Identification card (a biometric card) the only card eligible to register for mobile money and other financial services.

In addition to the above, in jurisdictions where it is easier to register for mobile money services without visiting appropriate registration centers to be identified, the incidence of mobile money fraud is likely to be high (INTERPOL, 2020). Also, mobile money fraud is higher in countries where there is a high rural population that lacks national identification regimes making it difficult to track criminal activities. To address this, mobile money service providers should put in place strict registration procedures to allow for easy tracking and tracing of mobile money users.

The mobile money industry is also besieged with non-standardized transaction processes in many jurisdictions, which is an important enabler of fraud. This is even exacerbated by the fact that almost all banks in developing countries have incorporated mobile money services into their portfolios (Markovich & Snyder, 2017). One way to promote standardization is to ensure that mobile money activities (e.g., registration and transaction procedures) are coordinated and harmonized in different jurisdictions. This is important because fraudsters employ different tactics across mobile money providers because of the differences in transaction procedures. This implies that there is an urgent need for mobile network providers to work closely with banks and other financial services that have more control over their operations. Banks for example have tight requirements for mobile money transactions, as they have sophisticated systems that can detect and safeguard funds against fraudsters (Narteh, Mahmoud, & Amoh, 2017), which could be beneficial to mobile network providers if they collaborate. For instance, mobile money providers and banks may set up unions to monitor fraud trends and share experiences on fraud management best practices. Currently, many mobile providers prefer to deal with fraud cases individually without consulting their counterparts in the sector (INTERPOL, 2020).

Further, inadequate education of users about the proper use of mobile money services contributes to the incidence of mobile money fraud. With effective education and communication, users will be in a good position to understand fraud trends as well as the strategies to put in place to mitigate them (Mudiri, n.d.-b). Given that mobile money is a recent phenomenon in many countries, those in the middle and upper classes (the literate) are not fully abreast with the full potential and the risks associated with mobile money services. This knowledge gap is even direr for those in the lower class, that is, the poor, illiterate and unbanked population. Mobile money fraud is higher in countries where there is a large number of illiterate because a bigger part of mobile money transactions requires users to read (Mudiri, n.d.-b). Mobile money service providers must sensitize all mobile money users about the activities of fraud and how to avoid becoming victims of fraud. This is important because fraudsters keep changing their tactics on regular basis and users of mobile money need to be abreast with their new tactics. To ensure this, there must be comprehensive fraud awareness and prevention programs using both print and electronic media. This could include among other things, agents' training and certification; education programs for new subscribers (e.g. keeping PIN secured); the use of road shows that focus on the interaction among providers, agents and subscribers to create public awareness as well as education programs for existing users (INTERPOL, 2020).

Another major enabler of fraud is weak internal controls. If mobile money operators have poor and porous internal controls that allow employees and agents to get away with their crimes, then the fight against fraud can take a rather long period to win (Akomea-Frimpong *et al.*, 2019; Rafay, 2021a). System congestions and access challenges may also facilitate the activities of fraudsters. Providers, therefore, need to implement controls that strike an appropriate balance between making the mobile money platform secure and at the same time user-friendly. Similarly, mobile money providers should investigate the character of those applying for jobs before they are employed.

Similarly, innovation is critical in the fight against fraud. Mobile money providers that use obsolete technologies are more likely to be vulnerable to fraud as compared to those with modern technologies. Providers of mobile money services must therefore work towards developing smart tools and technologies that are capable of limiting, detecting and stopping fraud. While mobile money providers may prioritise the development of new services for their clients, it is important they factor in the development of smart tools and technologies that are capable of generating big data on the activities of fraud for analysis (INTERPOL, 2020; Rafay, 2021b). If it becomes necessary, governments and donor organisations can assist to finance the development of smart tools and technologies, as there have to be robust anti-fraud response systems to secure the many users that rely on mobile money as their only means of financial control (Mudiri, n.d.-b).

Last but not least, the mechanisms for reporting fraud are inadequate and burdensome for the less savvy or isolated users. Central banks and relevant government institutions such as security agencies must provide enabling environments for mobile money providers to collaborate with them on a timely basis on fraud cases. In this regard, there must be a comprehensive fraud management system that should include cost-effective online reporting mechanisms, which must be accessible to the relevant security agencies. There is therefore the need to create security awareness as well as simplify the reporting process through dedicated service lines and online portals. Users of mobile money services must also report fraud cases promptly as well as assist in investigations to unravel fraudulent transactions (Buku and Mazer, 2017; INTERPOL, 2020).

CONCLUSION

This chapter has acknowledged that the mobile money sector has witnessed considerable growth in the last two decades partly because of the penetration of mobile telephony into most parts of the developing world. Mobile money is more dominant in Africa as compared to other parts of the developing world; and in Africa, East and West Africa have experienced the highest penetration of mobile money services. However, the growth of the sector is faced with one major challenge, mobile money fraud. This chapter examined the nature and forms of mobile money fraud as well as its effects on service providers and users.

This chapter has shown that mobile money fraud is increasingly becoming widespread in the developing world partly because of the rapid growth in registered mobile money accounts, transaction volumes and values. The sector is also becoming increasingly diversified, allowing for person-to-person, person-to-business, government-to-persons, and NGO-to-person transactions. The growth in mobile money fraud cases is also partly explained by factors such as high illiteracy, inadequate education on the activities of mobile money, weak regulatory frameworks, non-standardised transaction processes, weak internal control systems and inadequate mechanisms to report fraud.

It has also been demonstrated in this chapter that mobile money fraud takes several forms including those that are driven by agents, subscribers, non-subscribers, agents and employees of mobile money providers. The chapter argued that the activities of mobile money fraud if left unchecked can have adverse effects on subscribers, agents, and mobile money providers alike. Key among these negative effects are financial losses to subscribers, agents, and providers.

The chapter noted that while it may not be possible to eliminate completely the issue of mobile money fraud, some key strategies are important in reducing the phenomenon including collective action, implementing strong regulatory frameworks, standardisation of mobile money transaction processes, improving internal controls, experience sharing among relevant stakeholders, educating and building the capacity of mobile phone users on mobile money usage and the activities of fraudsters. As technology continues to improve (Rafay, 2019) so will the provision of mobile money services. At the same time, new forms of fraud will emerge with changes in the way mobile money services are provided. The chapter, therefore, contends that continuous monitoring is important for effective fraud mitigation. It is important to note that there is currently limited research on mobile money fraud partly because the service is fairly new in most parts of the developing world. More research is needed to understand the reasons for mobile fraud, how often it occurs, trends or patterns of the fraud, who are those involved in the fraud, and how effective the intervention is used to curb mobile money fraud, among others.

DECLARATION

The author declares that the manuscript follows ethical standards and there are no potential conflicts of interest with respect to the research, authorship and/or publication of this chapter.

DISCLAIMER

The contents and views of this chapter are expressed by the author in his personal capacity. It is not necessary for the Editor and the Publisher to agree with these viewpoints, and they are not responsible for any duty of care in this regard.

ACKNOWLEDGMENT

The author extends sincere gratitude to

- The Editor and the International Editorial Advisory Board (IEAB) of this book who initially desk reviewed, arranged a rigorous double/triple blind review process, and conducted a thorough, minute, and critical final review before accepting the chapter for publication.
- All anonymous reviewers who provided very constructive feedbacks for thorough revision, improvement, extension, and fine tuning of the chapter.
- All colleagues, assistants and well-wishers who assisted to complete this task.

REFERENCES

Afawubo, K., Couchoro, M. K., Agbaglah, M., & Gbandi, T. (2020). Mobile money adoption and households' vulnerability to shocks: Evidence from Togo. *Applied Economics*, *52*(10), 1141–1162. doi:10.1080/00036846.2019.1659496

Akomea-Frimpong, I., Andoh, C., Akomea-Frimpong, A., & Dwomoh-Okudzeto, Y. (2019). Control of fraud on mobile money services in Ghana: An exploratory study. *Journal of Money Laundering Control*, *22*(2), 300–317. doi:10.1108/JMLC-03-2018-0023

Andersson, S., & Naghavi, N. (2021). *State of the Industry Report on Mobile Money 2021, GSMA*. GSMA.

Bank of Ghana. (2015). *Guidelines for E-Money Issuers in Ghana*. Retrieved from https://www.bog.gov.gh/privatecontent/Banking/ E-MONEY GUIDE LINES-29-06-2015-UPDATED5.pdf

Boamah, E. F., & Murshid, N. S. (2019). "Techno-market fix"? Decoding wealth through mobile money in the global South. *Geoforum*, *106*, 253–262. doi:10.1016/j.geoforum.2019.08.012

Botchey, F. E., Qin, Z., & Hughes-Lartey, K. (2020). Mobile money fraud prediction-A cross-case analysis on the efficiency of support vector machines, gradient boosted decision trees, and Naïve Bayes algorithms. *Information (Basel)*, *11*(8), 1–20. doi:10.3390/info11080383

Buku, M., & Mazer, R. (2017). *Fraud in mobile financial services: Protecting consumers, providers and the system* (The World Bank - CGAP Brief No. 119208). Retrieved from https://documents.worldbank.org/en/publication/documents-reports/documentdetail/ 249151504766545101/fraud-in-mobile-financial-services-protecting-consumers-providers-and-the-system

Busuulwa, B. (2016). Mobile money fraud, crime rate increase in Uganda. *The EastAfrican*. Retrieved from https://www.theeastafrican.co.ke/tea/business/mobile-money-fraud-crime-rate-increase-in-uganda--1356614

Chatain, P. L., Zerzan, A., Noor, W., Dannaoui, N., & De Koker, L. (2011). *Protecting Mobile Money against FinancialCrimes: Global Policy Challenges and Solutions*. World Bank Publications. doi:10.1596/978-0-8213-8669-9

David-West, O., Iheanachor, N., & Umukoro, I. O. (2019). Mobile money as a frugal innovation for the bottom of the pyramid–Cases of selected African countries. *Africa Journal of Management*, *5*(3), 274–302. doi:10.1080/23322373.2019.1652023

Fitzhenry, W. (2022). Visualizing a timeline of mobile money fraud. *Cambridge Intelligence*. Retrieved from https://cambridge-intelligence.com/mobile-money-fraud/

INTERPOL. (2020). Mobile money and organized crime in Africa. *Enact Africa*. Retrieved from https://enactafrica.org/research/interpol-reports/mobile-money-and-organised-crime-in-africa

Khan, N., Rafay, A., & Shakeel, A. (2020). Attributes of Internal Audit and Prevention, Detection and Assessment of Fraud in Pakistan. *Lahore Journal of Business*, *9*(1), 33–58. doi:10.35536/ljb.2020.v9.i1.a2

Lepoutre, J., & Oguntoye, A. (2018). The (non-)emergence of mobile money systems in Sub-Saharan Africa: A comparative multilevel perspective of Kenya and Nigeria. *Technological Forecasting and Social Change*, *131*, 262–275. doi:10.1016/j.techfore.2017.11.010

Markovich, S., & Snyder, C. (2017). M-Pesa and mobile money in Kenya: Pricing for success. *Kellogg School of Management Cases*, *1*, 1–17. doi:10.1108/case.kellogg.2016.000221

Maurer, B. (2015). *How Would You Like to Pay?: How Technology Is Changing the Future of Money*. Duke University Press.

Merritt, C. (2011). Mobile money transfer services: The next phase in the evolution of person-to-person payments. *Journal of Payments Strategy and Systems*, *5*(2), 143–160.

Mudiri, J. L. (n.d.-a). *Fraud in Mobile Financial Services*. MicroSave. Retrieved from http://www.microsave.net/files/pdf/RP151_ Fraud_in_Mobile_Financial_Services _JMudiri.pdf

Nakitende, M. G., Rafay, A., & Waseem, M. (2021). Frauds in Business Organizations: A Comprehensive Overview. In A. Rafay (Ed.), *Handbook of Research on Theory and Practice of Financial Crimes* (pp. 21–38). IGI Global. doi:10.4018/978-1-7998-5567-5.ch002

Narteh, B., Mahmoud, M. A., & Amoh, S. (2017). Customer behavioural intentions towards mobile money services adoption in Ghana. *Service Industries Journal*, *37*(7/8), 426–447. doi:10.1080/02642069.2017.1331435

Rafay, A. (Ed.). (2019). *FinTech as a Disruptive Technology for Financial Institutions*. IGI Global. doi:10.4018/978-1-5225-7805-5

Rafay, A. (Ed.). (2021a). *Money Laundering and Terrorism Financing in Global Financial Systems*. IGI Global. doi:10.4018/978-1-7998-8758-4

Rafay, A. (Ed.). (2021b). *Handbook of Research on Theory and Practice of Financial Crimes*. IGI Global. doi:10.4018/978-1-7998-5567-5

Rafay, A. (Ed.). (2022). *Finance for Sustainability in a Turbulent Economy*. IGI Global. doi:10.4018/978-1-6684-5580-7

Rafay, A., & Khan, A. (2018). Synergy for sustainability in the upcoming telecommunication revolution: The Case of a developing economy. In A. Borchers (Ed.), *Technology Management in Organizational and Societal Contexts* (pp. 51–76). IGI Global. doi:10.4018/978-1-5225-5279-6.ch003

Compilation of References

Abdul-Ismail, A. (n.d.). *Corruption and its threats to the consolidation of democracy in Nigeria: The sharia perspective*. Bayero University.

Abdullahi, S. I. (2007). Essay on Corruption. Unpublished monograph, Kano Nigeria.

Abdullahi, S. I. (2019). Risk management and corporate governance: an Islamic perspective. In T. Azid, A. A. Alnodl, & M. A. Qureshi (Eds.), *Research in Corporate and Shariah Governance in the Muslim World: Theory and Practice*. Emerald.

Abeysekera, I. (2020). Intangibles disclosure on entrepreneurial small businesses' websites to influence stakeholders' impressions. *Australian Accounting Review*, *30*(1), 22–32. doi:10.1111/auar.12277

Abiloro, T. O., Olawole, A., & Adeniran, T. E. (2019). Corruption, income inequality, and economic development in Nigeria. *International Journal of Academic Research in Accounting, Finance and Management Sciences*, *9*(4), 304–319.

Abou-El-Sood, H., & El-Sayed, D. (2022). Abnormal disclosure tone, earnings management and earnings quality. *Journal of Applied Accounting Research*, *23*(2), 402–433. doi:10.1108/JAAR-07-2020-0139

Abraham, S., & Bamber, M. (2017). The Q&A: Under surveillance. *Accounting, Organizations and Society*, *58*, 15–31. doi:10.1016/j.aos.2017.04.001

Abshari, Z., Jenkins, G. P., Kuo, C. Y., & Shahee, M. (2021). Progressive taxation versus progressive targeted transfers in the design of a sustainable value-added tax system. *Sustainability*, *13*(20), 11165. doi:10.3390u132011165

ACFE. (2022). *Association of certified fraud examiners report to the Nations: Fraud trends and key takeaways*. Retrieved from https://www.acfe.com/-/media/files/acfe/pdfs/2012-report-to-nations.ashx

Achebe, C. (1988). *The trouble with Nigeria*. Fourth Dimension Publishers.

Açıkgöz, Ö. (2010). Osmanlı Para Politikasında Reform Çabaları:1800-1844 Dönemi Üzerine Bir Değerlendirm. *Uluslararası Yönetim İktisat ve İşletme Dergisi*, *6*(12), 36–55.

Adams, J. S. (1963). Toward an understanding of inequity. *Journal of Abnormal and Social Psychology*, *67*(5), 422–436. doi:10.1037/h0040968 PMID:14081885

Adams, J. S. (1965). Inequity in social exchange. In L. Berkowitz (Ed.). Advances in Experimental Social Psychology. Academic Press. doi:10.1016/S0065-2601(08)60108-2

Adegoke, A. O., Donga, M., Idi, A., & Abdullahi, B. (2018). An examination of drivers of financial development: Evidence in west African countries. *Pakistan Journal of Humanities and Social Sciences*, *6*(1), 132–143. doi:10.52131/pjhss.2018.0601.0038

Ades, A., & di Tella, R. (1997). The New economics of corruption: A survey and some new results. *Political Studies*, *45*(3), 496–515. doi:10.1111/1467-9248.00093

Ades, A., & Di Tella, R. (1999). Rents, competition, and Corruption. *The American Economic Review*, *89*(4), 982–993. doi:10.1257/aer.89.4.982

Adler, R., Mansi, M., Pandey, R., & Stringer, C. (2017). United Nations decade on biodiversity: A study of the reporting practices of the Australian mining industry. *Accounting, Auditing & Accountability Journal*, *30*(8), 1711–1745. doi:10.1108/AAAJ-04-2015-2028

Aerts, W. (1994). On the use of accounting logic as an explanatory category in narrative accounting disclosures. *Accounting, Organizations and Society*, *19*(4-5), 337–353. doi:10.1016/0361-3682(94)90001-9

Aerts, W. (2005). Picking up the pieces: Impression management in the retrospective attributional framing of accounting outcomes. *Accounting, Organizations and Society*, *30*(6), 493–517. doi:10.1016/j.aos.2004.07.001

Aerts, W., & Cheng, P. (2011). Causal disclosures on earnings and earnings management in an IPO setting. *Journal of Accounting and Public Policy*, *30*(5), 431–459. doi:10.1016/j.jaccpubpol.2011.03.006

Aerts, W., & Yan, B. (2017). Rhetorical impression management in the letter to shareholders and institutional setting: A metadiscourse perspective. *Accounting, Auditing & Accountability Journal*, *30*(2), 404–432. doi:10.1108/AAAJ-01-2015-1916

Afawubo, K., Couchoro, M. K., Agbaglah, M., & Gbandi, T. (2020). Mobile money adoption and households' vulnerability to shocks: Evidence from Togo. *Applied Economics*, *52*(10), 1141–1162. doi:10.1080/00036846.2019.1659496

AfricaNews. (2022). *Africa COVID-19 stats*. Retrieved from https://www.africanews.com/2020/06/29/coronavirus-in-africa-breakdown-of-infected-virus-free -countries/

Africa, C. D. C. (2020). *Corona virus disease 2019 (COVID-19)*. African Union. Retrieved from https://africacdc.org/COVID-19/

African Arguments. (2020). *Corona virus in Africa tracker: How many COVID-19 cases*. Retrieved from https://africanarguments.org/2020/06/29/coronavirus-in-africa-tracker-how-many-cases-and -where-latest/

Agbu, O. (2003). Corruption and human trafficking: The Nigerian case. *West Africa Review*, *4*(1), 1–13.

AGEA, E&Y Financial Letters. (2019). AGEA.

AGEA, E&Y Up Grade Procedure Services. (2014). AGEA.

AGEA, PwC Audit Reports 2011-2013. (n.d.). AGEA.

AGEA. PwC Special Report. (2014). AGEA.

Agenyi, E., & Ameh, I. E. (2009). Corruption in some public sectors: Implications for sustainable socio-economic development in Nigeria. *NASHER Journal*, *7*(1), 128–134.

Aghedo, I. & Osumah, O. (2013). Prospects and challenges of Anti-Corruption crusade in Nigeria's fourth republic. *Ilorin Journal of Business and Social Science, 15*(2).

Agoglia, C. P., Doupnik, T. P. S., & Tsakumis, G. T. (2011). Principles-based versus rules-based accounting standards: The influence of standard precision and audit committee strength on financial reporting decisions. *The Accounting Review*, *86*(3), 747–767. doi:10.2308/accr.00000045

Ahlström, H., & Monciardini, D. (2022). The regulatory dynamics of sustainable finance: Paradoxical success and limitations of EU reforms. *Journal of Business Ethics*, *177*(1), 193–212. doi:10.100710551-021-04763-x PMID:33642657

Ahmad, E., Ullah, M. A., & Arfeen, M. I. (2012). Does corruption affect economic growth? *Latin American Journal of Economics*, *49*(2), 277–305. doi:10.7764/LAJE.49.2.277

Ahmad, N. N. N., & Hossain, D. M. (2019). Exploring the meaning of climate change discourses: An impression management exercise? *Accounting Research Journal*, *32*(2), 113–128. doi:10.1108/ARJ-07-2016-0085

Ahmed, S. K. (2016). *European Union Somalia Gender Analysis Study*. Garowe: Somali Institute for Development and Research Analysis (SIDRA). Retrieved from https://sidrainstitute.org/wp-content/uploads/2018/04/Report_EU_Gender_Analysis_Somalia_Study-SIDRA_Final_2016.pdf

AICPA. (2022). *Updates*. Retrieved from https://www.ifrs.com/updates/aicpa/ifrs_faq.html#q3

Ainsworth, R. T. (2008). *MTIC (Carousel) fraud: Twelve ways forward; two ways' preferred'-has the technology-based administrative solution been rejected?* Boston University School of Law Working Paper, (08–10).

Ainsworth, R. T., & Alwohaibi, M. (2016). GCC VAT: The intra-gulf trade problem. SSRN *Electronic Journal*. Retrieved from https://ssrn.com/abstract=2916252 doi:10.2139/ssrn.2916252

AjekweC. (2017). Accounting Flexibility: Slippery Slope to Fraud? Retrieved from https://ssrn.com/abstract=2972726 doi:10.2139/ssrn.2972726

Ajekwe, C. (2021). Impact of Flexibility in Accounting on Financial Reporting. *European Journal of Accounting, Auditing and Finance Research*, *9*(3), 74–87.

Ajekwe, C. (2022). Application of professional judgement in international financial reporting standard. *European Journal of Accounting, Auditing and Finance Research*, *10*(7), 17–30.

Ajekwe, C., & Ibiamke, A. (2019). Disclosure of critical accounting judgments and key sources of estimation uncertainty in the financial statements of companies in Nigeria. *Journal of Finance and Accounting*, *7*(1), 22–31. doi:10.11648/j.jfa.20190701.14

Ajibewa, A. (2006). Democracy and corruption in Nigeria. In E. O. Ojo (Ed.), *Challenges of Sustainable Democracy in Nigeria*. John Archers.

Ajzen, I. (1985). From Intentions to Actions: A Theory of Planned Behavior. In Action Control. SSSP Springer Series in Social Psychology. Berlin: Springer. doi:10.1007/978-3-642-69746-3_2

Ajzen, I. (1991). The theory of planned behavior. *Organizational Behavior and Human Decision Processes*, *50*(2), 179–211. doi:10.1016/0749-5978(91)90020-T

Akdeniz, C., & Çatik, N. (2019). Parasal aktarım mekanizmalarının işleyişinde finansal koşulların önemi: Tvp-var modellerinden bulgular. *Pamukkale Üniversitesi Sosyal Bilimler Enstitüsü Dergisi*, *34*, 73–96.

Akgündüz, A. (Ed.). (1990). *Osmanlı Kanunnameleri ve Hukuki Tahlilleri:Osmanlı Hukukuna giriş ve Fatih devrikanunnameleri*. FEY Vakfı.

Akinola, M., & Mendes, W. B. (2008). The dark side of creativity: Biological vulnerability and negative emotions lead to greater artistic creativity. *Personality and Social Psychology Bulletin*, *34*(12), 1677–1686. doi:10.1177/0146167208323933 PMID:18832338

Akinpelu, O. (2020). COVID-19: How MTN, Telkom, Airtel and Safaricom are helping users cope with self-isolation. *Textnet.ng*. Retrieved from https://technext.ng/2020/03/26/COVID-19-how-mtn-telkom-airtel-and-safaricom-are-helping-users-cope-with-self-isolation/

Akomea-Frimpong, I., Andoh, C., Akomea-Frimpong, A., & Dwomoh-Okudzeto, Y. (2019). Control of fraud on mobile money services in Ghana: An exploratory study. *Journal of Money Laundering Control*, *22*(2), 300–317. doi:10.1108/JMLC-03-2018-0023

Akpınar, E., & Kasapbas, I. M. C. (2019). Association analysis between pharmacies and pharmaceutical companies in healthcare insurance systems. *Haliç University Journal of Science*, 2(1), 35–47.

Alavuotunki, K., Haapanen, M., & Pirttilä, J. (2019). The effects of the value-added tax on revenue and inequality. *The Journal of Development Studies*, *55*(4), 490–508. doi:10.1080/00220388.2017.1400015

AlBassam, B. A. (2013). The relationship between governance and economic growth during times of crisis. *European Journal of Sustainable Development*, 2(4), 1–18. doi:10.14207/ejsd.2013.v2n2p1

Ali, F., Rasoolimanesh, S. M., Sarstedt, M., Ringle, C. M., & Ryu, K. (2018). An assessment of the use of partial least squares structural equation modeling (PLS-SEM) in hospitality research. *International Journal of Contemporary Hospitality Management*, *30*(1), 514–538. doi:10.1108/IJCHM-10-2016-0568

Aliyu, S. U. R., & Elijah, A. O. (2008). *Corruption and Economic Growth in Nigeria: 1986–2007*. MPRA Paper No. 12504. Retrieved from https://mpra.ub.uni-muenchen.de/12504/

Allen, R., Helms, M., Takeda, M., & White, C. (2007). Porter's generic strategies: An exploratory study of their use in Japan. *The Journal of Business Strategy*, *24*(1), 69–90. doi:10.54155/jbs.24.1.69-90

Al-Sayani, Y. M., Mohamad Nor, M. N., & Amran, N. A. (2020). The influence of audit committee characteristics on impression management in chairman statement: Evidence from Malaysia. *Cogent Business and Management*, *7*(1), 1774250. doi:10.1080/23311975.2020.1774250

Aluko, Y. A. (2009). Corruption in Nigeria: Concepts and dimension. In D. U. Enweremadu & E. E. Okafor (Eds.), *Anti-corruption reforms in Nigeria since 1999: Issues, challenges and the way forward*. IFRA.

Amiram, D., Bozanic, Z., Cox, J. D., Dupont, Q., Karpoff, J. M., & Sloan, R. (2018). Financial reporting fraud and other forms of misconduct: A multidisciplinary review of the literature. *Review of Accounting Studies*, *23*(2), 732–783. doi:10.100711142-017-9435-x

Anand, V., Blake, E. A., & Joshi, M. (2004). Business as usual: The acceptance and perpetuation of corruption. *The Academy of Management Executive*, *18*(2), 39–53. doi:10.5465/ame.2004.13837437

Anderson, S. W., & Dekker, H. C. (2014). The role of management controls in transforming firm boundaries and sustaining hybrid organizational forms. *Foundations and Trends® in Accounting*, *8*(2), 75–141.

Anderson, J. C., & Gerbing, D. W. (1988). Structural equation modeling in practice: A review and recommended two-step approach. *Psychological Bulletin*, *103*(3), 411–423. doi:10.1037/0033-2909.103.3.411

Anderson, R. C., & Reeb, D. M. (2003). Founding family ownership and firm performance: Evidence from the S&P 500. *The Journal of Finance*, *58*(3), 1301–1328. doi:10.1111/1540-6261.00567

Andersson, S., & Naghavi, N. (2021). *State of the Industry Report on Mobile Money 2021, GSMA*. GSMA.

Andon, P., & Free, C. (2014). Media coverage of accounting: The NRL salary cap crisis. *Accounting, Auditing & Accountability Journal*, *27*(1), 15–47. doi:10.1108/AAAJ-02-2012-00936

Andvig, J. C., Fjeldstad, O. H., Weltzien, Å., Amundsen, I., Sissener, T. K., & Søreide, T. (2001). *Corruption. A review of contemporary research.* CRIStin. Retrieved from https://nmbu.brage.unit.no/nmbu-xmlui/handle/11250/2473686

Ansoff, H. I. (1975). Managing strategic surprise by response to weak signals. *California Management Review, 18*(2), 21–33. doi:10.2307/41164635

Antonucci, D. (2017). *The Cyber Risk Handbook: Creating and measuring effective Cybersecurity capabilities.* John Wiley & Sons. doi:10.1002/9781119309741

Arat, M. (1985). Kalp Para Nasıl Tanınır. *Türk NümizmatikDerneğiYayınları, 15*(1), 1–29.

Argyris, C. (1980). Making the undiscussable and its undiscussability discussable. *Public Administration Review, 40*(3), 205–213. doi:10.2307/975372

Armitage, C. J., & Conner, M. (2001). Efficacy of the theory of planned behavior: A meta-analytic review. *British Journal of Social Psychology, 40*(4), 471–499. doi:10.1348/014466601164939 PMID:11795063

Ashby, W. R. (1956). *An introduction to Cybernetics.* Chapaman & Hall. doi:10.5962/bhl.title.5851

Assay, B. (2023). Whistleblowing Policy against Corruption: The Case of Nigeria. In A. Rafay (Ed.), *Concepts and Cases of Illicit and Illegitimate Finance.* IGI Global. doi:10.4018/978-1-6684-8587-3.ch004

Asseraf, Y., Lages, L. F., & Shoham, A. (2019). Assessing the drivers and impact of international marketing agility. *International Marketing Review, 36*(2), 289–315. doi:10.1108/IMR-12-2017-0267

Atabo, A. (2022, January 7). Whistleblowing Policy: The gains, threats, losses and grief. *News Agency of Nigeria.* Retrieved from https://www.corruptionanonymous.org/ whistleblowing-policy-the-gains-threats-losses-and-grief/

Atia, M., & Herrold, C. E. (2018). Governing through patronage: The rise of NGOs and the fall of civil society in Palestine and Morocco. *Voluntas, 29*(5), 1044–1054. doi:10.100711266-018-9953-6

Austine, E., Charles, M., & Raymond, A. O. (2013). Corruption in Nigeria: A historical perspective. *Research Humanities and Social Sciences Journal, 3,* 16–19.

Autio, E., & Acs, Z. (2010). Intellectual property protection and the formation of entrepreneurial growth aspirations. *Strategic Entrepreneurship Journal, 4*(3), 234–251. doi:10.1002ej.93

Ayittey, G. (2002). *Biting their own Tails: African Leaders and the Internalist intricacies of the Rape of a Continent.* A Keynote address to SORAC.

Ayo, S. B. (1995). The Evolution of the Nigerian Local Government System. In A. M. Awokotun (Ed.), *New Trends in Nigerian Local Government.* Obafemi Awolowo University Press.

Ayres, I., Lingwall, J., & Steinway, S. (2013). Skeletons in the database: An early analysis of the CFPB's consumer complaints. *Fordham Journal of Corporate and Financial Law, 19,* 343. doi:10.2139srn.2295157

Azam, M. (2016). Does governance and foreign capital inflows affect economic development in OIC countries? *Journal of Economic Cooperation and Development, 37*(4), 21–50.

Azeez, O. (2019). Cybercrime cost Nigeria n288bn in 2018. *Business a.m.* Retrieved from https://www.businessamlive.com/cyber-crime-cost-nigeria-n288bn-in-2018/

Azmat, F., & Samaratunge, R. (2009). Responsible entrepreneurship in developing countries: Understanding the realities and complexities. *Journal of Business Ethics, 90*(3), 437–452. doi:10.100710551-009-0054-8

Babalola, A. A. (2019). *The elusive search for nation Nigeria*. Afe Babalola University Press.

Baglioni, A., & Colombo, L. (2011). The effects of imperfect auditing on managerial compensation. *International Review of Economics & Finance, 20*(4), 542–548. doi:10.1016/j.iref.2010.10.001

Balint, T., Bauer, M. W., & Knill, C. (2008). Bureaucratic change in the European administrative space: The case of the European Commission. *West European Politics, 31*(4), 677–700. doi:10.1080/01402380801905967

Banerjee, A., Mullainathan, S., & Hanna, R. (2012). *Corruption* (w17968). National Bureau of Economic Research. doi:10.3386/w17968

Banhamza, M. (2016, February 3). *EU/Morocco trade: How can a David engage in a win-win situation with a Goliath?* Retrieved from https://politheor.net/eumorocco-trade-how-can-a-david-engage-in-a-win-win-situation-with-a-goliath/

Bank of Ghana. (2015). *Guidelines for E-Money Issuers in Ghana*. Retrieved from https://www.bog.gov.gh/privatecontent/Banking/ E-MONEY GUIDE LINES-29-06-2015-UPDATED5.pdf

Baran, S. J. (2012). *Introduction to mass communication*. McGraw-Hill.

Barkema, H. G., Baum, J. A., & Mannix, E. A. (2002). Management challenges in new time. *Academy of Management Journal, 45*(5), 916–930. doi:10.2307/3069322

Barkemeyer, R., Comyns, B., Figge, F., & Napolitano, G. (2014). CEO statements in sustainability reports: Substantive information or background noise? *Accounting Forum, 38*(4), 241–257. doi:10.1016/j.accfor.2014.07.002

Barrales-Molina, V., Martinez-Lopez, F. J., & Gazquez-Abad, J. C. (2014). Dynamic marketing capabilities: Toward an integrative framework. *International Journal of Management Reviews, 16*(4), 397–416. doi:10.1111/ijmr.12026

Barrenechea, M. (2019, January 24). Les données ont une pierre angulaire: La confiance. *Globb Security. FR*. Retrieved from http://globbsecurity.fr/les-donnees-ont-une-pierre-angulaire-la-confiance-45128/

Barth, M. E. (2006). Including estimates of future in today's financial statements. *Accounting Horizons, 20*(3), 271–285. doi:10.2308/acch.2006.20.3.271

Barton, L. (1993). *Crisis in Organizations: Managing and communication in the heat of chaos*. South-Western Publishing Company.

Bastürk, F. H. (2020). Insurance Fraud: The Case in Turkey. In S. Grima, E. Boztepe, & P. J. Baldacchino (Eds.), *Contemporary Issues in Audit Management and Forensic Accounting*. Emerald. doi:10.1108/S1569-375920200000102009

Baumann, N. (2020). *Understanding COVID-19's impact on the insurance sector*. Deloitte. Retrieved from https://www2.deloitte.com/global/en/pages/about-deloitte/articles/covid- 19/understandingcovid-19-s-impact-on-the- insurance-sector-.html

Baumol, W. J. (1996). Entrepreneurship: Productive, unproductive, and destructive. *Journal of Business Venturing, 11*(1), 3–22. doi:10.1016/0883-9026(94)00014-X

Baxter, R., Bedard, J. C., Hoitash, R., & Yezegel, A. (2013). Enterprise risk management program quality: Determinants, value relevance and the financial crisis. *Contemporary Accounting Research, 30*(4), 1264–1295. doi:10.1111/j.1911-3846.2012.01194.x

Baytimur, S. (2016). Osmanlı devleti'nde kalpazanlık faaliyetleri ve uygulanan cezalar (1789-1808). *Bitlis Eren Üniversitesi Sosyal Bilimler Enstitüsü Dergisi, 5*(2), 56–72.

Bayuk, J. L., Healey, J., Rohmeyer, P., Sachs, M. H., Schmidt, J., & Weiss, J. (2012). *Cybersecurity policy guidebook.* John Wiley & Sons. doi:10.1002/9781118241530

BBC News. (2022). *Corona Virus: Tracking the Global Outbreak.* Retrieved from https://www.bbc.com/news/world-51235105

BBC. (2011). *Gang of 15 jailed for £250m VAT fraud.* Retrieved from https://www.bbc.com/news/uk-england-16262390

Beasley, M. S., Hermanson, D. R., Carcello, J. V., & Neal, T. L. (2010). Fraudulent Financial Reporting: 1997–2007: An analysis of U.S. public companies. *Association Sections, Divisions, Boards, Teams,* 453. Retrieved from https://egrove.olemiss.edu/cgi/viewcontent.cgi?article=1534&context=aicpa_assoc

Beattie, V., & Jones, M. (2002). Measurement distortion of graphs in corporate reports: An experimental study. *Accounting, Auditing & Accountability Journal, 15*(4), 546–564. doi:10.1108/09513570210440595

Beattie, V., & Jones, M. (2008). Corporate reporting using graphs: A review and synthesis. *Journal of Accounting Literature, 27,* 71–110.

Beattie, V., & Jones, M. J. (1999). Australian financial graphs: An empirical study. *Abacus, 35*(1), 46–76. doi:10.1111/1467-6281.00034

Beattie, V., & Jones, M. J. (2000a). Changing graph use in corporate annual reports: A time-series analysis. *Contemporary Accounting Research, 17*(2), 213–226. doi:10.1506/AAT8-3CGL-3J94-PH4F

Beattie, V., & Jones, M. J. (2000b). Impression management: The case of inter-country financial graphs. *Journal of International Accounting, Auditing & Taxation, 9*(2), 159–183. doi:10.1016/S1061-9518(00)00030-6

Becker, G. S. (1968). Crime and punishment: An economic approach. *Journal of Political Economy, 76*(2), 169–217. doi:10.1086/259394

Beebeejaun, A. (2019). The fight against international transfer pricing abuses: A recommendation for Mauritius. *International Journal of Law and Management, 61*(1), 205–231. doi:10.1108/IJLMA-05-2018-0083

Begley, T. A., & Purnanandam, A. (2021). Colour and credit: Race, regulation, and the quality of financial services. *Journal of Financial Economics, 141*(1), 48–65. doi:10.1016/j.jfineco.2021.03.001

Beissel, S. (2016). *Cybersecurity investments: Decision support under economic aspects.* Springer. doi:10.1007/978-3-319-30460-1

Bello-Imam, L. B. (2004). Corruption and national development. In I. B. Bellow-Imam & M. I. Obadan (Eds.), *Democratic governance and development management in Nigeria's fourth republic 1999-2003.* Centre for Local Government and Rural Development Studies Business.

Benazic, A. (2016). Primjena mehanizma obrnutog oporezivanja i njegovi učinci na troškove ispunjavanja obveze PDV-a u Europskoj uniji. *Porezni vjesnik, 2.*

Bennett, B. (2021). *Logically fallacious: The ultimate collection of over 300 logical fallacies.* Archieboy Holdings, LLC.

Bertelsmann Stiftung. (2018). *BTI 2018: Country Report – Somalia*. Gutersloh: Bertelsmann Stiftung. Retrieved from https://docslib.org/doc/9506976/bti-2018-country-report-somalia

Bhattacharya, A. (2022). Consumer, bank, and stock market reaction to CFPB's complaint data disclosure. *Journal of Financial Services Marketing*, 1–18. doi:10.105741264-022-00143-2

Birindelli, G., Trotta, A., Chiappini, H., & Rizzello, A. (2020). Environmental impact investments in Europe: Where are we headed? In *Contemporary Issues in Sustainable Finance* (pp. 151–175). Palgrave Macmillan. doi:10.1007/978-3-030-40248-8_7

BNDES. (2020). *Amazon fund*. Rio de Janeiro: The Brazilian Development Bank. Retrieved from https://www.bndes.gov.br/SiteBNDES/bndes/bndes_en/Institucional/Social_ and_Environmental_Responsibility/amazon_fund.html

Boamah, E. F., & Murshid, N. S. (2019). "Techno-market fix"? Decoding wealth through mobile money in the global South. *Geoforum*, *106*, 253–262. doi:10.1016/j.geoforum.2019.08.012

Bock, A. J., Opsahl, T., George, G., & Gann, D. M. (2012). The effects of culture and structure on strategic flexibility during business model innovation. *Journal of Management Studies*, *49*(2), 279–305. doi:10.1111/j.1467-6486.2011.01030.x

Boehm, F., & Sierra, F. (2015). *The gendered impact of corruption: Who suffers more-men or women?* Bergen: Chr. Michelsen Institute. Retrieved from https://www.cmi.no/publications/5610-the-gendered-impact-of-corruption

Boehm, F., & Lambsdorff, J. G. (2009). Corrupción y anticorrupción: Una perspectiva neo-institucional. *Revista de Economia Institucional*, *11*(21), 45–72.

Bolivar, V. J., & Baressi, J. (1995). Giving meaning to movement: A developmental study. *Ecological Psychology*, *7*(2), 71–97. doi:10.120715326969eco0702_1

Borselli, F. (2011). *Organised VAT Fraud: Features, Magnitude, Policy Perspectives* (Banca d'Italia occasional paper series, no. 106.). Retrieved from https://www.bancaditalia.it/pubblicazioni/qef/2011-0106/QEF_106.pdf

Bose, I., & Mahapatra, R. K. (2001). Business data mining – A machine learning perspective. *Information & Management*, *39*(3), 211–225. doi:10.1016/S0378-7206(01)00091-X

Botchey, F. E., Qin, Z., & Hughes-Lartey, K. (2020). Mobile money fraud prediction-A cross-case analysis on the efficiency of support vector machines, gradient boosted decision trees, and Naïve Bayes algorithms. *Information (Basel)*, *11*(8), 1–20. doi:10.3390/info11080383

Boudriga, A., Taktak, N. B., & Jellouli, S. (2009). Banking supervision and nonperforming loans: A cross-country analysis. *Journal of Financial Economic Policy*, *1*(4), 286–318. doi:10.1108/17576380911050043

Brachet, P. (1992). *Corruption & sous-développement au Maroc*. L'Harmattan.

Bradley, C. G. (2020). The consumer protection ecosystem: Law, Norms, and technology. *Denver Law Review*, *97*(1), 35.

Brazeal, D. V. (1993). Organizing for internally developed corporate ventures. *Journal of Business Venturing*, *8*(1), 75–90. doi:10.1016/0883-9026(93)90012-T

Brennan, N. M., Daly, C. A., & Harrington, C. S. (2010). Rhetoric, argument and impression management in hostile takeover defence documents. *The British Accounting Review*, *42*(4), 253–268. doi:10.1016/j.bar.2010.07.008

Brennan, N. M., Guillamon-Saorin, E., & Pierce, A. (2009). Impression management: Developing and illustrating a scheme of analysis for narrative disclosures - A methodological note. *Accounting, Auditing & Accountability Journal*, *22*(5), 789–832. doi:10.1108/09513570910966379

Brennan, N., & Gray, S. J. (2005). The impact of materiality: Accounting's best kept secret. *Asian Academy of Management Journal of Accounting and Finance*, *1*, 1–31.

Brenner, L., Meyll, T., Stolper, O., & Walter, A. (2020). Consumer fraud victimization and financial well-being. *Journal of Economic Psychology*, *76*, 102243. doi:10.1016/j.joep.2019.102243

Brinkmann, J. (2005). Understanding insurance customer dishonesty: Outline of a situational approach. *Journal of Business Ethics*, *61*(2), 183–197. doi:10.100710551-005-0278-1

Brivot, M., Cho, C. H., & Kuhn, J. R. (2015). Marketing or parrhesia: A longitudinal study of AICPA's shifting languages in times of turbulence. *Critical Perspectives on Accounting*, *31*, 23–43. doi:10.1016/j.cpa.2015.04.001

Brockett, P. L., Derrig, R. A., Golden, L. L., Levine, A., & Alpert, M. (2002). Fraud classification using principal component analysis of RIDITs. *The Journal of Risk and Insurance*, *69*(3), 341–373. doi:10.1111/1539-6975.00027

Brockner, J., Greenberg, J., Brockner, A., Bortz, J., Davy, J., & Carter, C. (1986). Layoffs, equity theory, and work performance: Further evidence of the impact of survivor guilt. *Academy of Management Journal*, *29*(2), 373–384. doi:10.2307/256193

Brown, G., Collins, R., & Thornton, D. (1993). Professional Judgment and Accounting Standards. *Accounting, Organizations and Society*, *8*(4), 275–289. doi:10.1016/0361-3682(93)90017-Z

Buchak, G., Matvos, G., Piskorski, T., & Seru, A. (2018). Fintech, regulatory arbitrage, and the rise of shadow banks. *Journal of Financial Economics*, *130*(3), 453–483. doi:10.1016/j.jfineco.2018.03.011

Buchanan, B. (2016). *The Cybersecurity dilemma: Hacking, trust and fear between nations*. Oxford University Press.

Bujaki, M., & McConomy, B. (2012). Metaphor in Nortel's letters to shareholders 1997-2006. *Accounting, Auditing & Accountability Journal*, *25*(7), 1113–1139. doi:10.1108/09513571211263211

Buku, M., & Mazer, R. (2017). *Fraud in mobile financial services: Protecting consumers, providers and the system* (The World Bank - CGAP Brief No. 119208). Retrieved from https://documents.worldbank.org/en/publication/documents-reports/documentdetail/ 249151504766545101/fraud-in-mobile-financial-services-protecting-consumers-providers-and-the-system

Bülbül, Y. (2013). *Osmanlı İktisat Tarihi*. Anadolu Üniversitesi Yayınları.

Burke, J. (2017). Somalis greet 'New Dawn' as US dual national wins presidency. *The Guardian*. Retrieved from https://www.theguardian.com/world/2017/feb/08/somali-presidential-election-won-mohamed-abdullahi-mohamed

Busuulwa, B. (2016). Mobile money fraud, crime rate increase in Uganda. *The East-African*. Retrieved from https://www.theeastafrican.co.ke/tea/business/mobile-money-fraud-crime-rate-increase-in-uganda--1356614

Button, M., Brooks, G., Lewis, C., & Aleem, A. (2017). Just about everybody doing the business? Explaining 'cash-for-crash' insurance fraud in the United Kingdom. *Australian and New Zealand Journal of Criminology, 50*(2), 176–194. doi:10.1177/0004865816638910

Buzan, B., & Hansen, L. (2009). *The Evolution of international security studies*. Cambridge University Press. doi:10.1017/CBO9780511817762

Caiden, N. (1998). Public service professionalism for performance measurement and evaluation. *Public Budgeting & Finance, 18*(2), 35–52. doi:10.1046/j.0275-1100.1998.01133.x

Caillier, J. G. (2015). Transformational leadership and whistle-blowing attitudes: Is this relationship mediated by organizational commitment and public service motivation? *American Review of Public Administration, 45*(4), 458–475. doi:10.1177/0275074013515299

Camargo, C. B., & Koechlin, L. (2018). Informal governance: Comparative perspectives on Co-optation, control and camouflage in Rwanda, Tanzania and Uganda. In African Cities and the Development Conundrum (pp. 78-100). Brill.

Campbell, J., & McCaslin, J. (2020). How Nigeria has responded to COVID-19 so far. *Council on Foreign Relations*. Retrieved from https://www.cfr.org/blog/how-nigeria-has-responded-COVID-19-so-far

Cardoso, R. L., Leite, R. O., & Aquino, A. C. B. (2018). The effect of cognitive reflection on the efficacy of impression management: An experimental analysis with financial analysts. *Accounting, Auditing & Accountability Journal, 31*(6), 1668–1690. doi:10.1108/AAAJ-10-2016-2731

Carè, R., Rania, F., & De Lisa, R. (2020). Critical success factors, motivations, and risks in social impact bonds. *Sustainability, 12*(18), 7291. doi:10.3390u12187291

Carifio, J., & Perla, R. (2007). Ten common misunderstandings, misconceptions, persistent myths and urban legends about Likert scale and Likert response formats and their antidotes. *Journal of Social Sciences, 3*(3), 106–116. doi:10.3844/jssp.2007.106.116

Carson, B. S. (2015, July 28). The perfect example of government overreach. *The Washington Times*. Retrieved from https://www.washingtontimes.com/news/2015/jul/28/ben-carson-perfect-example-government-overreach/

Carswell, A. T., & Bachtel, D. C. (2009). Mortgage fraud: A risk factor analysis of affected communities. *Crime, Law, and Social Change, 52*(4), 347–364. doi:10.100710611-008-9186-5

Carver, S. (2017, March 5). Somali elections: How women still fight for political space in African polls. *The Conversation*. Retrieved from https://theconversation.com/somali-elections-how-women-still-fight-for-political-space-in-african-polls-73213

Çetin, M. (2015). Risk yönetimi ve sigortacilik ilkeleri, sigorta ve riziko (Vol. 2). In Principles of risk management and insurance (Vol. 12). Pearson.

Çetin, M., & Ecevit, E. (2016). Vergi yükü ve ekonomik büyüme arasındaki ilişki: Türkiye ekonomisi üzerine ampirik bir analiz (1965-2013). *Namık Kemal Üniversitesi Sosyal Bilimler Metinleri. Ekim, 8*(30), 95–112.

CFPB. (2022). *Resources to help you avoid scams*. Retrieved from https://www.consumerfinance.gov/coronavirus/avoiding-scams/

Chaffey, D. (2010). Applying organizational capability models to assess the maturity of digital-marketing governance. *Journal of Marketing Management, 26*(3-4), 187–196. doi:10.1080/02672571003612192

Chalouat, I., Carrion-Crespo, C., & Licata, M. (2019). *Law and practice on protecting whistle-blowers in the public and financial services sectors* (Working paper 328). Geneva: International Labor Office. Retrieved from https://www.ilo.org/wcmsp5/groups/public/---ed_dialogue/---sector/documents /publication/wcms_718048.pdf

Chang, Y.-T., & Stone, D. N. (2021). Impression management in public sector audit proposals: Language and fees. *European Accounting Review*, 1–33. doi:10.1080/09638180.2021.1969260

Chatain, P. L., Zerzan, A., Noor, W., Dannaoui, N., & De Koker, L. (2011). *Protecting Mobile Money against Financial-Crimes: Global Policy Challenges and Solutions*. World Bank Publications. doi:10.1596/978-0-8213-8669-9

Check, N. A., Madise, T., Majozi, N., & Hamada, Y. (2019). *The Integrity of Political Finance Systems in Africa: Tackling Political Corruption* (International IDEA Policy Paper No. 20). Africa Institute of South Africa. Retrieved from https://www.idea.int/publications/catalogue/integrity-political-finance-systems-africa

Chen, Y., Wang, Y., Nervo, S., Benitez-Amado, J., & Kou, G. (2015). IT capabilities and product innovation performance: The roles of corporate entrepreneurship and competitive intensity. *Information & Management*, *52*(6), 643–657. doi:10.1016/j.im.2015.05.003

Chen, Z., Hu, J., Zhang, Z., Jiang, S., Han, S., Yan, D., Zhuang, R., Hu, B., & Zhang, Z. (2020). *Efficacy of hydroxychloroquine in patients with COVID-19: Results of a randomized clinical trial*. Renmin Hospital of Wuhan University.

Chiejina, N. (2021, June 27). Whistleblower policy yields N605b cash, others. *The Nation*. Retrieved from https://thenationonlineng.net/whistleblower-policy-yields-n605bn- cash-others/#:~:text=Whistleblower%20policy%20yields%20N605bn%20cash%2C%20others%20The%20Nation,billion%20in%20recovered%20funds%2C%20The%20Nation%20can%20reveal

ChijiokeUtomi, J. M. (2022, October 14). Nigeria @62: Corruption as war without end. *The Sun*. Retrieved from https://www.sunnewsonline.com/nigeria-at-62-corruption-as-war-without-end/

Chipkin, I. (2013). Whither the state? Corruption, institutions and state-building in South Africa. *Politikon*, *40*(2), 211–231. doi:10.1080/02589346.2013.798457

Cho, C. H., Hageman, A. M., & Jérôme, T. (2017). Eye-tracking experiments in social and environmental accounting research. *Social and Environmental Accountability Journal*, *37*(3), 155–173. doi:10.1080/0969160X.2017.1350588

Cho, C. H., Michelon, G., & Patten, D. M. (2012). Enhancement and obfuscation through the use of graphs in sustainability reports: An international comparison. *Sustainability Accounting. Management and Policy Journal*, *3*(1), 74–88. doi:10.1108/20408021211223561

Cho, C. H., Roberts, R. W., & Patten, D. M. (2010). The language of US corporate environmental disclosure. *Accounting, Organizations and Society*, *35*(4), 431–443. doi:10.1016/j.aos.2009.10.002

Cho, J., Krush, M. T., Walker, D., & Nowlin, E. L. (2023). An Examination of Student Loans, Partisanship and Complaining Behavior: The Consumer Financial Protection Bureau. *Journal of Consumer Satisfaction, Dissatisfaction & Complaining Behavior*, *36*(1), 1–18.

Chong, S., & Rahman, A. (2020). Web-based impression management? Salient features for CSR disclosure prominence. *Sustainability Accounting, Management and Policy Journal*, *11*(1), 99–136. doi:10.1108/SAMPJ-08-2018-0221

Choudhary, A., Ranjan, J. K., Sharma, P., & Asthana, H. S. (2022). Incorporating the outcomes of COVID-19 with other recent pandemic outbreaks on healthcare workers: A systematic review and meta-analysis. In N. Fagih & A. Forouharfar (Eds.), *Socioeconomic Dynamics of the COVID-19 Crisis: Global, Regional and Local Perspectives* (pp. 327–350). Springer. doi:10.1007/978-3-030-89996-7_15

Chukwuemeka, E. (2006). *Administration and politics in Nigeria: Past, present and issues*. Vinez Communications.

Chukwuemeka, E., Ugwuanyi, B. J., & Ewuim, N. (2012). Curbing corruption in Nigeria: The imperatives of good leadership. *African Research Review*, *6*(3), 338–358. doi:10.4314/afrrev.v6i3.25

Chuta, S. C. (2004). *Corruption in Nigeria*. Afro-Obis.

Cindori, S., & Zakarija, A. (2016). Prevencija prijevara u sustavu poreza na dodanu vrijednost u okvirima Europske unije. *Pravni vjesnik, 32*(3–4), 71–90. Retrieved from https://hrcak.srce.hr/179199

Clarke, M. (1989). Insurance fraud. *British Journal of Criminology*, *29*(1), 1–20. doi:10.1093/oxfordjournals.bjc.a047785

Clatworthy, M., & Jones, M. J. (2003). Financial reporting of good news and bad news: Evidence from accounting narratives. *Accounting and Business Research*, *33*(3), 171–185. doi:10.1080/00014788.2003.9729645

Clatworthy, M., & Jones, M. J. (2006). Differential patterns of textual characteristics and company performance in the chairman's statement. *Accounting, Auditing & Accountability Journal*, *19*(4), 493–511. doi:10.1108/09513570610679100

Clifford, S. (2019). Taxing multinationals beyond borders: Financial and locational responses to CFC rules. *Journal of Public Economics*, *173*, 44–71. doi:10.1016/j.jpubeco.2019.01.010

Cohen, J. R., Krishnamoorthy, G., Peytcheva, M., & Wright, A. M. (2011). *The impact of regulatory enforcement and principles-based accounting on auditors' judgments to curb aggressive reporting* (Working paper). Boston College, Northeastern University, and Lehigh University.

Cohen, J., Krishnamoorthy, G., & Wright, A. (2010). Corporate governance in the post-Sarbanes-Oxley era: Auditors' experiences. *Contemporary Accounting Research*, *27*(3), 751–786. doi:10.1111/j.1911-3846.2010.01026.x

Collier, M. W. (2002). Explaining corruption: An institutional choice approach. *Crime, Law, and Social Change*, *38*(1), 1–32. doi:10.1023/A:1019802614530

Compernolle, T. (2018). Communication of the external auditor with the audit committee: Managing impressions to deal with multiple accountability relationships. *Accounting, Auditing & Accountability Journal*, *31*(3), 900–924. doi:10.1108/AAAJ-05-2013-1356

Conseil Economique et Social. (2012). *La commande publique Levier stratégique de développement* [Public procurement Strategic lever for development verification]. Retrieved from https://www.cese.ma/media/2020/10/Avis-La-commande-publique-levier-strat%C3%A9gique-de-d%C3%A9veloppement-%C3%A9conomiqu e-et-social.pdf

Conway, S. L., O'Keefe, P. A., & Hrasky, S. (2015). Legitimacy, accountability and impression management in NGOs: The Indian ocean tsunami. *Accounting, Auditing & Accountability Journal*, *28*(7), 1075–1098. doi:10.1108/AAAJ-04-2012-01007

Cooper, S., & Slack, R. (2015). Reporting practice, impression management and company performance: A longitudinal and comparative analysis of water leakage disclosure. *Accounting and Business Research*, *45*(6-7), 801–840. doi:10.1080/00014788.2015.1081554

Corazza, L., Truant, E., Scagnelli, S. D., & Mio, C. (2020). Sustainability reporting after the costa concordia disaster: A multi-theory study on legitimacy, impression management and image restoration. *Accounting, Auditing & Accountability Journal, 33*(8), 1909–1941. doi:10.1108/AAAJ-05-2018-3488

Cordray, R., Thompson, D. E., & Peterson, C. L. (2020). *Consumer Financial Protection in the COVID-19 Crisis: An Emergency Agenda* (University of Utah College of Law Research Paper No. 370). University of Utah. Retrieved from https://papers.ssrn.com/sol3/papers.cfm?abstract_id=3569357

Cormier, D., & Magnan, M. L. (2005). From accounting to 'forecounting'. *Canadian Accounting Perspectives, 4*(2), 243–255. doi:10.1506/4CDJ-M98H-FH0Q-KQ1M

Corrigan, L. T., & Rixon, D. (2017). A dramaturgical accounting of Cooperative performance indicators. *Qualitative Research in Accounting & Management, 14*(1), 60–80. doi:10.1108/QRAM-08-2016-0060

Cortese, G., & Del Carlo, A. (2008). *La selezione del personale. Dalla ricerca all'inserimento in azienda: come scegliere il candidato migliore*. Raffaello Cortina Editore.

COSO. (2004). *Enterprise Risk Management: Aligning Risk with Strategy and Performance. Committee of sponsoring organizations of the Treadway Commission*. AICPA.

Costa, L. D. A., & Mainardes, E. W. (2016). The role of corruption and risk aversion in entrepreneurial intentions. *Applied Economics Letters, 23*(4), 290–293. doi:10.1080/13504851.2015.1071462

Cour des comptes. (2021). *Rapport relatif à l'audit des comptes des partis politiques et à la vérification de la sincérité de leurs dépenses au titre du soutien public: Année 2020* [Report on the audit of the accounts of political parties and the verification of the sincerity of their expenditure for public support: Year 2020]. Retrieved from https://www.courdescomptes.ma/fr/Page-27/publications

Courtois, C., & Gendron, Y. (2020). The show must go on! legitimization processes surrounding certified fraud examiners' claim to expertise. *European Accounting Review, 29*(3), 437–465. doi:10.1080/09638180.2019.1643753

Cressey, D. R. (1971). *Other Peoples' Money: A Study in the Social Psychology of Embezzlement*. Wadsworth Publishing.

Creswell, J. W., & Creswell, J. D. (2017). *Research design: Qualitative, quantitative, and mixed methods approaches*. Sage.

Creswell, W. J. (2019). Research Design: Qualitative, Quantitative, and Mixed Methods Approaches. *Sage (Atlanta, Ga.)*.

Crowder, M. (1978). *The story of Nigeria*. Faber and Faber.

Daka, T. (2022, November 22). Federal government says $1b stolen funds recovered since 2015, Okays anti-corruption document. *The Guardian*. Retrieved from https://guardian.ng/news/fg-says-1b-stolen-funds-recovered-since-2015-okays-anti-corruption-document/

Damooei, J. (2022). Lessons from COVID-19 and its impacts on reallocation of resources: a cross-country comparison in search of a global perspective. In N. Fagih & A. Forouharfar (Eds.), *Socioeconomic Dynamics of the COVID-19 Crisis: Global, Regional and Local Perspectives* (pp. 127–174). Springer. doi:10.1007/978-3-030-89996-7_7

Datasketch. (2019). *Welcome to open government—Datasketch Newsletter Open Gov #0*. Retrieved from https://www.datasketch.co/newsletter/open-government/issue-0-welcome/

Daudi, F., & Shindika, S. E. (2021). Reckoning frauds in Tanzania's insurance services: An ethical perspective. *International Journal of Innovative Science and Research Technology, 6*(3), 99–104.

Davidson, H. (2018, July 22). Timor-leste activists shocked by Australia's prosecution of spy witness K and lawyer. *The Guardian*. https://www.theguardian.com/world/2018/jul/22/timor-leste-activists-shocked-by-australias-prosecution-of-spy-witness-k-and-lawyer

Davidsson, P. (1995). Culture, structure and regional levels of entrepreneurship. *Entrepreneurship and Regional Development, 7*(1), 41–62. doi:10.1080/08985629500000003

David-West, O., Iheanachor, N., & Umukoro, I. O. (2019). Mobile money as a frugal innovation for the bottom of the pyramid–Cases of selected African countries. *Africa Journal of Management, 5*(3), 274–302. doi:10.1080/23322373.2019.1652023

Davis, M. A. (2009). Understanding the relationship between mood and creativity: A meta-analysis. *Organizational Behavior and Human Decision Processes, 108*(1), 25–38. doi:10.1016/j.obhdp.2008.04.001

Davison, J. (2015). Visualising accounting: An interdisciplinary review and synthesis. *Accounting and Business Research, 45*(2), 121–165. doi:10.1080/00014788.2014.987203

de la Feria, R., & Schoeman, A. (2019). Addressing VAT fraud in developing countries: The tax policy-administration symbiosis. *Intertax, 47*(11), 950–967.

De la Mora, D., & Garduño, J. (2017). The Road to Budget Transparency in Mexico. *International Budget Partnership*. Retrieved from https://internationalbudget.org/publications/road-to-budget-transparency-in-mexico/

de Soto, H. (2003). *The mystery of capital: Why capitalism triumphs in the West and fails everywhere else*. BasicBooks.

Dechow, P. M., & Skinner, D. J. (2000). Earnings management: Reconciling the views of accounting academics, practitioners, and regulators. *Accounting Horizons, 14*(2), 235–250. doi:10.2308/acch.2000.14.2.235

del Castillo, M., & Schifrin, M. (Eds.). (2022). *Forbes Blockchain 50 2022*. Retrieved from https://www.forbes.com/sites/michaeldelcastillo/2022/02/08/forbes-blockchain-50-2022/?sh=b20678331c6c

Dell, G., & McDevitt, A. (2018, September 12). Exporting Corruption: Progress Report 2018: Assessing Enforcement of the OECD Anti-Bribery Convention. *Transparency International*. Retrieved from https://www.transparency.org/en/publications/exporting-corruption-2018

Demaline, C. (2019). Disclosure characteristics of firms being investigated by the SEC. *Journal of Corporate Accounting & Finance, 30*(4), 11–24. doi:10.1002/jcaf.22412

Demaline, C. (2020). Disclosure readability of firms investigated for books-and-records infractions: An impression management perspective. *Journal of Financial Reporting and Accounting, 18*(1), 131–145. doi:10.1108/JFRA-10-2018-0094

Deman, S. (2009). *A strategic approach to global financial crises*. Retrieved from https://www.researchgate.net/publication/273448060_A_Strategic_Approach_to_Global_Financial_Crises

DeNichilo, N. (2013). *Le Metodologie innovative di reclutamento*. Tesi Magistrale Università degli studi Roma Tre.

DeNichilo, S. & Pedone, A. (2009). *The efficiency of the tax systems in Europe*. Università degli studi La Sapienza di Roma.

DeNichilo, S. & Regogliosi, C. (2011). *L'internal auditing in un organismo di diritto pubblico: il caso Agea*. Università degli studi Roma Tre.

DeNichilo, S. (2020b). Shadow Bank System in European Affairs: Measuring Capability (Discussion paper). European Association for Banking and Financial Law.

DeNichilo, S. (2021b), Management Accounting in European Affairs: a Memorandum Methodology for Formalize Audit Evidence. *Corporate Governance and Research & Development Studies, 1*, 153-171.

DeNichilo, S. (2020a). *Public Choice in European Affairs: Measuring Election Model. European Journal of Social Impact and Circular Economy*. University of Turin.

DeNichilo, S. (2020c). How Do Earnings Management Practices Distract International Environmental Funds? Empirical Evidence of European Development Funds in Italy. *GeoProgress Journal*, *7*(1), 87–101.

DeNichilo, S. (2021a). *Management Accounting in European Finance for Smart Tourism and Sustainable Destination: How Organizations Deficiency?* University of Turin.

DeNichilo, S. (2022). *How to resolve audit matters in European Affairs? Introduction to a sustainable management accounting under IAS 37*. University of Turin.

Derin, K. O. (2007). Leadership, governance and corruption in Nigeria. *Journal of Sustainable Development in Africa*, *9*(3).

Derrig, A. R. (2002). Insurance fraud. *The Journal of Risk and Insurance*, *69*(3), 271–287. doi:10.1111/1539-6975.00026

Devereux, M. P., Freedman, J., & Vella, J. (2012). Tax avoidance. SSRN *Electronic Journal*. Retrieved from https://www.researchgate.net/publication/350490406_Tax_Avoidance doi:10.2139/ssrn.3754562

Dhanani, A., & Kennedy, D. (2022). Envisioning legitimacy: Visual dimensions of NGO annual reports. *Accounting, Auditing & Accountability Journal*. Advance online publication. doi:10.1108/AAAJ-01-2020-4377

Didier, T., & Pinat, M. (2017). *The Nature of trade and growth linkages* (World Bank Policy Research Working Paper 8168). Washington, DC: World Bank.

Dike, V. E. (2001). *Democracy and political life in Nigeria*. Ahmadu Bello University Press.

Dike, V. E. (2003). *Nigeria and the politics of unreason: A study of the Obasanjo regime*. Adonis and Abbey Publishers.

Dilla, W. N., & Janvrin, D. J. (2010). Voluntary Disclosure in Annual Reports: The Association between magnitude and direction of change in corporate financial performance and graph Use. *Accounting Horizons*, *24*(2), 257–278. doi:10.2308/acch.2010.24.2.257

Dimant, E., & Tosato, G. (2018). Causes and effects of corruption: What has past decade's empirical research taught us? A survey. *Journal of Economic Surveys*, *32*(2), 335–356. doi:10.1111/joes.12198

Ding, K., Xu, H., & Yang, R. (2021). Taxation and enterprise innovation: Evidence from China's value-added tax reform. *Sustainability*, *13*(10), 5700. doi:10.3390u13105700

Dionne, G. (1984). The effects of insurance on the possibilities of fraud. *The Geneva Papers on Risk and Insurance. Issues and Practice*, *9*(3), 304–321. doi:10.1057/gpp.1984.18

Diouf, D., & Boiral, O. (2017). The quality of sustainability reports and impression management: A stakeholder perspective. *Accounting, Auditing & Accountability Journal*, *30*(3), 643–667. doi:10.1108/AAAJ-04-2015-2044

Dogarawa, A. B. (2007). Corporate failure: Accounting and auditing resolution. *Journal of Social and Management Sciences*, *12*(December), 120–127.

Donovan, D. (2022). *Map tracks coronavirus outbreak in near real time*. National Public Health Agencies. John Hopkins University. Retrieved from https://hub.jhu.edu/2020/01/23/coronavirus-outbreak-mapping-tool-649-em1-art1-dtd-health/

Dörry, S., & Schulz, C. (2018). Green financing, interrupted. Potential directions for sustainable finance in Luxembourg. *Local Environment*, *23*(7), 717–733. doi:10.1080/13549839.2018.1428792

Dou, Y., & Roh, Y. (2020). Public Disclosure and Consumer Financial Protection. SSRN *Electronic Journal*. Retrieved from https://papers.ssrn.com/sol3/papers.cfm?abstract_id=3647491

Douglas, E. (2017). Perceptions: Looking at the world through entrepreneurial lenses. In *Revisiting the Entrepreneurial Mind* (pp. 41–59). Springer. doi:10.1007/978-3-319-45544-0_4

Douglas, E. J., & Shepherd, D. A. (2002). Self-employment as a career choice: Attitudes, entrepreneurial intentions, and utility maximization. *Entrepreneurship Theory and Practice*, *26*(3), 81–90. doi:10.1177/104225870202600305

Dreher, A., & Gassebner, M. (2013). Greasing the wheels? The impact of regulations and corruption on firm entry. *Public Choice*, *155*(3), 413–432. doi:10.100711127-011-9871-2

Dudley, B. J. (1973). *Instability and political order: Politics and Crises in Nigeria*. Ibadan University Press.

Eckstein, D., Goellner, M., Blome, C., & Henke, M. (2015). The performance impact of supply chain agility and supply chain adaptability: The moderating effect of product complexity. *International Journal of Production Research*, *53*(10), 3028–3046. doi:10.1080/00207543.2014.970707

EDB. (2022). *Budget Highlights 2022/2023*. Economic Development Board, Mauritius. Retrieved from https://www.edbmauritius.org/edb-budget-corner

Edgar, V. C., Beck, M., & Brennan, N. M. (2018). Impression management in annual report narratives: The case of the UK private finance initiative. *Accounting, Auditing & Accountability Journal*, *31*(6), 1566–1592. doi:10.1108/AAAJ-10-2016-2733

Edwards, M. A. (2020). The Concept and federal crime of mortgage fraud. *The American Criminal Law Review*, *57*, 57.

Egwemi, V. (Ed.). (2012). *Corruption in Nigeria: Issues, Challenges and possibilities*. Aboki Publishers.

El Mesbahi, K. (2013). La prévention de la corruption au Maroc, entre discours et réalité [Corruption prevention in Morocco, between rhetoric and reality]. *Pouvoirs*, *145*(2), 83–97. doi:10.3917/pouv.145.0083

Ellinas, A., & Suleiman, E. (2008). The Reforming the Commission: Between modernization and bureaucratization. *Journal of European Public Policy*, *15*(5), 708–725. doi:10.1080/13501760802133179

Ellul, A., & Yerramilli, V. (2013). Stronger risk controls, lower risk: Evidence from U.S. bank holding companies. *The Journal of Finance*, *68*(5), 1757–1803. doi:10.1111/jofi.12057

El-Sayed, D., Adel, E., Elmougy, O., Fawzy, N., Hatem, N., & Elhakey, F. (2021). The influence of narrative disclosure readability, information ordering and graphical representations on non-professional investors' judgment: Evidence from an emerging market. *Journal of Applied Accounting Research*, *22*(1), 138–167. doi:10.1108/JAAR-06-2020-0115

ePortugal. (2020). *Government announces Simplex programme 2020-21*. Retrieved from https://eportugal.gov.pt/en/noticias/governo-apresenta-programa-simplex-2020-21

Erickson, M., Hanlon, M., & Maydew, E. (2006). Is there a link between executive equity incentives and accounting fraud? *Journal of Accounting Research*, *44*(1), 113–143. doi:10.1111/j.1475-679X.2006.00194.x

Ernst & Young. (2013). *Remarking financial services: risk management five years after the crisis. A survey of major financial institutions*. EY & Institute of International Finance. Retrieved from https://www.iif.com/portals/0/files/private/EY-Remaking_financial_services_Executive_ Summary_1.pdf

Erol, M. (1970). *Osmanlı İmparatorluğu'nda Kağıt Para*. TTK.

Estrin, S., Korosteleva, J., & Mickiewicz, T. (2013). Which institutions encourage entrepreneurial growth aspirations? *Journal of Business Venturing*, *28*(4), 564–580. doi:10.1016/j.jbusvent.2012.05.001

Etymonline.com. (n.d.). *Whistleblower*. Retrieved from https://www.etymonline.com/search?q=whistleblower

European Comission. (2021). *VAT gap in the EU: Report 2021*. Retrieved from https://taxation-customs.ec.europa.eu/business/vat/vat-gap_en

Europol. (2020). *Three arrested in Hungary in €1.4 million VAT fraud investigation*. Retrieved from https://www.europol.europa.eu/media-press/newsroom/news/3-arrested-in-hungary-in-%E2%82%AC14-million-vat-fraud-investigation

Evans, L., & Pierpoint, J. (2015). Framing the magdalen: Sentimental narratives and impression management in charity annual reporting. *Accounting and Business Research*, *45*(6–7), 661–690. doi:10.1080/00014788.2015.1039931

Evans, O. (2020). Fiscal discipline, financial development & economic growth in Nigeria. In C. I. Nwaogwugwu (Ed.), *Dynamics of Fiscal and Monetary Policies in ECOWAS Countries*. University of Lagos Press.

Everett, J., Neu, D., & Rahaman, A. S. (2007). Accounting and the global fight against corruption. *Accounting, Organizations and Society*, *32*(6), 513–542. doi:10.1016/j.aos.2006.07.002

Ezeogidi, C. (2020). A historical survey of corruption in Nigeria. SSRN *Electronic Journal*. Retrieved from https://ssrn.com/abstract=3563261 doi:10.2139/ssrn.3563261

Ezeoha, A., & Uche, C. (2005). *South Africa, NEPAD and the African Renaissance* (ASC Working Paper 64). African Studies Centre. Retrieved from https://vdocument.in/south-africa-nepad-and-the-african-south-africa-nepad-and-the-african-renaissance.html?page=1

Fagih, N., & Forouharfar, A. (2022). An Introduction to Socioeconomic Dynamics of the COVID-19 Crisis: Global, Regional and Local Perspectives. In N. Fagih & A. Forouharfar (Eds.), *Socioeconomic Dynamics of the COVID-19 Crisis: Global, Regional and Local Perspectives* (pp. 1–18). Springer. doi:10.1007/978-3-030-89996-7_1

Fairhurst, G., & Sarr, R. (1996). *The art of framing*. Jossey-Bass.

Faloore, O. O. (2010). The family and corruption in Nigeria. *Journal of Social and Policy Issues*, *7*(2), 84–89.

Falschlunger, L. M., Eisl, C., Losbichler, H., & Greil, A. M. (2015). Impression management in annual reports of the largest European companies: A longitudinal study on graphical representations. *Journal of Applied Accounting Research*, *16*(3), 383–399. doi:10.1108/JAAR-10-2014-0109

Fang, L., Pittman, J., Zhang, Y., & Zhao, Y. (2018). *Accounting standard precision, corporate governance, and accounting restatements*. Retrieved from https://www.fox.temple.edu/wp-content/uploads/2018/01/Zhang-Yinqi-Accounting-Standard-Precision-Corporate-Governance-and-Accounting-Restatements.pdf

Farooq, U., Nasir, A., & Quddoos, M. U. (2021). The impact of COVID-19 pandemic on abnormal returns of insurance firms: A cross-country evidence. *Applied Economics*, *53*(31), 3658–3678. doi:10.1080/00036846.2021.1884839

FATF. (2011). *Laundering the proceeds of corruption*. Financial Action Task Force. Retrieved from https://www.fatf-gafi.org/documents/documents/launderingtheproceedsofcorruption.html

Fawzy, L., & Dworski, L. (2011). *Emerging business online: Global markets and the power of b2b internet marketing*. Pearson Education Limited.

FBI. (2014). Investigating tax refund fraud. *Federal Bureau of Investigation*. Retrieved from https://www.fbi.gov/news/stories/investigating-tax-refund-fraud

FBI. (2018). *Cybercrime Statistics: Top ten countries in the world*. Internet Crime Complaint Centre, Federal Bureau of Investigation (FBI). Retrieved from https://www.ic3.gov/default.aspx

Ferrell, O. C., Fraedrich, J., & Ferrell, L. (2021). *Business Ethics: Ethical Decision Making and Cases*. Cengage Learning.

Fialho, A., Morais, A., & Costa, R. P. (2020). Impression management strategies and water disclosures – the case of CDP A-list. *Meditari Accountancy Research*, *29*(3), 568–585. doi:10.1108/MEDAR-08-2019-0542

Field, A. (2009). *Discovering statistics using SPSS* (3rd ed.). SAGE.

Fields, T. D., Lys, T. Z., & Vincent, L. (2001). Empirical research on accounting choice. *Journal of Accounting and Economics*, *31*(1-3), 255–307. doi:10.1016/S0165-4101(01)00028-3

Financial Times. (2016, May 10). *Three Nigerian bank CEOs questioned in anti-corruption drive*. Retrieved from https://www.ft.com/content/fa964f22-16ae-11e6-9d98-00386a18e39d

FindLaw Staff. (2021). *Tax Evasion vs Tax Avoidance*. FindLaw. Retrieved from https://www.findlaw.com/tax/tax-problems-audits/tax-evasion-vs-tax-avoidance.htm

Fischer, E. A. (2009). *Creating a national framework for Cybersecurity. An analysis of issues and options*. Nova Science Publishers.

Fisher, R., van Staden, C. J., & Richards, G. (2020). Watch that tone: An investigation of the use and stylistic consequences of tone in corporate accountability disclosures. *Accounting, Auditing & Accountability Journal*, *33*(1), 77–105. doi:10.1108/AAAJ-10-2016-2745

Fitzgibbon, W. (2019, July 23). *Treasure Island: Leak reveals how Mauritius siphons tax from poor nations to benefit elites*. International Consortium of Investigative Journalists. Retrieved from https://www.icij.org/investigations/mauritius-leaks/treasure-island-leak-reveals-how-mauritius-siphons-tax-from-poor-nations-to-benefit-elites/

Fitzhenry, W. (2022). Visualizing a timeline of mobile money fraud. *Cambridge Intelligence*. Retrieved from https://cambridge-intelligence.com/mobile-money-fraud/

Fjeldstad, O. H., Kagoma, C., Mdee, E., Sjursen, I. H., & Somville, V. (2020). The customer is king: Evidence on VAT compliance in Tanzania. *World Development, 128*, 104841. doi:10.1016/j.worlddev.2019.104841

Foohey, P. (2017). Calling on the CFPB for help: Telling stories and consumer protection. *Law and Contemporary Problems*, *80*(3), 177–210.

Foo, M. D. (2011). Emotions and entrepreneurial opportunity evaluation. *Entrepreneurship Theory and Practice*, *35*(2), 375–393. doi:10.1111/j.1540-6520.2009.00357.x

Fornell, C., & Larcker, D. F. (1981). Evaluating structural equation models with unobservable variables and measurement error. *JMR, Journal of Marketing Research*, *18*(1), 39–50. doi:10.1177/002224378101800104

Fragile States Index. (2019). *Fragility in the World 2019*. Retrieved from https://fragilestatesindex.org/

Franda, M. (2001). *Governing the internet: Emergence of an international regime*. Lynne Rienner Publishers. doi:10.1515/9781626373556

Frankel, J. A., & Romer, D. H. (1999). Does trade cause growth? *The American Economic Review*, *89*(3), 379–399. doi:10.1257/aer.89.3.379

Fraser, J. R., Simkins, B., & Narvaez, K. (2014). *Implementing Enterprise Risk Management: Case studies and best practices*. John Wiley & Sons.

Frimpong, A. I., Andoh, C., & Ofosu-Hene, D. E. (2016). Causes, effects and deterrence of insurance fraud: Evidence from Ghana. *Journal of Financial Crime*, *23*(4), 678–699. doi:10.1108/JFC-11-2015-0062

Frunza, M. (2019). *Value-added Tax Fraud*. Routledge.

Funmi, P. A., Omotayo, F. I., Isaac, O. I., & Olukayode, O. (2018). Bank fraud and its effect on Nigerian economy- a study of selected quoted banks. *European Journal of Accounting. Auditing and Finance Research*, *6*(8), 104–120.

Gaglio, C. M., & Katz, J. A. (2001). The psychological basis of opportunity identification: Entrepreneurial alertness. *Small Business Economics*, *16*(2), 95–111. doi:10.1023/A:1011132102464

Galal, S. (August 22, 2022). Social media penetration in Africa in 2022 by region. *Statista*. Retrieved from https://www.Statista.com/statistics/1190628/social-media-penetration-in-africa-by-region/#

Gámez Gutiérrez, J., Saiz-Álvarez, J. M., & Gil Ángel, G. (2017). A cognitive, emotional and behavioral assessment of Colombian entrepreneurs attitudes toward corruption. *Revista Universidad y Empresa*, *19*(33), 9–51. doi:10.12804/revistas.urosario.edu.co/empresa/a.4682

Gamson, W. A., & Modigliani, A. (1989). Media discourse and public opinion on nuclear power: A constructionist approach. *American Journal of Sociology*, *95*(1), 1–37. doi:10.1086/229213

Garba, T., & Abubakar, B. A. (2014). Corporate board diversity and financial performance of insurance companies in Nigeria: An application of panel data approach. *Asian Economic and Financial Review*, *4*(2), 257–277.

Garba, T., Bello, U., Abdullahi, H., & Abubakar, M. (2016). Institutions, natural resources and economic growth: An application of co-integration with structural break on Nigerian dataset. *Central Bank of Nigeria Economic and Financial Review*, *54*(4), 1–27.

García Osma, B., & Guillamón-Saorín, E. (2011). Corporate governance and impression management in annual results press releases. *Accounting, Organizations and Society*, *36*(4-5), 187–208. doi:10.1016/j.aos.2011.03.005

Garcia, E. G., & Maldonado, S. L. S. (2012). Reuse of public sector information in Spain: A solid foundation for a promising future. *Textos Universitaris de Biblioteconomia I Documentació, 29.*

Garcia-Bernardo, J., & Jansky, P. (2021). *Profit Shifting of Multinational Corporations Worldwide* (IES Working Papers 14/2021). IES FSV. Charles University.

Gartner. (2022). *Gartner forecasts worldwide public cloud end-user spending to reach nearly $500 billion in 2022.* Retrieved from https://www.gartner.com/en/newsroom/press-releases/2022-04-19-gartner-forecasts-worldwide-public-cloud-end-user-spending-to-reach-nearly-500-billion-in-2022

Gendron, Y., Brivot, M., & Guénin-Paravicini, H. (2016). The construction of risk management credibility within corporate boardrooms. *European Accounting Review, 25*(3), 549–578. doi:10.1080/09638180.2015.1064008

Gerbaudo, P. (2019). *The Digital party: Political organisation and online democracy.* Pluto Press.

Gettleman, J. (2017, February 7). Cash flows freely as Somalia holds 'fraudulent' election. *Irish Times.* Retrieved from https://www.irishtimes.com/news/world/africa/cash-flows-freely-as-somalia-holds-fraudulent-election-1.2966543#:~:text=Cash%20flows%20freely%20as%20Somalia%20holds%20%E2%80%98fraudulent%E2%80%99%20election,corruption%20Expand%20Swimmers%20among%20boats%20in%20Mogadishu%2C%20Somalia

Ghezzi, S. G. (1983). A private network of social control: Insurance investigation units. *Social Problems, 30*(5), 521–531. doi:10.2307/800269

Gibbins, M., & Mason, A.K. (1988). *Professional judgment in financial reporting.* CICA Research Study.

Gielnik, M. M., Frese, M., Graf, J. M., & Kampschulte, A. (2012). Creativity in the opportunity identification process and the moderating effect of diversity of information. *Journal of Business Venturing, 27*(5), 559–576. doi:10.1016/j.jbusvent.2011.10.003

Gill, K. M., Woolley, A., & Gill, M. (2005). Insurance fraud: The business as a victim? In M. Gill (Ed.), *Crime at work* (Vol. 1). Springer. doi:10.1007/978-1-349-23551-3_6

Gimpel, J. G. (2021). Citizen contacting in response to crisis: Voicing grievances to the Consumer Financial Protection Bureau. *American Politics Research, 49*(2), 198–214. doi:10.1177/1532673X20962414

Girling, J. L. S., & Staff, G. J. (1997). *Corruption, capitalism and democracy* (Vol. 11). Routledge.

Gitta, A., & Fröhlich, S. (2019, May 24). *Germany withholds aid money from Uganda.* Retrieved from https://www.dw.com/en/germany-withholds-aid-money-from-uganda/a-48862574-0

Global Cybersecurity Index. (2021). *Global Cybersecurity Index.* ITU Publications. Retrieved from https://www.itu.int/en/ITU-D/Cybersecurity/Pages/global-Cybersecurity-index.aspx

Global Open Data Index. (2016). *Place overview.* Open Knowledge Foundation. Retrieved from http://index.okfn.org/place.html

Global Witness. (2018, November 16). *DRC: Anti-Corruption organizations question make-up of candidate's campaign finance team.* Retrieved from https://www.globalwitness.org/en/press-releases/drc-anti-corruption-organisations-question-make-up-of-candidates/

Godfrey, J., Mather, P., & Ramsay, A. (2003). Earnings and impression management in financial reports: The case of CEO changes. *Abacus*, *39*(1), 95–123. doi:10.1111/1467-6281.00122

Gollwitzer, P. M., & Brandstätter, V. (1997). Implementation intentions and effective goal pursuit. *Journal of Personality and Social Psychology*, *73*(1), 186–199. doi:10.1037/0022-3514.73.1.186

Gollwitzer, P. M., & Sheeran, P. (2006). Implementation intentions and goal achievement: A meta-analysis of effects and processes. *Advances in Experimental Social Psychology*, *38*, 69–119. doi:10.1016/S0065-2601(06)38002-1

Gomes, C., Jin, Z., & Yang, H. (2021). Insurance fraud detection with unsupervised deep learning. *The Journal of Risk and Insurance*, *88*(3), 591–624. doi:10.1111/jori.12359

Gondwe, G. (2020). *Assessing the impact of COVID-19 on Africa's economic development*. UNCTAD. Retrieved from https://unctad.org/webflyer/assessing-impact-COVID-19-africas-economic-development

Gorsira, M., Denkers, A., & Huisman, W. (2018). Both sides of the coin: Motives for corruption among public officials and business employees. *Journal of Business Ethics*, *151*(1), 179–194. doi:10.100710551-016-3219-2

Goswami, Y., Kannan Asokan, K., & Arunasalam, K. (2022). Impact of frauds on the Financial Performance of Insurance Companies in India. *International Journal of Early Childhood Special Education*, *14*(3), 7490–7499.

Gouro, T. (2022). Extreme poverty rises in West Africa due to COVID-19 pandemic. *Relief Web*. Retrieved from https://reliefweb.int/report/world/extreme-poverty-rises-west-africa-due-COVID-19-pandemic

Government Accountability Project. (2018, 21 November). European parliament panel approves whistleblower protections for all EU countries. *Common Dreams*. Retrieved from https://www.commondreams.org/newswire/2018/11/21/european-parliament-panel-approves-whistleblower-protections-all-eu-countries

Government of Canada. PSIC. (2013, 10 September). *The servants disclosure protection act*. Retrieved from http://www.psic.gc.ca/eng/aboutus/psdpa

Government of Canada. PSIC. (2014). *Background, objectives, scope*. Retrieved from http://www.psic.ge.ca/ eng/content/background-objectives-scope

Graft, A., Verhulst, S., & Young, A. (2016, January). *Brazil's open budget transparency portal. Making public how public money is spent*. Omidyar Network. Retrieved from https://odimpact.org/files/case-study-brazil.pdf

Granger, C. W. J. (1969). Investigating causal relations by econometric models and cross-spectral methods. *Econometrica*, *37*(3), 424–438. doi:10.2307/1912791

Grant, W. B., Lahore, H., McDonnell, S. L., Baggerly, C. A., French, C. B., Aliano, J. L., & Bhattoa, H. P. (2020). Evidence that vitamin D supplementation could reduce risk of influenza and covid-19 infections and deaths. *Nutrients*, *12*(4), 988. doi:10.3390/nu12040988 PMID:32252338

Grasgruber, M., Otavova, M., & Semerad, P. (2013). Impacts of the application of the reverse charge mechanism of the value-added tax. *Acta Universitatis Agriculturae et Silviculturae Mendelianae Brunensis*, *61*(7), 2133–2141. doi:10.11118/actaun201361072133

Grewal, R., & Tansuhaj, P. (2001). Building organizational capabilities for managing economic crisis: The role of market orientation and strategic flexibility. *Journal of Marketing*, *65*(2), 67–80. doi:10.1509/jmkg.65.2.67.18259

Grichnik, D., Smeja, A., & Welpe, I. (2010). The importance of being emotional: How do emotions affect entrepreneurial opportunity evaluation and exploitation? *Journal of Economic Behavior & Organization*, *76*(1), 15–29. doi:10.1016/j.jebo.2010.02.010

Griffin, A. E., Colella, A., & Goparaju, S. (2000). Newcomer and organizational socialization tactics: An interactionist perspective. *Human Resource Management Review*, *10*(4), 453–474. doi:10.1016/S1053-4822(00)00036-X

Griffin, J. M. (2021). Ten years of evidence: Was fraud a force in the financial crisis? *Journal of Economic Literature*, *59*(4), 1293–1321. doi:10.1257/jel.20201602

Gross, A. G., & Harmon, J. E. (2016). *The Internet in the sciences and the humanities*. Oxford University Press.

Guessous, H. (2020, January 23). Morocco loses 7 places in 2019 corruption perceptions index. *Morocco World News*. Retrieved from https://www.moroccoworldnews.com/2020/01/291922/morocco-corruption-index

Guillamon-Saorin, E., Osma, B. G., & Jones, M. J. (2012). Opportunistic disclosure in press release headlines. *Accounting and Business Research*, *42*(2), 143–168. doi:10.1080/00014788.2012.632575

Gurdgiev, C. (2019). OECD-Led tax reforms: A prescription for a less competitive economy. SSRN *Electronic Journal*. Retrieved from https://ssrn.com/abstract=3406260 doi:10.2139/ssrn.3406260

Hadro, D., Klimczak, K. M., & Pauka, M. (2017). Impression management in letters to shareholders: Evidence from Poland. *Accounting in Europe*, *14*(3), 305–330. doi:10.1080/17449480.2017.1378428

Haendler, C., & Heimer, R. (2021). The Financial Restitution Gap in Consumer Finance: Insights from Complaints Filed with the CFPB. SSRN *Electronic Journal*. Retrieved from https://papers.ssrn.com/sol3/papers.cfm?abstract_id=3766485 doi:10.2139/ssrn.3766485

Hagberg, S., Kibora, L., Barry, S., Gnessi, S., & Konkobo, A. (2017). *Transformations sociopolitiquesburkinabè de 2014 à 2016: Perspectives anthropologiques des pratiques politiques et de la culture démocratique dans" un Burkina nouveau"*. Uppsala University. Retrieved from https://www.semanticscholar.org/paper/Transformations-sociopolitiques-burkinab%C3%A8-de-2014-%C3%A0-Hagberg-Kibora/d3e44808d5ffc8eb53006994d3f60892a044f397

Hagen, B., Zucchela, A., & Ghauri, P. N. (2018). From fragile to agile: Marketing as a key driver of entrepreneurial internationalization. *International Marketing Review*, *36*(2), 260–288. doi:10.1108/IMR-01-2018-0023

Hair, J. F., Risher, J. J., Sarstedt, M., & Ringle, C. M. (2019). When to use and how to report the results of PLS-SEM. *European Business Review*, *31*(1), 2–24. doi:10.1108/EBR-11-2018-0203

Haji, A. A., & Hossain, D. M. (2016). Exploring the implications of integrated reporting on organisational reporting practice: Evidence from highly regarded integrated reporters. *Qualitative Research in Accounting & Management*, *13*(4), 415–444. doi:10.1108/QRAM-07-2015-0065

Halvorsen, J. L., & Møkkelgård, P. J. (2018). *Financial literacy and other determinants of consumer complaint behavior: An empirical study utilizing the CFPB's complaint database*. Retrieved from https://openaccess.nhh.no/nhh-xmlui/handle/11250/2585500

Hamza, S., & Jarboui, A. (2022). CSR or social impression management? Tone management in CSR reports. *Journal of Financial Reporting and Accounting*, *20*(3-4), 599–617. doi:10.1108/JFRA-04-2020-0115

Harber, M., Marx, B., & De Jager, P. (2020). The perceived financial effects of mandatory audit firm rotation. *Journal of International Financial Management & Accounting*, *31*(2), 215–234. doi:10.1111/jifm.12115

Hassan, A. I. K., & Abraham, A. (2013). Computational intelligence models for insurance fraud detection: A review of a decade of research. *Journal of Network and Innovative Computing*, *1*, 341–347.

Hayden, S. (2019, April 6). Asylum for sale: Refugees say some U.N. workers demand bribes for re-settlement. *NBC News*. Retrieved from https://www.nbcnews.com/news/world/asylum-sale-refugees-say-some-u-n-workers-demand-bribes-n988351

Hayek, M. (2012). Control beliefs and positive psychological capital: Can nascent entrepreneurs discriminate between what can and cannot be controlled? *Journal of Management Research*, *12*(1), 3–13.

Hayes, R. M., Jiang, F., & Pan, Y. (2021). Voice of the customers: Local trust culture and consumer complaints to the CFPB. *Journal of Accounting Research*, *59*(3), 1077–1121. doi:10.1111/1475-679X.12364

He, G., Pan, Y., & Tanaka, T. (2020). The short-term impacts of COVID-19 lockdown on urban air pollution in China. *Nature Sustainability*, *3*(12), 1005–1011. doi:10.103841893-020-0581-y

Heintze, H., & Thielborger, P. (2016). *From cold war to cyber war: The evolution of the international law of peace and armed conflict over the last 25 years*. Springer. doi:10.1007/978-3-319-19087-7

Henn, C., Papageorgiou, C., Romero, J. M., & Spatafora, N. (2017). *Export quality in advanced and developing economies: evidence from a new data set* (World Bank Policy Research Working Paper 8196). Washington, DC: World Bank.

Henseler, J., Ringle, C. M., & Sarstedt, M. (2015). A new criterion for assessing discriminant validity in variance-based structural equation modeling. *Journal of the Academy of Marketing Science*, *43*(1), 115–135. doi:10.100711747-014-0403-8

Herdman, R. (2002). *Critical accounting and critical disclosures*. Speech by SEC Chief Accountant at Financial Executives International — San Diego on January 24, 2002. Retrieved from https://www.sec.gov/news/speech/spch537.htm

Heydari, M., Saeidi, M., & Danai, H. (2016). Examine the relationship between leadership style (based on likert theory) with job satisfaction of teachers in Shahed high schools for girls in Tehran in the academic year 2014-2015. *Mediterranean Journal of Social Sciences*, *7*(2), 224–224.

Heydari, M., Xiaohu, Z., Keung, L. K., & Shang, Y. (2020b). Entrepreneurial intentions and behavior as the creation of business: Based on the theory of planned behavior extension evidence from Polish universities and entrepreneurs. *Propósitos y Representaciones*, *8*(SPE2), e674.

Heydari, M. D., & Lai, K. K. (2019). The effect employee commitment on service performance through a mediating function of organizational citizenship behavior using servqual and collaborative filtering modeling: Evidence from China's hospitality industry. *Journal of Tourism & Hospitality (Los Angeles, Calif.)*, *8*(2), 1–10.

Heydari, M., Lai, K. K., & Xiaohu, Z. (2020a). *Risk Management in Public-Private Partnerships*. Routledge. doi:10.4324/9781003112051

Heydari, M., Lai, K. K., & Xiaohu, Z. (2021a). *Corruption, Infrastructure Management and Public–Private Partnership: Optimizing through Mathematical Models*. Routledge. doi:10.4324/9781003177258

Heydari, M., Xiaohu, Z., Lai, K. K., & Wang, S. B. (2019). Social-Psychology and Situational Elements Affecting Individual Social Behavior. *Journal of Hotel and Business Management*, *8*(2), 1–9.

Heydari, M., Xiaohu, Z., Lai, K. K., & Yuxi, Z. (2020c). Evaluation of organizational performance strategies. *Proceedings of the National Aviation University*, *82*, 77–93. doi:10.18372/2306-1472.82.14615

Heydari, M., Xiaohu, Z., Lai, K. K., & Yuxi, Z. (2021b). How might entrepreneurial activities affect behavior and emotions? *Proceedings of the National Aviation University*, *87*(2), 65–77. doi:10.18372/2306-1472.87.15722

Heydari, M., Xiaohu, Z., Saeidi, M., Lai, K. K., Shang, Y., & Yuxi, Z. (2020f). Analysis of the role of social support-cognitive psychology and emotional process approach. *European Journal of Translational Myology*, *30*(3), 1–17. doi:10.4081/ejtm.2020.8975 PMID:33117505

Heydari, M., Xiaohu, Z., Saeidi, M., Lai, K. K., & Yuxi, Z. (2020d). Entrepreneurship process as the creation of business by engaging family members: Based on the perceived emotion. *REICE: Revista Electrónica de Investigación en Ciencias Económicas*, *8*(15), 210–241. doi:10.5377/reice.v8i15.9955

Heydari, M., Xiaohu, Z., Saeidi, M., Lai, K. K., & Yuxi, Z. (2020e). Entrepreneurial cognition and effect on neuro entrepreneurship. *Gelpat Caderno Suplementar*, *3*, 1–27.

Hibou, B., & Tozy, M. (2009). La lutte contre la corruption au Maroc: Vers une pluralisation des modes de gouvernement? [The fight against corruption in Morocco: towards a pluralization of modes of government?]. *Droit Social*, *72*(2), 339–357. https://doi.org/10.3917/drs.072.0339

Higgins, C., & Walker, R. (2012). Ethos, logos, pathos: Strategies of persuasion in social/environmental reports. *Accounting Forum*, *36*(3), 194–208. doi:10.1016/j.accfor.2012.02.003

Higginson, N., Simmons, C., & Warsame, H. (2006). Environmental disclosure and legitimation in the annual report - evidence from the joint solutions project. *Journal of Applied Accounting Research*, *8*(2), 3–23. doi:10.1108/96754260680001048

Hilgers, M., & Loada, A. (2013). Tensions et protestations dans un régime semi-autoritaire: croissance des révoltespopulaires et maintien du pouvoir au Burkina Faso. *Politique Africanise*, *3*, 187-208. Retrieved from https://www.cairn.info/revue-politiqueafricaine-2013-3-page-187.htm

Hiltzik, M. (2015, July 23). Consumer protection: Why do republicans hate the CFPB so much? *Los Angeles Times*. Retrieved from https://www.latimes.com/business/hiltzik/la-fi-mh-cfpb-republicans-20150723-column.html

Hochberg, M. E. (2020). *Importance of suppression and mitigation measures in managing COVID-19 outbreaks*. doi:10.1101/2020.03.31.20048835

Hoerner, J., & Stephenson, P. (2012). Theoretical perspectives on approaches to policy evaluation in the EU: The case of cohesion policy. *Public Administration*, *90*(3), 699–715. doi:10.1111/j.1467-9299.2011.02013.x

Holm, C., & Zaman, M. (2012). Regulating audit quality: Restoring trust and legitimacy. *Accounting Forum*, *36*(1), 51–61. doi:10.1016/j.accfor.2011.11.004

Holtz, L. (2021). *COVID-19's Impact on overall health care services in Africa*. Brookings Institution.

Honson, S. (2009, August 6). *Corruption in Sub- Saharan Africa*. Council on Foreign Relations. Retrieved from https://www.cfr.org/backgrounder/corruption-sub-saharan-africa

Hossain, D. M., Alam, M. S., Mazumder, M. M. M., & Amin, A. (2020). Gender-related discourses in corporate annual reports: An exploratory study on the Bangladeshi companies. *Journal of Accounting and Organizational Change*, *17*(3), 394–415. doi:10.1108/JAOC-01-2020-0006

Hosseini-Nezhad, S., Safdar, S., Hosseini-Nezhad, P., & Luu, L. A. N. (2022). Psychological perspective on COVID-19. In N. Fagih & A. Forouharfar (Eds.), *Socioeconomic Dynamics of the COVID-19 Crisis: Global, Regional and Local Perspectives* (pp. 291–326). Springer. doi:10.1007/978-3-030-89996-7_14

Hrasky, S., & Jones, M. J. (2016). Lake pedder: Accounting, environmental decision-making, nature and impression management. *Accounting Forum*, *40*(4), 285–299. doi:10.1016/j.accfor.2016.06.005

Hruby, A. (2020). A rough road ahead for Nigeria. *Atlantic Council*. Retrieved from https://www.atlanticcouncil.org/blogs/africasource/a-rough-road-ahead-for-nigeria/

Huang, J., Sherraden, M., Sherraden, M. S., & Johnson, L. (2022). Effective finance to increase financial well-being for low-income families: Empirical examination and policy implications. *The Journal of Consumer Affairs*, *56*(4), 1638–1657. doi:10.1111/joca.12484

Huang, L., Ma, M., & Wang, X. (2022). Clan culture and risk-taking of Chinese enterprises. *China Economic Review*, *72*, 101763. doi:10.1016/j.chieco.2022.101763

Human Rights Watch. (2019, April 25). *Mozambique: Cyclone Victims Forced to Trade Sex for Food*. Retrieved from https://www.hrw.org/news/2019/04/25/mozambique-cyclone-victims-forced-trade-sex-food

Human Rights Watch. (2020). End internet shutdowns to manage COVID-19. *Human Rights Watch*. Retrieved from https://www.hrw.org/news/2020/03/31/end-internet-shutdowns-manage-COVID-19

Hutchinson, E., McKee, M., & Balabanova, D. (2019). What Drives Health Workers to Break the Rules and Use Public Resources for Private Gain? A Review of the Literature on sub-Saharan Africa. *LSHTM Research Online*. Retrieved from https://researchonline.lshtm.ac.uk/id/eprint/4659912/

IAIS. (2007). *Report on the survey on preventing, detecting and remedying fraud in insurance.* Basel: International Association of Insurance Supervisors. Retrieved from www.iaisweb.org/

IAIS. (2011). *Deterring, Preventing, Detecting, Reporting and Remedying Fraud in Insurance.* Basel: International Association of Insurance Supervisors. Retrieved from https://www.iaisweb.org/page/supervisory-material/application-papers/file/58019/application-paper-on-the-regulationand-supervision-ofcaptive-insurers

IASB. (2015). *IFRS Mission Statement*. International Accounting Standard Board. Retrieved from https://www.ifrs.org/content/dam/ifrs/about-us/our-history/2015-mission-statement.pdf?la=en

Ibendahl, G. (2018). *Comparing the financial ratios ROA and ROE.* Kansas State University Department of Agricultural Economics. Retrieved from https://agmanager.info /sites/default/files/pdf/ROA-ROE_2018_Ibendahl.pdf

ICAEW. (2006). *Measurement in Financial Reporting.* The Institute of Chartered Accountants in England & Wales. Retrieved from www.icaew.co.uk/bettermarkets

ICAEW. (2022). *Fraudulent financial reporting: Fresh thinking.* The Institute of Chartered Accountants of England and Wales. Retrieved from https://www.icaew.com/technical/thought-leadership/full-collection/audit-and-assurance-thought-leadership/fraudulent-fin ancial-reporting-fresh-thinking#:~:text=Fraudulent%20financial%20reporting%3A%20fresh%20thinking%20In%20this%20essay%2C,maximise%20the%20likelihood%20of%20identifying%20fraudulent%20financial%20reporting

IDEA. (2018). *Burkina Faso: Latest available data.* International Institute for Democracy and Electoral Assistance. Retrieved from https://www.idea.int/es/data-tools/country-view/61/55

IFRS. (2018). *Conceptual Framework for Financial Reporting 2018*. IFRS Foundation. Retrieved from https://www.ifrs.org/

Igbuzor, O. (2008). *Strategies for winning the anti-corruption war in Nigeria*. Action Aid.

Ikubaje, J. (2004). *Nigeria: Anti-corruption initiatives and the constitution*. Workshop on corruption in Nigeria, organized by Zero Corruption Coalition and the UNDP at Niimah Guest Palace, Kano, Nigeria.

Insurance Fraud Handbook. (2018). *Association of Certified Fraud Examiners*. Retrieved from https://www.acfe.com/uploadedFiles/ACFE_Website/Content/documents/Insurance-Fraud-Handbook.pdf

Internet World Stats. (2022). *Usage and population statistics: Internet penetration in Africa*. Retrieved from https://www.internetworldstats.com/stats1.htm

INTERPOL. (2020). Mobile money and organized crime in Africa. *Enact Africa*. Retrieved from https://enactafrica.org/research/interpol-reports/mobile-money-and-organised-crime-in-africa

IRA. (2020). *Insurance industry annual report*. Insurance Regulatory Authority. Retrieved from https://www.ira.go.ke/index.php/publications/statistical-reports/annual-reports

IRA. (2021). *Insurance industry annual report*. Insurance Regulatory Authority. Retrieved from https://www.ira.go.ke/index.php/publications/statistical-reports/annual-reports

IRS. (2022). *Types of Fraudulent Activities – General Fraud*. Internal Revenue Service. Retrieved from https://www.irs.gov/

Irungu, M. J. (2016). *Relationship between Fraud and Financial Performance of Insurance Companies in Kenya* [Unpublished MSC (Finance) Project]. University of Nairobi. Retrieved from http://erepository.uonbi.ac.ke/handle/11295/98963?show=full

ISACA. (2020). *Cybersecurity by the numbers: Increased attacks, rampant under reporting and the power of a fully staffed team*. Retrieved from https://www.ISACA.org/go/state-of-Cybersecurity-2020

Jacobson, L. (2015, Nov 14). Carly Fiorina Says Consumer Financial Protection Bureau has 'No Congressional Oversight. *Politifact*. Retrieved from https://www.politifact.com/factchecks/2015/nov/14/carly-fiorina/carly-fiorina-says-consumer-financial-protection-b/

Jain, A. K. (2001). Corruption: A Review. *Journal of Economic Surveys*, *15*(1), 71–121. https://doi.org/10.1111/1467-6419.00133

Jamal, K., & Tan, H. (2010). Joint effects of principles-based versus rules-based standards and auditor type in constraining financial managers' aggressive reporting. *The Accounting Review*, *85*(4), 1325–1346. doi:10.2308/accr.2010.85.4.1325

Jarus, O. (2020). 20 of the worst epidemics and pandemics in history. *LiveScience*. Retrieved from https://www.livescience.com/worst-epidemics-and-pandemics-in-history.html

Jeacle, I. (2008). Beyond the boring grey: The construction of the colourful accountant. *Critical Perspectives on Accounting*, *19*(8), 1296–1320. doi:10.1016/j.cpa.2007.02.008

Jeacle, I. (2014). "And the BAFTA goes to [...]": The assurance role of the auditor in the film awards ceremony. *Accounting, Auditing & Accountability Journal*, *27*(5), 778–808. doi:10.1108/AAAJ-03-2013-1252

Jeacle, I., & Carter, C. (2012). Fashioning the popular masses: Accounting as mediator between creativity and control. *Accounting, Auditing & Accountability Journal*, *25*(4), 719–751. doi:10.1108/09513571211225114

Jednak, D., & Jednak, S. (2019). Socially responsible financial markets. In *Financing Sustainable Development* (pp. 103–125). Palgrave Macmillan. doi:10.1007/978-3-030-16522-2_5

Jelčić, B., Lončarić H., Šimović, J., Arbutina, H., & Mijatović, N. (2008). *Financijsko pravo i financijska znanost*. Zagreb: Narodne Novine.

Johnson, N. F. (2009). *The ultiplicities of internet addiction: The misrecognition of leisure and learning*. Ashgate Publishing Company.

Jones, M. J. (2011). The nature, use and impression management of graphs in social and environmental accounting. *Accounting Forum*, *35*(2), 75–89. doi:10.1016/j.accfor.2011.03.002

Jones, M. J., Melis, A., Gaia, S., & Aresu, S. (2018). Does graphical reporting improve risk disclosure? Evidence from European banks. *Journal of Applied Accounting Research*, *19*(1), 161–180. doi:10.1108/JAAR-07-2016-0068

Joseph, T., & Ashkan, M. (2020). *International pulmonologists consensus on COVID-19*. Amrita Institute of Medical Sciences.

Jugnandan, S., & Willows, G. D. (2022). "It's a long story…" – impression management in South African corporate reporting. *Accounting Research Journal*, *35*(5), 581–597. doi:10.1108/ARJ-07-2021-0209

Jung, J., & Kim, J. B. (2021). Insurance fraud in Korea, its seriousness, and policy implications. Front. *Frontiers in Public Health*, *9*, 791820. doi:10.3389/fpubh.2021.791820 PMID:34869196

Kahn, T., Baron, A., & Vieyra, J. C. (2018, November). *Digital Technologies for Transparency in Public Investment: New Tools to Empower Citizens and Governments* (Discussion Paper No. IDB-DP-634). Inter-American Development Bank. doi:10.18235/0001418

Kamer, L. (2022a). Number of internet users in selected countries. *Statista*. Retrieved from https://www.Statista.com/statistics/505883/number-of-internet-users-in-african-countries/

Kamer, L. (2022b). Internet penetration in Africa. *Statista*. Retrieved from https://www.Statista.com/statistics/1124283/internet-penetration-in-africa-by-country/

Karhunen, P., Ledyaeva, S., & Brouthers, K. D. (2021). Capital Round-Tripping: Determinants of Emerging Market Firm Investments into Offshore Financial Centers and Their Ethical Implications. *Journal of Business Ethics*, 1–21. doi:10.100710551-021-04908-y

Karpoff, J. M. (2021). The future of financial fraud. *Journal of Corporate Finance*, *66*, 101694. doi:10.1016/j.jcorpfin.2020.101694

Kasoga, P. S. (2020). Does investing in intellectual capital improve financial performance? Panel evidence from firms listed in Tanzania DSE. *Cogent Economics and Finance*, *8*(1), 1–26. doi:10.1080/23322039.2020.1802815

Kautonen, T., Van Gelderen, M., & Fink, M. (2015). Robustness of the theory of planned behavior in predicting entrepreneurial intentions and actions. *Entrepreneurship Theory and Practice*, *39*(3), 655–674. doi:10.1111/etap.12056

Kautonen, T., Van Gelderen, M., & Tornikoski, E. T. (2013). Predicting entrepreneurial behavior: A test of the theory of planned behavior. *Applied Economics*, *45*(6), 697–707. doi:10.1080/00036846.2011.610750

Kavanagh, M., & McCarey, D. (2017). *All the president's wealth: the Kabila family business*. Congo Research Group. Retrieved from https://pulitzercenter.org/stories/all-presidents-wealth-kabila-family-business

Kayed, S., & Meqbel, R. (2022). (in press). Earnings management and tone management: Evidence from FTSE 350 companies. *Journal of Financial Reporting and Accounting*. Advance online publication. doi:10.1108/JFRA-10-2021-0373

Kazeem, Y. (2016, December 9). An 8 million dollar refugee fund scandal shows Buhari's anti-corruption drive in Nigeria is not going to plan. *Quartz*. Retrieved from https://qz.com/africa/858019/a-new-8m-scam-of-relief-funds-shows-nigerias-buhari-anti-corruption-drive-is-not-going-to-plan

Kemp, S. (2020a). *Digital 2020: April 2020 snapshots*. Retrieved from https://datareportal.com/reports/digital-2020-april-global-statshot

Kemp, S. (2020b). Digital trends 2020: Every single stat you need to know about the internet. *Global Web Index*. Retrieved from https://thenextweb.com/podium/2020/01/30/digital-trends-2020-every-single-stat-you-need-to-know-about-the-internet/

Kennedy, L. J., McCoy, P. A., & Bernstein, E. (2011). The consumer financial protection bureau: Financial regulation for the twenty-first century. *Cornell Law Review*, *97*, 1141.

Khan, N., Rafay, A., & Shakeel, A. (2020). Attributes of Internal Audit and Prevention, Detection and Assessment of Fraud in Pakistan. *Lahore Journal of Business*, *9*(1), 33–58. doi:10.35536/ljb.2020.v9.i1.a2

Khanna, K., & Irvine, H. (2018). Communicating the impact of the global financial crisis in annual reports: A study of Australian NGOs. *Australian Accounting Review*, *28*(1), 109–126. doi:10.1111/auar.12162

Kılıç, O. (1999). *16.Yüzyılın İkinci Yarısında Kalpazanlık Faaliyetleri. Osmanlı Ansiklopedisi*. Yeni Türkiye Yayınları.

Kiptoo, K., Kariuki, S. N., & Ocharo, K. N. (2021). Risk management and financial performance of insurance firms in Kenya. *Cogent Business & Management*, *8*(1), 1–17. doi:10.1080/23311975.2021.1997246

Kirchler, E., Maciejovsky, B., & Schneider, F. (2003). Everyday representations of tax avoidance, tax evasion, and tax flight: Do legal differences matter? *Journal of Economic Psychology*, *24*(4), 535–553. doi:10.1016/S0167-4870(02)00164-2

Kirzner, I. M. (1982). The theory of entrepreneurship in economic growth. Encyclopedia of Entrepreneurship, 272, 276.

Klassen, J., Lisowsky, P., & Mescall, D. (2017). Transfer pricing: Strategies, practices and tax minimization. *Contemporary Accounting Research*, *34*(1), 455–493. doi:10.1111/1911-3846.12239

Kleinig, J. (n.d.). *Whistleblower*. Retrieved from https://www.britannica.com/topic/whistleblower

Klitgaard, R. (1991). *Controlling corruption*. University of California Press.

Köbis, N. C. (2018). *The social psychology of corruption*. Vrije Universiteit.

Koçi (bey), & Danişman, A. Z. (1972). *Koçi Bey Risalesi, 1051/1641*. Ankara: Milli EğitimBakanlığı.

Kofler, G., Krever, R., Lang, M., & Staringer, C. (2020). *Controlled Foreign Company Legislation*. IBFD.

Köhler, A., Ratzinger-Sakel, N., & Theis, J. (2020). The effects of key audit matters on the auditor's report's communicative value: Experimental evidence from investment professionals and non-professional investors. *Accounting in Europe*, *17*(2), 105–128. doi:10.1080/17449480.2020.1726420

Koppl, R., & Minniti, M. (2003). Market processes and entrepreneurial studies. In *Handbook of Entrepreneurship Research* (pp. 81–102). Springer.

Kowal, A., & Przekota, G. (2021). VAT Efficiency—A discussion on the VAT System in the European Union. *Sustainability, 13*(9), 4768. doi:10.3390u13094768

KPMG. (2020). Government and institution measures in response to COVID-19. *KPMG*. Retrieved from https://home.kpmg/xx/en/home/insights/2020/04/nigeria-government-and-institution-measures-in-response-to-covid.html

Kredens, M. (2020). The Virus of desire. The life of passion. A COVID-19 Self-Help Erotic Book. Grupa Szeroka: Szeroka Street Publishing House.

Krueger, N. F. (2007). The cognitive infrastructure of opportunity emergence. In *Entrepreneurship* (pp. 185–206). Springer.

Krueger, N. Jr, & Dickson, P. R. (1994). How believing in ourselves increases risk taking: Perceived self-efficacy and opportunity recognition. *Decision Sciences, 25*(3), 385–400. doi:10.1111/j.1540-5915.1994.tb01849.x

Kshetri, N. (2019). Cybercrime and Cybersecurity in Africa. *Journal of Global Information Technology Management, 22*(2), 77–81. doi:10.1080/1097198X.2019.1603527

Kumarasinghe, S., & Samkin, G. (2020). Impression management and ancient Ceylonese rulers. *Accounting History, 25*(1), 5–26. doi:10.1177/1032373218802892

Lagoarde-Segot, T., & Paranque, B. (2017). Sustainability and the reconstruction of academic finance. *Research in International Business and Finance, 39*(B), 657–662.

Lai, M. M., Lein, S. Y., Lau, S. H., & Lai, M. L. (2016). Modeling age-friendly environment, active aging, and social connectedness in an emerging Asian economy. *Journal of Aging Research, 2016*, 2052380. doi:10.1155/2016/2052380 PMID:27293889

Lambsdorff, J. G., & Nell, M. (2006). Corruption: Where we stand and where to go. In M. Kreutner (Ed.), *The Corruption Monster: Ethik, Politik und Korruption*. Czernin.

Lash, N. A. (2003). *Corruption and economic development*. Layola University.

Lau, C. M., & Martin-Sardesai, A. V. (2012). The role of organisational concern for workplace fairness in the choice of a performance measurement system. *The British Accounting Review, 44*(3), 157–172. doi:10.1016/j.bar.2012.07.006

Lauletta, M., Rossi, M. A., Vieyra, J. C., & Arisi, D. (2019, November). *Monitoring Public Investment: The Impact of MapaRegalías in Colombia*. Inter-American Development Bank. doi:10.18235/0002014

Lawal, G. (2007). Corruption and development in Africa: challenges for political and economic change. *Humanity and Social Sciences Journal, 2*(1), 1-7.

Lee, O. K., Sambamurthy, V., Lim, K. H., & Wei, K. K. (2015). How does IT ambidexterity impact organizational agility? *Information Systems Research, 26*(2), 398–417. doi:10.1287/isre.2015.0577

Lee, S. Y., Florida, R., & Acs, Z. (2004). Creativity and entrepreneurship: A regional analysis of new firm formation. *Regional Studies, 38*(8), 879–891. doi:10.1080/0034340042000280910

Lepoutre, J., & Oguntoye, A. (2018). The (non-)emergence of mobile money systems in Sub-Saharan Africa: A comparative multilevel perspective of Kenya and Nigeria. *Technological Forecasting and Social Change, 131*, 262–275. doi:10.1016/j.techfore.2017.11.010

Leung, S., Parker, L., & Courtis, J. (2015). Impression management through minimal narrative disclosure in annual reports. *The British Accounting Review*, *47*(3), 275–289. doi:10.1016/j.bar.2015.04.002

Leventis, S., & Weetman, P. (2004). Impression management: Dual language reporting and voluntary disclosure. *Accounting Forum*, *28*(3), 307–328. doi:10.1016/j.accfor.2004.07.004

Levitin, A. J. (2009). Hydraulic Regulation: Regulating Credit Markets Upstream. *Yale Journal on Regulation*, *26*, 143.

Levitin, A. J. (2012). The consumer financial protection bureau: An introduction [Review]. *Banking and Finance Law*, *32*, 321.

Levitt, A. (1998). *The 'numbers game'.* Speech delivered at New York University Law and Business Centre. Retrieved from http://www.sec.gov

Li, X. (2022). *Bank Competition and Entrepreneurial Gaps: Evidence from Bank Deregulation.* Royal Economic Society. Retrieved from https://res.org.uk/wp-content/uploads/2022/11/11.pdf

Liang, T. (2020). *Handbook of COVID-19 prevention and treatment. Zhejiang*. Zhejiang University of Medicine.

Li, C., Lou, C., Luo, D., & Kai, X. (2021). Chinese corporate distress prediction using LASSO: The role of earnings management. *International Review of Financial Analysis*, *76*(C), 101776. doi:10.1016/j.irfa.2021.101776

Likert, R. A. (1952). A technique for the development of attitude scales. *Educational and Psychological Measurement*, *12*(2), 313–315.

Liñán, F., & Chen, Y. W. (2009). Development and cross–cultural application of a specific instrument to measure entrepreneurial intentions. *Entrepreneurship Theory and Practice*, *33*(3), 593–617. doi:10.1111/j.1540-6520.2009.00318.x

Liu, P., Li, H., & Guo, H. (2020). The impact of corruption on firms' access to bank loans: Evidence from China. *Economic Research-Ekonomska Istraživanja*, *33*(1), 1963–1984. doi:10.1080/1331677X.2020.1768427

Live Science. (2020). *Spanish Flu: The deadliest pandemic in history.* Retrieved from https://www.livescience.com/spanish-flu.html

Livingston, S. G. (1992). The politics of international agenda-setting: Reagan and North-South relations. *International Studies Quarterly*, *36*(3), 313–329. doi:10.2307/2600775

Ljubas, Z. (2019, July 24). *US: Another guilty plea in Mozambique financial scam.* Organized Crime and Corruption Reporting Project (OCCRP). Retrieved from https://www.occrp.org/en/daily/10304-us-another-guilty-plea-in-mozambique-financial-scam

Lo, W. Y. (2020). *International Transfer Pricing in a developing economy context: Perspectives from the taxpayers and the tax authorities* [PhD Thesis]. Lingnan University. Retrieved from https://scholars.ln.edu.hk/en/studentTheses/international-transfer-pricing-in-a-developing-economy-context-pe

Lodge, T. (2019). State Capture: Conceptual Considerations. In M. Meirotti & G. Masterson (Eds.), *State Capture in Africa: Old Threats, New Packaging?* EISA Publications.

Lohse, T., & Riedel, N. (2013). *Do transfer pricing laws limit international income shifting? Evidence from European Multinationals* (CESifo Working Paper Series No. 4404). Retrieved from https://www.cesifo.org/en/publikationen/2013/working-paper/do-transfer-pricing-laws-limit-international-income-shifting

Longhorn, M. (2015). *Country-by-Country Reporting: A Critical Analysis* [Master's Thesis]. Queensland University of Technology. https://eprints.qut.edu.au/84604/4/Monique_Longhorn_Thesis.pdf

Lopes, J., & Fletcher, C. (2004). Fairness of impression management in employment interviews: A cross-country study of the role of equity and Machiavellianism. *Social Behavior and Personality*, *32*(8), 747–768. doi:10.2224bp.2004.32.8.747

Loveday, B., & Jung, J. (2021). A current and future challenge to contemporary policing: the changing profile of crime and the police response. examples of policing fraud in two police jurisdictions: England and Wales and South Korea. *Policing. Journal of Policy Practice*, *15*(3), 1633–1650.

Lund, K. (2016). *Facilitating corporate entrepreneurial behavior: A study of corporate entrepreneurial behavior in corporate banking*. Turun Yliopisto.

Lu, Y., & Ramamurthy, K. (2011). Understanding the link between information technology capability and organizational agility: An empirical examination. *Management Information Systems Quarterly*, *35*(4), 931–954. doi:10.2307/41409967

Maclean, R., & Boley, T. (2019). Protests in Liberia over George Weah's failure to tackle corruption. *The Guardian*. Retrieved from https://www.theguardian.com/world/2019/jun/07/thousands-protest-in-liberia-against-failure-to-tackle-corruption

Mahyoro, A. K., & Kasoga, P. S. (2021). Attributes of the internal audit function and effectiveness of internal audit services: Evidence from local government authorities in Tanzania. *Managerial Auditing Journal*, *36*(7), 999–1023. doi:10.1108/MAJ-12-2020-2929

Maina, B. W. (2016). *The Effects of Financial Fraud and Liquidity on Financial Performance of Insurance Companies in Kenya* [Unpublished MBA Project]. University of Nairobi. Retrieved from http://erepository.uonbi.ac.ke/bitstream/handle/11295/99055/maina_The%20Effects%20of%20Financial%20Fraud%20and%20Liquidity%20on%20Financial%20Perform

Manes Rossi, F., Brusca, I., & Condor, V. (2021). In the pursuit of harmonization: Comparing the audit systems of European local governments. *Public Money & Management*, *41*(8), 604–614. doi:10.1080/09540962.2020.1772549

Mankiw, N. G. (2007). *Macroeconomics*. Worth publishers.

Manstead, A. S., Proffitt, C., & Smart, J. L. (1983). Predicting and understanding mothers' infant-feeding intentions and behavior: Testing the theory of reasoned action. *Journal of Personality and Social Psychology*, *44*(4), 657–671. doi:10.1037/0022-3514.44.4.657 PMID:6842361

March, J. G., & Olsen, J. P. (1996). Institutional perspectives on political institutions. *Governance: An International Journal of Policy, Administration and Institutions*, *9*(3), 247–264. doi:10.1111/j.1468-0491.1996.tb00242.x

Markovich, S., & Snyder, C. (2017). M-Pesa and mobile money in Kenya: Pricing for success. *Kellogg School of Management Cases*, *1*, 1–17. doi:10.1108/case.kellogg.2016.000221

Marques, M., & Pinho, C. (2016). Is transfer pricing strictness deterring profit shifting within multinationals? Empirical evidence from Europe. *Accounting and Business Research*, *46*(7), 703–730. doi:10.1080/00014788.2015.1135782

Marshall, A. (1890). *Principles of Economics: an introductory volume, book 4, ch. 6, version numérique*. McMaster University, Archive for the History of Economic Thought.

Martini, M. (2014). State Capture: An Overview, Anti-Corruption Helpdesk. *Transparency International*. Retrieved from https://www.transparency.org/files/content/corruptionqas/State _capture_an_overview_2014.pdf

Martins, A., Gomes, D., Oliveira, L., & Ribeiro, J. L. (2019). Telling a success story through the president's letter. *Qualitative Research in Accounting & Management*, *16*(3), 403–433. doi:10.1108/QRAM-03-2018-0018

Mathe, A. (2019). The misunderstood world of Cybersecurity in Africa. *Policy Centre for the New South.* Retrieved from https://www.policycenter.ma/opinion/misunderstood-world-Cybersecurity-africa

Mather, P., & Ramsay, A. (2007). Do board characteristics influence impression management through graph selectivity around CEO changes? *Australian Accounting Review, 17*(42), 84–95. doi:10.1111/j.1835-2561.2007.tb00446.x

Mather, P., Ramsay, A., & Steen, A. (2000). The use and representational faithfulness of graphs in Australian IPO prospectuses. *Accounting, Auditing & Accountability Journal, 13*(1), 65–83. doi:10.1108/09513570010316144

Mathew, R. E., Barnabas, O., Lawal, A. I., & Joseph, I. O. (2013). Analysis of corruption and economic growth in Nigeria. *Afro Asian Journal of Social Sciences, 4*(4), 1–19.

Matthysen, K., Spitaels, S., & Schouten, P. (2019). *Mapping artisanal mining areas and mineral supply chains in eastern DR Congo: Impact of armed interference & responsible sourcing.* International Peace Information Service. Retrieved from https://ipisresearch.be/publication/mapping-artisanal-mining-areas-mineral-supply-chains-eastern-drc/

Maurer, B. (2015). *How Would You Like to Pay?: How Technology Is Changing the Future of Money.* Duke University Press.

Mbaku, T. M. (2000). *Political Corruption and Bureaucratic in Africa: The Public Choice Perspective.* Kriag.

McClelland, D. C., & Winter, D. G. (1969). *Motivating Economic Achievement.* FreePress.

McCoy, P. A. (2018). Inside job: The assault on the structure of the Consumer Financial Protection Bureau. *Minnesota Law Review, 103*, 2543.

McGrath, R. G., & MacMillan, I. C. (2000). *The entrepreneurial mindset: Strategies for continuously creating opportunity in an age of uncertainty* (Vol. 284). Harvard Business Press.

McNally, M. A., & Maroun, W. (2018). It is not always bad news: Illustrating the potential of integrated reporting using a case study in the eco-tourism industry. *Accounting, Auditing & Accountability Journal, 31*(5), 1319–1348. doi:10.1108/AAAJ-05-2016-2577

Meeuwisse, R. (2015). *Cybersecurity for beginners.* Icutrain Ltd.

Melgar, N., Rossi, M., & Smith, T. W. (2010). The perception of corruption in a cross-country perspective: Why are some individuals more perceptive than others? *Economia Aplicada, 14*(2), 183–198. doi:10.1590/S1413-80502010000200004

Melis, A. (2004). On the role of the board of statutory auditors in Italian listed companies. *Corporate Governance, 12*(1), 74–84. doi:10.1111/j.1467-8683.2004.00344.x

Melis, A., & Gaia, S. (2011). Corporate governance in Italy: Normative developments vs. actual practices. In *Handbook on International Corporate Governance.* Edward Elgar Publishing. doi:10.4337/9781849808293.00010

Melloni, G., Caglio, A., & Perego, P. (2017). Saying more with less? Disclosure conciseness, completeness and balance in integrated reports. *Journal of Accounting and Public Policy, 36*(3), 220–238. doi:10.1016/j.jaccpubpol.2017.03.001

Melnychenko, R., Pugachevska, K., & Kasianok, K. (2014). Tax control of transfer pricing. *Investment Management and Financial Innovations, 14*(4), 40–49. doi:10.21511/imfi.14(4).2017.05

Mendez, C., & Bachtler, J. (2011). Administrative reform and unintended consequences: An assessment of the EU Cohesion policy 'audit explosion'. *Journal of European Public Policy, 18*(5), 746–765. doi:10.1080/13501763.2011.586802

Merkl-Davies, D. M., & Brennan, N. M. (2007). Discretionary disclosure strategies in corporate narratives: Incremental information or impression management? *Journal of Accounting Literature*, *27*, 116–196. https://ssrn.com/abstract=1089447

Merkl-Davies, D. M., & Brennan, N. M. (2011). A conceptual framework of impression management: New insights from psychology, sociology and critical perspectives. *Accounting and Business Research*, *41*(5), 415–437. doi:10.1080/00014788.2011.574222

Merkl-Davies, D. M., Brennan, N. M., & McLeay, S. J. (2011). Impression management and retrospective sense-making in corporate narratives: A social psychology perspective. *Accounting, Auditing & Accountability Journal*, *24*(3), 315–344. doi:10.1108/09513571111124036

Merritt, C. (2011). Mobile money transfer services: The next phase in the evolution of person-to-person payments. *Journal of Payments Strategy and Systems*, *5*(2), 143–160.

MFEPD. (2019a). *Budget Speech 2019: Embracing a brighter future together as a nation.* Ministry of Finance, Economic Planning and Development, Mauritius. Retrieved from https://mof.govmu.org/Documents/Documents/2019/2019_20budget speech.pdf

MFEPD. (2019b). *Annual Report 2019/2020.* Ministry of Finance, Economic Planning and Development, Mauritius. Retrieved from https://mof.govmu.org/Documents/Annual %20Report/MOFED_Annual_Report%20-%20FY%202020-2021.pdf

Micallef, M., & Bish, A. (2019, November 21). *After the storm: Organized crime across the Sahel-Sahara following upheaval in Libya and Mali.* Global Initiative against Transnational Organized Crime. Retrieved from https://globalinitiative.net/analysis/after-the-storm/

Mikeska, J. (1988). *Osmanlı Paralarının Sahteleri ve Taklitleri Üstüne Bazı Düşünceler.* Türk Nümizmatik Derneği Yayınları.

Miles, S., & Ringham, K. (2020). The boundary of sustainability reporting: Evidence from the FTSE100. *Accounting, Auditing & Accountability Journal*, *33*(2), 357–390. doi:10.1108/AAAJ-05-2018-3478

Mishkin, F. S. (1995). Symposium on the monetary transmission mechanism. *The Journal of Economic Perspectives*, *9*(4), 3–10. doi:10.1257/jep.9.4.3

Mishkin, F. S. (2013). *The Economics of Money, Banking and Financial Markets*. Pearson.

Mitusova, E. Y. (2021). Prospects of integration of operational control in the system of fiscal control. *Russian Economic Developments*, *7*, 49–56.

Miyazaki, A. D. (2009). Perceived ethicality of insurance claim fraud: Do higher deductibles lead to lower ethical standards? *Journal of Business Ethics*, *87*(4), 589–598. doi:10.100710551-008-9960-4

Mohamed, Z., & Stansfield, G. (2017). *What does the protected disclosures amendment act mean for whistleblowers and employers alike*? Cliffe Dekker Hofmeyr. Retrieved from https://www.lexology.com/library/detail.aspx?g=e9fc5039-f162-4609-bd1d-10e94ffe00da#:~:text=The%20PDA%20provides%20protection%20to%20whistleblowers%20in%20the,places%20further%20obligations%20on%20whistleblowers%20and%20employers%20alike

Momoh, Z. (2013). *Faces of Corruption in Nigeria, Jos.* New Africa Magazine.

Mordi, M. (2019). Is Nigeria really the headquarters of Cybercrime in the world? *The Guardian*. Retrieved from https://guardian.ng/news/is-nigeria-really-the-headquarters-of-Cybercrime-in-the-world/

Moreno, A., Jones, M. J., & Quinn, M. (2019). A longitudinal study of the textual characteristics in the chairman's statements of Guinness: An impression management perspective. *Accounting, Auditing & Accountability Journal, 32*(6), 1714–1741. doi:10.1108/AAAJ-01-2018-3308

Moriano, J. A., Gorgievski, M., Laguna, M., Stephan, U., & Zarafshani, K. (2012). A cross-cultural approach to understanding entrepreneurial intention. *Journal of Career Development, 39*(2), 162–185. doi:10.1177/0894845310384481

Morley, N. J., Ball, L. J., & Ormerod, T. C. (2006). How the detection of insurance fraud succeeds and fails. *Psychology, Crime & Law, 12*(2), 163–180. doi:10.1080/10683160512331316325

Moussa, T., Kotb, A., & Helfaya, A. (2021). An empirical investigation of U.K. environmental targets disclosure: The role of environmental governance and performance. *European Accounting Review*, 1–35. doi:10.1080/09638180.2021.1890173

MRA. (2019). *Guidelines for the Appropriate Use of Information contained in CbC Reports.* Mauritius Revenue Authority. Retrieved from https://www.mra.mu/download/GuideCBCR.pdf

MRA. (2020). Article. *MRA Technical Journal, 2,* 1-67. Retrieved from https://www.mra.mu/download/MRATechnicalJournal.pdf

MRA. (2022). *Double Taxation Avoidance Agreements.* Mauritius Revenue Authority. Retrieved from https://www.mra.mu/index.php/taxes-duties/international-taxation/double-taxation-agreements

Mubarak, M. (2017, February 7). State of Accountability in Somalia in 2016: Unrestrained Corruption. *Marqaati.* Retrieved from https://marqaati.org/en/2017/02/state-of-accountability-in-somalia-in-2016-unrestrained-corruption/

Mudiri, J. L. (n.d.-a). *Fraud in Mobile Financial Services.* MicroSave. Retrieved from http://www.microsave.net/files/pdf/RP151_ Fraud_in_Mobile_Financial_Services _JMudiri.pdf

Mukhtar, S., & Abdullahi, S. I. (2020). Do poverty, unemployment and sexual violence explain suicide rate in Nigeria: What the data says. *Journal of Conflict Resolution and Social Issues, 1*(1), 72–80.

Mulford, C. W., & Comiskey, E. E. (2002). *The financial numbers game: detecting creative accounting practices.* John Wiley and Sons Inc.

Nair, A., Rustambekov, E., McShane, M., & Fainshmidt, S. (2014). Enterprise risk management as a dynamic capability: A test of its effectiveness during a crisis. *Managerial and Decision Economics, 35*(8), 555–566. doi:10.1002/mde.2641

Nakitende, M. G., Rafay, A., & Waseem, M. (2021). Frauds in Business Organizations: A Comprehensive Overview. In A. Rafay (Ed.), *Handbook of Research on Theory and Practice of Financial Crimes* (pp. 21–38). IGI Global. doi:10.4018/978-1-7998-5567-5.ch002

Narteh, B., Mahmoud, M. A., & Amoh, S. (2017). Customer behavioural intentions towards mobile money services adoption in Ghana. *Service Industries Journal, 37*(7/8), 426–447. doi:10.1080/02642069.2017.1331435

Ndulue, J. (2003). Bank failure: Causes and prevention. *International Journal of Economic and Development Issues, 3*(1), 162–178.

Nègre, E., Verdier, M. A., Cho, C. H., & Patten, D. M. (2017). Disclosure strategies and investor reactions to downsizing announcements: A legitimacy perspective. *Journal of Accounting and Public Policy, 36*(3), 239–257. doi:10.1016/j.jaccpubpol.2017.03.003

Nelson, M. W. (2003). Behavioural evidence on the effect of principles- and rules-based standards. *Accounting Horizons*, *17*(1), 91–104. doi:10.2308/acch.2003.17.1.91

Neu, D. (1991). Trust, impression management and the public accounting profession. *Critical Perspectives on Accounting*, *2*(3), 295–313. doi:10.1016/1045-2354(91)90015-6

Neu, D. (1999). "Discovering" indigenous peoples: Accounting and the machinery of empire. *The Accounting Historians Journal*, *26*(1), 53–82. doi:10.2308/0148-4184.26.1.53

Ngai, E. W., Hu, Y., Wong, Y. H., Chen, Y., & Sun, X. (2011). The application of data mining techniques in financial fraud detection: A classification framework and an academic review of literature. *Decision Support Systems*, *50*(3), 559–569. doi:10.1016/j.dss.2010.08.006

Nnoli, O. (2003). *Introduction to Politics*. SNAAP Press Ltd.

Nohe, P. (2018). Re-Hashed: 2018 *Cybercrime Statistics: A closer look at the "Web of Profit*. Retrieved from https://www.thesslstore.com/blog/2018-Cybercrime-statistics/#:~:text=Re-Hashed%3A%202018%20Cybercrime%20Statistics%3A%20A%20closer%20look%20at,profitability%20to%20be%20in%20excess%20of%20%241.5%20trillion.

North Africa Post. (2020, September 16). *Corruption costs Moroccan economy up to 7% of GDP annually – Finance Minister*. Retrieved from https://northafricapost.com/43844-corruption-costs-moroccan-economy-up-to-7-of-gdp-annually-finance-minister.html

Nosheen, S., Sadiq, R., & Rafay, A. (2016). The Primacy of Innovation in Strategic Financial Management-Understanding the Impact of Innovation and Performance on Capital Structure. *Proceedings of the 2016 IEEE International Conference on Management of Innovation and Technology (ICMIT)*. 10.1109/ICMIT.2016.7605048

Nyagadza, B., Kadembo, E. M., & Makasi, A. (2020). Exploring internal stakeholders' emotional attachment & corporate brand perceptions through corporate storytelling for branding. *Cogent Business and Management*, *7*(1), 1816254. doi:10.1080/23311975.2020.1816254

Nye, J. S. (1967). Corruption and political development: A cost-benefit analysis. *The American Political Science Review*, *61*(2), 417–427. doi:10.2307/1953254

NYU. (2022). *The Governance Lab (The GovLab)*. NYU Tandon School of Engineering. Retrieved from https://engineering.nyu.edu/research-innovation/centers/governance-lab-govlab

Nzekwe, A. (1994). *Can Nigeria Survive*. Transafrican Links.

Obasanjo, O. (1994). Keynote address. In A. Mahadi, G. A. Kwanashie, & M. Yakubu (Eds.), *Nigeria: The state of the nation and the way forward*. Arewa House.

OECD. (2015a). *Designing Effective CFC Rules, Action 3- 2015 Final Report*. Organisation for Economic Co-operation and Development. Retrieved from https://www.oecd.org/publications/designing-effective-controlled-foreign-company-rules-action-3-2015-final-report-9789264241152-en.htm

OECD. (2015b). *Aligning transfer pricing outcomes with value creation, Actions 8-10 Reports*. Organisation for Economic Co-operation and Development. Retrieved from https://www.oecd.org/tax/aligning-transfer-pricing-outcomes-with-value-creation-actions-8-10-2015-final-reports-9789264241244-en.htm

OECD. (2016). *Macau (China), Mauritius and Ukraine join the inclusive framework on BEPS.* Organisation for Economic Co-operation and Development. Retrieved from https://www.oecd.org/tax/beps/macau-china-mauritius-and-ukraine-join-the-inclusive-framework-on-beps.htm

OECD. (2016a). *Preventing corruption in public procurement.* Paris: The Organisation for Economic Co-operation and Development. Retrieved from https://www.oecd.org/gov/ethics/Corruption-Public-Procurement-Brochure.pdf

OECD. (2016b). *Open government data review of Mexico: data re-use for public sector impact and innovation.* Paris: The Organisation for Economic Co-operation and Development. Retrieved from https://www.oecd.org/gov/digital-government/open-government-data-review-of-mexico-9789264259270-en.htm

OECD. (2020). *COVID-19 in Africa: Regional Socio-economic Implications and Policy Priorities.* Organisation for Economic Cooperation and Development.

OECD. (2020). *OECD/G20 Inclusive Framework on BEPS – Progress Report July 2019 – July 2020.* Organisation for Economic Co-operation and Development. Retrieved from https://www.oecd.org/tax/beps/oecd-g20-inclusive-framework-on-beps-progress-report-july-2019-july-2020.htm

Ogden, S., & Clarke, J. (2005). Customer disclosures, impression management and the construction of legitimacy: Corporate reports in the UK privatised water industry. *Accounting, Auditing & Accountability Journal, 18*(3), 313–345. doi:10.1108/09513570510600729

Ogundiya, I. S., & Baba, T. K. (2004). Electoral Violence and the prospects of democratic consolidation in Nigeria. Paper presented at the National Conference on Electoral Violence in Nigeria Organized by NPSA at Rock View Hotel, Abuja, Nigeria.

Ogundiya, I. S. (2009). Political corruption in Nigeria: Theoretical perspectives and some explanations. *The Anthropologist, 11*(4), 281–292. doi:10.1080/09720073.2009.11891117

Ogunshola, F. (2022, February 8). Protecting whistle-blowers via requisite legal framework. *New Telegraph.* Retrieved from https://www.newtelegraphng.com/?s=whistle-blowers

Ojo, O. (2007). A Political Economy Technique to comprehending Corruption and the obstacle of Human Development. In A. Aina (Ed.), *Corruption and the Challenge and Obstacle of Human Development.* Babcock University.

Okolie, D. O. (2007). *Nigeria government and politics: The changing scene.* John Jacobs Publishers.

Okonjo, J. (2021). International financial regulation and sustainable finance. In *Encyclopedia of Law and Development.* Edward Elgar Publishing. doi:10.4337/9781788117975.00044

Okonkwo, R. (2005). Corruption in Nigeria. In F. Anyika (Ed.), *African Humanities.* Afro-Orbis.

Oluikpe, N. (2018, December 24). Anti-corruption war: Stakeholders ruminate on role of media. *Daily Independent.*

Oluwole, B. (2022). Nigerians are the most addicted social media users in Africa - See how other countries rank. *Business Insider Africa.* Retrieved from https://africa.businessinsider.com/local/lifestyle/nigerians-are-the-most-addicted-social-media-users-in-africa-see-how-other-countries/7d93c98

Oluwole, B. (2022). Top 10 African countries with the highest number of internet users in 2022. *Business Insider Africa*. Retrieved from https://africa.businessinsider.com/local/markets/top-10-african-countries-with-the-highest-number-of-internet-users-in-2022/zm280z1

Omar, M., Nawawi, A., & Salin, A. S. A. P. (2016). The causes, impact and prevention of employee fraud: A case study of an automotive company. *Journal of Financial Crime, 23*(4), 1012–1027. doi:10.1108/JFC-04-2015-0020

Omilusi, M. (2019). *Buhari's change and challenges: Democratic transition and governance assessment in Nigeria.* Human & Organizational Resources Development Centre.

Omotola, J. S. (2006). 'Through a glass darkly': Assessing the 'new' war against corruption in Nigeria. *Africa Insight, 36*(3-4), 214-228.

Onwujekwe, O., Orjiakor, C., & Agwu, P. (2020). Coronavirus: corruption in health care could get in the way of Nigeria's response. *The Conversation.* Retrieved from https://theconversation.com/coronavirus-corruption-in-health-care-could-get-in-the-way-of-nigerias-response-136913

Onyango, S. (2022). Piling into a future $180 billion African internet economy. *Techcabal.* Retrieved from https://Techcabal.com/2022/03/09/piling-into-a-future-180-billion-african-internet-economy/

Onyeacholem, G. (2017, August 10). Malami and anti-graft agencies. *Nation (New York, N.Y.).*

Oppel, R. A., & Sorkin, A. R. (2001, November 9). Enron admits to overstating profits by about $ 600 million. *The New York Times.* Retrieved from https://www.nytimes.com/2001/11/09/business/enron-admits-to-overstating-profits-by-about-600-million.html

Orjiude, A. (2021, August 22). Eight banks lose N1.9bn to fraud in one year. *Punch.* Retrieved from https://punchng.com/eight-banks-lose-n1-9bn-to-fraud-in-one-year/

Orjiude, A. (2022, March 31). Four banks lost N1.77bn to fraud in 2021. *Punch.* Retrieved from https://punchng.com/four-banks-lost-n1-77bn-to-fraud-in-2021-says-report/

Osler, S. (2020). *Coronavirus Outbreak: All the secrets revealed about the COVID-19 pandemic: A complete rational guide of its evolution, expansion, symptoms and first defense.* Independently Published.

Otiso, N. H. (2021). The effects of fraud on performance of insurance industry: A critical review of literature. *International Journal of Management and Social Sciences, 9*(2), 60–76.

Ovuorie, T. (2022). Increased social media use puts African leaders on edge. *DW.* Retrieved from https://www.dw.com/en/increased-social-media-use-puts-african-leaders-on-edge/a-61303854

Öztel, M. (2018). Osmanlı Devleti'nde Kalpazanlık ve Sahte Para (1808-1914): Kalpazanlığı ve Sahte Paranın Tedavülünü BesleyenFaktörler. *Historical Studies (Melbourne, Vic.), 10*(1), 197–221.

Öztel, M. (2020). Counterfeit money in Circulation in the Ottoman Money Market (1811-1919). *Medeniyet Araştırmaları Dergisi, 5*(1), 1–23.

Öztel, M. (2020). Osmanlı Devleti'nin Kalpazanlıkla İmtihanı (1818-1921). *Belleten - Türk Tarih Kurumu, 84*(299), 315–356. doi:10.37879/belleten.2020.315

Öztel, M. (2020). Payitaht'ın Avrupalısı Beyoğlu'nda İdareci Olmak:Mutasarrıf Bahri Paşa'nın Zorgünleri. *Fatih Sultan Mehmet İlmi Araştırmalar*, *16*(1), 223–258.

Pakalın, M. Z. (1972). *Osmanlı Tarih Deyimleri ve Terimleri Sözlüğü*. Milli Eğitim Bakanlığı.

Palepu, K. G., Bernard, V. L., & Healy, P. M. (1996). *Business analysis and valuation using financial statements*. South-Western Publishing Company.

Pamuk, Ş. (1999). *Osmanlı İmparatorluğu'nda Paranın Tarihi*. TarihVakfı Yurt Yayınları.

Pao, T. I., Tzeng, L. Y., & Wang, C. W. (2014). Typhoons and opportunistic fraud: Claim patterns of automobile theft insurance in Taiwan. *The Journal of Risk and Insurance*, *8*(1), 91–112. doi:10.1111/j.1539-6975.2012.01498.x

Papachristou, L. (2018). *UK pulls aid to Zambia over corruption report*. Organized Crime and Corruption Reporting Project (OCCRP). Retrieved from https://www.occrp.org/en/daily/8598-uk-pulls-aid-to-zambia-over-corruption-report

Parada, L. (2020). Tax Treaty Entitlement and Fiscally Transparent Entities: Improvements or Unnecessary Complications? In J. Wheeler (Ed.), *The Aftermath of BEPS*. IBFD.

Parfet, W. (2000). Accounting subjectivity and earnings management: A preparer's perspective. *Accounting Horizons*, *14*(4), 481–488. doi:10.2308/acch.2000.14.4.481

Parker, L. D. (2016). From scientific to activity based office management: A mirage of Change. *Journal of Accounting & Organizational Change*, *12*(2), 177–202. doi:10.1108/JAOC-01-2015-0007

Parker, L. D., & Schmitz, J. (2022). The reinvented accounting firm office: Impression management for efficiency, client relations and cost control. *Accounting, Organizations and Society*, *98*, 101306. doi:10.1016/j.aos.2021.101306

Parker, L. D., & Warren, S. (2017). The presentation of the self and professional identity: Countering the accountant's stereotype. *Accounting, Auditing & Accountability Journal*, *30*(8), 1895–1924. doi:10.1108/AAAJ-09-2016-2720

Park, Y. (2014). A study on the strategies for reducing insurance crime. *Korean Police Studies Review*, *13*, 61–90.

Pashev, K. (2006). *Fighting VAT Fraud: The Bulgarian Experience* (CSD Working Paper No. WP 0606/2). Retrieved from https://mpra.ub.uni-muenchen.de/998

Patil, K. S., & Godbole, A. (2018). A survey on machine learning techniques for insurance fraud prediction. *Helix*, *8*(6), 4358–4363. doi:10.29042/2018-4358-4363

Perkiss, S., Bernardi, C., Dumay, J., & Haslam, J. (2021). A sticky chocolate problem: Impression management and counter accounts in the shaping of corporate image. *Critical Perspectives on Accounting*, *81*, 102229. doi:10.1016/j.cpa.2020.102229

Pesaran, M. H., & Shin, Y. (1999). An autoregressive distributed lag modelling approach to cointegration analysis. In S. Strøm (Ed.), *Econometrics and Economic Theory in the 20th Century: The Ragnar Frisch Centennial Symposium*. Cambridge University Press. 10.1017/CCOL521633230.011

Pesaran, M. H., Shin, Y., & Smith, R. J. (2001). Bounds testing approaches to the analysis of level relationships. *Journal of Applied Econometrics*, *16*(3), 289–326. doi:10.1002/jae.616

Pešout, P., & Andrle, M. (2011). Insurance fraud management as an integrated part of business intelligence framework. World Academy of Science, Engineering and Technology. *International Journal of Industrial and Systems Engineering*, *5*(11), 1387–1392.

Peterson, C. L. (2015). Consumer Financial Protection Bureau law enforcement: An empirical review. *Tulane Law Review*, *90*, 1057.

Petutschnig, M., & Resenig, K. (2019, January). Market reactions of multinationals to the OECD BEPS Action Plan. In *Proceedings. Annual Conference on Taxation and Minutes of the Annual Meeting of the National Tax Association* (Vol. 112, pp. 1-31). National Tax Association.

Peytcheva, M., & Wright, A. M. (2011). *The impact of principles versus rules-based accounting standards on auditor's process accountability, epistemic motivation, and reporting decisions* (Working Paper). Lehigh University and North-Eastern University.

Phan, P. H., Wong, P. K., & Wang, C. K. (2002). Antecedents to entrepreneurship among university students in Singapore: Beliefs, attitudes and background. *Journal of Enterprising Culture*, *10*(02), 151–174. doi:10.1142/S0218495802000189

Pihie, Z. A. L., & Akmaliah, Z. (2009). Entrepreneurship as a career choice: An analysis of entrepreneurial self-efficacy and intention of university students. *European Journal of Soil Science*, *9*(2), 338–349.

Pirson, M., & Turnbull, S. (2011). Corporate governance, risk management, and the financial crisis: An information processing view. *Corporate Governance*, *19*(5), 459–470. doi:10.1111/j.1467-8683.2011.00860.x

Pitrakkos, P., & Maroun, W. (2020). Evaluating the quality of carbon disclosures. *Sustainability Accounting. Management and Policy Journal*, *11*(3), 553–589. doi:10.1108/SAMPJ-03-2018-0081

Podlipnik, J. (2012). Missing trader intra-community and carousel VAT frauds - ECJ and ECTHR case law. *Croatian Yearbook of European Law & Policy*, *8*(1), 457–472. Retrieved from https://hrcak.srce.hr/94656

Pollack, J. M., Vanepps, E. M., & Hayes, A. F. (2012). The moderating role of social ties on entrepreneurs' depressed affect and withdrawal intentions in response to economic stress. *Journal of Organizational Behavior*, *33*(6), 789–810. doi:10.1002/job.1794

Poniatowski, G., Bonch-Osmolovskiy, M., Durán-Cabré, J. M., Esteller-Moré, A., & Smietanka, A. (2020). *Study and Reports on the VAT Gap in the EU-28 member states: 2019 Final report. CASE No. 500*. Retrieved from https://www.case-research.eu/files/?id_plik=6251

Porter, K. (2012). The complaint conundrum: Thoughts on the CFPB's complaint mechanism. *Brooklyn Journal of Corporate and Financial & Commercial Law*, *7*, 57.

Pouwels, A. (2021). *Missing Trader Intra-Community Fraud*. Affairs Directorate—General for Internal Policies PE 690.462—June 2021, Policy Department for Budgetary. Retrieved from https://www.europarl.europa.eu/RegData/etudes/BRIE/2021/690462/IPOL_BRI(2021)690462_EN.pdf

Power, M. K., & Gendron, Y. (2015). Qualitative research in auditing: A methodological roadmap. *Auditing*, *34*(2), 147–165. doi:10.2308/ajpt-10423

Praoyao, S., & Eugene, K. (2018). Institutions and financial development in African countries: An empirical analysis. *Business. Management and Economics Research*, *4*(5), 43–50.

Prettl, A. (2018). *Profit shifting and controlled foreign corporation rules – The thin bridge between corporate tax system.* Retrieved from https://papers.ssrn.com/sol3/papers.cfm ?abstract_id=3102553

Prettl, A., & von Hagen, D. (2022). Multinational ownership patterns and anti-tax avoidance legislation. *International Tax and Public Finance*, 1–70. doi:10.100710797-021-09719-5

Protected Disclosures Act. (2014). *A new era for whistleblowing in Ireland.* Retrieved from https://www.icsa.org.uk/ireland/knowledge-and-guidance/governance-and-directors/protected-disclosures-act-2014-a-new-era-for-whistleblowing-in-ireland

PSIC. (n.d.). *Tell us. You are protected.* Office of the public sector integrity commissioner of Canada. Retrieved from https://www.psic-ispc.gc.ca/

Public Protector South Africa. (2016). *State of Capture: A Report of the Public Protector* (Report No 6 of 2016/17). South African Government. Retrieved from https://www.gov.za/documents/state-capture-14-oct-2016-0000

PwC. (2008). *Principles-based Accounting Standards.* PriceWaterhouseCoopers. Retrieved from https://pwc.blogs.com/corporatereporting/files/principlesbased_accounting_standards.pdf

Rafay, A. (2022). Related Party Disclosures in Financial Reporting for Islamic Banks. *Journal of Islamic Accounting and Business Research, 13*(7), 997–1017. doi:10.1108/JIABR-03-2020-0066

Rafay, A. (Ed.). (2019). *FinTech as a Disruptive Technology for Financial Institutions.* IGI Global. doi:10.4018/978-1-5225-7805-5

Rafay, A. (Ed.). (2021a). *Money Laundering and Terrorism Financing in Global Financial Systems.* IGI Global. doi:10.4018/978-1-7998-8758-4

Rafay, A. (Ed.). (2021b). *Handbook of Research on Theory and Practice of Financial Crimes.* IGI Global. doi:10.4018/978-1-7998-5567-5

Rafay, A. (Ed.). (2022). *Finance for Sustainability in a Turbulent Economy.* IGI Global. doi:10.4018/978-1-6684-5580-7

Rafay, A. (Ed.). (2023). *Concepts and Cases of Illicit and Illegitimate Finance.* IGI Global. doi:10.4018/978-1-6684-8587-3

Rafay, A., & Ajmal, M. M. (2014). Earnings Management through Deferred Taxes Recognized under IAS 12: Evidence from Pakistan. *Lahore Journal of Business, 3*(1), 1–19. doi:10.35536/ljb.2014.v3.i1.a1

Rafay, A., Chen, Y., Naeem, M. A. B., & Ijaz, M. (2018). Analyzing the impact of Credit Ratings on Firm Performance and Stock Returns: An Evidence from Taiwan. *Indian Economic Review, 22*(3), 767–786. doi:10.22059/ier.2018.67452

Rafay, A., & Farid, S. (2017). Dynamic Relationship between Islamic Banking System and Real Economic Activity: Evidence from Pakistan. *Journal of King Abdulaziz University. Islamic Economics, 30*(2), 97–114.

Rafay, A., & Farid, S. (2018). Shariah Supervisory Board Report (SSBR) in Islamic Banks: An experimental study of Investors' perception and behaviour. *International Journal of Islamic and Middle Eastern Finance and Management, 11*(2), 274–296. doi:10.1108/IMEFM-07-2017-0180

Rafay, A., & Farid, S. (2019). Islamic Banking System: A Credit Channel of Monetary Policy – Evidence from an Emerging Economy. *Economic Research-Ekonomska Istrazivanja, 32*(1), 742–754. doi:10.1080/1331677X.2019.1579662

Rafay, A., & Khan, A. (2018). Synergy for sustainability in the upcoming telecommunication revolution: The Case of a developing economy. In A. Borchers (Ed.), *Technology Management in Organizational and Societal Contexts* (pp. 51–76). IGI Global. doi:10.4018/978-1-5225-5279-6.ch003

Rafay, A., Mohsan, T., & Sadiq, R. (2017). Structural Mix of Credit Portfolios in Islamic Banking System: Evidence from a South Asian Economy. In D. Mutum, M. M. Butt, & M. Rashid (Eds.), *Advances in Islamic Finance, Marketing, and Management: An Asian Perspective* (pp. 185–210). Emerald Group Publishing Limited. doi:10.1108/978-1-78635-899-820161010

Rafay, A., Sadiq, R., & Ajmal, M. M. (2016). The Effect of IAS-24 Disclosures on Governance Mechanisms and Ownership Structures in Pakistan. *Lahore Journal of Business*, *5*(1), 15–36. doi:10.35536/ljb.2016.v5.i1.a2

Rafay, A., Yasser, F., & Khalid, Z. (2019). Revaluation of Non-Current Assets under IAS-16: Possibility of any Managerial inducement - Evidence from a South Asian Economy. *DLSU Business and Economics Review*, *29*(1), 93–105.

Rahouma, K. H., Hamed, R., Aly, M., & Hamed, H. M. (2020). Challenges and solutions of using the social internet of things in healthcare and medical solutions. In A. E. Hassanien, R. Bhatnagar, N. M. Khalifa, & M. H. N. Taha (Eds.), *Towards Social Internet of Things (SIOT): Enabling Technologies, Architectures and Applications. Emerging Technologies for Connected and Smart Social Objects* (pp. 13–31). Springer. doi:10.1007/978-3-030-24513-9_2

Raman, R. (2018). *Global corruption: People pay $1 trillion in bribes every year*. Raman Media Network. Retrieved from https://www.ramanmedianetwork.com/global-corruption-people-pay-1-trillion-in-bribes-every-year/

Ramzan, M., Ahmad, I., & Rafay, A. (2020). Is Auditor independence influenced by Non-audit services? A stakeholder's viewpoint. *Pakistan Journal of Commerce and Social Sciences*, *14*(1), 388–408.

Ratcliffe, J. (2015, July 30). Abolishing the Consumer Financial Protection Bureau. *The Washington Times*. Retrieved from https://www.washingtontimes.com/news/2015 /jul/30/john-ratcliffe-abolishing-the-consumer-financial-p/

Raval, V. (2013). Human disposition and the fraud cycle. *International Journal of Applied Behavioral Economics*, *2*(1), 1–16. doi:10.4018/ijabe.2013010101

Ravichardran, T. (2018). Exploring the relationship between IT competence, innovation capacity and organizational agility. *The Journal of Strategic Information Systems*, *27*(1), 22–42. doi:10.1016/j.jsis.2017.07.002

Reding, A., Gorp, A. V., Cox, K., Walczak, A., Giacomantonio, C., & Hoorens, S. (2014). *Handling ethical problems in counter terrorism: An inventory of methods to support ethical decision making*. Rand Corporation. Retrieved from https://www.rand.org/pubs/research_reports/RR251.html

Reitano, T., & Shaw, M. (2015, June 11). *Fixing a Fractured State? Breaking the Cycles of Crime, Conflict and Corruption in Mali and Sahel*. Geneva: Global Initiative Against Transnational Organized Crime. Retrieved from https://globalinitiative.net/analysis/fixing-a-fractured-state-breaking-the-cycles-of-crime-corruption-and-governance-in
-mali-and-the-sahel/

Report, I. O. (2020). *The East Africa Insurance Outlook Report 2019/2020*. Deloitte. Retrieved from https://www2.deloitte.com/content/dam/Deloitte/ke/Documents /financialservices/ea_insurance_outlook_report_2019.pdf

Report, I. O. (2021). *The East Africa Insurance Outlook Report 2020/2021*. Deloitte. Retrieved from https://www2.deloitte.com/content/dam/Deloitte/ke/Documents /financialservices/ea_insurance_outlook_report_2020.pdf

République Française. (2015). *Bienvenue sur le site officiel d'information et de démarches administratives* [Welcome to the official website for information and administrative procedures]. Retrieved from https://www.service-public.fr/

Re, S. (2016). World insurance in 2015: Steady growth amid regional disparities. *Sigma*, *3*(1), 1–50.

Reurink, A. (2018). Financial fraud: A literature review. *Journal of Economic Surveys*, *32*(5), 1292–1325. doi:10.1111/joes.12294

Rheibay, J., & Chêne, M. (2016). *Gender and Corruption: A Topic Guide. Anti-Corruption Helpdesk.* Transparency International. Retrieved from https://knowledgehub.transparency.org /assets/uploads/kproducts/Topic_guide_gender_corruption _Final_2016.pdf

Riley, T. J., & Luippold, B. L. (2015). Managing investors' perception through strategic word choices in financial narratives. *Journal of Corporate Accounting & Finance*, *26*(5), 57–62. doi:10.1002/jcaf.22064

Rittinghouse, J. W., & Hancock, W. M. (2003). *Cybersecurity Operations Handbook*. Elsevier.

Rivas, M. F. (2013). An experiment on corruption and gender. *Bulletin of Economic Research*, *65*(1), 10–42. doi:10.1111/j.1467-8586.2012.00450.x

Rixen, T. (2013). Why reregulation after the crisis is feeble: Shadow banking, offshore financial centers, and jurisdictional competition. *Regulation & Governance*, *7*(4), 435–459. doi:10.1111/rego.12024

Roberts, C., Weetman, P., & Gordon, P. (2008). *International corporate reporting: A comparative approach* (4th ed.). Pearson Education Limited.

Rolle, L. (2010). *Risorse umane e benchmarking. Prassi eccellenti in aziende innovative*. Franco Angeli.

Rooijen, J. G. van. (2002). *Flexibility in financial accounting income strategies and earnings management in the Netherlands*. Retrieved from http://hdl.handle.net/11245/1.209698

Rosberg, A. G., & Knell, R. G. (2020). *How will this continue? Modelling interactions between the COVID-19 pandemic and policy responses*. Queen Mary University of London. doi:10.1101/2020.03.30.20047597

Rosner, R. (2003). Earnings manipulation in failing firms. *Contemporary Accounting Research*, *20*(2), 361–408. doi:10.1506/8EVN-9KRB-3AE4-EE81

Rowe, M., Wilcox, L., & Gadlin, H. (2009). Dealing with--or Reporting--"Unacceptable" Behavior. *Journal of the International Ombudsman Association, 2*(1), 52-64.

Rowe, M. (1993). Options and choice for conflict resolution in the workplace. In L. Hall (Ed.), *Negotiation: Strategies for mutual gain.* Sage.

Roy, P., Iwuamadi, K. C., & Ibrahim, J. (2020). *Breaking the cycle of corruption in Nigeria's electricity sector: A political settlements analysis* (Working Paper 20). ACE SOAS Consortium. Retrieved from https://eprints.soas.ac.uk/32532/1/ACE-WorkingPaper020-NigeriaPowerSector-200319.pdf

Sacer, I. M., Malis, S. S., & Pavic, I. (2016). The Impact of accounting estimates on financial position and business performance–case of non-current intangible and tangible assets. *Procedia Economics and Finance*, *39*, 399–411. doi:10.1016/S2212-5671(16)30341-0

Sahyoun, N., & Magnan, M. (2020). The association between voluntary disclosure in audit committee reports and banks' earnings management. *Managerial Auditing Journal*, *35*(6), 795–817. doi:10.1108/MAJ-05-2019-2279

Samaddar, R. (2020). Introduction: Borders of an epidemic. In R. Samaddar (Ed.), *Borders of an Epidemic: COVID-19 and Migrant Workers*. Mahanirban Calcutta Research Group.

Samkin, G., & Schneider, A. (2010). Accountability, narrative reporting and legitimation: The case of a New Zealand public benefit entity. *Accounting, Auditing & Accountability Journal*, *23*(2), 256–289. doi:10.1108/09513571011023219

Sánchez, J. C. (2009). Social learning and entrepreneurial intentions: A comparative study between Mexico, Spain and Portugal. *Revista Latinoamericana de Psicología*, *41*(1), 109–119.

Sandberg, M., & Holmlund, M. (2015). Impression management tactics in sustainability reporting. *Social Responsibility Journal, 11*(4), 677–689. doi:10.1108/SRJ-12-2013-0152

Sanghrajka, J. (2020). HMRC's Connect computer and investigations. *Taxation*. Retrieved from https://www.taxation.co.uk/articles/hmrc-s-connect-computer-and-investigations

Santiso, C. (2019). Révolution numérique et transformation de l'action publique [Digital revolution and transformation of public action]. *Politique Etrangere, 2*, 129–142. https://doi.org/10.3917/pe.192.0129

Sarasvathy, S. D. (2001). Causation and effectuation: Toward a theoretical shift from economic inevitability to entrepreneurial contingency. *Academy of Management Review, 26*(2), 243–263. doi:10.2307/259121

Sardeshmukh, S. R., Sharma, D., & Golden, T. D. (2012). Impact of telework on exhaustion and job engagement: A job demands and job resources model. *New Technology, Work and Employment, 27*(3), 193–207. doi:10.1111/j.1468-005X.2012.00284.x

Schick, A. (1998). Why Most Developing Countries Should Not Try New Zealand's Reforms. *The World Bank Research Observer, 13*(1), 123–131. https://documents1.worldbank.org/curated/en/597171468289000828/pdf/766180JRN0WBRO00Box374385B00PUBLIC0.pdf

Schipper, K. (2005). The introduction of international accounting standards in Europe: Implications for international convergence. *European Accounting Review, 14*(1), 101–126. doi:10.1080/0963818042000338013

Schleicher, T. (2012). When is good news really good news? *Accounting and Business Research, 42*(5), 547–573. doi:10.1080/00014788.2012.685275

Schleicher, T., & Walker, M. (2010). Bias in the tone of forward-looking narratives. *Accounting and Business Research, 40*(4), 371–390. doi:10.1080/00014788.2010.9995318

Schrand, C. M., & Zechman, S. C. (2012). Executive overconfidence and the slippery slope to financial misreporting. *Journal of Accounting and Economics, 53*(1–2), 311–329. doi:10.1016/j.jacceco.2011.09.001

Schumacher, S., & Kent, N. (2020). 8 charts on internet use around the world as countries grapple with COVID-19. *Pew Research Centre*. Retrieved from https://www.pewresearch.org/fact-tank/2020/04/02/8-charts-on-internet-use-around-the-world-as-countries-grapple-with-COVID-19/

SEC. (2003). *Study Pursuant to Section 108(d) of the Sarbanes-Oxley Act of 2002 on the Adoption by the United States Financial Reporting System of a Principles-Based Accounting System.* Securities and Exchange Commission. Retrieved from https://www.sec.gov/news/studies/principlesbasedstand.htm

Segovia, J., Arnold, V., & Sutton, S. G. (2009). Do principles- vs. rules-based standards have a differential impact on U.S. auditors' decisions? *Advances in Accounting Behavioural Research, 12, 61–84.* doi:10.1108/S1475-1488(2009)0000012006

Senogles, G., & Glowka, M. (2013). *Aggressive accounting versus fraudulent accounting*. Retrieved from https://www.financierworldwide.com/aggressive-accounting-vs-fraudulent-accounting/

Shadel, D., & Pak, K. (2017). *Under Fire: Military Veterans and Consumer Fraud in the United States*. AARP Research. doi:10.26419/res.00182.001

Shafer, W. E. (2009). Ethical climate, organizational-professional conflict and organizational commitment: A study of Chinese auditors. *Accounting, Auditing & Accountability Journal, 22*(7), 1087–1110. doi:10.1108/09513570910987385

Shalhoub, Z. K., & Al Qasimi, S. L. (2010). *Cyber law and cyber security in developing and emerging economies*. Oxford University Press. doi:10.4337/9781849803380

Shapero, A., & Sokol, L. (1982). *The social dimensions of entrepreneurship*. University of Illinois at Urbana-Champaign's Academy for Entrepreneurial Leadership Historical Research Reference in Entrepreneurship.

Sharif, M., Ansari, G. J., Yamin, M., & Fernandes, S. L. (2018). Reviews of the implications of vr/ar healthcare applications. In L. Dac-Nihuong, V. L. Chung, G. T. Jolanda, & N. N. Gia (Eds.), *Emerging Technologies for Health and Medicine* (pp. 3–15). Wiley. doi:10.1002/9781119509875.ch1

Sharma, C. (2021). Does corruption sand the wheels of financial sector development? Evidence from global panel data. *Journal of Financial Management. Markets and Institutions*, *9*(2), 1–32.

Sheldon, M. D., & Jenkins, J. G. (2020). The influence of firm performance and (level of) assurance on the believability of management's environmental report. *Accounting, Auditing & Accountability Journal*, *33*(3), 501–528. doi:10.1108/AAAJ-11-2018-3726

Shepherd, D. A., Patzelt, H., & Baron, R. A. (2013). I care about nature, but…: Disengaging values in assessing opportunities that cause harm. *Academy of Management Journal*, *56*(5), 1251–1273. doi:10.5465/amj.2011.0776

Shin, H. (2015). The Relationship between the Arab Spring Revolutions and Entrepreneurial Inhibitors, Enablers, and Activity in North Africa. In *Economics: Concepts, Methodologies, Tools, and Applications* (pp. 921–937). IGI Global. doi:10.4018/978-1-4666-8468-3.ch050

Shirley, M. (1996). *Bureaucrat in business: the economics and policies of government ownership*. The World Bank. Retrieved from https://documents.worldbank.org /en/publication/documents-reports/documentdetail/867101468780298811/bureaucrats-in-business-the-economics-and-politics-of-government-ownership#:~:text=Bureaucrats%20in%20 business%20%3A%20the%20economics%20and%20politics,also%20assesses%20why%20so%20few%20countries%20are%20reforming

Shivaprasad, V. M. (2019). *Analysis of customer complaint data of Consumer Financial Protection Bureau using different text classification methods*. Dublin Business School. Retrieved from https://esource.dbs.ie/bitstream/handle/10788/4224/msc_Shivaprasad_vm_2020.pdf?sequence=1&isAllowed=y

Shuaibu, M., Muhammad, H. M., Abdullahi, S. I., & Gwazawa, U. G. (2021). Impact of public debt on inflation and unemployment in Nigeria: An ARDL vector error correction model. *Noble International Journal of Economics and Financial Research*, *6*(5), 91–98. doi:10.51550/nijefr65.91.98

Siaplay, M. (2020). Rent-seeking in West Africa – How corruption affects economic growth and income inequality. *West African Financial and Economic Review*, *20*(12), 1–24.

Sidorova, E., Sebechenko, E., Kostyukhin, Y., Boboshko, D., Kostin, A., Kostina, O., & Vikhrova, N. (2021). Formation of a sustainable mechanism of preferential VAT taxation of exports as evidenced by the Russian Federation Practice. *Economies*, *9*(4), 190. doi:10.3390/economies9040190

Siggelkow, N. (2001). Change in the presence of fit: The rise, the fall, and the renaissance of Liz Claiborne. *Academy of Management Journal*, *44*(4), 838–857. doi:10.2307/3069418

Simon, H. A. (2013). *Administrative Behavior*. Simon and Schuster.

Šimović, H., & Deskar-Škrbić, M. (2020). *Ekonomika javnog sektora s hrvatskim primjerima*. Arhivanalitika.

Šimurina, N., Dražić Lutilsky, I., Barbić, D., & Dragija Kostić, M. (2018). *Osnove porezne pismenosti.* Zagreb: Narodne Novine.

Soderlund, W. C., Briggs, E. D., Najem, T. P., & Roberts, B. C. (2012). *Africa's Deadliest Conflict: Media Coverage of the Humanitarian Disaster in the Congo and the United Nations Response, 1997–2008.* Wilfrid Laurier University Press.

Solomon, J. F., Solomon, A., Joseph, N. L., & Norton, S. D. (2013). Impression management, myth creation and fabrication in private social and environmental reporting: Insights from Erving Goffman. *Accounting, Organizations and Society, 38*(3), 195–213. doi:10.1016/j.aos.2013.01.001

Solow, R. (1956). A contribution to the theory of economic growth. *The Quarterly Journal of Economics, 70*(1), 65–94. doi:10.2307/1884513

Soobaroyen, T., & Mahadeo, J. D. (2016). Community disclosures in a developing country: Insights from a neo-pluralist perspective. *Accounting, Auditing & Accountability Journal, 29*(3), 452–482. doi:10.1108/AAAJ-08-2014-1810

Spaventa, L. (2008). *Una crisi della nuova finanza.* Giuffrè Editore.

Sposato, P. (2010). *Valutazione e selezione del personale. Come scegliere e valorizzare il tuo staff ideale.* Bruno Editore.

Statista Research Department. (2022). *Countries with the highest number of internet users.* Retrieved from https://www.statista.com/statistics/262966/number-of-internet-users-in-selected-countries/

Statistics Mauritius. (2022). *National Accounts Estimates (2018 – 2021): December 2021 Issue.* Retrieved from https:// statsmauritius.govmu.org/Pages/Statistics/ESI/National_Accounts/NA/NAE_Dec21.aspx

Stevenson, H. H., & Jarillo, J. C. (2007). A paradigm of entrepreneurship: Entrepreneurial management. In *Entrepreneurship* (pp. 155–170). Springer.

Stiller, W., & Heinemann, M. (2021). *Do more harm than good? The optional reverse charge mechanism against VAT Fraud.* Retrieved from https://www.researchgate.net/publication/351904988_Do_More_Harm_than_Good_The_Optional_Reverse_Charge_Mechanism_against_VAT_Fraud

Suh, I., Sweeney, J. T., Linke, K., & Wall, J. M. (2020). Boiling the Frog Slowly: The Immersion of C-Suite Financial Executives into Fraud. *Journal of Business Ethics, 162*(3), 645–673. doi:10.100710551-018-3982-3

Sullivan, R. J. (2010). The changing nature of US card payment fraud: Industry and public policy options. *FRBKC Economic Review, 95*(2), 101–133.

Sunder, S. (2010). Adverse effects of uniform written reporting standards on accounting practice, education, and research. *Journal of Accounting and Public Policy, 29*(2), 99–114. doi:10.1016/j.jaccpubpol.2009.10.011

Sydserff, R., & Weetman, P. (2002). Developments in content analysis: A transitivity index and DICTION scores. *Accounting, Auditing & Accountability Journal, 15*(4), 523–545. doi:10.1108/09513570210440586

Tabakoğlu, A. (2016). *Osmanlı MaliTarihi.* DergahYayınları.

Tait, A. (1988). *Value-added Tax – International practice and problems.* International Monetary Fund.

Tankard, J. W. (2001). The empirical approach to the study of media framing. In S. D. Reese, O. H. Gandy, & A. E. Grant (Eds.), *Framing public life: Perspectives on media and our understanding of the social world.* Routledge.

Tanzi, V. (1998). Corruption around the world: Causes, consequences, scope, and cures. *IMF Staff Papers*, *45*(4), 559–594. doi:10.2307/3867585

Tauringana, V., & Mangena, M. (2014). Board structure and supplementary commentary on the primary financial statements. *Journal of Applied Accounting Research*, *15*(3), 273–290. doi:10.1108/JAAR-11-2013-0090

Tax Justice Network. (2020). *Financial Secrecy Index 2020*. Retrieved from https://fsi.taxjustice.net/en/

Teece, D., Peteraf, M., & Leih, S. (2016). Dynamic capabilities and organizational agility: Risk, uncertainty, and strategy in the innovation economy. *California Management Review*, *58*(4), 13–35. doi:10.1525/cmr.2016.58.4.13

Tekathen, M., & Dechow, N. (2013). Enterprise risk management and continuous realignment in the pursuit of accountability: A German case. *Management Accounting Research*, *24*(2), 100–121. doi:10.1016/j.mar.2013.04.005

Terra, B., & Kajus, J. (2021). *A Guide to the European VAT Directives*. IBFD.

Thiart, C., & Nel, G. F. (2018). An exploratory study of the effect of country-by-country reporting ambiguities on Johannesburg Stock Exchange-listed companies. *Suid-Afrikaanse Tydskrif vir Ekonomiese en Bestuurswetenskappe*, *21*(1), 1–8. doi:10.4102ajems.v21i1.2129

TI. (2006). *International global corruption report*. Transparency International.

Tillman, R., & Indergaard, M. (2007). *Control Overrides in Financial Statement Fraud: A Report to the Institute for Fraud Prevention*. Retrieved from https://www.researchgate.net/profile/Robert-Tillman-2/publication/241868976

TIRA. (2022). *Tanzania insurance quarterly performance for the three months period from 1st January to 31st March, 2022*. Tanzania Insurance Regulatory Authority. Retrieved from https://www.tira.go.tz

Titeka, K., & Thamani, J. (2018, December 18). How to get ahead in DR Congo politics: a flatterer's guide. *African Arguments*. Retrieved from https://africanarguments.org /2018/12/18/how-get-ahead-dr-congo-politics-guide/

Tiwari, R., & Buse, S. (2020). *Managing innovation in a global and digital world: Meeting societal challenges and enhancing competitiveness*. Springer. doi:10.1007/978-3-658-27241-8

Todd, J. D., Welch, S. T., Welch, O. J., & Holmes, S. A. (2000). The nature and characteristics of insurance agent fraud. *CPCU Journal*, *53*(3), 152–167.

Touhill, G. J., & Touhill, C. J. (2014). *Cybersecurity for executives: A practical guide*. John Wiley & Sons. doi:10.1002/9781118908785

Transparency International Rwanda. (2018a). *Gender-based corruption in public workplaces in Rwanda*. Retrieved from https://tirwanda.org/IMG/pdf/gender_based_corruption_1_.pdf

Transparency International Rwanda. (2018b). *Promoting Transparency and Accountability in Climate Change Finance in Rwanda*. Retrieved from https://tirwanda.org/IMG/pdf/climate_change_mapping_report_final.pdf

Transparency International Zimbabwe. (2013). *Enforcement of Anti-Corruption laws: Zimbabwe*. UNCAC Civil Society Review 2013. Retrieved from https://uncaccoalition.org/files/cso-review-reports/year2-zimbabwe-report.pdf

Transparency International Zimbabwe. (2019). *Gender and corruption in Zimbabwe: Debates and policy options*. Retrieved from https://www.tizim.org/gender-and-corruption-in-zimbabwe-debates-and-policy-options/

Transparency International. (2018a). *The Impact of land corruption on women: Insights from Africa*. Retrieved from https://www.transparency.org/news/feature/impact_of_land_corruption_on_women_insights_from_africa

Transparency International. (2018b). *Women, Land and Corruption: Resources for Practitioners and Policy-Makers*. Retrieved from https://www.transparency.org/en/news/impact-of-land-corruption-on-women-insights-from-africa

Transparency International. (2019). *Global Corruption Barometer Africa 2019: Citizen's Views and Experiences of Corruption*. Retrieved from https://www.transparency.org/whatwedo/publication/gcb_africa_2019

Transparency International. (2020). *CPI 2019: Sub-Saharan Africa*. Retrieved from https://www.transparency.org/news/feature/cpi_2019_sub_saharan_africa

Transparency International. (2021). *Corruption perceptions index*. Retrieved from https://www.transparency.org/en/cpi/2021

Transparency Maroc. (2020). *Rapport moral*. Retrieved from https://transparencymaroc.ma/transparency-maroc-lance-son-rapport-moral-au-titre-de-lannee-2020/

Tseng, L. M., & Kuo, C. L. (2014). Customers' attitudes towards insurance frauds: An application of Adam's equity theory. *Geneva Papers on Risk & Insurance*, *41*(11), 1038–1054. doi:10.1108/IJSE-08-2012-0142

Tseng, L. M., & Su, W. P. (2013). Customer orientation, social consensus and insurance salespeople's tolerance of customer insurance frauds. *International Journal of Bank Marketing*, *31*(1), 38–55. doi:10.1108/02652321311292047

Tukur, S. (2012, September 10). Nigerian banks aid corruption-EFCC. *Premium Times*. Retrieved from https://www.premiumtimesng.com/business/99682-nigerian-banks-aid-corruption-efcc.html

Turban, E., Sharda, R., Delen, D., & Efraim, T. (2007). *Decision support and business intelligence systems*. Pearson Education.

Turker, D., & Selcuk, S. S. (2009). Which factors affect entrepreneurial intention of university students? *Journal of European Industrial Training*, *33*(2), 142–159. doi:10.1108/03090590910939049

Tyner, K. (2009). *Literacy in a digital world: Teaching and learning in the age of information*. Taylor & Francis.

Uddin, A., Chowdhury, M. A. F., & Islam, N. (2017). Do socio-economic factors matter for the financial development of a Muslim country? A study in Bangladesh banking sector. *International Journal of Business and Society*, *18*(1), 59–78.

Uju, J. (2002). The military and corruption in Nigeria. In C. O. T. Ugwu (Ed.), *Corruption in Nigeria: Critical perspectives*. Academic Publishing Company.

UK Department for Business, Energy & Industrial Strategy. (2019, March). *Confidentiality clauses: Consultation on measures to prevent misuse in situations of workplace harassment or discrimination*. Retrieved from https://assets.publishing.service.gov.uk /government/uploads /system/uploads/attachment_data/file/783011/confidentiality-clauses-consultation.pdf

UN African Renewal. (2019). *Silencing the Guns in Africa*. UN department of Global Communication. Retrieved from https://www.un.org/africarenewal/sites/www.un.org. africarenewal/files/A_R33_3_EN_0.pdf

UN Commission on Human Rights. (2020). *Deliberate starvation and corruption hallmarks of conflict in South Sudan say UN human rights experts*. Retrieved from https://www.ohchr.org/EN/HRBodies/HRC/Pages/NewsDetail.aspx?NewsID=25583&LangID=E

UN Security Council. (2016). *Letter Dated 7 October 2016 from the Chair of the Security Council Committee Pursuant to Resolutions 751 (1992) and 1907 (2009) Concerning Somalia and Eritrea Addressed to the President of the Security Council*. S/2016/919.

UN Security Council. (2017). *Letter Dated 8 August 2017 from the Group of Experts on the Democratic Republic of the Congo Extended Pursuant to Security Council Resolution 2293 (2016) Addressed to the President of the Security Council*. S/2017/672/Rev.1

Unachukwu, G. C., Ojiakor, N., & Okafor, G. (2003). *Nigeria peoples and culture*. John Jacobs Classic Publishers.

UNECA. (2013). Tackling the challenges of Cybersecurity in Africa. *United Nations Economic Commission for Africa*. Retrieved from https://archive.uneca.org/publications/tackling-challenges-Cybersecurity-africa

UNECA. (2015). *Illicit financial flow: Report of the High Level Panel on Illicit Financial Flows from Africa*. Retrieved from uneca.org/handle/10855/22695

UNECA. (2020). *Policy Brief: Impact of COVID-19 in Africa*. *United Nations Economic Commission for Africa*. Retrieved from https://archive.uneca.org/publications/policy-brief-impact-COVID-19-africa

UNHCR. (2019, April 6). *UNHCR strongly rejects widespread allegations against workforce*. Retrieved from https://www.unhcr.org/news/press/2019/4/5ca8a2594/unhcr-strongly-rejects-widespread-allegations-against-workforce.html

US Department of Justice. (2019). *Three Former Mozambican Government Officials and Five Business Executives Indicted in Alleged $2 Billion Fraud and Money Laundering Scheme that Victimized U.S. Investors*. Retrieved from https://www.justice.gov/usao-edny/pr/three-former-mozambican-government-officials-and-five-business-executives-indicted

US Department of State. (2015). *Investment Climate Statement – Sudan*. Retrieved from https://2009-2017.state.gov/e/eb/rls/othr/ics/2015/244456.htm

Utah Insurance Department. (2022). *What is insurance fraud?* Retrieved from https://insurance. utah.gov/agent/fraud/what.php

Van Brederode, R., & Pfeiffer, S. (2015). Combating Carousel Fraud: The General Reverse Charge VAT. *International VAT Monitor, 26*, 146–157.

Van Der Meer, F. B., & Edelenbos, J. (2006). Evaluation in multi-actor policy processes: Accountability, learning and co-operation. *Evaluation, 12*(2), 201–218. doi:10.1177/1356389006066972

Van DoesumA.NellenF. (2021). *VAT in a Day*. Retrieved from https://ssrn.com/abstract=3867201

Van Wolleghem, P. G. (2022). Does administrative capacity matter? The absorption of the European Fund for the integration of migrants. *Policy Studies, 43*(4), 640–658. doi:10.1080/01442872.2020.1770209

Vandekerckhove, W. (2016). *Whistleblowing and organizational social responsibility: A global assessment.* Routledge. doi:10.4324/9781315547299

Vinšalek Stipić, V. (2020). Korporativno upravljanje i ekonomija trećeg puta. *Obrazovanje za poduzetništvo-E4E: znanstveno stručni časopis o obrazovanju za poduzetništvo, 10*(1), 132–146.

Vinšalek Stipić, V. (2022). The concept and importance of social audit for sustainable community development. *BH Ekonomski Forum, 16*(1), 151–165.

Viscelli, T. R., Hermanson, D. R., & Beasley, M. S. (2017). The integration of ERM and strategy: Implications for corporate governance. *Accounting Horizons, 31*(2), 69–82. doi:10.2308/acch-51692

Wadström, A., & Tetka, J. B. (2019). *Understanding land corruption as a basis for prevention: Findings from Liberia, Sierra Leone and Zambia.* Transparency International. Retrieved from https://www.transparency.org/en/publications/understanding-land-corruption-as-a-basis-for-prevention

Walker-Munro, B. (2021). Tax Enforcement in the Black Economy: Tackling disruptive Challenges. In A. Rafay (Ed.), *Handbook of Research on Theory and Practice of Financial Crimes* (pp. 356–380). IGI Global. doi:10.4018/978-1-7998-5567-5.ch019

Wang, L., Wang, Y., Ye, D., & Liu, Q. (2020). A review of the 2019 novel coronavirus (COVID-19) based on current evidence. *International Journal of Antimicrobial Agents, 55*(6), 105948. doi:10.1016/j.ijantimicag.2020.105948 PMID:32201353

Wang, Y., Zhang, D., Wang, X., & Fu, Q. (2020). How does COVID-19 affect China's insurance market? *Emerging Markets Finance & Trade, 56*(10), 2350–2362. doi:10.1080/1540496X.2020.1791074

Waterbury, J. (1973). Endemic and planned corruption in a monarchical regime. *World Politics, 25*(4), 533–555. https://doi.org/10.2307/2009951

Welch, C. E. (1987). The military and the state in Africa: Problems of political transition. In Z. Ergas (Ed.), *The African State in transition.* Springer. doi:10.1007/978-1-349-18886-4_9

Westermann, K. D., Cohen, J., & Trompeter, G. (2019). PCAOB inspections: Public accounting firms on "trial". *Contemporary Accounting Research, 36*(2), 694–731. doi:10.1111/1911-3846.12454

Whistleblowers Australia. (n.d.). *How to blow the Whistle?* Retrieved from http://www.whistleblowers.org.au/

White Paper. (2020). Cybersecurity trends 2019. *Eleven Paths.* Retrieved from https://www.elevenpaths.com/news-events/trend-reports/index.html

White, J. (2020, January 30). *Transfer pricing cases to watch in 2020.* Retrieved from https://www.internationaltaxreview.com/article/b1k3znjpb16b3v/transfer-pricing-cases-to-watch-in-2020

Widmalm, S. (2008). *Decentralisation, corruption and social capital: from India to the West.* SAGE. doi:10.4135/9788132100263

Willis, L. E. (2017). The consumer financial protection bureau and the quest for consumer comprehension. *RSF: The Russell Sage Foundation Journal of the Social Sciences, 3*(1), 74-93.

Woham, W. M. (2015). Supervisory control of discrete-event systems. Lecture Notes. Department of electrical and computer engineering. University of Toronto.

Wolfe, D. T., & Hermanson, D. R. (2004). The fraud diamond: Considering the four elements of Fraud. *The CPA Journal*, 38–42.

Wordorigins.org. (2021). *Whistleblower.* Retrieved from https://www.wordorigins.org/big-list-entries/whistleblower?rq=whistleblower

World Health Organization. (2020). African countries move from COVID-19 readiness to response as many confirm cases. *WHO Africa.* Retrieved from https://www.afro.who.int/health-topics/coronavirus-COVID-19

Wüstemann, J., & Wüstemann, S. (2010). Why consistency of accounting standards matters: A contribution to the rules-versus-principles debate in financial reporting. *Abacus, 46*(1), 1–27. doi:10.1111/j.1467-6281.2010.00304.x

Wu, T., Wang, D., Wang, R., Zhao, B., Tang, M., Zhang, S., & Nie, L. (2021). Pressure drops axial distribution uniformity of the particle bed in the radial bed. *Korean Journal of Chemical Engineering, 38*(8), 1578–1591. doi:10.100711814-021-0818-0

Xiaohu, Z., Heydari, M., Lai, K. K., & Yuxi, Z. (2020). Analysis and Modeling of Corruption among Entrepreneurs. *REICE: Revista Electrónica de Investigación en Ciencias Económicas, 8*(16), 262–311. doi:10.5377/reice.v8i16.10699

Xu, D. (2018). The convergence and divergence between China's implementation and OECD/G20 BEPS minimum standards. *World Tax Journal, 10*(3), 471–496.

Yang, J. H., & Liu, S. (2017). Accounting narratives and impression management on social media. *Accounting and Business Research, 47*(6), 673–694. doi:10.1080/00014788.2017.1322936

Yaru, M. A. (2009). Economic perspective of corruption in public sector: A theoretical explanation and lessons for Nigeria. *Ilorin Journal of Business and Social Sciences, 13*(2), 143–153.

Yekini, L. S., Wisniewski, T. P., & Millo, Y. (2016). Market reaction to the positiveness of annual report narratives. *The British Accounting Review, 48*(4), 415–430. doi:10.1016/j.bar.2015.12.001

Yildrim, I., & Rafay, A. (2021). Anti-Money Laundering in the Insurance Sector: The Turkish Case. In A. Rafay (Ed.), *Money Laundering and Terrorism Financing in Global Financial Systems* (pp. 108–127). IGI Global. doi:10.4018/978-1-7998-8758-4.ch005

Young, M. R. (2000). *Accounting irregularities and financial fraud.* Harcourt Inc.

Yuguda, I. (2012). Effective corporate governance for economic development in Nigeria. *Management in Nigeria, 48*(1), 6–17.

Yusuf, O. T. (2010). Brokers and the control of post contractual opportunism in the Nigerian insurance market. *Journal of Financial Crime, 17*(2), 223–239. doi:10.1108/13590791011033917

Yusuf, O. T. (2011). Brokers' incentives and conflicts of interest in the control of opportunism. *The Journal of Risk Finance, 12*(3), 168–218. doi:10.1108/15265941111136923

Zeng, X., Momin, M., & Nurunnabi, M. (2022). Photo disclosure in human rights issues by fortune companies: An impression management perspective. *Sustainability Accounting. Management and Policy Journal, 13*(3), 568–599. doi:10.1108/SAMPJ-06-2019-0243

Zhang, S., & Aerts, W. (2015). Management's performance justification and failure to meet earnings thresholds. *Accounting and Business Research, 45*(6-7), 841–868. doi:10.1080/00014788.2015.1048771

Zhao, H., Seibert, S. E., & Hills, G. E. (2005). The mediating role of self-efficacy in the development of entrepreneurial intentions. *The Journal of Applied Psychology, 90*(6), 1265–1272. doi:10.1037/0021-9010.90.6.1265 PMID:16316279

Zhao, J., Wei, G., Chen, K. H., & Yien, J. M. (2020). Psychological Capital and university students' entrepreneurial intention in China: Mediation effect of entrepreneurial capitals. *Frontiers in Psychology*, *10*, 2984. doi:10.3389/fpsyg.2019.02984 PMID:32038375

Zhao, L., & Atkins, J. (2021). Assessing the emancipatory nature of Chinese extinction accounting. *Social and Environmental Accountability Journal*, *41*(1-2), 8–36. doi:10.1080/0969160X.2021.1889386

ZhirovaG. (2017). *Tax Monitoring Development in Russia.* Regional Authorities, Local Self-Government and Civil Society: Mechanisms of Interaction. Saratov, 2017. C.80–82. Retrieved from https://ssrn.com/abstract=3167060

Zhu, X., Ao, X., Qin, Z., Chang, Y., Liu, Y., He, Q., & Li, J. (2021). Intelligent financial fraud detection practices in post-pandemic era. *The Innovation*, *2*(4), 1–11. doi:10.1016/j.xinn.2021.100176 PMID:34806059

Zizek, S. (2020). *Pandemic COVID-19 shakes the world.* OR Books. doi:10.2307/j.ctv16t6n4q

Zu, Y., Evans, C., & Krever, R. (2020). The VAT Compliance Burden in the UK: A Comparative Assessment. *British Tax Review*, *3*, 354–377.

Zywicki, T. (2013). The Consumer Financial Protection Bureau: Savior or menace. *The George Washington Law Review*, *81*, 856.

About the Contributors

Abdul Rafay is a practitioner cum academician. For more than 25 years, Mr. Rafay has been working as a freelance advisor, consultant & trainer to a wide variety of public & private sector national and multinational companies in the areas of Corporate Finance, Financial Policy & Implementation, Auditing & Assurance, Accountancy, Corporate Tax Management, Financial Technology, and System Consultancy. He has been providing consultancy to various industries including Textile, Auto Assembling, Footwear, Industrial/Agro Chemicals, Ice Cream/Dairies, Glass/Ceramics, Healthcare, Mining/Natural Resources, Packaging/Paper Sacking, Steel/Pipe Casting, Rice Processing, Brokerage/Co-operative Financing, Software Development, Real Estate, Printing/Publishing, and Construction/Civil Engineering, etc. Mr. Rafay is a Fellow member of the Institute of Chartered Accountants of Pakistan. He is also a member of various national and international professional bodies including the Institute of Internal Auditors (IIA), USA; Association of Certified Fraud Examiners (ACFE), USA. Since 2001, he has been a lifetime member of the Lahore Tax Bar Association. He has served as Co-regional Director (Founding) of Lahore-Islamabad Chapter of Professional Risk Managers International Association (PRMIA), Washington, USA (2011-2013). In 2012, he was nominated as Member: Education & Training Committee (ETCOM) of The Institute of Chartered Accountants of Pakistan (ICAP). He is also a member of ICAP's "Islamic Finance working group" which is closely in liaison with the State Bank of Pakistan and other stakeholders for Islamic Finance Accounting and Auditing Standards. He is an Alumnus of Rausing Executive Development Center (REDC), Lahore University of Management Sciences (LUMS), Pakistan. In 2014, International Finance Corporation (World Bank Group) selected him for Training of Trainers (ToT) for Corporate Governance Action Planning for SMEs. He is also an approved trainer for the Institute of Financial Markets of Pakistan (IFMP) established by the Securities and Exchange Commission of Pakistan (SECP), the corporate regulator. In 2013, his name got included in the list of "Certified Directors" as per Clause (xi) of The Code of Corporate Governance 2012 issued by SECP. Currently, he is on the board of a Listed Company as an Independent Director. For the last 27 years, Mr. Rafay has also been associated with teaching in some of the top business schools of Pakistan. His specialized subjects of interest include Strategic Corporate Finance, Financial Crimes, Financial Derivatives, Investments/Portfolio Analysis, International Financial Reporting Standards, Corporate Restructuring (Mergers & Acquisitions), Financial Statement Analysis & Corporate Taxation. He also served as an instructor in Civil Services Academy, Pakistan to train the CSS Officers selected by the Federal Public Service Commission of Pakistan (FPSC). Currently, he is a Professor of Finance & Accounting at the University of Management & Technology, Pakistan. He has published more than two dozen research papers in SSCI, ESCI and Scopus indexed journals published by reputed global publishers including Emerald, Sage, Taylor & Francis, and IGI Global. He contributed multiple chapters in Books edited by International Editors. For many years, he authored/edited multiple international books on FinTech, Islamic Finance, Financial Crimes, Money Laundering, Terrorism Financing, Energy Finance, and Environmental Finance published by IGI Global, USA.

* * *

Shafiu Ibrahim Abdullahi is a PhD candidate at the Department of Economics, Bayero University, Nigeria.

Clement Chiahemba M. Ajekwe holds a PhD in Accounting from Benue State University, Nigeria, and an MSc from the London School of Economics, UK. Currently, he is an Associate Professor of Accounting at Benue State University, Nigeria. He is a member of the Chartered Institute of Management Accountants of the United Kingdom and the Institute of Chartered Accountants of Nigeria. Dr. Ajekwe has more than thirty years of academic experience. He has taught undergraduate and graduate students and supervised undergraduate projects, Master's degree dissertations and PhD theses. Dr. Ajekwe is an accomplished researcher; he has several publications in peer-reviewed Journals and Chapters in Edited Books. In addition, he has had twelve years of professional management experience in corporate Nigeria.

Muhammad Mobeen Ajmal is a PhD candidate in China. Previously he did his Masters in Business Administration (Finance) from Lahore University of Management Sciences (LUMS), Pakistan. Currently, he is a faculty member at the University of Management & Technology, Pakistan. His research interests include Corporate Finance, Financial Technology and Islamic Finance.

Fábio Albuquerque holds a PhD in Economic and Business Sciences from the University of Extremadura, UNEX, Spain. Currently, he is an Assistant Professor at Lisbon Accounting and Business School, Portugal. His professional experience includes technical work in different entities in the areas of accounting, reporting and statistics, as well as the provision of consulting and business training services on international and national accounting and financial reporting standards and risk management in Auditing.

Benjamin Enahoro Assay holds a PhD in mass communication from Benue State University, Nigeria. Currently, he is a faculty member at Delta State Polytechnic, Ogwashi-Uku, Nigeria. He has published articles in scholarly journals and contributed chapters in several books, locally and internationally. His areas of research interest are journalism and media studies, information and communication technology and national development; international communication and comparative media studies, media, democracy and good governance, population and health communication, and public relations and advertising. He is a member of several professional bodies, including the African Council for Communication Education (ACCE) Nigeria chapter, the Advertising Practitioners Council of Nigeria (APCON), the Association of Communication Scholars and Professionals of Nigeria (ACSPN), Nigeria Institute of Public Relations (NIPR), National Association for Research Development (NARD), among others.

Ambareen Beebeejaun holds a PhD in International Tax Law from University of Mauritius. Previously she did LLM in International Business Law and ACCA. Currently she is a faculty member at the University of Mauritius. Her research interests include company law, insolvency law, tax law and corporate governance.

António Cariano has a master's degree in accounting and management of financial institutions. He is the Assistant Professor of Accounting at Lisbon Accounting and Business School (ISCAL) / Instituto Politécnico de Lisboa, Portugal, in the scientific area of accounting and auditing. António Cariano has been working for several financial institutions in accounting and financial reporting.

Stefano de Nichilo holds a PhD in Business Economics from University of Cagliari, Italy. Currently, he is a faculty member at the same university. His research interests include Creative Accounting, Fraud and Audit Alert. He possesses 10 years of experience as an advisor/consultant to Big Four accounting firms. He/she published more than 10 papers/book chapters/books.

Tochukwu Benedict Ezeifekwuaba holds an MSc in Oil and Gas Management from South America University, USA. He is a writer, freelancer, and independent researcher in Nigeria.

Mohammad Heydari holds a PhD and DSc. in Management Science & Engineering (MS&E) from Nanjing University of Science and Technology, China. His work has been supported by the Graham Munro Charitable Foundation, Wilfrid Laurier University, National Natural Science Foundation of China (NSFC), and Fundamental Research Funds for the Central Universities, China, etc. He worked as a scientist and an associate professor at the Business College, Southwest University in China. His CV has over 151 peer-reviewed papers, 16 textbooks, 45 book chapters, etc. He has pioneered many aspects of MS&E and won many awards nationally and internationally.

Busra Karataser holds a PhD in Economics from Tekirdağ Namık Kemal University, Turkey. Currently, he is an associate professor at the same university. His research interests include Economic systems.

Pendo Shukrani Kasoga holds a PhD in Business Administration from the University of Dodoma, Tanzania. Currently, she is a senior lecturer at the Department of Accounting and Finance at the University of Dodoma. Her research interests include financial services, corporate governance, and corporate finance. She possesses fifteen years of experience as an advisor and consultant to government, multinational, and local companies. She has published more than twenty papers and book chapters.

Kin Keung Lai holds a PhD from Michigan State University, USA. Currently, he is a distinguished Professor at the College of Economics, Shenzhen University, China, and an honorary professor at the Department of Industrial and Manufacturing Systems Engineering, Hong Kong University, Hong Kong. Before his post, he was the Chair Professor of Management Science at the City University of Hong Kong. Before his academic appointment, he was a Senior Operational Research Analyst for Cathay Pacific Airways and an Area Manager on Marketing Information Systems for Union Carbide Eastern. Professor Lai's main areas of research interest are operations and supply chain management, financial and business risk analysis, and modeling using computational intelligence. He has extensively published in international refereed journals on the above areas. He is the Founding Chairman of the Hong Kong Operational Research Society of Hong Kong and currently the President of the Asia Association on Risk and Crises Management. In 2009, Professor Lai was the Joon S. Moon Distinguished International Alumni Award of Michigan State University and was also appointed as the Chang Jiang Scholar Chair Professor by the Ministry of Education, China. In 2013, he was selected as a Fellow of the Asia Pacific Association of Industrial Engineering and Management Systems. In 2014, he was the recipient of the

Civil and Environmental Engineering Distinguished Alumni Award, from Michigan State University, USA. In 2017, Professor Lai was elected as the Academician of the International Academy of Systems and Cybernetic Sciences.

Xiaoyang Li holds a PhD in Economics. Currently, he is a Professor of Economics, at the College of Economics & Management, Southwest University, China.

Marie G. Nakitende holds a PhD in Management from Cardinal Stritch University, USA. Currently, she is Dean, of the Faculty of Business Administration and Management at Uganda Martyrs University, Uganda. She published many research papers in international journals.

Ali Polat holds a PhD from Marmara University, Turkey. Currently, he is an associate professor at Ankara Yıldırım Beyazıt University, Turkey. His research interests are International Economics, Banking and Financial Economics.

Hicham Sadok is a full professor at Mohamed V University in Rabat-Morocco. He teaches economics and finance and is interested in research themes in finance, development and technological management. He has published books and articles on related topics.

Adam Salifu holds a PhD in Development Studies from Western Sydney University, Australia. Currently, he is a Research Fellow at the University of Professional Studies, Accra. His research interests span a wide range of aspects of the sociology, economics, and politics of development including rural and agricultural transformation, food security, corruption, poverty reduction and social protection. He possesses over 10 years of experience as a consultant to both international and local NGOs in Ghana such as the International Food Policy Research Institute (IFPRI), Overseas Development Institute (ODI), International Labour Organization (ILO), DAI, UNICEF, Ghana Education Service (GES), Plan Ghana and the Accra-based Institute for Democratic Governance (IDEG). Dr. Adam Salifu has published more than 10 research reports, journal articles and book chapters.

Usman Sambo holds a PhD in Public Administration from the University of Maiduguri, Nigeria. Currently, he is a Senior Lecturer at the Department of Public Administration in Yobe State University Damaturu Nigeria. His research interest includes Corruption and Development Studies. He spent six years as Director of Administration, Federal Medical Centre Nguru, Yobe State Nigeria. He has published more than twenty (20) papers and book chapters both locally and internationally in reputable journals.

Kamal Kabiru Shehu holds an MSc from SRM University Chennai, India. Currently, he is a faculty member at the Department of Economics and Development Studies, the Federal University of Kashere, Gombe State, Nigeria.

Mukhtar Shuaibu holds a PhD. Currently, he is working as a faculty member at the Department of Social Sciences, Kebbi State Polytechnic, Dakingari, Nigeria.

Vinícius Stoltzemburg holds a Management degree from Instituto de Contabilidade e Administração de Lisboa (ISCAL) and a masters degree in Accounting also from ISCAL. Professionally, Vinícius is a

Tax Advisor at EY with specific knowledge and experience in tax services (tax consulting, tax auditing, tax compliance, tax due diligence, and accounting) provided to financial entities, including banks and insurance companies.

Babayo Sule holds a PhD in Political Science from Universiti Utara Malaysia. Currently, he is a Lecturer in the Department of Political Science, Faculty of Humanities Management and Social Sciences, Federal University of Kashere Gombe, Gombe State Nigeria. His research interest includes Political Economy, Political Theory, Security Studies, and Islamic Political Thought. He spent over thirteen (13) years as a Lecturer in the Department of Political in Gombe State University and the Federal University of Kashere Gombe where he holds several administrative positions including Faculty Exams Officer and Coordinator Postgraduate Studies. He has published over forty (40) papers and fifteen (15) book chapters and conference proceedings in local and international reputable journals.

Gunputh Suman is the holder of two PhDs in Law. Currently he is a Professor and Dean (Faculty of Law and Management) at the University of Mauritius. He is the Honorary Professor of University of Xiangtan in China. He is the Editor-in-Chief of the Just Africa Journal (Polokwane, South Africa). He is a member of the National Coordination Committee on issues of Human Rights and a member of the Environmental and Land Use Appeal Tribunal.

Amani Gration Tegambwage holds a PhD in Business Administration from the University of Dodoma, Tanzania. Currently, he is a senior lecturer at the Department of Business Administration and Management at the University of Dodoma. His research interests include service marketing and relationship marketing. He possesses seventeen years of experience as an advisor or consultant to government, multinational, and local companies. He has published more than twenty papers and book chapters.

Valentina Vinsalek Stipic holds a PhD from the Faculty of Economic Studies at the University of Modern Sciences - CKM in Mostar, Bosnia, and Herzegovina. Currently, she is a Professor at the Polytechnic "Nikola Tesla" in Gospic, Croatia. Her research interests include Corporate Social Responsibility and Financial management, Organizational Management, and SME. She possesses sixteen years of experience as a CFO in multinational companies. She has published more than 80 papers, ten teaching materials, and two books.

Mustapha Yusufu holds BSc and MSc in Economics from Modibbo Adama University of Technology, Yola, Nigeria. He is a PhD candidate at Modibbo Adama University, Yola. He published in local and international journals. Currently, he is a lecturer at the Federal College of Education, Yola, Nigeria.

Misbahu Ibrahim Zamfara is a lecturer in the Department of Sociology Gombe State University. He is engaged in teaching, research and community services. He has published numerous articles and book chapters in local and international journals and has attended several conferences locally and internationally. He is currently a PhD student.

Index

G

I

J

L

M

N

O

P

R

S

T

U

W

www.ingramcontent.com/pod-product-compliance
Lightning Source LLC
LaVergne TN
LVHW060359300926
849162LV00006B/1300

9781668450079